Racialized Commodities

RACIALIZED COMMODITIES

Long-Distance Trade, Mobility, and the Making of Race in Ancient Greece, c. 700–300 BCE

CHRISTOPHER STEDMAN
PARMENTER

OXFORD
UNIVERSITY PRESS

OXFORD
UNIVERSITY PRESS

Oxford University Press is a department of the University of Oxford.
It furthers the University's objective of excellence in research, scholarship,
and education by publishing worldwide. Oxford is a registered trade mark of
Oxford University Press in the UK and in certain other countries.

Published in the United States of America by Oxford University Press
198 Madison Avenue, New York, NY 10016, United States of America.

© Oxford University Press 2024

All rights reserved. No part of this publication may be reproduced, stored in
a retrieval system, or transmitted, in any form or by any means, without the
prior permission in writing of Oxford University Press, or as expressly permitted
by law, by license or under terms agreed with the appropriate reprographics
rights organization. Inquiries concerning reproduction outside the scope of the
above should be sent to the Rights Department, Oxford University Press, at the
address above.

You must not circulate this work in any other form
and you must impose this same condition on any acquirer

Library of Congress Cataloging-in-Publication Data
Names: Parmenter, Christopher Stedman, author.
Title: Racialized commodities : long-distance trade, mobility, and the making of race
in ancient Greece, c. 700–300 BCE / Christopher Stedman Parmenter.
Description: New York, NY: Oxford University Press, [2024] |
Includes bibliographical references and index.
Identifiers: LCCN 2024009141 (print) | LCCN 2024009142 (ebook) |
ISBN 9780197757116 (hardback) | ISBN 9780197757130 (epub)
Subjects: LCSH: Greece—Commerce—History—To 1500. | Race—Economic aspects. |
Greece—Ethnic relations—History—To 1500. |
Greece—History—146 B.C.-323 A.D.
Classification: LCC HF375 .P37 2024 (print) | LCC HF375 (ebook) |
DDC 382.0938—dc23/eng/20240315
LC record available at https://lccn.loc.gov/2024009141
LC ebook record available at https://lccn.loc.gov/2024009142

DOI: 10.1093/9780197757147.001.0001

Printed by Integrated Books International, United States of America

Contents

Preface ix

Abbreviations xiii

Introduction 1
    Introduction 1
    An Atlas of the Body 5
    From Ethnicity to Race 8
    The Horizons of Trade 13
    Summary of Chapters 21

Part I: *The World of the Elephantine Document*

1. A Short History of Natron 27
    Introduction 27
    Demand and Supply 29
    Buying and Selling 36
    The Ties That Bind 42
    Commodity Encounters 45
    Conclusion 51

2. Egypt in Your Hand 53
    Introduction 53
    Natron and Faience 57
    Biographies of Faience 59
    Sailors and Scarabs 63

	Voyaging with the Gods	68
	On the Trail of Sesostris	74
	The Script of the Heroes	81
	Conclusion	85
3.	From Ancestor to "Other"	87
	Introduction	87
	Afterlives of Faience	89
	Ethiopians and Egyptians	94
	An Aesthetic of Migration	97
	Consuming the Body	108
	Conclusion	121

Part II: Letters from the Pontus

4.	Journeys into Slavery	125
	Introduction to Part II	125
	Introduction to Chapter 4	127
	The "Biographical Turn"	128
	Slave Transits and Intraregional Mobility	134
	Shipwrecks and Law Courts	141
	Conclusion	149
5.	Slavery and the Balance of Trade	152
	Introduction	152
	Financing a Surplus: Metals, Minerals, Currency, and the Portable Arts	155
	Staples: Wine, Oil, Grain, and Fish	161
	Conclusion	168
6.	Inventing Whiteness	170
	Introduction	170
	Differential Treatment	174
	Reading the Skin	182
	Imagining the Steppe	194
	Conclusion	204

Postscript	206
Introduction	206
Familiarity Is Recognition	208
The Path Forward	211
Appendix 1: Quantifying the Natron Trade	213
Appendix 2: Catalogue of Greeks in Egypt, Seventh to Early Fifth Centuries BCE	225
Appendix 3:	233
Appendix 3.1: Aegyptiaca *Assemblages at Greek Sanctuaries, c. 700–525 BCE*	233
Appendix 3.2: Scarab Assemblages at Greek Sanctuaries, c. 700–525 BCE	234
Appendix 3.3: "Textual" Scarab Inscriptions from Large Assemblages	235
Appendix 3.4: "Textual" Scarab Inscriptions from Small Assemblages	235
Appendix 4: Five Large Scarabs from Late Geometric Greece	237
Appendix 5:	241
Appendix 5.1: Stone Head Scaraboids Distribution	241
Appendix 5.2: Stone Head Scaraboids Catalog	242
Appendix 5.3: Faience Head Scaraboid Distribution	247
Appendix 5.4: Faience Head Scaraboid Catalog	248
Appendix 6: Catalogue of Enslaved Journeys	255
Notes	259
Works Cited	321
Index	373

Preface

*donec ad haec tempora quibus nec uitia nostra nec remedia
pati possumus peruentum est*

Until things culminate in the present moment, when we can
neither endure our faults nor their cure.
(Liv. AUC 1.pr.9)

WHAT HAPPENS WHEN the revolution ends?

Time crawled in the weeks before my dissertation defense. Back in spring 2020, I had been commuting between New York, where I taught during the week, and Washington, DC, where my partner Antonia lived. I felt perversely relieved when the university closed on March 11th. Unlike New York, where fear was very real, Washington had taken on the mood of a carnival during the first week of the lockdown. As soon as Antonia's newsroom closed, her entire reporting team relocated to our living room to work the overnight shift. Two weeks in, someone decided it might be better not to work in person after all. By this point, unemployment had surged higher than the worst days of the Great Depression. That spring, I thought a lot about the former USSR where I had travelled a few times for research. Things held together until late 1991—then the bottom rusted out, the state collapsed, and in the following decade something like 3.4 million people died deaths of despair. Was this the year of *our* Chernobyl? Was our world soon coming to an end?

In the way that humanities dissertations take forever to write, I had been working on what would become *Racialized Commodities* for four years by the time the pandemic hit. Then the work became urgent. 2020 was a year of revolution. What revolutions need is a past: ancestries, genealogies, or exempla that might offer some guidance to things that might happen to come. For a brief moment, it felt like a wall had broken—elite institutions were suddenly avid to understand how *they* were implicated in the structures of power that stretched back hundreds of years. The whole project of history is to demonstrate how surface realities sit atop deep structures, and now the entire world was eager to learn, however earnest or fickle that interest might have been. This book is the result.

But the revolution failed in 2020. Since then, we have seen an authoritarian reaction that threatens to claw back gains made that year and far worse. In 2022, I was hired by the Ohio State University as member of a new faculty cohort whose work explores race, ethnicity, gender, and reconciliation. Within months, the state legislature took steps (so far unsuccessful) to ban teaching like mine at Ohio public institutions. Similar legislation succeeded in Florida, Texas, Indiana, and elsewhere. Today we stare down a future where any interrogation of the social order (past or present) might well become sole province of elite private universities—kleptocratic institutions that lack a social mission by default. If so, our work threatens to bolster the very forces so many of us had hoped to fight against.

What *Racialized Commodities* argues is that race was not a unique product of Atlantic modernity, nor are we alone in history for our ills. Race, or race-like constructions, have existed in many societies through time. In the period I study, racialized conceptions of human diversity took root because they rationalized certain structures of economic exploitation. There was nothing necessary about their existence, and there is no direct tie between ancient Greek ideas of race and those we have in America today. But as I argue elsewhere (2024a, 2024b), it was through the Early Modern and Enlightenment reception of these ideas that they reached modernity. I challenge the midcentury consensus that race and racism were first concocted by the heirs of Columbus as they sought to rationalize European expansion and the Transatlantic Slave Trade. Then and now, race is a social construct; the fact that race lacks any biological validity continues to do nothing to prevent racism from damaging human lives. Instead, the fact that race and racism once took different forms reminds us of the past's fundamental danger. We find a bottomless well of precedents and examples in the past; at any moment, one might be revived. Learning to read the past through the lens of the present reminds us to be on guard.

The first people I must thank are my dissertation committee: my outstanding supervisor, Barbara Kowalzig, and committee members Andrew Monson, Joan Breton Connelly, David Konstan†, and Clemente Marconi. Other faculty members who extended gracious assistance include Emilia

Barbiero, Raffaella Cribioret, Michael Peachin, David Sider, David Levene, and Laura Viidebaum.

I spent four semesters at the American School of Classical Studies at Athens, where I benefitted from the wisdom of Kevin Daly, Donald Haggis, Guy D. R. Sanders, Ioulia Tzonou-Herbst, and Tyler Jo Smith. At Oxford, I thank Nicholas Purcell and Irad Malkin. At Penn, my thanks go to Jeremy McInerney, Jamal Elias, and Dagmawi Woubshet. At Howard, I thank Molly Myerowitz Levine and Carolivia Herron. Many others I met elsewhere: Alexandra Villing, Dan-el Padilla Peralta, Denise McCoskey, Ian Moyer, Jackie Murray, Mathias Hanses, David Lewis, Patrice Rankine, Rebecca Futo Kennedy, Nandini Pandey, Shomarka O. Y. Keita, Najee Olya, and Julie Park.

Finally, I am enormously grateful for my new colleagues at Ohio State. Carolina López-Ruiz, Katie Rask, Sarah Iles Johnston, Gregory Jusdanis, Julia Nelson Hawkins, Tom Hawkins, James D. Moore, and Roxann Wheeler read my work with interest and provided me detailed feedback and encouragement—even before I first set foot in Columbus. For support editing the manuscript, I thank Alan Ross and Gillian Marbury. I am also grateful for the support for former department chair Anthony Kaldellis and current chair Mark Fullerton.

This project would not exist without the help of curators, archaeologists, site guards, archivists, and library staff all over the world. I thank curators at the Penn Museum, the Cyprus Museum, the archaeological museums at Andros and Delphi in Greece, and the Harvard Art Museums site guards and archaeologists at Kourion in Cyprus, Olbia in Ukraine, and Istros in Romania. I am grateful for the help of image licensing staff at the Museum of Fine Arts, Boston (Carolyn Cruthirds), the British Museum (Lucia Rinolfi), the Penn Museum (Evan Peugh), the Cyprus Museum (Giorgos Georgou), Lindy Crewe (Cyprus American Archaeological Research Institute), the Hellenic Ministry of Culture and Sports (Polyxeni Adam-Veleni, Maria-Xeni Garezou, Georgia Papadopoulou, Athanasia Psalti, and Krania Vasiliki), and the ASCSA Agora Excavations (Aspasia Efstathiou).

Special gratitude is due to staff members who have helped me along the line. At NYU, I thank Nancy Smith Amer, Maura Pollard, Maria Lampraki, and Polly Terzian. At Penn, I thank Sara Varney and Pamela Horn. Ioanna Damanaki at the American School helped me obtain permits. And finally, Khalid Jama at Ohio State facilitated the funding for this book.

I am greatly obliged to Stefan Vranka and Chelsea Hogue at Oxford University Press, as well as the essential work of this book's anonymous peer reviewers. My gratitude as well to copy-editor Rebecca Cain and production manager Dharuman B at NewGen Knowledge Works.

Thank you to my friends in no particular order: Philip J. Katz; Sam Holzman; Anne Duray; Eric Driscoll; Andrew Ward; Aimee Genova; Hannah Rich; Maria Papaioannou; Ari Zatlin; Calloway Brewster Scott; George Baroud; Stephanie Crooks; Rebecca Sausville; Andrea Pozzana; Del Maticic; Andreja Katancevic; John Baker; Maude Slingenberg; Dylan James; Victoria Fleck; Ben Davis; Ryan Franklin; Harry Eli Kashdan; Joel Pattison; Dennis Hogan; Chris Burke; Kelsey Rice; Kevin Kerr.

I received my AB at Hamilton College, where I studied under the guidance of Barbara K. Gold, Carl Rubino, Shelley P. Haley, and James B. Wells in Classics, Margaret Thickstun and Steve Yao in English, and Robert Paquette in History. At University of Oregon, I thank my MA supervisor, P. Lowell Bowditch; Christopher Eckerman, Mary K. Jaeger, Malcolm Wilson, Cristina Calhoon, and David Chamberlain. This book is dedicated to the memory of my high school Latin teacher, Merni Medley†.

I have gratitude for my parents, Pamela Parmenter and Tighe Stedman Parmenter; my sister, Natalie Michaelian Parmenter; my aunt, Prof. Carolyn Parmenter†; my grandparents, Patricia Parmenter, Prof. Charles Stedman Parmenter, Judy King, and George L. King II†; my aunt and uncle, Peggy and Jeff King; Meg†, Don, and Gordan Sillars.

I've spent half my life with Antonia Noori Farzan. My love for her has no bounds.

Abbreviations

Abbreviations of Latin and Greek texts follow the conventions of S. Hornblower et al., *The Oxford Classical Dictionary*, 4th ed., Oxford, 2012. Journal abbreviations follow the style of *The American Journal of Archaeology*. I have transliterated Greek proper nouns using their most familiar English forms. Hence *Miletus*, not Miletos, but *Samos*, not Samus.

AR	J. H. Breasted, *Ancient Records of Egypt: Historical Documents from the Earliest Times to the Persian Conquest*, 5 vols., Chicago, 1906.
Bergk	T. Bergk. 1878–82. *Poetae Lyrici Graeci*, 4th ed., 3 vols., Leipzig, 1878–82.
Bernabé	A. Bernabé. 1988–2006. *Poetarum Epicorum Graecorum: Testimonia et fragmenta*. 2 vols. Leipzig, 1988–2006.
BDAG	F. Montinari et al., *The Brill Dictionary of Ancient Greek*. Leiden, 2015.
BNJ	I. Worthington et al., *Brill's New Jacoby*, 2nd ed., 2016–ongoing. Updated project available at https://scholarlyeditions.brill.com/bnjo/.
CAD	M. T. Roth et al., *The Chicago Assyrian Dictionary*, 21 vols. Chicago, 1956–2010.
CGP	M. Dana, *La correspondance grecque privée sur plomb et sur tesson*, Munich, 2021.
CIL 4	C. Zangemeister et al., *Inscriptiones parietariae Pompeianae Herculanenses Stabianae*, 4 vols., Berlin, 1871–2020.
Dem. P.Mallawi	O. Zaghloul, *Frühdemotische Urkunden aus Hermupolis*, Cairo, 1985.
Diehl	E. Diehl, *Anthologica lyrica Graeca*, 2nd ed., Leipzig, 1936.
Domingo Foresté	D. Domingo-Foresté, *Aelian: Epistulae et fragmenta*, Stuttgart, 1994.
EGEF	C. Tsagalis, *Early Greek Epic Fragments*, 2 vols. Berlin, 2017.
FGrH	F. Jacoby et al., *Die Fragmente der griechischen Historiker*, 5 vols., 1923–ongoing.

Gernet	L. Gernet, *Fragments d'Antiphon le Sophiste*, Paris, 1923.
ID	F. Dürrbach et al., *Inscriptions de Délos*, 7 vols., Paris, 1926–72.
I.Eph.	H. Wankel et al., *Die Inschriften von Ephesos*, 8 vols., Bonn, 1979–84.
IG I^3 1	D. M. Lewis, *Inscriptiones Graecae I: Inscriptiones Atticae Euclidis anno anteriores*, 3rd ed., Berlin, 1981.
IG 2^2	J. Kirchner, *Inscriptiones Graecae II et III: Inscriptiones Atticae Euclidis anno posteriors*, 4 vols., Berlin, 1913–40.
IG 2^3 1	S. D. Lambert, *Inscriptiones Graecae II et III: Inscriptiones Atticae Euclidis anno posteriores*, 3rd ed., Berlin, 2012.
IG 9.1^2	G. Klaffenbach, *Inscriptiones Graecae IX,1*, 2nd ed., 2 vols., Berlin, 1968.
IG 11.2	F. Dürrbach, *Inscriptiones Graecae XI. Inscriptiones Deli*, Berlin, 1912.
IG 12^1	F. H. von Gaertringen, *Inscriptiones Graecae, XII. Inscriptiones insularum maris Aegaei praeter Delum*, Berlin, 1895.
IGCH	M. Thompson et al., *An Inventory of Greek Coin Hoards*, New York, 1973. Updated project available at http://coinhoards.org/.
IGDOP	L. Dubois, *Inscriptions grecques dialectales d'Olbia du Pont*, Geneva, 1996.
I.Lindos	C. Blinkenberg, *Lindos. Fouilles et recherches, 1902–1914. Vol. II, Inscriptions*, 2 vols., Copenhagen and Berlin, 1941.
IOSPE I^2	V. V. Latyshev, *Inscriptiones antiquae Orae Septentrionalis Ponti Euxini graecae et latinae*, 2nd ed., Petrograd, 1916.
I.Priene^2	W. Blümel and R. Merkelbach, *Die Inschriften von Priene*, 2nd ed., 2 vols., Bonn, 2014.
K-A	R. Kassel and C. Austin, *Poetae Comici Graeci*, 7 vols., Berlin, 1983–2023.
LGPN	R. Parker et al., *Lexicon of Greek Personal Names*, 7 vols., 1987–ongoing. Updated project available at https://www.lgpn.ox.ac.uk/.
LSJ	H.G. Liddell et al., *A Greek-English Lexicon*, 9th ed., Oxford, 1996.
L-P	E. Lobel and D. Page, *Poetarum Lesbiorum Fragmenta*, 2nd ed., Oxford, 1963.
M-L	R. Meiggs and D. M. Lewis, *A Selection of Greek Historical Inscriptions to the end of the Fifth Century B.C.*, Oxford, 1969.
M-W	R. Merkelbach and M. L. West, *Fragmenta Hesiodea*, Oxford, 1967.
O.Gardiner	J. Černy and A. H. Gardiner, *Hieratic Ostraca*, vol. 1, Oxford, 1957.
P.Cairo 65739	A. H. Gardiner, "A Lawsuit Arising from the Purchase of Two Slaves," *Journal of Egyptian Archaeology* 21.2 (1935): 140–46.
P.Cair.Zen.	C. C. Edgar, *Zenon Papyri, Catalogue général des antiquités égyptiennes du Musée du Caire*, 5 vols., Cairo, 1925–40.
PHST	D. Rehberger et al., *Peoples of the Historical Slave Trade*, 2018–ongoing. Updated project available at https://enslaved.org/.

P.Harris 1	P. Grandet, *Le papyrus Harris I (BM 9999)*, 2 vols., Cairo, 1994.
P.Mich. 5	E. M. Husselman, A. E. R. Boak, and W. F. Edgerton, *Michigan Papyri* vol. 5: *Papyri from Tebtunis*, part 2, Ann Arbor, 1944.
PMG	D. L. Page, *Poetae Melici Graeci*, Oxford, 1962.
P.Rainer 53	A. H. Gardiner, *Late Egyptian Miscellanies*, Brussels, 1937, pp. 137–39.
PSI 5	G. Vitelli and M. Norsa, *Papiri greci e latini*, vol. 5, Florence, 1917.
PTS 2098	A. L. Oppenheim, "An Essay on Overland Trade in the First Millennium B.C.," *Journal of Cuneiform Studies* 21: 236–54.
SAA	S. Parpola et al., *State Archives of Assyria*, 21 vols., Winona Lake, Indiana, 1987–2018.
SB 28	A. Jördens, *Sammelbuch griechischer Urkunden aus Ägypten*, vol. 28, Wiesbaden, 2013.
SEG	A. Chaniotis et al., *Supplementum Epigraphicum Graecum*, 64 vols., Leiden, 1923–ongoing.
SIG^3	W. Dittenberger, *Sylloge Inscriptionum Graecarum*, 3rd ed., Leipzig, 1915.
Snell	B. Snell, *Bacchylides: Carmina cum fragmentis*, Leipzig, 1958.
TAD	B. Porten and A. Yardeni, *Textbook of Aramaic Documents from Ancient Egypt*, 4 vols., Winona Lake, Indiana, 1986–99.
TASTD	D. Eltis et al., *The Transatlantic Slave Trade Database*, 1999–ongoing. Updated project available at https://www.slavevoyages.org/.
TCL 12	G. Contenau, *Contrats néobabyloniens I: Tiglath-phalasar III à Nabonide*, Paris, 1927.
WB	A. Erman and H. Grapow, *Wörterbuch der Aegyptischen Sprache*, 6 vols., Leipzig, 1926–50.
West	M.L. West, *Iambi et elegi Graece ante Alexandrum cantati*, 2nd ed., 2 vols., Oxford, 1989.
YOS 6	R. P. Dougherty, *Records from Erech: Time of Nabonidus (555–538 B.C.)*, New Haven, 1920.

MUSEUMS

Ashmolean	Ashmolean Museum, Oxford, UK
Berlin	Antikensammlung, Staatliche Museen zu Berlin, Berlin, Germany
BM	British Museum, London, UK
Louvre	Louvre Museum, Paris, France
MFA	Museum of Fine Arts, Boston, USA
MMA	Metropolitan Museum of Art, New York, USA
Penn Museum	University of Pennsylvania Museum of Archaeology and Anthropology, Philadelphia, USA
Princeton	Princeton Art Museum, Princeton, USA

PERIODS AND STYLES

Achaemenid	Achaemenid (27th) Dynasty (525–404 BCE)
Archaic	Archaic Period (700–480 BCE)
Classical	Classical Period (480–320 BCE)
EIA	Early Iron Age (1200–550 BCE)
EPC	Early Protocorinthian (720–690 BCE)
Hellenistic	Hellenistic Period (320–30 BCE)
Late Period	Late Period (664–332 BCE)
LBA	Late Bronze Age (1550–1200 BCE)
LG	Late Geometric (750–700 BCE)
LHIIIC	Late Helladic IIIC (1200–1075 BCE)
LPC	Late Protocorinthian (650–25 BCE)
Middle Kingdom	Middle Kingdom (2040–1802 BCE)
MPC	Middle Protocorinthian (690–50 BCE)
New Kingdom	New Kingdom (1550–1077 BCE)
Old Kingdom	Old Kingdom (2686–2181 BCE)
PC	Protocorinthian (720–625 BCE)
Ptolemaic	Ptolemaic (32nd) Dynasty (332–27 BCE)
Saite	Saite (26th) Dynasty (664–525 BCE)
Third Intermediate	Third Intermediate Period (1077–664 BCE)
WG	Wild Goat (650–550 BCE)

Introduction

Introduction

Nostalgia runs deep in Plato. For the generation that endured Athens' hard years in the 400s and 390s BCE—the counterrevolution, occupation, purges, and emigration—a sense of loss never felt distant. By the time that Plato was writing in the mid-fourth century, Athens had its empire back. Prospectors were again testing the mines of Laureion, and the city was wealthier than it had been in decades. But Plato was profoundly disturbed by the absence of so many from his youth. Like his contemporaries Xenophon and Lysias, Plato peopled his work with the men who died in those times—Polemarchos, killed in 404; Socrates, killed in 399; Phaedrus, dead in 393; many others in between. In 391 BCE, when his friend Theaetetus of Sounion appeared at the gates of Megara gravely wounded on a stretcher, a familiar pain returned to his heart.[1]

Plato's *Theaetetus* is set the day Theaetetus died. At the start of the dialogue, we encounter two Megarian philosophers, Euclides and Terpsion, waiting for the news. Euclides knew Theaetetus. Years prior, Theaetetus had studied with Socrates in Athens. On the morning of Socrates' trial in 399 BCE, Euclides witnessed a conversation between the two so moving that he wrote it down. As they mill about, Euclides pulls the transcript off the shelf and hands it to an enslaved attendant: "come boy, take the book and read" (*Theaet.* 143d1).[2] And so we are borne back to the past, when Socrates still lived, and Theaetetus was a child.

Socrates had spent the morning of his trial chatting with a mathematician named Theodorus of Cyrene. Socrates asked Theodorus whether he had any students. Yes, Theodorus answered. Beckoning toward a group of young men, he pointed out Theaetetus. Socrates perceived something immediately.

Tell him to come over, Socrates said, "So I can inspect how closely his face resembles my own!" (144d7).³ To put it bluntly, the boy was not handsome (οὐκ ἔστι καλός, 143e8). He had a flat nose and bulging eyes just like Socrates (143e9).⁴ Socrates dotes on the boy with a platitude—physical beauty is only skin deep, and what really matters is the soul (145b1). But clearly something deeper was at play. So much of our identities is wrapped up in the morphology of the face. Shortly before departing for his trial, Socrates is wistful. "If I only appeared to have normal eyes and a normal nose, and not a flat nose and great big bug eyes, wouldn't I look more like someone else?" (209c1).⁵ If he did, he would no longer be Socrates.

Faces, beauty, ugliness: Plato deploys these as framing devices in a dialogue largely concerned with other topics. But it is worth stopping to think about them. Depending who you were in Late Classical Athens, these things could mean an awful lot. To men in the stratum of Socrates and Theaetetus, little marks and blemishes made you an affable rogue. Theaetetus' father, after all, was a major landowner in Sounion (144d2). Citizens from the mining demes rested easy on the work of "barbarians" enslaved in the mines.⁶ Even though his inheritance had been squandered, ugly young Theaetetus inherited what counts: an "amazing freeness"⁷ that left his disposition unconcerned with money. But personal appearance meant something rather different to our enslaved internal narrator ("boy"), who could have found himself dispatched underground from any trifling offense. Few critics have ever been as conversant in the tropes of Athenian life as Julius Pollux, a Roman-era lexicographer who read Old Comedy closely. The comic mask "of a favored slave is distinguished by its hair," Pollux would write (4.154); the usual style is close-cropped. The nose is usually flat. (Figure I.1; see also Figure 6.1).⁸ The same visual *indicia* that made Theaetetus ugly rendered a fugitive visible from a mile away.

Racialized Commodities explores the material, social, and economic processes by which ancient Greeks came to ascribe meaning to human diversity. Over the long 400 years between circa 700 and 300 BCE, Greeks came up with various and often contradictory ways to explain why people looked different from one another: what it meant to have dark or light skin, a certain nose shape, curly hair, and so on. Sometimes these ideas were linked to the practice of physiognomy, the folk practice of making "inferences from human surfaces to human depths."⁹ At other times, imaginaries of the body were given clear social charge. "Dispositions follow bodily characteristics," writes an Aristotelian writer (*Physiogn.* 805a1);¹⁰ a person's somatics might tell you something about their cultural identity, the environment they grew up in, or whether someone was enslaved.¹¹ To critics from the eighteenth century until

FIGURE I.1 Drawing of white ground lekythos attributed to the Bosanquet Painter depicting free woman and enslaved attendant offering scented oil at funerary stele, c. 440 BCE. Berlin, Antikensammlung VI 3291. After Bosanquet 1899: pl. III. Public domain.

World War II, there was a simple way to read this logic: the Greek way of seeing the body prefigured the modern concept of race. (Such equivalences were convenient in an era when many scholars were open as to their own racial prejudice).[12] For understandable reasons, in the postwar era the pendulum swung far the other way.[13]

Scholars differ as to the consequences of reviving "race" as a paradigm for reading ancient societies. After all: race and racism are not mere biases and stereotypes, but "a historically specific ideology that emerged, took shape, and has evolved as a constitutive element within a definite set of social relations anchored to a particular system of production."[14] In the mid- to late twentieth century, pioneering Black leftists including Eric Williams (1911–81) and Cedric Robinson (1940–2016) came to see race and racism (indexed as anti-Blackness) as a key aspect of Atlantic modernity. But these scholars located its emergence somewhere between the end of feudalism and the rise of capitalism; whatever race-like systems existed in premodernity represented something else.[15]

In the past decade, premodernists have reopened the question, arguing that race should be defined loosely—perhaps, "the dominant group's refusal to recognize [its own] quality of humanity in a subaltern group,"[16] or a "structural relationship for the articulation and management of human differences."[17] Critics of the racial turn in the premodern humanities worry that such an approach decontextualizes a phenomenon intricately linked to the rise of global capitalism. If race is to be defined so broadly, what *doesn't* constitute race?[18] Yet as disciplinary historians make clear, race is something that lurks in every nook and cranny of our world. Very few paradigms used by historians are truly free of it.[19] If that is the case, we should be open-minded to the existence of race or race-like concepts in antiquity, seeing as big questions require long answers.

Racialized Commodities begins in the world of the Archaic Period. In the heat of Greece's remarkable commercial expansion in the seventh and sixth centuries BCE, the cadre of merchants who sailed between Saite Egypt and the Aegean circulated diminutive faience trinkets, known as *aegyptiaca*, bearing images of divinities, religious symbols, and carefully depicted foreign bodies (Chapters 1–3). Such objects were used in a variety of contexts, ranging from sincere religious devotion to (quite possibly) advertising. It was via these that the earliest images of the bodies that Greeks would come to label "Ethiopians" and "Egyptians" entered the visual vocabulary. In the last century of the Archaic Period, Greek views of foreign bodies began to turn from objects of reverence to symbols of consumption. Greek discourses on human diversity would be subsumed into the idea of the subhuman, menacing "barbarian" that proliferated following Achaemenid Persia's interventions in the Aegean between 499 and 49 BCE. From this point out, slavery begins to loom large in Greek explanations of human diversity. Anatomical difference became a convenient way to explain social hierarchy. It is from this context that stereotyped images of light-skinned, ruddy, and proverbially dim-witted forced laborers that the Greeks styled "Thracians" or "Scythians" in the fifth and fourth centuries would first emerge (Chapters 4–6).

Two millennia before the Transatlantic Slave Trade, anti-Blackness, or the rise (and fall) of race science, the ancient Greeks had generated their own meanings from human diversity. This rubric, which was always in flux, always contested, and always contingent, would fade from use as Archaic and Classical Greece melted into the Hellenistic and Roman worlds. But its roots were firm in the ground. As the intellectuals of the eighteenth- and nineteenth-century west sought to impose hierarchies on the natural world, they found rich precedents for their classifications in Classical texts.

An Atlas of the Body

Before examining the processes by which Archaic Greeks came to recognize and explain human diversity, it is worth spending a little more time at the end of the period covered by this book. When Plato in the *Theaetetus* sought to capture the distinct morphology of Socrates' face, he was using a vocabulary that had been honed over 300 years to capture the subtleties of human diversity. For the most part, it is banal. Noticing that someone else's face looks different from your own is not the stuff of race. Looking a little deeper, its contours suggest the "multiplicity of interlocking discourses" that are.[20]

Complexion and nose-shape were prime fixations of the anatomical vocabulary in the Classical Period. We hear of noses flat (σιμός) or hooked (γρυπός); skin complexions range from pale (λευκός) and ruddy (πυρρός) to honey-colored (μελίχλωρος), to dark (μέλας). In later periods—for instance, Ptolemaic Egypt—we see a much wider use of anatomical vocabulary. Ptolemaic notaries often took down physical descriptions of contract signatories, which gives us many descriptions of people with straight noses (εὐθύριν) and honey-colored skin (μελίχλωρος).[21] But in the Classical Period, authors are obsessed with abnormality. If you garner description, your body defies some norm.[22]

Sometimes, this language was merely descriptive. One Aristotelian writer appears to describe a sunburn as τὸ πυρρόν (*Prob.* 38.2.966b). Other times, it registered ideology. Classical authors quite frequently used skin color to meditate over issues of gender. Women were supposed to be fair, and men dark.[23] Male aesthetics were tied up in anxieties over leisure, wealth, and homosociality.[24] Hence the Old Comic playwrights constantly deploy skin color to lampoon women for being too masculine and men for being too feminine.[25] In Plato's *Republic* (5.474d7–e4), Socrates makes a point about moral relativism by carefully describing the faces of teenaged boys: some are flat-nosed (σιμός), others hook-nosed (γρυπόν); some are honey-skinned (μελιχλώρους), others are dark (μέλανας) or pale (λευκούς).[26] In this expression, boys' bodies were spaces of erotic possibility, a palette containing the entire morphology of the human form.

The earliest uses of the anatomical lexicon in the Classical Period come from what might be called ethnographic discourse.[27] Long before Plato, the mid-fifth-century trio of Aeschylus, Herodotus, and the author of the Hippocratic *Airs, Waters, Places* deploy the anatomical lexicon to closely describe the bodies of non-Greeks. Ethiopians and Egyptians are dark-skinned and flat-nosed; Scythians and Thracians are unusually light-skinned and prone to flush.²⁸ Derisive anatomical stereotypes were used in fifth-century Athens to describe the bodies of enslaved workers. *IG* I³ 1032 is a record of dozens enslaved rowers conscripted into the Athenian navy between 410 and 400 BCE. Many of their enslavers embarrassed them with pet-names that emphasized their physical difference: Σιμίας or Σῖμος (Flat-nose); Γλαυκίας (Gray-eyes); and one named Πύρρος (Ruddy).²⁹ Such names cannot be taken as evidence for origin or actual appearance. Rather, pet-names were an expression of ideology: "there were Greek slaves in Greece... but they were unfortunate accidents; ideological expressions were invariably formulated around 'barbarians.'"³⁰ A few decades after Plato, a fragment of Menander leaves us with the suggestion that the Ethiopian and Scythian physiognomy continued to be stigmatized into the Hellenistic Period.³¹

Indeed, if we step past the boundaries of circa 700–300 BCE, we get the sense that gendered and ethnographic uses of the anatomical lexicon proliferate among Hellenistic and Roman-era writers who, of course, were schooled in the canon of Archaic and Classical Greek literature. This can be seen in the work of two Hellenistic poets, Asclepiades of Samos and Theocritus of Syracuse, who worked under the patronage of Ptolemy II Philadelphus (r. 284–46 BCE) in Egypt. When Asclepiades handles the trope of light- and dark-skinned lovers (*AP* 5.210), he gives his love interest, a woman named Didyme, a common Egyptian name.³² "If she is dark-skinned (μέλαινα), who cares? So are coals—but when we heat them up, they glow like roses."³³ Theocritus deploys anatomical language widely.³⁴ For instance, take the singing farmer in *Id.* 10.26–28, who describes a female farmhand who catches his eye: "dear Bombyka, everyone calls you Syrian, thin, and sunburnt, but I alone call you honey-skinned (μελίχλωρον). Indeed, the violet is dark."³⁵ This trope would be borrowed by Roman-era authors in both Greek and Latin. It can be found in the novelist Longus (1.16.3);³⁶ Pollux (4.147) uses it to describe theater masks for light- and dark-skinned young men in Old Comedy.³⁷ When Latin writers adopt the trope, they specifically associate skin color and facial morphology with origin. Hence Lucretius (*DRN* 4.1155–1170),³⁸ Catullus (93.1–2),³⁹ Vergil (*Ec.* 2.14–18),⁴⁰ Martial (*Ep.* 4.42.1–10).⁴¹ The trope is even borrowed by amateur poets on the walls of Pompeii (*CIL* 4.1520,⁴² 4.6892).⁴³

So far, so good. Classical Athens possessed a lexicon to describe human diversity. It was frequently used to talk about gender (particularly the bodies of people who violated its norms) and non-Greeks. Hellenistic and Roman receivers of the anatomical lexicon used it to meditate over both. Might the anatomical lexicon be seen as one manifestation of a "structural relationship for the articulation and management of human differences?"⁴⁴ Historically, scholars have pointed to the lack of anything like scientific racism or Jim Crow to argue that race could not exist in antiquity.[45] Yet as early as the 420s BCE, we find a real desire in Classical Athens that a concept like race *should* exist. Without venturing too far into what the political philosopher Vanita Seth (channeling Quentin Skinner) has called the "mythology of prolepsis," one might say that Classical Athenians could easily imagine that physical appearance or ancestry *should* correlate with social status.[46]

The author of a fifth-century screed wrongly attributed to Xenophon laments the fact that citizens are banned from meting random punishment to enslaved people on the street. Why was that? Athenian citizens "don't dress any better than the slaves and foreigners—and aren't physically better looking either" (*Ps.-Xen. Ath. Pol.* 1.10).[47] In the middle of the fourth century, Plato (again using Socrates as his mouthpiece) argues that citizens of an ideal *polis* must be fooled into thinking that people are born into different social roles; intermarriage between classes should be restricted to maintain the purity of its citizenry (*Rep.* 3.415a–17b).[48] And at the end of the century, Aristotle laments nearly the same thing: you would think that an enslaved worker would have big arms (*Pol.* 1.1254b33) or at least descend from other slaves (*Pol.* 1.1255b1). In practice, neither appearance nor descent can tell you what a person's true destiny is.

Yet again, in the same text, Aristotle tells us that *no* barbarian is any better than a natural slave (*Pol.* 1.1252b8). If Classical Athenian writers lacked an idea of race, at least a few were stumbling precariously close to something like it.

At least these writers could admit their limits. By the turn of the third century, others were hard at work trying to a produce a world where physical difference carried social meaning. A generation after Aristotle composed his *Politics*, two or more of his unnamed students wrote a text known as the *Physiognomics*, a manual for reading a stranger's inner nature through outward appearance. Occasionally, these writers make assurances that physical appearance can determine someone's *true* origin.[49] In two passages, authors deploy the contrast of light and dark skin to make blanket statements associating the straight hair of Thracians (described as σκληρότριχες, *Physiogn.* 806b16–18) with courage. The excessively dark complexion (ἄγαν μέλανες) of Egyptians and Ethiopians symbolizes cowardice (*Physiogn.* 812a13–14). Aristotle himself had similar thoughts: curly hair (οὐλότριχες) is the sign of the Ethiopian, while straight hair (εὐθύτριχες) belongs to Thracians and Scythians (*Gen. an.* 5.782b25–35).

All told, our brief survey finds that fifth- and fourth-century Athenians frequently associated terms in the anatomical lexicon with specific places on the map. Athenians often associated physical appearance with place in the social hierarchy. Athenians were also capable of envisioning a system where physical appearance would be a fool-proof guarantor of social rank. To what extent might "race" be appropriate terminology for the real or putative coupling of appearance, culture, and rank? As we will find in the next section, the term works surprisingly well. Indeed, the idea that appearance, culture, and rank had some bearing on one another had deep roots in the culture of first-millennium Greece.

From Ethnicity to Race

For much of the past seventy years, historians of ancient Greece have been reticent to label Greek thinking about appearance, culture, and social rank as "race." In fact, the late 1990s–2010s boom in scholarship on ancient Greek "ethnicity" is predicated on the wholesale rejection of the term. In the decades before World War II, ancient historians had flirted with the idea that "race" was the main act of world history; the past might be seen as an interminable battle between different biologically defined groups, whether Romans and Jews, Blacks and whites, Nordics and Mediterraneans, and so on.[50] The atrocities of the war shocked intellectuals out of this mindset, at least when they spoke in public.[51] Indeed, in the postwar era race became less the province of biology than history, sociology, and other fields outside the natural sciences. This development energized a new generation of historians. Thus in his wildly influential 1944 *Capitalism and Slavery*, the left historian Eric Williams would theorize that race was a social construct made to rationalize the Transatlantic Slave Trade.[52] Efforts would emerge by the 1980s to try to push back the clock even further. Cedric Robinson, for instance, saw concepts of race at work in European feudalism.[53] Nonetheless, the line had to be drawn somewhere. If race had not existed since the beginning of time, it was necessary to pinpoint the place and time of its birth. Antiquity seemed to be off limits.

To a surprising extent, the unargued assumptions of prewar racialist scholarship never really exited the literature. Were you to ask an educated person in the 1930s what *race* meant, you might hear it defined through some untheorized combination of ancestry, anatomy, religion, territoriality, culture, or language.[54] In the leadup to the war, some Anglophone social scientists would call for the replacement of definitionally murky "race" with "ethnicity," "ethnicism," or their cognates.[55] "Ethnicity" would be put on firm methodological footing in the 1960s, when sociologists including Fedrik Barth would define the concept as a matter of a group's self-recognition of shared descent based on mutually accepted referents (language, religion, etc.) subject to constant contention and renegotiation.[56]

Yet in common parlance, ethnicity was transferred many of the same meanings that race held prior to the war.[57] And this was not merely a reading held by the unenlightened. Even the great anti-racist anthropologists of the postwar era often fossilized elements of the old racialism in new models.[58] It is in this sense that the sociologist Troy Duster calls racialism a paradigm never quite dispatched; it was "buried alive," waiting for revival in a day when people forgot the genocides of the midcentury.[59] (The post-2015 emergence of "genomic history" and neo-migrationism in Mediterranean archaeology suggests that such a day has come; but this topic cannot receive adequate treatment here).[60]

The fact that race survived only in the shadows means that few ancient historians have truly grappled with it. Around the turn of the millennium, ancient historians turned to the social sciences to embrace ethnicity as a paradigm for describing ancient Greek identity in a historically contingent, and non-essentialist, manner. Jonathan M. Hall theorized that Greeks in the Archaic Period saw the human community like a tree, sprouting branches to accommodate newcomers as distant relatives. Hall called this the "aggregative" logic of Greek ethnicity in the Archaic Period, which used ancestry as a metaphor to map the links between individual families, cities, or groups such as the Ionians and Dorians.[61] After the Persian Wars, the Greeks—and particularly the Athenians—began to define their ethnicity in terms of opposition. All Greeks shared a common Greekness; non-Greeks were "barbarians," perhaps only suited to be enslaved (e.g., Eur. *IA* 1400, quoted in Arist. *Pol.* 1.1252b8).[62] While the conceit of a universal human family did not totally exit the picture, fifth-century writers developed an interest in cataloging the cultural practices, physical environment, and physiognomies of "barbarian" peoples.[63] What was crucial to the "ethnicity" model was that there was nothing *essential* about Greek identity. "Greekness" was a historical phenomenon. In well-documented periods (i.e., Classical Athens), its transformations could be tracked from generation to generation.

There was and is much to like about the "ethnicity" paradigm. All forms of identity are social constructs. Nonetheless the "ethnicity" paradigm has its own blind spots. Foremost is that of social power. Up until the late 1990s, classicists had tended to envision Greek identity via the assumptions of midcentury structuralism. Following this logic, all identity is based on opposition. Thus one could not understand Athenian social structure without investigating how writers or artists depicted out-groups, namely women, foreigners, enslaved people. (The impact of the 1970s cultural turn was particularly evident here.)[64] As they made their intervention, Hall, Irad Malkin, and their contemporaries were very conscious that ancient texts were ideological documents. If statements about the "Other" could not be taken at face value, the ways that members of the in-group defined *their own* membership were potentially very rich. Malkin took a special interest in the intra-elite networks that linked together the distant shores of the "small Greek world."[65] Greek identity outside Classical Athens was a major fascination. (This raised a problem, since only in Classical Athens is there enough documentation enough to write a history of identity in the Archaic or Classical Periods with great detail).[66] In the 2000–10s, Greek historians told stories about collaboration, not conflict; diversity, not dichotomy; trade, not turmoil.[67]

But what about those out-groups? When we first encounter ethnonyms like "Egyptian," "Ethiopian," "Thracian," or "Scythian" in the Homeric poems, they denote people who belong more to myth than history. But in the sixth century, they become decidedly real, and in the fifth century, all of these groups became objects of intense ethnographic speculation. Joseph Skinner notes that even at the start of the sixth century, very detailed stereotypes of dark-skinned "Ethiopians" and bodysuit-wearing "Scythians" were ensconced in Greek iconography.[68] These groups cannot be studied through the lens of self-attestation, because every one of these terms is an exonym—a label affixed by Greek speakers onto another people. It is here that we encounter the less savory tendencies of the ancient Greeks. By the early fifth century, stereotypes of pale-complexioned "Thracians" and "Scythians" would be clearly implicated in the Greek slave trade with the north. Even the idea that Archaic Greek identity was completely "aggregative" or free of prejudice toward out-groups (as Erich Gruen dubiously argues)[69] is not beyond question.[70] When Classical Greeks themselves remembered the Archaic Period, it seemed self-evident that *their own* biases preexisted the Persian wars.

An example of this can be found in the *Theaetetus*. Plato writes that the early Greek philosopher Thales (b. 630–20 BCE) was so obsessed with looking at the stars that one day he fell into a well. "This χαρίεσσα and ἐμμελὴς Thracian slave girl mocked him"[71] (174a5). The adjective χαρίεσσα has a range of meaning from "refined" to "clever" to a term of endearment for a love interest. (This is how Theocritus uses it in *Id.* 10.26, quoted above.) Ἐμμελὴς is more inscrutable, meaning "suitable," "well-proportioned," or "in good taste." Plato also uses it elsewhere to mean "cheap."[72] *What sort of relationship* did Plato think Thales and the enslaved Thracian woman had?

Now, Plato's anecdote about presocratic philosophers and enslaved Thracians could be mere anachronism. But it should give us pause given how much closer Plato was to Thales than Thales is to us. (After all: fragments of Archaic poetry, e.g., Hipponax fr. 27 West, make it pretty clear that Phrygians, an Anatolian people frequently enslaved in the Classical Period, were already stigmatized in the Archaic.) Plato clearly believed that there was an association between being Thracian and enslaved in the late seventh century. We might dwell on this association by looking at the work of another early Greek philosopher dear to Plato. Nearly 200 years before Socrates' discourse on light and dark-skinned bodies in *Republic* 474d7–e4, Xenophanes of Kolophon (b. 570–60 BCE)[73] deploys almost the exact same metaphor:

ἀλλ' εἰ χεῖρας ἔχον βόες <ἵπποι τ'> ἠὲ λέοντες
ἢ γράψαι χείρεσσι καὶ ἔργα τελεῖν ἅπερ ἄνδρες,
ἵπποι μέν θ' ἵπποισι, βόες δέ τε βουσὶν ὁμοίας
καί <κε> θεῶν ἰδέας ἔγραφον καὶ σώματ' ἐποίουν
τοιαῦθ', οἷόν περ καὐτοὶ δέμας εἶχον <ἕκαστοι>.
Αἰθίοπές τε <θεοὺς σφετέρους> σιμοὺς μέλανάς τε
Θρῆικές τε γλαυκοὺς καὶ πυρρούς <φασι πέλεσθαι>.

But if horses or oxen or lions had hands, or could draw with their hands and accomplish such works as men, horses would draw the figures of the gods as similar to horses, and the oxen as similar to oxen, and they would make bodies of the sort which each of them had. Ethiopians say that their gods are flat-nosed and dark; Thracians that theirs are gray-eyed and ruddy.[74]

(Xenophanes fr. 13–14 Diehl)

What kind of associations did Xenophanes hold with Thracians or Ethiopians? Single fragmentary sources are a problem to work with. Because Xenophanes wrote in the Archaic Period, the conventional wisdom is that he was merely *interested* in otherwise neutral ideas of human diversity.[75] In *Racialized Commodities*, I argue something else. Seventh- and sixth-century Greeks were imaginative in coming up with explanations for why human bodies looked so different. This period, explored in Chapters 1–3, is very rich with depictions of the people whom Xenophanes calls "Ethiopians." In the sixth, fifth, and fourth centuries, Greeks become even more interested with the people whom Xenophanes called "Thracians." Chapters 4–6 cover how the growing Greek interest in Thrace, Scythia, and the lands around the Black

Sea were deeply enmeshed in the workings of the slave trade. The visualizations of foreign bodies that fascinated the mind of Archaic and Classical Greece circulated via an extensive network of trade that linked Greece with the Mediterranean's northern and southern bounds.

Race, as is understood in this book, was a social classification in Archaic and Classical Greece distinct from ethnicity. "Ethnicity" might be understood as how the Greeks thought of themselves; "race" could be imagined how Greeks explained the bodies and cultures of people believed to come from away.[76] I join a growing number of premodernists willing to see race as a concept active in the world before 1492. The move to reconsider the hard wall of chronology that separated a "racial" modernity from the "pre-racial" Middle Ages and Antiquity began around twenty years ago.[77] Early on, scholars hesitated in claiming that race or race-like constructions predated the Columbian exchange. Benjamin Isaac labelled ancient prejudices as "proto-racism"—bias lacking a theoretical frame.[78] (It is my opinion that the issue of framing is overdetermined. Eighteenth-century historians are adamant that western European intellectuals delayed theorizing race in any recognizable fashion until the 1780s—eighty years after the Transatlantic Slave Trade had reached industrial levels of brutality.)[79]

But as many of the scholars loosely gathered under the moniker of Critical Race Theory (CRT) would tell you, racism is not so much about theory as it is about outcomes, experiences, and trajectories.[80] Thus in the influential formulation of the Americanists Karen and Barbara Fields, racism represents "a theory and practice of applying a social, civic, or legal double standard" around the idea of race—an otherwise artificial idea that links social identity with ancestry.[81] Notably, the classicist Jackie Murray adapts Fields and Fields' definition to a premodern context by identifying several contexts in which this double standard might be applied, including dress, kinship restrictions, the application of legal disabilities to distinct groups, and tropes of monstrification.[82]

Racialized Commodities emphasizes the free-associative nature of race as a social construct. Indeed, contemporary theorists continue to disagree over which signifiers are most important in defining race. Fields and Fields, for instance, prefer definitions of race that foreground ancestry; they demote the role of visible anatomy to a subsidiary category they refer to as "bio-race."[83] Other theorists are adamant about the importance of somatics.[84] For the purposes of this book, I accept both somatics and ancestry claims as possible *indicia* for race as understood by the ancient Greeks. But as I hope to differentiate race as a meaningful concept in ancient Greece from ethnicity—which, as Hall understands, was *primarily* articulated through ancestry claims in ancient Greece—I will primarily focus on the former. Keeping in mind that the most important question that determines whether a group constitutes a *race* is one of treatment, we will continually return to the question of *how much* Greek constructions of difference impacted the lives of those so identified. As the Archaic Period melted into the Classical, they increasingly did.

As race-related scholarship has attained greater prominence in studies of the premodern world, we ought to venture forward with a fair bit of caution. When classicists first began to talk about race and racism in a serious fashion in the 2000s, it occurred largely in the worlds of Classical Reception—the emotive encounters between contemporary readers and ancient texts—and disciplinary history.[85] Here, the invocation of race stood on firm ground; race and racism are facts of our world, after all, and are things that shapes the lives of contemporary readers. Attempts to employ race as a coherent framework for understanding premodernity continue to be met with claims of theoretical imprecision.[86] (Such charges have frequently been levelled at definitions of premodern race such as that proposed by Geraldine Heng).[87] While I do not accept this critique, it is still worth taking seriously. If race constitutes innumerable "just-so stories with the potential to become self-fulfilling prophecies,"[88] then there will always be something evasive about it. (It is perhaps for this reason that Margo Hendricks speaks of race as a "bidirectional gaze . . . that looks inward even as it looks outward";[89] something easy to recognize in premodernity but hard to pin down.) When Socrates gazed upon the face of Theaetetus, he saw his own reflection in his eyes. Modernity has robbed us of the ability to look at the world without seeing race, even if we would rather not.[90]

If it is the case that the world that produced Thales or Xenophanes already had an ideology of race, we will need to identify the forces that produced it—the context that gave it meaning. Doing so requires a deeper look at the social and economic forces that produced human diversity in the eyes of Archaic Greece.

The Horizons of Trade

Racialized Commodities locates the emergence of an ancient Greek idea of "race" in the Aegean world's remarkable commercial expansion during the seventh and sixth centuries BCE. Understanding how and why "race" became a useful idea requires, then, an extended study of the mentality of the Archaic merchant.

The Greek world of the sixth century BCE was struck with a mania for the peoples thought to inhabit the edges of the earth. Around the turn of the sixth century, Arktinos of Miletus composed a faintly attested epic known as the *Aithiopis*, which portrayed the arrival of the hero Memnon in Troy with an army of Ethiopians. According to one reading, Achilles recruited an army of Scythians to counter them.[91] Ethiopians and Thracians were popular characters in Athenian Black Figure vase painting, which reached its apogee in the second half of the century. On fragments of two vases now in the Penn Museum, the painter Exekias (c. 540 BCE) portrays a bodysuit-wearing nomad watching his horse graze on the steppe. (Figure I.2, B). On two other vases, the hero Memnon leads club-bearing Ethiopians to Troy, one given the name of the Egyptian pharaoh Amasis (r. 570–26 BCE). (Figure I.2, A; 3.3). A few years prior, an artist known as the Busiris Painter (Figure 3.2) made Egypt his topic. His name-vase depicts a gigantic, nude Herakles taking the stance of the pharaoh smiting his enemies to slay a coterie of Egyptian priests, backed up by club-bearing attendants nearly identical to Exekias' Ethiopians.

FIGURE I.2 Two black figure amphorae attributed to Exekias, c. 545–30 BCE. **A:** Vase portraying scene from the Aithiopis. Club-wielding warrior named "Amasos" at viewer's left. Penn Museum MS3442; **B:** Vase portraying nomad and grazing horse. Penn Museum MS4873B. Photographs courtesy of the Penn Museum.

Indeed, the list of individuals art historians identify as Thracians, Scythians,[92] Egyptians, or Ethiopians[93] in sixth-century Athenian vase painting runs very long. Similar portrayals can be found in South Italian coroplastics,[94] Cypriot seal-carving,[95] or Greco-Egyptian faience.[96] These are the obvious predecessors of the "barbarians" that populated the fantasies of Classical Greece. In his important 2012 monograph, Joseph Skinner labels the proliferation of such images as Archaic Greece's "ethnic *imaginaire*."[97]

What do such images mean? We first must dispense with the notion that early Greek portrayals of non-Greeks are a mere record of contact.[98] Take the mid-sixth century depictions of the Ethiopians found in Xenophanes, Exekias, and the Busiris painter. Unique among the ethnographic repertoire of Archaic Greek art, the people identified by art historians as Ethiopians are not solely distinguished by their clothing, but by their physiognomy—particularly their nose shape and hair texture.[99] In the 1960–70s, the great African American classicist Frank M. Snowden Jr. assembled a catalog of such representations in his search of what Black life looked like in the ancient Mediterranean.[100] Arguing that ancient "Ethiopians" were synonymous to Black people in modernity, he compiled an extensive list of "Ethiopians" in the art of sixth-century Greece. To Snowden, they were realistically portrayed: in his (dated) parlance, Ethiopians were "black-skinned, flat-nosed, and wooly-haired."[101]

This approach finds little agreement today. Contemporary art historians do not regard vase painting as naturalistic.[102] In a recent book, Sarah Derbew draws attention to the palpable circularity in Snowden's logic, observing his use of modern Blackness (capitalized) to define black bodies (lowercase) in antiquity.[103] On the other hand, there is no doubt that the Ethiopians represent a special case given their anatomical difference from other stock characters of Greek vase painting. Moreover, Attic vase painters were very clearly influenced by figurations of the body that came from the Nile Valley.[104] Understanding how these visualizations of the body arrived in an Athenian workshop—and the work they performed there—requires a deeper investigation of trade and cross-cultural interaction in the Archaic Greek world.

Racialized Commodities takes many of its cues from the study of Blackness in the eighteenth-century Atlantic world. In his landmark 1985 *Sweetness and Power*, the anthropologist Sidney Mintz argued that the transatlantic trade in Caribbean sugar—a vast enterprise that intertwined captive labor from Africa and conquered land in the Americas with declining life expectancies in Europe—for the first time united the world in a political economy defined by mass consumption of a single commodity. Calling this approach "commodity biography," Mintz (following Eric Williams, Terence Hopkins, Immanuel Wallerstein, and others) argued that nearly every aspect of eighteenth-century political economy could be traced back to sugar and slavery.[105] In a 2011 monograph, Simon Gikandi extended this reading to aesthetics. Transatlantic capitalism produced new ways of visualizing the body: Black labor was employed in the production of a pure white substance that corroded the bodies of any it touched.[106]

European intellectuals did not know quite what to do with the visuality of Black bodies.[107] For Thomas Jefferson (1743–1826) and Edmund Burke (1729–97),[108] the ugliness of Black bodies offered *prima facie* proof of slavery's justice;[109] most noxiously, Isaac Teale (d. 1764) compared the body of an enslaved Black woman to Botticelli's Venus in the dark. (The cruelty of Teale's poem has been much discussed in the literature.)[110] Even abolitionists—from the German naturalist Johann Friedrich Blumenbach (1752–1840)[111] to the formerly enslaved Afro-British activist Ottobah Cugoano (c. 1757–post 1791) tended to side-step the question of whether beauty was truly relative.[112] The most effective use made by abolitionists of the Black body was as a mirror for the consumer, a way for the eaters of sugar to reflect on the ethics of consumption. Josiah Wedgwood's (1730–95) notorious anti-slavery medallions, mass-printed on teacups, saucers, brooches, and other media, presented the figure of a kneeling, enslaved Black man begging the viewer for his freedom: "AM I NOT A MAN AND A BROTHER?" (Figure 3.12). The consumer could be shamed into becoming a humanitarian.[113]

We cannot simply transplant the study of commodities and aesthetics in eighteenth-century Britain to ancient Greece. Whatever debates might have raged in the sixth century over the aesthetics of Ethiopian bodies are surely obscure now. Nonetheless, the increasingly obvious complexity of long-distance trade in Archaic Greece makes commodity biography a useful model to keep in mind when we talk about cultural change in the period. By the middle of the sixth century BCE, Greece had spent decades in the throes of sustained economic growth.[114] The overwhelming bulk of maritime trade was what Peregrine Horden and Nicholas Purcell (2000) famously characterized as *cabotage:* the itinerant trade in widely available commodities between adjacent regions. Nonetheless, a budding long-distance trade in higher-value commodities was clearly on the increase in the sixth century.[115] Archaeologists emphasize that the trade in rare, exceptional, or complexly produced items (and especially the portable arts) invited the consumers to reflect on their origin, former owners, and production.[116] Moreover, the embrace of writing as a technology invited a new level of sophistication into commerce, allowing for traders—even in remote areas to track expenses (*CGP* 23), debts (*CGP* 48), and record feuds (*CGP* 25).¹¹⁷ In places like Egypt, Greek merchants deftly engaged with complex local regimes of taxation (*TAD* C3.7).¹¹⁸

Racialized Commodities draws on evidence suggesting that long-distance trade tended to be dominated by a cadre of specialists.¹¹⁹ Sailing the length and breadth of the Mediterranean required specialized knowledge: seasons, winds, currents, labor, prices, and most critically, relationships of trust with local authorities.¹²⁰ Already in the Homeric poems we hear of elite seafarers like Mentes of Taphos (*Od.* 1.183–84) or Euenos, son of Jason (*Il.* 7.470–75), and by the sixth century we possess a short (but suggestive) list of celebrity merchants¹²¹ (Figure I.3). Sappho¹²² appears to have written several poems about her merchant brother, †Charaxos of Lesbos,¹²³ who is also mentioned by Herodotus (4.152); to these we can add †Sostratos of Aegina and Kolaios of Samos, referenced in the same passage.¹²⁴ Ceramicists have gathered a prosopography of traders (or perhaps, as Mario Torelli calls them, "*[famiglie] nei grandi traffici mediterranei*") attested by inscribed ceramic dedications at widely dispersed Mediterranean port sanctuaries in the sixth century—a

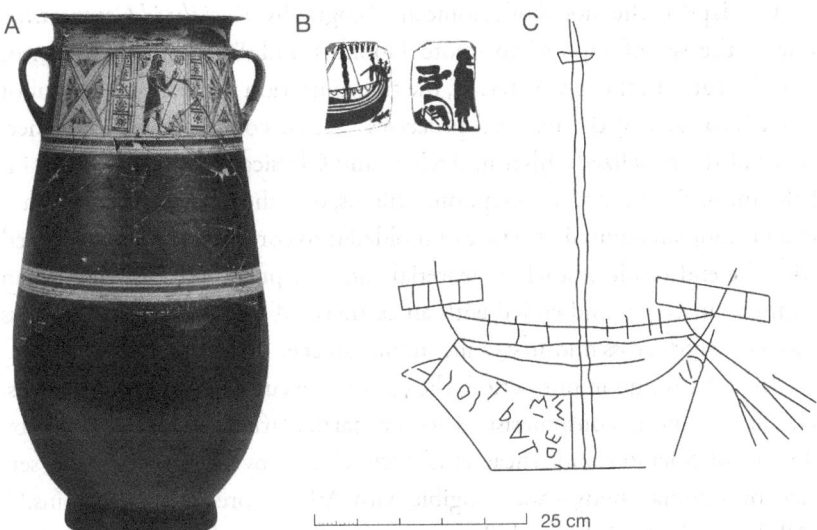

FIGURE I.3 Archaic Greek merchants. **A:** Situla excavated at Memphis, Egypt, sixth century BCE. Penn Museum 29-71-189. Photograph courtesy of the Penn Museum. **B:** Plaque from Penteskouphia, near Corinth, depicting merchant and ship, sixth century BCE. After Fraenkel 1891: pl. 8. Public domain. **C:** *Graffito* of merchant ship inscribed with name of †Sostratos, Vouliameni, Greece, sixth century BCE, after van de Moortel and Langdon 2017: fig. 17. Used with permission.

prosopography that includes some names remembered by Herodotus and other writers, including †Sostratos and Kolaios.[125]

The community of long-distance traders sat at the forefront of cultural and political developments in seventh- and sixth-century Greece.[126] Indeed, anxieties about merchants—and the new commodities, ideas, and wealth they brought with them—are fixtures of sixth-century Greek literature. The Theognidean corpus (a body of elegiac poetry datable between the seventh and fifth centuries BCE) sets the tone by treating merchants as worrisome social climbers, whose access to wealth threatened to destabilize the existing social order.[127] "We seek well-born (εὐγενέας) goats or asses or horses, and anyone wants his to descend from a good lineage ... yet a good man does not hesitate to marry a bad woman from a bad father, if he offers a big dowry ... they honor money, and good marries bad, and bad good: wealth mixes its way into the family line (γένος)" (Theog. 183–86, 89–90 West).[128] In particular, poets fixated on the very things they carried as corrosive tokens of a foreign culture. Archilochus despises elites who flaunt "the possessions of Gyges," (fr. 19 West); Phocylides opines that "an orderly polis is better than silly Nineveh" (fr. 5 West). With their access to foreign commodities and foreign wisdom, merchants threatened the city.

By adapting the model of commodity biography, *Racialized Commodities* traces "the set of inputs," to quote Hopkins and Wallerstein, "the prior transformations, the raw materials, the transportation mechanisms, the labor input into each of the material processes"[129] that conclude with the emergence of the racialized Other in Archaic and Classical Greece. When an inhabitant of sixth-century Kolophon, Miletus, or Athens gazed upon the face of an Ethiopian painted on a vase or molded into coroplastic, they were faced with the end result of a whole material and interpretive process that began with raw materials and ended with an aesthetic of the body. Such a process was writ large across mid-first-millennium Greece.

The later we go in our period, the clearer the cultural dynamic becomes. Discourses about consumerism become particularly well documented by the era of Socrates and Theaetetus' little chat. Anything—a good, a service, or a human body—was fungible with Athens' precious silver coins.[130] "All the products of the earth flow in upon us," vouches Thucydides' Pericles (2.38.2).[131] Both Thucydides and the Old Oligarch see access to goods as profoundly levelling:[132] "the masses have more enjoyment of these things than the elites and the wealthy," the latter writes (*Ps.-Xen. Ath. Pol.* 2.10).[133] Similar opinions are expressed by the poets Critias (fr. 2 West) and Hermippus (fr. 63 K-A). When slave labor enters the equation, such views become even more pointed. When Athenians tried to imagine the cultural backgrounds or the identities of the people they enslaved, they articulated their thought through that most precious commodity: silver.

Athens' might in the fifth and fourth centuries BCE was predicated on its near-monopoly over the production of silver, mined in both Attica and its holdings in the north Aegean. Silver was grotesquely exploitative, requiring a dedicated stream of enslaved laborers—usually from Thrace in the north—to mine it deep underground and smelt it on the surface out of lead-bearing ores. This was never lost to the writers of the fifth century. This is what Herodotus has to say about one of the lands where people were enslaved to work in Athens' mines:

Τῶν δὲ δὴ ἄλλων Θρηίκων ἐστὶ ὅδε νόμος· πωλέουσι τὰ τέκνα ἐπ' ἐξαγωγῇ. Τὰς δὲ παρθένους οὐ φυλάσσουσι, ἀλλ' ἐῶσι τοῖσι αὐταὶ βούλονται ἀνδράσι μίσγεσθαι, τὰς δὲ γυναῖκας ἰσχυρῶς φυλάσσουσι· καὶ ὠνέονται τὰς γυναῖκας παρὰ τῶν γονέων χρημάτων μεγάλων. Καὶ τὸ μὲν ἐστίχθαι εὐγενὲς κέκριται, τὸ δὲ ἄστικτον ἀγεννές· ἀργὸν εἶναι κάλλιστον, γῆς δὲ ἐργάτην ἀτιμότατον· τὸ ζώειν ἀπὸ πολέμου καὶ ληιστύος κάλλιστον.

Among the rest of the Thracians it is the custom to sell their children for export. They do not watch over the young women, who go for whichever man they want; their wives, however, they strictly guard, and buy them for a great price from the parents. To be tattooed is considered noble, and not tattooed humble; laziness is best, and least honored of all is the worker; living off war and brigandage is considered best (Hdt. 5.6.1-2)

Herodotus' fifth book begins with his ethnography of Thrace. Unlike his expansive coverage of Scythia in book four, the Thracian ethnography is a sketch: seven chapters in all (5.3–7), and nowhere quite as charitable. The Thracians are opposite of Greeks: they tattoo their bodies, live the life of thieves, honor not their women and children.[134] The Thracians are natural slaves: all their relationships are fundamentally commodifiable, reducible to that most precious commodity, silver coin (χρημάτων). As Timothy Taylor writes, this style of ethnography is nothing more than a "commodity digest."[135]

Then, take another writer of the fifth century. A decade after the defeat of the Persian fleet at Salamis, Aeschylus brought Xerxes' tragedy to the stage in our only surviving historical play, the *Persians* of 472 BCE. Amid the moans emanating from the women of the Persian court, we hear the truth of why the Persians lost. In 485 BCE, Athenian prospectors in the ancient mining region of Laureion hit the motherlode. Rather than distributing it to the people, the state kept the silver and used it to build its capacity—and in no way less consequential than investing in a navy (*Ps.-Aristot. Ath. Pol.* 22.7). These were the ships that defeated the Persians, and it was this spring of silver that made Athens free. No *Athenian* need sell their child for coin:

ἀργύρου πηγή τις αὐτοῖς ἐστι, θησαυρὸς χθονός
[...]
οὔτινος δοῦλοι κέκληνται φωτὸς οὐδ' ὑπήκοοι.

They [the Athenians] have a spring of silver ... they are neither slaves nor servants of any mortal. (Aes. *Pers.* 238, 242).

What Leslie Kurke calls a single, "relentlessly material"[136] logic pervades Aeschylus and Herodotus when they think about the peoples of the world. These two authors were separated by a momentous period of forty years—the rise of the Athenian Empire, the start of the Peloponnesian War, the coming of radical democracy, and so on. Yet shared between them is a calculation widely exhibited in the literature of Archaic and Classical Greece. The world and its people are commodities, to be purchased and made your own by the Greek invention of silver coin. Their bodies, cultures, and histories can be reduced to a singular logic of trade. We will return to this topic in particular in the latter part of this book.

Might this process have contributed to an idea of *race*? Keeping in mind the idea of differential treatment—the "theory and practice of applying a social, civic, or legal double standard based on ancestry"[137]—it arguably should. We might reflect on the line drawn at the beginning of the chapter between Theaetetus, the son of a miner, and the enslaved man ("boy") who serves as the unacknowledged internal narrator for the *Theaetetus*. The same commodity, silver, meant very different things for them. Theaetetus sat at one end of the chain of production; his leisurely existence was only possible because of the labor of enslaved, anonymous Thracians working deep underground. The unnamed slave had been purchased with this silver; he could be dispatched underground at any time.

To those who have adopted the moniker of premodern critical race studies, the fact certain premodern ideas of the body bear such a strong resonance with Atlantic-world conceptions of race presents the compelling case needed: in the perspective of Margo Hendricks, race presents a "bidirectional gaze ...

that looks inward even as it looks outward."[138] Critics who have peered into the beguiling eyes of Socrates have seen different things; I have been drawn to the hierarchies that gave them meaning.

Summary of Chapters

Part I of *Racialized Commodities*, entitled "The World of the Elephantine Document," offers a deep dive into the structures of trade underlaying the earliest Greek racializations of the people of Africa—known as Egyptians and Ethiopians in Greek parlance—in the seventh and sixth centuries BCE.

Following the model of commodity biography, I center my inquiry on the trade in a single commodity: natron, a mineral salt scraped from evaporated lakes around the edges of the Sahara. Around the middle of the first millennium BCE, Ionian traders sailed annually to the Nile Delta to load this commodity into their holds and return to the Aegean, where it was used in textile manufacturing, glassmaking, and other industries. (This progress is recorded in the so-called Elephantine document, an Aramaic-language trade register known formally as *TAD* C3.7.) Natron is a commodity that you have never heard of, a substance so modest that it escapes the view of any ancient author. But the tendrils of the natron trade were expansive in the culture of Archaic and Classical Greece. Using information from the Elephantine document, I trace the movements of the natron traders, demonstrating how these privileged individuals negotiated with both Egyptian and Greek economic authorities, transferred knowledge between both cultures, and carved out a comfortable lifestyle back home. Along the way, they popularized images of the people of Africa—emphasizing the physical difference of the African face—as a way of marketing commodities under their control, promoting the Nile Delta as a place of magic, exoticism, and esoteric wisdom symbolized in the morphology of its people.

Chapter 1 begins by offering a historical contextualization of the natron trade between Egypt and Greece. Building off two datasets—an appendix quantifying commodities listed in the Elephantine document, and a prosopography of Greek traders working in Late Period Egypt—I show how the bonds of commerce guided a small number of traders from the gates of Egyptian temples to the sanctuaries of major Greek cities.

Chapter 2 tracks the movement of these traders as they returned home. Archaic Greek seafarers popularized a type of religious offering known as *aegyptiaca*, or diminutive Egyptian religious symbols (scarabs, figurines, or amulets), some 6,000 of which have been excavated at a handful of sanctuaries. These objects, many of which were produced through an industrial process that required natron, were critical in popularizing images of Egypt, its culture, and the bodies of its people in late seventh- and early sixth-century Greece. Rather than seeing Egypt as "the Other," Greeks competed to display their affinity to Egypt, fabricating stories of pharaonic ancestors and Egyptian culture heroes.

Finally, in Chapter 3, I focus on a subset of these images, which depict strikingly African physiognomies in exquisite detail. Chapter 3 offers a biography of how the earliest imagery of Black bodies arrived in Greece, starting in amulet workshops outside Egyptian temples, following them to Greek sanctuaries, and then exploring how, in the modern period, these objects were interpreted as the earliest evidence for the category of a Black "race" by Classical archaeologists working during the era of racialism in the early twentieth century.

By around 550 BCE, Archaic Greece's racial imaginary possessed clear ideas of what an Egyptian or Ethiopian body was. These images, widely distributed from the poetry of Xenophanes to the vase painting of Exekias, were the exact same to first appear on *aegyptiaca*. By situating the appearance of this somatic imagery within discrete material and social processes, I shine light on one of the two poles of how race operated in ancient Greece. This is to say that the earliest images of an "African" race to appear in ancient Greece were not tools of oppression; rather they were an epiphenomenon of structured, long-distance trade between Greece and the powerful Saite Kingdom. But once Egypt was subsumed into the menacing Achaemenid Empire at the end of the sixth century, these images became distinctly negative. And with this change of circumstance, African difference had to be explained: Africans had dark skin because they lived close to the sun, or were cowardly because of the heat.

Part II, "Letters from the Pontus," turns from the south to the northern limits of the Greek world. In these chapters, I trace how Greek investigations into the light skin, hair, and eyes of people from the Pontic steppe—variously, and inconsistently, known as Scythians or Thracians—closely mapped onto the workings of the slave trade.

I begin in Chapter 4 by exploring the rise of the Greek slave trade along the northern coast of the Black Sea in the middle of the sixth century BCE.[139] Using an epigraphic corpus of thirty-seven letters inscribed by sixth-century slave traders onto lead tablets, I reconstruct synthetic life histories of individuals forcibly transformed into human commodities in newly founded Greek colonies. Building on methods developed by historians of slavery in the Atlantic world, I show that the experiences of enslaved people closely intersected with the ethnographic "knowledge"—presented by Herodotus, Hecataeus, and other Greek authors—about the cultures of the north.

Chapter 5 turns to the economics of the slave trade. Assembling three overlapping datasets—the distribution of coinage, amphorae, and shipwrecks—found along the coasts of the Black Sea, I trace the routes of the mariners who sailed between Athens and the Black Sea from the Late Archaic through the Classical Period. At the height of its empire and after, Athens created a deliberate trade surplus that left cities along the Black Sea in constant need to export bulk commodities in exchange for Athenian silver. Enslaved people were never the predominant export of Black Sea cities; rather, they represented a fallback strategy, a resource mobilized only in times of other shortage. The fact that the "human resource" produced in ancient slaving regions was only of secondary importance explains the general inconsistency of their racializations—especially when compared with the race regime of the Transatlantic Slave Trade.

Finally, in Chapter 6, I turn to the somatic indices that Classical Greeks associated with the people of the north. Two concepts are particularly common in ethnographic and medical writing: "whiteness" and "redness," both associated with Scythia and Thrace. I argue that these somatic indices were largely manufactured by Greek settlers in the north as a way of marking the people they enslaved as subhuman commodities, with particular skills, proclivities, and tendencies. Such marks on the body also served to make enslaved status "visible" to the naked eye. In the first half of the chapter, I trace how specific public spectacles in Classical Athens—namely evidentiary torture and public slave auctions—served to make race visible in a society where it was often *not*. The second half of my chapter returns to the frigid world of the steppe, searching for whether these indices were at all visible in the archaeologies of the people of the north. I argue that they do not. But the marketing that surrounded the slave trade encouraged many Greeks to believe they did.

PART I
The World of the Elephantine Document

I
A Short History of Natron

Introduction

On the [2]6th of [Phar]muthi they inspected for the [s]ea 1 [sh]ip of Protokles, Ionian, PSLD/RŠY. The silver, the customs [duty] (on) the value of the nat[ro]n which they took out to [the sea in it is si]lver, 6 karsh, 6 sh(ekels), 26 h(allurs), 2 q(uarters).[1]

ON AUGUST 7, 475 BCE, an Ionian merchant named †Protokles departed a port in the Nile Delta with a cargo of just over 15 tons of natron. His trip, and those of forty-two other merchants over a ten-month period, is only known because of the survival of an Aramaic-language customs register found at Elephantine in Egypt. Converting the 6 karsh, 6 shekels, 26 hallurs, 2 quarters silver he paid in export duties into 0.57 kg silver, we can arrive at a range of tonnages for the natron in his hold, depending on what its price was. In their annual visits to the delta, Ionian merchants like †Protokles brought to Egyptian authorities something they sorely lacked: silver, the internationally accepted medium of exchange in the eastern Mediterranean.[2]

Chapter 1 of *Racialized Commodities* offers a longitudinal survey of the trade in natron between Egypt and Greece in the mid-first millennium BCE. This chapter draws on two datasets collected at the end of this book, one that quantifies natron exports recorded in the Elephantine document, and a second that compiles a prosopography of the Greek community that followed this trade. (Named entries are marked with †.)[3] Silver and natron were only two of a bewildering number of commodities carried along on bottoms between Egypt and Greece in this period. Imported from Egypt were grain,[4] fibrous products like sails, rope, and tackle,[5] and wool;[6] Egypt imported oil, wine,[7] wood of whatever quality,[8] and medicinal earths.[9] But natron? The Elephantine document is nearly the only ancient documentary source to mention a trade in this commodity. Known to mineralogists as sodium bicarbonate decahydrate ($NaCO_3 \cdot 10H_2O$), this salty evaporite was scraped from dry lakebeds in Egypt's western desert and exported throughout the Mediterranean. It was used for textile bleaching, medicine, bathing, and—as we will explore more extensively in Chapters 2 and 3—early glassmaking.

Unpacking the mystery of why humble, unheralded natron figured so conspicuously in Egypt's balance sheet will lead us on a wide-ranging disquisition of the commercial, cultural, and religious ties that linked Egypt and Greece at the middle of the first millennium BCE. To Greeks, natron was a precious raw chemical with miraculous properties. But from the perspective of the Saite and Achaemenid governments, natron was what Regina Grafe calls a "loss leader":[10] a bulk, cheaply available commodity that could fill the holds of the Ionian ships on their return voyages. For them, the real function of the natron trade was to enable the collection of valuable customs duties in an additional Aegean commodity, silver. By the time of the Elephantine document, these revenues had become a small, but measurably significant, part of Egypt's annual tribute of 700 silver talents to the Achaemenids (Hdt. 3.91.2).[11]

At the beginning of his 1986 commodity biography of sugar, Sidney Mintz poetically envisioned the "mysteries" created by the transfer of commodities from one place to another:

> The chemical and mechanical transformations by which substances are bent to human use and become unrecognizable to those who know them in nature have marked our relationship to nature for almost as long as we have been human. Indeed, some would say that it is those very transformations that define our humanity. But the division of labor by which such transformations are realized can impart additional mystery to the technical processes. When the locus of manufacture and that of use are separated in time and space, when the makers and the users are as little known to each other as the processes of manufacture and use themselves, the mystery will deepen.[12]

The intermingling of commodities, institutions, and the people associated with each facilitated an unprecedented engagement between Greek and Egyptian cultures starting in the seventh century BCE. It created a tangible bridge over which Egyptian religious ideas, historiographies (Chapter 2), and imaginaries of the human body (Chapter 3) made themselves available to be appropriated in Greece. But as any use of the word "appropriation" implies,[13] borrowings flowed through specific channels and served specific purposes. Simply put, †Protokles could not *just* sail to Egypt. Along his keel travelled an enormously detailed body of knowledge. There was the question of demand. Who would buy natron in Greece, particularly when there were other commodities available with similar mineral properties? How did one navigate to the delta, where the annual flood of the Nile presented specific challenges and opportunities? And how did one negotiate with the great pylon temples of the delta that regulated trade under the Saite dynasty, or the "house of the king" (*byt mlk'*) that lorded over foreign trade under the Achaemenids? Facilitating each step of the process were a community of specialists, fixers, and interpreters who settled permanently in Egypt, married locally, and knew ways of the delta intimately. The history of how Greeks came to see Egypt and its people as mystical, exotic, and of a different substance than themselves flows through their activities.

This chapter begins by surveying our knowledge of natron from the ancient authors who described it most: the Greco-Roman medical tradition and Egyptian texts, where it is presented as a decidedly less exotic substance. In the following section, I explore the prosopography of the Egyptian natron trade, looking at how the structures of trust that bound Egyptian authorities with Greek merchants facilitated the speedy conveyance of the commodity—while also propagated Egyptian ways of seeing the world. Finally, in the concluding section I look at how natron figures in the ethnography of Herodotus, our most extensive chronicler of the Greek community in Egypt. As I argue, natron offered itself as a commodity "good to think with" when it came to imagining Egypt's culture. Used to purify the bodies of priests while alive, and preserve the body after death, natron (in the Greek imagination) occupied a special place in Herodotus' conception of Egyptian difference.

The basis for this chapter is collected in two appendixes: Appendix 1, which presents a quantification of the Greco-Egyptian natron trade, and Appendix 2, which collects the prosopography of Greeks in Egypt in the sixth and fifth centuries BCE.

Demand and Supply

We should begin with the question of our sources.

†Protokles' voyage was one of forty-two departures recorded in a document known today as the Elephantine papyrus (*TAD* C3.7). The Elephantine document is a palimpsest: at some point in the late fifth century BCE, it had been erased and reused to record the earliest extant version of the *Story of Aḥiqar*, a narrative relating the wisdom of its eponymous hero centuries earlier during the height of the Assyrian Empire.[14] First discovered in the early twentieth

century at the Achaemenid garrison town of Elephantine, the underlying text was published by Bezalel Porten and Ada Yardeni in 1993.[15] Underneath, Porten and Yardeni found traces of what remains the sole surviving customs register from all antiquity. This Aramaic-language document records export duties levied on some thirty-six Ionian and six Phoenician ships during year 11 of a fifth-century Achaemenid monarch, usually understood to be Xerxes. Some commentators identify the port in question as Naukratis, although this is far from certain.[16] The thirty-six captains of what the document calls Ionian ships came from the city of Phaselis (*ywny psldšy/pslršy*).[17] On entry, the Ionian captains paid a tax on ship size in gold, a flat tax in silver, as well as duty in silver on imported oil.[18] (Many ships carried in addition wine, wood, and empty transport amphorae, but these were not taxed.) Export duties were calculated in silver solely on the value of natron.[19] The six Phoenician ship captains pay their duties partially in kind.[20]

The centrality of natron in the Elephantine document was puzzling for a number of reasons. Natron is not an *unknown* commodity in our ancient sources, but it was not one commonly encountered. Antiquity's most extensive discussion of natron and its provenance is a confused narrative offered by the Roman Pliny the Elder (*NH* 31.46), who seems to believe it had metal-like qualities.[21] In fact, Pliny is most interested in natron as a kind of medicinal earth—a natural substance capable of curing ailments for unknown reasons.[22] Like other ancient medical writers, Pliny was prone to interpret the exotic provenance of medical commodities as the source of their power.[23] As such, geographical labels functioned as guarantees of "quality." The ancients policed these labels to the extent they could, but their ability to do so was shaky at best. At one point, an Aristophantic speaker (*Frogs* 709–13) mocks a bathhouse operator who tries to pass off the dregs (κονίας) of used-up "Kimolian earth" and pseudo-natron (ψευδολίτρου) as the real thing.[24] But how could he *really* tell?

Pliny's chapter, scattered asides in the Hippocratic texts, and even Aristophanes' thoughts together represent the bare remains of a whole ancient literature on natron that can be traced in some form at least as far back as the fifth century BCE.[25] At least one writer, Theophrastus (31.46.101), had authored a treatise solely on natron in the third century BCE (cf. Dio. Laert. 5.42.15). The fifth-century Hippocratic texts, not expressly referred to by Pliny, take contradictory positions on whether natron, alum, and other minerals were good. The author of *Airs, Waters, Places*, dating to the second half of the fifth century BCE, inveighs against the many people who think "springs from rocks . . . where there is hot water, or iron, copper, silver, gold, sulfur, alum, bitumen, or natron"[26] are healthy (*AWP* 7). "They are lying," the author harshly responds, "out of their lack of expertise in saline waters" (*AWP* 7).[27] Other Hippocratic texts seem to present the "debate" over natron and alum to one over identity. Laurence Totelin has observed that Hippocratic recipes frequently call for "Egyptian" mineral evaporates over local varieties precisely because they were more expensive; hence the "Egyptian salt" (Αἰγύπτιος ἅλς), "Egyptian alum" (Αἰγυπτίη στυπτηρίη), and "Egyptian natron" (Αἰγύπτιον νίτρον) repeatedly encountered in the corpus.[28] Making claims about the health benefits of rare and exotic substances was a way for elites to articulate identity against the background of a medical tradition that—devoid of modern science—could not ultimately promise better results for the rich than the poor.

Without pressing the matter too hard, medicinal narratives are only of limited use for a scholar interested in practical questions. Nearly absent from Pliny, the Hippocratic corpus, or other ancient sources are the basics. When was natron harvested? Who harvested it? What was the process? What was the price? We in fact lack a succinct discussion of these matters up until the colonial period, when European natural historians suddenly became *very interested* in Egypt's natural resources. C. S. Sonnini and Vivant Denon write:

> Natron may be found during the whole year, except at the period when the lakes cover the ground from which it is procured; but it is found in greatest abundance in August, the season when the lakes are of smallest size, and when the sunbeams have exerted the greatest influence in hardening the sediment. This month, therefore, is the period during which it is chiefly collected. It is separated from the ground with iron instruments, made for that purpose. It is carried on the backs of camels to Terané, a village upon the Nile, whence it is sent to Cairo, or to Rosetta: from the latter of which places it is carried to Alexandria, and thence to those foreign parts where it continues to be in demand. The purposes to which it is applied have already been mentioned. The quantity collected is usually twenty-five thousand quintals; though, were the demand increased, a much greater quantity could be procured. The usual price is from fifteen to eighteen medines the quintal.[29]

There is an obvious caveat here. Accounts of the natron trade by the European travelers who flocked to Egypt on the heels of Napoleon cannot be taken at face value. They were clearly interested in producing a map of Egypt's mineral wealth.[30] But their testimony contains key details about the preindustrial natron trade. The first is that natron has a specific seasonality: August is the harvest season.³¹ The second is that natron sources were utilized *opportunistically* and not *systematically*. But most important of all is that natron was a relatively common product found along the edges of the desert. During the twentieth century, many commentators drew on the medicinal narratives to interpret natron as a commodity with a specific *geography of production* in antiquity: Alfred Lucas and J. R. Harris, for instance, identified natron production centers mentioned by Pliny (31.46.111) and Strabo (17.1.23) with Kom el-Barnugi in the northwestern Nile Delta and the Wadi el-Natrun along its western edges.³² (Indeed, both of these sources were thoroughly harvested in the nineteenth and twentieth centuries.)³³ And these sites *probably were* certainly utilized in antiquity, as Roman glass kilns at the Wadi el-Natrun³⁴ and Kom el-Barnugi make clear.³⁵ But to say that natron in ancient Egypt only came from specific locales would be incorrect. Given the ephemeral techniques of salt-drying in antiquity, and the marshiness of the landscapes where it was carried out, we should not worry too much about our lack of an archaeology of ancient natron harvesting³⁶ (Figure 1.1). We have a good idea where it took place.

FIGURE 1.1 Abandoned soda-evaporation complex, Dale Dry Lakebed, California, March 2018. Photograph by author.

The better way to think about the provenance of natron is as ubiquitous commodity of ancient Egypt. Unlike in Greece and Rome, Egyptian authors only weakly identify provenance for mineral evaporites. Such provenance indicates that natron was a product of the desert fringe. A fifth-century Aramaic taxation document from Saqqara mentions "natron from the east."[37] Even earlier, the Middle Kingdom *Tale of the Eloquent Peasant* begins with its protagonist Khunanup, a peasant from the Wadi el-Natrun, loading his donkeys with salt and natron (secs. 2.3–4). When Khunanup travels to Herakleopolis to complain to the royal court that his trade goods had been stolen by an unscrupulous official named Nemtinakht, their response is pithy: "is this a cause for punishing Nemtinakht, on account of a little natron and a little salt?" (secs. 78–79).[38] Even when the commodities had been carried over at great effort over long distance they were not considered particularly valuable.

Nemtinakht's association of natron as a cheap thing like salt is rather typical. Three mineral evaporites are encountered with some regularity in ancient Egyptian texts. Indeed, natron comes a distant second to salt in its frequency in Egyptian texts. Natron appears as a trade good as early as the Old Kingdom, and its etymologies in other languages suggest that Egypt had long exported it in some quantity. The most typical Egyptian words for natron are *ḥsmn* or *nṯry*, which is derived from the verb "to purify," *nṯrd*.[39] The words for natron in other languages are formed off *nṯry*, including the Akkadian *nitiru/nitru*, Hebrew *neter*, Syriac *nethrû*, Aramaic *nitra*, Latin *nitrum*, and Greek νίτρον or λίτρον.[40] By the time of the New Kingdom, a third mineral evaporite, alum, begins to make occasional appearances in our sources. Although harvested in Egypt's western desert, alum has a foreign etymology. Alum was known as *'ibnw*, related to Akkadian *aban gabî* (*CAD* G s.v.). There is some thought that alum was considered by Egyptians to be a type of natron.[41]

Natron harvesting appears in two key Pharaonic texts in close association with salt, fishing, fowling, and gathering activities in the delta. *O.Gardiner 86*, a New Kingdom document sometimes considered scribal exercise, lists the assets of a real (or imagined) estate in the delta owned by the temple of Amun in Thebes.[42] A list of workers attached to the estate (81.12) details "cattle herdsmen, goat herds, shepherds, swine-keepers, [.] donkey grooms, *ptrw*-animal tenders, bird-keepers, fishermen, fowlers, vintners, salt workers (?), natron workers, papyrus [. . .] gatherers cutting in the thicket, rope makers, mat-makers (?)" in one place. Another document, *P.Rainer* 53, is a description of the nineteenth dynasty capital Pi-Rammeses and its resources by a scribe named Pbes. Listing the resources of the capital—fish, carobs (2.4), onions, leeks (2.5)—"its ships sail forth and moor, (so that) food and victuals are in it every day" (2.10)—the products of two special waters, salt (from the "waters of Horus") and natron (from the "*P3-ḥr* waters"), are included.[43] These same waters also provide rushes ("waters of Horus," 2.12) and flax ("*P3-ḥr* waters," 3.4). A twentieth-dynasty endowment inscription from the temple of Khnum at Elephantine explicitly groups natron and salt-gatherers with fishermen and fowlers (*AR* 4.148). Rather than appearing marked with geographical provenance, it seems possible, at least conceptually, to gather natron anywhere swampy, and perhaps anywhere salty.[44]

Natron and salt were common enough to have fit into the genre of scribal idealizations of the deltaic landscape that flourished in the New Kingdom.[45] *O.Gardiner* 28 fantasizes what it would be like to own an estate large enough to produce any possible resources that one could want, and even surplus to export overseas.[46] The similarity between the author of *O.Gardiner* 28 and visions of Hesiodic self-sufficiency (Hesiod's call in the *Works and Days* [631–32] to take the produce of one's farm and "haul your swift ship down to the sea and stow a convenient cargo in it, so that you may bring home profit")[47] belie the larger, and more difficult problem behind Lucas and Harris' search for the source of natron. The Egypt of *O.Gardiner* 28 was not fundamentally different from Hesiod's Greece: the basic commodities in circulation could be widely obtained, but were subject to periodic scarcities that encouraged redistribution.[48]

Our foray into early European and ancient Egyptian discussions of the natron trade helps us distance ourselves from the logic of connoisseurship so ingrained in the Greeks and Romans—as well as enables us to pick out useful details in Greek and Roman accounts. Vitruvius speaks of using only the "flower of natron" (*cum nitri flore*) for industrial purposes (7.11.1), a substance that only crystalized under precise conditions.[49] Harvesting salt, trona, and natron required evaporites to sit in piles after harvesting to gradually leech out impurities, as Pliny himself indicates (*NH* 31.46.105). And finally, a comparative angle can clarify issues in reading the very small number of documentary texts written in Greek that mention the natron trade. In a letter dating to August 31 (11 Epiph.), 250 BCE, a correspondent in a papyrus from the Zenon archive warns that he will have to shut down textile production unless more natron was obtained soon (*P.Cair.Zen.* 3.59304.4). This suggests that late summer—right as the natron harvest began—was a period when newly harvested natron lagged in replenishing the market.

We can find hints of this tension between supply and demand in the Elephantine document—as well as strategies taken by exporters to ensure a reliable supply (Figure 1.2). Natron exports were relatively stable over the

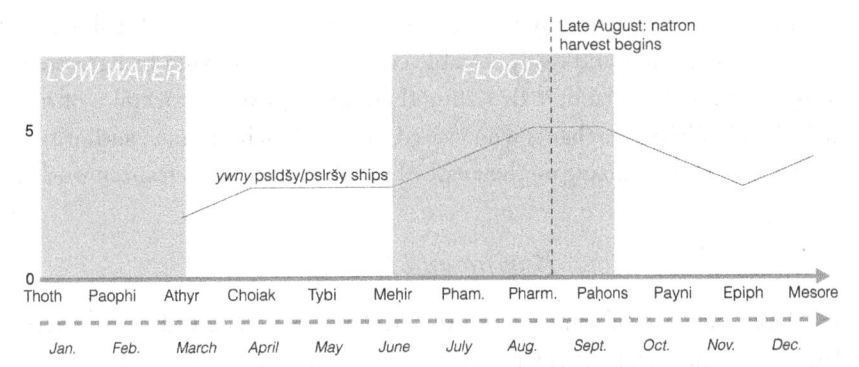

FIGURE 1.2 Arrivals of Ionian (*ywny psldšy/pslršy*) merchants in the Elephantine papyrus by month.

course of the year, only completely ceasing during the two winter months when low water made navigating the Nile Delta impossible.[50] The peak season was between the Egyptian months Phamenoth (June 13–July 14, 475 BCE) and Mesore (November 10–December 19, 475 BCE), when between five and six ships departed monthly to Greece with cargoes of natron. The increase in arrivals over the summer was due to the start of the Nile flood, which coincided with the height of the Mediterranean sailing season.[51]

But natron cargoes varied greatly even within the same month. Parmuthi (July 13–August 12, 475 BCE), at the height of the season, is the only month for which complete prices exist. The month begins with the departure of three ships, who buy natron taxed at an average of 0.95 kg silver. †Protokles and †Glaphyros, whose ships left at the end of the month, carried somewhat less. †Protokles, departing on 26 Parmuthi, paid an export duty of 0.57 kg silver, which was 69 percent of the month's average of 0.83 kg silver and 58 percent of the maximum recorded duty of 0.99 kg silver. †Glaphyros, departing on the 30th, paid 0.72 kg, or 87 percent of the average and 73 percent of the maximum (see Appendix 1 tbs. 1a–c for tabulation).

Is it the case that stockpiles were running out by the end of the month? The state of the manuscript is that we do not know individual levies for sea captains departing in Pachons, the following month. Although the Elephantine palimpsest is our only evidence, it appears that natron exports carried on in greater quantity during the second half of the year, as the annual harvest arrived in repositories, than in the first. The enormous storage magazines found at the Egyptian temples that loomed over Egypt's Mediterranean ports helped exporters compensate against the lag between the sailing season and natron's production cycle. Horden and Purcell's maxim summarizing the basic logic of

the Mediterranean economy fits well here: "diversify; store; redistribute."⁵²
Natron was an inert and easily storable commodity that could be harvested
using relatively little labor.⁵³ By selling their already extant stockpiles of natron to the Ionian merchants who visited the delta each summer, authorities
in Egypt were capitalizing on their ease of access to the Mediterranean world.

Buying and Selling

In March or April of some year in the Archaic Period, according to a very
late source, the merchant †Herostratos of Naukratis was caught up in a storm
off the Nile Delta.⁵⁴ He had just been in Paphos on Cyprus, where he had
purchased a figure of Aphrodite. When all hope was lost, she intervened to
save the ship:

> κατὰ δὲ τὴν τρίτην πρὸς ταῖς εἴκοσιν Ὀλυμπιάδα ὁ Ἡρόστρατος, πολίτης
> ἡμέτερος ἐμπορίᾳ χρώμενος καὶ χώραν πολλὴν περιπλέων, προσσχών
> ποτε καὶ Πάφῳ τῆς Κύπρου ἀγαλμάτιον Ἀφροδίτης σπιθαμιαῖον,
> ἀρχαῖον τῇ τέχνῃ, ὠνησάμενος ᾔει φέρων εἰς τὴν Ναύκρατιν. καὶ αὐτῷ
> πλησίον φερομένῳ τῆς Αἰγύπτου ἐπεὶ χειμὼν αἰφνίδιον ἐπέπεσεν καὶ [οὐ]
> συνιδεῖν οὐκ ἦν ὅπου γῆς ἦσαν, κατέφυγον ἅπαντες ἐπὶ τὸ τῆς Ἀφροδίτης
> ἄγαλμα σῴζειν αὐτοὺς αὐτὴν δεόμενοι. ἡ δὲ θεός (προσφιλὴς γὰρ τοῖς
> Ναυκρατίταις ἦν) αἰφνίδιον ἐποίησε πάντα τὰ παρακείμενα αὐτῇ μυρρίνης
> χλωρᾶς πλήρη ὀδμῆς τε ἡδίστης ἐπλήρωσεν τὴν ναῦν ἤδη ἀπειρηκόσι τοῖς
> ἐμπλέουσιν τὴν σωτηρίαν [διὰ τὴν πολλὴν ναυτίαν γενομένου τε ἐμέτου
> πολλοῦ], καὶ ἡλίου ἐκλάμψαντος κατιδόντες τοὺς ὅρμους ἧκον εἰς τὴν
> Ναύκρατιν. καὶ ὁ Ἡρόστρατος ἐξορμήσας τῆς νεὼς μετὰ τοῦ ἀγάλματος,
> ἔχων καὶ τὰς αἰφνίδιον αὐτῷ ἀναφανείσας χλωρὰς μυρρίνας, ἀνέθηκεν
> ἐν τῷ τῆς Ἀφροδίτης ἱερῷ, θύσας δὲ τῇ θεῷ καὶ ἀναθεὶς τῇ Ἀφροδίτῃ
> τἄγαλμα, καλέσας δὲ καὶ ἐφ' ἑστίασιν ἐν αὐτῷ τῷ ἱερῷ τοὺς προσήκοντ
> ας καὶ τοὺς οἰκειοτάτους ἔδωκεν ἑκάστῳ καὶ στέφανον ἐκ τῆς μυρρίνης, ὃν
> καὶ τότε ἐκάλεσε Ναυκρατίτην.

> During the 23rd Olympiad, Herostratos, a fellow-citizen of ours who
> roamed many lands as a trader, landed at Paphos on Cyprus and
> bought a statue of Aphrodite about a few feet high, ancient in craftsmanship. He took it with him to Naukratis when he left. They were
> coming close to Egypt when all of a sudden, a storm hit and they were
> not able to tell where land was. They all fled to the statue of Aphrodite
> begging her to save them. The goddess—she was after all a friend to

the people of Naukratis—suddenly intervened on behalf of the sailors begging for their lives, covering everything around her with green myrtle and filling the ship with the loveliest scent on account of all the vomit. When the sun came out, they saw the harbor and came into Naukratis. Herostratos disembarked from the ship with the statue and the green myrtle branches that had appeared so suddenly and offered them in the temple of Aphrodite, burning the branches for the goddess and dedicating the statue to her. Inviting his attendants (the sailors?) and family for a feast, he gave each a myrtle wreath, which he called "Naukratite." (Polycharmos *FGrHist* 640 F 1)

Polycharmos' story is an obvious etiology. (Leaving the fantastic details aside, Naukratis was not on the coast, and it was not remotely founded in time for the 23rd Olympiad of 688–85 BCE). But as a story, it is useful: the voyage of †Herostratos captures the kind of narrative of trade, disaster, and salvation at sea that widely circulated in the world of the Elephantine document.[55] These stories were intimately connected with the very real infrastructure that facilitated the trade in raw commodities between Egyptians and Greeks. Behind the legendary journeys of the great Archaic merchants—†Charaxos, Demaratus, Kolaios, †Sostratos, and (more dubiously) †Solon—sailed a detailed body of knowledge about when, where, and how to trade in ancient Egypt. This knowledge was critical in the Greek appropriation of Egyptian ways of seeing the world in the middle of the first millennium.

Long-distance trade in Late Archaic and Early Classical Greece was dominated by a relatively small, international clique. It is true that the vast majority of Mediterranean voyages in any period were local: as Hesiod advises his readers, spring is the time to "haul your swift ship down to the sea and put all the freight on board" (*WD* 672) and redistribute the commodities you have for the ones you do not.[56] Horden and Purcell called this mode of transport *cabotage*.[57] But other mariners specialized in long-distance trade. These were the men known in the Roman Period as the *ochlos nautikos*, members of a transient maritime counterculture that sat at an uneasy distance from the regulated world of the *polis*.[58] Long-distance mariners congregated at a handful of major Mediterranean ports, including Gravisca in Italy and Naukratis in Egypt, and their dedications clustered at some even more exotic locations including Snake Island[59] and Bejkush[60] in the Black Sea and Palagruža[61] in the Adriatic. As Elizabeth Greene (2018) has surveyed, kitchen wares found in Late Archaic and Early Classical shipwrecks leave us with the strong suggestion that the same ships habitually sailed the same long-distance

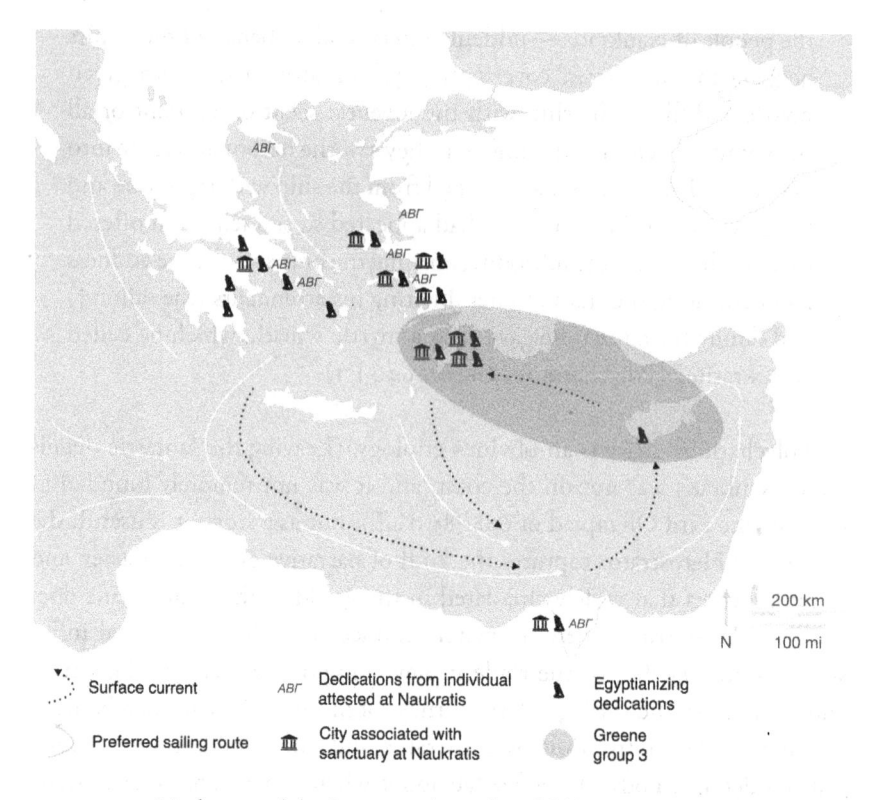

FIGURE 1.3 Naukratis and the Aegean in the sixth and fifth centuries BCE. Assemblages of Greco-Egyptian *Aegyptiaca*—the topic of Chapter 2—are only mapped if they number thirty or more objects.

routes. The vessels that form her Group 3 of Late Archaic/Early Classical shipwrecks (Figure 1.3) sailed regularly between East Greece, Cyprus, and perhaps the Levant and Egypt.[62] Such regular voyages might be confirmed by the two visits made by a merchant named †Glaphyros to Egypt in the Elephantine document, only a few months apart.

Few Mediterranean ports loom larger in our understanding of trade in Archaic and Classical Greece than Naukratis. Naukratis was one of two cities founded along the Nile's Canopic branch during the Saite Period that served as taxation bottlenecks to monitor and control Greek access to the Nile.[63] Right at the river-mouth sat the waterlogged city of Thonis-Herakleion, where a massive pylon temple to Amun-Gereb greeted travelers coming over the sea. The dynastic capital of Sais was located a short distance from Naukratis by canal.[64] Although Herodotus attributes the foundation of Naukratis to the wily pharaoh Amasis (Eg. Ahmose, r. 570–26 BCE), archaeological evidence suggests that the city was founded right around the time Greek traders began sailing to the delta in numbers circa 620 BCE under Psammetichos II (Eg. Psamtik I, r. c. 664–10 BCE).[65] It was one of several foreign merchant quarters to form in the shadow of Egyptian temples in the Late Period.[66] Greek merchants arriving anywhere else in the delta were compelled to make a long and costly diversion there.[67]

Naukratis is unusual among the ports frequented by long-distance merchants in the Archaic Period in featuring relatively permanent trading infrastructure.[68] Naukratis was a "house of the port" (*pr-mryt*), where taxes on imported and exported commodities were collected by temple officials.[69] The first customs officials here were appointed under Psamtik II (r. 595–89 BCE), when we hear of an individual named Neshor holding the title of "Agent of the Gate of the Foreign Countries of the Great Green Area."[70] The reign of Amasis has produced more evidence for state supervision of foreign trade. One Nachtohorheb appears to have held Neshor's office during this period.[71] Another set of officials who monitored foreign trade, known as "Overseers of the Antechamber" (*ḏm ḏ-rȝ rwt*), are known from sealings; one named Ahmes-sa-Neith was active at Naukratis.[72] Finally, an official named †Neferpre-sa-Neith, son of *Grḫs*, known from an inscribed *naophoros* statue (Hermitage 8499) dedicated by him later in life, was supervisor over Naukratis during the year 561 BCE under Amasis.

More surprising was the very substantial infrastructure built by Greeks at this foreign port. A line of Greek sanctuaries lined the waterfront north of the massive Egyptian temple of Amun Re-Baded, which anchored the city.[73] Established on land donated by the Pharaoh for the benefit of "those who did not want to live in Egypt" (Hdt. 2.178.1), these sanctuaries served as a kind of home-away-from-home for visitors. The largest of them, the Hellenion, was controlled by a consortium of Greek cities, while others were subsidiary cults tied to the worship of Samian Hera and Zeus Hellenios on Aegina.[74] The sanctuary of Aphrodite featured a notable Cypriot presence.[75] Many of the Greek cities most heavily invested in Naukratis hosted sanctuaries in their own territory where Egyptianizing religious dedications, known as *aegyptiaca*, were dedicated in large numbers at the turn of the sixth century. Such practices, which were once interpreted as a kind of mariner's religion,[76] will be discussed in much greater depth in Chapter 2.

As at Gravisca and Palagruža, visitors to the Naukratis sanctuaries were enthusiastic dedicators: excavators in the late nineteenth century collected some 2,800 inscribed sherds from the site, originally part of vessels dedicated during feasting. Among these inscriptions were found the names of a large number of dedicators, among which were individuals named †Hyblesios, †Lethaios, †Sostratos, and †Zoilos, who might be identifiable at other ports.[77] Naukratis was the locus of an entire leisure literature—featuring boastful captains and deceptive sex workers (discussed further in Chapter 3)—that would eventually reached the ears of Polycharmos.[78] Perhaps inspired by Polycharmos' story, the excavator Ernest Gardner dubiously reconstructed on inscription mentioning a dedicator named †Kaiqos to read Εἰ]ς Να[ύ]κρατιν [ἀφικόμεν]ος [Ἀφροδίτη]ι Καῖqο[ς ἀνέθηκεν, "Kaiqos dedicated to Aphrodite when he came to Naukratis." And indeed, coming to Naukratis was a momentous occasion. It was then that business could begin.

Up to the Achaemenid invasion in 525 BCE, the Egyptian state institution Greek merchants dealt with most were the temples. Egyptian temples evolved into massive, fortified repositories for commodities over the Third Intermediate and Late Periods, inhabited semi-permanently by priests and their dependents.[79] Barry Kemp's likening of them to the acropolises of Greek cities is apt: in the flat landscape of the Nile Delta, they served functions of storage, administration, taxation, arbitration, and defense.[80] In addition to exercising state functions, temples had a long tradition of entrepreneurship, employing captains to sell commodities under their control and attracting merchants from as far away as the Levant.[81] Their economic activities left an outsized record, both in documents and archaeologically: although it is certain that ships docked up and down the waterfront, the monumental quay at the temple of Amun Re-Baded at Naukratis is the only permanent docking installation found yet by excavators.[82]

Temples were not simple extensions the state in ancient Egypt. Although they were crucial sites of state administration, as religious foundations they were technically separate from the Pharaoh.[83] At the start of his reign, Pharaoh Psamtik I (r. c. 664–10 BCE) had consolidated his power by granting vast tracts of land in the western delta to the temple of Amun Re at Thebes.[84] The temple of Neith at Sais also demanded substantial concessions, and several of its officials sat in positions of power through the history of the regime.[85] The reality of these grants meant that when the state attempted to tax foreigners entering the western delta, it was forced to balance the exercise of state authority with longstanding prerogatives of the temples. Evidence for the tensions between temples and state over customs revenue can be found in a pair of matching basalt stele erected at the massive pylon temples of Amun-Gebed and Amun Re-Baded at Thonis-Herakleion and Naukratis during the reign of Necatanebo I (r. 379–60 BCE). The stelae dedicate 10 percent of import duty on Greek ships sailing into the Canopic mouth of the Nile to the domain of Neith at Sais. In her recent edition of the text, Anne-Sophie von Bomhard argues that this arrangement was likely a revival of a tax concession first granted under the Saite kings.[86]

The massive disruption caused by the Achaemenid invasion of 525 BCE raises questions about the extent to which Saite fiscal practices continued into the late sixth and fifth centuries BCE.[87] The taxation formulae of the Elephantine papyrus were obvious Achaemenid creations: under the Persians, fiscal authority was removed from the temples and centralized under the "house of the king" (Arm. *byt mlk*). The vocabulary used in the document is almost exclusively the language of Persian imperial administration.[88] Indeed, Herodotus appears to suggest that Naukratis was no longer the sole site of state regulation of trade during his visit in the 430s BCE (2.179.1).[89] Nonetheless, the name of the *ad valorem* export tax levied on natron (*tšy*) appears to be an Egyptian word (derived from Demotic *t3 šyyet*, "customs duty").[90] Might this reflect a longer continuity in how both the Saite and Achaemenid states regulated the export trade in natron?

If so, we can track the evolution of the Greco-Egyptian natron trade over a period of several hundred years, reflecting an uneasy cooperation among temples, the state, foreign merchants, and two different dynasties of Egypt. The earliest references to natron exports from Egypt are more or less incidental: in a letter from Assyrian Nineveh, dating to between 672 and 69 BCE (*SAA* 16.82), we hear about a hapless clerk named Marduk-šarru-uṣur who had lost track of a quantity of Egyptian alum and natron from temple storage.[91] The picture changes substantially in the latter half of the seventh century, under the reign of Psamtik II. There is, for instance, some suggestion that Sappho's brother †Charaxos was involved in an early iteration of the natron trade. (She herself mentions natron [λίτρον] in a single word fragment [189 L-P].)[92] By the middle of the sixth century, the trade in mineral evaporites between Egypt and elsewhere would become much more advanced. In 551–50 BCE, a merchant named Nadin-aḫi led two caravans from somewhere in the Levant to Sumeria, carrying dyes, copper, and Egyptian alum.[93] Around 548 BCE, Herodotus (2.180) reports that the pharaoh Amasis dedicated 1,000 talents of alum (the equivalent of 27 tons) to the temple of Apollo at Delphi. The Greek settlers at Naukratis added to this an additional 20 minae (a paltry 11.42 kg).

It is impossible to say how important the trade in mineral evaporites was in Archaic Naukratis compared with the exchange of other commodities. But it was clearly present, and growing in importance. If the natron trade represented in the Elephantine document was a strategy by temple or state authorities to raise silver for the Achaemenid government, it was in all likelihood an exchange that had been pioneered a century earlier under the Saites. The men involved in it were sitting on a pile of generational knowledge.

The Ties That Bind

What enabled the quick and problem-free voyages of †Protokles and †Glaphyros in the eleventh year of a fifth-century Achaemenid monarch were a network of interpersonal relationships over a century in the making. Yesterday and today, the border is a menace. Even well-heeled Egyptians were prone to view customs agents with trepidation.[94] Ionian merchants in fifth-century Egypt had an advantage in this regard: they could rely on an ancestral class of †"translators" to speed their entries and exits from port. The end result of this system was the perhaps unusual speed at which the natron trade operated. In a world of interminable port delays, natron merchants could expect to spend eleven days in port or less (Table 1.1).

Table 1.1 Port stays in the Elephantine document

Captain	Arrive	Depart	Days in port
Unknown	30 Athyr	10 Choiak	10
Unknown	18 Tybi	x Meḥir	12+
Tmt-- son of *--sy*	20 Meḥir	10 Phamenoth	20
Myrsilos	x Paḥons	10 Paḥons	9-
---gwt---	7 Paḥons	18 Paḥons	11
Panteleon son of Moschos	10 Paḥons	22 Paḥons	12
[---] son of Yriglos	[15] Paḥons	27 Paḥons	12
----gl[s]	[15+] Paḥons	30 Paḥons	15-
Timokedes son of Mikkos	9 Payni	17 Payni	8
[--] son of *-mn*	[10+] Payni	21 Payni	11-
Unknown	17 Payni	26 Payni	9
Unknown	20 Payni	27 Payni	7
Šwmn, son of *Šmnds*	2[0+] Payni	[30] Payni	10
Charisthenes son of Prytkm	[x Mesore]	9 Mesore	9-
Iokles	[x Mesore]	[10] Mesore	8-
Phanes	[x Mesore]	2[2] Mesore	11+
Unknown	12 Mesore	25 Mesore	13
		Avg. days in port	11

Port stays in the age of sail tended to be long. Aside from the physical time it took to load and unload ships, negotiations with authorities, bargaining, crew hiring, reprovisioning, and waiting for a good wind all took time. At certain points in Mediterranean history, attempts were made to limit port delays; the Byzantine-era Rhodian sea law, for instance, penalized merchants who held captains in port for over twenty days.[95]

Some people got to skip the line. One New Kingdom record portrays the benefits—as well as the limitations—of showing up to port with the backing of a temple. *P. Turin* 2008 + 2016 relates the voyage of a ship operated by the first prophet of the temple of Amun in Thebes on a trip to lower Egypt to exchange textiles for sesame oil.[96] The ship additionally carried a coterie of specialists, including scribes, temple officials, and other merchants, or *šwty*, who engaged in other trade for the temple's benefit along the side, including in fish, salt, and reeds.[97] The trading world portrayed in *P. Turin* 2008 + 2016 was highly ritualized, involving days of waiting, specific personnel, and the involvement of religious authorities. Recording their progress day by day, the ship's scribe records their stay in Memphis as twelve days (rt. II.23) while their stay in the following port at the Pylons of the House of Osiris, a day's sail away, was seven (rt. III.15). In both ports, trade could only begin after days of waiting. At Memphis, nothing happens until the arrival of the 'Staff of Amun' on the seventh day, after which trading begins (rt. I.14). At the Pylons of the House of Osiris, it is not until the third day when a party leaves the ship to go to the temple (rt. III.3).

Was this *really* as fast as things could go? We might take perspective from a second tranche of fifth-century documents also preserved from Elephantine. In the letters of Makkibanit, an Aramaean mercenary and small-time merchant resident in Syene, we see trade portrayed as both happenstance and sharply constrained by the costs involved in transportation and communication. Thus we see him in one letter asking his sister in Syene for a small quantity of wool in exchange for a quantity of silver.[98] In another, he asks his father Psami to send northward enough leather to make a single garment and some barley in exchange for fancy striped textiles and scented oils. The problem is that "[I] have not found a man to bring them to you."[99] Not much later, Makkibanit writes to his sisters Tarou and Tabi to complain that "nothing is brought to us from Syene . . . Sheil [another individual] has not dispatched me a letter or anything else."[100] Of course, Makkibanit was a mercenary by profession and not in Egypt primarily to trade. Nevertheless, the limitations in his activities show the benefits of having the sanction and support of a major institutional actor. This support was not something just any foreigner could access.

Greco-Egyptian trade in the sixth and fifth centuries BCE was dependent on a class of people that Herodotus calls †Translators (Ἑρμηνέες), whom he describes (2.154.2) as Egyptians who had been taught to learn Greek during the first generation of settlement.[101] These figures are a minor presence in the Greek epigraphy of the fifth century BCE. Two fragmentary decrees from Lindos issued as late as 411 BCE (*SIG*³ 110, 110 app.) single out a pair of men for honors, one named †Damoxenos "living in Egypt" (ἐν Αἰγύπτωι οἰκέοντα), and the other †Deinias, a translator (ἑρ[μα]νέα), who carries the ethnic Αἰγ[. There is very good reason to read it as "Egyptian" over other suggestions.[102] Additionally, several men of the late fifth century with Greek names specifically identify themselves as Egyptian, from Naukratis, or other Egyptian cities. A pair of graffiti inscribed on the walls of the Osiris temple at Abydos a pair of Greeks identify themselves as †Chariandros of Memphis, son of Straton and †Timarchos of Daphnis, both using Egyptian—and not Greek— cities as their ethnonyms. The fifth-century Attic grave stele of †Dionysios, son of Parmenon, found at Naukratis, uses the city's name as an ethnic as well (Διονύσιος Παρμένοντο<ς> | Ναυκρατίτης). Farther afield, The †Apollos, son of Thalinos, who was commemorated by an Egyptianizing "false door" funerary marker with a Greek inscription in Naukratis, and †Exekestos, son of Charon, who had a similar monument in Saqqara, might belong in this group as well.

That the descendants of mixed marriages occupied a space as privileged intermediaries in Greco-Egyptian trade is not particularly surprising. This phenomenon is widespread in global trading diasporas, from the *dragomans* of the eastern Mediterranean to the Eurafricans of west Africa's Atlantic coast.[103] What is exceptional is the extent to which the children of these mixed marriages—and sometimes, people who were not Egyptian at all— attained positions of power within the first generation of Greek settlement in the delta. The earliest, and probably most famous, was a Saite official known in death as †Wahibre-em-achet, son of *Irkskrs* (Arkeskares or Alexikles) and †*Sntt* (Zenodote), who presided as "Chancellor of Upper Egypt" (*ḥtm-bity*) at Thebes. †Wahibre-em-achet was buried in elite fashion at the end of the seventh century, complete with inscribed *ushabtis*, a canopic jar, and a monumental stone sarcophagus. Around the same, a mysterious individual known †Pedon, son of Amphinnes, dedicated an inscribed statue at an unknown Ionian sanctuary, claiming to have been given command of "gold and a city on account of my excellence" (χρύσεογ καὶ πόλιν ἀρετῆς ἕ | νεκα) by Psamtik II.[104] An early Demotic papyrus from Hermopolis, written on 6 Parmouthi, fifteenth year of Apries (575 BCE), lists a priest with the Greek name of †Ariston in an unclear position of authority at the temple of Thoth. And finally, we have very clear evidence that individuals of Greek descent had authority over trade with Greeks in Naukratis. †Neferpre-sa-Neith, son of *Grḥs*, is attested as supervisor over a city during the year 561 BCE explicitly identified as Nokrodj, the Egyptian name for Naukratis. His non-Egyptian patronymic and has been read variously as †Qerches, Korax, or Korakos. The likelihood that †Neferpre-sa-Neith's father was a Greek or Carian immigrant is high.

Even a simple prosopography barely scratches the surface of the very substantial integration of people of Greek descent into Egyptian culture in the sixth and fifth centuries BCE. Despite the official xenophobia of the Egyptian state—a xenophobia that became notably pronounced in early sixth century Egypt, after Greek mercenaries intervened in the civil war between Apries (Eg. Wahibre, r. 589–70 BCE) and Amasis—Egypt had a long tradition of integrating migrants.[105] Moreover, we are passing over the rather large numbers of people from the borderlands of the Greek world (particularly the Anatolian region of Caria) who came with the Greeks to Egypt and assimilated to an even greater extent.[106] When Herodotus arrived in Egypt, he encountered a community that felt rooted in the country, and had developed an entire historiography that related the stories of Homeric heroes, wandering sages, and mercenaries in the seventh century.[107] The point is that by the time of the voyages recorded in the Elephantine document, and certainly by the time of Herodotus, there were a very large number of Aegean migrants in Egypt who regarded Egypt as *their* country—and who themselves were involved in the mediation and supervision of trade.

Commodity Encounters

The Greco-Egyptian natron trade was embedded in an entire international ecosystem that guided the commodity from the hands of peasants in the western desert—people like Khunanup, in the *Tale of the Eloquent Peasant*, whose cargo was so remorselessly stolen from him—to the holds of †Protokles, †Glaphyros, and their unnamed crews. Natron mostly passed along this journey unheralded, since to Egyptians it was cheap stuff and to Greeks only commented upon in medical contexts. But every now and then, this commodity does come to the surface. For the conclusion of this chapter, I will explore how two members of the wider Greek community in Egypt interacted with this miraculous commodity. These men are the sixth-century priest, †Ariston, and Herodotus, who visited Egypt 150 years later. Both men shared an intimate knowledge of one of the most curious and culturally specific uses natron was put to, mummification. Their very different engagement with the use of natron in the preservation of animal and human bodies shows the unexpected ways that the traffic in material things helped to make Egypt's culture such a "mystery" (to use the words of Sidney Mintz) in the Greek imagination.

On August 11, 575 BCE, the scribe Inaros urgently wrote to †Ariston, an official of unclear standing at the temple of Thoth in Hermopolis. A sacred ibis had died in the Fayum and needed to be embalmed:

> Letter of the servants of the priest of Thoth, the twice great, the lord of Hermopolis, to Ariston *(3rstn)*. May Thoth, twice Great, the Lord of Hermopolis, live long! We have sent the priest of Thoth *P3 td nhm ʿn*, the son of *Ḏḥwtḏ m ḥtp*, with the servants of the ibis of Hermopolis to the district of El-Fayum to bring the ibis for his funeral in Hermopolis, his resting place. May Ariston do good for Thoth, the twice great, the Lord of Hermopolis, to cause one to hear the words that will be said when they come to the Ibis. So wrote the servant, the scribe of the treasury, the writer of letters Inaros, son of *P3ḏ f t3w ʿ.wḏ is*, in year 15 of Apries, 6 Pharmuthi.[108]

†Ariston is a mysterious figure in the literature. It is true that Inaros' letter to †Ariston is one of the earliest texts written in Demotic; but this aside, nothing else about the letter—barring †Ariston's name itself—seems out of the ordinary for what it is. In fact, he was not even the *only* Greek to work at an Egyptian temple in the early sixth century BCE. (As Egyptian officials of rank, both †Wahibre-em-achet—who was himself mummified—and †Neferpre-sa-Neith must have served rotations as *wʿb* priests,[109] while †Pedon's inscribed dedication shows clear engagement with Late Period priestly biographies.)[110] Nonetheless, actually *seeing* a Greek at work at an Egyptian temple makes †Ariston an interesting figure to think with. In the imagination of Herodotus, animal worship was one of the single most alienating aspects of Greek culture. Animal cults were one of the characteristic developments of the Late Period,[111] and Herodotus uses his description of them to emphasize Egypt's foreignness:

> Ἐοῦσα [δὲ] Αἴγυπτος ὅμουρος τῇ Λιβύῃ οὐ μάλα θηριώδης ἐστί· [...]
> Μελεδωνοὶ ἀποδεδέχαται τῆς τροφῆς χωρὶς ἑκάστων καὶ ἔρσενες καὶ θήλεαι τῶν Αἰγυπτίων, τῶν παῖς παρὰ πατρὸς ἐκδέκεται τὴν τιμήν. Οἱ δὲ ἐν

τῇσι πόλισι ἕκαστοι εὐχὰς τάσδε σφι ἀποτελέουσι εὐχόμενοι τῷ θεῷ τοῦ ἂν
ᾖ τὸ θηρίον· ξυροῦντες τῶν παιδίων ἢ πᾶσαν τὴν κεφαλὴν ἢ τὸ ἥμισυ ἢ τὸ
τρίτον μέρος τῆς κεφαλῆς, ἱστᾶσι σταθμῷ πρὸς ἀργύριον τὰς τρίχας· τὸ δ᾽
ἂν ἑλκύσῃ, τοῦτο τῇ μελεδωνῷ τῶν θηρίων διδοῖ· ἡ δ᾽ ἀντ᾽ αὐτοῦ τάμνουσα
ἰχθῦς παρέχει βορὴν τοῖσι θηρίοισι. Τροφὴ μὲν δὴ αὐτοῖσι τοιαύτη ἀποδέδ
εκται. Τὸ δ᾽ ἄν τις τῶν θηρίων τούτων ἀποκτείνῃ, ἢν μὲν ἑκών, θάνατος ἡ
ζημίη, ἢν δὲ ἀέκων, ἀποτίνει ζημίην τὴν ἂν οἱ ἱρέες τάξωνται. Ὃς δ᾽ ἂν ἶβιν
ἢ ἴρηκα ἀποκτείνῃ, ἤν τε ἑκὼν ἤν τε ἀέκων, τεθνάναι ἀνάγκη.

Egypt is not a country of many animals although it borders on Libya
... both men and women from Egypt are chosen as their guardians
for raising each kind, which the son inherits from his father. People in
each town, when they pay their vows, pray to the god to whom the animal is dedicated, shaving all or one half or one third of their children's
heads, and weighing the hair in a balance against a sum of silver; then
the weight in silver of the hair is given to the female guardian of the
creatures, who buys fish with it and feeds them. Thus, food is provided for them. Whoever kills one of these creatures intentionally is
punished with death; if he kills accidentally, he pays whatever penalty
the priests appoint. Whoever kills an ibis or a hawk, intentionally or
not, must die for it. (2.65.2–5)

Ἀπάγονται δὲ οἱ αἰέλουροι ἀποθανόντες ἐς ἱρὰς στέγας, ἔνθα θάπτονται
ταριχευθέντες, ἐν Βουβάστι πόλι. Τὰς δὲ κύνας ἐν τῇ ἑωυτῶν ἕκαστοι πόλι
θάπτουσι ἐν ἱρῇσι θήκῃσι. Ὡς δὲ αὕτως τῇσι κυσὶ οἱ ἰχνευταὶ θάπτονται.
Τὰς δὲ μυγαλᾶς καὶ τοὺς ἴρηκας ἀπάγουσι ἐς Βουτοῦν πόλιν, τὰς δὲ ἴβις ἐς
Ἑρμέω πόλιν.

They take away dead cats to sacred buildings in the city of Bubastis,
where they are embalmed and buried; they bury female dogs in sacred
coffins in their own cities; mongoose are buried just like the dogs. They
take shrews and falcons to Buto and ibises to Hermopolis. (2.67.1)

It is worth pointing out here that Herodotus is hardly as derogatory in his
mention of animal cults as some of his successors would be.[112] Nonetheless,
this is Herodotean ethnography at its most oppositional. Egyptians worship animals as gods; slaughtering one is murder; animals get tombs; and, of
course, they commodify their sacrifices with silver. Being an animal priest is
a hereditary profession. It would have greatly surprised Herodotus to learn

that in the first generation of Greek settlement, some of those priests were just like him.

150 years separate †Ariston and Herodotus. Their parallel encounters with the world of the temples—†Ariston an insider, and Herodotus an outsider—brought with them competing perspectives. †Ariston was one of the many Greeks who had ingratiated themselves to the Saite state at the height of its power; when Herodotus visited Hermopolis a century later, he was guided by the descendants of †Ariston and his colleagues, whose stories bristled at Achaemenid rule.[113] As they passed through the same spaces, witnessed the same rituals, and encountered the same commodities, they would inhabit different conceptual worlds. For †Ariston, natron was the essential substance that, when used in its ritual context, purified mind and body and made one closer to the gods. For Herodotus, it was a bare commodity. All Egyptian sacrifices could be measured in silver.

Herodotus' description of animal cult uses an Egyptian ritual to focalize on the issues of silver imports, labor relations, and social hierarchy. Leslie Kurke argues that Herodotus' discussions of silver and gold "pry open the seemingly guileless surface" of the text and find the value system underpinning it.[114] Kurke reads Herodotus' observations on other cultures, such as the alleged Egyptian custom of expressing sorrow for killing a sacred animal by shaving a child's head and selling the hair to the priests for silver (2.65.3), as a sort of running commentary on the politics of commoditization and mass/elite tensions in the Greek *polis*. Kurke's approach necessitates looking at Herodotus' narrative in terms of commodities, noting the "relentlessly material vein" that pervades it.[115] Natron occupies a similar place in Herodotus' Egyptian narrative. If we look at his description of animal embalming, we can identify a single thread that leads us all the way back to the world of the port, with its Greek merchants, haughty administrators, and promiscuous band of camp followers. The priests take silver as payment. And to embalm the dead animal, they needed natron.

Facilities for raising and embalming sacred animals in their thousands existed outside almost every major Egyptian temple in the Late Period.[116] †Ariston's journey to embalm the sacred Ibis would have taken him to the western extreme of the Nile plain, where Hermopolis' animal cemeteries were located at the desert edge. This enormous subterranean facility was home to the remains of thousands of animals, most having been raised for the exact purpose of mummification.[117] Going into temple storage, †Ariston or his attendants would have found the commodities they needed for the process. In his canonical description of mummification (2.87–88), Herodotus lists the commodities needed as natron, unguents, palm wine, and linen.[118] A sense of the portions involved comes from *P.Harris* 1, where one sanctuary was given 2,396 cups of natron (sec. 55b.8), measuring just 0.12 l. each.[119] Analysis of animal mummies—and some human mummies as well—shows that priests and embalmers economized resources when they could, mixing up animal hair and teeth with dirt and sand to create single "mummies," or burning the flesh and "mummifying" the bones to save natron.[120]

Thus Herodotus might have had good reason to doubt the altruism of the priests. The money-grubbing nature of the priests comes to the fore in one of the set-pieces of his Egyptian ethnography, his extended description of human mummification in 2.86–87. (Herodotus' parallel description of human taxidermy, found in his ethnography of Scythia in 4.71–72, will be discussed in Chapter 6.)[121] Immediately when a corpse is brought in, the embalmers present three choices to the customer, starting with the best quality (σπουδαιοτάτην), then moving on to two lower grades, one that is "lower in quality" (ὑποδεεστέρην), and then "cheapest" (εὐτελεστάτην, 2.86.1). Each has successively better access to commodities, with the highest grade receiving palm wine, spices, myrrh, cassia, and gum (2.86.2); the middle grade receiving cedar oil (2.87.1); and the lowest grade nothing at all (2.88.1). The commodity they all share, however, is natron, which is mentioned at least three times in the passage (2.87.2, 2.87.3, and 2.88.1).[122]

†Ariston, though probably knowledgeable of the phenomenon of fake animal mummies, would have held rather different views on embalming. Only a single person of Greek ancestry, †Wahbire-em-achet, is definitively known to have been embalmed in Egypt after death, although given their status it is certain that †Neferpre-sa-Neith, †Pirapia, and †Ariston would have as well. The Carian *choachyte* †*Pdrwihy* is directly attested to have functioned as an auxiliary to the economy of death. For elites, proper burial in Egypt was a central aspiration, and anything else was lamentable.[123] Migrants to Egypt who joined elite circles underwent the process, too. Both Jacob (*Gen.* 50.2) and Joseph (*Gen.* 50.26) were mummified, the latter receiving Egyptian burial.

Burial lay at the center of an entire industry, connected with the temples, that conditioned Herodotus' decision to portray the embalming as a commercial process. Egypt's elaborate funerary cultures were in part linked to a principle of Egyptian case law, first defined by Janssen and Pestman, known as the "law of the Pharaoh." In this, a father's inheritance went to the child who tended to the father's tomb. For this and other reasons, funerary rites seem to have taken up a substantial portion of private spending in the Egyptian economy.[124] The laborers and craftsmen at twentieth dynasty Deir el-Medineh, for instance, generated income so large from recirculating grave goods from old tombs that it drew judicial attention.[125] These same laborers were heavily involved in the funerary economy, as the presence of faience *ushabti* figurines from the site's assemblage, inscribed with all but the name of the dead, testifies. A surviving bill of sale (BM EA10800) shows temple workshops selling them for profit to private individuals.[126] Expenditures connected to the "law of the Pharaoh" were conspicuous down to Herodotus' time. A sixth-century BCE archive of choachytes from Thebes testifies to both the large fees charged by funerary businessmen in maintaining ancestral tombs, the length to which they would go (even violence) to maintain contracts, and the profits they extracted.[127]

The language of Herodotus' description of mummification draws specific attention to the commercial and self-interested aspects of the process, removing any hint of the sacred. He uses words for fish pickling (ταριχεύω) five times in the passage (2.86–88), and the image is not lost.[128] Davidson notes that the language of pickling and salt fish is heavily embedded in a discourse on luxury and class relations in Classical Athens.[129] Herodotus' Egyptian narrative as a whole—mediated through merchants as it was—draws heavy attention to Egyptian forms of commerce, and Kurke has seen circulating in Herodotus' writing hints of an aristocratic critique of market trade.[130] The sixth-century pharaoh Amasis, whose narrative dominates much of Herodotus' second book (2.162–74), raises particular issues with his commodification of things—his own dignity, among other things—that do not belong on the market. Herodotus' implication is that Egyptians themselves circulate in a funerary market with their own commodities. If Scythian royal mummification rituals are marked by the use of the "human commodity"—made clear through the sacrifice of over a hundred associates and slaves with the king—Egyptian burial rites are marked through a distinct over-commercialization and use of Egypt's commodity, natron. The excessive amount of the commodity used—so extensive that the excess was bagged and kept in tombs—would not have escaped Herodotus' notice.[131]

Herodotus' commodity encounters bring out the nakedly commercial in Egyptian culture where it would not have been visible to Egyptians, or noteworthy to assimilating Greeks. If we look even at Herodotus' description of the life †Ariston would have lived, we can see commodities at every step. Priests spent their rotations in the temple physically conditioning themselves into a state of ritual purity. Ubiquitous as it was, in a sacral context, natron was regarded as a ritually pure substance—the verb for "to purify" is *ntrd*—and when on duty, priests would have encountered it frequently over the course of the day.[132] Priests were required to drink water mixed with natron for days in order to advance through the successive chambers of the temple, as the charges against priests who failed to do so in *P.Turin* 1887 reveal. They cleaned their cups every day with natron (Hdt. 2.37.1), only wore clean white linen, bleached with natron (2.37.2), and bathed four times a day, probably with natron (2.37.4).

The association between natron with temple rituals and the bodies of the priests gave natron a surprising visibility in Greek visualizations of Egypt and its culture. A comparison might be found in the ideological uses that imported, white, granular commodities were put to in the Anglo-American world during the eighteenth and nineteenth centuries. As Mintz notes, it was rarely lost on contemporary critics of the transatlantic sugar trade that the whitest of substances had been produced by enslaved Africans in the tropics. Sugar refiners used the process of settling—by packing raw sugar into vertical, cone-shaped vessels—to separate out dense, molasses-infused treacle from white, granular sugar. The latter was actually an inferior product, offering fewer calories by weight in an undernourished age; nevertheless, the very whiteness of the finished product encouraged European customers to consume without thinking about the race of the people who made it.[133] Consuming substances can also lead consumers to think about their own bodies. Kim Stringfellow finds that one borax manufacturer in early twentieth-century America appealed to customers' fears about issues of race, gender, and class, to market their product: one pamphlet written for women encourages readers to apply borax directly to the skin to remove freckles and lighten it.[134]

I am not claiming that Greek observations of how the priests used natron to condition their spiritual state formed the sole rock upon which the entire structure of an ethnography was built. Rather, natron represents something like a shared *topos* around which Greeks and Egyptians—there for business—exchanged cultural knowledge in the physical space of the temple. Both sides had ample reason to distrust each other; on the other hand, their relationships were maintained by skilled interlocutors, like the †"Translators" of Naukratis, and potentially even shared descent. Once either party had stepped out of this shared space, the process of imagination could begin.

Conclusion

This chapter has drawn a commodity biography that traced natron from a mineral evaporite scraped from the desert floor to a cultural commodity that figured conspicuously in Greek imaginings of Egypt in the sixth and fifth centuries BCE. Along the way, I have emphasized the role of people—priests, peasants, merchants, and the Greco-Egyptian community of Naukratis—in the production and conveyance of this commodity. In so many ways, it is an odd story: natron is so rarely mentioned in texts either Egyptian or Greek. But as I have argued, natron is an absent presence that pervades interactions between both sides. Without the Elephantine document, we would know far less about the strings that held them together.

In the coming chapters, we will examine how the consumption of natron in the Aegean produced a host of cultural phenomena that would be difficult to imagine from the perspective of the delta. The most curious of these would, ultimately, result in the production of a kind of racial imaginary, that would use products manufactured using natron as a matrix to imagine the Egyptian body. It is no coincidence that the earliest images of black bodies in the repertoire of Greek art would be produced using this African commodity. The end result of this truly mysterious transformation would be the vocabulary Greeks developed to describe these images back to Egypt.

2

Egypt in Your Hand

Introduction

It seemed to me that the mysteriousness that accompanied me seeing, at one and the same time, cane growing in the fields and white sugar in my cup, should also accompany the sight of molten metal or, better, raw iron ore, on the one hand, and a perfectly wrought pair of manacles or leg irons, on the other. The mystery was not simply one of technical transformation, impressive as that is, but also the mystery of people unknown to one another being linked through space and time—and not just by politics and economics, but along a particular chain of connection maintained by their production.[1]

"THE MYSTERIOUS CHARACTER of the commodity-form lies simply in the fact that the commodity reflects the social characteristics of men's labor," writes Marx; "through this exchange, the products of labor become commodities, things at the same time sensually supernatural (*sinnlich übersinnlich*) and social."[2] In two different ways, and a century removed from each other, Sidney Mintz and Karl Marx arrived at a similar definition of a commodity. Commodities reflect societies that make them; when a consumer holds the finished product in their hands, they might be put in a direct relationship with the people who made it. Yet as we saw in the previous chapter, such relationships are rarely as straightforward as either author makes them out to be. Commodity biographies are not, simply put, stories about how commodities connect people. Rather, they are about people *disconnected* by the very same networks that enable the flow of material between them. Each step along the commodity chain produced very discrete forms of knowledge: how and when to harvest natron; how to store, pack, and ship it; and how to negotiate with the authorities into whose hands it fell. But for the most part, most of this knowledge stayed in its immediate link.

The previous chapter argued that what bits and pieces of Egyptian knowledge reached Greece came through the hands of privileged intermediaries who worked closely with local economic institutions, in different periods the temples or the state. Chapters 2–3 of *Racialized Commodities* explore how such individuals repackaged knowledge circulated in these encounters into a kind of exoticized, fictive Egypt that reached wide appeal in Greece between circa 725 and 525 BCE. Over these two centuries, Egyptian religious symbols, devotional practices, and iconographies were widely embraced and emulated across the Greek world. These objects and practices—some genuine imports, others "invented traditions"[3]—lay the basis for Egypt's transformation in the Greek imagination into a kind of race apart, with its own distinct human morphologies, ecological conditions, and deep history. By emulating Egypt, people in Archaic Greece were attempting to lay claim to this heritage in a period when Egypt was the preeminent kingdom facing the eastern Mediterranean. It was with its own *sinnliche Übersinnlichkeit* that the natron trade would lay the groundwork for the earliest racializations of Egypt in the west.

Properly speaking, our narrative predates the formal start of the natron trade. As Phoenician seafarers sailed west during the early first millennium BCE, they brought with them the custom of depositing Egyptianizing scarabs, amulets, and figurines in the graves of women and especially children.[4] These practices, as Carolina López-Ruiz writes, were a central part of the "orientalizing kit" that Phoenicians transferred across the Mediterranean, from Cyprus to Italy to Spain.[5] A trickle of this material had arrived in Greece during the post-Mycenaean period; it increased in popularity during the Early Iron Age, particularly in the most Phoenician-facing areas of the Aegean, including Crete and Euboea. But then, in the mid-seventh century BCE, the pattern changed. The foundation of Egypt's Saite dynasty circa 664 BCE was followed by the mass migration of Greeks to the Nile Delta; a generation later, this community was concentrated at Naukratis.[6] Between 650 and 575 BCE, the Phoenicianizing custom of including scarabs or amulets in burials mostly disappears in Greece. Instead, the vast bulk of *aegyptiaca* were dedicated at a handful of Aegean sanctuaries[7] (Figure 2.1). And then it stopped: the practice of dedicating Egyptianizing votives comes to a halt even before the Saite collapse in 525 BCE. Almost no Egyptianizing objects appear at all in the Aegean between the Late Archaic and Hellenistic Periods.[8]

The story of *aegyptiaca*'s rise and fall in turn-of-the-sixth-century Greece is a tale about long-distance trade, Egypt's cultural imprint far outside its borders—and humble, unheralded natron. Only a vanishingly small proportion of *aegyptiaca* in the first-millennium Mediterranean was ever produced in Egypt; the stuff was almost always manufactured by foreigners. In the Phoenician world, workshops on Cyprus and the Levant predominate.[9] *Aegyptiaca* in the Aegean are generally believed to have been produced at workshops in East Greece, particularly Rhodes, starting around 650 BCE and at Naukratis after 575 BCE.[10] Indeed, access to natron was critical in the production of Egyptianizing dedications. Some 90 percent of objects found in the Aegean were manufactured from faience, a brightly colored, low-fired vitreous substance related to glass, consisting of powdered silica, mineral pigment, and natron used as flux.[11] Despite its documentary invisibility, it appears certain that natron was being exported throughout the Mediterranean generations before the date of the Elephantine document. For most of antiquity after circa 700 BCE, natron was the predominant flux used in glassmaking.[12] By circa 500 BCE, workshops for vitreous materials as far away as Crimea were reliant on Egyptian natron.[13]

Aegyptiaca thus present an oddity in the history of Greek religion. Faience-making was reliant on an international commodity chain undocumented in

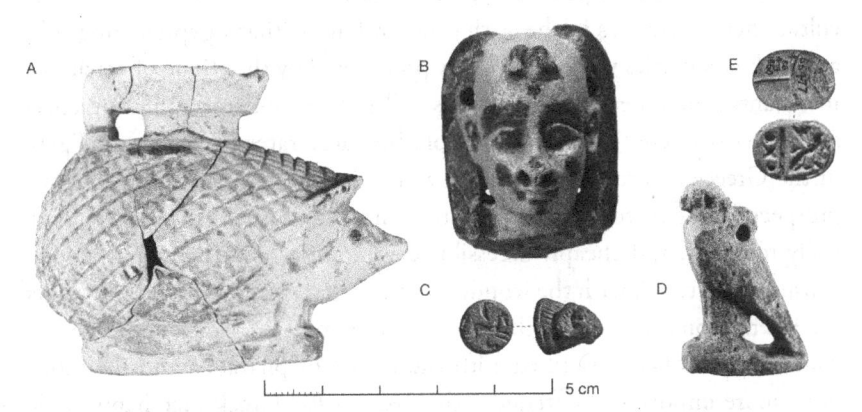

FIGURE 2.1 Greco-Egyptian faience. **A**: Hedgehog aryballos from Kourion, Cyprus. Penn 54-28-6. Photograph courtesy of the Penn Museum. **B**: Head of fragmentary figure of woman. Princeton y1954-119. Photograph courtesy of the Princeton Art Museum. **C**: BM Scaraboid in shape of ram's head from Naukratis, Egypt. 1886,0401.1692. Photograph © Trustees of the British Museum. All rights reserved. **D**: Amulet of a falcon from Naukratis, Egypt. MFA 86.811. Photograph © 2024 Museum of Fine Arts, Boston. **E**: Scarab from Naukratis, Egypt, inscribed with name of Psamtik I (r. 664–610 BCE). BM 1886,0401.1650. Photograph © Trustees of the British Museum. All rights reserved.

our written sources, stretching from the temples of the Nile Delta to the early peripteral sanctuaries of East Greece. No ancient author mentions their use.[14] Yet they partake in a much larger category of religious trinkets that have been well studied in comparative contexts. As the Nigerian anthropologist Akinwumi Ogundiran writes, such small, transitory devotional objects offered worshippers a "critical medium through which the meanings, purposes, anxieties, and aspirations of human condition . . . were articulated and contemplated"—meanings that, critically, transform as objects changed hands between parties.[15] With our lack of literary evidence, it remains difficult to tease out the meanings of *aegyptiaca*. Nathan Arrington and Matthew Skuse have separately noted that factors as concrete as supply and as idiosyncratic as personal aesthetics might be determinative in shaping how people in Archaic Greece understood scarabs, amulets, and other Egyptianzing devotional objects.[16] So, well over a century after they first came to the attention of scholars, faience *aegyptiaca* remain evidence without a narrative—a vast body of material testifying to a mania for Egyptian culture in the late seventh- and early sixth-century Aegean detached from the existing narratives of Greece's political, cultural, and social development.

Aegyptiaca are a graveyard of scholarly ambition. Despite the vast bibliography they have attracted, very few accounts have held up to much scrutiny.[17] This chapter charts a different course. Reading the rise and fall of Greek Egyptomania against the proliferation of Phoenician and Egyptian culture hero narratives in the sixth century, I argue that Egyptianizing cults at Greek sanctuaries were deliberately propagated by the clique of privileged merchants who traded with Egypt—as well as their emulators. These practices and narratives were employed as part of a broader strategy of valorizing Egypt in the Greece's cultural imagination to bolster the political and economic prospects of the merchant class. By importing these visually distinct, symbolically resonant, and cheaply accessible commodities, merchants put regular consumers in touch with the wonders of the delta. And we should not forget the international context of this encounter. By putting Greek consumers in contact with tokens inscribed with the names of pharaohs and divinities, none more important or frequent than Amun Re, Greek merchants could persuade their trade partners in Egyptian sanctuaries that they were allies in the effort of extending the territory of the god to the world's distant corners.[18]

If you were to ask a citizen of Miletus, Samos, or Corinth who their ancestors were around the year 600 BCE, you might hear a story of the city's foundation by the pharaonic army of King Sesostris, or of ancient heroes who had gone to Egypt and come home. For proof, you might have been directed to the stunning array of blue-green faience strung around the altar at a sacred precinct; scarabs, figurines, and amulets, all inscribed with mysterious hieroglyphs. Decades before Greeks learned to see Egypt's culture as alien and foreign, its people culturally or physically different from themselves, Egypt was the land of the ancestors, a fabulously wealthy kingdom whose patronage was channeled through the hands of the merchants. †Protokles and his fellow natron captains of 475 BCE were far too young to have traversed the Mediterranean when it was an Egyptian pond. But the routes they travelled had been blazed in this period, mapped by a geography of myth, ritual, and patronage. Long before Greeks saw themselves as a race of their own, faience scarabs and amulets helped them visualize themselves sons of the Nile.

Natron and Faience

We should begin with an investigation of the material itself (Figure 2.2). The overwhelming majority of Egyptian or Egyptianizing objects deposited at Greek sanctuaries between circa 725 and 525 BCE were manufactured from faience. Faience is a low-fired vitreous substance comprising powered silica, alkali flux, and mineral colorants. Mixed cold into a paste, it was pressed into molds and then fired in a kiln. With its bright blue and green colors, its odd luminosity, and its unusually smooth glaze, faience was a miraculous substance. Ancient authors regarded it as synthetically produced stone, and magical for that reason. Theophrastus, writing in the Hellenistic Period but pointing to an earlier tradition, highlights the Egyptian "biography" of the material as an intrinsic part of its appeal. "Those who write the history of the kings of Egypt state . . . [that they] first made artificial κύανος [blue] in imitation of the natural kind"; he notes, differentiating "manufactured" (σκευαστὸς) and "natural" (αὐτοφυῆ) varieties of blue stone, such as lapis lazuli (*On Stones* 55); "κύανος [blue] was sent as tribute from Phoenicia and as gifts from other quarters, and some of it was natural and some had been produced by fire."[19]

Faience-making is ancient. The earliest predecessor of faience, glazed steatite, appears in Egypt between 2575 and 465 BCE.[20] Although faience does not have to be fused at as high a temperature as glass, ancient craftsmen still had difficulty in building kilns that could reach such high temperatures.[21] The solution was to add an alkali flux, which brought down the melting point of the silica matrix to around 1100 degrees Celsius. Up until the end of the Bronze Age, this was typically sourced from the ashes of hardwood trees or plants that grew in salty soil.[22] Natron took the place of potash in Egyptian glass and faience-making during the LBA/EIA transition.[23]

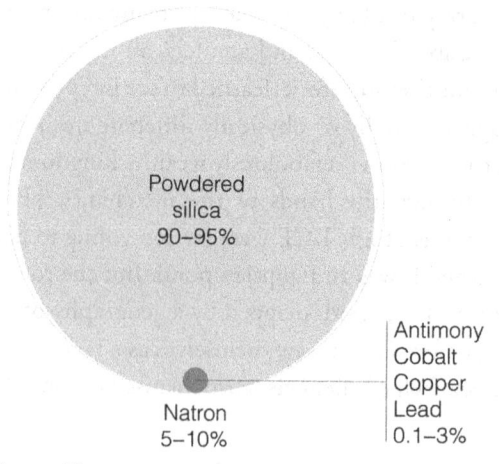

FIGURE 2.2 Makeup of faience.

Powdered silica 90–95%

Natron 5–10%

Antimony
Cobalt
Copper
Lead
0.1–3%

The reasons for the adoption of natron in glass- and faience-making are obscure. The Libyan pharaohs of the twenty-second and twenty-third dynasties began to consolidate the western desert under Egypt's control, a trend that would continue into the Saite Period; this might have made harvesting natron easier than the multi-step process of extracting alkali from potash.[24] Even glassmaking industries in Roman Europe depended on desert natron, despite the fact that potash could be obtained locally in most places. It took the collapse of Mediterranean mobility in the late centuries of the first millennium CE to encourage a return to using potash.[25]

Natron used in ancient glassmaking varied drastically in quality, as the same salt pans could produce trona, thermonatrite, nahcolite, thenardite, and halite in the same year, depending on weather conditions. One study suggests that Roman glassmaking required as much as a ton of natron per ton of the finished product.[26] Because of impurities, far more alkali substances had to be put into the mix than were strictly necessary for the reaction, which is why such great percentages of impurities such as lime or halite appear in many artifacts.[27] Still, natron/silica ratios could not have approached 1:1 in seventh- and sixth-century Mediterranean faience. Most objects were not vitrified in entirety, and the many pieces described by scholars as of "glazed composition" were only vitrified on the exterior, leaving a crumbly core in the middle.[28] Recent estimates suggest that pieces found in the Mediterranean average 5 percent alkali by weight, although midcentury analysis performed by Lucas and Harris found evidence for Egyptian faience with alkali content as high as 20 percent.[29]

Biographies of Faience

Archaic Greece's mania for dedicating faience was long in the making. Although faience "trinkets" were ubiquitous in Egypt as early as the First Intermediate Period (c. 2181–55 BCE), vitreous objects only make sporadic appearances in the graves of their foreign trade partners until the very end of the second.[30] People on Crete were actually making a locally distinctive variety of faience objects, such as the Knossos house models, during the Middle Minoan Period, but these goods only circulated on the island.[31] The first real hint of faience's future popularity in the Aegean comes from the Late Helladic IIIC cemetery at Perati in Attica, where excavators found some forty-nine scarabs and amulets of various materials; Sarah Murray finds their appearance so unusual that she convincingly argues these were burials of migrants from the eastern Mediterranean.[32]

Faience grave goods hold an unusual prominence in EIA Greece. Drawing on published data, Murray estimates that faience makes up some 48 percent of *all* surviving individual imports in the Protogeometric period and 37 percent in the Geometric.[33] From the Middle Protogeometric Period on, the main center of activity was Lefkandi on Euboea. Like Perati, Lefkandi was home to a community of merchants whose Mediterranean wanderings put them in touch with the culture of burying women and children with amulets that was already common in Cyprus and the Levant. Phoenician merchants were certainly present there.[34] During the early phases of the Geometric Period, these imports begin to be found more widely; the most sensational of these is perhaps the necklace of circa 1,100 faience segment beads found in the Early Geometric tomb of the so-called rich lady in the Athenian Agora (Figure 2.3).[35]

For all the prominence of faience in the material culture of EIA Greece, neither Homer, Hesiod, nor any of the cyclic poets ever mention it. This is odd considering how much attention they lavish on the ivory, gold, silver, amber, textiles, and bronzes exchanged between heroes. Partly, this might be because we have not properly looked for it in the poems. Another reason, however, is that faience was a relatively new entry in the system of elite values. As Ian Morris pointed out almost forty years ago, elites of the EIA sought to emulate the material culture of the LBA; faience, which barely appears in Mycenean burials, did not carry the ideological heft of other materials.[36] Both Murray and Jan Paul Crielaard have associated the culture of wearing amulets with the cosmopolitan seafarers of the ninth and eighth centuries. By burying their children with a miraculous commodity made in Egypt and the Levant,

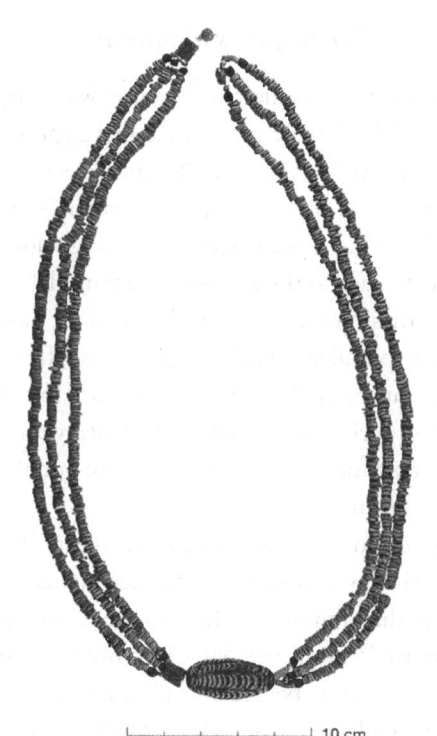

FIGURE 2.3 Necklace of faience segment beads and glass pendant from the grave of the "rich lady" in the Athenian Agora. Early Geometric Period. Adapted from ASCSA Agora Excavation photograph 2012.02.1060. Ephorate of Antiquities of Athens City, Ancient Agora, ASCSA: Agora Excavations © Hellenic Ministry of Culture and Sports/ Hellenic Organization of Cultural Resources Development (HOCRED).

EIA merchants signaled horizons of their world that differed greatly from their land-based (and landholding) neighbors.³⁷

Around 725 BCE, the practice of including goods in graves went into rapid decline across the central Aegean.³⁸ Sanctuaries emerged as the main center of dedicatory activity. Faience and glazed steatite scarabs, amulets, and figurines appear at sanctuaries across Greece during the LG Period, including at sites like Delphi (Figures 3.6–3.7) or Apollo Daphnephoros at Eretria, where dedications of *aegyptiaca* are unknown in the subsequent period.³⁹ The sporadic "Phoenician" and "Levantine" scarabs published in unstratified contexts at Perachora and Artemis Orthia represent the early beginnings of faience assemblages already beginning to take shape at the end of the eighth century.⁴⁰ Anton Bammer's excavation of an LG *peripteros* at Ephesus in the late 1980s might represent a similar case, where flooding preserved *in situ* a heterogenous variety of amulets and scarabs decorating the base of a cult statue.[41]

The Ephesian Artemision is one of three sanctuaries where assemblages of *aegyptiaca* were not swept up in later cleaning and disposal. Ayia Irini on Cyprus—where sanctuaries were also repositories of faience trinkets—offers an additional case where flooding has preserved objects *in situ*; there, an inundation of the Cypro-Archaic I Period (700–600 BCE) left in place scarabs strung along the interior wall of the altar temenos.[42] Cypriot votary sculptures often feature worshippers wearing scarabs and seals strung as necklaces.[43] A further instance comes from the ruins of temple III at Old Smyrna, believed to have been destroyed by the Lydians under Alyattes circa 600 BCE. There, the scatter of faience objects in debris in the northwestern corner of the cella might indicate that objects had been either displayed or kept in storage as a group until rummaged through by soldiers.[44]

But the more typical case is that faience objects are found in secondary contexts. At the Samian Heraion, home of the largest and most diverse collection of *aegyptiaca* in the entire Mediterranean, a vast quantity of faience appears to have been deposited haphazardly over a fifty-year period beginning in the late seventh century east of the Rhoikos Altar.[45] Scarabs, amulets, and figurines were deposited in a similar fashion at the temple of Aphaia on Aegina.[46] At other sites, faience assemblages appear to have remained visible through the whole Archaic period. Most of the faience material at Perachora was probably buried during the fourth century, although some deposits clearly date to the Archaic Period.[47] Objects from Lindos were recovered from two massive votive deposits on the acropolis that date no later than the end of the fifth century.[48] At both the Argive Heraion and Sounion, *aegyptiaca* were unearthed and redeposited during fifth-century levelling operations. At the latter, fifth-century workers seem to have carefully deposited classes of objects into different contexts.[49] A remarkable 16-meter-deep *bothros* at the temple of Aphrodite on Zeytintepe at Miletus, still published only in part, contains an assemblage dated between 680 and 630 BCE by ceramics.[50]

If we look at the totality of Egyptian or Egyptianizing objects dedicated at Greek sanctuaries during the seventh and sixth centuries—ranging from the official dedications made by the pharaohs themselves to gifts of a single scarab—we find that assemblages have a remarkable uniformity. Faience constitutes 95 percent of the Egyptianizing offerings at the twelve Archaic sanctuaries with the largest published assemblages[51] (Appendix 3.1; Figure 2.4). Lower ratios sometimes indicate closer relationships between a sanctuary and the delta. The survival of over 200 bronze figurines at Samos is exceptional,

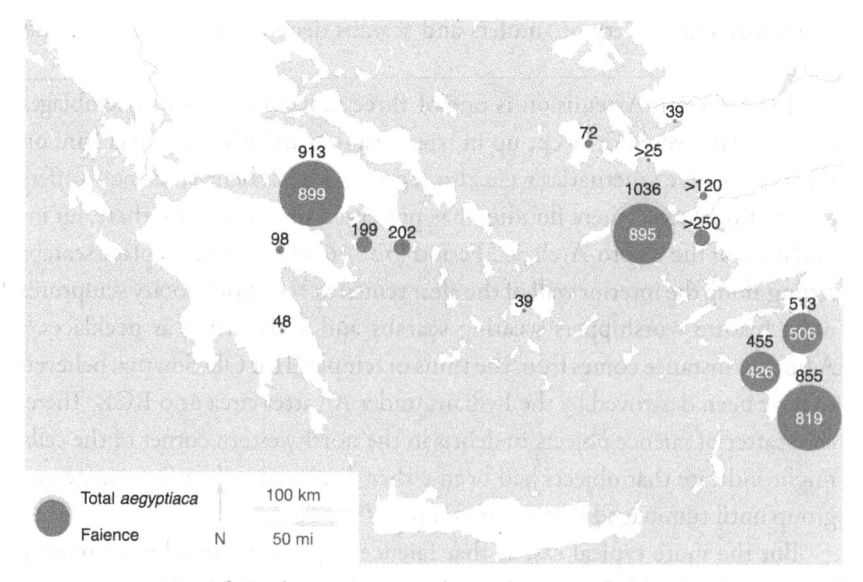

FIGURE 2.4 Map of Greek sanctuaries with Egyptianizing dedications showing total size of assemblage and proportion faience. Detailed data is given in Appendix 3.1.

but we know that the Samian Heraion benefitted from direct Saite patronage (Hdt. 2.182.2).[52] The Egyptianizing assemblage at Old Smyrna both features a relatively low proportion of faience and is relatively early; it notably lacks, for instance, the Naukratis-made scarabs, figurines, and vessels so typical of sixth-century assemblages. But even sanctuaries with high percentages might show unusual tendencies. The three Rhodian sanctuaries received both direct pharaonic patronage (Hdt. 2.181) and mercenary dedications (†Smyrdes, †Unnamed), even though the vast majority of surviving votives are faience. Yet among the dedications at the temple of Athena at Ialysos were faience inlays to a lost wooden chapel dedicated by Necho II and unique *senet* set.[53]

The establishment of mass production in east Greece ushered in a wave of standardization visible after circa 650 BCE. Virginia Webb has proposed a three-stage typology for categorizing faience vessels and figurines at Archaic Greek sites during the seventy-five-year period when the material reaches the height of its popularity (Figure 2.5).[54] Starting in the second quarter of the seventh century, artisans made carefully crafted imitations of Egyptian cosmetic vases for a limited customer base in the east Aegean. By the start of the sixth century, both the production and appeal of faience had massively expanded; at the same time, the repertoire shrinks to anthropomorphic figurines and aryballoi in imitation Corinthian and plastic shapes.[55]

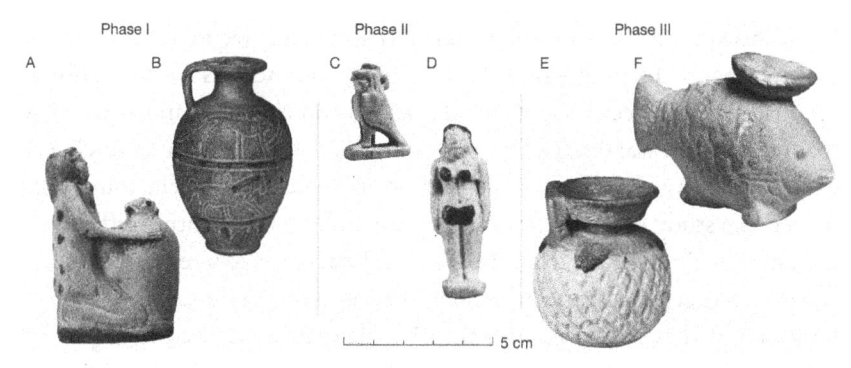

FIGURE 2.5 Webb's phasing of Greco-Egyptian faience figures and vessels. **A:** Vessel of the Leopard Spot Group depicting woman kneeling with vessel. Princeton y1954-100. Photograph courtesy of the Princeton Art Museum. **B:** Ovoid aryballos. MMA 17.194.2273. **C:** Falcon amulet. MMA 74.51.4497. **D:** Female figure. MMA 17.194.2398. **E:** Spherical aryballos. MMA 17.194.2277. **F:** Tilapia aryballos. MMA 41.162.122. Photographs of objects in the Metropolitan Museum of Art published under CC0 1.0 Universal public domain dedication.

Scarabs and amulets are more difficult to date, but over this period there is a discernible shift from types common in the Cypro-Phoenician world to more crudely shaped varieties that feature a limited repertoire of pseudo-hieroglyphs.[56] Some amount of Aegean-style faience even found consumers in Cyprus,[57] North Africa,[58] and Iberia.[59] In this odd way, by the first quarter of the sixth century, Greeks were centrally involved in the production and dissemination of specific kinds of "Egyptian" material culture across the wider Mediterranean.

Sailors and Scarabs

John D. S. Pendlebury (1904–41) is best associated with the study of Crete and Egypt at the end of the Bronze Age, but his earliest work was on faience in EIA and Archaic Greece. Having excavated with Petrie at Amarna in 1928, Pendlebury returned to Greece later that year with an eye for explaining why so many Egyptian artifacts had been found at Archaic sanctuaries. In his first book, *Aegyptiaca* (1930), he argued that sailors were responsible: "the dedications and deposits here are the honest treasures and 'lucks' of Attic sailors," he writes of faience dedicated at sanctuaries of Athena and Poseidon at Sounion, "brought from a far country, not amulets brought to place in a tomb with some hope of benefits for the dead, but 'curios' dedicated in thankfulness to Poseidon by the living."[60]

In this and his abortive study of *aegyptiaca* from Perachora (his opinions are given by the Egyptologist T. G. H. James, who used his notes to publish the material two decades after his death),[61] Pendlebury expanded his view that many of the scarabs, figurines, and amulets that sailors carried to Greece were Bronze Age heirlooms.[62] Pendlebury provided a coherent frame that shaped the study of *aegyptiaca* for the remainder of the century, effectively marginalizing *aegyptiaca* from the historical narrative of Greek art. Faience "curios" at Greek sanctuaries were souvenirs, and their dedicators had little or no idea how they were used in their original contexts. Carried to Greece by humble sailors, they did not participate in the narrative of Greek artistic and cultural development.[63]

Pendlebury's interpretation put an end to what had been an active discourse on the influence of Egypt on Greek culture around the turn of the twentieth century. During his watershed excavations at Naukratis in 1884, Petrie had claimed to find what he called a "factory of glazed pottery" in the south central part of the site, now dated to circa 600–570 BCE[64] (Figure 1.5). In earth tinted a "yellowish colour, apparently owing to the decomposition of some matter thrown away with the rubbish from the factory,"[65] Petrie found some 678 molds (Figure 2.6) for making scarabs as well as lumps of raw pigment and copper slag.[66] Petrie quickly realized that many of the artifacts there were of the exact same types found at other Mediterranean sites, particularly on Rhodes. Drawing attention to what he deemed to be the poor

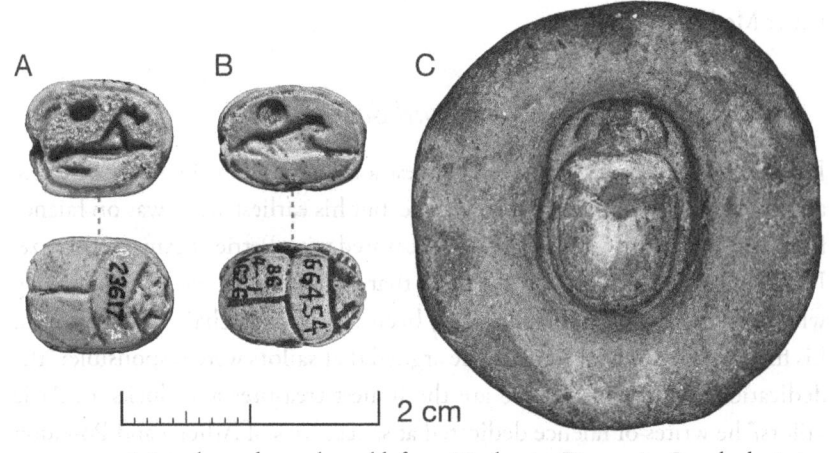

FIGURE 2.6 Scarabs and scarab mold from Naukratis, Egypt. **A:** Scarab depicting lion and sun-disk. BM 1886,0401.1625. **B:** Scarab depicting lion and sun-disk. BM 1886,0401.1626. **C:** Scarab mold. BM 1965,0930.902. All photographs © Trustees of the British Museum. All rights reserved.

quality of the hieroglyphic inscriptions on scarabs he found, Petrie argued that Naukratis faience was the work of Greeks imitating Egyptian models for deliberate export: "the un-Egyptian character of many of the types is evident, and those at the end are distinctly done by men more familiar with Greek vase-painting than with hieroglyphics."[67] With this gesture, Petrie inserted the scarabs of Naukratis into a model of colonial entrepreneurship, with Greek artisans making "Egyptian" pieces for export abroad.[68]

Pendlebury's "sailor thesis" represented a rejection of a dialogue that had grown out of Petrie's discovery, which had tended to present scarabs and amulets—even if debased—as products of multicultural industry that had been distributed across the Mediterranean in the hands of Greek entrepreneurs, sea captains, or wealthy Phoenician or Egyptian visitors to the Aegean. The years immediately following Petrie and his successors' excavations at Naukratis saw great interest in faience material.[69] Excavators of major Archaic faience assemblages in the Aegean at Aphaia on Aegina, the Argive Heraion, the Ephesian Artemision, Artemis Orthia in Sparta, both temples of Sounion, and Lindos on Rhodes[70] rushed to include their material as products of Petrie's workshop.[71] Already by 1906, the German scholar F. W. von Bissing had recognized that Naukratis could not be the only site of production and hypothesized that an earlier one had existed on Rhodes; this view was widely accepted by continental scholars, although evidently ignored by Pendlebury.[72] Inflected by colonialism as Petrie's views were, he and other early excavators shared a belief that Greeks and Egyptians jointly inhabited a cultural and commercial space during the seventh and sixth centuries BCE. Rather than a reflection of the inadvertent discoveries of social outcasts, faience *aegyptiaca* were key to understanding trade among elites in the Archaic Period.[73]

The overwhelming concentration of *aegyptiaca* at sanctuaries of cities with direct ties to Naukratis, such as at Samos, Miletus, or Rhodes, should have offered Pendlebury the first indication that faience predominantly travelled over structured networks. But further evidence comes from the nature of the objects themselves. Conspicuous in the very heterogenous Egyptianizing material found in the period before the founding of Naukratis—the eighth and early seventh centuries—are faience amulets fashioned in the shape of the Memphite gods, especially Nefertem, Sekhmet, the dwarfish Pataikoi, and the bandy-legged, leonine Bes. These are especially common on Rhodes, which had a local tradition of Phoenician colonization and remained in contact with the Levant through the EIA. In recent years, these have been thought to signal the mediation of Greek trade with Egypt through Tyre, which had established a trading quarter in the vicinity of Ptah's temple in Memphis.[74] Herodotus notes that Tyrians decorated the prows of their ships with wooden carvings of the Pataikoi (3.37.2), while Bes was another favored maritime god;[75] one much later Memphite hymn commemorates him as "thou dwarf of heaven, / thou big-faced dwarf / with high back / with weakly legs, lion of the ship of the Phoenix."[76]

Although amulets in the shape of the Memphite gods continue to appear at Greek sites through the Egyptianizing phase, during the middle of the seventh century *aegyptiaca* associated with the deities of the western delta—home of the twenty-sixth dynasty's capital at Sais and nearby Naukratis and Thonis-Herakleion—begin to displace the Memphite gods. By far the most important of these was Amun Re. Psamtik I had donated land in the region to the priests of Thebes at the outset of his reign, and the main temples at both Naukratis and Thonis-Herakleion were to Amun Re.[77] In 2018, Aurélia Masson-Berghoff presented the conclusive argument that the bulk of scarabs excavated from Naukratis were inscribed with cryptographic renderings of the name Amun Re[78] (Figure 2.7). Instead of the illiterate scribblings imagined by Petrie and his successors, the scarabs of Naukratis carried the name of Naukratis' patron god, whose credentials as a maritime divinity are

Hieroglyph	Gardiner	Transliteration	Description
	V30	nb	basket
	Z2	-	plural stroke
	M17	i	reed
	Y5	mn	senet board
	N5	rꜥ	sun-disk
Translation:		Lord Amun Re	
	M17	i	reed
	E13	mjw	cat
	N5	rꜥ	sun-disk
Translation:		Amun Re (cryptogram)	
	G13	m	owl
	Y5	mn	senet board
	N5	rꜥ	sun-disk
Translation:		Amun Re (cryptogram)	

FIGURE 2.7 Cryptographic and acrophonic scarab readings.

well developed.[79] Rather than objects made primarily for export, the products of the Naukratis faience workshops were typical of a Late Period Egyptian city. Most of the production was meant for immediate consumption at the nearby sanctuary.[80]

The relationship between the temples of Ptah at Memphis and Amun Re in the delta—who served as major institutional actors in directing foreign trade—and the dissemination of faience "trinkets" should make us reconsider how much Greek dedicators of *aegyptiaca* were aware of their cultural background. This is to say, there is good reason to believe that Greek dedicators knew where *aegyptiaca* came from, and perhaps even what they signified. A version of this, in fact, has always been maintained by continental scholars including Günther Hölbl, Gisèle Clerc, and Panagiotis Kousoulis, who—free from the shadow of Pendlebury—have long assumed that foreign users of scarabs and amulets knew what they meant. All three draw a link between Bes and the Pataikoi's protective powers over childbirth and the association between *aegyptiaca* and women and children's graves across the Mediterranean.[81] On the other hand, Arrington and Wengrow express caution as to how much users of *aegyptiaca* outside Egypt really knew what they signified; Greeks and Egyptians, after all, had little direct contact until the late seventh century.[82] It is here that we especially feel the absence of literary evidence.

Yet in light of Masson-Berghoff's republication of the Naukratis scarabs, it is time to restore scarabs and other creations of faience to their role as intercultural emissaries—functionaries in trade, not symptoms of. A trio of reinscribed dedications found in Egypt make it clear that some Greek dedicators in the Archaic and Classical Periods could correctly infer the meaning of specific hieroglyphic phrases. A bronze Isis statuette rededicated by one †Pythermos, son of Neilon, carefully refers to the identity of the statue, making clear that †Pythermos knew he was dedicating to the goddess (τῆς Ἔσιος ἄγαλμα). †Sokydides' early fifth-century offering of a bronze bull figurine to Apis attempts to recreate an Egyptian votive formula in Greek. His inscription, τōι Πανεπι μ' ανεστασε Σōqυ|[δι]δης, "Sokydides has dedicated me to the son of Apis," conflates the Egyptian definite article *p3* (transliterated as Πα) with the name of Apis himself.[83] But the most notable is a sixth-century dedication (Figure 2.8) made by †Melanthios of a bronze-sheathed statue base with separate hieroglyphic and Greek inscriptions. The Egyptian inscription asks for Amun's benefactions for an otherwise unknown name (*t3 Imn ʿnḫ B r s3*, "may Amun give life to *Brs*"). The Greek inscription correctly identifies that the sheath was originally an offering to Amun, syncretically translating the name to "Theban Zeus" (τῶι Ζηνὶ Θηβαί|ωι ἄκαλμα).

FIGURE 2.8 Dedication of Melanthios to "Theban Zeus." MMA 21.2.65. Photographs of objects in the Metropolitan Museum of Art published under CC0 1.0 Universal public domain dedication.

These sophisticated, cross-cultural acts of translation and dedication testify to the shortcomings of Pendlebury's model. If Greeks active in Egypt were able to correctly read and recontextualize Egyptian material culture, why should their correspondents back in the Aegean not have been able to? Rather than the detritus left by the tramps of the sea, the dispersion of faience *aegyptiaca* found at Greek sanctuaries during the period of peak dedications—between circa 650 and 575 BCE—is better understood as a coherent strategy of building alliances, on the behalf of knowledgeable and highly mobile elites, between the Egyptian temples they traded with and sanctuaries in their home cities. Through their dispersion of scarabs, figurines, and amulets, they were creating a conceptual geography of their travels centered in the great Amun Re temples of the western delta. For their fellow citizens, a world anchored in the faraway delta opened new possibilities made possible through the consumption of their goods. And if they could not access them, then imitations would do well.

Voyaging with the Gods

In his 2000 *Archaeology as Cultural History*, Ian Morris makes the provocative claim that the Orientalizing phase of the eighth and seventh centuries BCE was a "class phenomenon"; through their manipulation of imported goods, elites of the period overawed the locally rooted peasantry with their ties to "the gods, the heroes, and the east."[84] Although Morris and Kurke's class-conflict reading of Archaic Greek history has seen some pushback on theoretical grounds,[85] other critics have targeted its central premise: that elites, with their imported luxuries, withdrew from the city to enjoy them in private worlds of their own.[86] Sarah Murray and Nathan Arrington show that the occurrence of foreign exotica in Early Iron Age graves does not correlate with other signifiers of elite status, such as the presence of precious metals.[87] Arrington argues that the Protoattic vase-painting style of seventh century Athens in fact emerged from the sub-elite appropriation of "foreign" and "elite" styles.[88] Moreover, as elites moved their wealth from family tombs to public display at sanctuaries during the early eighth and seventh centuries, foreign objects entered into public view as never before. Seeing rare and imported objects on display at sanctuaries was part of the regular—and not elite—experience of living in a Greek city by the beginning of the seventh century. The merchants who could procure these goods accrued for themselves a new type of power within the *polis* community.[89]

Marketing Egyptianizing "trinkets" to a wide audience helped to smooth the arrival of sea captains with loads of goods into port. The travails of Ionian captains were hardly at an end when they left the tax collectors of Naukratis or Thonis-Herakleion in their wake. Greek cities extracted the bulk of their revenues from port duties, and it was well understood that cities maintained absolute right to reject incoming shipments.[90] The example of Late Archaic Kyzikos might be typical: in granting a respected non-citizen named Manes, son of Medikes, an exemption from customs duties (*ateleia*), it still required him to pay a harbor fee, taxes on using scales or selling horses, and an enormous 25 percent sales tax on slaves (*SIG*^{3} 4). Citizens appear to have had the right to enter their own ports with some portion of their cargoes tax-free; nevertheless, our conception of the rights assumed to come with citizenship might be overdetermined, especially in a world without identity credentials and on ships with heterogenous crews.[91] Malkin, for instance, has assumed that most of the merchants who list themselves as from Phaselis in the Elephantine document were lying about their identities, drawing on the "flags of convenience" that frustrate contemporary state efforts to regulate sea commerce.[92] Just like in the delta, sea captains needed help greasing the gears to make sure their commodities could be sold at all, whether in their home cities or that of a neighbor.

One strategy merchants might have used to generate trust was to directly dedicate some of the commodities in their holds at local or Panhellenic sanctuaries. We see hints of this in Herodotus' report that the pharaoh Amasis dedicated a shipload of alum at Delphi in 548 BCE (2.180). It is worth noticing that the merchants of Naukratis added a small quantity of their own—an amount weighing perhaps 11.42 kg—on top of it. Horden and

Purcell call such acts *thesaurisation*, or the transformation of a banal good into a sacred commodity through the act of dedication.[93] Direct donations of either raw alum or natron seem, however, to have been relatively rare. A rare additional example comes between 165 and 57/6 BCE, when one Apollonios dedicated a χοίσκον of natron—perhaps as much as 2.3 kg.—at Delos (*ID* 1403 Bb1.94).[94] Natron donated at Hellenistic Delos appears to have been used to keep sacred buildings clean.[95]

On the other hand, faience *aegyptiaca* were routinely dedicated at Greek sanctuaries. Mass produced and inscribed with mysterious hieroglyphic messages, faience *aegyptiaca* might have—at least in part—provided symbolic capital for merchants to persuade citizens of their home cities that their commerce with Egypt brought benefits to people other than themselves. Catherine St.-Pierre Hoffmann and Theodore Brisart (2010) have in fact argued that faience *aegyptiaca* represented a miniaturization and popularization of the type of unique, hyper-expensive eastern import dedicated by elites at Greek sanctuaries in the eighth and early seventh centuries. By publicly dedicating scarabs or figurines at a sanctuary, merchants might have been able to send an inexpensive message that they could put the citizen community as a whole in touch with wealthy trade partners across the sea—all without leaving their homes.[96]

We should begin with the question of how circulating faience trinkets might have generated trust between merchants and their interlocutors. Merchants in ancient Greece were often considered untrustworthy. The aristocratic writers collected under the name Theognis of Megara labelled merchants among the *kakoi*, the low-born individuals who challenged elite rule over the city with disastrous results: "the merchants are in charge, bad men ruling over good, and I'm afraid" (φορτηγοὶ δ' ἄρχουσι, κακοὶ δ' ἀγαθῶν καθύπερθεν. / δειμαίνω), one writes in a candid moment (679–80 West).[97] Such a label clearly did not apply to all merchants; as Kurke notes, long-distance traders in particular appear to have dodged the curses thrown at them by elite writers.[98] In fact, the writers of the Theognidean corpus often deploy metaphors of commerce, deal making, and trust building to express their uncertainty about class and status in the contemporary *polis*. "Trust few men when you attempt important enterprises, lest one day, Kyrnos, you get pain beyond cure. A trustworthy man is worth his weight in gold and silver," we see one Theognidean writer advise (75–77 West).[99] At another point, a Theognidean writer uses the metaphor of a seal used to guarantee the quantity of a product to figuratively "sign" his verses: "let a seal, Kyrnos, be placed on these verses. Their theft will never pass unnoticed, nor will anyone take something worse in exchange when that which is good is at hand" (19–21 West).[100]

Theognis' usage of the *sphragis* as metaphor is a strange one. Although sealing might be known in the fifth century,[101] very few seal impressions are known from anywhere in the Greek world until the beginning of the fourth century, when the practice of stamping amphorae becomes widespread.[102] The exception to this is at Naukratis, where stamped *bullae* were routinely affixed to shipments of commodities by Egyptian administrators.[103] Where seals would have been commonly encountered in the sixth century were at major sanctuaries, particularly at Perachora on the Gulf of Corinth and throughout east Greece, where temples collected thousands of Egyptian scarabs. Could the seals referred to here be scarabs in the hands of merchants? Without outright endorsing this reading, I present it as a space where we could viably envision the practice of dedicating *aegyptiaca* as a backdrop.

The circulation of small, mass-produced trinkets as a way of building trust between trade partners is widely paralleled in global merchant cultures. One example are the so-called shell currencies that proliferated during the era of European colonialism. Beginning in the sixteenth century, Portuguese, Dutch, and later English merchants imported something in the region of ten billion cowrie shells from the eastern Indian Ocean to west Africa, where they became privileged adornment worn by local participants in the slave trade. Cowries rapidly became inexpensive for both parties who transacted over slaves, but their circulation itself—as well as subsequent recirculation within west Africa—took on symbolic and eschatological dimensions that served to bolster relationships of trust, kinship, and loyalty.[104] The production of shell currencies was a coordinated effort across the Atlantic world. Three thousand miles away, William Bradford, longtime governor of the Plymouth colony, bewailed the transformations that the colonists' mass production of *wampumpeag* (the regional shell currency that preexisted colonization) to facilitate the trade in furs had wrought on the culture of their Indian neighbors.[105] Bradford's self-serving lament treats the phenomenon as though it were unidirectional (from colonists to natives), and its ultimate effect was the destruction of native culture. But as scholars have made clear, the production and circulation of *wampumpeag* facilitated new strategies of exchange and diplomacy, enabling chiefs with close relationships with Europeans to accrue greater political power *without* resorting to the depravity and violence that Bradford mourns.[106]

But in certain ways, shell currencies represent an imperfect model. Even though users might often have known who made them and where they came from, by the nineteenth century they had become so generic that they did not *necessarily* represent a specific relationship. Cowries, for instance, were recontextualized in unpredictable ways in their host societies, and their use long outlasted the mechanisms that brought them there. This was never the case in Greece, where *aegyptiaca* were largely confined to the spatial context of the sanctuary, were regularly disposed of after dedication, and rapidly went out of use in the middle of the sixth century. The use of *aegyptiaca* was directly connected to the activities of the merchants who brought it from Egypt.

Perhaps a better parallel from the Black Atlantic can be found in Brazilian Candomblé, an Africanizing religious practice that attained wide popularity in Brazil during the early nineteenth century. As J. Lorand Matory has chronicled, during the early nineteenth century, the newly independent Brazil began to expel large numbers of manumitted, urban-dwelling ex-slaves to the coast of west Africa. Leveraging their fluency in Portuguese, ancestral ties on the coast, and patronage connections with their former masters, many established themselves as transatlantic merchants.[107] Over the following century, merchant heroes such as Joaquim Francisco Devodê Branco (1856–1924), Martiniano Eliseu de Bomfim (1859–1943), and Filisberto Américo Souza (d. 1933) bankrolled the establishment of temples in Bahia to west African deities whose worship they learned during their travels[108] (Figure 2.9). Africanizing religions had existed consistently in Brazil since the opening of the slave trade in 1551, but what gave Candomblé its appeal was the promise of new and ongoing contact with religious authorities "on the coast" (*a costa*). The ability of this "transnational class" to import the kola nuts, black soap, cloth, and cowries demanded by the gods—in addition to their bulk cargoes of palm oil—made their religious knowledge especially persuasive. "Their public personae," Matory writes, "their travels, their wares, and the profitability of those wares to local retailers allowed them to chart new and persuasive symbolic geographies."[109]

Matory's work puts merchants at the center of a transnational religious world that spanned both sides of the Atlantic. As long as they could guarantee the flow of sacralized commodities from west Africa to Brazilian temples, they maintained their position as leaders of a spiritual community. Adopting this as a model requires accepting that it is, in itself, a model; so far, Archaic Greece has produced no direct evidence for this very specific mode of spiritual leadership. But the image of travelling ritual specialists—"wandering charismatics" in the phrasing of López-Ruiz—has loomed large in scholarly understandings of Greek-Phoenician interaction in the seventh and sixth centuries.[110] Moreover, the theoretic pilgrimage was a trope of sixth-century

FIGURE 2.9 The foundation of Ilê Axé Opô Afonjá in Salvador was bankrolled by the merchant Joaquim Francisco Devodê Branco (1856–1924). Under the supervision of *Mãe* Aninha (1869–1938), it became a model for "pure" African worship in Brazil. Photograph by Jurema Oliveira, Wikimedia Commons. Public domain.

wisdom figures; †Solon himself was traditionally held to have travelled to Egypt in search of the secrets of good government.[111] If seafarers were directly involved in the making or transference of cults in Archaic Greece, it would be privileged, intercultural actors like the merchants we should look for agency with, and not Pendlebury's anonymous sailors.

So far, I have argued that dedicating (or making available for dedication) large quantities of faience at Greek sanctuaries might have helped to smooth relations with local authorities when merchants came to port. But if this case holds up, there is good reason to see the reverse happening as well. Purchasing and exporting inscribed scarabs and amulets might *also* have helped to improve merchants' relations with the Egyptian authorities on which they depended. By dispersing the name of the Memphite gods or Amun Re of the western delta throughout the Mediterranean, merchants were helping to incorporate distant lands under the domain of the Egyptian gods. In doing so, they were laying the groundwork for an overlapping network of faith that linked the Mediterranean's northern and southern shores.

Egyptians commonly subsumed entire territories under control of specific temples.[112] During the difficult years of the twenty-first dynasty (1069–945

BCE), the Theban priest Wenamun voyaged to Byblos with a specific goal in mind: to obtain cedar to build the royal bark of Amun. Protected by his personal god (Amun-on-the-Road, *Imn t3 mtn*), Wenamun arrives in Byblos after an eventful voyage. In his unilateral demand to king Zekerba'al for the cedar, he assigns Amun Re a huge conceptual geography: "There is not any ship on the river that does not belong to Amun! His is (also) the sea! And his is the Lebanon which you think 'It is mine!'"[113] Wenamun's difficult voyage long predated the travels of merchants like †Charaxos in the opposite direction, but his demands of commodities from Zekerba'al—who in no way viewed himself as an Egyptian subject—can be taken as typical. The fantasy of the good life written on *O.Gardiner 28* in the same period ("your fisherman brings fish. Your ship is come from Khor [Syria] loaded with all manner of good things")[114] shares the same view that Egypt was at the end of the world's commodity chains: foreigners owed it things, and Egyptians consumed them.

This exchange of divinities along the lines of mobility situated the natron trade in what—with different goals in mind—Dionisius Agius (2017) calls the "spiritscapes" or what Irad Malkin (2011) and Barbara Kowalzig (2018) have called the "religious networks" that subsume routes of maritime passage under the supervision of the gods. When captains arrived in port with luminous blue and green scarabs and figurines—even if *actually* produced on nearby Rhodes—they held out the promise to average members of the city that they, too, could hold in their hands a token of the pharaoh and his gods. In introducing loads of faience to Greek sanctuaries, merchants skewed the class dynamic of the Archaic *polis* strikingly in their favor, cementing the importance of Egypt in the Greek imagination for centuries to come.

On the Trail of Sesostris

The model I have proposed so far in this chapter depends a crucial factor: that masses of worshippers in Greek cities understood that faience "trinkets" had some link with the Saite regime. As I have repeatedly emphasized, no surviving author provides the essential, unambiguous testimony we need to make anything more than an argument based off likelihoods. But what if this were not *quite* the case? In the following section, I present the argument that the mania for collecting *aegyptiaca* at Greek sanctuaries was actually the background for genealogical tales linking worshippers with "Egyptian" or "Phoenician" ancestors during the sixth century. Juxtaposing genealogical myth against the corpus of Egyptian inscriptions and pseudo-inscriptions found on scarabs at Greek sanctuaries shows surprising levels of engagement between the two.

At the dramatic height of Aeschylus' *Suppliants*, an Egyptian herald confronts the chorus of the Danaids, who had fled Egypt with their father Danaus in the hope of escaping an arranged marriage to the sons of Aegyptus (825–910). "I revere the gods of the Nile" (τοὺς ἀμφὶ Νεῖλον δαίμονας σεβίζομαι, Aes. *Supp.* 922), he says, and "do not fear the native gods [in Greece]—they didn't raise me, nor did they offer me sustenance" (οὔτοι φοβοῦμαι δαίμονας τοὺς ἐνθάδε· / οὐ γάρ μ' ἔθρεψαν, οὐδ' ἐγήρασαν τροφῇ, 893–94). Aeschylus' herald was speaking in hyperbole, but the memory of such people could not have been far off. Just as many in Archaic and Classical Greece thought their ancestors were Dorian or autochthonous, others thought they had descended from Kadmos, Danaos, or other primordial wanderers.[115] "All Greece," Hecataeus of Miletus wrote in the first half of the fifth century, "was once a colony of barbarians" (*FGrHist* 1 F 119). Indeed, Hecataeus' Miletus radiated several myths of this type.[116] Herodotus claims that the pre-Socratic Thales was a descendent of Kadmos, a point on which he was repeatedly cited in antiquity.[117] An even more obscure tradition surrounds one Kadmos of Miletus, a hypothetical early historian who is not cited by any author before Diodorus in the first century BCE. The *Souda* associates with him the invention of prose and the alphabet.[118]

Similar tales are known from other east Greek cities. One genealogical tradition, first found in the epic poet Asios in the sixth century, claims that Samians were descended from Ankaios, son of Phoinix.[119] Herodotus claims that another Phoinix settled Thasos with Phoenicians (6.47); since Homer (*Il.* 14.321–22) lists a Phoinix as father of Europa, there is some thought this ubiquitous Phoinix is another name for Kadmos.[120] Panyassis, uncle of Herodotus, apparently wrote that the nymph Smyrna, namesake of the city, was the daughter of an Assyrian king.[121] Herodotus himself (2.182.2) states that the sanctuary at Lindos was founded by Danaos in his flight from Egypt. A second tradition associates Ialysos—another sanctuary that featured direct pharaonic dedications—with Kadmos and his Phoenicians.[122]

As Sarah Morris has so conclusively demonstrated, Greek tales of wandering Phoenician culture heroes were ancient. In the first half of the first millennium BCE, Phoenician merchants were frequent visitors to the Aegean, leaving behind a trail of toponyms, portable arts, and the narratives that would eventually coalesce into the cosmogonies recorded in the Homeric and Hesiodic poems.[123] Yet not all of these stories were of the *same* antiquity. Around the turn of the sixth century, two new culture heroes enter the picture: Danaos, mythical father of the suppliant maidens, and the conquered Pharaoh Sesostris, who was held to have colonized the entire world with his armies in the distant past.[124] These stories would have long lives; among their most avid readers were African American scholars in the era of abolition, who used these stories to argue for Africa's historical priority *over* Greece. (It is from this discourse that figures like Danaos and Sesostris were introduced to Martin Bernal).[125] In their own historical context around 600 BCE, these tales served something of an analogous purpose, offering those who told them prestigious ancestors who lived in deep antiquity. As I will argue here, narratives of Egyptian culture heroes were promulgated and circulated by members of Egyptianizing cults in Greece in search of traditions of their own. But rather than merely an "invented tradition," these tales presented a calculated borrowing from oral narratives about ancient conquering pharaohs in circulation in Late Period Egypt. In fact, the use and display of scarabs inscribed with pharaonic names in Greek sanctuaries represents some of the earliest evidence we have for the so-called Demotic Cycle.

Sesostris is unique among the foreign culture heroes that populate the imaginary of the seventh century in being generally held to be a real historical figure. Manetho (*FGrHist* 609 F 2) equates him to Senusret III, the twelfth-dynasty pharaoh who ruled between 1878 and 39 BCE.[126] According to Herodotus (2.102–7), Sesostris leads an army as far as the Black Sea, leaving behind "dark skinned and curly haired" (μελάγχροές εἰσι καὶ οὐλότριχες) descendants who circumcise their male children. Herodotus claims that Sesostris carved a pair of monumental reliefs on the roads between Ephesus and Phocaea and between Smyrna and Sardis, the latter of which was identified with the Karabel reliefs in the nineteenth century.[127] Dismissing observations from earlier authors (2.106.5),[128] Herodotus offers the completely spurious translation "I conquered this land on the strength of my shoulders" (Ἐγὼ τήνδε τὴν χώρην ὤμοισι τοῖσι ἐμοῖσι ἐκτησάμην, 2.106.4).

Much is uncertain about when the Sesostris myth first sets in. The earliest explicit reference to the mythical pharaoh might be a fragment of the poet Hipponax, written around 540 BCE. In his 1881 edition of the poet, Bergk emended a difficult recounting of the monuments of Asia Minor (fr. 15 Bergk = 42 West) to include the alleged monument of Sesostris, based on Herodotus' placement of it in the region. Such evidence is hardly conclusive.[129] But even if monuments of Sesostris are not to be found in Hipponax, the myth still appears to have *at least* a late sixth-century vintage. Askold Ivantchik has argued that the Milesian colonists along the northern shores of the Black Sea during the Archaic Period might have actually interpreted Scythian funerary stelai as Egyptian victory monuments.[130] Otherwise, there is some thought that stelai erected by the Persian monarch Darius I (r. c. 522–486 BCE) during his campaign along the northwestern Black Sea coast in 514–12 BCE might have been deliberately passed off after his defeat as monuments of an invented, ancient pharaoh Sesostris.[131]

It is here that the trail, by conventional evidence, goes cold. Greek tales of Sesostris represent the earliest evidence for what Egyptologists call the Demotic Cycle, an expansive, semi-connected sequence of prose narratives that circulated in Late Period and Hellenistic Egypt.[132] These tales—which among other things may or may not display the influence of Homer[133]— relate the achievements of world-conquering pharaohs in the distant past and the heroic defense of the Nile Delta by the delta chieftains of the Third Intermediate Period. Yet if, as Ivantchik thinks, the Greek colonists of the Black Sea had access to the Sesostris myth by the end of the sixth century BCE, it must have been in circulation many decades before Herodotus visited the region.[134] Evidence from inscriptions found on *aegyptiaca* at Greek sanctuaries—and the lively, fictive, and inaccurate ways they were interpreted by Greeks—might militate for an early sixth-century date when the conquests of Sesostris entered the imagination of Greece.

The Egyptianizing assemblages at Archaic sanctuaries present a massive, repetitive, and largely unexplored body of epigraphy, all written in Egyptian hieroglyphs. In fact, if taken as a whole, these hieroglyphic inscriptions make up a sizable percentage of *all* epigraphy from the Archaic Aegean. The vast majority of inscriptions appear on scarabs, which make up 39 percent of published *aegyptiaca* at Greek sanctuaries. (Appendix 3.2). About one in seven scarabs found at sites across the Mediterranean carry a royal title or name of an Egyptian pharaoh. (Appendixes 3.3–4). Pharaonic names served several purposes in the repertoire of scarab inscriptions. On the face of it, they could be seen as political propaganda, the names of men like Psamtik or Apries who upheld the cosmic order (Figure 2.10). (Such a reading once led scholars to see scarabs as valuable tools for dating Greek ceramics.)[135] Yet also prominent in the record are the names of Pharaohs that had been long, long dead. Take the commonly encountered *praenomina* of two New Kingdom pharaohs, Tuthmosis III (*mn ḫpr Rʿ*) (r. 1479–25 BCE) or Amenophis III (*nb mȝʿt Rʿ*) (r. 1388–51 BCE). To some extent, these names served a political agenda; both pharaohs had been venerated by the Nubian, or twenty-fifth dynasty (744–656 BCE), which styled them precedents for its own imperial ambitions.[136] But even this explanation is probably insufficient. In the Late Period, both pharaohs were popularly used to cryptographically render the name of Amun Re.[137]

Then there are the pharaohs whose names are more difficult to explain in our scarab assemblages. Senusret III is foremost among these: his praenomen, *kh' kȝ Rʿ*, appears in at least three Archaic Greek sanctuaries, deposited long before Herodotus was born.[138] Senusret III had a reputation long before he

Hieroglyph	Gardiner	Transliteration	Description
	Y5	mn	senet board
	L1	ḫpr	scarab
	N5	rʿ	sun-disk
Translation:		Thuthmose III	
	Y5	mn	senet board
	D28	k3	arms upraised
	N5	rʿ	sun-disk
Translation:		Thuthmose III	
	V30	nb	basket
	H6	m3ʿt	feather
	N5	rʿ	sun-disk
Translation:		Amenhotep III	
	V29	w3ḥ	swab
	F34	ib	heart
	N5	rʿ	sun-disk
Translation:		Psamtik I	

FIGURE 2.10 Common royal names on scarab cartouches from Greek sanctuaries.

became a valorized figure in the Demotic cycle; among other things, he was the pharaoh of the canonical *Tale of Sinhue*. But the appearance of his name in the repertoire of Late Period scarabs appearing outside Egypt suggests that his conquests resonated long before that. Indeed, by the time Herodotus related his tales of Sesostris, the personal name *s n wsrt* (the nomen of the three pharaohs Senusret) was spreading in popularity in Egypt. The late pharaoh Necatanebo, whose reign was contemporaneous with the earliest surviving cyclic papyri, would even adopt the praenomen of Senusret I, *ḫpr k3 Rʿ*, as his own.[139]

Scarabs and vessels carrying the cartouche of Bakenranef (r. c. 725–20 BCE; Hellenized as Bocchoris) present another case where *aegyptiaca* offer evidence for the circulation of myths about the pharaohs outside Egypt. Bocchoris was the short-lived twenty-fourth-dynasty king based in Sais; as the ancestor of Psamtik I, the Saite regime promoted his reputation as a wise pharaoh.[140] A few inscriptions of his praenomen, *w3ḥ k3 Rʿ*, had already made it to Etruria and Pithekoussai by the seventh century, where they are the foundation of the local site and ceramic chronologies.[141] By the time of Manetho in the third century and Hecataeus of Abdera in the second, he was considered a legendary lawgiver; subsequently he is also the king who expelled Moses and is associated with a prophecy given by a lamb.[142] Bocchoris' sad end at the hands of the Kushite Shabaka is related by Manetho, a hostility hinted at by the representation of bound Nubian prisoners on the faience vessel bearing his name found at Tarqunia in Etruria.[143]

The presence of such obscure pharaonic names in the Mediterranean offers the tantalizing but indecisive hint that Greeks were participants in what Moyer (2011) has called Late Period Egypt's negotiation with its past. We should be clear that this evidence represents little more than a trace; thousands of inscribed scarabs were in circulation in the Archaic Mediterranean, and the number discussed here is in single digits. Nonetheless, they deserve to be added to the same dossier that makes Herodotus our earliest literary attribution for the very Egyptian tales of the Demotic cycle.

Yet at least one question remains. To what extent would Greeks have been conscious of the meanings inscribed on scarabs dedicated in their sanctuaries? Could they have identified the names of Senusret III or Bakenranef? The makeup of scarab corpora at Greek sanctuaries suggests that dedicators of *aegyptiaca* recognized them as textually inscribed objects whose meanings were subject to interpretation. Even if they lacked the ability to *read* hieroglyphs, they *were* capable of producing "translations" akin to Herodotus' attempt to read the feats of Sesostris in the Luwian hieroglyphs of the Karabel inscription. (And this leaves aside the existence of specialists like †Pythermos or †Melanthios, who clearly *could* read hieroglyphs). If scarab assemblages were created through informed behavior—and not the unpredictable activities of Pendlebury's sailors—then they present a hitherto unheralded space where worshippers at Greek sanctuaries constructed notions of the past, ancestry, and their relationships with a fabulous kingdom across the sea.

My survey finds that dedicators at sanctuaries with assemblages of over circa 100 scarabs, such as Perachora and the sanctuaries of Rhodes, preferred to dedicate scarabs that had impressions that could be read in Egyptian without resorting to cryptography (Appendix 3.3–4). These include the names of gods, pharaohs, royal titles, or magical phrases. I define these as "text," not because readers of Egyptian hieroglyphs would have recognized them as inherently *more* textual than pictorial scenes that include hieroglyphs as part of a decorative scheme,[144] but because readers of an alphabetic script—Greek—might have seen them as textual characters, regardless of whether they could be read.

At sites with fewer than a hundred scarabs, ratios are inconsistent. At some sites (the sanctuaries of Chios; the Argive Heraion) worshippers appear to have preferred "textual" impressions; at others (the temples of Sounion) they did not. The ratios found at large assemblages might well reflect a form of collective wisdom, whether at the direction of worshippers who had sailed to Egypt or via local traditions of "reading" dedications made by the pharaohs themselves, like Herodotus' attempt to "read" Sesostris' "inscriptions" in Ionia. Small collections were much more likely to have been steered by the aesthetic preferences of a single individual.[145] *Aegyptiaca* frequently were carried to sanctuaries strung on single necklaces, where impressions would have been highly visible; this was the case, for instance, at, the Paros Delion.[146] Another example comes from an exceptional grave dated to circa 545–40 BCE in Taranto, in southern Italy, where an individual chose to be buried with 157 scarabs strung on three necklaces carefully deposited in a ceramic vessel[147] (Figure 2.11). These show a high degree of seriality, repeating the same impressions as many as twenty-four times. An exceptional 67 percent of these cannot directly be translated as an inscription.

	Hieroglyph	Gardiner	Transliteration	Description
 x24		E14	-	dog
		N5	rꜥ	sun-disk
 x16		M17	i	reed
		G13	m	owl
		N5	rꜥ	sun-disk
 x11		M17	i	reed
		Y5	mn	senet board
		N5	rꜥ	sun-disk
		M17	i	reed
		N5	rꜥ	sun-disk
 x10		G5	ḥrw	falcon
		Y5	mn	senet board
		N5	rꜥ	sun-disk
 x5		F35	nfr	heart/windpipe
		F34	ib	heart
		N5	rꜥ	sun-disk

FIGURE 2.11 Repeated impressions on scarab necklaces from Taranto grave 1, after Hölbl 1979 2, tf. 118/3, 121/1, 128/2, and 133/4.

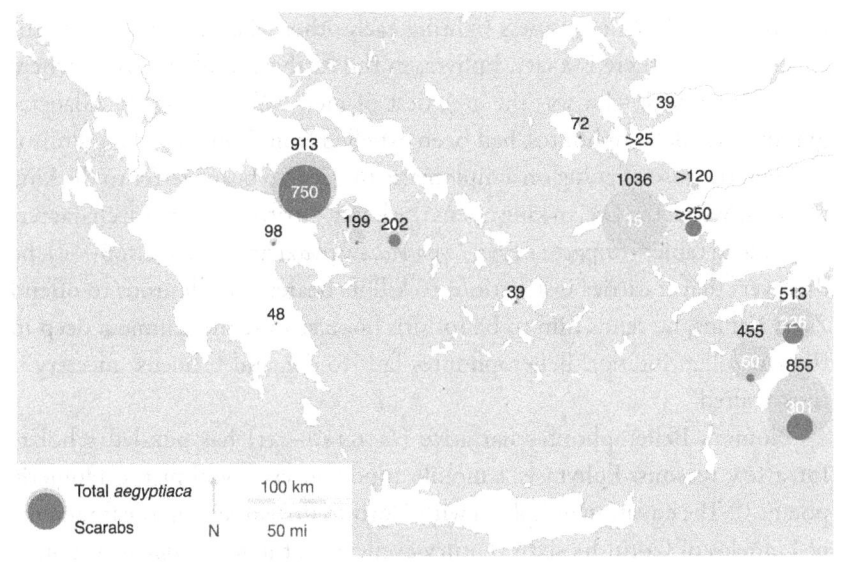

FIGURE 2.12 Map of Greek sanctuaries with scarab dedications showing total size of assemblage and proportion scarab. For full data from small assemblages, see Appendix 3.2.

The inconsistencies of excavation technique and our very small knowledge of the scarab "supply" in Archaic Greece makes me cautious in pursuing the argument that some Greeks could and others could not "read" hieroglyphs any further than this point. But the Taranto necklaces raise the possibility that some Greeks who liked scarabs collected them on principles that veered close to personal aesthetics, while groups of people who collected them at sanctuaries exchanged knowledge about how to "read" them. To conclude this chapter, I want to turn to turn to a group of worshippers in the Peloponnese where scarab collecting took place on an outsized level at the turn of the sixth century. Despite their lack of formalized trading relationships with Naukratis, worshippers at Corinth's sanctuary to Hera at Perachora gathered the largest single assemblage of inscribed scarabs in the entire Mediterranean (Figure 2.12). I argue that worshippers who dedicated scarabs at Perachora used their possession of these distinctive "trinkets" to lay claim to genealogical ties with Egypt that rivalled those of the cities of east Greece.

The Script of the Heroes

Diomedes and Glaucus' confrontation on the battlefield before the walls of Troy ended in a famous de-escalation. As the heroes poised for combat, the pair exchanged genealogies, discovering that their grandfathers were friends and that they had no business fighting each other. Glaucus begins with his ancestry first. "There is a city, Ephyra, in the furthest nook of Argos, where Sisyphos reigned, who was the greediest of men" (*Il.* 6.152–53).[148] Glaucus' grandfather, Bellerophontes, had been expelled from Ephyra by king Proitos through the ruse of going on a diplomatic mission to bear a letter to the king of Lycia. When the Lycian king opens the letter, "written in baneful characters on a folded tablet" (σήματα λυγρὰ / γράψας ἐν πίνακι πτυκτῷ, *Il.* 6.168–69), he discovers that it carries instructions to kill its bearer. Not desirous to offend Zeus Xenios, he sends him to be forlorn hope against the Chimera deep in the Anatolian interior. Bellerophontes fails to die, and Glaucus' ancestry is thus assured.

Homer's Bellerophontes narrative (*Il.* 6.144–211) has puzzled scholars for a few reasons. Ephyra is a mobile toponym even within the Homeric poems.[149] The equation of Ephyra with Corinth first appears in the fragments of Eumelos of Corinth's sixth century cyclic epic, the *Korinthiaka*, although there is some thought the association goes back earlier. By the fifth century, Pindar had squarely located Bellerophontes in Corinth (*Ol.* 13).[150] The story's reference to σήματα λυγρὰ is by far the earliest literary reference to writing in Greece. Although scholars have equivocated whether these "baneful characters" are in fact writing, there is a growing amount of evidence for a culture of writing in the late eighth century when the poem was probably composed.[151]

The problem is that none of the conventional evidence for early writing comes from Corinth or its environs. The earliest writing in Greece appears in the areas most frequented by visiting Phoenicians, on Crete and along the Euboean networks that stretched between Al Mina, Pithekoussai, and the North Aegean.[152] By the end of the sixth century, Greeks generally understood that the "Phoenicians" had invented it. Two Cretan inscriptions, one from the middle of the century and one from its end, refer to letters as ποινικήια.[153] Herodotus' story about the origins of the alphabet *both* gives credit to the "Phoenicians" (παρὰ τῶν Φοινίκων τὰ γράμματα, "letters from the Phoenicians") and locates them on Euboea, where some of them settled (5.57–58).[154] The discovery of Phoenician inscriptions and early Greek abecedaria in the same levels at Eretria makes this one of many instances where Herodotus has his finger on the truth.[155] Yet Corinth was not well connected into the networks the early alphabet travelled along. Evidence for resident Phoenicians in early Corinth remains only a supposition.[156] Corinth's epigraphical culture is poorly represented through the end of the Archaic Period, and only one LG inscription is known at all.[157] The most damning evidence, however, is that Corinth's Archaic alphabet is far closer in resemblance to those of Argos, Attica, and Ionia than the Euboean world or even the rest of the Peloponnese. Though scholars are now cautious with diffusionary models of the Greek alphabet—Nino Luraghi, for instance, has argued that cities *consciously* used their alphabets as symbols of local identity—it is probably the case that Corinthians were not among the earliest adopters of the alphabet.[158]

Corinth's adoption of Bellerophontes' journey to Asia Minor in the *Iliad* formed one facet of a larger reorientation of Corinth's local mythological traditions in the direction of Ionia in the seventh and sixth centuries. Sixth-century Corinthians would not have seen the σήματα λυγρὰ he was carrying as the same "Phoenician letters" that, to people on Crete or Euboea, were evidence for visits by Levantine traders in the distant past. Rather, the ancient "letters" Corinthians identified in their own territory were Egyptian hieroglyphs. During their excavation of Corinth's maritime sanctuary at Perachora in 1929–30, Payne and Pendlebury uncovered an assemblage of at least 750 inscribed Egyptian or Egyptianizing scarabs, which they dated to the Protocorinthian Period (725–625 BCE). But unlike the sanctuaries of Rhodes or the Samian Heraion, which highlighted their direct connections with the Saite state through display of pharaonic or mercenary dedications, only a handful of Egyptian inscriptions from Perachora actually came from Egypt. The overwhelming majority of them were produced by Egyptianizing faience workshops in the east Aegean and Naukratis.[159] Archaic Corinthians used imitation "Egyptian" goods to lay claim to a past just as glorious that the children of Sesostris in east Greece. The association among myth, letters, and faience helped Corinthians visualize an ancestry that ran, via Bellerophontes, through Ionia and ultimately to Egypt.[160]

That the alphabet was a space for contesting ideas of ancestry is already clear in the sixth century.[161] Although the "Phoenician" tradition about its origins is by far the best represented in ancient sources, it had serious rivals from the outset.[162] One of its major competitors was a "native" tradition that claimed the alphabet was either invented by Greeks or was a gift of the gods. Stesichoros is paraphrased (*PMG* fr. 213) claiming that Palamedes, hero of the Trojan War, invented letters in the first half of the century.[163] Aeschylus ascribed their invention to Prometheus (*PB* 454–61).[164] The most frequently attested competitor to the "Phoenician" story, however, is a tradition associated with Miletus that identified Danaos the Egyptian, rather than Kadmos the Phoenician, as the person who brought letters to Greece. The earliest hints of this tradition are preserved by a scholiast to the Hellenistic grammarian Dionysius Thrax, who claims that Hecataeus of Miletus (*FGrHist* 1 F 20) was among several Milesian writers, including Dionysius and Anaximander, to assert that letters were first brought to Greece by Danaus rather than Kadmos.[165]

All of this makes it plausible that Corinthians, by the turn of the sixth century, could have seen the "baneful characters" on Belleropontes' tablet as the same mysterious characters that were hoarded at Perachora. Political impetus existed for such readings under the reign of Periander (d. c. 585 BCE), who both aggressively courted ties with the eastern Aegean and under whom Corinthians began to consolidate local mythology into a coherent narrative. Both might be visible in Eumelos' identification of Homeric Ephyra, and its hero Bellerophontes, with Corinth. Periander established political relations, sometimes close, with Thrasyboulos, tyrant of Miletus (Hdt. 5.92f–g, Ar. *Pol.* 5.8.7.1311a); Pisistratos, tyrant of Athens (Hdt. 5.95); and Alyattes, king of Lydia (Hdt. 3.48). Kypselid-era relations between Corinth and the Saites in Egypt are much less well known. Aristotle (*Pol.* 5.9.22.1315b) reports that Periander's short-lived successor was a nephew named Psammetichos, son of Gordias, whose name scholars have assumed represented a diplomatic effort to court Egypt.[166] But as early as 1922, years before the excavations at Perachora revealed the depths of Archaic Corinth's fascination with Egypt, Percy Ure suspected that the real point of Periander's "Egyptianizing tendencies" was to solidify a cultural relationship with the Milesians, who had direct access to Egypt.[167]

Ionian merchants resident in Corinth represent the group most likely to have brought *aegyptiaca* to the city. Corinthian demand for east Greek finewares was not high during the seventh and sixth centuries; what little has been excavated is limited to plain or banded cups.[168] But the tight concentration of most east Greek ceramic imports in a single building in the Archaic city's Agora led a previous generation of excavators to posit the existence of a commercial establishment for foreign traders. The proposed dates of the complex, 580–60 BCE, match the height of Egyptianizing dedications at Perachora across the water.[169] Likewise, although some amount of Corinthian pottery is present at Naukratis, Corinth was not part of the city's founding consortium, and its surviving prosopography presents no links with Corinth.[170]

It appears likely that both the embrace of the trans-Aegean hero Bellerophontes and an invented "Egyptian" past served the immediate purpose of bolstering the political position of the tyrannical Kypselid regime. The Ionian merchants drawn in during this period brought new and evocative goods that allowed the city's rulers to claim they had put Corinthians in touch with the prosperous world of eastern Mediterranean trade. Corinth's fascination with Egypt and tenuous claims to "Egyptian" ancestry faded with the collapse of the Saite regime in 525 BCE, leaving only its attempt to identify with the Homeric story of Bellerophontes to posterity. The flimsiness of Corinth's claims to "Egyptian" heritage explains why, unlike elsewhere, Corinth's Egyptianizing phase was simply forgotten—never to be mentioned by any Classical or Hellenistic author, and buried at Perachora.

Conclusion

If you were to do a tour of the Aegean's most prosperous cities around the year 600 BCE, you would be greeted by a panoply of claims—our ancestors were Kadmos and the Phoenicians, *ours* were Egyptian. A century before the earliest Greek historians would take up the pen, people in the Aegean saw themselves as children of outsiders. As proof, a subset of them took up the art of collecting evocative, brightly colored faience in their sanctuaries, which could be credibly pointed to as evidence the pharaoh was *here*. In a way, they were not wrong. The collecting habit had been propagated by the very merchants who did business with the Delta, and whose travels to distant Egypt put them in touch with a kingdom far wealthier and more powerful than anything the Aegean had ever seen. *Aegyptiaca* greased the gears of business on that side of the encounter, too, convincing the priests of the Delta that they were trading with Amun's domains across the sea.

In this chapter, I presented a new interpretation to explain the dispersion of Egyptianizing faience scarabs, amulets, and figurines at Greek sanctuaries during the seventh and sixth centuries BCE. I contextualized the circulation of *aegyptiaca* within the larger trade in natron, the key material involved in their manufacture, between Egypt and Greece. By dedicating brightly colored and evocatively shaped *aegyptiaca* at Greek sanctuaries, merchants helped to negotiate a new form of symbolic capital that would facilitate the trust between themselves and their local customers. Long after the height of Aegean Egyptomania between circa 650 and 575 BCE, worshippers at Greek sanctuaries would continue to circulate narratives that explained the abundance of Egyptian dedications through genealogies, the travels of the heroes, and even visiting pharaohs themselves. In this way, the natron trade helped to generate an overlapping convergence of Greek and Egyptian culture through the sixth century.

Yet the cracks were already starting to emerge in this "Egyptian Mediterranean." Some hint of it can be found the much-later description of Sesostris' army offered by Herodotus: "dark-skinned and wooly-haired" (μελάγχροές εἰσι καὶ οὐλότριχες) (2.104.2). If the Greek Egyptomania of the late seventh and earlier sixth centuries was predicated on an idea of common ancestry and descent, things would move in a markedly different direction in its latter half—a period when the powerful Saite dynasty collapsed and Egypt was taken into the Achaemenid fold. Instead, Egypt would come to be seen as a domain of difference, a land with an alien climate inhabited by people biologically and culturally Other to Greece.

In the following chapter, I will continue my analysis of *aegyptiaca* by focusing on a particular and very notable subset of Greco-Egyptian faience that show evidence for this transformation. A significant number of scarabs, amulets, and figurines portrayed human bodies with strikingly racialized features. By the end of the sixth century, Greeks inhabiting the cities that were most networked with Egypt had begun to develop theories to explain the physical differences between people who lived on the northern and southern shores of the Mediterranean. These would become among the racialized images of "Othered" bodies that would be swept up into the idea of the "barbarian" in fifth-century Greece.

3

From Ancestor to "Other"

Introduction

Ida Mae had watched people do it all her life and knew how it was done . . . above her was an entire economy she could not see but which ruled her days and determined the contours of her life. There were bankers, planters, merchants, warehouse clerks, fertilizer wholesalers, seed sellers, plow makers, mule dealers, gin owners. A good crop and a high price made not much improvement to the material discomforts of Ida Mae's existence but meant a planter's wife could "begin to dream of a new parlor carpet and a piano" and a salesman of farm implements could be "lavish with more expensive cigars than he smoked last year." On Wall Street, there were futures and commodities traders wagering on what the cotton she had yet to pick might go for next October. There were businessmen in Chicago needing oxford shirts, socialites in New York and Philadelphia wanting lace curtains and organdy evening gowns. Closer to home, closer than one dared to contemplate, there were Klansmen needing their white cotton robes and hoods.[1]

IN HER 2010 *Warmth of Other Suns*, Isabel Wilkerson traces the interwoven life histories of three Black emigrants who left the segregated southern United States in the first half of the twentieth century for Chicago, New York, and Los Angeles. Between circa 1915 and 1970, six million African Americans departed north and west in a movement that became known as the Great Migration.[2] Racial apartheid in the south was designed to keep the cost of commodity extraction low. Its cornerstone was racism: in keeping workers like Ida Mae Gladney, whom Wilkerson profiles, in a state of constant fear, the leaders of the New South guaranteed that labor would be cheap and free from agitation. Black emigrants found many of the same dangers waiting for them in their new homes. A campaign of racial terror swept the north and Midwest in the immediate aftermath of the First World War, fueled by portrayals of sexual violence instigated by African Americans on stage, film, radio, and mass-market paperbacks.[3]

In the two decades that followed, the federal government would direct job guarantees and housing subsidies to many of the white ethnic communities that had entered the twentieth century in a conditions no less impoverished than the American south.[4] The result was that by World War II, the divide between Black and white ossified and widened in American life. Foreign migrants from the Mediterranean, eastern Europe, and west Asia gained admission into a white racial elite.[5] Domestic migrants from the south remained locked in a permanent, racialized underclass. Adolph Reed Jr. puts it succinctly: anti-Black racism was "a historically specific ideology that emerged, took shape, and has evolved as a constitutive element within a definite set of social relations anchored to a particular system of production."[6]

If the bearing of Jim Crow and its afterlives on Egypt and Greece in the first millennium does not seem immediately obvious, one must recall the sheer power that white supremacy held over the study of the ancient world at the turn of the twentieth century.[7] This chapter grapples with how to engage with the structures it left us. When we left off in the previous chapter, Saite Egypt was the preeminent kingdom of the eastern Mediterranean; many people in the Aegean looked to Egypt as home of their ancestors and their gods, and not an alien Other. Merchants who sailed there came back wealthy; they showered their fellow citizens with benefactions. But at some point around the middle of the sixth century, Egypt lost its hold on the Greek imagination. Around the same time, new images of its people enter the repertoire, identifiable by body, behavior, and costume. A Homeric ethnonym, Ethiopian, was attached to this image, and when it enters into our awareness in the poetry of Xenophanes (fr. 14 Diehl), it appears fully fledged. As late as World War II, many critics treated Greece's Ethiopians as a simple facsimile for Blackness, as though the racial order of Atlantic modernity was transhistorical.[8] In the postwar period, this reading was adapted to anti-racism.[9] Yet the interpretive problem remained: how do we read black bodies in antiquity without the lens of Blackness?[10] As Sarah Derbew writes, we might not be able: "black people are in dialogue with, but not a replica of, Black people."[11]

Thus writing a history of Ethiopians in sixth-century Greece requires a parallel history of how Ethiopians became Black in the scholarship of the twentieth century. This chapter chronicles how Greco-Egyptian faience became the mechanism by which visualization of the Nile Valley's peoples entered into the Greek imagination; their racialization might be regarded as an ultimate product of the Greco-Egyptian natron trade. At the same time, we will retrace a twentieth-century dispute between two American critics—the white art historian Grace Hadley Beardsley (1896–1966) and Black classicist Frank M. Snowden, Jr. (1911–2007)—who sought to use these images to tell competing stories of migration, racism, or the lack thereof in classical antiquity. Though their interpretations of Greco-Egyptian faience are polar opposites, they shared one thing in common: what the ancient Greeks thought about human diversity had some bearing on modernity. Race could not be a central facet of American life if it were not eternal.

A holistic view would find a much less teleological narrative. I argue that "Ethiopians" burst into the imaginary of sixth-century Greece as thinkers like Xenophanes felt an increasing need to explain human diversity. If Greeks in the Early Iron Age conceived of the human body as malleable and unpredictable, people in the sixth century needed causes to explain why some people had dark skin and others pale. Greece's turn-of-the-century Egyptomania had popularized images of the Nile Valley's people through the lens of consumption; as we saw in the previous chapter, there was an entire industry dedicated to producing Egyptianizing votives. Thus from the start, Greeks were prone to see a people who were not exploited by them as, somehow, commodities. (This situation thus differs from the Thracians and Scythians, who are the focus of Chapters 4–6 of this book.)

Yet even as sixth-century Greeks increasingly came to see the peoples of Africa as different from themselves, these portraitures were rarely derogatory, at least not yet. The final transformation of "Ethiopians" and "Egyptians" from ancestors to the Other was a postscript to the history of faience; a century after its decline in Greece, the imaginary it introduced would be transformed, in the wake of the Persian wars, into the body of the Other.

Afterlives of Faience

For over half a century, the study of black people in antiquity was dominated by a single scholar: Frank M. Snowden Jr.[12] Over a career that spanned from Great Depression to the turn of the millennium, Snowden presented a tripartite thesis about the racial dynamics of ancient Greece and Rome:

a. Greeks and Romans were "white";[13]
b "Ethiopians" (Snowden's term for people called Αἰθίοψ, *Aethiops*, μέλας, *fuscus*, and *niger* in Greek and Latin) were a defined racial group equivalent to American "blacks";[14] and
c. Greek and Roman societies lacked "color prejudice."[15]

Snowden's argument was very much an argument about the present. Growing up in a family of Civil Rights activists, Snowden spent most of his career as professor, and later dean, at Howard University in Washington, DC. Between 1948 and the early 1960s, Snowden additionally served multiple terms overseas as a political appointee in the United States Department of State. Snowden's service reached its apogee under the hawkish administrations of Harry S. Truman and Dwight D. Eisenhower, when he served at US Embassy, Rome, as press monitor (1949–50) and cultural attaché (1954–56), and as delegate to two early conferences to the United Nations Educational, Scientific and Cultural Organization (UNESCO) in 1958 and 1960.[16] The State Department actively facilitated his research as a diplomatic tool. In his rarely cited political and propaganda writings, he openly presented Greece and Rome as models of multiracial empires that lacked racial discrimination; the United States was following their example as it (slowly) worked to abolish Jim Crow.[17] Ancient expressions of bias, social stratification, or oppression lacked the organization of modernity. At various points, other scholars disputed Snowden's characterization. Notable here are both the Barbadian classicist Lloyd Thompson (1932–97), who recognized Snowden's curious restraint, as well as Martin Bernal (1937–2013), who excoriated Snowden as an establishment lackey.[18] But Snowden wielded immense political and institutional power, which he freely directed toward his critics. Benjamin Isaac's much-criticized failure to engage with his work in *The Invention of Racism in Classical Antiquity* was almost certainly as much an act of *avoidance* as *erasure*.[19]

The political economy that surrounded Snowden's reading of Blackness in antiquity can be traced through his interpretation of a single class of artifacts. These are Archaic head scaraboids, a subset of Greco-Egyptian faience introduced in the previous chapter. Figure 3.1 presents a group of faience head-shaped scaraboids, and molds for making them, that Snowden argues were evidence of cross-racial encounters in Archaic Greece. Naukratis is the only known production site.[20] Each depicts the same, or almost the same, face: an individual with short, curly hair, a broad nose, wide cheeks, and full lips. All are approximately the same size, between one and two centimeters in diameter. The finished examples are pierced horizontally to be worn as a

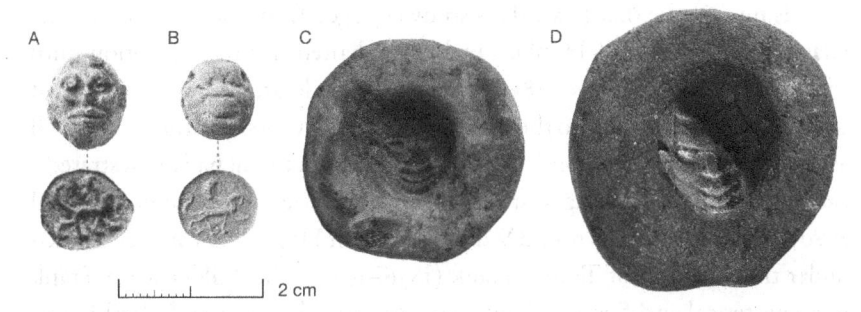

FIGURE 3.1 Head-shaped scaraboids and scaraboid molds from Naukratis, Egypt. **A:** Head-shaped scaraboid depicting right-facing quadruped. MFA 88.873. **B:** Head-shaped scaraboid depicting right-facing quadruped. MFA 88.872. **C:** Mold for head-shaped scaraboid. MFA 88.1064. **D:** Mold for head-shaped scaraboid. MFA RES.87.182. All photographs © 2024 Museum of Fine Arts, Boston.

pendant, an outward-looking, realistic face hanging between the neck and chest of its wearer. Scaraboid B is bright blue; A retains only traces of its original greenish hue.

What were these heads intended to portray? In his monograph-length contribution to the Menil Foundation's *Image of the Black in Western Art* (1976), Snowden presents these representations as product of interactions between Greeks and Egyptians in Naukratis. He writes:

> Greek residence in Naukratis stimulated the interest of sixth-century Greek artists in the Negro and that the city and its environs were a center from which such interest radiated to various parts of the Greek world . . . they must have passed on to their friends and fellow artists information about the physical characteristics of the people of the country as well as descriptions of visual portrayals of Negroes.[21]

And indeed, scholars writing in Snowden's wake have been unanimous in describing them as "Nubian," "Ethiopian," "Black," "Black African," "African," or (regrettably) "Negroid."[22] But this was not always the case. The British archaeologist W. M. F. Petrie (1853–1942), who first excavated the Naukratis head molds, simply labeled them molds for "heads."[23] The scarabs only enter the academic literature as Black ("Negroes") in a 1929 monograph written by Grace Hadley Beardsley (1896–1966), who received her doctorate at Johns Hopkins University in Baltimore in 1922. She was one of several white scholars of the period to show great interest in alleged ancient representations of Africans.[24]

It is no mistake that Beardsley's study emerged from Johns Hopkins. The Classics Department at Hopkins had been chaired from its inception until 1915 by Basil Gildersleeve (1831–1924), a Confederate reprobate who had turned the department into the center of American Classical Studies—as well as a hotbed of racial reaction.[25] Members of the department had orchestrated a campaign of harassment against Black members of the American Philological Association in the years around World War I.[26] At Hopkins, Beardsley studied under the direction of Tenney Frank (1876–1939). Like Gildersleeve, Frank was a hysterical anti-Semite; Frank's greatest contribution to scholarship was an influential 1916 article in the *American Historical Review* blaming the collapse of the Roman Empire on "Oriental" migrants.[27] All of this was situated in the urban context of Baltimore, a massive industrial city with a nearly bottomless hunger for labor. Up until World War I, it was a major locus for migrants from eastern Europe. After the war halted European migration, it became one of the destination cities of the Great Migration. Baltimore's white population orchestrated two anti-Black pogroms in 1919 alone. The July 1919 pogrom in nearby Washington, DC, was many times larger.[28] This context transparently motivates Beardsley's reading of the Naukratis scarabs.[29] Africans in antiquity were outsiders and subalterns, and this was how the scarabs were to be interpreted. "Sufficiently ugly to be prophylactic," she writes, "the Greeks of Naucratis probably enjoyed them fully as much as we do."[30]

It is not as though Beardsley's monograph went unchallenged.[31] Writing in the *Journal of Negro History*, William M. Brewer excoriated the book, at one point comparing Beardsley's rhetoric to the ravings of Alabama Senator James "Cotton Tom" Heflin (1869–1951) on the Senate floor. (This was no idle comparison: in 1908, "Cotton Tom" brutally murdered a Black man on a Washington streetcar. He routinely issued graphic threats to anti-segregationists in Congress. He is also the father of Mother's Day.)[32] Two decades later, W. E. B. Du Bois (1869–1963) recalled Beardsley's book as "a stupid combination of scholarship and race prejudice which Johns Hopkins University published."[33] Dismissed, ignored, or quickly forgotten by white scholars, Beardsley's book represented a threat to the Black intelligentsia: if Greece and Rome were the origin of Western civilization, Beardsley had produced a narrative where they were always marginal.[34]

The debunking of Beardsley was critical in the arc of Snowden's career. Snowden's family had all the markings of what Du Bois had called the "talented tenth." Snowden was born in 1911 to a career civil servant in the Virginia Tidewater; his parents, who were extensively networked in the Civil Rights movement, would move north to Boston in the early stages of the Great Migration. (In 1932, W. E. B. Du Bois would even be forwarded a personal letter written by Snowden's father advertising the achievements of his exceptional son.)[35] Snowden Jr. attended integrated schools in Boston; matriculating at Harvard, he would earn his AB (1933), AM (1934), and PhD (1944) in succession, interrupted by his research in Italy and service during the war.[36] Soon after receiving his doctorate (his Latin-language dissertation surveyed evidence for slavery in Pompeii), Snowden was courted by Du Bois, who hoped to cultivate him in challenge to Beardsley. And, indeed, this would become his singular contribution to the literature. But whether out of frustration with Du Bois' imperious attitude toward him, or his innate establishmentarian politics, Snowden would travel in a very different direction from his radical elder. Snowden accepted the patronage of the federal government, developed a vocal anti-communism, and devoted himself to the cause of gradual progress on Civil Rights.[37]

In the "debate" between Snowden and Beardsley over the meaning of Blackness in Archaic Greece, we see perspectives from two sides of the Great Migration. ("Debate" belongs in scare quotes, because the two scholars never corresponded or met. Despite her racial animus, Snowden was consistently politic toward Beardsley's work—until his later career when he erases her from his footnotes.) Snowden makes Beardsley's evidence serve an opposite agenda. Migration is a net positive in history; Black people were not comic relief in Greece and Rome but serious contributors to society, and their bodies were respectfully portrayed by (white) artists. Naukratis was where the Greeks, transparent stand-ins for northern and midwestern whites, learned to see an "Ethiopian" race. The faience trinkets manufactured there exported its dynamic to the rest of the world.

I will have more to say about their antagonism later, since in many ways their argumentation represents two sides of the same coin; what unites them is both a positivistic style of reading ancient evidence, and a presentism that sees antiquity as the history of the moment. As Denise McCoskey notes, there is no essential strand that requires ancient images of the "Ethiopian" to end logically in the images of Blackness promulgated in the era of the Transatlantic Slave Trade.[38] Yet between them, for a contemporary viewer, is an inescapable *resonance*. There is no seeing ancient images of Blackness without reference to the present.

Without leaving aside our issues of interpretation, I want to return to the question of how people envisioned black bodies at the very tail end of our period, the mid- to late sixth century that gave us Xenophanes, Exekias, and the Busiris painter. Today, there are very few people who would accept Snowden's assertion that these images were naturalistic; as François Lissarrague writes, images are "a discourse other than the discourse of language" and must be understood contextually.[39] Yet the prevailing interpretations have not been wholly satisfying. Lissarrague, Claude Bérard, and other Francophone scholars who revolutionized the study of vase painting in the late 1980s tended to prefigure black bodies as the Other.[40] Is such a reading true? Before proceeding, it is worth returning to Heng's rubric for reading race in premodernity: a "structural relationship[s] for the articulation and management of human differences,"[41] one that transforms ideas of appearance or ancestry into a palpable thing. It is hard to see this at work at the end of the sixth century.

Rather, I believe what we are witnessing was the emergence of a discourse within Late Archaic Greece that takes place after the twilight of the Egyptianizing moment that burned bright decades earlier. Around 600 BCE, thousands of people across Greece believed they *were* Egyptian; Egypt's gods were the gods of their ancestors. Long-distance traders were religious functionaries. Saite Egypt's long political decline over the sixth century took away much of the material basis for this belief. By the tail end of the century, Egypt had become the focus of an interest distinctly ethnographic in nature. Looking at the immense human diversity of the Nile Delta, some Greek artists, writers, and thinkers divided its people in two: Egyptians and Ethiopians.

Ethiopians and Egyptians

Around 550 BCE, an artist known to scholars as the Busiris Painter put the finishing touches on a polychrome hydria, excavated at Ceveteri in Italy and now in Vienna.[42] On one side he depicted our earliest surviving version of the mythical Egyptian pharaoh, Busiris. Busiris was a Greek construction; taking his name from the prominent Late Period cult center in the central Delta, myths of a malevolent Egyptian pharaoh who (in the distant past) sacrificed foreigners to his gods circulated among the Greek community in Egypt. Herakles was subjected to this treatment while on a visit to Egypt; he interrupts his parade to the altar by breaking loose and slaughtering the pharaoh and all his men. Herodotus (2.45.1) regarded it as a vindicationist slander passed between Greeks resident in Egypt.[43]

At any rate, the artist who painted the story a century earlier demonstrates a very real engagement with Egyptian iconographic conventions. On one side of the vase, we are treated to a monstrous Herakles, slaughtering a coterie of white-robed Egyptian priests who had attempted to sacrifice him to their

FIGURE 3.2 Illustration of Caeretan hydria by the Busiris Painter depicting Herakles fighting Egyptian priests and Egyptian soldiers, c. 550 BCE. Kunsthistoriches Museum, Vienna 3576. After Furtwängler and Reichhold 1904-32 vol. 1 pl. 51. Public domain.

gods (Figure 3.2). The artist makes a clear visual quotation of the motif of the pharaoh smiting his enemies from the canon of Egyptian art.[44] He also portrays Herakles' skin as red, the skin color most typically associated with Egyptians in Egyptian painting. Following a convention of polychrome vase painting, the artist alternates the skin, clothing, and hair colors of the men he portrays.[45] The priests are given alternating patterns of either black skin and tan or red hair or tan skin and black or red hair. On the other side of the vase, five soldiers with black skin and black hair, all armed with clubs, march to assist.[46] The vase deliberately aims to capture Egypt's human diversity: the priests range in skin color, hair color, and face shape, while the soldiers are all depicted using a register very similar to Exekias' portrayals a few decades later (Figure I.2, B, Figure 3.3). This represents a deliberate choice. Other Greek vase painters who portrayed Egyptianizing scenes—for instance, the Laconian artist of the Arkesilas cup, dating circa 565–50 BCE—made the conscious choice *not* to portray Egyptians as physically different from themselves.[47]

In Snowden's telling, the men on the back of the Busiris hydria were Ethiopians, an ancient racial classification that he posited were synonymous with Black people in the United States.[48] But the actual moment when Ethiopians become visually identifiable in Greek art is very unclear. In Homer, the Ethiopians were pious people who lived in two groups at the edges of the world, where the sun rises and sets (*Od.* 1.22–26). As Edith Hall writes, "ethnicity was scarcely an issue in the archaic literary world of the heroes,"[49] and there is truth in this: the Homeric narrators show very little interest in

FIGURE 3.3 Black Figure table amphora by painter Exekias depicting Achilles fighting Penthesileia and Memnon with Ethiopians, c. 535 BCE. BM 1849,0518.10. Photograph © Trustees of the British Museum. All rights reserved.

personal appearance outside of specific moments. Snowden would identify one of these moments as the earliest portrayal of a Black person in Greek literature: a minor figure named Eurybates,[50] whom Odysseus (in disguise) describes to the swineherd Eumaeus as "round-shouldered, dark of skin, and curly-haired" (*Od.* 19.246–48).[51] But this description is neither linked to a genealogy, a geography, or a race. This is simply what Eurybates looks like.[52]

We have some reason to believe that somatic difference creeps into the picture in the seventh century, but this is slight. The pseudo-Hesiod author of the *Catalogue of Women* twice refers to "countless black men" (ἀπε]ιρεσίων Μελάνω[ν) and "Kronos' sons, the black men and great-hearted Ethiopians" (τοῦ δ' υἱοῖ] Μέλανές τε καὶ Αἰ[θ]ίοπες μεγάθυμοι) as residents of the edge of the world (fr. 150.11 M-W); at another point they are listed as residents of the world's end with the Libyans and Scythians (fr. 150.15 M-W). Apparently, Archilochus (Pollux 2.23 = Archilochus fr. 238 West) called Ethiopians "wooly-haired" (τρίχουλον). But this one word, quoted by the lexicographer Pollux, is all we have of the poem, and it cannot stand as reliable evidence.[53]

In fact, if we are searching for visual depiction or description of "Ethiopians" in any medium before the middle of the sixth century, we run dry very quickly. This was known to Snowden, as well as the author of a 1988 continuation volume (Vassos Karageorghis' *Blacks in Ancient Cypriot Art*);[54] these scholars both presuppose the existence of the "Ethiopian" in Homeric Greece and, recognizing the lack of evidence, supply material culture from Egypt or Cyprus to fill the gap.[55] Simply put, any "Ethiopian" in Greece pre-550 BCE is not an "Ethiopian" at all. Rather, we are looking at a range of strategies for depicting human diversity in the eastern Mediterranean, including the Nile Delta, that largely predates any system of geographic, cultural, or racial description in Greece. These depictions greatly interface with iconographic conventions that rode the sea lanes between Egypt, Cyprus, Assyria, and elsewhere.

Both Ethiopia and an idea of blackness would become distinct entities in the mind of fifth-century Greece. As Derbew surveys through her readings of Aeschylus, Herodotus, and subsequent authors, the trope of blackness served its own purposes in the Classical imaginary.[56] Limiting our inquiry to the sixth century, I will use the evolution of Greco-Egyptian faience as a genre for tracing how Greeks learned to see "race" when viewing Egyptian bodies.

An Aesthetic of Migration

Full fathom five thy father lies;
Of his bones are coral made;

Those are the pearls that were his eyes;
Nothing of him that doth fade,
But doth suffer a sea-change
Into something rich and strange.
Sea-nymphs hourly ring his knell:
Ding-dong.
Hark! now I hear them—ding-dong, bell.[57]

Dedications of foreign imports—well-wrought cauldrons, luxuriant textiles, random scraps of metal, interesting rocks, and mass-produced trinkets—began to pile up at Greek sanctuaries at the end of the eighth century. Through the Early Iron Age (c. 1100–700 BCE), elites circulated expensive luxuries to articulate their social status. The gifts that Menelaus and Helen received of two silver bathtubs, two tripods, ten talents of gold, golden distaff, and the wheeled silver vessel with golden fringes from King Polybios of Egyptian Thebes offered lasting proof of their distant travels and far-flung alliances.[58] The rise of sanctuaries as centers of wealth accumulation in the Late Geometric Period (c. 760–700 BCE) challenged the existing elite's monopoly over the symbolic capital objects could provide. Herodotus makes this loss of control one of the hallmarks of a sanctuary dedication: once the original dedicator was no longer present, it was easy for others to reappropriate their offerings (1.54, 3.47).[59] To visit a Greek sanctuary at the start of the seventh century was to walk through a museum without labels, an assemblage of objects clearly from far away but without known origins. The miraculous creations stored there offered "something rich and strange" (as Ariel sings) to worshippers, pointing to fantastic kingdoms that lay across the sea.

This section argues that the early representations of what Snowden and his continuators identified as "blacks" in Greek art are better understood as part of an aesthetic of the body in the EIA Mediterranean engendered by migration, instability, and a distinct *lack* of association between human diversity and culture. Presenting a small group of head-shaped seals at from LG contexts in Greece as products of the same workshop (Appendix 4), I argue that the imageries they bear—crudely rendered hieroglyphs, warrior scenes, animals, pharaonic cartouches, and Nilotic vegetation—appealed to the desire of dedicators to envision themselves as participants in a cosmopolitan and unstable seafaring world. This aesthetic transformed worshippers' uncertainty about Mediterranean cultural geography into a celebration of the unstable borders between people, beasts, and gods.[60] When Menelaus wrestles Proetus on the shores of Egypt the *Odyssey* (4.456–59), Homer imagines all these forms combined in a single being: "at first he turned into a bearded lion, then a serpent, then a leopard, then a boar, then flowing water, and finally a tree, high and leafy."[61] In the same way, when the false Odysseus describes the physical appearance of his herald Eurybates (*Od.* 19.246–48), it is in the context of seafaring. Later Greeks would have been driven to explain this difference with a cultural label, but for Homer such a visualization of the body is another possibility of a sea that easily conjures up stranger things.

The earliest diminutive head-shaped objects to circulate the eastern Mediterranean were weights. The end of the Bronze Age saw several weight standards in use in the eastern Mediterranean.[62] The weight sets used to arrive at equivalences were themselves art objects, often carved or cast into shapes including geese, ducks, cows, and human heads.[63] Already during the LBA these had become a medium for artisans to project the morphologies of the body encountered by traders. One lead-filled ivory example from Enkomi on Cyprus (Figure 3.4, A), for instance, models a woman's head, while a contemporary example from Kalavassos-Ayios Dhimitrios uses dark bronze to model what its excavator interpreted as African physiognomy (Figure 3.4, B). Complete weight sets already appear in graves as early as thirteenth century BCE, when one set was deposited in Tomb 11 at Kalavassos-Ayios Dhimitrios.[64] Jan-Paul Crielaard has identified three widely dispersed graves at EIA Lefkandi in Greece, Palaephos-Skales on Cyprus, and Achziv in Israel

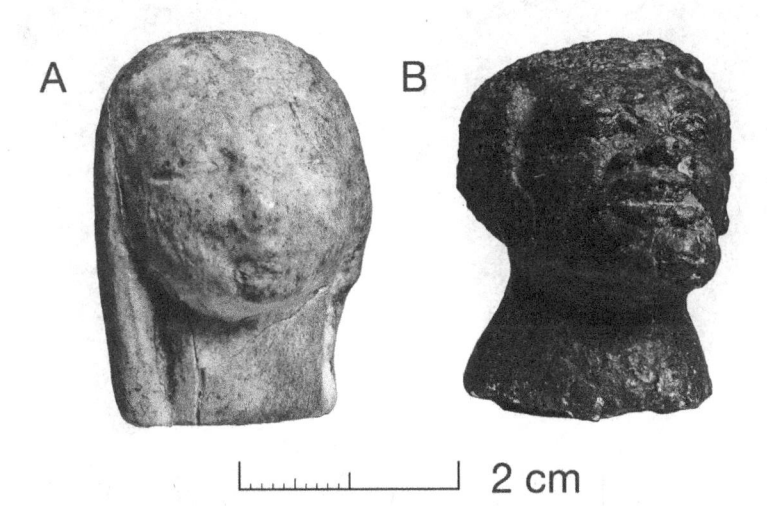

FIGURE 3.4 Late Bronze Age head-shaped weights from Enkomi and Kalavasos-Ayios Dhimitrios, Cyprus. **A:** Nicosia Enk. 59.145; **B:** Nicosia K.-A.D. 454. Photographs by author. Published with permission of the director of the Department of Antiquities, Republic of Cyprus.

containing very similar assemblages of balances, weights, and Phoenician pottery.[65]

The symbolic value of these objects grew as the political systems of the Mediterranean broke down in the eleventh century BCE. Imagery that had circulated on weights during the Bronze Age migrated to the stone, glazed steatite, and faience devotional trinkets that were the calling card of the transnational merchants of the EIA.[66] What had started out as wistful adornment began to take on a life of its own.

Starting in the eighth century, amulets in the shape of human heads begin to appear in number on Cyprus.[67] The vast majority of the forty-four examples catalogued in Appendixes 5.1–2 come from the cemeteries of Amathus on the south coast, where they were probably produced. Cypriot head pendants appear in three types, depicting individuals with pointed, Assyrian-style beards (Figure 3.5, B), cross-scored headdress that reaches the lower forehead (Figure 3.7, A, 3.8, D), and Africanizing features (Figure 3.5, A). (In Appendix 5, I separate these into categories of "headdress," "physiognomic," and "bearded.") Most were carved from dark-colored serpentine,

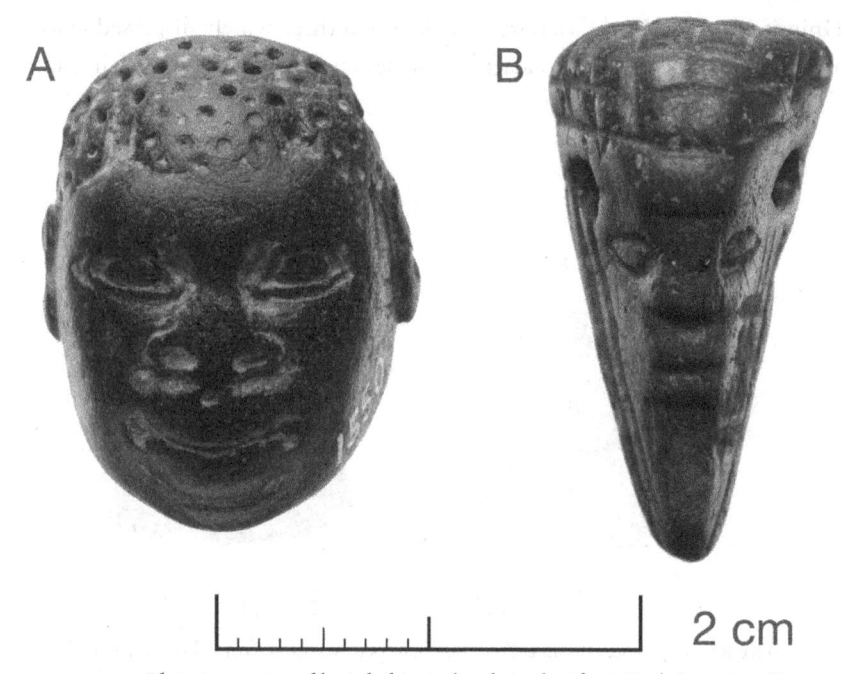

FIGURE 3.5 Physiognomic and bearded stone head amulets from Early Iron Age Cyprus. A: MMA 74.51.5010; B: MMA 74.51.5011. Photographs of objects in the Metropolitan Museum of Art published under CC0 1.0 Universal public domain dedication.

although a small number were made from glazed steatite (Appendix 5.2 nos. 7–10) or ivory (Appendix 5.2 nos. 22, 34). Context at Amathus gives little sense that dedicators differentiated between varieties; all three types appear on necklaces strung with faience *wedjet* eyes, hippopotamus pendants, and Pataikos amulets.[68] One necklace featured two faience demon-faces with a steatite physiognomic head;[69] another was made up of four bearded heads.[70] Contemporary sculpture on Cyprus depicts women and children weighed down with heavy amulet necklaces. On these, heads appear to have been popular choices as center pendants (Figure 3.8 below), but this practice does not appear consistently in the Amathus burials.[71]

Very few head amulets produced on Cyprus during the eighth and seventh centuries were exported off the island.[72] The fact that the bulk of these seals have blank seal-faces might explain why. Cypro-Levantine glyptic styles were popular across the Mediterranean during the EIA. The blank seal-faces of bearded-head amulets and many physiognomic amulets did not appeal to that sensibility. On the other hand, most of the headdress amulets feature the full range of Cypro-Levantine glyptic. With the assortment of hieroglyphs, animals, hunters, and divinities carved on the back and mysterious bearded faces on the front, these offered foreign audiences a canvas to project their own narratives upon.

Questions of provenance and distribution once dominated publications of Anatolian, Levantine, Cypriot, and Egyptian objects found at Greek sanctuaries. More recent years have seen scholars turn to contextual interpretations of sanctuary dedications, questioning how a visual audience understood imagery in place.[73] This approach has most typically been taken in regard to monumental objects—cauldrons, portable sculpture, textiles—but seals and other diminutive arts drew in attention as well. With rich detail crammed into a small space, these focalized the attention of viewers in the miniature worlds they contained.[74] This range of stimuli encouraged worshippers to reflect on their own positions in a world of things sourced from near and far, large and small, positioning them in relation to ancestors, foreign kingdoms, and—if slightly more democratized in the past—the world of the elite who had access to both. For this reason, sanctuary attendants attempted to control what images were available through curating their positions and disposing what was no longer useful underground.[75] New acquisitions of rare and expressive objects—however they arrived—might both complement and express tension with objects already on display.

Head scarab A (Figure 3.6) and scarab B come from an eighth- to sixth-century votive deposit discovered during early excavations at Delphi. The

FIGURE 3.6 Early Iron Age scaraboid from Delphi, Greece (Scaraboid A, Delphi Museum inv. no. 31231). Rights to the depicted object, which is subject to the jurisdiction of the Ephorate of Antiquities of Phokis, belong to the Hellenic Ministry of Culture and Sports (Law 4858/2021). © Hellenic Ministry of Culture and Sports/Hellenic Organization of Cultural Resources. Photograph by author.

two scarabs were the only faience objects to come from the sanctuary.[76] Head scarab A depicts a violent scene of a round-shielded warrior facing off against two zoocephalous creatures with square shields. They are set against a background of Nilotic vegetation and surrounded by a border of vegetative hieroglyphic signs reading *rn* ("name"), probably chosen because it resembles the vegetation also depicted on the impression.[77] Scarab B depicts a peaceful scene of antelope grazing in front of vegetation, with the ground rendered as a hatched *nb* basket.

Imagery of Nilotic vegetation and round-shielded warriors appealed to stylistic preferences expressed by worshippers at Delphi in their selection of objects with similar motifs in other media. A contemporary silver Cypro-Phoenician bowl also found at site depicts an Assyrianizing city siege scene, pitting a round-shielded warrior, some archers, a pair of charioteers, and sappers against a city defended by bowmen.[78] Warriors in different headdresses, including Egyptian-style wigs and pointed Assyrian caps, attempt to scale ladders and kill the inhabitants. Cypro-Phoenician bowls depicting warriors in different garbs—Egyptianizing, Assyrianizing, and some with helmets and round shields—appear in in Greece and were especially popular in Italy during the period.[79]

FIGURE 3.7 Two Early Iron Age scarabs from Zagora, Andros, Greece. **D:** Scaraboid D from Zagora (Andros Museum inv. No. 1300). **E:** Scarab E from Zagora (Andros Museum inv. nos. 1324). Photographs by author. Rights to the depicted objects, which are subject to the jurisdiction of the Ephorate of Antiquities of the Kyklades, belong to the Hellenic Ministry of Culture and Sports (Law 4858/2021). © Hellenic Ministry of Culture and Sports/Hellenic Organization of Cultural Resources. Photographs by author.

Although both seals from Delphi employ hieroglyphs as part of their decorative scheme, neither bears a legible inscription. Scarab C (Figure 3.9) from an LG grave in Attica and scarabs D and E (Figures 3.7, D, E) from the eighth-century sanctuary at Zagora all feature designs primarily made using hieroglyphs—although only scarab E, inscribed with the praenomen *mn ḫpr R‘* of the LBA pharaoh Thuthmosis III alongside a *pschent*-wearing sphinx and an *ankh*, carries a legible phrase. Both the Delphi and the Zagora pair appear to have been sorted based off their size (A and B are unusually large, measuring over 4 cm in length, while D and E both measure 1.7 cm) and hieroglyphic scheme (hieroglyphs are not conspicuous in A and B, while they dominate the scenes in D and E). It is more difficult to arrive at the preferences behind the selection of scarab C, since it was found in a grave and its archaeological

FIGURE 3.8 Votary figure of boy wearing head pendant from Ayia Anna, near Kourion, Cyprus. Late fifth century BCE. MMA 74.51.2311. Photograph published under CC0.1.0 Universal public domain dedication.

context was not recorded. If this group of scarabs arrived in Greece together, as I will argue below they did, then these physical characteristics might have been central in how they ended up dispersed to where they are.

Scarabs A, C, and D all take the shape of headdress amulets. These are rare in eighth-century Greece (Appendix 5.2 no. 5 is of the same type but somewhat different workmanship), although several faience examples appear during the following century (Appendix 5.3). Although each of their original excavators resisted incorporating these scarabs under the label "African" or its equivalent,[80] more recent scholars have been less reticent.[81] The problem is that the features scholars point to as proof—hair, noses, and lips—are either indistinct or are clearly a piece of apparel. Scarab A, for instance, appears to be wearing a headpiece. One faience mold from Naukratis appears to model the hair as a feathered headdress.[82] In fact, the faces of headdress amulets most

FIGURE 3.9 Large Early Iron Age scarab from Attica (head scaraboid C). Harvard Art Museums/Arthur M. Sackler Museum 1960.628. Photograph © President and Fellows of Harvard College.

closely resemble the obscure wearers of reed-and-feather hats that appear as Egypt's seaborne enemies on the walls of Ramesses III's LBA temple complex at Medinet Habu or on the covers of anthropoid coffins at EIA Beth Shean in modern Israel.[83] Images of similar feathered-headdress wearers appear throughout the eastern Mediterranean over the EIA, including on Cyprus, where there was a brief fad for portraying disembodied heads wearing unusual headdresses during the seventh century (Figure 3.10).[84]

What head seals at early Greek sanctuaries might have actually evoked for their viewers was something else: their own travels. Representations of mariners wearing what appear to be spiky or feathered helmets appear in Greece as early as LHIIIC and remain common in ship scenes on pottery through the Geometric Period (Figure 3.11).[85] Although their presence in the eastern Mediterranean during the EIA has been overstated, Assyrian royal sources repeatedly complain about seaborne *Iamanaja* raiders coming from the west.[86] Mercenaries have been given an outsized role in the recirculation and repurposing of war booty as sanctuary dedications at the start of the seventh century.[87] While there remains considerable disagreement over their importance, both sporadic raiding and mercenary service loomed large in the imagination of eighth- and seventh-century Greece.[88] As much of the Near East was engulfed in Assyria's wars of expansion during the seventh

FIGURE 3.10 Bichrome V vase depicting frontal face. Sixth century BCE. Nicosia B 388. Photograph by author. Published with permission of the director of the Department of Antiquities, Republic of Cyprus.

century, Greeks imagined themselves as participants both through the piratical wanderings of the Achaean heroes and city-siege narratives, the greatest of which was the *Iliad* itself.[89]

Both the solitary face carved on the back of scarab A and the narrative scene of round-shielded warriors facing zoocephalous men appealed to a context of instability, seafaring, and periodic depredation. Lone Wriedt Sørensen has argued that images of the disembodied head were politicized during the first centuries of the first millennium as the conquering Assyrians employed

FIGURE 3.11 Drawing of Late Helladic IIIC crater from Kynos, East Locris, Greece. After Wachsmann 2000: 115, Figure 6.13. Illustration used with permission.

beheading as a weapon of terror across the near east. Assyrian relief carvers paid careful attention to the heads of enemy soldiers when depicting city-sieges to foreground the gruesome decapitations that inevitably followed.[90] Zainab Bahrani notes the dexterity with which Assyrian artisans adopted the artistic styles of Assyria's victims—a borrowing that became particularly charged during the reigns of Esarhaddon (r. 681–669 BCE) and Ashurbanipal (r. 668–27 BCE), when Assyrian artists repurposed longstanding Egyptian representations of Nubian bodies as standard representations of Egyptians themselves.[91] In the inscriptions Esarhaddon commissioned to memorialize his sack of Thebes in 667 BCE, the Assyrian monarch gloated about deporting Egyptian artists and craftsmen. He also makes a series of pointed comments about the physical appearance of the pharaoh Taharqa and his family, all members of a dynasty with roots in Nubia to the south. "His wives, his sons, and [his] daughters, [whose . . .] skin, like his, was black as pitch."[92] These politicized representations the body tricked out slowly into the Mediterranean world, and we are hindered in establishing a timeline by our fuzzy dating of early archaeological excavations and the Homeric poems.

If the circulation of physiognomic amulets in Cyprus and Greece during the eighth and seventh centuries indicates anything, it points to an emerging logic of the body at the end of the EIA. Rather than distinct representations of "races" or "ethnicities," as Snowden and his successors were inclined to think, head-shaped trinkets promoted an idea that the body *had* morphology, but not yet that that morphology could be assigned a geographic or cultural origin. Head amulets possessed an aura of interchangeability, potentially representing a range of physiognomic identities in a world of movement. Dedicators might have even identified themselves with these images, as was the case of the round-shielded warriors of Delphi. Zoocephalous men, bearded men in weird hats, and bronze-armed warriors were all likely to be encountered at the distant reaches of the corrupting sea.

Consuming the Body

Some had them inlaid in gold in the lids of their snuffboxes. Of the ladies, some wore them in bracelets, and others had them fitted up in an ornamental manner as pins for their hair. At length the taste for wearing them became general, and thus a fashion, which usually confines itself to worthless things, was seen for once in the honourable office of promoting the cause of justice, humanity and freedom.[93]

Josiah Wedgwood's (1730–95) medallion for the Society for Effecting the Abolition of the Slave Trade was ubiquitous across the British Atlantic the early 1790s (Figure 3.12). Starting in 1787, Wedgwood and his imitators churned out tens of thousands of medallions of a chained Black man on his knees begging the viewer for his freedom, reproduced on various media.[94] Two decades later, Thomas Clarkson (1760–1846), the leader of the society, reflected on its success. Through reproducing the image, members of the society forced a middle-class audience of sugar consumers to reflect on their role in propagating the suffering of enslaved Africans in the West Indies. Middle-class consumers led the charge against the West Indian block in Parliament, eventually leading to the abolition of the slave trade in 1808.[95] They bankrupted them, too. Images of suffering bodies persuaded them to redirect their consumption toward new, "free" sources of sucrose processed from the sugar beet in continental Europe.[96] Once this had happened, images of suffering Black people lost their polite appeal; although slavery would persist in British territories for decades longer, middle-class commiseration for the fate of enslaved Africans was short-lived.

Small, portable objects like Wedgwood's anti-slavery medallions taught middle-class English to *visualize* the effects of their own choices on the bodies of others. In reproducing imagery of the racialized body—a racialization

FIGURE 3.12 Anti-slavery medallion, Wedgwood Manufactory. 1787. Art Institute of Chicago 1912.326. CC0 Public Domain Designation.

that *specifically drew attention* to the foreignness of enslaved Africans—they instructed wielders that a common humanity transcended visual somatics.[97] Wedgwood's world, of course, is not the period of our study; but in a similar light, we can see how small, portable objects, wielded in intensely personal ways, encouraged practices of reflection and consideration among their users. In the eighth and seventh centuries BCE, the line between demons, humans, and gods was blurry; all were part of the larger family of living creatures traced, for instance, in the *Odyssey*, or the Hesiodic *Catalogue of Women*. The sea was a miraculous place where you could run into a Polyphemus or Eurybates alike.

This section looks at the moment that this worldview began to fall apart. In this, we return to Naukratis, the multicultural emporion surveyed in Chapter 1, and that Snowden saw as the cradle for ancient multiracialism. Surveying Greco-Egyptian faience likely manufactured along the networks that linked Naukratis, Rhodes, and wider east Greece, I argue that the specific visualizations we see in Greco-Egyptian faience of the human body responded to specific material conditions of the trade in natron and other commodities. I draw particular attention to the service economies that surrounded Archaic ports, particularly the sex trade. The imaginings of the human body to rise from these settings increasingly encouraged the wielders of Greco-Egyptian faience back in the Aegean to see Egyptians as bearers of a distinct, somatic, alterity. By the end of Greek Egyptomania in the second quarter of the sixth century BCE, some in Greece would be prepared to identify people who possessed these visual qualities as natives of a region beyond Egypt, as would Xenophanes, Exekias, and the Busiris Painter. Through these means the image of the "Ethiopian" would be born.

Starting in the last quarter of the seventh century, faience workshops in east Greece began producing a new type of nude, anthropomorphic figures out of faience that blended Egyptian and Greek portraitures of the body. Christened "mixed-styled figures" by Virginia Webb, they often carry animals, musical instruments, and ceramic vessels (Figure 2.5, D; Figure 3.13). Artisans at Naukratis followed and began making their own versions around the turn of the century.[98] Mixed-style figures appeared so alien to early scholars that some believed they were the primary vector of the *kouros* posture from Egyptian and Cypriot stone-carving to Greece.[99] The majority are either nude male *aulos* players or women in an Astarte posture. In both cases, their breasts, genitals, and pubic triangles are disproportionately large and marked with brown paint[100] (Figure 2.5, D; Figure 3.13, A). Indeed, their sexualization is one of the characteristics that marks these faience figures products of an intercultural exchange. Male nudity is a calling card of Greek art of the sixth century, but rare in Egypt. Nude female figures were, on the other hand, commonly encountered across the eastern Mediterranean.[101]

Due to their conspicuous stylization, Webb labels some of these figures as Greek representations of "Africans"[102] (Figure 3.13, B, C). As is often the case, such a characterization is difficult to justify. Their facial details, after all, were for the most part quickly rendered with schematic lines on a glob of wet faience. Artisans often paid more attention to the implements their figures carried as the details of the body itself. Such attention can be seen on a small subset of figurines that convey non-Egyptian ceramics used for carrying wine. One example from Naukratis (Figure 3.13, C) is a nude woman kneeling and presenting a Phoenician-style torpedo amphora. Another (Figure 3.13, B) is a nude man holding a more carefully rendered amphora of the same type.[103]

Mixed-style figurines were distinct products of what Ian Moyer (2011) has called the "double hermeneutic" that characterized Greco-Egyptian

FIGURE 3.13 Greco-Egyptian mixed-style faience figures. **A:** Mixed-style figure of woman holding *dinos* and new year's flask from Rhodes, Greece. MMA 17.194.2397. Published under CC0 1.0 Universal public domain dedication. **B:** Mixed-style figure of woman holding amphora from Naukratis, Egypt. BM 1888,0601.44. Photograph © Trustees of the British Museum. All rights reserved. **C:** Mixed-style figure of woman holding amphora Naukratis, Egypt. BM 1888,0601.46. Photograph © Trustees of the British Museum. All rights reserved.

interactions in the seventh and sixth centuries BCE. During the Late Period, faience artisans at the east delta cities of Bubastis, Tanais, and Busiris produced nude female figures carrying baskets, New Year's flasks, and imported Greek ceramics, including *dinoi* and amphorae.[104] The production of ceramic figures in similar shapes would continue through the Hellenistic period.[105] Herodotus reports that ritualized female nudity (2.60.2), self-flagellation (2.61.1), and wine consumption (2.60.3) were crucial parts of festivals to Isis at Busiris and Bastet at Bubastis. Wine itself was a commodity imported in great quantity from the Levant. When Herodotus comments that Greeks had learned a great deal from these festivals (2.58.1), he (perhaps inadvertently) draws attention to the intercultural nature of Late Period delta festivals: bringing people and commodities together from far afield, they offered something recognizable to everyone. Mixed-style figures and figures produced for dedication at east delta sanctuaries are not easily discernible; some number of the former made it back to Greek sanctuaries.[106]

Indeed, faience figures appear to have been dedicated with some regularity at the three Rhodian sanctuaries, the Samian Heraion, and the sanctuaries of Apollo and Aphrodite at Naukratis (Figure 3.14). In Greece, only figurines from Samian Heraion have documented archaeological context, where they appear to have been deposited east of the Rhoikos Altar over a fifty-year period.[107] Single deposits at the sanctuaries of Aphrodite and Apollo

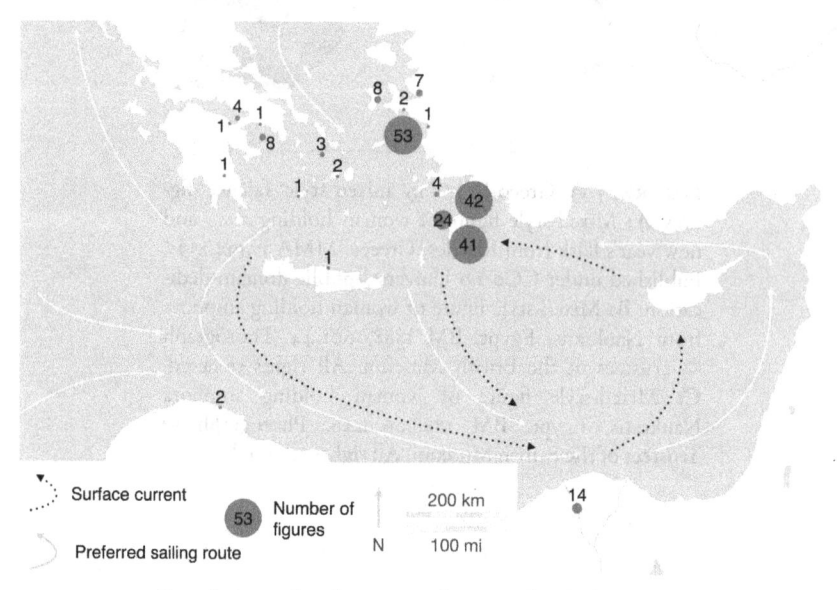

FIGURE 3.14 Distribution of anthropomorphic mixed-style figurines after Webb 1978.

at Naukratis appear to have contained a large number of figurines.¹⁰⁸ At the Apollo sanctuary, layer AΠ4-5 contained some twenty figurines, fourteen of which were anthropomorphic of various kinds, dating between circa 600 and 540 BCE; the latter layer contained nothing else. Petrie's recording is sporadic, and Webb indicates that the total number of figurines found across the Naukratis sanctuaries was considerably higher.¹⁰⁹

What meanings might dedicators at the Samian Heraion or the Rhodian sanctuaries—far from the delta—attach to these brightly colored, voluptuous faience figures? Herodotus' description of wine and nudity at the east delta festivals might prove a useful guide. Naukratis was a major center of the sex industry in Archaic and Classical Greece; Herodotus (2.34–35) reports lurid myths about the sixth-century sex worker †Rhodopis/Doricha, who was based off the lover of Sappho's brother †Charaxos in her poetry. When the Greek sanctuaries of Naurkatis were first excavated at the end of the nineteenth century, excavators were quick to identify the many women known from their epigraphical corpus as sex workers who had dedicated ceramics.¹¹⁰ It is uncertain to what extent the Greek sanctuaries of Naukratis served as a center for prostitution; Herodotus notes that both Greeks and Egyptians viewed intercourse at sanctuaries as unclean (2.58.1), and at any rate brothels are notoriously elusive in the archaeological record.¹¹¹ But as the central spaces where sailors ritually feasted, caroused, and dedicated to the gods who had brought them safely to Egypt, it is here that we should locate the port's sexual economy—even if not its consummation.

Non-Greeks appear to be disproportionately represented among in the prosopography of sex workers known from the Greek sanctuaries of Naukratis.¹¹² Aside from the Thracian †Rhodopis/Doricha, we find common pseudonyms used by sex workers in Classical Greece, including †Archedike, †Mikkis, and †Doris. The inscribed sherd of a vessel dedicated by a woman named †Iunx might also represent another sex worker. To these we should add some extremely unusual inscriptions. One patron carved an extended *Lieblingsinschrift* for a woman with the Egyptian name †Tamynis (*vac* Γοργίας φιλεῖ [...]νιν καὶ Τάμυνις Γοργίαν φιλ[), which its original publisher, Beazley, thought was rather romantic.¹¹³ An interesting case are three sherds of Chian chalices pre-painted with the *dipinto* †Aigyptis, "Egyptian woman."¹¹⁴ These vessels, produced in a batch abroad, came to Naukratis as premade *Lieblingsinschriften*. If later parallels from Classical Athens are of any use, these almost certainly refer to enslaved sexual labor.¹¹⁵ A final oddity is an Attic skyphos foot inscribed by †Ariston, who announces he is excited to go to the baths. The only partially legible inscription is drawn

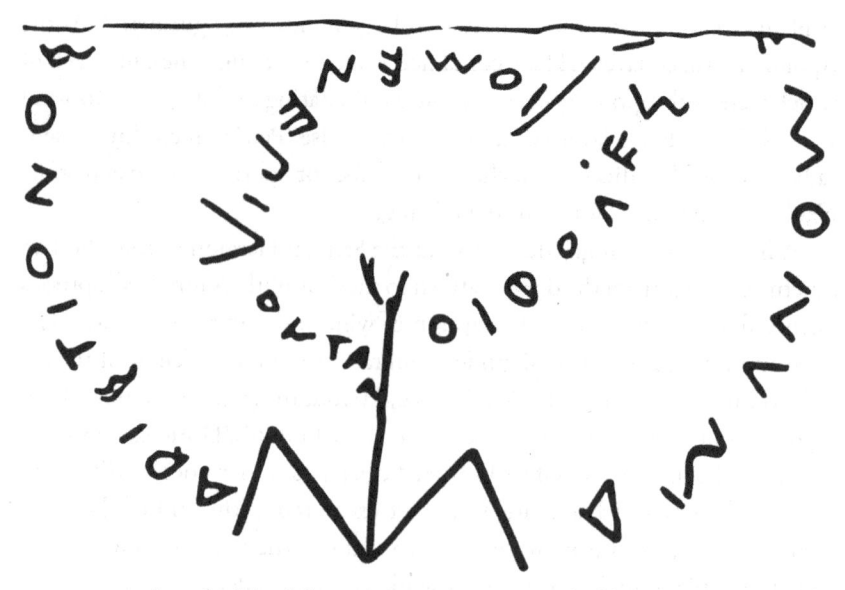

FIGURE 3.15 Inscribed sherd from Naukratis, Egypt, inscribed by Aristion. After Edgar 1907. Public domain.

in a circle around a crude stick-drawing of a woman in missionary position (Figure 3.15).

The association drawn between sex work, non-Greeks, and the Greek sanctuaries of Naukratis in the Greek imagination suggests that when people at Greek sanctuaries were viewing or dedicating faience nude figurines, they were thinking of non-Greek bodies. With their voluptuous features, striking nudity, and Greek wine vessels in their hands, they were designed by the artisans of Rhodes to evoke the idea of the pleasure economy Greeks could participate in if they sailed to the Nile Delta. Like the Chian vessels pre-painted with the name †Aigyptis for dedication at a Greek sanctuary in Naukratis, mixed-style figurines both presented the "Other" as different from Greeks while at the same time an object of consumption. We are not yet at the point where these bodies become distinctly black, Ethiopian, or otherwise. Rather, what is important to see is that these bodies possessed a *distinct* somatic borne from the mechanisms of trade.

By far the most striking—and most studied—portrayal of "Othered" bodies in Archaic Naukratis are the head scarabs, which we began this chapter with. Between circa 600 and 570 BCE, the workshop identified by Petrie as the Naukratis "scarab factory" produced head-shaped scaraboids out of faience[116] (Figures 2.6, 3.1, 3.16). Some 131 head-shaped molds are known from

FIGURE 3.16 Molds for head-shaped scaraboids and head-shaped scarboid from Naukratis, Egypt. **A**: BM 1896,0610.15; **B**: BM 2012,5020.1; **C**: BM 1886,0401.1691. Photographs © Trustees of the British Museum. All rights reserved.

the site.[117] These can be added to some sixty-four finished examples, not all of which were manufactured at Naukratis[118] (Appendix 5.3). Typologically, the head scaraboids can be divided into two overarching categories, both of which derive from the eighth- and seventh-century head amulets that circulated on Cyprus. Headdress scaraboids comprise forty-four of the finished examples, although only a single mold is from Naukratis (Figure 3.16, C). Physiognomic faience scaraboids, all of which closely resemble the physiognomic head amulets from Archaic Cyprus, make up twenty finished examples, as well as the vast majority of the Naukratis molds (Figure 3.1, Figure 3.16, A). But the physiognomic molds carry quite a degree of variation. Some seventeen of the so-called African head molds present a heavily stylized rendering of the leonine dwarf god, Bes, who bore distinctive forehead cicatrices and other markings[119] (Figure 3.16, B).

Who was the intended audience for the Naukratis head scaraboids? Petrie had interpreted the products of the Naukratis "scarab factory" through the lens of the colonial souvenir trade, with Greek artisans settled in Naukratis making little representations of the native people to sell to visitors.[120] Beardsley and Snowden assimilated the head scarabs in the American racial narrative, making them white depictions of Black bodies. Yet the answer appears to lie in neither of these approaches. In her recent republication of the "scarab factory," Masson-Berghoff notes that the vast majority of faience made at Naukratis appears to have been destined for use within the city itself,

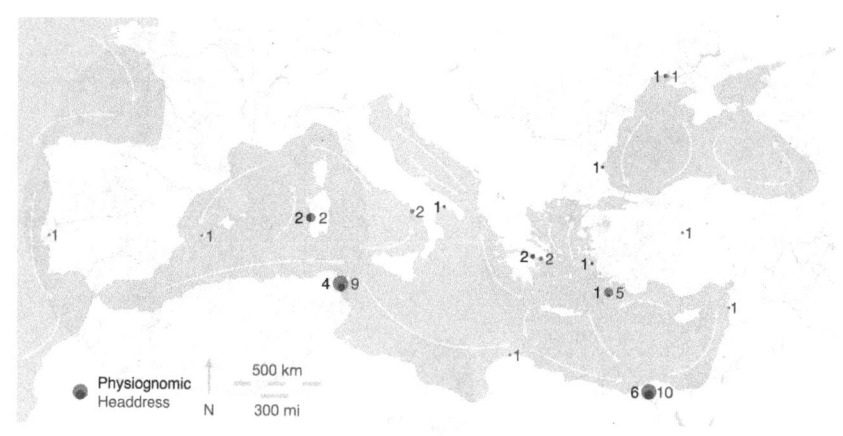

FIGURE 3.17 Distribution of faience head scaraboids.

either as personal devotional items or for dedications at the local sanctuary of Amun Re-Baded.[121] Indeed, Bes, was a popular god in the western delta during the Late Period, where he was worshipped in his capacity as son of Neith, whose cult was based at Sais.[122]

Bes' association with the Black body might also explain the distribution of head scaraboids in the wider Mediterranean (Figure 3.17). Head scaraboids have only been found in ones and twos across the Greek world. No examples come from Cyprus at all. In fact, the largest concentration of Naukratis head scaraboids outside Naukratis is found at the sixth-century Dermech-Douïmès cemetery in Carthage, where a third of all graves contained scarabs (Appendix 5.4 nos. 4–10, 49–52). Several Egyptian dwarf gods including Bes had been adopted by Phoenician sailors as tutelary gods at the middle of the first millennium BCE. Likewise, masking rituals—involving individuals wearing grotesque masks to inspire religious awe—were a longstanding part of Phoenician funerary practices.[123] The predilection for brightly colored amulets depicting frontal faces would survive in the Phoenician world long after it had disappeared in Greece. In the second half of the sixth century, Phoenicians would switch to pendants made from rod-formed glass.[124]

All told, then, the origin of the imagery presented by the Naukratis head scaraboids is somewhat more complex than what either Snowden or Karageorghis argued. It is not as though the head scaraboids did not convey a new imagery of the human body to Greece; it is plausible they could have, even though few examples have been recovered from the Aegean. It is more a matter of the purposes they served in Naukratis. For worshippers of the cult of Neith, they circulated imagery akin to that of Bes, their fierce leonine protector. For the Phoenicians who showed a real interest in head scaraboids, they circulated the frightful—but religiously inspired—imagery of the mask. Head scaraboids were components of a pan-Mediterranean culture of visualizing the body in which human diversity was linked to factors *other* than geography, behaviors, or cultures.

But if—in the spirit of Snowden and Karageorghis—we are looking for how Greco-Egyptian faience *might have served* as a vector of images of the "Ethiopian" body to Greece, there are some more likely candidates. These are faience janiform and quad-form oil vessels, or aryballoi, which have one foot each in the cosmopolitan Mediterranean of the late seventh century and the rise of the Athenian ceramic industry in the mid-sixth (Figure 3.18). These vessels, which are made in the shape of multiple human heads fused into a single object, borrow heavily from the imaginary of the EIA Mediterranean. They juxtapose disembodied heads of animals and demons with human faces clearly borrowed from the iconographies of Assyria and Egypt.[125] Produced on Rhodes after circa 600 BCE,[126] some nine examples of these had been catalogued by Webb's work in the 1970s, a number that has slightly increased in subsequent years.[127] The close similarities in workmanship between certain of these—for instance, the grimacing demons on Figures 3.18 A, B, the Egyptian ladies on Figures 3.18 A, D, or the Nubians on Figures 3.18 C, E—raise the possibility (at this point not yet proven via material testing) that they are products of the very same artisans. The small number and uncertain provenance of these vessels make it difficult to establish patterns of distribution; as of now, it seems that they followed the general pattern of other Greco-Egyptian faience, with a small plurality of objects coming from Rhodes, and others vaguely attributed to contexts in Italy, Cyprus, and elsewhere.[128]

Faience head vessels have raised issues of interpretation very similar to those that have attended the head scaraboids. A striking number of them portray black people, and these depictions very clearly overlap with demons, such as the sharp-toothed Africanized demon in Figure 3.18, A. Curators at the Metropolitan Museum have inconsistently labelled the head in Figure 3.18, E as "Bes," raising the same issue we saw earlier with the depiction of forehead cicatrices on some of the Naukratis head scaraboid molds. The point, of course, was that these depictions are fluid. Aryballoi were vessels for perfumed oils, often imported from far away, that improved the smell and appearance of the body.[129] As such they lent themselves to depictions of the human form in all its capacities.[130] Around the same time as the janiform and quad-form vessels were being made, ceramicists in Rhodes and Corinth were

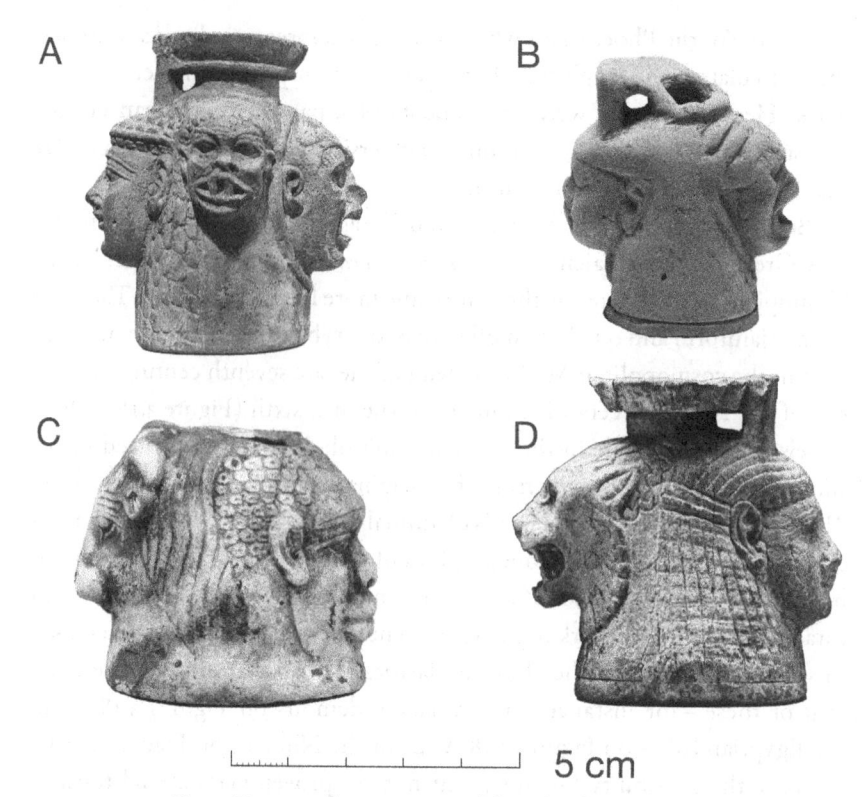

FIGURE 3.18 Greco-Egyptian faience. **A**: Quad-form head aryballos. MMA 1992.11.59. Photograph by author. **B**: Janiform head aryballos from Kourion, Cyprus. Penn 1954-28-229. Photograph courtesy of the Penn Museum. **C**: Janiform head aryballos. MMA 2008.546. Photographs of objects in the Metropolitan Museum of Art published under CC0 1.0 Universal public domain dedication. **D**: Janiform head aryballos from Rhodes, Greece. Getty Villa 91.AI.25. Photograph courtesy of the J. Paul Getty Museum.

experimenting with head-shaped aryballoi,[131] while some potters on Euboea developed a weird fixation with feet.[132] This anatomical interest seems to have appeared on shapes meant for different venues, as well: Lissarrague, for instance, has identified a group of Black Figure Athenian painters who rendered disembodied arms, legs, hands, and feet on hoplite shields.[133]

Faience janiform and quad-form aryballoi present a clear precursor to a much better-known body of objects. These are the so-called janiform ceramic vessels made in mid- to late sixth-century Attica. (Figure 3.19). Janiform vessels are some of the most recognizable products of late sixth-century Greece; endlessly reproduced on the covers of books[134] or fliers for lectures on race in ancient Greece, they remain remarkably little understood. They represent a subset of the much larger class of head-shaped ceramics meant for pouring

From Ancestor to "Other"

FIGURE 3.19 Janiform ceramic *kantharos*, c. 510-480 BCE. MFA 98.926. Photograph © 2024 Museum of Fine Arts, Boston.

wine, a type that take obvious precedent in Rhodian and Corinthian aryballoi earlier in the century. Janiform vessels made in Attica were exclusively made for drinking wine; they come in the shape of *oinochoai*, for pouring wine, or more commonly, two-handled *kantharoi* for drinking.[135] In Derbew's recent count, ninety-five of these vessels now exist.[136]

As is so often the case with Attic ceramics, Lissarrague's (1995) contextualist approach remains the dominant way janiform vessels are read. Circulating images of (presumed Greek) women, beasts, gods (Herakles or Dionysos), and black people, they alternate images of beautiful Greek bodies with the alien, non or sub-human, Other. Derbew questions this approach. In her recent revaluation of the so-called Janiform vessels, Derbew points out the complete lack of male Greek heads in the corpus; in essence, each one of these vessels portrays an Other, whether by the rubric of gender, divinity, or phenotype. Derbew situates double-headed vessels in the world of what Fiona Hobden has called "ethnographic play" in the *symposion*.[137] Seeing as all the janiform vessels are large enough to hide the face of the person drinking, Derbew sees them as a type of mask; when the symposiast drank, he transformed into the face on the opposite side of the cup, whether woman, god, or foreigner.[138]

Derbew's reading is a persuasive one, at least to me; as we will see in Chapter 6, the *symposion* was to a great extent the central venue in which human difference was imagined and articulated in Late Archaic Greece. But it does not explain the uses of our Greco-Egyptian faience aryballoi, which ceased to be manufactured at least a generation before Attic artists put their hands to manufacture janiform vessels. Our lack of archaeological context for nearly the entire corpus of faience head aryballoi is immensely damaging here. Teleology binds our interpretation of these objects to a much greater extent than the anthropomorphic figures or the scaraboids.

Taken together, the three groups of portable faience objects discussed in this section—mixed-style figurines, head scaraboids, and janiform or quad-form vessels—presented three different routes by which portraitures of black bodies arrived in the imaginary of sixth-century Greece. The distribution of mixed-style figurines was closely linked to the routes of long-distance trade between Saite Egypt and east Greece. These figurines, with their strikingly eroticized portrayals of male and female bodies, can be associated with the sex industry that flourished alongside the trade in natron and other commodities. Head scaraboids, although produced in great quantity, had only a limited distribution within the Greek world. Their main consumers appear to have been Phoenicians in the western Mediterranean, who closely associated them with tutelary gods such as Bes. Nevertheless, they were produced at workshops in Naukratis that certainly also produced goods for export to the Greek world, and the iconographies they circulated travelled within such routes. Finally, janiform and quad-form vessels present a case where imagery of black bodies seems to have made the transition from the Egyptianizing world of the early sixth century to Attic vase painting decades later. Each of these imageries made themselves available to the writers and artists of the Late Archaic Period who were developing Greece's earliest ideas of blackness.

Conclusion

The narrative laid out so far in this chapter concludes around 550 BCE, just as faience dedications were dropping out of style at Greek sanctuaries. Whatever imageries of the "African" body appeared at these sites still remained ambivalent at this point, straddling the border between human and supernatural. But something changes around 550. Black Figure vase painters in Athens began painting individuals with marked "Ethiopian" features on sympotic vessels that had been absent in Corinthian and east Greek ceramics. Exekias portrayed the Ethiopian hero Memnon in the company of black people, but not black himself; Xenophanes imagined that Ethiopians and Thracians imagined the gods looked just like themselves, as would (in the same situation) lions and cattle. With one foot still in the world of the *Odyssey*, where Menelaus plausibly wrestled the shapeshifting Proetus on the shores of Egypt, both Xenophanes and Exekias locate the human body on a spectrum of people, beasts, and gods. Xenophanes' overriding point is that religious beliefs are relative; it does not actually matter what people look like, because they all share a common belief in the gods.[139] But in linking the morphology of the body to a human geography, Xenophanes and Exekias herald in a new way of thinking about appearance in ancient Greece, making a precise link between human diversity, geography, and ancestry.

Over the past three chapters, I argued that the emergence of Greece's racial imaginary around the turn of the sixth century was a direct result of the Saite dynasty's organization of directed trade between Egypt and the Aegean after circa 625 BCE. Their development of a trade in low-value, bulky natron focalized a scattered assemblage of stereotypes, judgments, and observations that had been floating around the eastern Mediterranean for centuries into a coherent set of knowledge. When Greeks involved in the trade imagined Egypt, they saw a powerful, sacred, and exotic kingdom that might have even been home to their ancestors. When they reflected on Egypt's human diversity, they focalized on Egypt's *difference*. Out of this process emerged the idea of an "Ethiopian" race. Images of the black body circulated on faience *aegyptiaca* alongside a repertoire of gods, demons, and animals, all made using commodities themselves extracted from Egypt. These imageries would long outlive the Egyptianizing phenomenon itself.

This study sheds light on the surprising directions a commodity biography can take us. In *Sweetness and Power*, Sidney Mintz wondered at the great mystery that united "cane growing in the fields and white sugar in my cup ... raw iron ore, on the one hand, and a perfectly wrought pair of manacles or leg irons, on the other."[140] What miracle of capitalism makes so banal a substance that unites the labor of people separated by borders, continents, oceans, and fate? What the natron trade gives us is an even more extreme example made possible by time. This ancient commerce in a commodity only known to us from a few scraps of evidence appears to have provided the context in which Greeks first established their iconography of black bodies. Through a chain of transmission, reception, and appropriation, these images arrived in our time, decontextualized and given new meanings in entirety. The ancient Greeks did not come up with an idea of racial Blackness particularly meaningful to us; theirs was a blip on the radar, nothing compared with the monstrous anti-Blackness of Atlantic modernity. But because ancient Greece meant something to the eighteenth century's inventors of race, the images the Greeks produced gained value. And so an entirely ancient phenomenon was incorporated into modernity. In an odd way, the alkali taste of natron lingers in our mouths.

In Part II of *Racialized Commodities*, I turn to the other half of Xenophanes' formulation: Thracians. As Greeks increasingly moved into the world of the Black Sea in the sixth century BCE, they came into contact with new cultures, regimes of power, and visualizations of the body. The racial imaginary that would emerge out of this development was linked with a phenomenon that has only been discussed peripherally so far: slavery. How the slave trade shaped Greek ideas of race will be the subject of the remainder of this book.

PART II

Letters from the Pontus

4
Journeys into Slavery

Introduction to Part II

During the summer or fall of some year during the third quarter of the sixth century BCE, a captive named *Phaylles was put on board a ship departing Borysthenes (modern Berezan, Ukraine) on the Bug/Dnieper Liman. Everything known about his life comes from his sales receipt, inscribed on a lead tablet found at Phanagoria on the modern Kerch Strait in Russia:

ὁ παῖς : οὗτος *vac.* | ἐ Βορυσθενέος | ἐπρήθη : ὄνομα : | αὐτῶι : Φαύλλης, | ἑωυτὸ : θέλομεν : | [.]+[.(.)]++Λ/Δ[.]σθαι. *vac.*

This slave here was sold out of Borysthenes, his name is Phaylles. We wish him to be . . . (*CGP* 49)

The journey of *Phaylles from Borysthenes to Phanagoria is hardly an outlier. Millions of free people were tricked, captured, or abducted into slavery in the over one thousand years of classical antiquity. From the perspective of the documentary record, almost all these experiences have been lost. But due to the unique epigraphical practices of the Greeks who settled the northwestern coast of the Black Sea in the sixth century BCE, we are able to partially reconstruct the life histories of *Phaylles and other individuals enslaved in the region. (Their names, marked with an *asterisk, are listed in the prosopographical catalog of Appendix 6). To a much greater extent than elsewhere, the Greeks of the Black Sea inscribed documents—including receipts, letters, and legal records—on durable materials such as lead and terracotta. A growing corpus of at least sixty-five merchant letters are known from the Pontus, dating between the middle of the sixth century BCE and the

Hellenistic Period.¹ Of these, thirty-seven letters were written by men who dealt in slaves.

What does it mean to reconstruct a historical lived experience? Critical theorists from Gayatri Chakravorty Spivak in the 1980s to Saidiya Hartman recently have taken a pessimistic outlook on the project of social history. As Hartman writes, one can produce a critical fabulation of lives captured in the documentary record—an "[imagining of] what might have happened or might have been said or might have been done"—but it will always remain a *fabulation*.² In the 2000s and 2010s, historians of the Transatlantic Slave Trade grappled with a problem that might seem strange to classicists, who are used to scarce evidence. These historians found themselves suffocated by the sheer abundance of the slave trade's documentation—a record that did little to capture the feelings and emotions of people listed in its pages.³ Both the promise and peril of microhistory is the belief that vignettes about the little people of history—people like *Phaylles—might tell larger stories. It is with understanding of our limits that we advance.

Part II of *Racialized Commodities* uses the Black Sea letters as a jumping-off point to explore the entanglement of the Pontic slave trade with the emerging idea of race in Late Archaic and Classical Greece. I argue that Greece's transformation of what Moses Finley called a "slave society" during the mid-first millennium BCE laid the groundwork for the racialization of the slave trade's victims as light-skinned, dim-witted, and easily enslavable "Thracians" or "Scythians."⁴ If we were to accept Karen and Barbara Fields' definition of racism as "a social, civic, or legal double standard" of persons "based on ancestry," it would seem relatively straightforward to label Greek attitudes toward enslaved people as a form of racism.⁵ After all, the ancient Greeks concocted all sorts of tales about the lands where enslaved people came from. They associated specific cultural and somatic tropes with enslaved people. We also know that the ancient Greeks treated enslaved people badly. Nonetheless, ancient historians have long been hesitant to see ancient slavery as a racialized phenomenon. "Roman attitudes towards ex-slaves," Peter Hunt writes recently, "could be hostile and tinged with ethnic chauvinism. They were not linked to skin color nor were they as systematic as modern racism."⁶ Such is a representative view.⁷

My argument in "Letters from the Pontus" runs to the contrary. As men like *Phaylles were marched to the coast, loaded onto ships, and taken away, they were sundered from their previous identities as fathers, sons, and husbands, and marked as something else: σώματα, the typical Greek expression for enslaved bodies. As Finley argued decades ago, even in the "absence of the skin-color stigma," the language used to describe this transformation looked awfully racialized. Greeks typically saw enslaved workers as childlike (literally a παῖς in the case of *Phaylles), deracinated, and otherwise subhuman.[8] Part II of *Racialized Commodities* sets out a three-step process by which enslaved captives were turned into racialized commodities in the world of Archaic and Classical Greece. I begin in this chapter by using the Black Sea merchant letters to reconstruct the individual paths taken by captives, drawing special attention to the ways our documentary sources conflict with Greek literary accounts of the Pontus. In Chapter 5, I turn to the economic forces that drove the trade in slaves, arguing that Athens' perennial surplus of silver led to a constant need for Pontic cities to export cheap goods—and most notably, enslaved laborers. Finally, in Chapter 6, I focalize squarely on the institutions in Greek cities—particularly Athens, our best-documented case—that specifically worked to transform people into racialized commodities.

Introduction to Chapter 4

This chapter begins by tracing the routes taken by captives between their homelands in the interior and slavery on the coast in search of a "bottom-up" perspective on the expansion of chattel slavery in the Archaic Greek world.[9] By comparing reconstructions of the journeys that enslaved people took through the region with descriptions of how to navigate it found in Herodotus, the Archaic poets, and later geographers, I argue that Greek geographical and cultural speculations about the Black Sea coast encoded generations of accumulated commercial knowledge about where, when, and how to acquire the region's most sinister export.

I draw upon a prosopographical catalog of seventeen captives or groups of captives (marked with an *asterisk) known from both documentary evidence and literary accounts, whose names are collected, with short bibliography, in an appendix at the end. I begin by evaluating the role of the North Black Sea coast in supplying captives bound for Aegean Greece, situating the disproportionate evidence that survives from the region in terms of recent scholarship about the workings of the ancient slave trade. The following section traces the individual movements of enslaved people along the intraregional economic and cult networks that linked the cities of the Pontus together. Next, I explore the role of Greek law in entrapping victims into the slave trade—even as Greek sources from as early as the seventh century sought to portray endemic "barbarian" warfare as the main driver of enslavement. I conclude by contextualizing the real-life histories of captives with literary narratives of the legendary slaves *Rhodopis, *Aesop, and *Salmoxis, whose long-distance travels by sea indoctrinated them into the world of their masters.

The stark differences revealed between real and fictional life histories—and the emphasis on cultural transformation, barbarian violence, and long-distance travel in the latter—demonstrate the extent to which slavery served as the background for how Greek writers imagined Scythians, Thracians, and the races of the Black Sea world.

The "Biographical Turn"

Few aspects of Greek and Roman societies rouse as much interest as the slave trade. Yet, until very recently, few have devoted much attention to recovering the voices of the people caught in its gears.[10] This can partially be attributed to the dearth of available sources. Moses Finley, whose work introduced ancient historians to the advances made in the study of the Transatlantic Slave Trade during in the second half of the twentieth century, lamented our lack of "relevant documentation" for the "slave psychology" in antiquity compared with the nineteenth century.[11] As Keith Bradley (1987) and others would later show, Finley's pessimism here was not quite warranted. Nevertheless, Finley's comments reflect his close engagement with then-contemporary scholarship on New World slavery. The publication of Eric Williams' *Capitalism and Slavery* in 1944 spurred a general reevaluation of the profitability, transnationality, and modernity of the Atlantic plantation complex over the following decades.[12] But it was only in the 1970s that scholars began to turn to the actual experiences of slaves themselves, and even their sources—slave autobiographies, plantation diaries, and especially the oral histories recorded by the Federal Writers' Project during the 1930s—posed major issues of interpretation.[13] It was for all of these reasons that Finley's influential narrative about the rise of slavery and the slave trade in Archaic Greece between circa 700 and 500 BCE took a somewhat schematic and Athenocentric form, which at least could be correct in general if imprecise at close range.

Finley's narrative goes as follows. Until the reforms of the Athenian lawgiver Solon in 594/3 BCE (fr. 36.8–15 West), anyone could potentially be enslaved. But with Solon's call to exclude people who could speak the Attic dialect from enslavement, Solon forced the Athenians to look for slaves elsewhere. This development was paralleled in other cities, especially Chios, where hints of democratic governance are contemporary with the rise of the slave trade.[14] Greeks turned to the hinterlands to find captive laborers, and especially the Black Sea, as Finley argued in 1962. The dichotomy between native citizen and enslaved outsider created three of the central and unique binaries of classical civilization: citizen versus noncitizen, free versus enslaved, and, on a more abstract level, Greeks versus barbarians.[15]

Finley's model has continued to hold, despite its very obvious shortcomings.[16] Part of its appeal is that, thanks to the paring down of the early history of Greek slavery into a set of deliverables, Greek slavery could easily be mobilized equally as evidence for a political argument (as Mohamad Nafissi argues was Finley's purpose) or to situate ancient Greece into a comparative history of global slaveries.[17] This reductionist impulse set the tone for the equally macrohistorical narratives that have gradually displaced Finley. For instance, Edward Harris (2012) and David M. Lewis (2018) argue that slavery in Classical Greece actually exhibited many points of commonality with forms depicted in the Homeric poems: how different were the slave barons of Classical Athens, they ask, from Homer's heroes? In both cases, elite wealth was predicated on owning hundreds of slaves. Lewis goes further to argue that Greek "slave systems," rather than being particularly Greek, were regional variants of a system of subjugating labor that was shared with Assyria, the Persian Empire, and other eastern Mediterranean societies. In a similar vein, Jeffrey Fynn-Paul (2009) situates ancient Greece within what he calls a "greater Mediterranean slave system," a set of norms and institutions that includes at its poles the empires of ancient Mesopotamia and the Atlantic plantation complex. In all of these systems, personal status was based on a firm divide between people deemed "enslavable"—usually outsiders—and those allowed to benefit from their work. Where medieval and early modern slave traders derided their captives as "infidels," and eighteenth- and nineteenth-century slave traders legitimated their activities on the principle of race, in antiquity the enslaved were "barbarians"—regardless of their origins.[18]

But what about the experiences of people enslaved themselves? Even with our scarcity of primary sources, enslaved people left a bigger mark in the record than most scholars usually permit. As I will argue in the following sections of this chapter, the Greek colonies along the northern coast of the Black Sea offer a unique case where we not only have an abundance (relatively speaking) of evidence for the expansion of the slave trade during the sixth century, but also a case where this evidence touches particular victims with names, identities, and histories.

Finley was hardly the first to argue that the northern Black Sea coast was an important source for captive labor in ancient Greece. Nevertheless, there remains a real question as to how significant a source it was.[19] Our earliest reliable description of the Black Sea slave trade dates only to the third century BCE, when Polybius states that the quantity of human bodies led off to slavery there (τὸ τῶν εἰς τὰς δουλείας ἀγομένων σωμάτων πλῆθος) exceeds anywhere else in the world (4.38.4–5). Two centuries later, Strabo (11.2.3) praises the quality of enslaved laborers in his description of a slave market at the mouth of the river Don. But evidence that Athens and other Aegean cities were ever dependent on the Black Sea as a source for enslaved labor is much shakier. Surviving lists from Classical and Hellenistic Greece show that proportions of slaves with typically northern names (Thraix, Pyrrhos) or ethnonyms (Getic, Scythian) varied considerably depending on time and place. Likewise, even ancient sources recognized that using names to determine the origins of enslaved people was difficult at best.[20] Slaves labeled "Thracian" could have come alike from Aegean Thrace or the regions around the Black Sea; "Phrygian" was a label applied to captives marched from the interior to markets on both the Propontis and Ionia. For all the ink spilled by Plato, Aristotle, and other Athenian writers over the "ethics" of slavery itself, none of them paid anything more than perfunctory attention to where captives came from and how they got there.

For the most part, our knowledge of the Black Sea slave trade before Polybius derives from the heavily ideological descriptions of the region's peoples found in fifth- and fourth-century authors.[21] None of these offers as straightforward a description of the slave trade as Polybius does, but all imply its work. Classical writers depict the northwest Black Sea as a kind of slave coast, with underlying cultural dynamics that guaranteed a steady flow of captives.[22] Innumerable Thracians—the most populous nation in the world, according to Herodotus (5.3)—and nomadic, slave-raiding Scythians populated a shadowy region where the harbors iced in during the winter and lines between Greek and barbarian were often unclear. The coast was home to "the dumbest of all peoples" (ἔθνεα ἀμαθέστατα), Herodotus notes (4.46); but he excludes the noble Scythian horsemen assumed by Greeks to deliver their slaves from his appraisal. Herodotus' Scythian ethnography begins (4.2) with a discussion of native slaving practices in the far north. At several points he quotes Scythians claiming that anyone less radically free than a Scythian must be a slave (4.20, 4.128, 4.142). The hyperbolic liberty of the Scythians contrasts sharply with the easy enslavability of the Thracians, who sell their children to foreigners for gold (5.6). Later sources report that people up the Danube traded captives for salt (Men. fr. 891 K-A; Pollux 7.14); in an obscure passage, Aristophanes describes people with tattooed faces as "Istrian" (fr. 90 K-A).[23] In the words of Aristotle's pupil Clearchus, Thracians associated the mere idea of their Scythian neighbors with slavery (Ath. 12.524c1–f4).[24]

The discovery of commercial letters and sales receipts documenting the early Black Sea slave trade has raised major questions about the reliability of these narratives. Y. G. Vinogradov (1998) and Nadia Gavriljuk (2003) read the letters synthetically with literary evidence, arguing that the journeys of *Phaylles and other slaves were representative of a larger trade. Greece needed manpower to feed its growing economy in the sixth century; the search for slaves might even have explained why Greeks settled in the region. On the other hand, recent scholarship on early trade between the Aegean and the Mediterranean's borderlands is characterized by a backlash against "commodity hunger" as an explanation for Greek expansion.[25] While no one doubts that sixth-century Greece must have required a real infusion of manpower to match the growth of its economy—mining, viticulture, milling, smelting, and weaving are all labor-intensive—there were much closer "sources" of human capital than the distant reaches of the Black Sea. A survey of known Greek slave markets operating in the late Archaic and Classical Periods shows that most were located equidistant from slaving regions in the interior of Anatolia and Thrace and the major centers of "consumption" along the coast of Asia Minor, the islands, and Attica (Table 4.1).

Both literary and documentary sources confirm the short-distance orientation of the slave trade in the Archaic and Classical Periods. Markets were ephemeral; one of the several monthly "circles" (*kykloi*) met in the Athenian Agora, for instance.[26] Both East and North Aegean cities benefited from sporadic slave raiding in the interior, as when Achilles sold poor *Lykaon in Lemnos (*Il.* 21.40), when Hipponax spoke of Soloikoi and Phrygians sold in Miletos to grind barley (fr. 27 West), or when Xenophon sold some of his captives at Perinthos on the Propontis (*An.* 7.4). At least during the late Archaic Period, there was still a robust slave trade *from* Greece *to* its "barbarian" neighbors. Periander of Corinth, according to Herodotus (3.48), punished the Corcyreans by demanding that one hundred of their sons be sent to Anatolia to be castrated (their liberation by the slave-trading Samians speaks to the fact that Solon was not the only person in sixth-century Greece to squirm at exporting Greeks). The Carian prisoner of war *Hermotimos of Pedasos was hardly that lucky. He was castrated on Chios by Panionios the slave dealer and re-exported to Lydia (Hdt. 8.104). But, according to Herodotus, he at least took his revenge.

One of the major contributions of the letters is that they show that the slave trade in the Black Sea followed the same general principles as in the Aegean: people captured from its shores were more likely than not to remain in the Pontus. Of the twenty-three individuals or groups in my appendix,

Table 4.1 Attested or likely slave markets in Archaic and Classical Greece

Slave market	Evidence
East Aegean	
Chios	Hdt. 8.104–6 (5th cent. BCE); Thuc. 8.40 (5th cent. BCE); Aristophanes fr. 556 K-A (5th cent. BCE); Theopomp. *FGrHist* 115 F 122 (4th cent. BCE); Ael. fr. 74a–h Domingo-Foraste (unclear).
Ephesos	Aristophanes fr. 556 K-A (5th cent. BCE); *Life of Aesop* (W) 20 (unclear); Varro *Ling.* 8.9 (1st cent. BCE).
Klazomenai	Aristophanes fr. 556 K-A (5th cent. BCE).
Miletos	Hipponax fr. 27 West (6th cent. BCE); island in harbor named Perne; Brückner et al. (2017: 886) argue derived from πέρνημι.
Samos	Hdt. 2.134 (5th cent. BCE); Hdt. 4.95 (5th cent. BCE); *Life of Aesop* (W) 20 (unclear).
Sardis	Hdt. 3.48 (5th cent. BCE); Hdt. 8.104 (5th cent. BCE).
North Aegean	
Abdera	*SEG* 47.1026 slave transit tax (3rd cent. BCE).
Abydos	Aristophanes fr. 556 K-A (5th cent. BCE).
Ainos	Antiph. 5.20 (5th cent. BCE).
Amphipolis	*SEG* 28.537 slave trader funerary stele (1st cent. CE).
Byzantion	Polyb. 4.38 (3rd cent. BCE); Ael. fr. 74a–h Domingo-Foraste (unclear).
Cyzicus	*SIG*^{3} 4 slave transit tax (6th cent. BCE).
Lemnos	Hom. *Il.* 21.40 (8th cent. BCE?).
Pagasai	Hermippos fr. 63 K-A (5th cent. BCE).
Perinthos	Xen. *An.* 7.4 (4th cent. BCE).
Black Sea	
Istros	Aristophanes fr. 90 K-A (5th cent. BCE); *SEG* 23.381 = *IG* 9.1^2 4.1778 (3rd cent. BCE); Pollux 7.14 (unclear). Hind 1994 argues for representation of slaves on 5th–4th cent. BCE coinage.
Myrmekeion	*CGP* 46 (4th cent. BCE).
Odessos	*SEG* 23.381 = *IG* 9.1^2 4.1778 slave list from Rheneia (3rd cent. BCE).
Olbia/ Borysthenes	*CGP* 49 receipt (6th cent. BCE); *SEG* 48.998 (6th c. BCE) merchant letter; *CGP* 25 (6th c. BCE) *sulan* dispute, writer enslaved, slave trader; *CGP* 26 (6th c. BCE) *sulan* dispute, slave trader.
Phanagoria	*CGP* 49 receipt (6th cent. BCE); *CGP* 48 letter (5th cent. BCE).
Sinope	Strabo 12.3.1 (3rd cent. BCE); Diog. Laer. 6.95–99 (3rd cent. BCE); *IG* 12^1 465, 466a, 467 slave tombstones (3rd cent. BCE); see Avram 2007: 246.
Tanais	Strabo 11.2.3 (2nd cent. CE); Ael. fr. 74a–h Domingo-Foraste (unclear).

only one (the *Colchian girl) had to endure the long-distance voyage from the Black Sea as described by Polybius and Strabo. It is also notable that the slave trade in the north appeared within a generation of Greek settlement. But what remains truly distinct about the Pontic slave trade is that it has produced records of transactions that are contemporary with or even predate the largely anecdotal literary evidence. Using these, it is possible to reconstruct the diverse paths individual slaves took into the "slave system" from the perspective of enslaved people themselves—not their masters.

My inquiry here takes advantage of what Joseph C. Miller has heralded as the "biographical turn" in the study of the Transatlantic Slave Trade since the 2000s.[27] Historians have harnessed powerful datasets like the *Transatlantic Slave Trade Database (TASTD)* to track the voyages of individual slave ships along the Middle Passage, as well as the records of their captains, owners, and insurers. In the late 2010s, the *Peoples of the Historic Slave Trade (PHST)* database and its forerunners enabled historians to trace the movement of individual enslaved and formerly enslaved people from archive to archive.

As I noted earlier, we are still dealing with the consequences of this work. As Saidiya Hartman notes in her oft-cited 2008 essay, the availability of so much data might lead us to reproduce the judgements of the violent men who created it.[28] Nonetheless, Lisa A. Lindsay and John Wood Sweet argue that even given the relative scarcity of direct testimony from enslaved people, using the records of the slave trade to reconstruct their mobility can "reveal unexpected comparisons and connections, [cause us] to reconsider facile abstract distinctions between slavery and freedom, and to explore common dynamics that undergird local phenomena and personal experiences dispersed in space and time."[29] The biographical turn focuses squarely on the agency of enslaved people. For instance, we might ask how enslaved people manipulated their presence in the archival record. To what extent did enslaved people have a hand in producing knowledge about their cultures as reflected in the records of their masters?[30] And how can maritime geography encode the experiences of people forced to cross it unwillingly?

In the same way, reading the tension between our literary and documentary evidence for the Black Sea slave trade in the Archaic and Classical Periods reveals the whole range of perils and opportunities faced by people caught up in the trade. In the following sections, I track the trajectories of slaves on the move between the Black Sea and the Aegean in the sixth century, situating their movements within larger patterns of mobility in the region. Where Greek cities established mechanisms to draw in commerce—whether through cultic networks, manipulating coinage, or privileged taxation arrangements—they also drew in streams of the enslaved. Mobility presented enslaved people with surprising opportunities to exert agency, while raising the risk for the free that they might find themselves in chains. The responses of the free people around them to these possibilities, especially in the remote north, shaped how Greeks would come to view their "barbarian" neighbors over the *longue durée*.

Slave Transits and Intraregional Mobility

Authority has its downsides. In a letter addressed to a priest in Olbia inscribed around 500 BCE on the back of a sherd, his counterpart in Berezan lists his grievances. Hirophos, another religious official, had fasted too much and was ill; at Chalkeie, a nearby sacred place, the priestesses were upset. The sacred grove at Hylaie, across the estuary from Olbia, had been overrun by horsemen, maybe Scythians. And adding to other troubles, all the slaves had run away after a shipwreck. Only *one, belonging to Metrophanes (Μητροφάνεως ἱρός), remained after the loss to attend to the rituals:[31]

[- - - c.9 - - τῶι ἀγω]νοθέτῃ μέλι καὶ κριὸ[ν - - c.11 - - -]
[- - - -c.14 - - - - ν]ῦν ὡς ἐπιτέλλεις πέμπ[ω - - c.9 - - -]
[- - c.10 - - - παντ]ὸς τόπους θεοποιήτους περιε[- - c.9 -]
[- c.9 - - διὰ γὰ]ρ ἄκρην λίη<ν ἔ>καμε Ἱρόφως νησ[τείην καὶ]
[- - - c.13 - -] δικαίως. ἐν τῇ Χαλκηίῃ αἱ γυ[ναῖκές εἰσι]
[ἐν τραχῆι πολ]λῆι. ἐνθεῦθεν ἐς τὴν Ὑλαίη[ν διέβην]
[- - c.12 - -] αὖτις οἱ βωμοὶ βεβλαμμένο[ι εἰσί]
[- - c.10 - - Μ]ητρὸς Θεῶν καὶ Βορυσθέ<νεος> καὶ Ἡρακλ[έους - -]
[- - c.8 - μ]ετὰ τὸ ναυάγιον οἱ δοῦλοι καταδρα[μόντες - -]
[- c.9 - - τ]ῇ ἱρουργίῃ Μητροφάνεος ἱρὸς ἐλίπετ[ο- - -]
[- c.10 - - τ]ῶν πιτύων κακαὶ τῶν δένδρων διηκόσια
[- - c.12 - ο]ἱ θηρευταὶ τῶν ἵππων ηὑρήκασι μετὰ κινδύνων πολ[λῶν

... I am sending to the *agonothetes* honey and a ram... as you request ... (I have inspected?) all the places made by the gods... because, following an excessive fasting, Hirophos was ill... rightly so. In the Chalkeie the women (are in great agitation?)... Thence (I moved) towards Hylaie... the altars have again been damaged... of the Mother of the Gods and Borysthenes and Herakles... after the shipwreck the slaves have run away (?)... (only) the sacred slave of Metrophanes was left in the religious service... of the pines and (?) of the (?other) trees two hundred (had been damaged?) the hunters of the horses have found with many dangers...³²

This section means to situate the voyages of *Phaylles, *Melas' enslaved woman, *Aristonymos' slave, and the *captives in the Priest's Letter within the patterns of mobility that bound the region (Figure 4.1). I argue that the logistics of the slave trade were deeply encoded in Greek navigational knowledge of the Black Sea, recoverable from the surviving itineraries of Herodotus, Strabo, Ps.-Skylax, and Arrian.

The lacunose Priest's Letter situates the movement of priests, captives, and commodities within a closely bound geography circumscribed by dangerous outsiders. From about the middle of the sixth century BCE, the Milesian colonists of the northwest Black Sea—founders of cities including Istros, Olbia, and Borysthenes between the mouths of the Danube and the Dnieper and Pantikapaion on the Kerch Straits—extended a tightly knit series of sacred landmarks along the prevailing sea routes that guided merchants on voyages both within the Black Sea and out past the Bosporus to the Aegean and beyond.³³ By the end of the century, the most important shrines to Achilles, Apollo, and Aphrodite at Istros, Leuke, Olbia, Berezan, Pantikapaion, and Phanagoria were graced by marble Ionic temples facing southeast toward the sea.³⁴ Olbia and Borysthenes' network of shrines—"beacons," as Alla Bujskikh calls them³⁵—marked the major routes through the region. Despite occasional doubts about the significance of Greek colonization in the region before the fourth century, an abundance of evidence—ranging from the commercial documents to coin hoards, votive dedications, and the spread of Ionic architecture—points to the frequency of movement between the region's cities and the ties that bound them to the wider world.³⁶

The Black Sea basin is largely shut off from the Mediterranean. Its unusual hydrology is caused by the disparity between the fresh water that streams into the region after the Eurasian snowmelt between April and July and the much smaller amount of salt water that enters into the sea through the Hellespont and the Bosporus.³⁷ Traditional navigation followed the sea's two cyclonic currents, which rotate counter-clockwise and meet along a meridian that extends between modern Mys Sarych on the Crimea (a headland known in antiquity as *Kriou Metopôn*, the Ram's Brow) and the Anatolian coast at ancient Themiscyra, west of Sinope. Both Herodotus (4.86) and Ps.-Skylax (68) list this place as a point to cross the sea northward, which could be done with the flow of the current against the summer's prevailing northern winds. Strabo (7.4.3) notes that from the center of the sea both promontories can be seen at

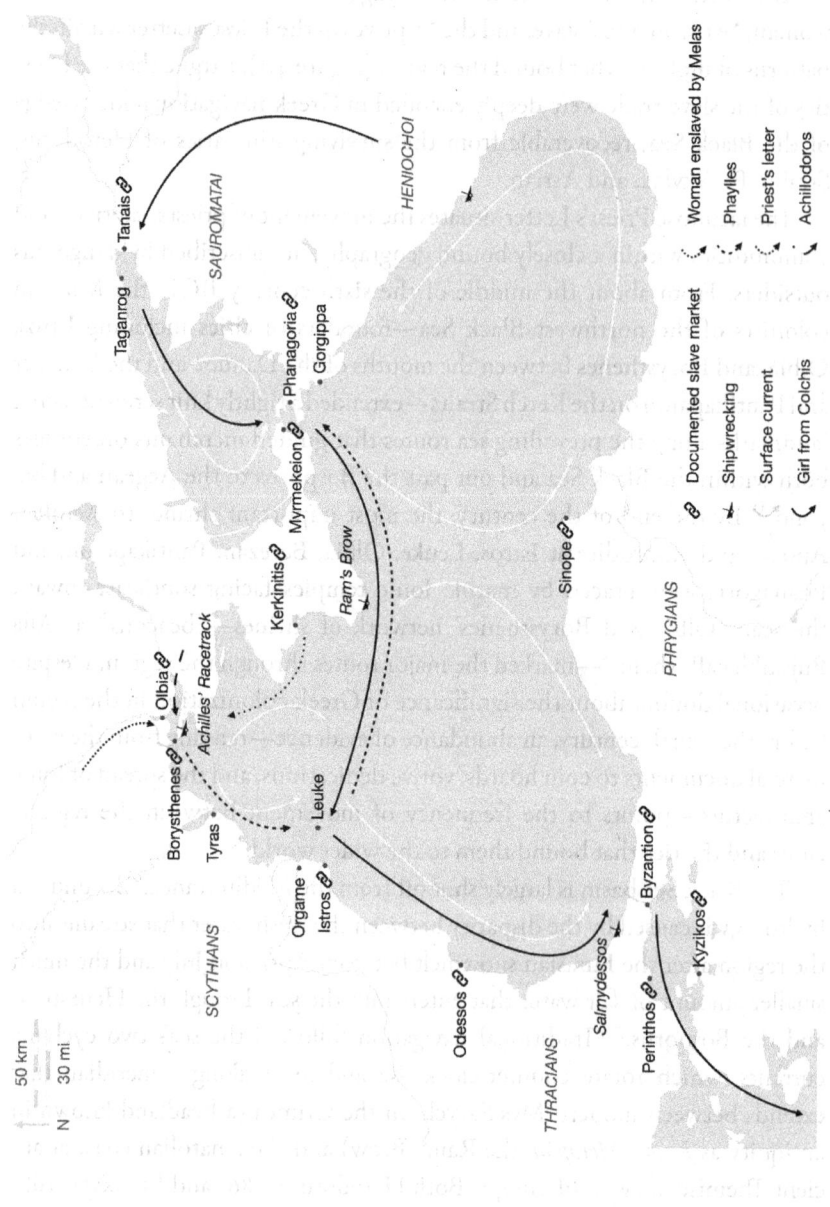

FIGURE 4.1 Map of routes taken by enslaved captives in Appendix 6.

once.[38] The Milesian colony at Sinope marked the southwestern point in a circular voyage taken along the Black Sea's western gyre between the Bosporus, northern Anatolia, Crimea, and the western coast of the Black Sea. When Anglo-American navigators were first admitted into the basin by the Ottomans at the end of the eighteenth century, they were surprised by the persistence of a traditional three-month summer itinerary taken by local merchants along this route. Sailing offshore using instruments was much faster.[39]

The meridional route between Sinope and Crimea was important from an early point in the Greek settlement of the region, despite the absence of much colonial activity in the western Crimea itself until the foundation of Chersonesos in the fifth century.[40] The Ram's Brow was the starting point for a smaller and weaker gyre in the shallow waters of the sea's northwestern corner set in motion by the outflow of the rivers Danube (ancient Ister), Dniester (Tyras), Bug (Borysthenes), and Dnieper (Hypnais; see Hdt. 4.47). This heavily colonized region provides us with the best record of interregional mobility preserved from the Archaic Period. It is here that *Phaylles and other captives would have met annual traffic of people and goods both within the region and beyond.

Let us begin following them upstream, whence they probably came. As in other regions of colonization, there was relatively little settlement on the coasts of the Bug/Dnieper Liman until the arrival of Greek migrants at the end of the seventh century.[41] By the turn of the fifth century, the two cities of Olbia and Borysthenes were surrounded by a dense scattering of rural agricultural outposts only vaguely referred to by Herodotus, who praises the grain-growing capacity of the countryside and alludes to "Scythian farmers" living as far as an eleven days' sail upstream (4.17–19). Herodotus' mentions of what lay farther upstream are even hazier; he comments that nobody can go farther upstream than Gerrhus on the Dnieper, where the Scythians bury their kings, about a forty-day journey north (4.53, 4.71).[42] Beyond this region, where the barren steppe gives way to trees, was the urban site of Belskoye, associated by archaeologists with Herodotus' wooden city of Gelonos. Scholars tend to assume the major slaving region was here, based on the precedent of Genoese and Tatar slaving in the late medieval and early modern periods.[43]

The number of Greeks to ever reach this region is unclear. Herodotus claims that the Gelonoi inhabited one of several of what he calls "Helleno-Scythian" settlements in the far interior.[44] It is unclear what Herodotus means by this. On the other hand, judging by the volume of Greek sympotic wares found in the forest steppe from the seventh century on, it seems that elites in the region engaged in Greek-style drinking rituals, which Herodotus might allude to with his repeated mentions of the Scythian proclivity for wine.[45] The continual appeal of Greek-style drinking was demonstrated by the sensational find of fifteen gold-plated bronze vessels from Attica dating to the fifth and fourth centuries in a sunken canoe at Peshchannoe on a tributary of the river Dnieper, five hundred kilometers north from the sea.[46] Drinking vessels and the wine they were used for have plausibly been identified as the commodities Greeks traded for slaves, but not much is known about the circulation of either within the interior.[47] The elites at Trakhtemirov, a fortified settlement south of modern Kyiv on the Dnieper, seem to have enjoyed wine drunk from Wild Goat vessels; this town seems to have been sacked at some point in the period, possibly by steppe nomads.[48] There were many ways to be enslaved.

An *enslaved woman procured from a merchant named Melas, attested in another commercial letter from Berezan dating to 540–535 BCE, likely shared the same origins as *Phaylles and the *slaves of the Priest's Letter. All might have come from the forest-steppe, but we cannot track their journeys that far north. When we first encounter them in the letters, they are already enslaved, perhaps in the agricultural region between there and the Greek cities of the coast. One of the persistent concerns of the Black Sea letters is relations between town and countryside, as landowners based in town correspond with family members or agents in the field.[49] This is the scenario where we meet the (falsely) enslaved *Achillodoros pleading for help from his family in the countryside and where, two centuries later, we find a slave in the countryside of Gorgippa on the Kerch Strait being told to dig out a garden.[50] In a poorly preserved directive dating to the third quarter of the sixth century, a Berezan-based writer instructs one of his cronies to bring him *Melas' enslaved woman as well as "other things there" (τῶν γὰρ | ἐνθένδε ἄTα) to wherever he was based, presumably in the city (*CGP* 23). A similar scenario is known from a recently published fifth-century letter sent by one Pistros to a merchant named Aristonymos at Phanagoria, which includes a captive (ἀνδράποδον) among a list of debts owed by Aristonymos to his partners.[51] As is the case for both *Melas' and *Aristonymos' slaves, we know nothing about *Phaylles' origins before he appears in the documentary record. His rare, non-Greek name (only attested here in *LGPN*) suggests he was a first-generation slave. *Melas' enslaved woman might have been caught up in one of the prevailing currents of Mediterranean slavery, which was the concentration of enslaved women in central places where they might be forced to weave or process grain, or into prostitution. Slave traders did pay attention to the gender of their captives; in *Achillodoros' letter, enslaved men and women are listed separately as part of his confiscated property (δόλος καὶ δόλας, l. 6). What little Herodotus tells us about labor and gender in Scythia suggests that these slaves were born in societies with gender norms markedly different from the world they were compelled to enter.[52]

At this point we lose track of *Melas' enslaved woman. The *slaves of the Priest's Letter were aboard a ship headed from elsewhere to the Bug/Dnieper Liman when it wrecked. *Phaylles' journey to Phanagoria, on the other hand, can be traced down along the coast. When *Phaylles left Berezan in the last quarter of the sixth century, it was still a city of crude dug-out dwellings designed to withstand the winter, when the surrounding waters froze. The earliest monumental buildings on the island date to around his lifetime.[53] Starting in the mouth of the liman, *Phaylles' captors would have set out due southwest, passing three important sanctuaries linked to Olbia and referenced in the Priest's Letter. Two of these were on headlands immediately opposite Berezan: the Achilles sanctuary at Beikush and the sacred grove, Hylaia. Beikush had particularly strong connections with the maritime route southward toward the Bosporus. There, navigators and other worshippers dedicated dozens of ceramic disks inscribed with dedications to Achilles, etchings of snakes, and hastily carved pictures of ships. A further Achilles sanctuary featuring similar dedications existed at Achilles' Racecourse on the Tendra spit, twenty-six kilometers south-southeast of Berezan.[54] Southbound ships would not have visited here, as longshore drift along this part of the coast flows north. A few days' journey down the coast, another Achilles cult existed at Tyras, the Milesian colony about thirteen kilometers inland from the mouth of Dniester, later the site of the Genoese and Turkish slaving fortress Akkerman.[55]

The central navigational and sacral node of the North Black Sea was the isle of Leuke, known in modern times as Zmeinyy (Snake Island) and in the nineteenth century by its Greek name, Fidonisi. Little is known of the archaeology of the island, as it was cleared in the second quarter of the nineteenth century and the remains of its temple were spoliated to build the present lighthouse.[56] Located some forty kilometers off the present Sulina mouth of the Danube, Leuke was the central point where the west Pontic gyre and weaker currents of the northwest Black Sea met. Virtually all southward journeys from Crimea and the northwest Black Sea stopped here on their voyage south; by the fifth century it features both in Pindar ("Achilles holds the shining island [of Leuke] in the Euxine," *Nem.* 4.49–50) and Euripides as the major landmark on homeward voyages to the Aegean.[57] The assemblage of votive coins from the island attests to the diverse homelands of the merchants who stopped there.[58] Intraregionally, the island had importance in that eastward voyages from the Bug/Dnieper Liman would have picked up the eastward current here; in historical times, it was also where vessels staged to prepare for the dangerous journey into the Danube mouth.[59] In ancient times, this was the site of Istros and its adjacent Milesian colonies, the former of which was likely an important slave market (see Table 4.1).

The reasons why Achilles represented such an important navigational god to the Milesian colonists of the northwestern Black Sea are obscure. There is only late evidence for an Achilles cult in Miletos, and scholars have rejected the longstanding idea that it was syncretized with a local god in the north.[60] Jonathan Burgess has proposed that Achilles' prominence in the region was consolidated by the shared experience of long-distance voyages from the Aegean up through the Hellespont and into the Black Sea; along the way the voyagers would have passed one of several tumuli in the Troad to have been identified with that of Achilles, which in the *Odyssey* is described as sited on "projecting headland by the broad Hellespont ... seen from far over the sea" (*Od.* 24.82–83).[61] Indeed, the most frequent travelers into the Black Sea during the earliest period of colonization appear to have been from the Greek cities of North Ionia and the Propontis, where cults of Achilles appear by the early sixth century.[62] Substance-wise, however, the reincorporation of Achilles into the religious landscape of the far north seems to have something additional to do with both the "cargoes" that passed by his most important sanctuary. Could the Greeks of the north have specifically molded Achilles in the image of their frightening and extreme Scythian neighbors as a slaving god?

The early history of the association between Achilles and Scythia is shady at best. According to Proclus, Arktinos of Miletos' cyclic epic, the *Aithiopis*, presented Achilles leading the forces of the far north to Troy against Memnon the Ethiopian, who led an army from the south.[63] The earliest preserved linkage appears in the early sixth century in an enigmatic fragment of Alcaeus of Lesbos in the North Aegean, who refers to an "Achilles lording over the Scythians" (Ἀχίλλευς ὁ τὰς Σκυθίκας μέδεις, fr. 354 West). Alcaeus' phrasing is closely mirrored by the language deployed on ostraca dedicated to Achilles in the Black Sea in the following century; one fifth-century ostracon from Leuke was dedicated by Glaukos son of Posideios to "Achilles, lording over Leuke" (Γλαῦκός με ἀνέθηκεν Ἀχιλλῆι Λευκῆ<ς> μεδέοντι, παῖ(ε)ς Ποσιδῆο, *IGDOP* 48b). Another early fifth-century ostracon from Tyras is dedicated to [--]ΛΕΙ | ΣΚΥ[--], restored by its editor as a dedication to Achilles lord of Scythia.[64]

It seems plausible that the activities of Scythian nomads of the sea's north shore brought to mind Achilles' atrocious behavior in the later stages of the

Iliad. During his rage in book 21, Achilles stumbles upon *Lykaon son of Priam, whom he had previously captured and sold into slavery on Lemnos for a hundred oxen (*Il.* 21.79). Slaughtering *Lykaon in cold blood and gloating that he will never be properly buried, Achilles proceeds to clog the Scamander with corpses, kill Hector, abuse his body, and sacrifice twelve Trojan boys on the pyre when he finally commemorates Patroklos (*Il.* 23.22–23). Now, as commentators have noted, Herodotus' ethnography of Scythian culture in the fifth century—our main source on Scythian culture—is filtered through various lenses, including comparisons with the cultures of Egypt and Sparta.[65] But among their many idiosyncrasies in Greek eyes the Scythian commitment to slave raiding, mutilating corpses, human sacrifice (Hdt. 4.62), and a radical conception of personal freedom all mirror Achilles' character. By the fourth century, when local traditions of metalworking become established in the region, Achilles even shows up in Greco-Scythian iconography.[66]

So far we have accompanied *Phaylles on half his voyage. The remaining course was east, to Phanagoria. This part of the trip, across a spate of open water and then the rocky headlands of the Crimea, represented the easy part of the trip, and could potentially have even taken place late in the season; this part of the Black Sea does not freeze, and the prevailing southerly winds of autumn and early winter potentially offered a smoother ride than was typically the case in the summer.[67] Little of this coast was settled by Greeks in the sixth century; perhaps these conditions allowed early myths to accrue (cf. Hdt. 4.103) that the local people looked out for Greek sailors to sacrifice from the high cliffs.[68] As the elevation profile lowered toward the east, *Phaylles' captors would have brought him along fertile agricultural lands dotted with Scythian kurgans; one fifth-century document from this region shows local Greek merchants paying them taxes in an unclear context.[69] Finally, entering into the Kerch Straits, the ship would have spotted the great Ionic temple on a hill above Pantikapaion to their left and the approach to the swampy land of the Kuban peninsula on the right, where Phanagoria was. The seafloor beneath the crowded roadstead where they anchored waiting for the southward current to slack would have been littered with the refuse of countless ships that came before.[70] This is where we take leave of *Phaylles.

Shipwrecks and Law Courts

Slavery is a form of violence: "The permanent, violent domination of natally alienated and generally dishonored persons," in Orlando Patterson's classic formulation.[71] Yet, for all the violence inherent in slavery's very definition, many slaves found themselves in chains for reasons other than warfare. In this section I argue that, as early as the sixth century, Greek writers focused on barbarian violence as the driver of the "slave supply" along the Black Sea coast as a way of displacing very real anxieties that Greeks themselves could (and did) end up in bondage among the Other. As the letters show, not only were judicial or pseudo-judicial proceedings in Greek colonies an important mechanism for enslavement, but non-Greeks themselves often had access to them as plaintiffs. If the categories of "free" and "Greek" were increasingly becoming aligned in the Aegean world, along the Black Sea one day's slaving captain could become cargo the next.

The Black Sea was a perennially alien space in Greek thought. In Homeric times, Strabo wrote that "this sea was not navigable, and was called the Axine (Ἄξεινος) because of its wintery storms and the ferocity of the tribes that lived around it" (7.3.6). The Scythians in particular "sacrificed strangers, ate their flesh, and used their skulls as drinking cups." Strabo's account builds heavily off of Herodotus', but the general picture is consistent with other ancient sources: "Many of the tribes have a ready proclivity towards murder and cannibalism, especially ... the Heniochoi," Aristotle wrote (*Pol.* 8.4, 1338b19–22), drawing attention to one group absent in Herodotus but conspicuous in other authors.[72] Greek anxieties about shipwreck and enslavement focused to the greatest extent on three points along the coast. The Heniochoi dwelt along a rocky and dangerous stretch somewhere between modern Sukhumi and Novorossiysk, where no regional power ever maintained control.[73] Human sacrifice and opportunistic enslavement are first associated with the Taurians at modern Mys Sarych on the Crimea in the fifth century, as Athenian interests consolidated in the region. But by far the earliest associations focalized on Salmydessos in the southwestern corner of the Black Sea, thought by Jan Stronk to be the notorious "false entrance" of the Bosporus near modern Karaburun. The opportunistic slaving of the local Thracians was proverbial. The victims, of course, were Greek.[74]

The cases of the Greek slave traders *Achillodoros and Apatorios, who were detained with their "cargoes" by non-Greek plaintiffs at Olbia and Berezan in the second half of the sixth century, shed light on the poorly known role of the law in supplying Greek slave markets.[75] By displacing the risk of enslavement to the "barbarians" who dwelt around prominent navigational landmarks and by making their victims Greek, migrants from the Aegean consolidated a sense of group identity that linked the ability to travel by sea with freedom—while the "barbarians" lurking on the coast were both slave-masters and potential slaves themselves.

The earliest description of an identifiable Black Sea landmark comes from Hipponax in the sixth century, who squarely locates it within a calculus of sea travel, enslavement, and ethnicity. Hipponax's wish that his opponent be greeted kindly by "top-knotted Thracians" when he washes up on the shore at Salmydessos is typical. "May he vomit much seaweed and may his teeth chatter while he lies on his face like a dog at the edge of the surf," he writes; "there he will have full measure of a multitude of woes, eating the bread of slaves" (fr. 115.4–8 West).[76] Tropes involving bread, grinding grain, and barbarian peoples were familiar in Archaic poetry: Hesiod prescribes how much bread an enslaved ploughman should eat (*WD* 442); in Hipponax's own description, captured Solokoi and Phrygians can expect to grind barley for bread if sold at Miletus (fr. 27 West). Archilochus (fr. 42 West) likens the image of a slave grinding grain both to fellatio—hinting at the abuse that slaves faced daily—and to cultural practices in their homelands: "she was bent over, working hard, just like a Thracian or Phrygian sucks up beer through a straw."[77] Hipponax's image of a Greek grinding grain on barbarian shores reverses this trope: if in Greece being Thracian and Phrygian was synonymous with being enslaved, Greeks should expect the same treatment if captured abroad.

While Greeks probably did fall victim to occasional piracy and kidnapping along the coast, we have little evidence that this happened with the frequency that our literary sources claim. The letters offer a different sort of threat. *Achillodoros' letter, dating between 550 and 500 BCE from Berezan, lays out an ambiguous situation where the writer has been detained with his cargo:

Outside: Ἀχιλλοδώρο τὸ μολί-
βδιον παρὰ τὸμ παῖδα
κἀναξαγόρην.

Inside: ὦ Πρωταγόρη, ὁ πατήρ τοι ἐπιστέλλε. ἀδικέται
ὑπὸ Ματασυος· δολōται γάρ μιγ καὶ τō
φορτηγεσίο ἀπεστέρεσεν. ἐλθὼμ παρ' Ἀναξαγό|(<-)ρην
ἀπήγησαι· φησι γὰρ αὐτὸν Ἀναξαγόρεω
5   δο̃λον ἔναι μυθεόμενος· "τἄμ' Ἀνα<ξα>γόρης ἔχε
καὶ δόλος καὶ δόλας κοικίας". ὁ δὲ ἀναβῶι τε
καὶ οὔ φησιν ἔναι οὐδὲν ἑωυτῶι τε καὶ Ματας<υι>
καὶ φησιν ἔναι ἐλεόθερος καὶ οὐδέν ἔναι ἑωυτ<ῶ>ι
καὶ Ματα{τα}συ<ι>· ἒ δε τι αὐτῶι τε κἀναξαγόρηι, αὐτοὶ
10   οἴδασι κατὰ σφᾶς αὐτός. ταῦτ' Ἀναξαγόρη λέγεν
καὶ τῆ γυναικί. ἕτερα δέ τοι ἐπιστέλλε· τὴμ μητέρα
καὶ τὸς ἀδε<λ>φεός, <ο>ἵ ἐσσιν ἐν Ἀρβινάτηισιν, ἄγεν ἐς
τὴμ πόλιν·
αὐτὸς δε γ' ὁ νεορὸς ἐλθὼμ παρὰ μιν <ἰ>θύωρα καταβήσεται.

Achillodoros' piece of lead, to his son and Anaxagoras.
Protagoras, your father sends instructions to you. He is being wronged by Matasys, for he is enslaving him and has deprived him of his cargo-carrier [or: of his position as a carrier; or: of the shipment]. Go to Anaxagoras and tell him the story, for he [Matasys] asserts that he [Achillodoros] is the slave of Anaxagoras, claiming: "Anaxagoras has my property, slaves, both male and female, and houses." But he [Achillodoros] disputes it and denies that there is anything between him and Matasys and says that he is free and that there is nothing between him and Matasys. But what there is between him and Anaxagoras, they alone know. Tell this to Anaxagoras and the (his?) wife. Besides, he sends you these other instructions: take the (your?) mother and the (your?) brothers, who are among the Arbinatai, to the city. The ship-guard himself [or: Euneoros himself], having come to him, will go directly down [or: down to Thyora].[78]

The nature of *Achillodoros' encounter has been subject of debate since his letter's first publication by Vinogradov in the 1970s. In his letter, *Achillodoros writes his son Protagoras to say that he has been enslaved (δολῶται) by another merchant with the Iranian name Matasys.[79] Matasys appears to claim that *Achillodoros is a slave belonging to another merchant, Anaxagoras, and has seized him with the moveable goods, houses, and *slaves he was in charge of. *Achillodoros tells Protagoras to go out into the countryside, where his family lives among the Arbinatai of the northwest Crimea, and find help. He also asks for help from Anaxagoras, whose relationship with him is not clear. Nearly all scholars agree that Matasys' basis for seizing *Achillodoros is that the former believes the latter actually is enslaved.[80] (This might have been a reasonable guess; Melas, for his part, appears to have had an *enslaved business agent.)

*Achillodoros' case closely resembles a second letter from Olbia dating to the turn of the fifth century:

Outside: Ἀπατόριος
Λεάνακτι
Inside: Λήνακτι Ἀπατόριος· : τὰ χρήματα σισύλημαι ὑπ᾽ Ἡρακλείδεω τō Ε[ὀ]θήριος : κατὰ δύναμιν τὴν σὴν : μὴ ἀπολέσω τὰ χρήματα : τὰ γὰρ χρήμ]ατα σὰ ἐφάμην ἔναι : καὶ Μένων : ἔφατό : σε ἐπ[ι]θέναι ἑωυτῶι : καὶ τ[ἄ]<λ>λα ὅσα σὺ αὐτῶι ἐπέ-

5   θηκας καὶ π[ρὸ]ς ἔφατο {σ'} ἐμοὶ σὰ τὰ χρήματα ἐνῆν :
    ἰὰν ἐπιθε-
    ίης διφθέρια π[ρὸς] Ἡρακλείδην καὶ Θαθαίην : τὰ χρήματα σ-
    ἐο ΥΣ ὁπό[σο, ἀποδ]όσε· : κ͂ενοι γάρ φασιν : ὅ τι σὸν
    ἔχοσιν ἀποδώ-
    [σεν] τὸ : συλη[θὲν ὄλ]ον ἑπτὰ καὶ εἴκοσιν στατῆρες. vacat
    [τί? θε]ή̣σ̣ε̣ς̣; περὶ τῶν οἰκιητέων Θυμώλεω (sic)
10 (- - c.10-11 - - Ἐό?]θυμίωι : αὐτωι μοι οὐκ οἶδα ἢν {ε} γένηται ἔο
    Vacat.

Apatorios to Leanax.
To Leanax, Apatorios. I have had the goods confiscated by Herakleides, son of Eotheris; by your influence I will not lose the goods. For I said the goods were yours, and Menon said that you had entrusted to him also the other things that you have entrusted to him, and he added that the goods that I had were yours. If you would send the records to Herakleides and Thathaie(s) (Oathaie?), how much(?) your goods(?) . . . for they say they will hand over what they have of yours. The total of goods seized is twenty-seven staters. What will you decide? Concerning the slaves of Thymoleos . . . to Eothymios; as to myself, I do not know if it is going to end well.[81]

Unlike *Achillodoros, Apatorios does not make the claim that he has been enslaved. He had been detained and his goods (and possibly *slaves) impounded by Herakleides through *sulan* (σισύλημαι), a common pseudo-judicial maneuver allowing a plaintiff to confiscate goods from a defendant.[82] Apatorios asks Leanax to send records to Herakleides and a partner whose non-Greek name has been restored both as Thathaiên and as Oathaiên in the accusative.[83] The phrasing of Apatorios' letter presents a somewhat more transparent legal situation than *Achillodoros' does, with a clear sense of *why* Apatorios has been apprehended and the mechanisms necessary to clear the shipment (producing documents). Like in the *Achillodoros letter, one of the plaintiffs appears to be non-Greek.

*Achillodoros' and Apatorios' letters together offer a perspective on the use of the law as a tool for entrapping people into the Greek slave trade or rerouting those already lost. According to Diogenes Laertius, Olbia permitted freedmen and their families to be sold back into slavery for violations of the law; the peripatetic philosopher *Bion of Borysthenes, son of a formerly enslaved fish-salter and prostitute, suffered this fate after his father failed to pay taxes.[84] The bulk of what we know about (re)enslavement through the courts comes from late Classical Athens. From the time of Solon in the early sixth century, Athenian law seems to have all but precluded the judicial enslavement of free citizens.[85] On the other hand, enslavement continued to present a very real threat for non-citizens. Resident aliens could be enslaved as a punishment for falsely claiming to be a citizen or failing to pay taxes; enslavement could also occur if a young man, when applying to enroll as a citizen at the age of eighteen, was found to be a non-citizen.[86] A list of about three hundred slaves whose free status was challenged and proven in court exists from the 320s BCE (*IG* 2² 1553–78). Through a maneuver known as *dike apostasiou*, former masters could bring cases challenging the manumission of a freedman on the basis of not fulfilling unspecified obligations, or, as R. Zelnick-Abramowitz suspects, failing to repay a predatory loan for manumission.[87] Other cases involved the heirs of a deceased master attempting to reclaim a legally manumitted individual. Both proceedings imply a level of brazenness on the part of the plaintiffs, something that is backed up by comparative evidence.[88] We have additional evidence for another legal procedure that could technically be initiated by others to free a falsely enslaved individual, but our only attestations for it involve masters staging impromptu "liberations" of their own slaves, who might be compelled to testify against them under torture.[89] Without citizen friends to sponsor a defense, the deck was stacked against the detained.[90]

Both *Achillodoros' and Apatorios' letters present the case of rival merchants using litigation to intercept a cargo of *slaves, and in the former's case kidnap the master as well. Based on his name and his family in the countryside, *Achillodoros might actually have been a freedman and even of non-Greek origin, which would explain why he was so vulnerable despite his local connections.[91] If that is the case, then the *Achillodoros letter presents a situation very different from what could possibly be encountered in Athens: non-Greeks enslaving each other in a Greek city on the basis of Greek law, all within a generation of Solon's reforms in Athens that had explicitly linked the concept of freedom from slavery with citizenship.

There is good reason to believe that slave markets all around the Black Sea both enabled non-Greek slavers to obtain legal standing and facilitated the predatory environment that allowed Matasys, Herakeides, and Thathaie(s) or Oathaie to press their claims. The letter from Phanagoria presents a similar case; there, a merchant named Aristonymos (*CGP* 48) is reminded that he owes a *slave and a gold stater to a man with the Thracian name of Sapasis, which implies that the latter had the right to enforce his debts.[92] We know that other northern slave markets awarded status to non-Greek slave traders from an early point. Cyzicus, for instance, granted *ateleia* to Manes son of Medikes and to the descendants of Aisopos in the last quarter of the sixth century, all of whom have Phrygian names.[93] Herodotus comments on the elaborate residence of the Scythian king Scyles in Olbia (4.79), and Matasys and Thathaie(s)/Oathaie might have been other Scythian slavers resident in town. Tymnes, the commercial agent of the Scythian king Ariapithes, lived in Olbia full-time in the fifth century (Hdt. 4.76). Non-Greeks made up an unclear proportion of Olbia's total population.[94] Byzantion, another prominent slave market, was relatively open in granting citizenship to wealthy foreigners, and its onomastics show a heavy concentration of Thracian names.[95] There is not nearly enough evidence for us to frame the internal politics of Pontic cities along the lines of ethnicity, but what we see from the letters is that both Greeks and non-Greeks in the region had the ability to use the law to pursue their enemies, which is a good measure of civic standing.

Finally, litigation and criminal prosecution were important mechanisms for increasing supply in times of high demand in other historical slaving regions. Roquinaldo Ferreira has noted that the Eurafrican itinerant traders (*sertanejos*) who trafficked between the coastal cities of Portuguese Angola and the interior often used the legal system to ensnare their own porters or trade partners and ship them to the coast during times of high slave prices, accusing them of theft or other capital offenses.[96] In the many cases where enslaved people successfully challenged their enslavement in court before being shipped off to Brazil, it was precisely through leveraging their ties with local African rulers. By claiming they were the property of another, they required that the phony charge against them be dismissed. Similar maneuvers are known from other slaving zones, such as in eighteenth-century Ghana, where factory-based English merchants who opportunistically seized the kin of their trading partners might find themselves besieged until they retrieved the person of interest from the Caribbean—presuming he or she survived the voyage.[97] Neither of these represents the precise situation that *Achillodoros faced, but his attempt to reach out to his family in the interior shows him leveraging local (and potentially non-Greek) ties in order to make a defense. The references to Scythian armies lurking outside the walls in our sources (e.g., Hdt. 4.75) demonstrate that coastal merchants of any ethnicity needed to be careful.

The negotiations involved in freeing *Achillodoros did not extend to the nameless *captives under his or Apatorios' control. As Fynn-Paul 2009 observes, the greater Mediterranean system was predicated on a careful binary division between enslavable and non-enslavable peoples, and, like *Phaylles or

*Melas' enslaved woman, the slaves casually referenced in the *sulan* letters fit into the former category. A hint of the fate they awaited comes from one of the few surviving fragments of what perhaps was the earliest literary representation of the area in Greek, the *Arimaspeia* of Aristeas of Prokonessos. This mysterious poem, listed by Herodotus (4.11–15) as one of his main sources and said to have been written an implausible 240 years before his time, involved the metaphysical journey of the poet from his home in the Propontis to the most distant reaches of the steppe.[98] There he met the nomadic Issedones, whose unending battle was against the griffons who lived at Eurasia's heart. At a poignant moment excerpted by Longinus, Aristeas seems to speak from the voice of his nomad interlocutors in expressing incredulity at Greeks who arrived in ships:[99]

θαῦμ' ἡμῖν καὶ τοῦτο μέγα φρεσὶν ἡμετέρῃσιν.
ἄνδρες ὕδωρ ναίουσιν ἀπὸ χθονὸς ἐν πελάγεσσι·
δύστηνοί τινές εἰσιν, ἔχουσι γὰρ ἔργα πονηρά·
ὄμματ' ἐν ἄστροισι, ψυχὴν δ' ἐνὶ πόντῳ ἔχουσιν.
ἦ που πολλὰ θεοῖσι φίλας ἀνὰ χεῖρας ἔχοντες
εὔχονται σπλάγχνοισι κακῶς ἀναβαλλομένοισι.

Now this too is a great wonder in our hearts. Men dwell in the water, away from land, in the sea; they are wretched, for they have harsh toils; eyes on the stars, they have a heart in the sea. Often stretching their hands up to the gods, they pray for their turbulent hearts.[100]

The hatred of Black Sea locals toward ships is a recurrent topos in Greek doxography. Diogenes Laertius has the Scythian sage Anacharsis make a few witty quips about the fallacy of seafaring ("On being asked what kind of ships were the safest, he replied, 'Those which are hauled up on shore'").[101] The type of northerner represented by the wise Anacharsis or the noble Issedonean lord was the same who might engage in ritualized feasting with Greek migrants. But the fear of ships is a sentiment probably more appropriate to the countless victims that the nomads delivered to Greek sea captains. After all, fear of ships and hatred of the sea is a near constant in eighteenth- and nineteenth-century slave autobiographies.[102] The Greeks who navigated the Black Sea gyre would have been alert to the voices of the people on board. So when they themselves approached what could be dubious interactions with Scythian and Thracian merchants, it was their own slaves' perspectives they used to vocalize those fears. The end result of this was inscribed in Greek memories of the coast.

Conclusion

If reading the Black Sea letters side by side with literary descriptions of the Black Sea world illustrates how much ancient authors overhyped the risk of enslavement from piracy or shipwreck, then what tensions might they reveal when we compare the letters with literary narratives about slaves themselves? To conclude this chapter, I explore some of the promise—and peril—that literary accounts of enslaved people offer for understanding slavery in the Archaic Period. One case offers an especially good example:

> Διονύσιος τοὔνομα, ἔμπορος τὸ ἐπιτήδευμα δολιχεύσας πολλοὺς πολλάκις πλοῦς, τοῦ κέρδους ὑποθήγοντος, καὶ πορρωτέρω τῆς Μαιώτιδος ἐκκουφίσας, ὠνεῖται κόρην Κόλχον, ἣν ἐλήισαντο Μάχλυες, ἔθνος τῶν ἐκεῖ βαρβάρων. ὑπάγοντος αὐτὸν τοῦ πλούτου καὶ ἐπὶ μᾶλλον ὑποθήγ οντος. Διονύσιος τοὔνομα ἔμπορος τὸ ἐπιτήδευμα, δολιχεύσας πολλοὺς πολλάκις πλοῦς, περιβάλλεται πλοῦτον εὖ μάλα ἁδρόν. ὁ τοίνυν Διονύσιος καταγράφων ἑαυτῷ λύτρα πλεῖστα ὑπὲρ τῆς κόρης, ἢ χρυσίον πάμπολυ, ἢν ἀπόλοιτο αὐτή. τινὰς παραλαβὼν ἁδροῦ μισθοῦ ἐς Βυζάντιον ἐλθεῖν πείθει. εἶτα τῆς ὑστεραίας προσέσχε τῇ Χίῳ, καὶ ἀποβάντες ἐντυγχάνουσι τῇ κόρῃ πιπρασκομένῃ. ὁ δὲ ἔπραττε κακῶς, καὶ πᾶσα ἡ οἰκία αὐτοῦ ἐνόσει, καὶ τὰ τῆς ἐμπορίας ἐπικερδῆ ἥκιστα αὐτῷ ἦν. θυγάτηρ δὲ ἥπερ ἦν οἱ τῶν ἐκείνου μηχανῶν τε καὶ ἐπιβουλῶν ἀμαθής, ἐξάντης γίνεται τοῦ κακοῦ.

There was a man named Dionysius, merchant by trade, who frequently went on long voyages out of a desire for profit. Weighing anchor up past Maiotis, he bought a Colchian girl, whom the Machlyes, a tribe of barbarians there, had carried off. Having brought in money for himself and excited by his worst impulses, the man named Dionysus, who was a merchant by trade and frequently went on long voyages, increased his already great wealth. Now Dionysius had taken a large ransom payment on behalf of the girl, or anyway a lot of gold, if she were redeemed. Taking some persons, he persuaded them for the price of a hefty fee to come with him to Byzantion. On the following day he went to Chios, and disembarking, they came upon the girl as she was being sold. But for this he fared badly, and his whole household fell ill, and when that happened the profits of trade were least of all to him. Although his daughter was ignorant of his contrivances and plots, she met with misfortune regardless.[103]

This account, preserved in badly garbled form by Aelian, goes something as follows: Dionysios, a Chian captain, had apparently accepted money to ransom a *Colchian girl who had been captured by the barbarian Machyles and put up for sale at the mouth of the Don. Instead, he voided his agreement, pocketed the money, and took her back to Chios, where divine providence made his family suffer the consequences.

The *Colchian girl's voyage out of the Black Sea closely resembles the Hellenistic and Roman slaving routes given by Polybius (4.38.4–5) and Strabo (11.2.3). Although Aelian is a late author, at its kernel lies an ancient story, since the earliest revenge plots involving evil Chian masters date at least to the fifth century. As Herodotus (8.104–5) reports, the eunuch dealer Panionios had once bought a Carian prisoner of war named *Hermotimos of Pedasos, castrated him, and sold him to the Lydians. A few years later, *Hermotimos came back with his Persian friends and did the same to Panionios' sons. Other East Greek master/slave tales follow a similar pattern, although they result more in comeuppance than revenge. *Rhodopis the Thracian was owned by the slave merchant Xanthos of Samos before being bought by Sappho's brother Charaoxos and taken to Naukratis, where she found eternal fame. This same Xanthos was also remembered as the proverbially stupid owner of the Thracian or Phrygian moralist *Aesop in the novelistic accounts that circulated about his life as early as the fifth century BCE. The last member of this group, *Salmoxis the Thracian, was claimed by the Greeks of the Black Sea to have been a slave of Pythagoras on Samos. Returning to the Black Sea, he so beguiled his fellow Thracians with his new knowledge that they worshipped him as a god. *Salmoxis' story, which even Herodotus (4.95) notes is a Greek travesty of Thracian religious habits, probably scratches the surface of the reverse migrations of freed slaves northward after being redeemed. Our knowledge of these, however, is limited to an elusive reference to *Thracians manumitted from slavery in Athens, accompanied by Herodes, on a ship to Ainos in Antiphon's namesake speech.

Like stories about barbarians and shipwrecks, narratives about crafty slaves were central to how east Greek slaveowners and the far-flung communities that supplied them conceptualized their place in the world. By aestheticizing the most gruesome parts of enslaved life into a learning experience, crafty slave narratives presented slavery as a type of apprenticeship into a new society.[104] The experience of travel focalizes the slave's rebirth. Even when the journey is not long—*Hermotimos was a Carian on Chios—the journey into slavery meant a total break from the slave's previous life, often marked in sexual terms. Although Aelian's *Colchian girl shows relatively little agency over her situation, the others turn their complete severance from their homelands into an opportunity to learn new skills: *Aesop gains command over the language of Greek philosophy, while his contemporary *Rhodopis finds power in sex, and *Salmoxis uses his experience to become a god.

Reconstructing enslaved journeys allows us to separate out the cruel laughter and concealed fears of the master class found in our surviving slave narratives from the real experiences of slaves in the Black Sea. For *Phaylles or *Melas' enslaved woman, slavery offered nothing like the opportunities it did for the fictional or quasi-fictional *Rhodopis or *Salmoxis. Nevertheless, each part of the record holds equal importance in understanding how the Mediterranean slave system expanded into the Black Sea world. Disconnected from the evolving cultural norms that limited who was subject to enslavement in the Aegean, Greek slave traders in the Black Sea had learned to see the world through the eyes of their captives from the outset.

In this chapter, I have shown that most enslaved captives in the earliest period of Greek slavery in the north travelled only short distances, that they appear only in dispassionate references to goods in commercial documents, and that masters themselves could be enslaved using the same legal mechanisms that they used to obtain their cargoes. The contradictions and anxieties borne out by this commerce were writ large in the geography of the region, as Greek sea captains circulated a working knowledge of how to navigate it that displaced its biggest threats to its most desolate stretches. I argue that Greek migrants in the north were sensitive to the experiences of enslaved people, over time coming to adopt their fears as their own—even though it was Greeks themselves who benefitted from their abuse. Knowledge of how to secure deals with local partners and most quickly transport slaves from one place to another underlay the earliest attempts by Greeks in the region to differentiate Greeks from barbarians.

5

Slavery and the Balance of Trade

Introduction

> *February 14 the 1785*
> *about 5 am in aqua Landing with great fog morning so*
> *I hav see my Boostam yams canow com hom with yams so*
> *I have pay Captin Savage 1000 yams for 100 Coppers and at*
> *12 clock night Captin Brown Teder go way with 430 slaves.*[1]

ON JULY 28, 1784, the ship *Lion* departed Liverpool for Calabar in present-day Nigeria under the command of one Captain John Burrows. Arriving in Calabar with forty men, the *Lion*'s crew would dwindle to twenty-five as she rode at anchor until August of the following year. Burrows had provisions for 600 captives; months of negotiations with Calabar merchants yielded 344, of whom 315 survived to be disembarked in Grenada in the West Indies on October 26, 1785. Additional cargoes included 427 elephant tusks and two chests of pepper.[2] The *Lion* departed for home on February 27, 1786, and arrived in Liverpool on April 11 after a voyage of twenty-two months.

The cruelest irony of the Transatlantic Slave Trade is its recording.[3] Almost nothing has come down from the hands of its survivors.[4] But in terms of data, voyages like that of the *Lion* in 1784–86 are incredibly *well* documented. In the *Lion*'s case, we have *Lloyd's Register* and Liverpool port records, collated by the editors of the *Transatlantic Slave Trade Database* (*TASTD*).[5] The surgeon Alexander Falconbridge (c. 1760–92), who would one day become an abolitionist, encountered Burrows and his crew at Calabar, recording in his journal that Burrows sheltered mutinous white sailors from another slave ship.[6] But some of the most crucial records are not European. Above I have quoted the journal of Antera Duke (d. post-1788), a slave trader of Efik ethnicity who

Racialized Commodities. Christopher Stedman Parmenter, Oxford University Press. © Oxford University Press 2024.
DOI: 10.1093/9780197757147.003.0006

was one of the African rulers of Calabar. Duke was fluent in the ways of the Europeans. He made the Europeans ride in the delta for months as he raided the interior for captives, compelling them to sweeten their terms as disease ate at the crew. If it is the English who reported the *Lion*'s cargo from Liverpool, Duke is the man who recorded what the deals were in west Africa: metal and textiles for captives, ivory, food, and spices. It is his accounting that enables us to reconstruct the Transatlantic Slave Trade, in part, from both ends.

We lack almost any documentation for the slave trade in ancient Greece. Although it is no longer accepted that ancient merchants had no use for recordkeeping,[7] ancient Greek commercial documents are almost a *lacuna*— the sum total include a single customs register,[8] a single contract,[9] a few dozen merchant letters,[10] and an estate archive.[11] Ancient sources almost never present economic data in a centralized fashion.[12] But evidence for a far more informal means of accounting is widespread. This is what, in the eighteenth century, would have been called a "balance of trade": an idea of how much one territory is trading with another, and the concordant assumption that imports and exports should be balanced in such a way to supplement economic autarchy.[13] No city in Classical Greece produced more evidence for such a logic than Athens. Athens ran a trade surplus almost entirely dependent on a single commodity, silver, that was fungible for almost everything: grain, lumber, enslaved bodies. In the fifth century, Athens enforced its economic dominance through compulsion, fielding its colossal navy to predate upon its neighbors unless they agreed to route trade through the Piraeus using Athenian currency.[14] In the fourth century, Athens turned congenial, offering merchants access to financing, arbitration, and maritime labor in exchange for assurance that they would carry grain to Athens.[15] Basic understanding of imperial finance was widespread in Athenian society, and this is reflected by the abundance of discussions on the matter in fourth century writing on household economics.[16]

Literary narratives about the ancient slave trade are marked with this kind of informal accounting. In his description of life along the River Rhône in the sixth century BCE, Diodorus Siculus (5.26–27) claims that northern peoples were so barbarous that the only commodity they had to trade for wine were slaves.[17] Polybius tells a very similar story about the Pontic slave trade during the Hellenistic Period:

πρὸς μὲν γὰρ τὰς ἀναγκαίας τοῦ βίου χρείας τά τε θρέμματα καὶ τὸ τῶν εἰς τὰς δουλείας ἀγομένων σωμάτων πλῆθος οἱ κατὰ τὸν Πόντον ἡμῖν τόποι παρασκευάζουσι δαψιλέστατον καὶ χρησιμώτατον ὁμολογουμένως· πρὸς δὲ περιουσίαν μέλι, κηρόν, τάριχος ἀφθόνως ἡμῖν χορηγοῦσι. δέχονται γε μὴν τῶν ἐν τοῖς παρ' ἡμῖν τόποις περιττευόντων ἔλαιον καὶ πᾶν οἴνου γένος· σίτῳ δ' ἀμείβονται, ποτὲ μὲν εὐκαίρως διδόντες, ποτὲ δὲ λαμβάνοντες.

For those commodities which are the first necessaries of existence, cattle and slaves, are confessedly supplied by the districts round the Pontus in greater profusion, and of better quality, than by any others: and for luxuries, they supply us with honey, wax, and salt-fish in great abundance; while they take our superfluous stock of olive oil and every kind of wine. In the matter of grain there is a mutual interchange, with them supplying or taking it as it happens to be convenient. (Polyb. 4.38.4–5)

And this dismissiveness toward the periphery is hardly unique. One Demosthenic orator (35.35) describes a trade in Aegean wine for Black Sea commodities too trifling to name.[18] In the first century CE, the Roman geographer Strabo (7.4.6, 11.2.3) lays out a balance sheet of Black Sea hides, captives, and fish for Aegean clothing, wine, and grain. Each of these authors dismisses the exports of the civilized world as cheap stuff (περιττευόντων ἔλαιον καὶ πᾶν οἴνου γένος, Str. 11.2.22); the nomads had no idea their goods were so valuable. What was the point of having such a bounty when all one got for it was coldness (ψύχη), poverty (ἀπορίας), and isolation (δυσεπίμικτοι τοῖς ἄλλοις)? This dismissiveness is so profound that it might well be seen as a kind of legitimization for compelled migration from the uncivilized north.

This chapter reads ancient speculations about the balance of trade might against the backdrop of nondocumentary evidence—namely the distribution of coinage, amphora handles, and shipwrecks—to reconstruct the economics of the ancient slave trade between Greece and the Black Sea in the Classical Period. Reconstructing the balance sheet of the Black Sea slave trade allows us to better situate the lived experiences of *Phaylles, *Achillodoros, and the other individuals we met in the last chapter. One surprising conclusion is the extent to which the slave trade was not the primary business of most of the merchants involved in it. Rather, it was a way for merchants—both from the Pontus and Athens—to *balance* their account books in years when the other saleable commodities were scarce.[19] By contextualizing the place of the slave trade within the much better-documented flow of staple commodities between the barbarian north and the Mediterranean, this study adds to a growing body of scholarship that uses distinctive commodities (coins, shackles, glass beads, and decorative ceramics) to map the movement of captive labor in premodern Europe.[20]

The first half of this chapter will approach the issue of financing, focusing especially on Athens' control of silver resources in the Aegean. In the second half, I explore how Pontic cities used enslaved captives to balance exports of staple commodities, especially grain, in the face of Athens' massive trade surplus. Tracing the paths taken by merchants from Athens to the north will allow us to find the spaces and routes across which slavery thrived in Classical Greece.

Financing a Surplus: Metals, Minerals, Currency, and the Portable Arts

πρῶτον μὲν ἐνθένδ' ἡλίου πρὸς ἀντολὰς
στρέψασα σαυτὴν στεῖχ' ἀνηρότους γύας·
Σκύθας δ' ἀφίξῃ νομάδας, οἳ πλεκτὰς στέγας
πεδάρσιοι ναίουσ' ἐπ' εὐκύκλοις ὄχοις,
ἑκηβόλοις τόξοισιν ἐξηρτυμένοι·
οἷς μὴ πελάζειν, ἀλλ' ἁλιστόνοις πόδας
χρίμπτουσα ῥαχίαισιν ἐκπερᾶν χθόνα.
λαιᾶς δὲ χειρὸς οἱ σιδηροτέκτονες
οἰκοῦσι Χάλυβες, οὓς φυλάξασθαί σε χρή,
[...]
ἰσθμὸν δ' ἐπ' αὐταῖς στενοπόροις λίμνης πύλαις
Κιμμερικὸν ἥξεις, ὃν θρασυσπλάγχνως σε χρὴ
λιποῦσαν αὐλῶν' ἐκπερᾶν Μαιωτικόν·
ἔσται δὲ θνητοῖς εἰσαεὶ λόγος μέγας
τῆς σῆς πορείας, Βόσπορος δ' ἐπώνυμος
κεκλήσεται. λιποῦσα δ' Εὐρώπης πέδον
ἤπειρον ἥξεις Ἀσιάδα.

First, from this spot, turn yourself toward the rising sun and make your way over untilled plains; and you shall reach the Scythian nomads, who dwell in thatched houses, perched aloft on strong-wheeled wagons and are equipped with far-darting bows. Do not approach them, but keeping your feet near the rugged shore, where the sea breaks with a roar, pass on beyond their land. On the left hand dwell the workers in iron, the Chalybes, and you must beware of them, since they are savage and are not to be approached by strangers [...] just at the narrow portals of the harbor, you shall reach the Cimmerian isthmus. This you must leave with stout heart and pass through the channel of

Maeotis; and ever after among mankind there shall be great mention of your passing, and it shall be called after you the Bosporus. Then, leaving the soil of Europe, you shall come to the land of Asia. (*Ps.*-Aes. *PB* 707–15, 29–35)

No region of the Mediterranean is as remote as the Kerch Strait. Here at the edge of the world, the water smells fresh, and the strong current—running up to 5 knots southward during springtime in Eurasia—impedes northern passage. South of that are 200 miles of open water, which with luck—and with wind—could be crossed overnight from the Anatolian coast.[21] Northward lies the brackish Sea of Azov, the ancient Maeotic Lake, which reaches a depth of 46 feet only at its very center. Fed by the roaring flow of the river Don from the northeast and bordered by the hypersaline *Syvash*—the Russian "rotten sea"—on its west, the sea is turbid, unpredictable, and subject to rise and fall due to the *seiche* effect of the wind. Parts of the sea freeze in winter; in all other seasons it provides some of the best fishing anywhere. Ionian cities including Klazomenai (Strb. 11.2.4) had established fishing colonies here in antiquity.[22] On both sides of the Kerch Strait—the ancient Cimmerian Bosporus, named after Io's passage—lay the Bosporan Kingdom, with its temples, tumuli, and hybridized culture that blended Greece and the steppe, Europe and Asia.

Despite ample working evidence for local ironworking at Berezan and other sites, there is not much evidence that Greeks first came to the Black Sea for metals.[23] But if his description of the iron-working Chalybes is off-the-mark, the author of the *Prometheus Bound* captures something of the rationale for Greek voyages to the Black Sea. The Cimmerian Bosporus was the central objective of nearly all long-distance traffic to the Black Sea. For hundreds of years in antiquity, the roadstead at Ak-Burun—the promontory facing the harbor of Pantikapaion, modern Kerch—was where ships rode things out when the fierce north current clashed with the south wind, waiting either to return home or for a window to proceed north to marketplaces along the Don. In 2017, Russian archaeologists working at the Kerch Strait found an underwater sherd scatter measuring some 75,000 m^2, deposited underwater during breakwater construction in the Middle Ages. The ceramics, still undergoing publication, date from the earliest moments of Greek trade in the region in the sixth century BCE all the way to the seventh century CE.[24] Among them was perhaps their most spectacular discovery: a mold-made, terracotta figural head, datable to the end of the fifth century BCE, that had either been mounted as an antefix on a building or (less convincingly) on a ship, as a figurehead[25] (Figure 5.1).

FIGURE 5.1 Russian archaeologist Sergei Olkhovsky poses with the Ak-Burun head at the Kerch Strait bridge construction site, 2017. After Olkhovsky 2018: 249, fig. 6. Olkhovsky's excavation might be described as *wildly illegal* by the laws of the west. It contravenes at least the following: the Ukrainian Law of August 14, 2014 No,. 1644-VII; 1954/1999 Hague Conventions for the Protection of Cultural Property in the Event of Armed Conflict; the 1972 UNESCO Convention Concerning the Protection of the World Cultural and Natural Heritage; and the 2001 UNESCO Convention for the Protection of the Underwater Cultural Heritage (Babin 2020).

The relationship between the Greek colonies of the Black Sea coast and the wider Mediterranean in antiquity has been a central question since the dawn of archaeology in the region in the eighteenth century.[26] The re-emergence of the North Black Sea as a zone of interstate conflict has seen archaeology mobilized to answer these questions, particularly by Russian archaeologists working in territories unilaterally annexed from Ukraine in 2014. Archaeometric analysis of the Ak-Burun head has been deployed to answer these questions. While testing on the Ak-Burun head remains preliminary, there is some suggestion that the clays used in its making came from Puglia in Italy. (This would make sense, given that coroplastics is an art of West Greece.)[27] The lead clamps used to hold the piece together came from the mines of Laureion.[28]

The Ak-Burun head thus, and perhaps uniquely for a single object, lays bare some of the logic of international trade in the fourth century BCE. Art objects were objects of trade, with their own geographies of demand and supply too specific to be the focus of this chapter.[29] But analyzing their components can lay bare the much larger flow of staple commodities along which they travelled.[30]

Chief among these is Attic lead. Lead from Attica was a major trade good in antiquity: starting in the sixth century, it is found everywhere from Sparta to Naukratis in the Nile Delta to the Kerch Strait.[31] A substantial quantity of this commodity travelled around the Mediterranean as ship components, in the form of anchors and lead sheathing to prevent fouling.[32] Although there were many silver and lead mines across the Aegean, production in the fourth century was heavily centralized in Athens: vast quantities were produced as byproduct of Athens' most important commodity, silver.[33] Silver mining was an industry with huge emotional resonance for Athenians: the discovery of a new seam at Maroneia in 485 BCE had enabled Athens to finance a fleet to meet the Persian invasion five years later (*Ps.-Aristot. Ath. Pol.* 22.7). (In 472 BCE, the poet Aeschylus would outright state that silver bought Athens its freedom.)[34] But no Athenian writer tarried much to think about its costs. The processes of mining, washing, smelting, and cupellation exposed enslaved laborers to massive amounts of lead.[35] Life was short in the Lavreotiki.[36] In fact, given the huge turnover of labor required to meet the demands of the mine concessionaries, the greatest profiteers of the mining business were contractors who leased enslaved labor to the mines. These individuals were known to enslave hundreds of men, women, and children.[37]

All of this is to say that the voyage of the Ak-Burun head was, in some sense, tracing in reverse the transformation of Pontic labor to Athenian coin. Indeed, the two industries—slaving and silver—shared a set of actors and financing. Wealthy mine concessionaries were known to contribute financing for voyages to the Pontus (Dem. 37.6), while some large enslavers were mocked as "red-faced" and "Scythian" by their critics.[38] The Athenian Empire of the fifth century had striven to make its drachma the reserve currency of the Aegean, forcing its allies to use the drachma over local currency and giving Athenians outsized purchasing power wherever they went. ("In most port cities," Xenophon would write, "merchants have to take on a return cargo because the local coinage is of no use elsewhere; at Athens, however ... even if merchants do not want to load up with a return cargo of goods, by exporting the coinage they will be exporting an excellent item of trade"; *Poroi* 3.2.)[39] Indeed, slave prices in Athens were low by comparative ancient standards.[40] But maintaining this purchasing power meant ensuring that the imbalance of trade—with Athenian drachmas buying up the world—was ever tilted in its favor.

Currency exchanges were a particular risk in far-flung regions, like the Black Sea. Generally speaking, ancient coinage tended to gravitate back to the city of issue; but the periodic *dysconnectivity* of the Pontus disrupted this trend, as is dramatically illustrated by an early Hellenistic hoard of Olbian coinage found in central Asia.[41] Thus Athens, its merchants, and its Black Sea trade partners conspired together to keep the Black Sea a separate currency zone from the Aegean.[42] During the Peloponnesian War, Athens had tried to enforce the Coins, Weights, and Measures decree on its Pontic allies, which would have required them to use the drachma for foreign trade. But this quickly lapsed.[43] What appears to have replaced it was a preference to keep Athenian silver out of the Pontus—and indeed, it is almost never found there. One fourth-century shipping contract for a voyage from Athens to the Black Sea requires its signatories convert a cash loan into wine in the North Aegean before proceeding to the Pontus (*Ps.*-Dem. 35.10–13, quoted below). If currency had to be used, merchants typically converted their Athenian drachmas to the Cyzicene stater (*Ps.*-Dem. 36.23), which had dominated the cash ecosystem of the Pontus since the invention of coinage in the sixth century.[44]

Pontic cities made a great effort to draw in Cyzicene staters carried by Athenian traders. Pantikapaion used a coinage standard easily convertible with both Athens and Cyzicus, which facilitated direct voyages there from the Thracian Bosporus.[45] Olbia attempted to underbid Pantikapaion, posting a decree at Hieron on the Thracian Bosporus that offered an even more attractive conversion rate between Cyzicus and its own currency.[46] (Its own currency, which was widely distributed in its hinterland, was mostly valueless bronze)[47] (Figure 5.2). The end result of this system was one of exploitation. Elites in Pontic cities kept a courtesy amount of silver close to home for their own purposes;[48] but their own goods were so cheap to outsiders that they had to export constantly to meet their thirst for oil and wine. Exploitation radiated through the countryside. The simple term for this is colonialism.[49]

In a roundabout fashion, then, the lead clamps from Ak-Burun testify to the wider, often unseen ways that Athens' access to precious metals shaped trade across the wider Mediterranean world. Lead, a byproduct of silver, was a hanger-on in the trade that silver facilitated. Much similar could be said of other minerals and metals that appear along Pontic trade route. Slaves were said to be so cheaply obtainable along the Danube that they could be obtained for salt.[50] There was a substantial trade in stone—both incidental (as in the case of the ships' ballast that ended up used to build a fourth-century seawall in Pantikapaion,[51] or the Achaemenid decree that ended up in fill at Phanagoria)[52] and deliberate, as in the export of marble for use in temple building at Istros, Olbia, Pantikapaion, and Phanagoria.[53] But such cargoes were never consistently a trade good. The precious metals that financed the slave trade between the Pontus and the Aegean rarely crossed the Bosporus. We should now turn to the staples alongside which captives moved.

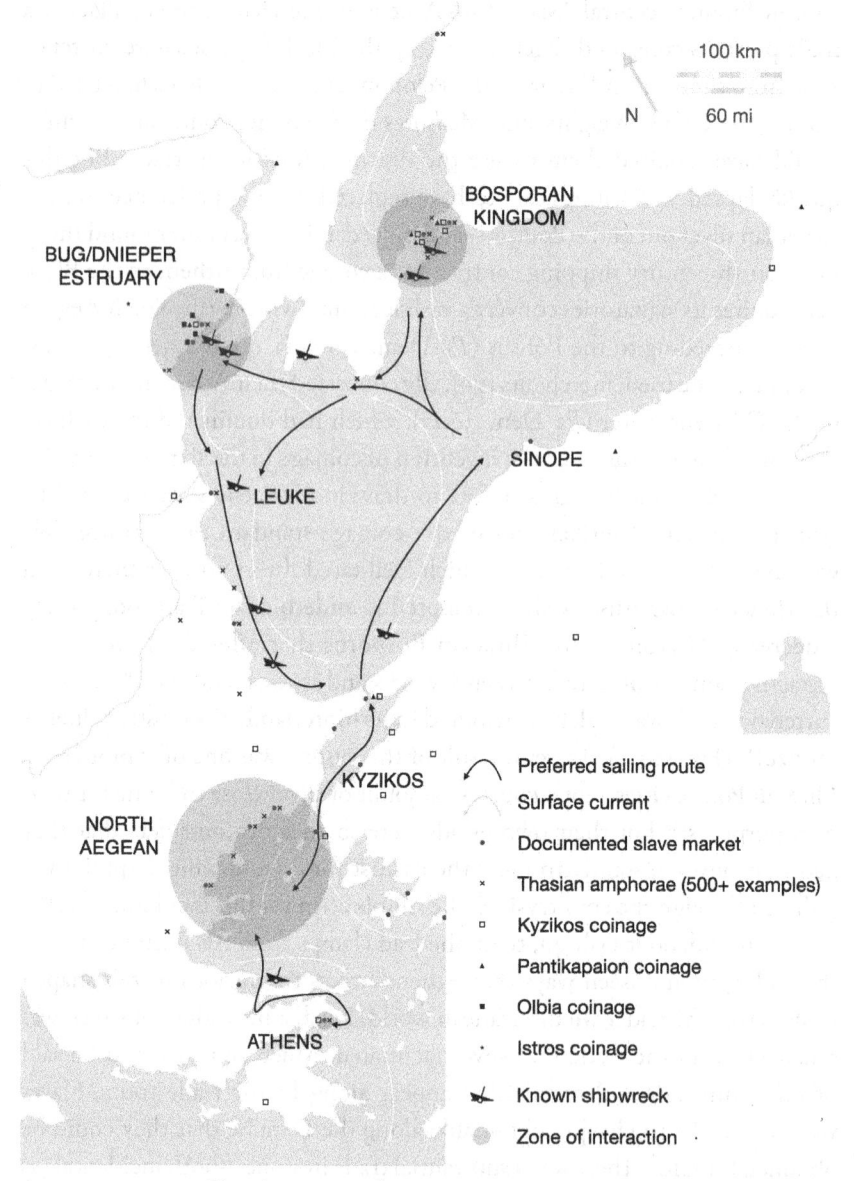

FIGURE 5.2 Map of fourth-century Athenian trade with the Black Sea. Mapping of slave markets after Parmenter 2020: fig. 1; Thasian amphorae, after Tzochev 2016; coinage after *IGCH*; shipwrecks after above, pp. 11–12.

Staples: Wine, Oil, Grain, and Fish

Ἐδάνεισαν Ἀνδροκλῆς Σφήττιος καὶ Ναυσικράτης Καρύστιος Ἀρτέμωνι καὶ Ἀπολλοδώρῳ Φασηλίταις ἀργυρίου δραχμὰς τρισχιλίας Ἀθήνηθεν εἰς Μένδην ἢ Σκιώνην, καὶ ἐντεῦθεν εἰς Βόσπορον, ἐὰν δὲ βούλωνται, τῆς ἐπ' ἀριστερὰ μέχρι Βορυσθένους, καὶ πάλιν Ἀθήναζε, ἐπὶ διακοσίαις εἴκοσι πέντε τὰς χιλίας, ἐὰν δὲ μετ' Ἀρκτοῦρον ἐκπλεύσωσιν ἐκ τοῦ Πόντου ἐφ' Ἱερόν, ἐπὶ τριακοσίαις τὰς χιλίας, ἐπὶ οἴνου κεραμίοις Μενδαίοις τρις χιλίοις, ὃς πλεύσεται ἐκ Μένδης ἢ Σκιώνης ἐν τῇ εἰκοσόρῳ ἣν Ὑβλήσιος ναυκληρεῖ. ὑποτιθέασι δὲ ταῦτα, οὐκ ὀφείλοντες ἐπὶ τούτοις ἄλλῳ οὐδενὶ οὐδὲν ἀργύριον, οὐδ' ἐπιδανείσονται. καὶ ἀπάξουσι τὰ χρήματα τὰ ἐκ τοῦ Πόντου ἀντιφορτισθέντα Ἀθήναζε πάλιν ἐν τῷ αὐτῷ πλοίῳ ἅπαντα. σωθέντων δὲ τῶν χρημάτων Ἀθήναζε, ἀποδώσουσιν οἱ δανεισάμενοι τοῖς δανείσασι τὸ γιγνόμενον ἀργύριον κατὰ τὴν συγγραφὴν ἡμερῶν εἴκοσιν, ἀφ' ἧς ἂν ἔλθωσιν Ἀθήναζε, ἐντελὲς πλὴν ἐκβολῆς, ἣν ἂν οἱ σύμπλοι ψηφισ αμενοι κοινῇ ἐκβάλωνται, καὶ ἄν τι πολεμίοις ἀποτείσωσιν·

Androkles of Sphettos and Nausikrates of Karystos lent to Artemon and Apollodoros, both of Phaselis, three thousand drachmae in silver for a voyage from Athens to Mende or Skione, and thence to Bosporus—or if they so choose, for a voyage to the left parts of the Pontus as far as the Borysthenes, and thence back to Athens, on interest at a rate of two hundred and twenty-five drachmae on the thousand; but, if they should sail out from Pontus to Hieron after the rising of Arktouros at three hundred on the thousand, on the security of three thousand jars of wine of Mende, which shall be conveyed from Mende or Scione in the twenty-oared ship of which Hyblesios is owner ... they agree to bring back to Athens in the same vessel all the goods put on board in Pontus as return cargo. [...] And if they do not enter Pontus, but remain in the Hellespont ten days after the rising of the dog-star, and disembark their goods at a port where the Athenians have no right of reprisals, and from thence complete their voyage to Athens, let them pay the interest written into the contract the year before. (*Ps.*-Dem. 35.10–13)

Fifth- and fourth-century Athens survived on imported grain. Decades after the height of its fifth-century empire—when Pericles had encouraged Athens to "Suppose we were islanders: we would be impregnable!" (Thuc. 1.143.5)[54]—the resurgent city deployed a mixture of incentive and compulsion to keep grain flowing even in times of scarcity. From around third quarter of the fifth century BCE, the northern Black Sea coast became what Peregrine Horden and Nicholas Purcell call a "dispersed hinterland" for Athens, functioning as a countryside linked to the city via a bridge of ships.[55] The ruling Spartakid dynasty of Pantikapaion, which grew to dominate much of Crimea and the Taman peninsula, thrived on its close ties with Athens. But depending on such a far-flung region as the Black Sea was not without risks. The Black Sea was distant, and merchants sailed at the mercy of war (which closed the Thracian Bosporus in 513, 480, 404, 339, and 220 BCE), instability, and the weather. The corpus of commercial litigation surrounding voyages between Athens and the Pontus—such as the shipping contract, from the Pseudo-Demosthenic *Against Lakritos*, quoted here—shows the existence of what might be considered an annual triangle trade that leveraged Athens' access to Mediterranean commodities (namely wine and oil) to supply the city with grain (Figure 5.2). Drawn to Athens by its markets, expertise, and its friendly legal regime, merchants used their access to Laureion silver to purchase commodities (notably wine from the northern Aegean); trade for grain, captives, and hides in the far north; and return to the Aegean in the narrow window—July and September—when transits between the Black Sea and the Aegean were possible.[56]

As a well-documented example of long-distance, state-directed trade, the Black Sea grain trade between Athens and the Kerch Straits has aroused considerable interest over the years, particularly in the context of debates over the complexity of the ancient economy.[57] The flow of grain to Athens was enmeshed in the trade in at least five other commodities: silver, which has already been answered for, and wine, oil, and salt-fish, which will be addressed below. Slaves represented something like a sixth spoke of the wheel, which could be flexibly added or subtracted from other commodities. The ships that plied the routes from Athens to Pantikapaion were themselves often crewed with enslaved sailors (Dem. 25.32, Ps.-Dem. 33.8) or oarsmen (*IG* 2³ 1.298 l. 60), a fact that cannot be removed from the viability of this trip as a slaving route. More to the point, captives might stand in for other commodities of the steppe whenever the region erupted in paroxysms of violence, which was frequently. In this way, the integration of the far north into the Mediterranean landscape made every encounter with the wider world a potential site of the slave trade.[58]

A striking example of this comes from a voyage made by Lampis, a formerly enslaved business agent employed in the Bosporan Kingdom by a merchant named Dio (Λάμπιδι τῷ Δίωνος οἰκέτῃ ἐν Βοσπόρῳ) in the year 327/26

BCE (Dem. 34.5).[59] Lampis was the owner (ναυκλήρου) of a ship that regularly sailed between the Kerch Straits and Piraeus (Dem. 34.7). On his voyage north to the Kerch Straits that year Lampis had taken on unspecified goods belonging to another freedman, Phormion, who joined the voyage as supercargo. (The resulting lawsuit features Phormion as defendant, sued by a lender named Chryssipos, another freedman named Kittos, and a Phoenician trader named Theodoros.) Lampis and Phormion had arrived in Pantikapaion during a time of war between the Bosporan king Pairisades (r. 342–10 BCE) and the Scythian nomads. Wartime meant little demand for either Lampis' or Chryssipus' products. Phormion elected to unload his cargo anyway and stay behind until the market recovered. Lampis, on the other hand, decided to head back home, loading up his ship well over capacity with an unusual cargo. In his lawsuit against Phormion, Chryssipos describes what happens next: the ship floundered right off what is now Ak-Burun. On deck, Lampis—who, along with some of his enslaved crewmembers, had survived—had loaded excess of 1,000 hides. Below, he might have been carrying as many as 300 enslaved prisoners (Dem. 34.10). Their lives were lost to the sea.[60]

Up until the end, aspects of Lampis' voyage seem utterly typical of Athenian trade with the Black Sea in the mid-fourth century. Shipowners depended on financing; freedmen were prominent commercial actors;[61] the voyage had three legs, with the ship departing with silver from Athens, converting to wine in North Aegean cities like Mende, Skione, Thasos, or Skopelos, and purchasing grain, hides, or captives in Crimea. A variation often seen in these voyages, albeit not represented in the literary evidence, is the substitution of olive oil for wine.[62] Our relatively few literary references to the olive oil trade in the Black Sea are belied by occasional quips—made by none other than Xenophon, who was more than occasionally involved in the slave trade himself (*Anab.* 7.4)—that people in the region lacked it (*Anab.* 6.4.6, 6.6.1, both describing Bithynia in northern Anatolia). The Mossynoikoi in the southwestern Pontus were so impoverished that they used dolphin blubber for fat (5.4.28).[63] One Hippocratic author (*De sem.* 51.11) offers a detailed explanation[64] for how the Scythians separate butter fat from milk.[65]

The material trail left by Athens' grain merchants—who, as we have seen, easily doubled as slave merchants—accord very closely with our literary evidence. These are mapped together in Figure 5.2. To start, at least ten Classical shipwrecks are known either from literary or archaeological evidence along the route between Athens and the north (Table 5.1): at Alonissos in the Sporades, where ships transited between the North Aegean and the Euboean Gulf;[66] at Ak-Burun;[67] near Theodosia;[68] at the Donuslav inlet, near Yevpatoriya; two

Table 5.1 Classical shipwrecks along shipping route between Athens and the Black Sea

Location	Date	Evidence	Estimated amphora capacity	Estimated tonnage	Attested cargo	Publication or discussion
Alonissos, Greece	425–400 BCE	Archaeological	4,200	100+	1,000 amphorae observed on surface	Hadjidaki 1996
Eregli, Turkey	300–275 BCE	Archaeological		12–15	50-60 amphorae observed on surface	D. Davis et al. 2018
Ak-Burun, Ukraine	350/49 BCE	Literary			1,000 hides; 300 captives	Dem. 34.10; Lewis 2022
Feodosia, Ukraine	c. 340 BCE	Literary	3,000	c. 200	80 amphorae wine, 12 amphorae salt-fish, 3 bundles hides	Ps.-Dem. 35.31; Lewis 2022
Donuslav, Ukraine	c. 400 BCE	Archaeological	3,000	100	20 amphorae recovered	Blavatskiy and Peters 1969
Kinbrun Spit A, Ukraine	c. 400 BCE	Archaeological	3,000	100	10 + amphorae recovered	Geramisov et al. 2018
Kinbrun Spit B, Ukraine	500–400 BCE	Archaeological				Gerasimov et al. 2018: 189
Zmiinyi, Ukraine	400–300 BCE	Archaeological	3,000	100	800 amphorae observed on surface	Tereshenko 2013
Varna, Bulgaria	487–277 BCE	Archaeological			20-30 amphorae observed on surface, some containing salt-fish	Lund and Gabrielsen 2005: 164.
Burgas, Bulgaria	410–380 BCE	Archaeological				Pacheco-Ruiz et al. 2019: 11–12

wrecks off the Kinbrun spit, at the mouth of the Bug-Dnieper Estuary;[69] at Zmiinyi, or Snake Island, off the Sulina mouth of the Danube;[70] near Varna, ancient Odessos;[71] and in deep water off Herakleia Pontica, modern Eregli.[72] Other misfortunes are known that did not result in disaster. The contract in *Ps.*-Dem. 35.10–13 mentions the risk of a ship being confiscated in a Pontic port; this reality is vouched for in an Attic inscription dating between 330/29–328/27 BCE (*IG* 2³ 1.367), which describes the plight of a Cypriot grain merchant named Herakleides of Samos, whose sails had been seized in port by authorities in Herakleia Pontica (mod. Eregli). The Athenians had dispatched officials to get his sails back.

Next comes evidence from amphorae, the packaging of trade. From the fifth-century Alonissos shipwreck, we have at least 4,200 amphorae, the majority of which came from Skopelos and Mende.[73] Over 800 amphorae from Skopelos are documented on the fourth-century wreck at Snake Island.[74] Most important is the vast and well-studied corpus of stamped amphora handles from Thasos.[75] Thasian amphora, which carried the island's distinctive wine, are not well known in the Aegean or eastern Mediterranean outside the northern Aegean. But for the first three-quarters of the fourth century, Thasian amphorae appear in great quantity all along the Black Sea, in particular in the Bosporan Kingdom, the Bug/Dnieper estuary, and the stretch of coast between the mouth of the Danube and Odessos, modern Varna in Bulgaria.[76] Mapping these together with our literary and numismatic evidence compensates for the curious silence in documentary sources such as merchant letters[77] (Figure 5.3).

Both the litigation surrounding Lampis' abortive voyage from the Crimea and the merchant letters make clear that captives were frequently taken as supplementary, but rarely primary, cargoes on trading voyages.

In fact, Lampis' voyage appears to be an extreme case of a common practice in the Black Sea slave trade. Lampis "could not ship the goods because his trash was unsaleable" (οὐκ ἂν δύναιτο ἐνθέσθαι εἰς τὴν ναῦν τὰ χρήματα· ἄπρατον γὰρ εἶναι τὸν ῥῶπον, Dem. 34.10). Instead of loading the goods he had set out to carry, Lampis took advantage of Pairisades' war on the Scythians. Hides were available, perhaps because the Bosporan king had seized cattle from the nomads. And so were captives. If, as David Lewis (2022) argues, the manuscript reading of "300 bodies" (τριακόσια σώματα) should be taken over later emendations, Lampis might have taken advantage of a sudden spike in the number of captives for sale.[78] (Similar spikes are visible in the records of the Medieval Genoese and Venetian slave trades in the same regions).[79] This opportunism might also explain why the ship was not correctly

FIGURE 5.3 Photogrammetric image of early fourth-century BCE shipwreck preserved on seafloor off Burgas, Bulgaria, in the anoxic layer of the water column, 2,112 m below the surface of the Black Sea, after Pacheco-Ruiz et al. 2019: 14, fig. 19. Image produced by Rodrigo Pacheco-Ruiz, University of Southampton. Used with permission. Vessels of this size were far smaller than the ship of Dem. 34. But they made up the majority of traffic along the Black Sea coast.

balanced, leading to disaster. This same logic appears on a much smaller scale in a number of the merchant letters. At the start of the fifth century, a merchant named Pistos corresponded with an agent in Phanagoria on the Taman Peninsula, asking for payments of debts both in cash and an enslaved person (*CGP* 48). Between 325–300 BCE, a merchant named Oreos requested an agent resident in Myrmekeion on the Kerch Strait to dispatch him a consignment of cloth along with a slave (*CGP* 46). On the other side of the document, he instructs a subaltern named Kerkion to pick up a cargo of salt-fish if available.

In fact, the one staple commodity that enslaved people most closely resembled were salt-fish. Fisheries are a subject of great interest by commodity historians of the Atlantic, where Grand Banks cod was used to finance the trade in woolens between Spain and England in the Early Modern Period.[80] The production of smoked and salted fish for export along the Sea of Azov tended toward increased complexity through the Classical Period, with the appearance of dedicated manufactories, ceramics, and signs of vertical integration between Bosporan producers and their agents working in Athens.[81] It was also manufactured in the Bug/Dnieper estuary.[82] Indeed, the lands beyond the Turkish straits were celebrated for producing fish by the comic poets: "Sing to me, Muses having homes on Olympus, about what Dionysus captains on the wine dark sea," sings a speaker in Hermippus' *Basket-Carriers*: "from the Hellespont mackerel and other sorts of dried fish" (fr. 63.5 K-A).[83] The bulk of fish appear to have been transported dried or smoked in baskets (ἐν σαργανίσαν, Kratinos fr. 44 K-A), although clearly some were fermented into fish sauce.[84] Some sources refer to salt-fish as an opportunistic addition to existing cargo. One merchant letter from Kerkinitis, dating to the fifth century (*CGP* 36), appears to refer to salt-fish stacked in a cargo hold like planks (τὸς ταρίχος ἐς οἶκον | συνκόμισον καὶ σφήκ(ια) ἴσα). Artemon and Apollodoros, the merchants lambasted by the Demosthenic orator in *Against Lacritus*, picked up "eleven or twelve ceramic containers (ταρίχους κεράμια) of fish sauce" (*Ps.*-Dem. 35.34) as well as two bundles of goat hides.

The likening of the trade in salted fish and enslaved captives was powerful in structuring fifth- and fourth-century Athenian thought.[85] Fish were also one of the most frequently circulated images of the Black Sea. The two most important currencies of the Black Sea were the staters of Cyzicus and Pantikapaion. Both currencies changed their iconography with extreme frequency, and images of fish were among their most common legends.[86] At other times, these currencies borrowed from a Scythian imaginary. One issue from Cyzicus, for instance, improbably depicts a Scythian, kneeling next to a tuna, adjusting the flail and bow-case (*gorytos*) he wears around his waist.[87] The flail and *gorytos* were frequently reproduced symbols of manhood in Scythian art; in the imagination of Herodotus (4.2–3) and the comic playwrights, these became implements used to regulate and torment slaves[88] (Figure 5.4). But the casual linkage of the Black Sea, the fish trade, and the slave trade ran even deeper. As James Davidson notes, the sexual harassment or outright assault of enslaved Thracian women is one of the enduring tropes of Athenian comedy. With great frequency they were likened to salt-fish.[89]

Perhaps the greatest testament to the way the slave trade intermixed in the quotidian reality of trade between Greece and the Black Sea comes in the fragments of Aristophanes' lost *Cargo Ships*, which featured a chorus of anthropomorphized vessels. As in Hermippus' play, we have cargo manifests. One fragment consists of a list of grain (fr. 428 K-A),[90] one a list of fishes (fr. 430 K-A),[91] one a list of milling implements (fr. 431 K-A), one a mention of a city at the mouth of the river Phasis of modern-day Georgia (fr. 443 K-A), and one an apparent mention of the bakery slaves who could have been additional cargo as well (fr. 427 K-A).[92] If Athens' long-distance trade with the Black Sea was not expressly constructed to obtain enslaved captives, what it

FIGURE 5.4 Stater of Cyzicus depicting Scythian kneeling next to tuna. CNG Coin ID 147045. Image: Classical Numismatic Group. Used with permission.

produced was a stream over which they easily flowed. Evidence for this was pervasive.

Conclusion

High on a promontory above the right bank of the Dnieper, around 550 BCE, an act of hideous violence was about to unfold. Starting in the last quarter of the seventh century, elites up and down the rivers that emptied into the Black Sea had taken up a taste for a new commodity: wine, served in elaborately painted ceramics from Greece.[93] At the same time, Greek settlement of the region's estuaries attracted nomads from the northern Caucasus who soon developed similar tastes.[94] What would happen in Trakhtemirov was repeated across the border between the forest and the steppe in the sixth century: an attack of nomads on a settled community, a shower of Scythian arrowheads, and the survivors taken captive.[95] Marched down to the rivers, loaded onto canoes, and brought to the sea, these would be the first of countless victims enslaved here over the ages.[96]

This chapter has attempted to put together a balance sheet for Greece's, and particularly Athens', slave trade in the Black Sea in the fifth and fourth centuries BCE. In many ways, doing so represents the reverse of my objective in the previous chapter; this exercise effectively flattens the human topographies of suffering, longing, and endurance that are the prevalent interest in the contemporary study of slavery. As Jennifer Morgan writes, "the archival silences around the lived experiences of enslaved woman . . .

are themselves the technologies that rendered those women as outside history."[97] But a very different question faces us, in the absence of anything like the abundance of data in the *TASTD*. By attempting to construct the economic motivations behind Greece's stripping its hinterlands of people, are we further obfuscating the measured silences that pervade the subject of our last chapter, the letters from the Pontus? Simply put—if we could put a number on the masses of people stolen from the Black Sea to Greece, would it actually tell us anything?

My answer to this is yes; but arriving at these estimates will be the work of other scholars, and not myself.[98] There is room for telling stories big and small. For now, assembling the big picture helps to break through the inky darkness of the mines of Laureion; the means by which slavery shaped the economic rationality of writers who usually have little or nothing to say about it, for instance Isocrates in the *Panegyricus*, or Thucydides' Pericles. As we have become increasingly prone to wax poetically about Classical Athens' achievements in standard of living, it is worth keeping its calculus of death in mind.[99]

6
Inventing Whiteness

Introduction

Ἀκούετ', ὦ ἄνδρες Ἀθηναῖοι, τοῦ νόμου τῆς φιλανθρωπίας, ὃς οὐδὲ τοὺς δούλους ὑβρίζεσθαι ἀξιοῖ. τί οὖν πρὸς θεῶν; εἴ τις εἰς τοὺς βαρβάρους ἐνεγκὼν τὸν νόμον τοῦτον, παρ' ὧν τὰ ἀνδράποδ' εἰς τοὺς Ἕλληνας κομίζεται, ἐπαινῶν ὑμᾶς καὶ διεξιὼν περὶ τῆς πόλεως εἴποι πρὸς αὐτοὺς ὅτι 'εἰσὶν Ἕλληνές τινες ἄνθρωποι οὕτως ἥμεροι καὶ φιλάνθρωποι τοὺς τρόπους ὥστε πόλλ' ὑφ' ὑμῶν ἠδικημένοι, καὶ φύσει τῆς πρὸς ὑμᾶς ἔχθρας αὐτοῖς ὑπαρχούσης πατρικῆς, ὅμως οὐδ' ὅσων ἂν τιμὴν καταθέντες δούλους κτήσωνται, οὐδὲ τούτους ὑβρίζειν ἀξιοῦσιν, ἀλλὰ νόμον δημοσίᾳ τὸν ταῦτα κωλύσοντα τέθεινται τουτονὶ καὶ πολλοὺς ἤδη παραβάντας τὸν νόμον τοῦτον ἐζημιώκασιν θανάτῳ,' εἰ ταῦτ' ἀκούσειαν καὶ συνεῖεν οἱ βάρβαροι, οὐκ ἂν οἴεσθε δημοσίᾳ πάντας ὑμᾶς προξένους αὐτῶν ποιήσασθαι;

Athenians—listen to the *humanity* of the law, a law that protects even slaves from assault. By the gods, think what this means! Suppose someone described it to the barbarians who export slaves to Greece— suppose that praising you and going into detail about the city, he told them, "There are some Greeks so totally humane and mild that, even though they have so often been wronged by you—even though they have in their very nature an underlying, ancestral hatred toward you— nevertheless they think it inappropriate to do violence (ὑβρίζειν) even to any of the slaves acquired for a price. In fact they established a law in the assembly forbidding it, and they have punished many transgressing it with death." If the barbarians heard these words and understood them correctly, don't you think they would make you all *proxenoi* in *their* assembly? (Demosthenes [*Against Meidias*] 21.48–50, my translation)

In 350 BCE, Demosthenes of Paiania dragged a rival named Meidias to court on a charge of *hubris* for slapping him at a parade. This was a grave doing, Demosthenes told the jury—for in Athens, it is illegal even to assault a slave.[1] Now, for any enslaved person in Demosthenes' earshot, this would have been a surprise. Abuse was the great constant of enslaved life. But in staking out his position, Demosthenes tells a tale. The barbarians are just like us; they deliberate in their own assembly (δημοσίᾳ), and they decided to sell us their own citizens as slaves. If they *knew* they were being abused in Athens, they would have stopped!

Life among the "barbarians" and slavery: these were two topics familiar to Demosthenes. Born in 384 BCE, Demosthenes inherited a fortune at the age of seven. As he reports in the *Against Aphobos* of 366 BCE, his patrimony included a sword factory, a furniture factory, commodities used at both, maritime loans, and fifty-three enslaved artisans (Dem. 27.9–11). The acquisition of this fortune traces an entire history of mobility, enslavement, and Athenian trade with the Black Sea in the fifth and fourth centuries BCE. Demosthenes' father was a businessman who had married the daughter of a prosperous trader named Gylon. At the end of the Peloponnesian War, Gylon had been exiled and taken up residence somewhere on the Taman peninsula, where he appears to have married a local woman. Demosthenes quite possibly had "barbarian" ancestry through his maternal grandmother.[2]

This was no secret to his enemies. In the reckoning of his rival Aeschines (Aesch. 3.172), he was "Scythian by ancestry" (Σκύθιν δὲ τὸ γένος), and ineligible for citizenship.[3] Indeed, it was pretty common for rich Athenians to attract the same insinuation throughout the history of the democracy. The law of 451/50 BCE restricted Athenian citizenship to those with four Athenian grandparents. Because it was only sporadically enforced, many Athenians would be entrapped by the purges that followed its reimposition in 403 and the 380s BCE.[4] In a world of inconsistent recordkeeping, any personal feud could result in a tribunal over one's γένος, a word translatable as ancestry, origin, or race.[5] Informants were on the prowl for the scantiest evidence of foreign ancestry—maybe your grandfather had an accent (Dem. 57.18), *maybe* you were adopted (Dem. 21.149).[6] This environment incentivized a certain surveillance of the body.[7] As Xenophon would write, two of the wealthiest Athenians—and greatest slaveowners—in anyone's memory were Hipponikos and Nicias (*Poroi* 4.14). They were not beyond accusation. Hipponikos was "red-faced" (ἐρυθρὸν τῆι ὄψει) and "ruddy" (διὰ τὸ πυρρὸν), "Scythian" in the imaginations of the comic poets Cratinus[8] and Eupolis.[9] Aristophanes (*Ecc.* 427–29) mocked Nicias—who kept an astounding one thousand people enslaved in the mines—for his pale face (λευκός).[10] Yet no one went after these men.

What made it possible for rich Athenians to laugh it off when a mere *insinuation* of foreignness could be so ruinous to a regular citizen? The answer, according to Susan Lape (2010), is the racialized logic of Athenian citizenship. In theory, membership in the state was predicated on genetic lineage over wealth, reputation, or prowess. But in practice, citizenship operated on what Barbara and Karen Fields have called (in a modern context) a "social, civic, or legal double standard based on ancestry"[11] by which the law treated the same acts differently depending on the actor. Even full-blooded Athenian citizens lost their citizenship periodically; when they did it could be retrospectively explained by some deficiency of their blood.[12] If we think of race as what Adolph Reed Jr. calls a "just-so story"[13]—a narrative that serves a specific purpose, and nothing more—then the internal contradictions of the Athenian citizenship regime make sense. The *point* of racialized hierarchies are the glaring and inconsistent disparities they produce, disallowing for one person what is allowed for another. Regular Athenians were policed for what their elites got away with. Thus when the comic poets pointed out the obvious signs of "barbarian" ancestry on the faces of the rich, it was a way of capitalizing on the anti-elite resentment that so energized Athenian democracy.

Which brings us back to Demosthenes' case against Meidias. In his appeal to the jurors, Demosthenes situates Athens at the center of a geography of enslavement that emanated outward from the Agora to the edges of the world. Through the cooperation of Greeks and barbarians, Athenians had access to the racialized commodities they encountered each day in the Agora—people visibly recognizable by their pale skin,[14] ruddy complexion,[15] tattoos,[16] short[17] or straight hair,[18] and shabby dress.[19] As the lexicographer Julius Pollux would so vividly describe an Old Comedy slave mask (4.149), "red hair, spread out above the brow, furrowed eyebrows . . . he is red-haired and his hairline is receding, which magnifies his brows"[20] (Figure 6.1). But these images were not simple representations of reality; they were objects of ideology, meant to solidify the positions of the elite men who circulated them, to emphasize the difference of outsiders, and to always keep in question the γένος of the red-haired citizen, or man whose complexion seemed a little pale.

This chapter explores the specific institutional contexts in which Classical Athenians produced, circulated, and propagated a distinctly Athenian understanding of race. I begin in the first section by examining the institutional structures that produced, in the words of Fields and Fields, "social,

FIGURE 6.1 Ceramic comic mask representing an enslaved Thracian, Hellenistic Period (Fitzwilliam Museum, Cambridge Gr.67.1984). Note red hair, white skin, and flat nose. Fitzwilliam Museum, Cambridge Gr.67.1984. Photograph © The Fitzwilliam Museum, Cambridge.

civic, or legal double standard based on ancestry." Touring the public spaces of Classical Athens from the perspective of an enslaved person, I argue that the Athenian state leveraged shocking public spectacles—slave auctions and evidentiary torture—as a way of reifying the often-fuzzy boundary between free and enslaved persons. In so doing, Athenians presented the difference between freedom and slavery as natural—meting out differential treatment for the same acts to people on the basis of ancestry.

The following section examines attempts made by fourth-century Athenian writers to produce somatic criteria by which an enslaved person might be identified. Theorists settled on two terms—"paleness" (ἡ λευκότης) or "ruddiness" (τὸ πυρρόν)—as lexica for enslaved Thracian or Scythian bodies. At this point, we should be clear that the biodeterminism of Classical Athens was never unanimously agreed; ancient Greece produced no concept equivalent to Atlantic world Blackness. Indeed, both terms had a range of other uses, ethnographic, gendered, medical, and otherwise. Nonetheless, we might be willing to see the Athenian effort to define a servile "whiteness" as a kind of stumbling toward race.

Finally, I return to the world of the Black Sea, where Demosthenes' maternal grandfather made his fortune. I argue that Athenian definitions of "whiteness" took their origin among the Greek settlers of the Pontic Steppe. I argue that there is little reason to believe—as Demosthenes vouched—that the "barbarians" were self-consciously selecting a class of their members to sell to Athens. Rather, the Greeks of the Black Sea imposed their own fictive categories of somatic and cultural difference upon the steppe peoples as a form of marketing. The stereotypes that figured Thracians as pale-skinned, red-haired slaves and Scythians their enslavers instead emerged out of the Greek hunger for human bodies. As a member of the broader Pontic community, Demosthenes understood the dynamic well.

The racialization of Thracians and Scythians into human commodities served to mystify the workings of a commodity chain that dealt very different benefits to the parties involved. For Demosthenes' jurymen, it was the comfort in living in the imperial city; knowledge that to be Athenian was to consume the world. This was psychological. Despite the real question of his patrimony, Demosthenes was the person actually given license to consume the world's wealth. And for the people involved—those unfortunate Thracians—there were no benefits to speak of. We are only left with the grotesque image of their faces, pale-skinned, red-haired, and different as they were. Which is to say, in a phrase, racialized commodities.

Differential Treatment

Of Kephisodoros, a metic living in Peiraieus:

Tax	Sale price	Item
2 dr.	165 dr.	Thracian woman
1 dr. 3 ob.	135 dr.	Thracian woman
2 dr.	170 dr.	Thracian man
2 dr. 3 ob.	240 dr.	Syrian man
1 dr. 3 ob.	105 dr.	Carian man
2 dr.	161 dr.	Illyrian man
2 dr. 3 ob.	220 dr.	Thracian woman
1 dr. 3 ob.	115 dr.	Thracian man

Tax	Sale price	Item
1 dr. 3 ob.	144 dr.	Scythian man
1 dr. 3 ob.	121 dr.	Illyrian man
2 dr.	153 dr.	Colchian man
2 dr.	174 dr.	Carian child
1 dr.	72 dr.	Little Carian child
3 dr. 1 ob.	301 dr.	Syrian man
2 dr.	151 dr.	Melitenean man *or* woman
1 dr.	(≥) 85 dr. 1 ob.	Lydian woman[a]

[a] *IG* I³ 421 col. i frg. b 33–49, trans. after Osborne and Rhodes 2017: 431–33.

Our story begins nearly four decades before Demosthenes' birth. Athens was in crisis in September 414 BCE when a group of officials known as the Poletai erected eleven stelae in the southeast corner of the Agora.[21] Standing outside the temple of the Eleusinian deities Demeter, Kore, and Iakkhos, each stele listed property confiscated from fifteen men who had been condemned the previous year (Figure 6.2, A). These were the Hermokopidiai. Days before the departure of the Athenian fleet to Sicily, a group of aristocrats and rich metics had been accused and convicted of religious impropriety that included smashing the herms and mocking the Eleusinian Mysteries. Some Athenians took this as a signal flare for a coup (Thuc. 6.27–28). In all, twenty-three men would be executed or forced into exile, their property carefully recorded—with appropriate tax—and auctioned off. These events darkly forbode Athens' staggering losses in Sicily and the successful aristocratic coup of 411 BCE.[22]

If the targets of the purges of 415–14 BCE were primarily wealthy, consequences fell hard on the men and women enslaved by the accused. Athenian legal procedure appears to have required enslaved witnesses be tortured before producing testimony. Both prosecution and defense leaned heavily on the words of slaves.[23] Some enslaved witnesses escaped torture by dispensation of the assembly: the orator Andocides, who was one of the accused, angrily laments that a pair of slaves named Andomachos and Lydos received immunity (ἄδεια) for betraying their enslavers (1.12–13, 17–20).[24] But most others were not so lucky. Andocides murdered one of his slaves to prevent his testimony (Lys. 6.22). He offered over others to be tortured by the prosecution in full knowledge they knew nothing (And. 1.64).[25] And, of course, there was the traumatic end result of all of this: an auction of forty enslaved people. Sale disarticulated whatever social ties enslaved people had

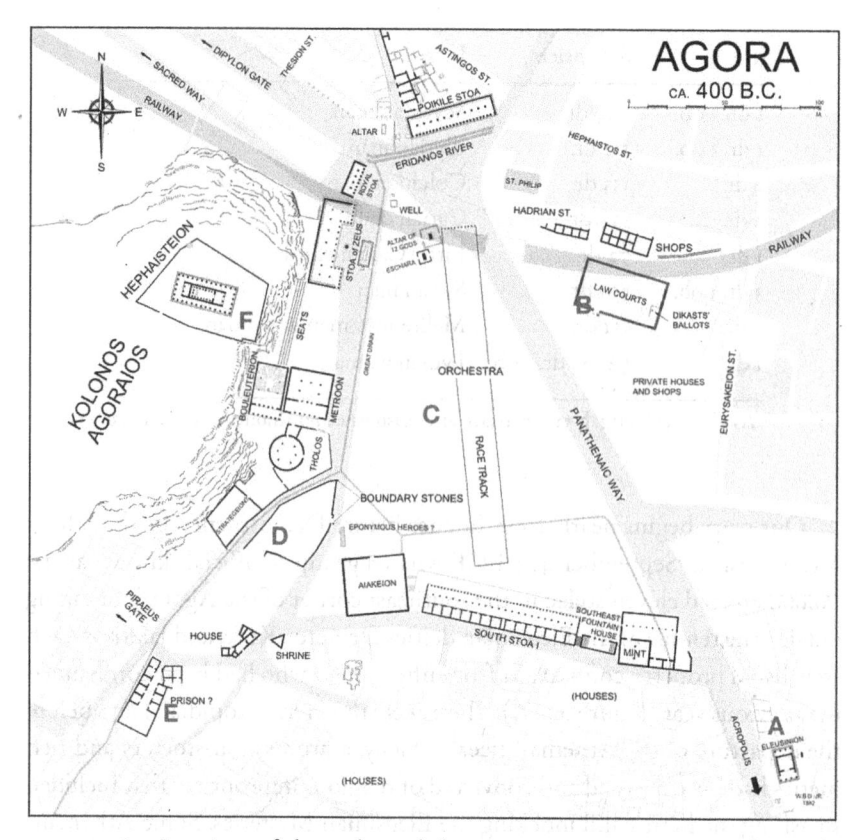

FIGURE 6.2 Locations of slave sales and slave torture in Attic oratory and comedy. **A:** Eleusinion; **B:** Helaia; **C:** Possible locations for *kykloi;* **D:** Poletereion; **E:** Prison; **F:** Hephaesteion. Map after ASCSA Agora image 2011.04.0038. Courtesy American School of Classical Studies at Athens: Agora Excavations.

managed to make with other members of the household, re-alienating them as commodities on the market.[26]

Andocides' indignant account of the persecutions of 415 BCE is a good place to begin our search for positive evidence that the institutions of the slave trade acted as sites of race-making in ancient Greece, enacting a "social, civic, or legal double standard based on ancestry."[27] In resolving the crisis of the Hermokopidai, the Athenians turned to two institutions to reconstitute their social structure, differentiating innocent from guilty and free from enslaved. The first was the slave market, a terrifying spectacle held regularly in the Agora. The second was rarer and more spectacular: evidentiary torture, the practice of tormenting an enslaved person in order to "cure" their testimony. Even if the guilty were all citizens, the Athenian state was dead-set in making sure the line between free and enslaved could not be crossed opportunistically in a time of unrest.

The juxtaposition of the law courts with slave markets was occasionally remarked by the orators. Take Demosthenes' prosecution of Stephanos, an accomplice of the wealthy freedmen Phormion and Pasion. Speaking from the Helaia (Figure 6.2, B), located in the northeastern corner of the Agora,[28] Demosthenes bellows:

Ἄξιον τοίνυν, ὦ ἄνδρες Ἀθηναῖοι, καὶ Φορμίωνι τῷ παρασχομένῳ τουτονὶ νεμεσῆσαι τοῖς πεπραγμένοις, τὴν ἀναίδειαν τοῦ τρόπου καὶ τὴν ἀχαριστίαν ἰδόντας. οἶμαι γὰρ ἅπαντας ὑμᾶς εἰδέναι, ὅτι τοῦτον, ἡνίκ' ὤνιος ἦν, εἰ συνέβη μάγειρον ἤ τινος ἄλλης τέχνης δημιουργὸν πρίασθαι, τὴν τοῦ δεσπότου τέχνην ἂν μαθὼν πόρρω τῶν νῦν παρόντων ἦν ἀγαθῶν.

It makes sense to resent Phormion for his accomplishments seeing his ingratitude and shamelessness . . . if, when he was up for sale, he'd been bought by a cook or some other workman, he'd have learned *that* trade instead of being a man of wealth. (Dem. 45.71)

This vivid portrayal of Phormion being sold as a slave was not hyperbole. There were actual slave auctions not even one hundred yards across the Agora.[29] Stirring up indignation among the free citizen jury, he continues: "Don't think, 'oh, but this one is some Syros or Manes [stereotypical slave names], but this one is Phormion'—the thing is the same! They are slaves, and he was a slave too; you are masters, and so was I."[30] Even after manumission, slavery was an indelible state; the barbarian lurked beneath the robes of every freedman. It is this permanent association of ancestry, legal status, the body, and a geography of power that makes it worth thinking whether—and if so, how—slaves were considered to be a *race*.

To be sure, the idea that every slave was a barbarian was common enough in Classical Greece. In his mid-fourth-century *Politics*, Aristotle gave it its canonical form: an enslaved worker was "a kind of a breathing piece of property" (κτῆμά τι ἔμψυχον, *Pol.* 1.1253b32).[31] The perfect slave was the barbarian, since in barbarian societies power is based on domination rather than cooperation; the relationship between master and slave was theoretically no different (*Pol.* 1.1252b). But real life is considerably messier. Even though barbarians are servile in general, anyone could be a slave by disposition; there is no way to identify a slave from appearance (*Pol.* 1.1254b33) or descent alone (*Pol.* 1.1255b1).[32] This means it is realistic that people free by nature (φύσει) could end up enslaved by chance (*Pol.* 1.1255a1). But generally speaking, the condition of enslavement lent *ipso facto* proof one deserved to be enslaved (*Pol.* 1.1255a1–2). Aristotle crowns his argument by quoting Euripides (*Pol.* 1.1252b8 = Eur. *IA* 1400), who writes, "it is appropriate for Greeks to rule over barbarians."[33] While not wholly endorsing this position, Aristotle appears satisfied in using the status of barbarian as a proxy for disposition.

We should be clear that Aristotle's theory was hardly the predominant ancient interpretation of slavery. It was contested by other Classical writers,[34] who emphasize the humanity of enslaved people.[35] But Aristotle's line of thought mapped onto a certain logic that we see in circulation whenever slaves or freedpeople found themselves into the public sphere. (A grim testament to this was the Athenian practice of marking the graves of enslaved people with epitaphs that omitted their name but included an ethnonym—sometimes with the addition of a word like χρηστός, meaning "useful").[36] In his attack on Phormion—one of the rare freedmen to become a citizen in Athens—Demosthenes puts this logic into words: he was a "Greek instead of a barbarian, a wealthy man rather than a slave" (45.73).[37] Demosthenes invites his (free) audience to follow Phormion's progress backward from an enfranchised citizen into a slave on the block.

Slave markets were regular events in the Athenian Agora. This might come as a surprise, given that they rarely had a specialized architecture; indeed, the program of the American archaeologists who have excavated the Agora since the 1930s has been to locate every single other Athenian institution in a specific locale.[38] References to slaves standing on temporary platforms (τράπεζα) suggest the difficulty of identifying a slave market as specific *place*; almost anywhere around the Agora would do.[39] Coffles of bound captives must have been a relatively common sight for Athenians doing public business.[40] (This notwithstanding the rareness of individuals specifically identified as slave traders in the record.)[41]

Yet for all their invisibility in the archaeological record, slave markets are relatively well-known as institutions. Enslaved people were risky commodities: capable of getting sick, escaping, or revolting, the purchase of a slave involved inspection, warranties, and ample documentation.[42] Greek cities tended to regulate them heavily.[43] Late sources report that auctions for slaves, livestock, and agricultural implements, known as *kykloi* ("circles"), took place in the Agora on the first of the month (Figure 6.2, C). (It must be no coincidence these were the same high-value commodities auctioned off in *IG* I^3 421–30.)[44] Contemporary references to slaves put up for sale tend to be comic.[45] "Five slaves and a yoked pair of oxen!" barks an auctioneer in the comic Alcaeus (fr. 14 K-A).⁴⁶ "I see myself, by the gods, stripped down in the *kykloi*, hurried about the circle and sold," imagines slave being punished in Menander (Fr. 150 K-A).⁴⁷ "What an ill-starred day it was then, when the auctioneer called 'this man's price?' for me!" (Aristoph. fr. 339 K-A).⁴⁸ The same trope appears in Demosthenes, who elsewhere had invoked a similar image of Phormion put up on the block. "A slave bought yesterday"⁴⁹ (19.209) is one epithet he uses for a not particularly intelligent person.⁵⁰

Thus if we were to look for two precise sites in the Agora where some sales might have taken place, two sites in the Agora stand out in particular. The first was at the office of the Poletai in the southwestern corner of the Agora (Figure 6.2, D), where they posted commodities to be auctioned off by the state outside on whited boards (Ar. *Ath. Pol.* 47.2).⁵¹ There is indirect evidence that slaves might have been auctioned on the "selling stone" (ὁ πρατήρ λίθος, Pollux 3.126) in front of their building.⁵² Another place is in front of the Eleusinion (Figure 6.2, A), where the slave lists of 414 BCE were monumentalized. This is entirely speculative, but if slaves belonging to those accused of profaning the Mysteries were auctioned there, it might show some realization on the part of the Athenians how frightful these spectacles really were.⁵³

A second institution of race-making was evidentiary torture (Table 6.1). Evidentiary torture (βάσανος) is a disputed topic among scholars of Athenian judicial procedure.⁵⁴ Despite the apparent informality with which it was inflicted—it could technically take place anywhere, and it appears to have especially been used to terrorize slaves with close access to their enslavers' affairs (particularly women)⁵⁵—it was usually preceded by several formal steps. Torturers had to ascertain the enslaved status of the victim, explicitly couched in claims of descent.⁵⁶ Slaveowners had clear incentives to prevent it from happening, or at least moderate it if it did, since torture was understood to be traumatic and damaging, and to produce dubious testimony.⁵⁷ One possible solution was to have the torture done in public, where witnesses could see that the process was conducted "fairly" (Dem. 53.25, 54.28). The oratorical corpus gives us three locations where public torture took place. The first, and probably most surprising, is in the Helaia itself (Figure 6.2, B); if Demosthenes' racist screed against Phormion seemed bad enough, both Aeschines (2.126) and a Pseudo-Demosthenic speaker (47.12) offer to have a slave tortured right in front of the jury in the middle of trial.⁵⁸ Publicly owned slaves were tortured by the Eleven—public officials responsible for executions—in their headquarters in the southeastern corner of the Agora (Dem. 53.23) (Figure 6.2, E).⁵⁹

Table 6.1 Torture of enslaved witnesses for evidence in Attic legal oratory

Offers by plaintiff or defendant to torture enslaved witness: 13	Aes. 2.126–28 (4th cent.); And. 1.22; And. 1.64 (5th cent.); Ant. 2.8; Ant. 6.23–24 (5th cent.); Dem. 29.11–12; Dem. 29.38; Dem. 30.27–30; *Ps.*-Dem. 46.21; Dem. 53.22–25; Dem. 54.27–30 (4th cent.); Lys. 7.34–38 (4th cent.); Isae. 8.10–14 (4th cent.)
Demands by plaintiff or defendant to torture enslaved witness: 14	Ant. 1.6–13; Ant. 5.30 (5th cent.); Dem. 29.13–14; Dem. 30.36–37; Dem. 37.27; Dem. 37.42; Dem. 45.61; Dem. 48.16–17, 18; *Ps.*-Dem. 49.57–58; *Ps.*-Dem. 59.21–25 (4th cent.); Lys. 1.18; Lys. 4.10–17; Lys. 6.22 (4th cent.); Isoc. 17.15–16 (4th cent.); Lyc. 1.28–35 (4th cent.)
Total offers or demands: 28 (25 speeches)	
Offers or demands rejected: 15 (54%)	Aes. 2.126–28 (4th cent.); Ant. 1.6–13; Ant. 6.23–24 (5th cent.); Dem. 29.13–14; Dem. 30.27–30; Dem. 30.36–37; Dem. 37.27; *Ps.*-Dem. 46.21; *Ps.*-Dem. 49.57–58; Dem. 54.27–30; *Ps.*-Dem. 59.21–25 (4th cent.); Lys. 4.10–17; Lys. 7.34–38 (4th cent.); Isae. 8.10–14 (4th cent.); Lyc. 1.28–35 (4th cent.)
Slave torture performed: 6 (22%)	And. 1.22; And. 1.64 (5th cent.); Ant. 1.20; Ant. 5.30 (5th cent.); Dem. 37.42; Dem. 48.16–17, 18 (4th cent.)
Slave torture averted: 5 (18%)	Dem. 45.61; Dem. 53.22–25 (4th cent.); Lys. 1.18; Lys. 6.22 (5th cent.); Isoc. 17.15–16 (4th cent.)

But the most surprising location for public torture was on temple grounds. We know this from an account of evidentiary torture—or rather, an instance of evidentiary torture averted by a hair—that turns darkly comedic. In Isocrates' *Trapezeticus*, an unnamed speaker attempts to prosecute Pasion for fraud and seeks testimony from a slave. At first, Pasion attempts to claim the slave in question (named Kittos) was a freedman and ineligible for torture (17.14). After this is proven false, plaintiff and defendant agree to hire torturers and have the man publicly put on the rack next to the Hephaisteion (Figure 6.2, F) (Ἑλόμενοι δὲ βασανιστὰς ἀπηντήσαμεν εἰς τὸ Ἡφαιστεῖον).[60]

The two parties continued to squabble as the torturers tied Kittos to the rack (17.15). Ultimately the torturers decide to back out because the unnamed speaker and Pasion could not agree on terms (17.16).[61]

Kittos made a miraculous escape. But his case raises a troubling picture: even if far from an everyday event, evidentiary torture must have been familiar enough as a spectacle in the Athenian Agora. In fact, what Kittos' escape alerts us to is a whole geography of the Agora that was entirely different from what either free citizen experienced. Entering the marketplace from the northwest (walking toward the Acropolis on the Panathenaic way), an enslaved observer might have seen the Hephaisteion peeking up above the landscaping on the right, which made the site where Kittos escaped torture weirdly Edenic (Figure 6.2, F).[62] On her left were the law courts (Figure 6.2, B), where torture was also conducted. If she were walking on the first of the month, she might have seen different *kykloi* in the open spaces on both sides (Figure 6.2, C), replete with goats, sheep, and slaves, all bound. If not, she might have wandered past the Poletai's whited boards (Figure 6.2, D) and screams from the prison of the Eleven farther south (Figure 6.2, E). And on her way out, following the road to the southeast, she would have walked by a ghoulish monument on her left. These were the Hermokopidai stelae (Figure 6.2, A). Here at the Eleusinion, carved perfect *stoichedon*, were listed dozens of slaves, with price and sales tax, by gender, profession, occasionally name, and almost always γένος or ἔθνος.

Γένος, ἔθνος, and their Latin equivalent, *natio*, possessed variable meanings in ancient slave transactions. The Hermokopidai auction inscriptions include γένος more than any other detail.[63] Antiquity's canonical formulation of the role of γένος/ἔθνος/*natio* in slave sales comes late, at the hand of the third-century CE Roman jurist Ulpian, who mandated that slave-dealers disclose the *natio* of a slave being sold: "the slave's race may often induce or deter a purchaser; therefore, we have an interest in knowing the race" (*Dig.* 21.1.31.21).[64] Knowing the *natio* of a slave served as a kind of guarantee for behavior, skills, vulnerability for disease, or aptitude to run away. Ulpian's prescription is kind of a codification of centuries of slave-market procedure. Both Greek and Roman source complain that slave-dealers routinely renamed slaves to conceal their origins.[65] But despite the importance accorded to γένος or *natio*, ancient sources are actually rather disorganized in listing the stereotypes associated it. Unlike in later periods—for instance, in the medieval Arab world or the eighteenth-century Caribbean—antiquity produced no manuals to assist prospective enslavers in selecting certain races.[66] Rather, these judgments are dispersed freely through the literary record:[67] Thracians were proverbially stupid (Hdt. 4.46.2) and sold their children cheaply (Hdt. 5.6.1), and were the slaves of the Scythians, who made them wear embarrassing haircuts (Clearchus ap. Ath. 12.524c1-f4). Particularly worthless slaves came from Thessaly (Hermippus fr. 63.19 K-A) or Macedonia (Dem. 9.31). Thracian women were sexually available (Archippos fr. 27 K-A); light-skinned slaves were cowardly (Ps.-Aristot. Oec. 1.5.5.1344b12-14). Even if names only indicated a particular γένος unreliably, certain ones—Lydos, Geta, "Syros or Manes" (Dem. 45.86)—practically indicated enslaved status.[68] Most importantly, slaveowners should not enslave multiple individuals from the same ἔθνη.[69]

What we might take from this exercise is this. Two institutions of Athenian race-making—slave auctions and evidentiary torture—had distinct geographies visible in the Agora, the cradle of the Athenian state. On the streets of Athens, slaves and free were easily confused; many citizens had blood relatives who were enslaved (think of the slaves listed as "home-born" in the Hermokopidai stelae),[70] and more than a few metics like Phormion—and even citizens—had enslaved backgrounds.[71] But in the political space of the Athenian Agora, free and enslaved were separated out again, with signs of their condition made visible on their bodies. Demosthenes' plea to the jurors to imagine Phormion on the auction block and Menander's mockery of a naked slave in the *kykloi* helped to produce the illusion that underlies Aristotle's doctrine of natural slavery. Their pristine visions of free and enslaved were sporadically made vivid by the spasms of violence that slave auctions or evidentiary torture enacted. Ancient Athenians commanded a ruthless machine for enacting difference, and its daily operation shaped slave life in innumerable ways. If race is to be constituted as a "social, civic, or legal double standard based on ancestry," enslaved people in ancient Athens clearly met this standard.

Reading the Skin

> *A logical consequence of the slave-outsider equation is racism, a term I insist on despite the absence of the skin-color stigma; despite the variety of peoples who made up the ancient slave populations; despite the frequency of manumission and its peculiar consequences. The issue is not a concept of "race" acceptable to modern biologists or of a properly defined and consistently held concept, but of the view commonly taken in ordinary discourse, then as now. There were Greek slaves in Greece, Italian*

slaves in Rome, but they were unfortunate accidents; ideological expressions were invariably formulated around "barbarians," outsiders who made up the majority in reality.[72]

In his 1980 *Ancient Slavery, Modern Ideology*, Moses Finley argues that ancient slavery was a fundamentally racialized institution. No—ancient slavery was not the slavery of the Atlantic world, with its guiding narratives of white supremacy over Black labor. But if we part from a narrowly biodeterministic conception of race (an understanding still very widespread in the late 1970s), we can see the principle at work. Race operated through differential treatment of different people for the same offense—imagined differences of ancestry or the body made tangible by the law. With one or two exceptions,[73] Finley was nearly alone among twentieth-century ancient historians in seeing ancient slavery as a racialized institution. In fact, the objection that ancient slavery *could not have been* racialized was popularized at the exact moment of the Civil Rights Movement.[74] Post-Finley surveys of ancient slavery are typically prefaced with some kind of denial that race or racism can be used as a lens for interpretation.[75]

But if we were to adopt Finley's standard, we would find no shortage of evidence for racism in the working of the slave system. Classical Athens used hideous spectacles like slave auctions or evidentiary torture to mete out the line between slave and free. But these were distinct moments. Once they ended, things eased their way back to the normal equilibrium of carve-outs, exceptions, and rule-bending that made enslaved life endurable, and allowed some to pass as free. As the Old Oligarch wrote—perhaps in a moment of bitter exaggeration,[76] but an interesting comment nonetheless—the borderline between people enslaved and free was difficult to make out in everyday life:

ἐσθῆτά τε γὰρ οὐδὲν βελτίων ὁ δῆμος αὐτόθι ἢ οἱ δοῦλοι καὶ οἱ μέτοικοι καὶ τὰ εἴδη οὐδὲν βελτίους εἰσίν. [. . .] εἰ νόμος ἦν τὸν δοῦλον ὑπὸ τοῦ ἐλευθέρου τύπτεσθαι ἢ τὸν μέτοικον ἢ τὸν ἀπελεύθερον, πολλάκις ἂν οἰηθεὶς εἶναι τὸν Ἀθηναῖον δοῦλον ἐπάταξεν ἄν.

[Athenians] are no better dressed than slaves and metics, nor are they any more handsome . . . if it were customary for a slave (or metic or freedman) to be struck by one who is free, you would often hit an Athenian citizen by mistake on the assumption that he was a slave. (Ps.-Xen. *Ath. Pol.* 1.10)

For this reason, a number of theorists in Classical Greece attempted to extend the physical stereotypes circulated around the Agora, the courts, or the theatre into a theory of race that might be applied generally. If we define race with the bias of teleology, this effort failed, as it produced nothing like the grand race theories of the late nineteenth century.[77] But if we approach this effort on its own terms, it offers an interesting outline how race-making worked in a premodern context. One of the intractable problems of slavery, Aristotle wrote in the *Politics* (1.1254b33), was that someone's biological aptitude to be enslaved was rarely visible. Less-discerning theorists of slavery would have disagreed.

We should begin by returning to the great enslavers so effectively mocked by the comic poets: the "red-faced" Hipponikos, "pale-faced" Nicias, "Scythian" Demosthenes. Roughly speaking, Archaic and Classical Greeks associated a pair of somatic terms with the peoples of the north. These were ἡ λευκότης and τὸ πυρρόν. The former can be translated as "whiteness," The latter, "redness," indicates either the propensity to flush, having red hair, or both. The former term had something of a prehistory in association with female beauty, a distinction not lost among the new meanings acquired with slavery.[78] Τὸ πυρρόν was a relative latecomer, appearing neither as adjective nor abstract noun before Xenophanes of Kolophon made his famous claim that the Thracians were "gray-eyed and ruddy" (fr. 13–14 Diehl). Together, they formed an ethnographic pair. In his canonical description of life on the steppe, Hippocrates (*AWP* 20) describes the Scythians as both "white" and "red": "The Scythians are a red race on account of the cold, and not on account of the heat of the sun; but the lightness of their skin is burned by the cold and becomes red."[79]

Πυρρ- and its cognates were far more commonly employed to describe the complexion of enslaved northerners than the feminine-gendered ἡ λευκότης.[80] The chorus of Aristophanes' *Frogs*, complaining about the bronze currency issued by Athens during the emergency of 405 BCE, makes a potent comparison:

Τῶν πολιτῶν θ' οὓς μὲν ἴσμεν εὐγενεῖς καὶ σώφρονας
ἄνδρας ὄντας καὶ δικαίους καὶ καλούς τε κἀγαθοὺς
[. . .]
τοῖς δὲ χαλκοῖς καὶ ξένοις καὶ πυρρίαις
καὶ πονηροῖς κἀκ πονηρῶν εἰς ἅπαντα χρώμεθα

Of the citizens, those we know to be well-born and wise men, just and beautiful and good . . . we despise them, and instead make use of bronze money and foreigners and red-headed [slaves] and worthless sons of worthless fathers for everything. (Aristophanes, *Frogs*, 728–29, 730–31)

Leaving aside Aristophanes' pointed use of εὐγένος here—something that surely must hearken back to Theognis' (190 West) complaints about wealth corrupting the γένος of a good family—we have the simple use of a color term to stand in for enslaved people.[81] In fact, the comic poets tend to use Pyrrhos and Pyrrhias (among other names) as shorthand to refer to enslaved characters.[82] Nearly every one of the male slave masks catalogued by the lexicographer Pollux (4.148–50) is identified as "red."[83] And these practices existed to some extent in real life: *IG* 1³ 1032, which lists slaves conscripted by the Athenian navy between 410–404 BCE, includes five individuals named Σιμίας or Σῖμος ("flat-nose," sometimes associated with African somatics but often slaves in general),[84] one named Γλαυκίας ("gray-eyes"), and one named Πύρρος ("ruddy").[85] But as Kostas Vlassopoulous has emphasized, the poets' uses of these names were more prescriptive than descriptive. Of the hundreds of enslaved persons identifiable in the record of fifth- and fourth-century Athens, the vast majority had names indistinguishable from regular citizens.[86] For the poets, and for a minority of slaveowners, rechristening a slave with a demeaning name translatable as "Red," "Redhead," or "Ruddy" was a way of producing a more convenient reality.

If fair skin and ruddiness were insufficient in making status visible, there were always other marks an enslaver could inflict on the body. When the comic poets imagined enslaved bodies, they saw a whole world of deformity: marks of torture, shabby clothes, bad haircuts, baldness, and tattoos.[87] These tended to overlap neatly with determinations of ἡ λευκότης and τὸ πυρρόν. We can see this in the fragments of Eupolis' *Golden Race*, a comedy first performed in 424 BCE, which runs an extended metaphor between Athens under the guidance of the demagogue Kleon with a barbarian kingdom ruled by slaves along the Black Sea.[88] In a description of the citizens of this *polis* at the beginning of the play, Eupolis presents a constellation of physical deformity, shabby dressing, and Thracian physiognomy:

{Α.} δωδέκατος ὁ τυφλός, τρίτος ὁ τὴν κάλην ἔχων,
ὁ στιγματίας τέταρτός ἐστιν ἐπὶ δέκα,
πέμπτος δ' ὁ πυρρός, ἕκτος ὁ διεστραμμένος·
χοῦτοι μέν εἰσ' ἑκκαίδεκ' εἰς Ἀρχέστρατον.
ἐς τὸν δὲ φαλακρὸν ἑπτακαίδεκ'. {Β.} ἴσχε δή.
{Α.} ὄγδοος ὁ τὸ τριβώνιον ἔχων.

A: The blind man is twelfth: the one with the hump is thirteenth; the tattooed guy is fourteenth, and the πυρρός [red-head or person prone to flush] is fifteenth; the cross-eyed fellow is sixteenth. These men in fact make up sixteen up to Archestratus, but seventeenth up to the bald guy.
B: Now hold on!
A: The guy wearing the rough cloak is eighteenth.
(Eupolis fr. 298 K-A, trans. Storey 2011)

And Eupolis was hardly alone. Life in "barbarian-land" (γῆ βάρβαρος) was a popular trope of drama in the 420–10s.[89] ("A land where a barbarian rules over barbarians," as Euripides describes the Crimea).[90] Of all these markers, tattoos attracted a particular scorn: they represented a permanent mark that could be applied to the body to mark social death.[91] Hence the glee with which the comic poets bandied them about. The Cloud Cuckoo Land of Aristophanes' *Birds* might have been fictional, but even here are Carians and Phrygians tattooed (760–65). A tattooed runaway is dragged off by a slave dealer in a confusing fragment of Eupolis' *Kolakes* (fr. 172 K-A).[92] Platon (fr. 202 K-A) accused the demagogue Hyperbolus (himself occasionally accused of being Phrygian) of being tattooed; in his fragmentary *Babylonians* Aristophanes apparently accused the entire citizenry of Samos for being tattooed as well after enfranchising formerly enslaved people (fr. 71b K-A).

Some hay has been made about the lack of a clearly visible biodeterminism in these tropes. Yes, so this thinking goes; the ancient Greeks held various negative opinions about the physical appearance of enslaved Thracians, but if you press upon these constructions *even slightly*, they give way into a morass of contradictions.[93] And, indeed, this is true. Dive at any depth into the Greek language of the body and you will swim in inconsistencies, overlaps, and tepid rationalizations. (For example, what motivated the Aristotelian writer of *Problems* 38.2.966b to claim that fishermen, who spend all day outside in the hot sun, have τὸ πυρρόν like the pale-skinned Scythians? What does Hippocrates mean when he says that people in the far west have εὔχροά, or "healthy complexion" [*AWP* 5], while people in the east are ἀχρόους, "pale?" [*AWP* 6].) But this is to downplay the "just-so" nature of race as narrative. Even at the *height* of race science in the early twentieth century, critics railed at its inconsistencies. It took nearly three decades for Franz Boas' (1858–1942) critique of racialism to take hold in the first half of the twentieth century; it arguably only did because race science became politically inconvenient and lost its use, and not because race science was intrinsically flawed.[94] And if we reflect on the origins of the white supremacist synthesis in the eighteenth century, we will find a surprising *lack of urgency* in scientifically theorizing race until the Transatlantic Slave Trade had passed its historical halfway point.[95]

So if we are going to think about Thracians and Scythians as racialized groups in Classical Greece, the better approach is to think in terms of what these images accomplished. And, as we have seen, they accomplished an awful lot. We can divide the usage of these tropes into two categories.

The first, broadest, and least marked might be what we could call the physiognomic tradition that began in Classical Athens. At its simplest, physiognomy was the association of permanent, inexorable moral characteristics with the human body. Physiognomy was one of antiquity's longest-lived and best-attested arts, beginning in earnest with the Hippocratic writers and carrying on through reception into the Middle Ages.[96] As Maude Gleason writes, "everyone who had to choose a son-in-law or a travelling companion, deposit valuables before a journey, or make a business loan became perforce an amateur physiognomist: he made risky inferences from human surfaces to human depths."[97] And if physiognomy sounds like the various racial pseudo-sciences we encounter in the eighteenth and nineteenth centuries, there is a reason: the racial theories of the Comte de Buffon (1707–88), Thomas Jefferson (1743–1826), Johann Friedrich Blumenbach (1752–1840), Friedrich Tiedemann (1781–1861), and Samuel George Morton (1799–1851) were all mined to different extents from ancient ethnographic and natural-historical writing.[98] But as a practice, physiognomy tended to be free-associative rather than strictly analytic. As the author of the pseudo-Aristotelian *Physiognomics* wrote (805a), there were three real ways to apply the science of physiognomy. You could (I) compare someone with an animal they looked or acted like; in this case, maybe you have τὸ πυρρόν because you are crazy like a fox. You could (II) use appearance to read inner emotions; cowards have dark skin. Or, maybe you are (III) light or dark-skinned because you are (at heart) a Thracian or an Ethiopian, which would bump us back to rubric II: Thracians are brave and Ethiopians cowardly.

So rather than making clear associations between human diversity and its causes, we should look at the corpus of physignomical writers as a place where tropes were collected and circulated.[99] Because physiognomy was such a well of commonplaces—particularly ones borrowed from comedy—they enabled anyone to dip their ladle in when searching for "evidence" to confirm a bias.[100] As such, physiognomy often did a good job of using somatic imagery to inscribe the social order on the body. Sometimes this imagery circulated in relatively unmarked ways. This is clearly the case when Socrates, in Plato's

Republic (5.474d7–e4), makes a point about visual contrast by juxtaposing the bodies of dark (μέλανας) or light-skinned (λευκοὺς) male lovers. But when the lexicographer Pollux uses the exact same imagery to describe the theatrical masks of Old Comedy, the imagery becomes a little more marked:

ὁ δ' ἁπαλὸς νεανίσκος, τρίχες μὲν κατὰ τὸν πάγχρηστον, πάντων δὲ νεώτατος, λευκός, σκιατροφίας, ἁπαλότητα ὑποδηλῶν. τῷ δ' ἀγροίκῳ τὸ μὲν χρῶμα μελαίνεται, τὰ δὲ χείλη πλατέα καὶ ἡ ῥὶς σιμή, καὶ στεφάνη τριχῶν.

The tender young man has hair good for all uses, and is the youngest of all; he is light-skinned as he was brought up in the shade, and he hints at tenderness. The peasant is dark in his color, his lips broad and his nose flat, and he has a wreath of hair. (Pollux 4.147)

The fact that physical appearance could tell a story about one's status, class, or race made physiognomy a marketable skill. The first individual credited with making physiognomy a profession was one Zopyros the Thracian, an anti-celebrity of the fifth century. Zopyros was an enslaved Thracian who at some point was allowed education by his owner, Pericles. According to Plato (1 *Alc.* 122b), Zopyros was then let loose to supervise the miseducation of Alcibiades. Setting him on fire might have been the subject of Strattis' *Burning of Zopyros* (frs. 9–10 K-A);[101] Plato's associate, Phaedo of Elis, apparently wrote an essay excoriating him.[102] Zopyros' infamy endured among readers of ancient philosophers. In two different places, Cicero (*Fat.* 10–11, *Tusc. Disp.* 4.80–81) stages fictive encounters between Zopyros and Socrates, both of which end with Socrates demonstrating that character is not predestined by the appearance of the body.[103] Cicero's negative description of Zopyros ("he was derided by the rest") is in accord with his derogatory portrayal in fifth-century sources and indicates that someone "who offered himself up to read people's characters by means of the body, eyes, face, and brow" was seen as a charlatan even then.[104]

Now, it is important to point out that Classical Greece's natural historians, like their physiognomist camp-followers, understood that there was no one cause of skin color. One's skin color could change for various reasons. Light skin color—often described with synonymous terms ὠχρότης or λευκότης (pale skin), or ἐρυθρός or πυρρός (ruddy skin)—could be an obvious sign of ill health, the "result of long sickness or heat," as Aristotle writes in the *Categories* (9b24).[105] On the other hand, the tradition of using skin color to read someone's inner emotional state was as old as Homer.[106] "That there are many changes of skin color because of emotion is clear," Aristotle wrote (*Cat.* 9b11–12), "when someone is embarrassed, he turns red (ἐρυθρός), and when someone is afraid, he turns pale (ὠχρός), etc."[107]

But in the vernacular traditions well represented in the pseudo-Aristotelian corpus, we get a better sense of how this understanding was typically applied. Take one example that appears in the pseudo-Aristotelian *Physiognomica*, a text that circulated early in the Hellenistic Period.[108] The author of this text (which, in fairness, actually consists of *two* treatises joined together) expands his reading of skin color as sign of inner emotional state to draw linkages with a range of signifiers that include gender, animality, and race. These are supposed to be predictive of behavior:

Οἱ ἄγαν μέλανες δειλοί· ἀναφέρεται ἐπὶ τοὺς Αἰγυπτίους, Αἰθίοπας. οἱ δὲ λευκοὶ ἄγαν δειλοί· ἀναφέρεται ἐπὶ τὰς γυναῖκας. τὸ δὲ πρὸς ἀνδρείαν συντελοῦν χρῶμα μέσον δεῖ τούτων εἶναι. οἱ ξανθοὶ εὔψυχοι· ἀναφέρεται ἐπὶ τοὺς λέοντας. οἱ πυρροὶ ἄγαν πανοῦργοι· ἀναφέρεται ἐπὶ τὰς ἀλώπεκας.

Excessively dark-skinned people are cowards; e.g. Egyptians and Ethiopians. Excessively light-skinned people are cowards; e.g. women. But the skin color right in the middle of these makes people brave. Light-haired people are strong of heart, e.g. lions. Excessively red-haired people are criminals; e.g. foxes. (*Ps.*-Aristot. *Phys.* 812a13–14)

There is nothing consistent here; what the author is doing is rather arbitrarily drawing on images that populated an imaginary. But the language clearly operated in some reference to slavery. We know this because another Aristotelian writer uses this exact same lexicon, and even the exact same phrasing (particularly the repetition of οἱ ἄγαν) to advise a potential slaveowner what sort of people he should enslave:

Γένη δὲ ἂν εἴη πρὸς τὰ ἔργα βέλτιστα <τὰ> μήτε δειλὰ μήτε ἀνδρεῖα ἄγαν. Ἀμφότερα γὰρ ἀδικοῦσι. Καὶ γὰρ οἱ ἄγαν δειλοὶ οὐχ ὑπομένουσι καὶ οἱ θυμοειδεῖς οὐκ εὔαρχοι.

The races best-disposed to work are neither excessively cowardly nor brave; both extremes do evil, since the cowardly do not abide slavery well, while the high-spirited are hard to govern. (*Ps.*-Aristot. *Oec.* 1.5.5.1344b12–14)

It is worth repeating that any search of the Aristotelian corpus for the language of the body will find numerous instances of this; it will also find many things that do not fit so cleanly. Aside from learning that fishermen have τὸ πυρρόν, we also hear from the author of the pseudo-Aristotelian *Problems* that old people are darker-skinned (μελάντεροι) than young people (38.10.967b), athletes are pale-skinned (ἄχροοι) but moderate exercise gives you good complexation (εὔχροοι) (38.5.967a), and that skin color is actually a product of fluid retention (38.3.966b–67a).

But then there are more tantalizing hints. "Concerning work in the mills—why do those who work with barley become pale-skinned?"[109] (Ps.-Aristot. 38.10.967b). The Aristotelean writer's answer is that barley is unhealthy to work with. This is obviously true: ancient authors from Lysias (1.18) to Apuleius (*Met.* 9.12) to the Antipater of Thessalonica (*AP* 9.418) treat millwork as uniquely degrading and unhealthy, and bioanthropology has provided ample evidence to illustrate why.[110] From almost the moment slaves were given ethnonyms in Greek literature—recall Hipponax's comment about enslaved Phrygians in Miletus (fr. 27 W)—they are associated with millwork.[111] As the enslaved speaker of a comedy by Menander (*Asp.* 243–45) says:[112] "We Thracians, though, we're men, unique—the Getic tribe, by Apollo—yes, real men. That's why we fill the grain-mills."[113] Slavery returns to the picture.

This brings us to our second group of Classical thinkers who theorized whiteness. These were the writers working in what might squarely be called the ethnographic tradition, most importantly the Hippocratic writer of *Airs, Waters, Places*, and Herodotus. Both authors resided in a cultural milieu that sought to lay out biological explanations for social difference.[114] Like the physiognomic writers, ethnographic writers reflect a clear understanding that skin color had no one solitary cause. And like the physiognomic writers, our fifth-century ethnographers were prone to disagreement or contradiction. But on the other hand, Hippocrates and Herodotus share an occasionally exhibited interest in the slave trade. In fact, as Timothy Taylor, Thomas Harrison, and I have separately argued, the use of slavery as an explanatory device reappears through their narratives.[115] Their explanations for ἡ λευκότης and τὸ πυρρόν are shaped likewise.

If you were to ask most people in late fifth-century Athens why Scythians or Thracians had such light skin, you would receive some shade of the following answer. Scythians, as Hippocrates had said (*AWP* 20), lived far from the sun; therefore, they are pale and ruddy. This was a simple explanation, and had ample precedent. Homer often describes skin color as the result of sun exposure, a detail that comes out when warriors strip the corpses of their victims.[116] And this explanation remained viable long into the era of the physiognomical texts. (In the simple formulation of the author of the *Problems* [38.8.667b]: "the sun makes people dark-skinned" [τοὺς δ' ἀνθρώπους ὁ μὲν ἥλιος μελαίνει].)

Yet in the fifth century, we see that it receives a fair amount of pushback. Herodotus' approach to Scythian skin color was largely culturalist: yes, Scythians looked *different* from Greeks, but this was because of things they did, and not because of the natural environment. Such a position is in accord with the stance he takes elsewhere.[117] Indeed, skin color does not even appear to have mattered very much to Herodotus' evaluation of the people of the north. At one point, Herodotus appears to accredit Scythian "whiteness" to women's beauty rituals:

Αἱ δὲ γυναῖκες αὐτῶν ὕδωρ παραχέουσαι κατασώχουσι περὶ λίθον τρηχὺν τῆς κυπαρίσσου καὶ κέδρου καὶ λιβάνου ξύλου, καὶ ἔπειτα τὸ κατασωχόμενον τοῦτο παχὺ ἐὸν καταπλάσσονται πᾶν τὸ σῶμα καὶ τὸ πρόσωπον . . . ἅμα δὲ ἀπαιρέουσαι τῇ δευτέρῃ ἡμέρῃ τὴν καταπλαστὺν γίνονται καθαραὶ καὶ λαμπραί.

Their women pound cypress and cedar and frankincense wood on a rough stone, adding water also, and with the thick stuff thus pounded they anoint their bodies and faces . . . when on the second day they take off the ointment, their skin becomes clear and bright (καθαραὶ καὶ λαμπραί). (Hdt. 4.75.3)

Indeed: Herodotus' Scythians were obsessed with marking social status with body modification. They blind their slaves (4.2), drink the blood of their victims, and turn their skulls into drinking cups (4.65; Figure 6.3), and sacrifice enslaved retainers to their dead kings (4.71–72). Some of them make coats out of human skin. The best part are the hands: they "take off the skin, nails and all, from their dead enemies' right hands and make covering for their quivers; human skin, as it turns out, is thick and shining, one might say the brightest in whiteness (λαμπρότατον λευκότητι)" (Hdt. 4.64.3–4).[118] If Scythian women prided themselves on their own whiteness, Scythian men ghoulishly pinned strips of their enemies' whitened skin to their *gorytoi*—the combination bow-case and quiver carried by every Scythian man—to mark their personal triumph over outsiders. To Herodotus, "whiteness" is the result of a social process that can only be explained by looking seriously at Scythian society.

FIGURE 6.3 Illustration of gold applique for hat depicting two Scythians with scalped human head from Kurdzhips Kurgan, Adygea Republic, Russia. Fourth century BCE. After Minns 1913: 233, fig. 126. Public domain.

Absent from either Herodotus or the Hippocratic writer's interpretation of the Scythian body was any understanding that skin color was transmissible via heredity. (Heredity did, in fact, exist in the awareness of the Classical Period, but it was a dim light.)[119] But one thing they share is an occasional interest in using slavery to explain human diversity. This is particularly the case for the Hippocratic writer. For instance: a common trope of Classical ethnography was that Thrace was overpopulated,[120] while Scythians could barely reproduce themselves.[121] In the telling of *Airs, Waters, Places*, Scythians tended toward infertility (πολύγονον δὲ οὐχ οἷόν τε εἶναι) because horse-riding gave men shortened torsos; boys and women were overweight from sitting in the wagons and never doing work (*AWP* 21). How does the Hippocratic writer draw a proof? Look at the very different fertility patterns of women *enslaved* by the Scythians. They get pregnant if a man even touches them (*AWP* 21).[122] In this, we see fingerprints of one of Old Comedy's most troubling commonplaces: the sexual availability of enslaved women from the north.

And who might these women be? Building on Herodotus and the Hippocratic writer, one of Aristotle's students developed an explicit racial geography of the north—a geography that largely explained *how* and *where* these Old Comedy tropes came to be. In a passage summarized by Athenaeus, the ethnographer Clearchus nearly explained how many of Thrace's cultural practices—tattooing, cropped hair—came about as a direct result of Scythian slave raiding.

> τρυφήσαντες δὲ καὶ μάλιστα δὴ καὶ πρῶτοι πάντων τῶν ἀνθρώπων ἐπὶ τὸ τρυφᾶν ὁρμήσαντες εἰς τοῦτο προῆλθον ὕβρεως ὥστε πάντων τῶν ἀνθρώπων εἰς οὓς ἀφίκοιντο ἠκρωτηρίαζον τὰς ῥῖνας· [ἀφ'] ὧν οἱ ἀπόγονοι μεταστάντες ἔτι καὶ νῦν ἀπὸ τοῦ πάθους ἔχουσι τὴν ἐπωνυμίαν. αἱ δὲ γυναῖκες αὐτῶν τὰς Θρᾳκῶν τῶν πρὸς ἑσπέραν καὶ ἄρκτον [τῶν] περιοίκων γυναῖκας ἐποίκιλλον τὰ σώματα, περόναις γραφὴν ἐνεῖσαι. ὅθεν πολλοῖς ἔτεσιν ὕστερον αἱ ὑβρισθεῖσαι τῶν Θρᾳκῶν γυναῖκες ἰδίως ἐξηλείψαντο τὴν συμφορὰν προσκαταγραψάμεναι τὰ λοιπὰ τοῦ χρωτός, ἵν' ὁ τῆς ὕβρεως καὶ τῆς αἰσχύνης ἐπ' αὐταῖς χαρακτὴρ εἰς ποικιλίαν καταριθμηθεὶς κόσμου προσηγορίᾳ τοὔνειδος ἐξαλείψῃ. πάντων δὲ οὕτως ὑπερηφάνως προέστησαν ὥστε οὐδένων ἄδακρυς ἡ τῆς δουλείας ὑπουργία γιγνομένη διήγγειλεν εἰς τοὺς ἐπιγινομένους τὴν ἀπὸ Σκυθῶν ῥῆσιν οἵα τις ἦν. διὰ τὸ πλῆθος οὖν τῶν κατασχουσῶν αὐτοὺς συμφορῶν, ἐπεὶ διὰ τὸ πένθος ἅμα τόν τε τῶν βίων ὄλβον καὶ τὰς κόμας περιεσπάσθησαν, παντὸς ἔθνους οἱ ἔξω τὴν ἐφ' ὕβρει κουρὰν ἀπεσκυθίσθαι προσηγόρευσαν.

[The Scythians] lived so outrageously that they outstripped all mankind in their rush towards degeneracy; they came to such a point of *hubris* that they cut off the noses of anyone they came across. [. . .] Their wives used to tattoo the bodies of Thracian women who lived in the northwest [region of Thrace bordering Scythia], pin-pricking their skin with the points of their fibulae. This is why, years later, the wives of the Thracians who had been tattooed covered up the marks of their shame by tattooing the rest of their skin, so that their original tattoos, when incorporated [into the design of another tattoo], might be passed off as ornament. [The Scythians] lorded over all other peoples so arrogantly that the burden of slavery—something grievous by its very nature—has subsequently been called "a Scythian command." On account of the number of disasters that befell [the Thracians]— they were stripped of both their happiness and even their hair because of their misfortune—people of every other tribe called having one's hair cut for the purpose of shame "ἀπεσκυθίσθαι." (Clearchus ap. Athenaeus 12.524c1–f4)

More explicitly than either Herodotus or the Hippocratic writer, Clearchus uses "the business of slavery" (ἡ τῆς δουλείας ὑπουργία) as a lens for examining the lives of Thracians and Scythians in their homelands. By making Thracians proud of their humiliation at the hands of the Scythians, Clearchus naturalizes their subordination to outsiders. He also adds an additional comment absent from Herodotus: the Scythians cut the Thracians' hair to add to the embarrassment, which Clearchus explains in his gloss for the rare Greek word ἀποσκυθίζομαι. Through their practices of caring for the body, the Thracians present themselves as natural slaves of both the Greeks to the south and the Scythians to their east.

Taken together, we might see the ethnographic tradition of explaining Thracian and Scythian bodies as a predecessor to the physiognomic tradition that flowered in fourth-century Athens. Realistically, they coexisted, overlapped, and emphasized each other's contradictions. What remained constant was the overarching linkage between the peoples of the north, human diversity, and the condition of being enslaved. That Hipponikos was "red-faced," or Nicias was "pale," or Demosthenes was "Scythian" did *not* mean they were suddenly vulnerable to being enslaved. That was plainly not true. But for their enemies, rivals, or simply envious fellow citizens, their visible *slavishness* stood right out. And this is what made the linkage between enslavement with ἡ λευκότης and τὸ πυρρόν so potent. The construction of the anatomical Thracian or Scythian was a distinct form of race-making in Classical Greece. When processed through formal *institutions* of race-making—public auction, evidentiary torture, or otherwise—these signifiers became something identifiable as race.

Imagining the Steppe

A century before Demosthenes' birth, and hundreds of miles north, the sun had set on another man (Figure 6.4).

A: [Μνῆμ' ἀρετῆς ἐστ]ηκα, λέγω δ' ὅτι τῆλε πόλε[ως πρὸ]
[οὐλόμενος κεῖτ]αι Λέωξος ὁ Μολπαγόρε[ω]
B: [Λεώξο μνῆμ]ά εἰμ[ι | τõ Μολπαγόρ]εω

A: I stand as a memorial of excellence, I say that Leoxos, son of Molpagores, was slain far from the city. B: I am the monument of Leoxos, son of Molpagores. (*SEG* 41.616)[123]

Around 480 BCE, a young man named Leoxos, son of Molpagores, set out into the steppe from Olbia never to return. Explanations differ as to

FIGURE 6.4 Proposed reconstruction of Leoxos stele from Olbia, c. 480 BCE. Formerly Kherson Regional Museum, Ukraine. In October 2022, internet reports claimed that the contents of the Kherson Regional Museum had been expropriated by the Russian army and relocated to the National Reserve of Tauric Chersonesos, Sevastopol, Crimea. A photograph published in *The New York Times* on November 22, 2022, shows the empty display stand that formerly held Leoxos. Drawing by M. M. Kobylina; after Koshelenko, Kurglikova, and Dologorukov 1984: 289, tb. 99.

why. According to the great Soviet historian Y. G. Vinogradov, Leoxos died fighting for his city's independence: chafing at the "Protektorat" established over their city by Scythian nomads, the Olbians dispatched a failed expedition to shake them off. Unable to offer a proper burial, Leoxos' family erected a cenotaph, depicting the Scythian who killed him on the other side.[124] In the reading of Jochen and Kirsten Fornasier, the Leoxos stele was a product of the "Schnittpunkt der Kulturen" between Scythians and Greeks; the monument portrays the same individual dressed in different costumes, a member of a bicultural class and skilled intermediary between the Mediterranean and the steppe.[125]

Though separated by over a century, the performance of twoness on the Leoxos stele resonates in a strange way with Demosthenes' appeal to an Athenian jury in 350 BCE (21.48–51), when he asked them to imagine a "barbarian assembly" choosing to export slaves. Born in the 380s, Demosthenes did not grow up in a time when it was fashionable to galivant in the costume of a Scythian prince; given how many of Demosthenes' rivals stigmatized his "Scythian γένος" (e.g., Aesch. 3.172), maybe that option was never attractive, anyway. Instead, whatever double consciousness Demosthenes *had* manifests instead through his use of metaphor. To Demosthenes, the barbarian world is a reflection of Greece, even if distorted;[126] slavery is legitimate in Athens because it is rooted in the social structure of the steppe. In order to perpetuate that hierarchical relation, it is incumbent upon Athenians to understand and respect life among the "barbarians."

For the final section of this chapter, I argue that privileged, bicultural men like Demosthenes, Leoxos, and the mysterious Zopyros were largely responsible for creating and propagating the image of the racialized Thracian or Scythian in Classical Athens. These authors presented the Thracian or Scythian captive laborer as an authentic product of the steppe; their cultures, as Herodotus surmised (5.6.1), were machines for enslaving people. As we will see, this was not true: any survey of steppe archaeology will quickly reveal that slavery is very difficult to identify in the material culture left by the nomads. Rather, these ideas were (in the terminology of Eric Hobsbawm) "invented traditions" that gave their wielders a certain cultural and political cache.[127] When Athenian authors deployed concepts like "whiteness" or "redness" to describe the bodies of enslaved people, they were embracing a rhetoric concocted by the Greeks of the Pontus.

We should begin with some general comments on how scholars approach the question of social structure in the cultures of the ancient Pontic steppe. Despite thirty years of serious engagement, eastern and western traditions continue to approach issues of cultural contact, change, and identity very differently. Vinogradov was product of a Russophone archaeology steeped in its distinct mode of cultural historicism: cultures advanced through stages of material progress, and conflicts arose between and within societies at different stages.[128] To this day, there remains a general tendency to take Herodotus and other Greek ethnographers at their word, rather than as fabulists, or wielders of the "ethnographic mirror."[129] Moreover, in prerevolutionary Russia and the Soviet Union alike, the encounter of Greek settlers with Scythian nomads was seen as a central event in the history of the nation.[130] After the USSR's vivisection in 1991, this interest was repackaged into a kind of transnational nationalism known as "Eurasianism," which has flourished with the occasional support of the Russian and Kazakh states.[131] Control over Greek antiquities and Scythian archaeological sites thus became a legitimating discourse for conflict in the years between Russia's annexation of Crimea in 2014 and invasion in 2022. As Vladimir Putin himself wrote in the preface to a 2021 publication of Greek archaeological sites in Crimea, "Crimea... dictated by history itself, was to be together with Russia."[132] At time of writing, Leoxos' monument, previously held in the regional archaeological museum in Kherson, Ukraine, has been expropriated by the Russian Army.

Early in the Soviet period, it was generally assumed that Scythians, like Greeks, passed through a uniform "slave mode of production" on their way to the Middle Ages. This idea, which originated in the work of Friedrich Engels (1820–95), gained currency in Soviet historiography during the Stalin period, although it was not fully accepted by professional academics.[133] Like so much else, this dogmatism loosened with Stalin's death. Instead, slavery was to be seen as a dynamic and changing force in history, worth understanding in the terms of societies that practiced it. In the first post-Stalin issue of *Soviet Archaeology*, V. D. Blavatskiy (1954) laid out something like a new mission statement for the study of Scythian social structure. He states that Greek settlement had violently destabilized Scythian society; even if forms of slavery predated the first contact, it was intercourse with the Greeks that produced chattel slavery for the first time.[134] Blavatskiy argued that proper study of the ancient Pontic steppe would mean reading Herodotus' ethnographic account of the steppe against findings from excavations. But the limits of this approach were clear. Archaeology itself was ill-equipped to answer historical questions. It could, however, help confirm specific observations of Scythian society we find in the texts.[135]

The problems of this approach are obvious. We are, in essence, held at the mercy of Herodotus and the other Greek ethnographers—and, as we have seen, these writers were very keen to look at Scythian society through the lens of slavery. Indeed, Herodotus openly credits interested parties in the Black Sea slave trade for information: the "Greeks of the Black Sea" whom he names as informants in 4.8.1–2 and elsewhere; Scythians themselves (4.8.1); most importantly of all, a single named individual: Tymnes (4.76.6), commercial agent of the Scythian king Skyles resident in Olbia.[136]

In Herodotus' mind, slavery among the Scythians could be broken down into two categories: enslaved insiders and enslaved outsiders, each with their own roles. The group most visible in his account were prisoners of war, who were by definition outsiders. Herodotus begins his narrative with an account of how Scythians blind some prisoners of war and use them to churn milk (4.2), following the logic that as blind men they would be unable to escape on the limitless steppe.[137] Some were so integrated into Scythian family life that their children might have become a permanent underclass (4.3–4); others were dispatched as human sacrifices (4.62.3). Herodotus makes an additional, oblique, reference to bought slaves (4.72.2), indicating the presence of a market.

Enslaved insiders were reserved for special "duties." Scythians mark the one-year anniversary of the king's death by sacrificing fifty of the king's best former slaves—"these are native Scythians, because the king has no bought slaves, but chooses people to serve him from among his subjects"[138] (4.72.2). Afterward, the victims are rendered into grotesque human scarecrows around the tumulus (Figure 6.5). We are left with the conclusion that the slavery that existed in Scythia before the arrival of the Greeks comprised both insiders and outsiders; if Herodotus is correct, the only enslaved people identifiable in the record, the retainers found sacrificed at Scythian elite burials, were all insiders.[139]

Given the clearly interested nature of our narrative sources, there is a certain flimsiness involved in relying on them to paint a picture of Scythian society. Even Herodotus, who recognizes that Scythian identity comprises many subgroups (4.19–20, 4.24.1, 4.46.1), is cautious in drawing up an ethnic map of the steppe. Contemporary scholars follow him in preferring units like "clan" or "band" over "ethnicity."[140] Likewise, even *Scythian-made* portrayals of Scythian society fail to depict clear lines between "insiders" and "outsiders." Starting in the fourth century, a school of gold-workers flourished

FIGURE 6.5 Diorama of Scythian human sacrifice at royal tomb, following Herodotus 4.71–72. Ukrainian National Academy of Sciences Museum, Kyiv. Photograph by author.

in the region between Crimea and the rivers Dnieper, Don, and Kuban on the mainland. So-called Greco-Scythian metalwork drew on an iconographic vocabulary originating from Achaemenid Persia, distant Siberia, and Greek anatomical realism. The scenes of combat, horse-taming, feasting, and personal hygiene depicted on metal objects have long been understood to portray Scythian life through the eyes of elite Scythians.[141]

But the world portrayed on these objects shows little evidence for social rank, "ethnic" differentiation, or other hierarchies.[142] The world that is portrayed is of almost exclusively elite men who ride horses, carry flail and *gorytos*, and style their hair with fierce individuality. Outsiders to the warrior elite, and even women, are almost never portrayed.[143] Case in point are a pair of golden objects from two fourth-century burial mounds in the region that Herodotus calls Gherros (4.71): a cup from Gaimanova and a comb from Solokha, both located along the former rapids of the Dnieper in modern Ukraine.[144] Both portray scenes of social subordination—but all within the elite class. The Gaimanova cup, now in the Museum of Historical Treasures in Kyiv, depicts a pair of feasting Scythians in repose receiving an older man on his knees, touching his beard in a gesture of submission, while a boy sits on an inflated wine-skin in the background. All are portrayed wearing identical clothing, leading one to suspect this represents the resolution of a conflict between members of the same group.[145] The Solokha comb (Figure 6.6) depicts a pair of horsemen—one dismounted because his horse is dead—fighting against a foot soldier with a crescent-shaped shield. All are similarly bearded and wearing the ubiquitous Scythian pantsuit, but all carry different combinations of weapons and armor. Although Caspar Meyer's assertion that the footman is Thracian appears generally accepted, the differences between the figures are extremely slight. Other objects that might potentially depict social gradation, such as the cup from Tolstaya Mogila depicting husbandry work, do not seem to distinguish between any of the figures based on rank, body, or any other visible index aside from age.[146]

Thus, as it stands, we have little reason to believe that Greek slave traders—as Demosthenes suggested in his speech *Against Meidias*—were simply feeding off class or status distinctions that existed naturally within societies of the north. Rather, the racialized scheme of Scythian and Thracian, insider and out, was a product of Greeks *interpreting* the cultures of the steppe and mobilizing styles, symbols, and ideas for their own benefit. For Demosthenes, this appropriation simply meant internalizing the idea that the slave trade was just; barbarian elites were sending their own people to work

FIGURE 6.6 Golden comb from Solokha Mogila, Ukraine, depicting horseman and foot solder fighting another foot soldier. Fourth century BCE. Hermitage Дн.1913-1/1. Alamy Stock Photograph.

for wealthy Greeks like himself. But if we were to turn back a century, the world of Leoxos, we would see a different style of appropriation. In the same late sixth-century years that east Greek Egyptophiles were producing fictive biographies linking their ancestors to the ancient conquests of the pharaohs, enthusiasts of the steppe were producing their own fictive worlds, taking on the airs of a Scythian horse-lord. Here lie the origins of the conceit hard at work throughout Classical narratives of the steppe: *all Greeks* are Scythians. Enslaved people were Thracian.

The years between 510 and 500 BCE saw a boom in representations of individuals in nomad attire on Athenian ceramics. In his 1990 catalogue, François Lissarrague identifies as many as 700 potential "Scythians" in Attic vase painting, with very few outliers pre- or post-dating this interval.[147] "Scythians" on early Red Figure vases are often difficult to identify, because by convention there was no distinction drawn between Scythians and Persians.[148] And as Ashkold Ivantchik argues, it might have been convention to portray *all* archers as Scythians.[149] Typical accoutrement include a bow, *gorytos*, a decorated pantsuit, and a distinctive, pointed hat known as a *kidaris*.[150] These items migrate around the vase-painter's *imaginaire* in a free-associative manner. For most of sixth century, Amazons were depicted as light-skinned women in hoplite armor; around 525 BCE, painters working in the Black Figure technique began depicting them in full Scythian kit.[151] At other times, the *kidaris* is worn by male symposiasts or athletes pretending to be lords of the steppe. This custom, known as ethnographic play, was popular at the end of the sixth century. An amphora painted by Euthymides at the turn of the sixth century BCE depicts athletes under the supervision of an older man changing into Scythian gear (Figure 6.7). On the other hand, drunk symposiasts might imagine they could see the world through the eyes of the "Other" courtesy of the psychotropic effects of wine.[152] It is probably this custom that produced the incessant trope that Scythians were drunkards.[153] As the much later Strabo (7.3.7) would emphatically state, this trope was clearly incorrect. For Homer (*Il.* 13.5–6) and Hesiod (fr. 150.15–16 M-W), the Scythians were a nation of upright milk-drinkers. It was the Greek introduction of wine that corrupted them.[154]

Thus over a century before Demosthenes, and decades before Herodotus, we see Athenian artists hard at work creating their own distinct vision of Scythian culture, practically unmoored from earlier traditions. The *kidaris* gives it away. Scythians became popular in Greek vase painting in the years after Darius I of Persia's disastrous foray into the Pontic Steppe in 514–12 BCE, leading an army that comprised many east Greeks and nomads alike.

FIGURE 6.7 Drawing of red-figure amphora attributed to Euthymides depicting training athletes (top) and partially clad man surrounded by archers (Munich 2308). After Furtwängler and Reichhold 1904–32: vol. 2, pl. 81. Public domain.

This is almost certainly why the *kidaris* portrayed in Red Figure so closely resembles portrayals of Scythian tributaries in Achaemenid stone-carving.[155] When Scythians portrayed *themselves*, they were usually hatless, drawing attention to their flowing, individualistic hairstyles[156] (Figure 6.6). We have the strong suggestion that in a period when elite Greeks showed enthusiasm for all things Persian, they were imagining the world of the steppe through Persian eyes.[157] When Leoxos' family chose to commemorate him in "Scythian" dress around 480 BCE, they embraced an iconography of Scythian difference that had its origins far away.

When Greek symposiasts donned the *kidaris*, they had a certain type of Scythian in mind. This was not the anonymous ΣΚΕΥΘΗΣ ΧΡΗΣΤΟΣ buried without his name recorded in fifth-century Attica, almost certainly enslaved.[158] Rather, they were ravenous Scythian lords, terrorizing the Thracian girls who served them drink. This trope continued to have currency long after the ethnographic play of the Late Archaic symposium had been swept aside by the jingoism of the fifth century. One of the places it survived was in the tropes surrounding a controversial group of foreigners resident in Classical Athens: the corps of Scythian archers. According to Andocides (3.5), Athens had purchased a corps of enslaved Scythian archers around 446 BCE, during the peace with Sparta. Scholars have downdated their arrival, given that we lack evidence for their presence before 425 BCE.[159]

Explanations for their function vary. The common assertion that they were delegated routine policing power—powers that would have been outrageous for one citizen to bear over another—seems questionable given the thinness of our sources.[160] But one task they certainly had was to police Athenians with no rights to speak of: slaves. In Aristophanes' *Lysistrata* of 411 BCE, Lysistrata and the women of Athens seize the Acropolis and are attacked by the corps of archers. After repulsing them, she issues a taunt: "what did you expect? Did you imagine that we were slaves, or did you think that women can't show courage?" (*Lys.* 463–65).[161] A fragment of Eupolis' *Officers* features a speaker calling for an archer to come drag a female character off to be auctioned (fr. 273 K-A).[162] And in Aristophanes' *Women at the Thesmophoria*, we see a dim-witted Scythian archer acting not much differently from symposiasts wearing the *kidaris*. When one of Euripides' relatives is caught by a Scythian archer after violating the sanctity of the *Thesmophoria*, Euripides comes up with a plan to trade his kinsman for an enslaved dancing girl (ἡ παῖς) (1172–1216). Aristophanes' audience is treated to the spectacle of what if an *actual* Scythian with an exaggerated accent found his way into the *symposion*, and not just Greeks playing dress-up.[163]

So when Eupolis (perhaps in 424 BCE)[164] and Cratinus (at a date unknown) castigated the great enslaver Hipponikos for his red, Scythian-like complexion, there were *actual Scythians* resident in Athens whose language, behaviors, and appearance could serve as reference. Hipponikos kept a thousand of his fellow beings enslaved in dire bondage, bodies wracked by exposure to lead; if any escaped, there were archers ready to drag them back. The method developed by the Thracian Zopyros could discern the ones more successful in hiding. Thus when Herodotus left for his expedition to the steppe in the 420s BCE, he had a basic understanding of the dynamics of the steppe based on the racialized structures of Athenian slavery. Whatever questions he might have had for Tymnes and other interlocutors were predicated by the assumption that Scythians had some outsized role in the commodity chain that yielded enslaved people.

Which brings us back to Demosthenes' use of the "barbarian world" trope in his prosecution of Meidias in 350 BCE. As we have seen throughout this chapter, Demosthenes was keen to use the specter of slavery to remind jurors of their power; as citizens, it was in their power to judge the fate of the unfortunates dragged before them. ("They are slaves . . . you are masters," as he says in 45.71.)[165] Most of them would have been fully aware how fragile that privilege was, and some might have even found themselves on the wrong side of the tribunal in the past. Demosthenes himself would have been vulnerable had he not been so wealthy, aggressive, and litigious. For all these reasons, it benefitted him to create the image in the jury's head of the barbarian world as a kind of double to Greece. The whole world was made up of citizen's assemblies tasked with the job of purging their own societies. Athens and the north stood in cooperation, with the latter relieving the former of its undesirables. And who would know better than a half-barbarian?

Conclusion

In this chapter, I have argued that slavery in Classical Athens was a fundamentally racialized institution. Borrowing from the theorists Karen and Barbara Fields, I demonstrated that slavery represented a "social, civic, or legal double standard based on ancestry"[166] in that Athenian public institutions meted out differential treatment to individuals on the basis of imagined γένος, In the following section, I explored sources that included Old Comedy, the Aristotelian physiognomy tradition, and the ethnography of the fifth century to show that Athenians squarely associated two somatic indices, referred to as ἡ λευκότης and τὸ πυρρόν, with enslaved people from the north. Finally,

I explored the narratives through which Athenians came to explain Thracian and Scythian difference. The idea that northerners represented a distinct race of man was a product of Athenian social tensions. Its fiercest defenders were men like Demosthenes, whose own membership in the Athenian γένος was questionable at best.

Postscript

Introduction

Over the previous six chapters, I argued as follows: between circa 700 and 300 BCE, fragments of an idea of race percolated through the Aegean world. These were attached to discrete structures. Ideas of blackness (given the label "Egyptian" or "Ethiopian") travelled along the routes of an institutionalized, long-distance trade in natron and other commodities between Greece and Saite Egypt. Concepts of whiteness (assigned ethnonyms "Thracian" or "Scythian") were rooted in the slave trade conducted with nomads living north of the Black Sea. After the end of our period, this language remained in place, circulating widely within the practice of physiognomy. Indeed, the astounding popularity of physiognomy as a technology for evaluating a person's moral characteristics might be seen as its ultimate legacy. But because physiognomy was so malleable, almost nobody agreed how the signs of the body should be interpreted; it would never sprout into a full-on theory of race.[1] If we were to write history in the *longue durée*, we might identify eighteenth-century race-making as its ultimate legacy; Carolus Linnaeus, for instance, defined the four races of the world using a Latin vocabulary borrowed from Lucretius, Vergil, and other appropriators of Greek's anatomical lexicon.[2]

In that, we should be clear what distinguishes ancient Greece's race-making from that in later periods. In Greek ideas of blackness, we have a concept different from that which arose in the Atlantic world: it was associated with the power, prestige, and institutions of a great African kingdom, Egypt. Greek ideas of whiteness, on the other hand, have something uncanny about them: they clearly emerged out of a slave trade, and the tropes associated with it are shockingly familiar. In ancient Greece's idea of race, we recognize something familiar in a society much unlike our own.

This word—*recognition*—is the sticking point in a mounting critique of the study of race in the premodern world. Until recently, those of us who study race in the premodern world have faced overwhelming skepticism. For generations, scholars have believed that race was a core product of modernity, and particularly one experience—the Transatlantic Slave Trade.[3] *Ipso facto* race and racism did not exist in premodernity.

Like many who work on race in premodernity, my trajectory into this field was shaped by the dominance of Frank M. Snowden Jr.'s narrative about race in antiquity. Snowden's dominance had begun to break in the 2010s, as race and race-making became topics of pervasive interest in the modern humanities. When I accessed Snowden's personal papers in 2019, I hoped to situate his work in twentieth-century history to an extent it had not been previously.[4] Snowden's fundamental point was that *nothing* is permanent in the world; the banal racism he faced every day of his own life was not the inevitable outcome of history. Premodern Critical Race scholars have approached the question of racism in world history from a different perspective. When Geraldine Heng defines race as a fundamentally amorphous idea—a relationship of power construed in reference to ideas of the body or ancestry—she is writing in an era when racism has transformed from an open power structure (e.g., Jim Crow) to something often veiled in deniability.[5] Social scientists would largely back this definition.[6] The study of race in antiquity is no less shaped by our positionality than it was fifty years ago.

Still, there is a danger in malleable definitions. If race can be identified at work in almost any power structure, what *isn't* race? In a 2020 article in *History and Theory*, Vanita Seth raises two objections to attempts to locate race in premodernity. The first, borrowing from the British intellectual historian Quentin Skinner, is that the search for origins is, in itself, fallacious—a "mythology of prolepsis" that seeks to identify concepts in the past that could not be effectively vocalized by people who lived in it.[7] Just because something looks familiar—for instance, pseudo-scientific reasoning behind Aristotle's definition of natural slavery—does not mean it is. Seth's second point deals more with rhetoric. Many proponents of Premodern Critical Race Studies have sought to establish their arguments as *non-falsifiable*. Seth sees this position as an outcome of the very real aggression non-white scholars have faced in humanities disciplines, but argues that this position is nonetheless insufficient, labelling Premodern Critical Race Studies more "a politics" than a theory.[8] (Seth goes on to situate premodern race studies as response to institutional priorities, and an attempt to rationalize the study of premodernity to our modernist colleagues—two points that certainly feel true.)[9]

Seth's critique is worth listening to; she is also far from alone in making it. To conclude *Racialized Commodities*, I would offer a brief response.

Familiarity Is Recognition

I brought back to Athens, to their homeland founded by the gods, many who had been sold, one legally another not, and those who had fled under necessity's constraint, no longer speaking the Attic tongue, as wanderers far and wide are inclined to do. And those who suffered shameful slavery right here, trembling before the whims of their masters, I set free.[10] *(Solon fr. 36.8–15 West)*

A logical consequence of the slave-outsider equation is racism, a term I insist on despite the absence of the skin-color stigma; despite the variety of peoples who made up the ancient slave populations; despite the frequency of manumission and its peculiar consequences. The issue is not a concept of "race" acceptable to modern biologists or of a properly defined and consistently held concept, but of the view commonly taken in ordinary discourse, then as now. There were Greek slaves in Greece, Italian slaves in Rome, but they were unfortunate accidents; ideological expressions were invariably formulated around "barbarians," outsiders who made up the majority in reality.[11]

It may be useful to note once again what we should and should not be looking for in Greece and Rome; Greek and Roman antiquity did not know the sort of racism that Western civilization developed in the nineteenth and twentieth centuries, since they had no concept of biological determinism. There was no nationalism in the modern sense in the Graeco-Roman world, nor was there any concept that a specific ethnic group should live within defined borders.[12]

One of the bedrocks of the *status quaestionis* on ancient slavery, we learned in Chapter 4, goes as follows. At the start of the sixth century BCE, the Athenian statesman Solon took control of the city and rewrote the laws. He banned the citizens of his city "founded by the gods" from being enslaved; he describes Athenians as anyone who spoke the Attic tongue. In the same poem, he speaks of freeing the Attic soil from the slavery of mortgages. In just a few lines we find a constellation of language, soil, religion, and freedom neatly packaged up. As Francis Hargrave pleaded evocatively in the *Somerset* case of 1772: "the air in England is too pure for a slave to breath."[13]

Our second passage comes from Moses Finley, in his *Ancient Slavery and Modern Ideology* (1980); we encountered this passage earlier in Chapter 6. To Finley, ancient biases toward enslaved people should be taken as a form of racism, because they systematically understood unfree people as social outsiders. Race is not skin color or nose shape, like prewar biologists might have thought; it is a socially constructed category. And, more to the point, racism was part of *his own* experience. His permanent exile from American academia after 1955 was in no small part due to his racialization as a Jewish leftist in the 1930s.[14]

And then there is Benjamin Isaac. Solon might assimilate language, soil, religion, and freedom, but there was no such thing as nationalism in antiquity; this was an invention of modernity. Neither could we interpret as "race" the idea that specific peoples (including the famously autochthonous Athenians) possessed special ties to the ground they inhabited.[15] What we are seeing in Solon, Herodotus, or other ancient writers is an uncanny resemblance. *Antiquity was different.*

Across his *Invention of Racism in Classical Antiquity* (2004), Isaac reads resemblances between ancient and modern behaviors as mere coincidences; we might call such actions *proto-racism* to distinguish them from the present.[16] Like Snowden, Isaac is troubled by the many instances of bias, prejudice, and identarian violence carried out in antiquity; nonetheless, both agree they could *not* represent racism.[17] In this, both Isaac and Snowden were doing what historians are trained to do: make sense of the past *in its own terms*, which means being willing to jettison contemporary presuppositions. This mode of learning is what we associate with modern, professional historiography, which recognizes that reality was not always how we perceive it now.[18]

Yet from time to time, we run up against the edges of this way of thinking about the human past. At what point does it not become a kind of special pleading to define things out of existence that sit in front of your own eyes?[19] This is probably what led Finley to accept the quasi-racial nature of ancient slavery, despite the fact that his own doctoral supervisor William Westermann (1873–1954) had strenuously argued it had nothing to do with race.[20] Of course, there is the matter of how Finley was using the term *race*: he was clearly deploying it in a descriptive, and not analytical, way, and he deliberately distanced himself from the so-called science of race, which in the

1970s was held in deep disrepute. Nonetheless, his use of the term is notable, particularly because almost the entire field of ancient slavery studies continues to agree with Westermann to this day. Scholarship had banished "race" because it was defined equivalent to the ethos of Nazism, Apartheid, or Jim Crow. As Adolph Reed Jr. writes in his memoir, this is the real tyranny of race: any recognition of a racial dynamic anywhere is reducible to an uncanny reflection of the way things used to be.

> Indeed, now and again, as the business class car on Amtrak fills up, I flash on Homer Adolph Plessy's attempted 1892 trip from New Orleans to nearby Covington... and imagine the conductor ordering me to give up my seat for a white passenger. But that's only scar tissue. There's no chance that the regime will return, at least not on terms familiar to its survivors.[21]

If anything, midcentury attitudes toward the question of race in antiquity offer an interesting register of how inconsistent "professional" historiography could be on such an emotive issue as race. In Chapter 3, we covered Snowden's extensive dialog with Grace Hadley Beardsley, whose *Negro in Greek and Roman Civilization* (1929) was the book Snowden set out to rebut. Snowden was a professional; his argument was backed up by a meticulous catalog of primary sources. Beardsley, on the other hand, marshalled almost no evidence in stating that ancient Black people "were slaves... without question."[22] She did not need to; the lion's share of classicists and Egyptologists also assumed this was true.[23] It was Snowden, in fact, who faced the higher burden, even though his argument (from an evidentiary perspective) should have been intuitive. Yet even his work (as Lloyd Thompson would later point out) was marked by a certain affectation; it was with little evidence that he assumed Black life in antiquity had shades of the American middle class."[24]

Both were, in fact, combining a *professionalizing* attitude toward the study of history with a more intuitive, and pre-professional, type of interpretation. Isn't modernity the fruit of antiquity? All Beardsley had to do was assume that the way things are *now* is how they always were. Snowden's argument, which posited a rupture between antiquity and the present out of which racism was invented, was much more difficult. The goal of Premodern Critical Race Studies has been to prove such a rupture did not exist.

My point here is that disconnecting our own sense of positionality from the study of history is a problem: it embraces an objectivity even the natural sciences have troubles maintaining sometimes.[25] As Shelley Haley writes, it is ridiculous to pretend modern readers do not find stakes in the ancients.[26] And at any rate: there are many social formations we accept in antiquity, that the ancients lacked words for. We speak of gender, the economy, religion, or socio-economic class; even English lacked a word for ethnicity until the 1930s. To fastidiously avoid the language of race in examining the distant past is a hypercorrection.

The Path Forward

By raising this objection, I do not mean to play down the very real risk of anachronism, nor to claim continuities that do not exist. Greece and Rome had very different racial ideas than would emerge in the modern world. My overwhelming emphasis in *Racialized Commodities* has been on the discreteness of race in Archaic and Classical Greece; their reception in modernity is another story.

To conclude, then—in my estimation there is a continued need for studies that examine how, when, and where ideas of race came into and out of being across the ancient world. I have raised the point that physiognomic texts might be one place to look at the continued import of race from antiquity into the Middle Ages, but this surely represents a different project from that carried out here. The next few years will see many promising studies on particular aspects of race and antiquity—both in modernity's reception, but also in images of the Black body in ancient Greece and Rome. The relationship between the study of the ancient world and prewar race science is seeing increasing attention as new advances in the study of the human genome have enabled scientists to map ancient migrations—using the same methodological frameworks overturned by Snowden and other anti-racist scholars. As this work goes forward, the reality that the ancient world had concepts of race interdependent with our own, but chronologically differentiated, will become widely accepted.

APPENDIX I

Quantifying the Natron Trade

Introduction

In *The Making of the Ancient Greek Economy* (2016), Alain Bresson interprets the Elephantine document as evidence that the Greek textile industry relied on a trans-Mediterranean supply chain at the start of the Classical Period.[1] Invoking David Ricardo's (1772–1823) Theory of Comparative Advantage, he argues that Egypt and Greece respectively concentrated on a single part of the productive process to increase overall production. Egyptians extracted raw minerals needed for processing, and Greeks focused on the advanced work of weaving, bleaching, and dyeing. Even though both parties were already able to locally obtain nearly all the raw materials necessary for cloth manufacture, by dividing their labor they increased their overall efficiency.[2]

Bresson's deployment of Ricardo is speculative. (As we saw in Chapter 2, some of our strongest evidence for natron use in Greece is in fact in building maintenance, not textile manufacture.) And, indeed, we lack knowledge of what the natron recorded in the Elephantine document would eventually be used for. Nonetheless, Bresson's comparatism remains compelling. We have many records attesting to the fact that natron, alum, and other mineral evaporites were exported from Egypt in quantity around the middle of the first millennium BCE (Chapter 1 above). Herodotus (2.37, 49) saw the habit of wearing blindingly white textiles during religious rituals as one of Egypt's unique contributions to Greece. It is quite likely there was *something* going on. The purpose of this appendix is to deploy quantification to determine whether natron was being moved in such a quantity to make a transnational commodity chain viable.

Appendix 1

Natron and Alum

We should begin with a technical explanation of the role played by our two mineral evaporites in the textile industry. Natron and alum can be used to, respectively, bleach and mordant textiles (the latter is the process of making the surface of a thread "sticky" to receive dye). When dissolved in water and heated, natron ($NaCO_3 \cdot 10H_2O$) reacts to produce a weak solution of sodium hydroxide (NaOH), which bleaches cloth.[3] Powdered alum ($KAl[SO_4]_2 \cdot 12H2O$) was used as a mordant for fixing dyes. Alum reacts with the surface of threads to allow them to absorb color.

Natron and alum are persistently reported together in our ancient sources; this is largely because of their usage in textile production, although both were believed to have medicinal properties as well (Chapter 1 above). Despite being grouped together in sources, alum had a geography of production quite distinct from natron. Alum was widely available in the Mediterranean world. Linear B texts from Pylos, Tiryns, and Knossos dating to the thirteenth century BCE record alum locally produced in Greece.[4] Aegean sources of alum continued to be exploited through the Classical Period.[5] On Lemnos, for instance, alum was extracted from volcanic deposits.[6] Indeed, alum is conspicuously underreported in Egyptian sources until the Late Period, when extraction appears to have begun in the western desert. There, alum was mined from ancient lake deposits in Egypt's Kharga and Dakleh Oases buried beneath a few feet of sand.[7] Unlike the seasonal lakes that produce natron and halite, alum sources do not flood seasonally, and there is no annual harvest cycle. Despite the number of alum deposits around the Mediterranean, very few were consistently exploited, meaning that supply remained susceptible to cornering and supply shocks.[8]

Nonetheless, from our earliest Mesopotamian sources for the trade in mineral evaporites from Egypt, we see these two commodities linked together. They were clearly exported from the western Nile Delta to Greece in tandem in the Late Period (Hdt. 2.78). So even though Greeks had no shortage of local supply, alum developed an association as an Egyptian commodity.

Quantifying the Natron Trade

One of the challenges of claims like Bresson's comes from our lack of hard data. In her study of the Early Modern *bacalao* trade between England and Spain, Regina Grafe uses price data—collected both from Basque ports in northern Spain and inland markets—to show how the Spanish interior progressively became more integrated with North Atlantic markets over the seventeenth century.[9] Ancient historians, on the other hand, have repeatedly emphasized the fragmentation and *dis*-integration of ancient markets. The monument of this approach was Peregrine Hordern and Nicholas Purcell's *Corrupting Sea*, which argues that Mediterranean economies only approached any level of price integration through the actions of small actors—*caboteurs* who piloted their own small ships—within maritime "microregions."[10] Only under the high

Appendix 1

Roman Empire does this dynamic change, with the rise of the *annona* system that kept a handful of cities (mainly Rome and Constantinople) constantly supplied with African grain.[11]

The natron trade between Saite and Achaemenid Egypt and Greece was an early outlier to this trend. Like the Roman *annona*, it was almost certainly facilitated by a state.[12] Coming from that perspective, arriving at an estimate of the size and scale of the trade offers a way of gauging how meaningful the natron trade was in the overall picture of Mediterranean trade in the mid-first millennium BCE. As Neville Morely writes, the point of quantification is always in providing a narrative: once you establish a scale of things, it becomes more realistic to characterize the overall significance of a phenomenon.[13]

Estimating the tonnage carried by vessels in the Elephantine document is not straightforward.[14] Total export duty figures for natron in the Elephantine palimpsest only exist for two discontinuous months on the Egyptian calendar, Pharmuthi (July 18–August 16, 475 BCE; KV2:13-25) and Payni (September 16–October 15, 475 BCE; KV3:16-EV1:9), as well as partial figures for Epiph (October 16–November 14, 475 BCE; EV1:10-EV2:11) (Tables A1.1a–c). In Pharmuthi, five Ionian ships exported natron taxed the equivalent of 4.2 kg of silver, or 0.84 kg per ship.[15] In Payni, four Ionian ships exported natron taxed either 1.6 or 2.4 kg in silver depending on the text, averaging either 0.4 or 0.6 kg per ship.[16] In Epiph, three Ionian ships exported an amount of natron that was taxed the equivalent of at least 0.6 kg per ship.[17]

It would be possible to calculate the tonnage of natron exported per ship if we knew the price that Ionian merchants paid for it. The document shows that Ionian captains paid in silver weighted in local units rather than barter. The problem is that we lack reliable data: no legible natron price survives from any period of Egyptian history. The best approximation might be the price of salt, which we know a little more about: salt and natron were often harvested together, sold by the same merchants, and both regarded as low value.

Table A1.1a Duty charged on natron exports in Pharmuthi

Departure date	Captain	Taxed cargo	Export duty
x Pharmuthi	]*mn*[…	natron	0.89 kg silver
x Pharmuthi	Spitaka	natron	0.97 kg silver
21 Pharmuthi	[…]*kles*	natron	0.99 kg silver
26 Pharmuthi	Protokles	natron	0.57 kg silver
30 Pharmuthi	Glaphyros	natron	0.72 kg silver
Converted dates		total	4.14 kg silver
July 18–August 16		average	0.83 kg silver

Table A1.1b Duty charged on natron exports in Payni

Departure date	Captain	Taxed cargo	Export duty
17 Payni	Timokedes, son of Mikkos	natron	
21 Payni	PN son of *-mn*	natron	
26 Payni		natron	0.05 + kg silver
27 Payni		natron	
Converted dates	total		1.6/2.4 kg silver
September 16–October 15	average		0.4/0.6 kg silver

Table A1.1c Duty charged on natron exports in Epiph

Departure date	Captain	Taxed cargo	Export duty
x Epiph	Glaphyros	natron	0.05 + kg silver
x Epiph	*Š---*	natron	
x Epiph	*Hpw---*	natron	
Converted dates		total	1.84 + kg silver
October 16–November 14		average	0.6 + kg silver

The handful of extant salt prices from ancient Egypt are divided by a period of over a millennium. Natron circulated volumetric units including *khar* (sacks or skins) or *dbt* (bricks, lumps, or bars) in pharaonic Egypt; in the Roman period it was sold in fractions of artabas. The earliest is found in *P.Turin* 1907/8 III, dating between 1069 and 945 BCE. This values salt at two copper weight unit *deben* per volumetric *oipe*, or the equivalent of 1 g silver per 20.74 kg salt at the standard metallic conversion ratio for the period.[18] Converting using natron's specific gravity, 1 g silver would buy 13.7 kg natron.[19]

The next available salt price comes from the Roman period, in a grant of monopoly to salt merchants at Tebtynis dating to 47 CE.[20] This document (*P.Mich* 5.245) lists three grades of salt, respectively priced at 2.5 ("good," τὸ καλὸν), 2 ("light," τὸ λεπττὸν), and 1.5 silver obols ("lightest," τὸ λεπττότερον) per 1/10 of a volumetric *artaba*.[21] This gradation is curious; as discussed in Chapter 1, the same lakebeds produced natron, halite, nahcolite, and other evaporites. Natron's specific gravity is considerably lighter than halite's. Moreover, sampling of Late Period mummies demonstrates that even skilled professionals only had a limited ability to control the ratio of natron to other evaporite minerals.[22] This means that the "lightest" salt sold at Tebtynis probably contained high proportions of other evaporites such as natron. Its price could stand in for a real natron price. 1/10 of an artaba—2.71 l—would be the equivalent of 3.86 kg natron. Converted, 1 g silver would buy 3.57 kg natron.

The problem with this pair of isolated prices is that they are products of two different systems of valuation. Abstractly, the 74 percent collapse in silver's purchasing power indexed to natron between the twenty-first dynasty and 47 CE is massive (Figure A1.1). Copper's purchasing power drops 92.6 percent. This reflects the general decrease in the purchasing power of metals in Egypt over the first millennium, particularly from circa 220 BCE onward.[23] But no semblance of a cash economy existed in the pharaonic period, when silver was relatively rare and even copper *deben* were not used for most transactions.[24] Although the earliest Greek coin hoards in Egypt are contemporaneous with the Elephantine document, outright monetization—driven by the compulsory payment of taxes in coinage—only set in under the Ptolemies. Value ratios between silver and copper continue to be roughly stable into the third century BCE, when the Ptolemaic regime adjusted them downward.[25]

For these reasons I extrapolate three sets of possible figures for natron prices, using P.Turin 1907/8 III (TableA1.2a), P.Mich 5.245 (Table A1.2b), and an average of the two, which is 1 g silver = 8.64 kg natron (TableA1.2c). I regard the last of these as the most representative, since it is based on the traditional ratio of 100:1 silver to copper, but reflects a world in which the quantity of circulating metals has increased. But it is worth noting that the latter (Table A1.2c) is still an arbitrary number. Most transactions in Egypt were paid for in kind even in the Hellenistic and Roman periods. Indeed, the fact that Ionian ships were taxed in silver—rather than in kind, like Phoenician

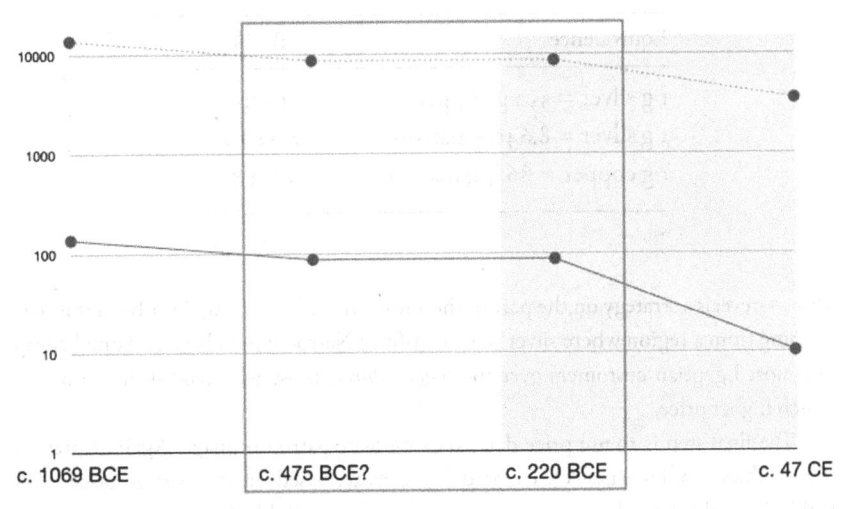

FIGURE A.1 Estimated natron prices in silver and copper, c. 1069 BCE–47 CE. Boxed area represents period of early coin circulation in Egypt. Area shaded in grey represents era of monetization. The period c. 220 BCE is when silver and copper ratios begin to diverge. Data drawn from Table. A1.2c.

Table A1.2a Price equivalences using price in *P.Turin 1907/8 III* (1069–945 BCE)

Equivalence	Ratio
1 g silver = 100 g copper	100:1
1 g silver = 13,700 g natron	13,700:1
1 g copper = 137 g natron	137:1

Table A1.2b Price equivalences using price in *P.Mich* 5.245 (47 CE)

Equivalence	Ratio
1 g silver = 350 g copper	350:1
1 g silver = 3,570 g natron	3,570:1
1 g copper = 10.2 g natron	10.2:1

Table A1.2c Price equivalences using avg. of Tables A1.2a–b

Equivalence	Ratio
1 g silver = 350 g copper	100:1
1 g silver = 8,640 g natron	8,640:1
1 g copper = 86.4 g natron	86.4:1

ships—reveals a strategy on the part of the authorities of extracting silver from travelers coming from a region where silver was plentiful.[26] Natron would have remained cheap for most Egyptian customers over the *longue durée*; those who paid in metal paid a much higher price.

The final step is to use price data to extrapolate natron tonnage. Again, I present three tables (Tables A1.3a–c). I regard Table A1.3c, based on the average price from Table A1.2c above, as the most representative. Following Table A1.3c, if the export duty were an implausible 100 percent of price, then the average ship in the Elephantine document, paying 0.83 kg duty in silver, would carry 7,171.2 kg in natron. If the duty were 25 percent—a figure paralleled in the Ptolemaic kingdom[27]—then the average

Appendix 1

Table A1.3a Estimated annual natron exports using price in *P.Turin 1907/8 III* (1069–945 BCE)

	At 100% duty	At 50% duty	At 25% duty
1 ship	11,371 kg	22,742 kg	45,484 kg
36 ships	409,356 kg	818,712 kg	1,637,424 kg
1 g silver = 13.7 kg natron			

Table A1.3b Estimated annual natron exports using price in *P.Mich* 5.245 (47 CE)

	At 100% duty	At 50% duty	At 25% duty
1 ship	2963.1 kg	5,926.2 kg	11,852.4 kg
36 ships	106,671 kg	213,342 kg	426,684 kg
1 g silver = 3.57 kg natron			

Table A1.3c Estimated annual natron exports using avg. of Tables A1.3a–b

	At 100% duty	At 50% duty	At 25% duty
1 ship	7,171.2 kg	14,342 kg	28,684 kg
36 ships	258,163 kg	516,312 kg	1,032,624 kg
1 g silver = 8.64 kg natron			

cargo could have been 28,684 kg per ship. That would yield an annual total of some 1,032,624 kg natron in exchange for 29.88 kg silver. This is my preferred annual figure.

At this point it is worth reiterating that these figures must be taken with caution. But as I will argue in the following paragraphs, independent data show that annual exports in the area of 1,000 tons of natron were realistic at the start of the fifth century BCE.

Mineral evaporites had been exported in small quantities from Egypt as early as the seventh century BCE. Sources from Assyria, Babylon, and Greece offer some indication of what individual shipments looked like, albeit no register of annual exports like the Elephantine document (Table A1.4). Our earliest source, Marduk-šarru-uṣur's letter of 672–69 BCE, lists the equivalent of 303 kg natron and 909 kg alum missing from a storeroom. The manifests of Nadin-aḫi's caravans from to Uruk in 551–50 BCE list two

Table A1.4 Egyptian evaporite mineral exports, 672–475 BCE: individual shipments

	Marduk-šarru-uṣur, 672-669 BCE	Nadin-aḫi, 551 BCE	Nadin-aḫi, 550 BCE	Naukratis, after 548 BCE	Amasis, after 548 BCE	Ionian/Phaselite merchants, 475 BCE
alum	909 kg	133 kg	133 kg	11.42 kg	27,000 kg	
natron	303 kg					28,684 kg

shipments of Egyptian alum of 133 kg each, out of total cargoes of about a ton. Finally, in 548 BCE, the merchants of Naukratis offer the temple of Apollo at Delphi a paltry single mina (11.42 kg) of natron.

These shipments represent different orders of scale. At the very bottom goes the tiny donation of the people of Naukratis to Delphi after 548 BCE. This small amount might accurately represent a single shipment of natron or alum transported from the western desert carried on the back of a single peasant, like Khunanup in the *Tale of the Eloquent Peasant*. Nadin-aḫi's two shipments in 551 and 550 BCE are a sum of these; his cargoes were destined for temple storerooms like the one that Marduk-šarru-uṣur had mismanaged a century earlier.

The difference between these fairly small quantities and the massive numbers recorded starting in the middle of the sixth century has to do with the Egyptian state's degree of involvement. Amasis' gift of 100 talents (27 tons) of alum to Delphi after 548 BCE and the probable average cargo (28.7 tons) carried by the ships of the Elephantine document are about the same size (this statistic makes Herodotus' report of Amasis' donation look trustworthy). The average Greek ship of the Elephantine document could carry as much as 60 tons of cargo, making these quantities just under half of an individual ship's capacity.[28] The data at our disposal is extremely scrappy, and indeed too tenuous to make as bold a claim as one might like. But if the estimates are trustworthy, then we should date the rise of a structured, state-directed export trade in evaporite minerals from Egypt back to the middle of the sixth century. In that case, Naukratis almost certainly would have been center of the trade. (The structures of foreign trade at Naukratis are discussed in greater detail in Chapter 2 below.)

Estimating Production

What percentage of Egypt's annual natron production might the 1,032 tons possibly annually exported to Greece at the start of the fifth century BCE represent? This is a tricky question, but it is worth asking because it can help us imagine the cost—in manhours, in productive capacity, and in overall effort—of the natron trade to Greece's Egyptian

Appendix 1

trade partners. In this section I briefly review available data from ancient Egypt and comparative statistics from the nineteenth century to conclude that producing natron for export to Greece required minimal effort on the part of Egyptians. The arrival of Greek merchants with bags of silver during the sixth century represented a massive windfall for both the temples and the state.

As should be expected, no annual production statistics exist from ancient Egypt for any commodity, including grain. In the pharaonic period minerals like copper, gold, and building stone, all frequent presences in the documentary record, were state property and their access was controlled.[29] On the other hand, natron, salt, alum, and other evaporites were relatively common; there is no proof that the Ptolemaic monopolies on producing them predated the Macedonian conquest.[30] Evidence for the informal quarrying of gypsum in the western desert dating as early as the Old Kingdom shows the extent of Egyptian resource gathering beyond the Nile Valley that evades documentary mention.[31]

The closest we have to a production statistic for mineral evaporites comes from *P.Harris* 1, the record of Ramesses III's colossal dedications to the temples in 1155 BCE. Commodities listed in the document came from the pharaoh's private (*khato*) land; the disruption in pay to Ramesses' workmen at Deir el-Medina in the same year might indicate that his donations strained his capacity.[32] Among the document's difficulties is that it lists natron and salt both discreetly and as mixtures with uncertain ratios; natron, salt, and alum are reckoned in units of both volume and mass. In Table A1.5, I present a range of possible tonnages for each commodity. I arrived at these figures by converting quantities listed in *P.Harris* 1 into metric units of mass using the specific gravities of natron and halite.

These conversions indicate that at the end of the New Kingdom, the pharaoh's lands could produce between 683.8 and 1,738.4 tons of natron and 1,954.2-4,228.4 tons of salt.[33] Alum, uncommon in Egypt before the Late Period, appears in much smaller quantities. It is worth repeating that these figures do not indicate Egypt's total annual production; rather, they are useful in offering a perspective on how many commodities were immediately at the pharaoh's disposal. If we add to these numbers the commodities that were available to the state through additional labor, taxation, or other forms of requisition, then it is becomes very realistic that the Egyptian state could have annually dispensed with circa 1,000 tons of natron for export.

Table A1.5 Royal donations of mineral evaporites to temples in *P.Harris 1*

	Alum	Natron	Salt	Natron and salt mix	Total natron	Total salt
Min		418.6 t	844.7 t	1,706.4 t	683.8 t	1,954.2 t
Max	12.7 t	730.8 t	1,503.9 t	3,172.2 t	1,738.4 t	4,228.4 t

Comparative export statistics from the early nineteenth century show merchants exporting natron from Egypt's western desert in nearly the same quantity. European demand for natron had picked up during the late eighteenth century, when natural scientists in both Britain and France unsuccessfully explored the use of imported substances to improve efficiency in textile production. "India, Syria, and Egypt... knew the efficiency of natron... for combining with and carrying off the colouring matters with which cloth is stained," wrote David Brewster in the *Edinburgh Encyclopedia*; "but though those nations appear to have early acquired the art of bleaching, the progress they made in it when compared with the advantages which some of them enjoyed, was very inconsiderable."[34] Manufactures at Rouen in the 1770s failed in their attempt to revive the use of natron in textile bleaching, but glassmakers in Venice were more successful in employing it as a flux for the first time in Europe since the collapse of the Roman Empire.[35] Travelers to Egypt during the Napoleonic wars, including Sonnini, Denon, and Dearborn, testify fairly modest natron exports; the figure that Dearborn gives passing through Rosetta in the western delta is 30,000 quintals of Alexandria, the equivalent of 1095.6 tons.[36] Annual alum exports in the same period were much smaller, reaching 1,000 kantars, equivalent to 45 tons.[37]

Natron production took place at this artisanal level across the world's deserts until the middle of the nineteenth century. The demand for natron, soda ash (Na_2CO_3), and other mineral evaporites exploded during the later phases of the first industrial revolution, when they began to be used in manufacturing paper, soaps, bricks, and in metal processing. Early production statistics from the American west—the era just before machines began to be employed in the process of extraction—show that only a handful of workers could harvest vast quantities of natron (Fig. A1.2). Using traditional

FIGURE A.2 Borax harvesting, Searles Valley, CA, 1880. Photograph by Payne, Stanton, & Co., Los Angeles. Borax ($Na_2B_4O_7$) is not found in North Africa but was harvested alongside trona, thernadite, and halite. Photograph courtesy California Historical Society MSP-1933_006. Public domain.

evaporation and scraping techniques, the Nevada Soda Ash Company was able to produce between 360 and 450 tons annually between the late 1860s and early 1870s. With only five laborers, their harvest season was limited to summer and early fall.[38]

We can use statistics from the Nevada Soda Ash Company to arrive at yield per laborer; in a bad year the company averaged 72 tons of soda ash per workman, while in a better year they averaged 90. But these estimates for yield per laborer cannot be transposed either to ancient or eighteenth-century Egypt, given that workmen in nineteenth-century America almost certainly ate better and had access to metal tools, draft animals, and wagons. The American workmen were paid wages and dedicated all of their time to production; studies of artisanal harvesting in Africa's Sudan show that laborers even camping at isolated salt pans were engaged in a variety of activities.[39]

What this exercise shows instead is a cluster of likelihoods. The first is that natron exports from late Saite and early Achaemenid Egypt only totaled a small percentage of Egypt's total production. The second is that exports could have been roughly equivalent to what Egypt exported at the turn of the nineteenth century. The third is that the workforce required to produce this material was not large, even if production took place on a more casual level than it did in nineteenth-century Nevada. If selling already stockpiled natron to Greek merchants offered a cheap and easy way for the Saite state to capitalize on their existing resources, once Egypt fell under Achaemenid rule, it transformed into a method for authorities to raise the silver they needed to pay their share of the tribute to Susa.

APPENDIX 2

Catalogue of Greeks in Egypt, Seventh to Early Fifth Centuries BCE[1]

Aigyptis: Known from *dipinti* on three Chian chalices, sixth century: *vac*? Αἰγυπτὶς ἀν (BM 1924,1201.755 + 808);]τὶς ἀν[(Ashmolean AN1896-1908-G.114.7); and]υπτ<ὶ>ς ἀ[(BM 1924,1201.809). See D. Williams 2013: 44; Johnston 2015a: 44.

Anaxanor of Ialysos: Abu Simbel inscription (M-L 7 G); see Bernand and Masson 1957: 12–13.

Antimenidas of Mytilene, brother of Alcaeus: Alcaeus fr. 370 L-P. Attested at Ashkelon "fighting with the Babylonians" (601 BCE); Fantalkin and Lytle (2016) argue he was on the Egyptian side.

Apollos, son of Thalinos: "False door" funerary marker, Cairo JE27753. Ἀπολλῶτος| τ˜ο Θαλίνο. See Johnston 2015b: 2 no. 2; Villing 2015b: 234–35.

Archidike: Hdt. 2.135.5, Ath. 13.596d, Ael. 12.63; inscribed sherd BM 1911,0606.17. Unclear dating. Subject of popular songs. Her name also found on inscribed early fifth-century Attic sherd from Naukratis].χεδίκη *vac.* (Johnston); also single fifth-century *Lieblingsinschrift*. See Möller 2000: 200; Demetriou 2012: 141; Johnston 2015a: 44.

Archon, son of Amoibichos: Abu Simbel inscription (M-L 7 A); see Bernand and Masson 1957: 8. Possibly brother of Python (M-L 7 D). Amoibichos is not attested elsewhere.

Ariston: Base fragment of Attic cup (Cairo JE38360) inscribed Ἀρίστονος[---------]. μ' ὄνυμα || ἴομεν ἐπὶ λουτρὰ οἰφόλεσι[, "Ariston's my name ... let's go to the baths, to [...]!" Inscribed in two concentric circles around crude stick drawing of woman in missionary position, head facing toward center. See Edgar 1907; Venit 1988: no. 397, pl. 83; Johnston 2015a: 77.

Ariston 2, priest of Thoth: Demotic papyrus fragment from Hermopolis west, *Dem. P.Mallawi* 480. Name given as *3rstn*. His position of authority is unclear; Zaghoul argues "ein höherer Beamte." 6 Pharmuthi, fifteenth year of Apries (August 11, 575 BCE). See Zaghloul 1985: 23–31; Vittmann 2003: 158; Agut-Labordère 2012: 297; Kaplan 2015: 403–4.

Chariandros of Memphis, son of Straton: Abydos temple graffito, dated mid-fifth century by letterform. Identifies himself as Μεμφίτης; see Timarchos above. See Jeffery and Johnston 1990: 359 no. 54; Bresson 2000: 77–78; Kaplan 2015: 404.

Charisthenes or Charystion, son of *Prytkm*²: *TAD* C3.7 Jr1:2, Ev2:13; Yardeni 1994 tb. 2 no. 37. *Krystin bn Prytkm.* Captain of *spynh rbh* (large) ship. Arrives during Mesore and departs 9 Mesore after a stay of nine or fewer days. Briant and Descat (1998: 65) restore name to Charisthenes or Charystion. Father might not have been Greek.

Charaxos, of Mytilene, brother of Sappho: "Brothers Poem" (Obbink 2014, 2016), Hdt. 2.134–35, Posidippus *AG* 6.207. The publication of the "Brothers Poem" provided direct testimony that Charaxos was active in Egypt, as Herodotus and Posidippus claim later; Sappho's isolated mention of λίτρον (fr. 189 L-P) hints at his cargo. Said to have manumitted Rhodopis. See Vasunia 2001: 82–87, Obbink 2014; Raaflaub 2016: 138–39; Bowie 2016: 161–63. On the ethical mess left behind by Obbink, see Higgins 2020.

Damoxenos, son of Hermon: proxeny decree from Lindos (*SIG*³ 110 app., *SEG* 32.1586), 440–11 BCE. "Damoxenos, son of Hermon, living in Egypt" (Δαμόξενον Ἕρμωνος ἐν Αἰγύπτωι οἰκέοντα). Bought in Cairo. See Bresson 2000: 35; Möller 2000: 190; Malkin 2011: 85; Demetriou 2012: 124–25.

Deinias, son of Pytheas: proxeny decree from Lindos (*SIG*³ 110, *I.Lindos* 16, *IG* 12¹ 760), 411–407 BCE. "Deinias, son of Pytheas, an Egyptian in Naukratis, translator" (Δει[ν]-si-]αν Πυθέω Αἰ|[------ τ]ὸν ἐγ Ναυκράτ|[ιος] ἑρ[μα]νέα). Editors are unanimous in restoring ethnic as Αἰγ[ύπτιον; Figueira (1988: 543–44) argues that Deinias is a refugee from Aegina in the service of Naukratis. In the early 1980s, Bresson (reprinted in Bresson 2000: 35) proposed the alternative restoration Αἰγ[ύπτιον; although Figueira (1988: 547–48) rejects this reading on grounds of likelihood (and not for textual reasons per se), Bresson's reading has defenders including Möller (2000: 190–91), Malkin (2011: 86–87), and Demetriou (2012: 126–27). It is worth noting that the late fifth-century Athenian comic playwright Strattis mocks a Δεινίας Αἰγύπτιος as a wealthy, perfume-wearing merchant (fr. 34 K-A). This evidence, not cited in the original debate, makes Bresson's reading much more likely.

Dionysios, son of Parmenon: Attic grave stele, fifth century BCE. *IG* 2² 9984. Διονύσιος Παρμένοντο<ς> | Ναυκρατίτης. See Möller 2000: 189.

Doris: Body sherd of Attic cup. Δωρὶς φίλτ[ρον (?) Ἀφροδίτηι (Johnston). Mid-fifth century. See Gardner 1888: 66 no. 798 pl. 21; Demetriou 2012: 141 n. 193; Johnston 2015a: 44.

Exekestos, son of Charon: "False door" funerary marker, Saqqara, fifth century BCE. Ἐξηκέστο(υ) εἰμὶ το(ῦ) Χάρωνος. See Lacaze, Masson, and Yoyotte 1984: 137 n. 34a; Vittmann 2003: 227, abb. 113.

Glaphyros 1: *TAD* C3.7 DDr8:9, Kv2:22; Yardeni 1994 tb. 2 no. 20. Captain of *'swt* (small) ship. Arrives in Pharmuthi and leaves 30 Pharmuthi. Possibly the same as Glaphyros 2 below; see Briant and Descat 1998: 65.

Glaphyros 2: *TAD* C3.7 Gr2:15, Ev.1:11; Yardeni 1994 tb. 2 no. 31. Captain of *'swt* (small) ship. Arrives 5 Epiph and departs later that month. Possibly the same as Glaphyros 1 above; Braint and Descat 1998: 65.

Helesibios of Teos: Abu Simbel inscription (M-L 7 B); see Bernand and Masson 1957: 15.

Herostratos of Naukratis: Ath. 15.18.675f–676c = Polycharmos *FGrHist* 640 F 1. Polycharmos implausibly dates Herostratos to the 23rd Olympiad (684–80 BCE), long before the foundation of Naukratis. Stronk 2010 (*BNJ* s.v.) argues that this fragment references the *Kham(a)sin* season of March and April, a fifty-day period of heavy southerly winds. This season was well within the navigational year recorded in the Elephantine documents. See Yoyotte 1991/92: 636; Möller 2000: 186; Jenkins 2001: 163; Demetriou 2012: 141-42; Ross Thomas 2015a: 27; Villing 2015a: 9.

Hpw-[. . .]: *TAD* C3.7 GGr11:20, Ev2:3; Yardeni 1994 tb. 2 no. 35. Captain of *spynh rbh* (large) ship. Arrives during Epiph and departs later that month.

Hyblesios: Rim fragment of Attic lip cup (BM 1888,0601.243) from Hera sanctuary inscribed *vac* Υβλησ[(Johnston), mid-sixth century; another inscribed name Ύλη[σ] on a WG amphora (BM 1965,0930.725) might refer to the same person. Demetriou and Johnston argue this is the same Hyblesios who dedicated an Attic cup at Gravisca, also to Hera and was probably Samian; a (different?) Samian Hyblesios is buried in Kyme in the late sixth century. Rare name later appears as captain in fourth cent. *Ps.*-Dem. 35. See Torelli 1982: 314–15, 319; Demetriou 2012: 79; D. Williams 2013: 44; Johnston 2015a: 50–51, 78.

Iokles, son of Š[. . .]: *TAD* C3.7 Jr1:26, Ev2:15; Yardeni 1994 tb. 2 no. 38. Captain of *'swt* (small) ship. Arrives during Mesore and departs [10] Mesore after a stay of ten or fewer days.

Itoana (?): funerary stele, private collection. Two registers depict prothesis scene (top) and deceased before Osiris (below). Greek inscription in between registers indicates gender. Name is possibly Carian, but inscription too poorly preserved to properly reconstruct name. See Vittmann 2003: 228–29, abb. 114.

Iunx: Body sherd of Chian chalice, BM 1924,1201.621. Inscription read Ἴ]υνξ ἀ[νέθηκε by Gardner, who expressly identifies her as a sex worker. See Gardner 1888: 63 no. 712; Demetriou 2012: 141; Johnston 2015a: 44.

Kaiqos: Three inscribed dedications, two on Chian chalices; *vacat* καιqος μ[. . .]θηκην (BM 1888,0601.188a–b), *vacat* καιqος μ[. . .]θηκην (BM 1888,0601.191; both readings by Johnston). A third inscription now lost reported along rim of limestone perirhanterion, published by Johnston as]ην |]ς Ναυκρατιν |]. Και κο[but inventively restored by Gardner as Ει]ς Να[ύ]κρατιν [ἀφικόμεν]ος [Ἀφροδίτη]ι Καῖqο[ς ἀνέθηκεν; see Gardner 1888: 66 no. 795; Johnston 2015b: 6 no. 5.

Krithis: Abu Simbel inscription (M-L 7 E); see Bernand and Masson 1957: 18.

Lethaios: Two inscribed sherds: Attic kylix (BM 1910,0222.120) inscribed]. Λαθαιο. [and East Greek cup (BM 1886,0401.112) with inscription given as]λης Λε[by Johnston. Several inscribed sherds with the name Lethaios/Lathaios have appeared from Mende on the Thermaic Gulf and Gravisca, Tarquinia, and Veii in Italy. Johnston alternatively argues for a trading family, or more likely a potonym; see Torelli 1982: 310, 315; Johnston 2010: 470–74; 2015a: 48; Demetriou 2012: 81. If it is the latter, then cf. Aigyptis above.

Mandrippos: Shoulder fragment of Chian vase inscribed]ανδιπ(π)ος μ, sixth century (BM 1886,0401.503). Name known from contemporary dedications at Ialysos (*SEG* 53.818) and Miletus; see Johnston 2015a: 48.

Melanthios: Sheathing for wooden statue base with separate Greek and hieroglyphic inscriptions (*SEG* 27.1106), MMA 21.2.65. Egyptian inscription reads *t3 Imn ʿnḫ B-r-s 3*, "may Amun give life to *Brs*" (Masson). Greek inscription reads [Με]λάνθιός με | ἀνέθηκε τῶι Ζηνὶ Θηβαί|ωι ἄκαλμα: "Melanthios dedicated me, a statue to Zeus in Thebes." See Masson 1977: 53–57; Jeffery and Johnston 1990: 358 no. 49; Vittmann 2003: 230–31, abb. 115; Vlassopoulos 2013: 159.

Metrodoros, son of Apollonides from Miletus: Funerary marker, Cairo JE31183. Μητροδώρου: εἰμὶ: σῆμα: τὠπολλωνίδεω: Μιλησίο. Identifies city ethnic of father but not himself. See Johnston 2015b: 3 no. 2.

Mikis: Body sherd of Chian chalice, BM 1924,1201.824. Inscribed Μῑκὶς ἀν[έθηκεν (Johnston). Sixth century. Several *Lieblingsinschriften* exist for the male diminutive of this name, Mikion; see Klein 1898: 52, 136; on Mikis, Gardner 1888: 64 no. 745 pl. 21; Demetriou 2012: 141 n. 193; Johnston 2015a: 44.

***Mrgs*, son of *Pq*[. . .]:** *TAD* C3.7 Br1:7, Kv1:2; Yardeni 1994 tb. 2 no. 4. Captain of *ʾswt* (small) ship. Arrives 2 Choiak and departs later that month.

Myrsilos: *TAD* C3.7 DDr9:18, Kv3:2; Yardeni 1994 tb. 2 no. 21. Captain of *spynh rbh* (large) ship. Arrives early Pahons and leaves [10] Pahons after stay of around nine days. Name restored to Myrsilos (Lydian?) by Briant and Descat 1998: 65.

Neferpre-sa-Neith, son of *Grḫs* (Qerches, Korax, or Korakos): Inscribed *naophoros* statue, St. Petersburg 8499. See Yoyotte 1991/92: 643. Possibly supervisor of Naukratis (Nokrodj); see Möller 2000: 10; Vittmann 2003: 220; Villing 2015a: 21. Tenth year of Amasis, 561 BCE.

Pabis of Colophon: Abu Simbel inscription (*M-L* 7 F); possibly short for Pambios. See Bernand and Masson 1957: 19.

Panteleon, son of Moschos: *TAD* C3.7 Er2:11, Kv3:7; Yardeni 1994 tb. 2 no. 23. Captain of *ʾswt* (small) ship. Arrives 10 Pahons and departs 22 Pahons after stay of twelve days. Restored to Panteleon by Briant and Descat 1998: 65. An individual named Moschos dedicates a little master cup to Hera in mid-late sixth cent. Gravisca; see Torelli 1982: 309.

***Pdrwihy* (?), son of *ʾIpdy*:** Carian funerary stele, Florence 2507. Fourth year of Apries (587/6 BCE). Identified as choachyte. Ray includes in catalogue of individuals with probably Carian names. See Ray 1998: 132; Vittmann 2003: 158–59.

Pedon, son of Amphinneos: Inscribed statue from Priene (*SEG* 37.994), Private collection. Claims Psammetichos "gave me a city and a bracelet for good service, gold, and a city on account of my excellence" qὧι βα-|| σιλεύς ἔδoq' ὠιγύπ-|| τιος: Ψαμμήτιχο-|| ς: ἀριστήριια ψίλιό-|| ν τε χρύσεογ καὶ || πόλιν ἀρετῆς ἕ-|| νεκα. A Chian chalice rim fragment from Naukratis inscribed Πηδω[(BM 1966,0930.26) might date to late seventh century but seems unlikely to refer to same person. Moyer argues Pedon's inscription mimics priestly autobiographies, a flourishing genre in Saite Egypt. Piccolo notes that neither Pedon nor Amphinneos' names are otherwise attested in *LGPN* and suggests Egyptian etymology. See Sahin 1987; Masson and Yoyotte 1988; Hölbl 2007: 449; Moyer 2011: 57–58; Johnston 2015a: 49; Piccolo 2019.

Peleqos, son of Eudamos or Oudamos: Abu Simbel inscription (M-L 7 A); see Bernand and Masson 1957: 9 Possibly *nom de guerre* "Axe." Abel and Bechtel suggested false identity for Archon's weapon (as though the axe inscribed its own name). Dillon (1997) suggests Οὐδάμο ("nobody") for the otherwise unattested Εὐδάμο, a joke based of *Od.* 9.366, 369, and 408.

Phanes 1 of Halikarnassos: Hdt. 3.4. Betrays Psamtik III for Cambyses in 525 BCE. See Kaplan 2003: 11; 2015: 406.

Phanes 2: *TAD* C3.7 Jr2:5, Ev2:17; Yardeni 1994 tb. 2 no. 29. Captain of *spynh rbh* (large) ship. Arrives during Mesore and departs 2[2] Mesore after a stay of at least eleven days. Particularly common name in Egypt; see Phanes 1 above and Phanes 3 below.

Phanes 3, son of Glaukos: Attic dinos fragment (BM 1886,0401.677-79) inscribed *vac* Φανης με ανεθηκε τωπολλων[. . . .]λησιωι ο Γλαυqο *vac* (Johnston), "Phanes, son of Glaukos dedicated me to Milesian Apollo." Schlotzhauer argues this is the same as Phanes 2 but dismissed by Johnston. See Torelli 1982: 317; Johnston 2015a: 49; on Apollo Milesios, Demetriou 2012: 59.

Pigres the Carian: Polyaenus 7.2. Involved in Psamtik's coup; informed Psamtik that Carians wear feathers on their heads. Part of Memphis named "Karomemphitai" after him; see Kaplan 2003: 11; 2015: 406.

Pirapia, son of *Khaa-s-n-Mut*: Fragment of *naophoros* statue? (only known through drawing) with one Greek and three hieroglyphic inscriptions. Probably from Memphis. Longest Egyptian inscription reads "the *imakhou* (with) Osiris Piratji (or Pirapi), beget by Khaa-s-n-Mut, just of voice" (Lacaze, Masson, and Yoyotte). Greek inscription with nearly unique letter forms reads Πιραπια ἠμί. Editors believe the name is Lycian or other Anatolian. Earliest Greek inscription to offer translation of hieroglyphs. Date is not clear, possibly early sixth century. See Lacaze, Masson, and Yoyotte 1984: 132–37; Vittmann 2003: 228–29, abb. 115.

Protokles: *TAD* C3.7 DDr7:9, Kv2:20; Yardeni 1994 tb. 2 no.19. Captain of *spynh rbh* (large) ship. Arrives in Pharmuthi and departs 26 Pharmuthi.

Psammetichos, son of Theokles: Abu Simbel inscription (M-L 7 A); see Bernand and Masson 1957: 7. Possibly had an Egyptian mother; see Vittmann 2003: 220 with parallels. Pharaonic names were common among emigrants in Egypt; hence the possible second generation Greco-Egyptians named Neferpre-sa-neith (throne name of Psamtik II; see Vittmann 2003: 220) and Wahibre-em-achet. We also see Aramaeans named Wahpre (Porten et al. 2011 no. B1 = *TAD* A2.1) and Psami (Porten et al. 2011 no. B4 = *TAD* A2.4) in the fifth-century Makkibanit archive.

Psammetes: Abu Simbel inscription (M-L 7 F); possibly short of Psammetichos. See Bernand and Masson 1957: 20 and entry for Psammetichos above.

Pythermos, son of Neilon: Bronze statuette of Isis with Horus child with Greek inscription. Cairo JE 36571. Πυθρμός με ὁ Νε(ί)λωνος ἐλύσατο τῆς Ἐσιος ἄγαλμα, "Pythermos, son of Neilon, consecrated me, a statute of Isis." Late sixth century. Skon-Jedele has argued that Pythermos and Neilon were members of a long-lasting Greco-Egyptian family with Samian origins; their descendants might have been epigraphically active as late as the Hellenistic period. See Masson 1977: 57–61; Jeffery and Johnston 1990: 358 no. 50; Skon-Jedele 1994: 1422; Vittmann 2003: 231–32.

Python, son of Amoibichos: Abu Simbel inscription (M-L 7 D); see Bernand and Masson 1957: 17. Possibly brother of Archon (M-L 7 A). Amoibichos is not attested elsewhere.

Rhodopis or Doricha the Thracian: Hdt. 2.134–35, Strb. 17.1.33, Ath. 13.596d, Posidippus *AG* 6.207, *SEG* 13.364. Legendary; between late seventh and mid-sixth centuries. Owned by Iadmon son of Hephaistopolis of Samos, also owner of Aesop; sold and brought to Egypt by Xanthos of Samos. Herodotus both claims she was manumitted by Charoxos of Lesbos, brother of Sappho (late seventh/early sixth cents.), but also lived in time of Amasis (mid-sixth cent.). Herodotus also reports dedications at Delphi; late sixth-century offering base inscribed ἀνέθη]κε Ῥοδ[ῶπις is potentially hers (*SEG* 13.364). Rhodopis is a popular in sixth- and fifth-century *Lieblingsinschriften* and appears on several vessels, although doubtfully a sherd from Naukratis published Ροδ[-- by Petrie; see Klein 1898: 47 Rodopis s.v. nos. 1–2; Petrie 1886: 62 no. 531. On Rhodopis stories, see Kurke 1999: 220–27; Möller 2000: 199; Vasunia 2001: 82–87; Demetriou 2010: 67–70; 2012: 141; on slavery in Aesop myths, Kurke 2011: 61–63.

Sktrsl bn Srtn **([*Sktrsl*] son of Straton?):** Inscription in Saudi Arabia. Name with -*ol* ending is likely Carian, but father has Greek name. Fought with neo-Babylonians against Necho II? Dismissed by Fantalkin and Lytle 2016: 108–10.

Smyrdes (Rhodes): Two inscribed statue fragments from Kameiros, Rhodes E7020 and G2649/14341. Latter inscribed -]δης με ανε[θηκε - - -, restored by Jeffery as [Σμυρ]δης. Former said to have name of Smyrdes and unrelated hieroglyphic inscription. See Jeffery and Johnston 1990: 348–49 no. 10 (another possible dedication no. 11?), Boardman 1980 [1964]: 142–43 fig. 167; Skon-Jedele 1994: 1989–90 no. 3011; Ebbinghaus 2006: 195–96; Hölbl 2007: 449.

Sokydides: Bronze Apis bull figurine (BM 1898,0225.1) with Greek inscription τōι Πανεπι μ' ανεστασε Σōqυ|[δι]δης, "Sokydides has dedicated me to the son of Apis." Πα is rendering of Egyptian definite article *p3*. Early fifth cent. See Masson 1977: 61–63; Jeffery and Johnston 1990: 358 no. 52; Vittmann 2003: 231–32 abb. 117.

Solon of Athens: Fr. 28 West in Plut. *Solon* 26.1; Hdt. 1.29, Plut. *de Iside* 10 and Diod. 1.96. States that he stood at Νείλου ἐπὶ προχοῆισι, Κανωβίδος ἐγγύθεν ἀκτῆς, "the mouth of the Nile, near the headland of Canopus." Solon is the only of several Archaic wisdom figures, including Pythagoras and Thales, to have authored a surviving record of his visit. See Moyer 2011: 58–59; Villing 2015a: 5.

Somenes/Sumenos/Somenos, son of Simonides: *TAD* C3.7 Cr2:3, Kv1:13; Yardeni 1994 tb. 2 no. 8. Captain of *spynh rbh* (large) ship. Arrives 16 Tybi and departs later that month.

Sostratos: Three inscribed dedications from Naukratis: a complete WG lekane with female protome (BM 1888,0601.456) inscribed vac Σωστρατος με ανεθηκεν τηφροδιτηι[(Johnston); large body sherd of WG lekane inscribed Σω (BM 1888,0601.460.k); Chian kantharos fragment inscribed]οστρ.[(BM 1924,1201.783). All late seventh century. Torelli argued this Sostratos was the grandfather of Sostratos, son of Leodamas, the Aeginetian trader mentioned in Hdt. 4.152.5; Torelli attributes anchor from Gravisca inscribed Σόστρατος to him. Van de Moortel and Langdon (2017) publish a sixth-century inscription from Vouliagmeni, Attica (facing Aegina) portraying a merchant ship labelled Σοστρατος ειμί [μι]. Langdon (personal comment) reports the existence of two additional Late Archaic inscriptions naming Sostratos in the environs of Vouliagmeni. Some caution is warranted here: Sostratos is a common name in Aegina, Attica, and elsewhere. See Torelli 1982: 318; Möller 2000: 57, 178; Johnston 2010: 474; 2015a: 49; Demetriou 2012: 80–81; D. Williams 2013: 44; van de Moortel and Langdon 2017: 400, fig. 17.

Spitaka: *TAD* C3.7 DD15:5, Kv2:16; Yardeni 1994 tb. 2 no. 17. Captain of *spynh rbh* (large) ship. Arrives in Pharmuthi and departs later that month. Briant and Descat (1998: 65–66) note Iranian name.

Šwmn, son of Šmnds: *TAD* C3.7 Kr4:12, Ev1:2; Yardeni 1994 tb. 2 no. 30. Captain of *qnrt*ᵒ ship. Arrives after 20 Payni and leaves 30 Payni after a stay of at most ten days. Briant and Descat (1998: 65–66) propose emendation to *Šw(pr)mn* for Greek name Symphoron or Sympheron. The former is known from single sherd of a Chian Kantharos at Naukratis inscribed Σύμφορο[(BM 1911,0606.12). *Šwmn*'s is the only Phoenician ship in Elephantine documents to have captain with Greek name. Kuhrt (2007) suggests *Šmnds* is for Greek Simonides.

Tamynis: Body sherd of Attic bowl, Ashmolean AN1896-1908-G.141.48. Last quarter of fifth century. Inscription given vac Γοργίας φιλεῖ [. . .]νιν καὶ Τάμυνις Γοργίαν φιλ[by Johnston. "Gorgias writes his tetrameter, and reads it to Tamynis, his little Egyptian friend, who is no scholar;" thus Beazley 1927: 352 fig. 3. See Johnston 2015a: 44.

Teaos: Funerary marker, Naukratis, found in secondary deposition at Dioskouroi temple (BM 1886,0401.1). Dated early fifth century by letterform. See Jeffery and Johnston 1990: 358 no. 53; Johnston 2015b: 2 no. 1.

Telephos of Ialysos: Abu Simbel inscription (M-L 7 C); see Bernand and Masson 1957: 16.

Timarchos of Daphnis: Abydos temple graffito, dated first half of fifth century by letterform. Τιμάρχος || ὁ Δαφναιτ || ˉες. Identifies self as from Daphis; see Chariandros. See Jeffery and Johnston 1990: 358 no. 51; Bresson 2000: 77–78; Kaplan 2015: 404.

Timokedes, son of Mikkos: *TAD* C3.7 Kr2:23, Kv3:17; Yardeni 1994 tb. 2 no. 26. Captain of *ˀswt* (small) ship. Arrives 9 Payni and departs 17 Payni. Briant and Descat (1998: 65) also offer Timachidas son of Makos.

***Tmt*—[. . .] son of *–sy*:** *TAD* C3.7 Dr3:8, Kv2:3; Yardeni 1994 tb. 2 no. 12. Captain of *spynh rbh* (large) ship. Arrives on 20 Mehir and departs 10 Phamenoth after stay of twenty days.

Unnamed (Rhodes): Inscribed statue from Rhodes; unpublished hieroglyphic inscription said to use military title. See Kousoulis 2017: 43 εικ. 10.

Wahibre-em-achet, son of *Irkskrs* (Arkeskares or Alexikles) and *Sntt* (Zenodote): Stone sarcophagus, Leiden 1383; see Grallert 2001. Posthumous "beautiful name." His name is given with slight differences in other items from his tomb: Wahibre-em-achy, son of *Sntty* (Zenodote): Canopic jar, Stockholm 98–101; given title "Chancellor of Upper Egypt" (*ẖtm-bity*); Wahibre-em-achy, son of *Sdy* (Zenodote); *Ushabtis* from Saqqara, Stockholm 18046. Grallert stylistically dates to reign of Psamtik I. Agut-Labordère argues for Amasis on basis of Neferpre-sa-Neith's dedication. See Grallert 2001: 186; Vittmann 2003: 203; Ebbinghaus 2006: 196; Agut-Labordère 2012: 301.

Zoilos, son of Kleiostratos?: Name appears on eighteen sherds, all sixth century, discussed in Johnston. Fourteen are *dipinti* and four are graffiti; sixteen on various Chian shapes. Johnston and Williams believe Zoilos was a ceramics trader in the model of the Chians Aristophantos and Damonidas, whose work appears commonly at Aegina. A nineteenth dedication from ancient Plinthine is a stone disk inscribed]Ζώιλος με ἀν[-----]Κλειοστρ[, restored "Zoilos, son of Kleiostratos dedicated me" by Johnston, who is not confident it is the same person. The name is commonly Samian. A Zoilos dedicates a mid-sixth-century little master cup at Gravisca; see Torelli 1982: 312, 314; Demetriou 2012: 81; D. Williams 2013: 44; Johnston 2015a: 42–43; 2015b: 12; Villing 2015b: 231.

[. . .]*kles*: *TAD* C3.7 DDr6:10, Kv2:18; Yardeni 1994: tb. 2 no. 18. Captain of *spynh rbh* (large) ship. Arrives in Pharmuthi and departs 21 Pharmuthi.

--*gwt*--: *TAD* C3.7 Er1:15, Kv3.4, Yardeni 1994: tb. 2 no. 22. Captain of *spynh rbh* (large) ship. Arrives 7 Pahons and departs 18 Pahons after stay of eleven days.

[. . .], son of Ergilos or Yrgilos: *TAD* C3.7 Er2:17, Kv3:9; Yardeni 1994 tb. 2 no. 24. Captain of *spynh rbh* (large) ship. Arrives [15] Pahons and departs 27 Pahons after stay of twelve days. (Briant and Descat 1998: 65) prefer Carian Yrgilos to unusual Greek Ergilos.

. . .*gl[s]*: *TAD* C3.7 Kr1:16, Kv3:12; Yardeni 1994 tb. 2 no. 25. Captain of *ˀswt* (small) ship. Arrives after 15 Pahons and departs 30 Pahons. Potentially same name as the father of [. . .] above.

[----]: Abu Simbel inscription (M-L 7 E); see Bernand and Masson 1957: 18.Fig. A.1, Fig. A.2

APPENDIX 3

Appendix 3.1: *Aegyptiaca* **Assemblages at Greek Sanctuaries, c. 700–525 BCE[1]**

	Total	Faience	Percentage faience
Perachora[a]	913	899	92%
Argive Heraion	98	97	99%
Artemis Orthia	48	48	100%
Sounion (both)[b]	202	202	100%
Aegina (both)	199	198	99%
Paros	39	37	95%
Smyrna[c]	39	31	79%
Erythrai[d]	>25	>25	
Chios (both)	72	66	92%
Samos[e]	1,036	895	86%
Ephesus[f]	>120	>120	
Miletus[g]	>250	>250	
Lindos	855	819	96%
Kameiros	445	426	96%
Ialysos	513	505	98%
Total	**4,861**	**4,621**	**95%**

[a]The *aegyptiaca* from Perachora had a difficult publication history, and the true number might be significantly higher; see Skuse 2021: 43–51.

[b]Skon-Jedele (1994: 174–85) publishes sixty-two objects collated from Stais (1917) and Pendlebury (1930), all faience. Theodoropoulou-Polychroniadis (2015: 74–78, 273–79) mentions the existence of at least 202 items, all faience, but her decision to publish a randomly chosen "selection" of the total without museum inventory numbers means the total number is uncertain. Already in 1930, Pendlebury notes that many objects from Stais' excavation had gone missing.

c Akurgal 1983: 101–5, tf. 135–36; Cook and Nicholls 1998: 22–26, pls. 20–21.

d *Aegyptiaca* from the sanctuary of Athena at Erythrai remains unpublished. For brief mention of objects from Erythrai, including bronze and faience, see Leclant 1980: 418 with figs. 63–64; Hölbl 1985: 39; 2007: 455–56. A much smaller amount of material seems to come from Phokaia, and Klazomenai; see discussion in Hölbl 2007: 450.

e These numbers are from Skon-Jedele 1994. Webb's two recent publications of the faience from Samos (2016, 2021) add a great quantity of new objects. Webb 2016 counts 606 faience objects, some of which were already published by Skon-Jedele. Webb 2021 adds to this number 2,277 faience fragments. Because Skon-Jedele includes non-faience *aegyptiaca,* and because Webb's new catalogues are necessarily incomplete, I have preferred her numbers here for the sake of consistency; readers should be aware that publications from Samos are ongoing.

f No comprehensive publication exists for *aegyptiaca* from Ephesus. Some ninety individual faience objects are published by Hogarth (1908: 202–8) and discussed by Hölbl (1978). An additional eighteen objects from Bammer's excavations are published by Hölbl (1999). Twelve more objects from the project are published by Seipel (2008: 193–210).

g At least 250 scarabs were known from the 16-meter-deep *bothros* on Zeytintepe as of 2014; see Hölbl 1999; 2014: 190. Hölbl has additionally published a large number of stone, bronze, and faience figurines and vessels with inventory numbers, but a complete count awaits his final publication.

Appendix 3.2: Scarab Assemblages at Greek Sanctuaries, c. 700–525 BCE

	Total	Scarab	Percentage scarab
Perachora	913	750	82%
Argive Heraion	98	45	46%
Artemis Orthia	48	28	58%
Sounion (both)[a]	202	150	74%
Aegina (both)	199	28	28%
Paros	39	27	71%
Smyrna	39	2	5%
Erythrai	>25		
Chios (both)	72	21	29%
Samos[b]	1,036	15	1%
Ephesus	>120		
Miletus	>250	>250	
Lindos	855	301	35%
Kameiros[c]	445	60	13%
Ialysos	513	226	44%
Total	**4,861**	**1,878**	**39%**

a Of the objects published by Stais (1917), Pendlebury (1930), Skon-Jedele (1994: 174–85), and Theodoropoulou-Polychroniadis (2015: 74–78, 273–79), only seventy independent objects can be identified. The total number of scarabs and scaraboids given by Stais is 150. That number is used here to offer a total of >202, but Figures 2.4, 2.12 use 70 + as a total.

[b] Skon-Jedele (1994: 1591–97, nos. 2289–97) provides a total of eight scarabs. Webb 2016: 95–98 publishes four more. Webb 2021: 33 adds an additional three.

[c] Kameiros was excavated by Salzmann and Biliotti in 1859 (Salzmann 1875). The provenance of their finds (including whether objects come from the votive deposit on the acropolis or from the cemetery at Makri Langoni) is uncertain. Here I include all objects listed by Skon-Jedele (1994).

Appendix 3.3: "Textual" Scarab Inscriptions from Large Assemblages[2]

	Perachora	Lindos acropolis	Ialysos acropolis	Kition (site II)	Carthage necropolis	Average
Royal (**text**)	11	13	11	17	20	14.4
Divine (**text**)	42	24	26	39	60	38.2
Other (**text**)	2.5	12	8			4.5
Pictorial (**non text**)	36	21	38	33	14	28.4
% **Text**	55.5	49	45	56	80	57.1
% **Non-text**	36	21	38	35	19	29.8
Illegible	7	30	14	10	1	12.4
# total	750	301	226	103	423	1,803

Appendix 3.4: "Textual" Scarab Inscriptions from Small Assemblages

	Argive Heraion	Artemis Orthia	Sounion (both)	Chios Phanai	Taranto G. 1	Tharros (Cara)	Average
Royal (**text**)	16	14	9	38	12	15	17.3
Divine (**text**)	55	7	16	24	35	7	28.8
Other (**text**)					0.5		0.1
Pictorial (**non text**)	16	25	66	14	49	68	47.6
% **Text**	71	21	25	62	37	32	49.6
% **Non-text**	16	25	66	14	49	68	47.6
Illegible	15	57	9	24	14	0	23.8
# total	45	28	70+	21	157	41	362

APPENDIX 4

Five Large Scarabs from Late Geometric Greece

Style

This appendix identifies five scarab seals from LG contexts in Greece of similar material and workmanship as a group. All are manufactured from glazed steatite and share the same color, ranging from grey to white to pale green. Three of these are carved in the shape of a frontal-facing human head wearing a stylized headpiece and a beard. All are pierced longitudinally to be worn as amulets. This appendix should not be treated as an exclusive list; there are other additions that I have not seen in person.[1]

a. All share a rough carving style, with deep and broad incising to allow for interior carving to glaze during the cementation process and visible tool markings.[2] Repeated motifs, such as hieroglyphs, are rendered inconsistently or are visibly asymmetrical.

b. All employ hieroglyphs in their decorative scheme. A and D possibly make use of the hieroglyphs *r* (D21) and *n* (N35) to form a border around the scene.[3] Three examples (B, D, and E) include an unevenly drawn *nb* basket (V30) in the exergue.[4] C employs the symmetrically balanced *khepher* scarab (L1) and winged uraei. The impression of D is mostly taken up by the squatting figure of Ma'at (C10).

c. Individual scarabs in the group share common rendering of vegetation (plants rendered as spades or branches on A and B) and heads (facial detail represented as a V-shaped visor in A and D).

d. The scarabs are inconsistent in size. Scarabs A and B from Delphi measure over 4 centimeters in length; D and E from Andros are diminutive. Scarab C from Attica is nearly 3 centimeters in profile.

e. Head scarabs A, C, and D all share indentations at the edges of their headbands.

f. The *khepher* scarab carved on the back of head scarab C closely resembles the back of scarab B, featuring deeply inscribed, hatched lines marking off the abdomen and thorax and triangles marking retracted wings.

The subject matter varies between the familiar and unique. B, an animal grazing before a papyrus brake, is a motif familiar on Cypriot bowls.[5] Motifs in C and D, respectively depicting a large squatting Ma'at figure and a *khepher* scarab flanked by winged uraei, are commonly encountered in eastern Mediterranean seals.[6] E bears the praenomen of Tuthmosis III (*mn ḫpr Rᶜ*) over a couchant sphinx.[7] A, featuring zoocephalous creatures facing off against a man in armor, is nearly unique.

The style of the seals has been variously described as "Phoenician," "gréco-phénicien," "chypriote," and, perhaps accurately, "East Mediterranean imitation of an earlier Egyptian model."[8] Scholars in recent years have demonstrated the cosmopolitanism of imagery on seals, making it difficult to associate style with regional or ethnic origin.[9] Egyptian imagery was widely emulated across the Levant during the Bronze Age and the mid-first millennium. Cyprus was an intermediate destination for goods and imagery between the Levant and the Aegean through the early first millennium.[10] Cypro-Levantine styles were particularly influential in the Aegean in the eighth and seventh centuries.

Context and Dating

Only a single example here was found in a primary funerary context. The scarab from Attica (C) was discovered by David Robinson in an undisclosed tomb in southeastern Attica inside a LG Attic skyphos.[11] Corroded bronze adhering to both sides of the scarab indicates that other objects in the tomb were not published by Robinson. An additional unpublished scarab from Aigio was found in a similar context.[12]

The Delphi (A, B) and one of the Zagora (D) scarabs were found in votive deposits at sanctuaries.

The scarabs from Delphi were excavated from a deposit in an area of the site between the Bouleterion, the Treasury of the Knidians, and its facing exedra, at a depth of between 20 and 40 centimeters beneath the sacred way. Pierre Amandry grouped a variety of Near Eastern and Geometric objects discovered in the area during excavations in July 1893 (including head scaraboid A) and July 1939 (including scarab B) as a single Geometric votive deposit, including bronze fibulae, several Near Eastern seals, an inscribed trinacia shell, and a Corinthian crater.[13] The Zagora head scaraboid (D) was one of two excavated by Cambitoglou, Birchall, Coulton, and Green at Zagora on Andros in 1969. It comes from a votive trench cut down to bedrock south of the Archaic temple that contained a range of eighth- to sixth-century material.[14] The site's publishers dated the head scarab stylistically to the seventh century, which was the era that most *aegyptiaca* arrives in the Aegean, but a comparison with objects of similar style in securely dated funerary contexts might allow for them to be moved to the turn of the seventh century.

Appendix 4

The other scarab from Zagora (E) was excavated from a securely dated LG domestic context.[15]

Catalogue

A head scarab from Delphi:
   4.3 cm l; 3 cm w; 1.9 cm h
   glazed steatite
   votive deposit near Knidian Treasury
   Delphi Museum 31231
   Bibliography: Perdrizet 1908: 25 fig. 100–100a

B scarab from Delphi:
   4.8 cm l; 3.4 cm w
   glazed steatite
   votive deposit near Knidian Treasury
   Delphi Museum
   bibliography: Amandry 1944: 50 fig. 11; Skon-Jedele 1994: 879 no. 1246; Gorton 1996: 78 no. 1

C head scarab from Attica:
   4.8 cm l; 3.8 cm w; 2.8 cm h
   glazed steatite
   burial in SE Attica; found inside LG skyphos (Harvard 1960.281)
   Harvard 1960.628
   bibliography: Robinson 1949: 310–11 no. 7; Langdon 1993: 188–89 no. 73; unpublished XRF analysis by Harvard Art Museums in 1993

D head scarab from Zagora:
   1.7 cm l; 1.2 cm w; 0.8 cm h
   glazed steatite
   votive deposit south of Geometric temple
   Andros Museum 1300
   bibliography: Cambitoglou 1981: 91 no. 296; Cambitoglou et al. 1988: 235 no. 1300

E scarab from Zagora
   1.6 cm l; 1.1 cm w; 0.5 cm h
   glazed steatite
   geometric house
   Andros Museum 1324
   bibliography: Cambitoglou 1981: 72 no. 187; Cambitoglou et al. 1988: 235 no. 1324; Skon-Jedele 1994: 983 no. 1394

APPENDIX 5

Appendix 5.1: Stone Head Scaraboids Distribution

	Headdress	Physiognomic	Bearded	Total
Amathus	1	4	10	15
Attica	1			1
Carthage		1		1
Delphi	1			
Idalion	1		1	
Kourion	1	1		2
Lefkandi	1			1
Pyrga	1			1
Salamis			1	1
Tyre		1		1
Zagora	1			1
No provenance	11	6	1	17
Total	**18**	**14**	**12**	**44**

Appendix 5.2: Stone Head Scaraboids Catalog[1]

Catalog number	Type	Site	Material	Obverse	Bibliography	Museum
1	Headdress	Amathus	Serpentine	Blank	Clerc 1991: 67	Limassol (Amathus T. 232/97)
2	Headdress	Attica	Glazed steatite	Winged *khepher* beetle with falcons and *Ma'at* feathers	Robinson 1949 no. 7; Langdon 1993: 188–89	Harvard 1960.628
3	Headdress	Delphi	Glazed steatite	Man in armor with round shield and spear approaching two dog-headed men with square shields; nilotic vegetation and antelope in background; border of hieroglyphic characters?	Perdrizet 1908: figs. 100–100a	Delphi (inv. no. 31231)
4	Headdress	Kourion	Serpentine	Horse-group motif	Karageorghis 1988: 17 no. 7; Reyes 2001: 36 no. 6 fig. 31	MMA 74.51.4393
5	Headdress	Lefkandi	Glazed steatite	Male figure with caprid	Sherratt 2010: 131 tb. 6.1; Arrington 2015 tb. 2 46.26	Eretria (Toumba T 46.26)
6	Headdress	Pyrga	Serpentine	Standing griffin, linear border	Reyes 2001: 38 no. 7	Nicosia 1960. xi-21.26

7	Headdress	Zagora	Glazed steatite	Seated goddess Ma'at; border of reeds and ovals; *nb* basket	Cambitoglou 1981: no. 296	Andros (inv. no. 1300)
8	Headdress	No provenance	Glazed steatite	Ma'at feather, bee, and uraeus	Giustozzi 2016: 112 no. 1	Naples Rm XXI case 49
9	Headdress	No provenance	Glazed steatite	Cartouche *mn ḫpr Rʿ*	Hall 1913: no. 765	BM EA 46248
10	Headdress	No provenance	Glazed steatite	Cartouche *mn ḫpr Rʿ* with winged solar disk, two Ma'at feathers, and *nb* basket	Hall 1913: no. 796	BM EA 27048o
11	Headdress	No provenance	Serpentine	Horse group	Reyes 2001: 38 fig. 32a	Ashmolean 1914.59
12	Headdress	No provenance	Serpentine	Horse group; unusual seal with head carved in profile	Reyes 2001: 38 fig. 32b–c	Geneva 20449
13	Headdress	No provenance	Serpentine	Standing two-winged deity in long robe and headdress carrying scepter; object with rounded top in front	Reyes 2001: 39 no. 12	Nicosia D.62
14	Headdress	No provenance	Serpentine	Striding lion	Reyes 2001: 210 fig. 534	Geneva 20452
15	Headdress	No provenance	Serpentine	Kneeling bull and palm leaf	Eisen 1940: no. 125	MMA 1985.357.35
16	Headdress	No provenance	Serpentine	Horned animal with branch	Eisen 1940: no. 126	
17	Headdress	No provenance	Serpentine	Deer fleeing hunter, vegetation	Vollenweider 1983: 57 no. 89	Geneva 20449
18	Headdress	No provenance	Serpentine	Man chasing goat	Zazoff 1983: 69 pl. 13,1	Munich, Slg. Arndt Nr. 1110

(*continued*)

Appendix 5.2: Continued

Catalog number	Type	Site	Material	Obverse	Bibliography	Museum
19	Physiognomic	Amathus	Serpentine	Winged uraeus	Karageorghis 1988: 19 no. 11; Clerc 1991: 25; Reyes 2001: 36 no. 4 fig. 29	Limmasol (Amathus T. 242/76)
20	Physiognomic	Amathus	Serpentine	Quadruped	Karageorghis 1988: 19 no. 10; Clerc 1991: 19; Reyes 2001: 37 no. 5 fig. 30	Limmasol (Amathus T. 236/60)
21	Physiognomic	Amathus	Serpentine	Blank	Reyes 2001: 209 no. 528, fig. 527	MMA 74.51.5010
22	Physiognomic	Amathus	Ivory	Blank	Karageorghis 1989: 798 fig. 43; Reyes 2001: 209 no. 529, fig. 528	Limmasol (Amathus T. 542)
23	Physiognomic	Carthage	Serpentine	Blank	Vercoutter 1945: no. 908	
24	Physiognomic	Idalion	Serpentine	Blank	Reyes 2001: 210 no. 532 fig. 529a	MMA 74.51.1361

25	Physiognomic	Kourion	Serpentine	Blank	Karageorghis 1988: 15 no. 6; Reyes 2001: 210 no. 533 fig. 530	Episkopi (Kourion St. 871)
26	Physiognomic	Tyre	Serpentine	Spirals and loops	Walters 1926: no. 314 Reyes 2001: 38 no. 8 fig. 33	BM 1886,0909.2
27	Physiognomic	No provenance	Serpentine	Deer attacked by lion from behind, hatched border		Ashmolean 1891.624
28	Physiognomic	No provenance	Serpentine	Bird with object on either side	Karageorghis 1988: 39 no. 31; Reyes 2001: 38 no. 9 fig. 34	BM 1899,1101.1
29	Physiognomic	No provenance	Serpentine	Winged griffin, hatched border	Vollenweider 1983: 116 no. 158; Karageorghis 1988: 18 no. 9; Reyes 2001: 39 no. 10 fig. 35	Geneva 20451
30	Physiognomic	No provenance	Serpentine	Two quadrupeds, linear border	Karageorghis 1988: 17 no. 8; Reyes 2001: 39 no. 11 fig. 36	Paris Bib. Nat. (= de Clercq 2577)
31	Physiognomic	No provenance	Serpentine	Running goat with head turned back	Vollenweider 1983: 116 no. 156; Reyes 2001: 211 fig. 532	Geneva 20448
32	Physiognomic	No provenance	Serpentine	Striding griffin	Vollenweider 1983: 116 no. 157; Reyes 2001: 211 fig. 533	Geneva 20450

(*continued*)

Appendix 5.2: Continued

Catalog number	Type	Site	Material	Obverse	Bibliography	Museum
33	Bearded	Amathus	Serpentine	Blank	Karageorghis 1973: 622 fig. 145; Reyes 2001: 34 fig. 28a	Limmasol (Amathus T. 550/70)
34	Bearded	Amathus	Ivory	Blank	Karageorghis 1989: 801 fig. 42; Reyes 2001: 34 fig. 28b	Limmasol (Amathus T. 550/70)
35	Bearded	Amathus	Serpentine	Blank	Boardman 1991: 162 pl. 5 no. 1	Limmasol (Amathus T. 142/70)
36	Bearded	Amathus	Serpentine	Blank	Boardman 1991: 162 pl. 5 no. 2	Limmasol (Amathus T. 200/169)
37	Bearded	Amathus	Serpentine	Blank	Boardman 1991: 162 pl. 5 no. 3	Limmasol (Amathus T. 232/50)
38	Bearded	Amathus	Serpentine	Blank	Boardman 1991: 162 pl. 5 no. 4; Reyes 2001: 34 fig. 28c	Limmasol (Amathus T. 297/810.4)
39	Bearded	Amathus	Serpentine	Blank	Boardman 1991: 162 pl. 5 no. 5; Reyes 2001: 34 fig. 28c	Limmasol (Amathus T. 297/810.5)
40	Bearded	Amathus	Serpentine	Blank	Boardman 1991: 162 pl. 5 no. 6; Reyes 2001: 34 fig. 28c	Limmasol (Amathus T. 297/810.6)
41	Bearded	Amathus	Serpentine	Blank	Boardman 1991: 162 pl. 5 no. 7; Reyes 2001: 34 fig. 28c	Limmasol (Amathus T. 297/810.7)
42	Bearded	Amathus	Serpentine	Blank	Reyes 2001: 34 n. 21	BM 1894,1101.415
43	Bearded	Salamis	Serpentine	Blank	Karageorghis 1970: 168; Reyes 2001: 210 no. 531 fig. 534	
44	Bearded	No provenance	Serpentine	Blank		MMA 74.51.5011

Appendix 5.3: Faience Head Scaraboid Distribution

	Headdress	Physiognomic	Total
Aegina		1	1
Amrit	1		1
Apollonia Pontica		1	1
Athens		1	1
Berezan		1	1
Carthage	9	4	13
Conca	2		2
Gordion	1		1
Ialysos	1		1
Ibiza	1		1
Kameiros	3	1	4
Lindos	1		1
Naukratis	10	6	16
Olbia	1		1
Porto do Sabugeiro	1		1
Perachora		2	2
Samos	1		1
Taranto		1	1
Tharros	2	2	4
Tocra	1		1
No provenance	10		10
Total	**44**	**19**	**63**

Appendix 5.4: Faience Head Scaraboid Catalog

Catalog number	Type	Site	Color	Obverse	Bibliography	Museum
1	Headdress	Amrit	Blue	Winged lion striding right	Gorton 1996: 123 XXXIV.A.15	BM EA 48120
2	Headdress	Carthage	White	Horus wearing pschent, uraeus, *nb* basket	Vercoutter 1945 no. 455; Gorton 1996: 44 XV.A.36	
3	Headdress	Carthage	Blue	Couchant lion, three gods, *nb* basket	Vercoutter 1945 no. 452; Gorton 1996:: 6 XXVI.A.16	
4	Headdress	Carthage	White	Crocodile on shrine with Ma'at feather	Vercoutter 1945: no. 456; Gorton 1996: 119 XXXIII.A.42	
5	Headdress	Carthage	White	Titulature for golden Horus name (*ḥr nbw*) with god holding scepter	Vercoutter 1945 no. 459; Gorton 1996: 119 XXXIII.A.44	
6	Headdress	Carthage	Blue	Thoth with Horus falcon over open mouth (*wr*, meaning "the great")	Vercoutter 1945 no. 458; Gorton 1996: 123 XXXIV.A.11	
7	Headdress	Carthage	Blue	Couchant sphinx crowned with Pschent holding water jar; Horus falcon and Uraeus	Vercoutter 1945 no. 462; Gorton 1996: 123 XXXIV.A.12	
8	Headdress	Carthage	Blue	Couchant sphinx crowned with sun disc holding water jar	Vercoutter 1945 no. 463; Gorton 1996: 123 XXXIV.A.13	
9	Headdress	Carthage	Blue	Falcon-headed sphinx with Ankh	Vercoutter 1945 no. 464; Gorton 1996: 123 XXXIV.A.14	

10	Headdress	Carthage	Blue	Bes holding a lion crowned with a Uraeus in each hand; sky with rain above, *nb* basket below	Vercoutter 1945: no. 465; Gorton 1996: 136 XXXIX.3	
11	Headdress	Conca	White	Illegible	Hölbl 1979: 2 no. 683	Rome, Villa Giulia
12	Headdress	Conca	White	Man pointing right with animal	Hölbl 1979: 2 no. 684	Rome, Villa Giulia
13	Headdress	Gordion	White	Winged lion striding right	Dusinbere 2005: cat. no. 23 fig. 147a–b	
14	Headdress	Ialysos	White	Date palm with two monkey above *nb* basket	Skon-Jedele 1994: no. 4710	Rhodes (inv. no. Σ75)
15	Headdress	Ibiza			Vives y Escudero 1917: 107 no. 657	
16	Headdress	Kameiros	Blue	Cartouche *nfr-ỉb-Rꜥ* ?	Hall 1913: no. 2589; Skon-Jedele 1994 no. 3215; Gorton 1996: 119 XXXIII.A.45	BM 1861,0425.15
17	Headdress	Kameiros	Blue	Goat eating flower	Walters 1926: no. 262; Gorton 1996: 119 XXXIII.A.46	BM 1861,0425.16
18	Headdress	Kameiros	Red	Winged lion striding right	Walters 1926: no. 298; Gorton 1996: 119 XXXIII.A.47	BM 1861,0425.14
19	Headdress	Lindos	Blue	Cartouche *mn-kꜣ-Rꜥ*	Blinkenberg 1931: 1371; Skon Jedele 1994: no. 3824; Gorton 1996: 4 XXV.B.22	
20	Headdress	Naukratis	White	Winged lion striding right	Petrie 1886: pl. 37 no. 26; Gorton 1996: 97 XXVIII.A.116	BM EA 66445
21	Headdress	Naukratis	White	Papyrus flower and two buds	Petrie 1886: pl. 37 no. 4; Gorton 1996: 99 XXVIII.A.169	BM EA 66432

(*continued*)

Appendix 5.4: Continued

Catalog number	Type	Site	Color	Obverse	Bibliography	Museum
22	Headdress	Naukratis	Red	Scorpion	Petrie 1886 pl. 37 no. 9; Gorton 1996: 100 XXVIII.A.203; Masson-Berghoff 2018: 19 fig. 43	Louvre E8056 bis.2
23	Headdress	Naukratis	White	Duck with sun disc ($z\underline{3}\ R^c$, "Son of Re") with Maàt feather	Petrie 1886 pl. 37 no. 83; Gorton 1996: 102 XXVIII.B.36	
24	Headdress	Naukratis	Blue	Winged sphinx	Petrie 1886 pl. 37 no. 133; Gorton 1996: 106 XXXIII.C.8	BM EA66507
25	Headdress	Naukratis	Blue	Winged goddess with two snakes	Petrie 1886 pl. 37 no. 141; Gorton 1996: 124 XXXIV.B.24	
26	Headdress	Naukratis	White	Two crocodiles	Petrie 1886 pl. 37 no. 11; Gorton 1996: 130 XXXVI.35	BM EA66437
27	Headdress	Naukratis	Blue	Illegible	Gardner 1888 pl. 18 no. 59; Masson-Berghoff 2018: 5 fig. 2	MFA 88.726
28	Headdress	Naukratis	White	Winged figure with two cobras	Petrie 1886 pl. 37 no. 141; Gorton 1996: 124 XXXIV.B.24	BM EA 66513
29	Headdress	Naukratis	Blue	Couchant sphinx	Petrie 1886: pl. 37 no. 142; Gorton 1996: 123 XXXIV.A.16	BM EA 66514
30	Headdress	Olbia	Blue	Two animals	Touraïeff 1911 fig. 2; Alekseeva 1975: 40 pl. 9.1; Parmenter 2019: 20 n. 37	Hermitage Oa.1908-2726
31	Headdress	Porto do Sabugeiro		Cartouche $mn-k\underline{3}-R^c$ with two wedjet eyes	Harrison 1988: 351 fig. 86	

32	Headdress	Samos	Brown	Duck with sun disc (*s3 Rʿ*, "Son of Reʿ") with *Maʿat* feather	Webb 2016: 99 no. 167	Kassel Antikenssamlung S 79a
33	Headdress	Tharros	White	Horus falcon wearing Atef crown over *nb* basket	Hölbl 1986: 2 Tb. 124/1	Cagliari
34	Headdress	Tharros	White	Unspecified hieroglyphic	Hölbl 1986: 2 Tb. 124/3	Cagliari inv. no. 19685
35	Headdress	Tocra	White	Two facing antelopes with vegetation, solar disks, and schematic x	Boardman and Hayes 1966: 165 no. 92; Gorton 1996 XXXIV.B.23	
36	Headdress	No provenance	Glazed steatite	Cartouche *mn ḫpr Rʿ*	Hall 1913: no. 765	BM EA 46248
37	Headdress	No provenance	Glazed steatite	Cartouche *mn ḫpr Rʿ*	Hall 1913: no. 796	BM EA 27048o
38	Headdress	No provenance	Blue	Cartouche *mn ḫpr Rʿ*	Hall 1913: no. 1238	BM EA 41864
39	Headdress	No provenance	Blue	Cartouche *mn ḫpr Rʿ*	Hall 1913: no. 1239	BM EA 48788
40	Headdress	No provenance	Green	*Rʿ ḫpr* between two *Maʿat* feathers	Hall 1913: no. 1240	BM EA 38571
41	Headdress	No provenance	Green	Cartouche *mn ḫpr Rʿ*	Hall 1913: no. 1241	BM EA 30629
42	Headdress	No provenance	White	Cartouche *mn ḫpr Rʿ*	Hall 1913: no. 1888	BM EA 16917
43	Headdress	No provenance	White	*mn Rʿ* over *t* surrounded by pattern of open mouths	Hall 1913: no. 2535	BM EA 45777
44	Headdress	No provenance	Green	*mn ḫpr* with *Maʿat* feather		MMA 1926.7.177

(continued)

Appendix 5.4: Continued

Catalog number	Type	Site	Color	Obverse	Bibliography	Museum
45	Physiognomic	Aegina	Blue	Couchant winged lion	Furtwängler, Fiechter, and Thiersch 1906: 433 no. 19; Skon-Jedele 1994 no. 1302	Aegina (inv. no. 228)
46	Physiognomic	Apollonia Pontica	Blue	Griffin striding right	Baralis, Panayatova, and Nedev 2019: cat. 195.	Sozopol (inv. no. 3694).
47	Physiognomic	Athens	Blue	Lion attacking bull	Spier 1992: 15 no. 8	Getty 85.AN.370.5
48	Physiognomic	Berezan	Blue	Griffin striding right	Bolshakov and Ilyna 1988: fig. 2 no. 29, tb. 1 no. 6; Solovyev 2005: no. 204; Parmenter 2019: 20 n. 31, fig. 2	Hermitage Б-79.179
49	Physiognomic	Carthage	Brown	Cartouche W_3h-ib-R^c with Bastet cat	Vercoutter 1945 no. 451; Gorton 1996: 97 XXVIII.A.117	
50	Physiognomic	Carthage	Green	i-mn nb ("Lord Amun Re")	Vercoutter 1945 no. 457; Gorton 1996: 119 XXXIII.A.43	
51	Physiognomic	Carthage	Grey	Quadruped striding right with vegetation	Vercoutter 1945: no. 461	
52	Physiognomic	Carthage	White	Illegible	Vercoutter 1945: no. 466; Gorton 1996: 127 XXXV.8	
53	Physiognomic	Kameiros	Green	s htp Sbk ("Offered to Sebek")	Hall 1913: no. 193	BM 1861,0425.17

54	Physiognomic	Naukratis	White	Cartouche *mn ḫpr Rˁ*	Petrie 1886: pl. 37 65; Gorton 1996: 105 XXVIII.B.151
55	Physiognomic	Naukratis	White	Winged lion striding right wearing Pschent	Gardner 1888 pl. 18 no. 55; Gorton 1996: 97 XXVIII.A.114 BM EA 35981
56	Physiognomic	Naukratis	Brown	*mn Rˁ* with Horus falcon	Petrie 1886 pl. 37 no. 100; Gorton 1996: 97 XXVIII.A.115 BM EA 66493
57	Physiognomic	Naukratis	Blue	Winged lion facing right	Gardner 1888 pl. 18 no. 60; Masson-Berghoff 2018: 5 fig. 2 MFA 88.726
58	Physiognomic	Naukratis	Blue	Winged lion striding right	Gardner 1888: pl. 18 no. 61; Gorton 1996: 126 XXXIV.C.13 MFA 88.872
59	Physiognomic	Naukratis	Blue	Seated goddess *Maʿat* with *nb* basket	Gardner 1888 pl. 18 no. 32; Gorton 1996: 119 XXXIII.A.21 or A23 Chautauqua, NY (lost)
60	Physiognomic	Perachora	Blue	Illegible	James 1962: no. D65; Skon-Jedele 1994L no. 0293
61	Physiognomic	Perachora	Blue	Winged lion couchant	James 1962: no. D501; Skon-Jedele 1994 no. 0862
62	Physiognomic	Taranto	White	*mn Rˁ*	Hölbl 1979: 2 no. 1220 Taranto (inv. no. 117.274)
63	Physiognomic	Tharros	Blue	Unspecified	Hölbl 1986: Tb. 124/2 Cagliari
64	Physiognomic	Tharros	Blue	Unspecified	Hölbl 1986: Tb. 124/4 Cagliari

APPENDIX 6

Catalogue of Enslaved Journeys

Enslaved Captives Known from Documents

Achillodoros: *CGP* 25; previous edition *SEG* 26.845. Author of lead letter from Berezan, circa 550–500 BCE; for description of the text see Dana 2021: 114–16. Achillodoros was held captive and deprived of his cargoes, including male and female captives, by a rival merchant named Matasys. Vinogradov (1971, *editio princeps*) and Gallavotti (1990: 156) express the minority opinion that δολõται should be read as δολοῦται (to defraud) rather than δουλοῦται (to enslave), but this has not been accepted; for the latter reading, see Bravo 1974: 124–25. On the role of Achillodoros' wife or other family members in trade, see Eidinow and Taylor 2010: 38; on whether he was Anaxagoras' agent, see Bravo 1974; Lintott 2004: 342; E. M. Harris 2013: 113–17; Dana 2021: 383–91. For further comment see L. Dubois 1996: 50–55 no. 23; J.-P. Wilson 1997–98: 36–39; Heinen 2001a: 490–92; Avram 2007: 239; Fischer 2016: 54; Lamont 2023: 3–5.

Achillodoros' captives: See entry for *Achillodoros. Eidinow and Taylor (2010: 38–39) comment on the frequency of instructions to or about slaves in the letters. The *captive belonging to Aristonymos, the *enslaved woman belonging to Melas, and *Thymoleos' slaves also change hands in payment for debt.

Fugitives from Priest's Letter: *CGP* 28; previous editions *SEG* 42.710, 51.970. Referenced in a letter from Olbia inscribed on the back of a Fikellura sherd dated to c. 500 BCE; for description of the text see Dana 2021: 142–43. L. Dubois (1996: 55–64 no. 24) downdates the letter to c. 400, but this has not been accepted. The *editio princeps* is Rusjaeva and Vinogradov (1991: 201--2); Bravo (2001) suspects the document was later reused for ritual purposes; for recent discussion, see Dana 2021: 147–48.

Metrophanes' captive: See entry for *fugitives from Priest's Letter. Likely a consecrated slave consecrated to the god. This form of quasi-manumission is well attested in the Hellenistic period; for summary, see Zanovello 2018: 130.

Phaylles: *CGP* 49; previous edition *SEG* 48.1012. Subject of a lead letter from Phanagoria, c. 530–510 BCE; for description of the text see Dana 2021: 209. Phaylles is traded in Berezan in exchange for a cancellation of debt; this is the earliest known sales receipt for a slave in the Greek world. See Vinogradov 1998: 160–63 no. 3; Dana 2007: 87–88; Avram 2007: 239; Tsetskhladze 2007a: 316; Eidinow and Taylor 2010: 38; Fischer 2016: 54; Lamont 2023: 8–9.

Captive belonging to Aristonymos: *CGP* 48; *editio princeps* Zavojkina and Pavlichenko 2016. Subject of a letter from Phanagoria, c. 450–400 BCE. Pistros writes to Aristonymos to inform him of his debts to Sapasis, including a gold stater and a slave (ἀνδράποδον). Sapasis is a non-Greek name; see Matasys in the entry for *Achillodoros. These captives' situation is possibly similar to that of *Melas' enslaved woman and *Thymeleos' slaves. See Lamont 2023: 4.

Enslaved woman belonging to Melas: *CGP* 23; previous edition *SEG* 48.911. Referenced in a lead letter from Olbia, c. 540–535 BCE; her situation is possibly similar to that of *Thymeleos' slaves and *Aristonymos' slave. For description of the text see Dana 2021: 106–7. For further discussion see Vinogradov 1998: 154–56 no. 1; Avram 2007: 239; Eidinow and Taylor 2010: 38–39.

Enslaved business agent belonging to Melas: *CGP* 23. Dana argues (2021: 108) on the basis of the *Phaylles letter that l. 2's παι should be read as vocative of παῖς, "boy." If so, it is possible that this individual could be an enslaved business agent.

Captives belonging to Thymoleos: *CGP* 26. Referenced in lead letter from Olbia, c. 500 BCE; their situation is possibly similar to that of *Melas' slave woman and *Aristonymos' slave. For further comment see J.-P. Wilson 1997–98: 38–40; Vinogradov 1998: 157; Dana 2007: 75–76; Avram 2007: 239. Eidinow and Taylor (2010: 38–39) comment on the frequency of instructions to or about slaves in the letters.

Enslaved Captives Known from Literary Sources

Aesop: Hdt. 2.134–35; Aristophanes *Birds* 471; *Vitae* G and W. Aesop's earliest appearance is in either Aristophanes or Herodotus, where he is the slave of Xanthos of Samos, also owner of *Rhodopis. *Vita* W 20 lists his place of sale as Ephesus. He was later manumitted and killed by the Delphians. It is not known how early Aesop was considered to be a historical figure; his eagle and fox fable appears without attestation as early as Archil. fr. 174 West. Herodotus gives Aesop a Thracian origin; the *Suda* (Perry 1952: 215 no. 3) notes disagreement over whether he was Phrygian, Lydian, or a Thracian from Messembria on the Black Sea. *Vitae* G and W list his ethnicity as Phrygian; see Andreeva 2017: 606–7. Kurke (2011: 13) describes him as a "mobile, free-floating figure in ancient culture." For extended discussions see Perry 1952; Kurke 2011; Forsdyke 2012: 61–65; Fischer 2013: 554–55.

Bion of Borysthenes: Diog. Laert. 4.46. Son of a formerly enslaved fish-salter and prostitute, suffered this fate after his father failed to pay taxes. After his family was sold at Olbia, Bion was bought by a *rhêtor* "on account of [his] youth and graciousness" (νεώτερον ὄντα καὶ εὔχαριν, Diog. Laert. 4.46), instructed in philosophy, freed, and allowed to emigrate to Athens to make a living. See Blavatsky 1954: 30, no. 10.

Colchian girl: Aelian fr. 71 Hercher = fr. 74a–h Domingo-Foraste; the badly garbled text has been reconstructed from *scholia* by editors. She was originally from Colchis and was captured by the Machyles, bought by Dionysios of Chios on the Sea of Azov, and sold on Chios. Narratives of invidious East Greek masters date to as early as the fifth century; see entries for *Aesop and *Hermotimos. For discussion see Blavatskiy 1954: 47; Avram 2007: 244; Tsetskhladze 2007a: 316; Fischer 2016: 56.

Hermotimos of Pedasos: Hdt. 8.104–5. A Carian prisoner of war bought by Panionios of Chios, castrated, and sold in Sardis; later he was a prized eunuch of Xerxes. He lures Panionios and his sons to Sardis, where he has the latter castrated. Eunuch dealers feature conspicuously in ancient attacks on slave dealers: e.g., Suet. *Dom.* 7.2, Mart. 9.5; for further discussion see Harrill 1999: 111–13; Braund 2007b: 15–16.

Lycaon, son of Priam: *Il.* 21.30–135. Achilles captures Lykaon and sells him for a hundred oxen on Lemnos; he is ransomed by his family. Days later he is murdered by Achilles after his plea for clemency is rejected on the battlefield. Simone Weil presented Lykaon's murder as the central exhibit in her study of violence in the *Iliad*; see Weil 1965: 7–8, 18–22, 25.

Rhodopis or Doricha the Thracian: Hdt. 2.134–35; Strabo 17.1.33; Ath. 13.596d; Posidippus AG 6.207; *SEG* 13.364. Legendary; between late seventh and mid-sixth centuries. She was owned by Iadmon son of Hephaistopolis of Samos, also owner of Aesop; she was sold and brought to Egypt by Xanthos of Samos. Herodotus claims that she was manumitted by Charoxos of Lesbos, brother of Sappho (late seventh/early sixth cent.), but also that she lived in time of Amasis (mid-sixth c.). Herodotus reports that she dedicated at Delphi; a late sixth-century offering base inscribed ἀνέθη]κε Ῥοδ[ῶπις is potentially hers (*SEG* 13.364). Rhodopis is a popular in sixth- and fifth-century *Lieblingsinschriften* and appears on several vessels, although doubtfully a sherd from Naukratis published Ῥοδ[-- by Petrie; see Petrie 1886: 62 no. 531. On Rhodopis stories see Kurke 1999: 220–27; Möller 2000: 199; Vasunia 2001: 82–87; Demetriou 2012: 141; on slavery in Aesop myths, Kurke 2011: 61–63.

Salmoxis: Hdt. 4.94–96, Strabo 7.3.5. Herodotus relates a tale from the Greeks of the Pontus who claim that Salmoxis, a Thracian of the Getae tribe, was the slave of Pythagoras on Samos. He returned home to beguile his countrymen into thinking he was a god. Strabo makes the additional claim that he visited Egypt; see entry for *Rhodopis. The case that Thracian religion was shaped by the returnees is plausible.

Matory (2005: 64) notes the importance of freedman returnees in Afro-Brazilian religious movements. This case, however, appears to be religious libel. For further discussion see Eliade and Trask 1972; Braund 2008: 257–59.

Freedmen accompanied by Herodes: Antiph. 5.20. The speaker in *On the Murder of Herodes* mentions that Herodes was accompanying some Thracian freedmen from Athens who had been ransomed to Ainos in the North Aegean. They were joined by additional Thracians who had been manumitted. The "reverse" slave trade in returnees is poorly studied; for analogous cases from nineteenth-century Brazil, see Law and Mann 1999: 318–22.

Notes

INTRODUCTION

1. Nails 2002: 275.
2. Ἀλλά, παῖ, λαβὲ τὸ βιβλίον καὶ λέγε.
3. Πάνυ μὲν οὖν ... ἵνα κἀγὼ ἐμαυτὸν ἀνασκέψωμαι ποῖόν τι ἔχω τὸ πρόσωπον·.
4. προσέοικε δὲ σοὶ τήν τε σιμότητα καὶ τὸ ἔξω τῶν ὀμμάτων.
5. Ἀλλ' ἐὰν δὴ μὴ μόνον τὸν ἔχοντα ῥῖνα καὶ ὀφθαλμοὺς διανοηθῶ, ἀλλὰ καὶ τὸν σιμόν τε καὶ ἐξόφθαλμον μή τι σὲ αὖ μᾶλλον δοξάσω ἢ ἐμαυτὸν ἢ ὅσοι τοιοῦτοι.
6. Citizens from the mining demes are disproportionately represented in fourth-century triarchy lists; see Crosby 1950: 205.
7. πρὸς τὴν τῶν χρημάτων ἐλευθεριότητα θαυμαστός.
8. τὸ δὲ παράψηστον θεραπαινίδιον διακέκριται τὰς τρίχας, ὑπόσιμον δ' ἐστὶ.
9. Gleason 1996: 55.
10. αἱ διάνοιαι ἕπονται τοῖς σώμασι.
11. Lape 2010: 186.
12. Parmenter 2024a; e.g. Morton 1842: 65; Holmes 1850: 194.
13. "Greek and Roman antiquity did not know the sort of racism that western civilization developed in the nineteenth and twentieth centuries, since they had no concept of biological determinism" (Isaac 2004: 37).
14. Reed 2013: 49.
15. E. Williams 1994 [1944]: 7–29; Robinson 2000 [1983]: 9.
16. J. Murray 2021: 144.
17. Heng 2018: 3.
18. Seth 2020: 363.
19. Tanner 2010; McCoskey 2012; Matić 2018; Padilla Peralta 2021; McCoskey 2021; Greenwood 2022a.
20. Heng 2018: 3.

21. The Ptolemaic practice of *eikonismos* has a fascinating history, albeit after the period of this book. I hope to discuss this practice further in a forthcoming article. Starting in the late third century BCE, Ptolemaic notaries recorded the personal appearance of contract signatories using a vocabulary culled from the Greek anatomical lexicon of the Classical Period. While prewar racialist historians saw this practice as an early form of biometrics, scholars today agree that physical descriptions were meant to aid the enforceability of contracts. A typical notarial follows a set form, e.g., Hermias, son of Asklepiades, Persian of the reserve force, around twenty-five years of age, tall ([εὐμεγέθ]ης), of honey complexion (μελίχρως), curly haired (κλ[αστ]ὸς), long of face (μακροπρόσωπος), and of straight nose (εὐθύ[ριν]) who was recorded in *SB* 18.13168 in 123 BCE. On the history of this practice, see Clarysse 1991: 48–55; DePauw 2011: 190–92; Yftach 2019: 83.
22. Dee 2004: 162.
23. Albeit complications raised by Eaverly 2013: 4–7.
24. Davidson 1998: 159–67.
25. "She's reasonably dark, like me, with eyebrows that meet in the middle" (μείξοφρυς / μέλαιν' ἐπιεικῶς κατ' ἐμέ) vouches an unknown character in Pherecrates (fr. 187 K-A). Aristophanes' *Women at the Thesmophoria* is a particularly rich source of erotic color discourse. One lover is judged for her complexion. (406): "the girl's color does not please me at all" (τὸ χρῶμα τοῦτό μ' ἀρέσκει τῆς κόρης). Meanwhile, our protagonist, the tragedian Agathon, gets to have it all ways: he is described scornfully by a kinsman first as "the dark-skinned, strong one" (ὁ μέλας, ὁ κρατερός) (31) and later as "pale" and "soft" (λευκός . . . ἁπλός) (191–92). In the *Women in the Assembly*, Praxagora boasts that in a world turned upside down, men will have to sleep with old women first to access the "most beautiful and fairest" (καὶ καλλίστη καὶ λευκοτάτη) (699); but new opportunities will be available for "flat-nosed and ugly men" (τοῖς γὰρ σιμοῖς καὶ τοῖς αἰσχροῖς) (705).
26. A. Cohen 2011: 480–81.
27. Cf. Skinner (2012: 14–19), who defines ethnography as a mode of discourse, rather than specific genre.
28. Aeschylus describes Egyptians as a "dark, sun-struck race" (μελανθὲς / ἡλιόκτυπον γένος), *Supp.* 155–56; a "dark dream" (ὄναρ μέλαν), *Supp.* 890; and dark people" (κελαινὸν φῦλον), *PB* 808. Herodotus describes Egyptians as dark-skinned (μελαίνας, 2.55.1; μελάγχροες, 2.104.2) and curly haired (οὐλότριχες, 2.104.2); Ethiopians have dark skin (μέλαινα, 3.101.1) and curly hair (οὐλότατον τρίχωμα ἔχουσι πάντων ἀνθρώπων, 7.70.2); Scythians have very light skin (λαμπραί, 4.75.3). The Hippocratic author describes Scythians as light skinned (ἡ λευκότης) and ruddy (Πυρρόν, πυρρή, *AWP* 20); both Scythians and Egyptians are "homogenous in regard to the beauty of their bodies" (Περὶ δὲ τῶν ὡρέων καὶ τῆς μορφῆς . . . ἔοικεν αὐτὸ ἑωυτέῳ, *AWP* 19).
29. Robertson 2008: tb. 5.2.
30. Vlassopoulos 2010: 124; quote is from Finley 1980: 118.

31. τί τῶν λεγόντων εἰσὶ δυσγενέστεροι; / ὃς ἂν εὖ γεγονὼς ᾖ τῇ φύσει πρὸς τἀγαθά, / κἂν Αἰθίοψ ᾖ, μῆτερ, ἐστὶν εὐγενής. / Σκύθης τις· ὄλεθρος· ὁ δ᾽ Ἀνάχαρσις οὐ Σκύθης; ("What of those who say some people are low-born? Who is born so well in regards to all the finer qualities—mother, even if he is an Ethiopian he is wellborn. What about the Scythian? Is he low-born? Wasn't Anacharsis a Scythian?" Men. fr. 835.10–14 K-A) This passage clearly reflects animus toward both Ethiopians and Thracians; see L. Thompson 1989: 181–82.

32. Alan Cameron argues (1995: 233–39) this Didyme was the Egyptian lover of Ptolemy II described in Athenaeus 576e = *FGrH* 234 F4, thus dating Asclepiades (named in Theoc. *Id.* 7.40) decades older than Theocritus. Snowden (1992) argues against this precise definition but states she must be an Ethiopian, not an Egyptian, because of her skin-tone (καὶ ἄνθρακες).

33. εἰ δὲ μέλαινα, τί τοῦτο; καὶ ἄνθρακες· ἀλλ᾽ ὅτε κείνους / θάλψωμεν, λάμπουσ᾽ ὡς ῥόδεαι κάλυκες.

34. Theocritus deploys the language of the body widely. The protagonists of *Idylls* 3, 6, and 11 are spurned lovers (in *Idylls* 6 and 11, identified as the Cyclops Polyphemus) moping over their physical flaws. These are identified as unusually prominent chins (καλὰ μὲν τὰ γένεια *Id.* 3.9, προγένειος *Id.* 6.36), flat noses (σιμός, *Id.* 3.8; πλατεῖα δὲ ῥίς, *Id.* 11.33), noticeable lips (ἐπὶ χείλει, *Id.* 11.33), and hairy brows (λασία μὲν ὀφρὺς ἐπὶ παντὶ μετώπῳ, *Id.* 11.32).

35. Βομβύκα χαρίεσσα, Σύραν καλέοντί τυ πάντες, / ἰσχνάν, ἁλιόκαυστον, ἐγὼ δὲ μόνος μελίχλωρον. / καὶ τὸ ἴον μέλαν ἐστί

36. Ἀγένειός εἰμι, καὶ γὰρ ὁ Διόνυσος· μέλας, καὶ γὰρ ὁ ὑάκινθος· ἀλλὰ κρείττων καὶ ὁ Διόνυσος Σατύρων <καὶ> ὁ ὑάκινθος κρίνων. Οὗτος δὲ καὶ πυρρὸς ὡς ἀλώπηξ καὶ προγένειος ὡς τράγος καὶ λευκὸς ὡς ἐξ ἄστεος γυνή. ("I am boyish but so is Dionysus; dark, but so is the hyacinth; but Dionysus is better than the satyrs and the hyacinth is better than white lilies. He [Dorkon] is reddish like the fox, big-chinned like the goat, and fair like a townswoman").

37. ὁ δὲ μέλας νεανίσκος νεώτερος, καθειμένος τὰς ὀφρῦς, πεπαιδευμένῳ ἢ φιλογυμναστῇ ἐοικώς. ὁ δ᾽ οὖλος νεανίσκος μᾶλλον νέος, ὑπέρυθρος τὸ χρῶμα· αἱ δὲ τρίχες κατὰ τοὔνομα· ὀφρῦς ἀνατέταται, καὶ ῥυτὶς ἐπὶ τοῦ μετώπου μία. ὁ δ᾽ ἁπαλὸς νεανίσκος, τρίχες μὲν κατὰ τὸν πάγχρηστον, πάντων δὲ νεώτατος, λευκός, σκιατροφίας, ἁπαλότητα ὑποδηλῶν. τῷ δ᾽ ἀγροίκῳ τὸ μὲν χρῶμα μελαίνεται, τὰ δὲ χείλη πλατέα καὶ ἡ ῥὶς σιμή, καὶ στεφάνη τριχῶν ("The dark-skinned youth is younger, hair settled on his brow, in appearance like to an educated person or an athlete. The curly-haired youth is very young, reddish in skin-color; his hair is in accord with his name, rises from his face, and there is a pucker in his face. The tender young man has hair good for all uses, and is the youngest of all; he is light-skinned as he was brought up in the shade, and he hints at tenderness. The peasant is dark in his color, his lips broad and his nose flat, and he has a wreath of hair").

38. *multimodis igitur pravas turpisque videmus / esse in deliciis summoque in honore vigere. / atque alios alii inrident Veneremque suadent / ut placent, quoniam foedo*

adflictentur amore, / nec sua respiciunt miseri mala maxima saepe. / nigra melichrus est, inmunda et fetida acosmos, / caesia Palladium, nervosa et lignea dorcas, / parvula, pumilio, chariton mia, tota merum sal, / magna atque inmanis cataplexis plenaque honoris. / balba loqui non quit, traulizi, muta pudens est; / at flagrans, odiosa, loquacula Lampadium fit. / ischnon eromenion tum fit, cum vivere non quit / prae macie; rhadine verost iam mortua tussi. / at nimia et mammosa Ceres est ipsa ab Iaccho, / simula Silena ac Saturast, labeosa philema. / cetera de genere hoc longum est si dicere coner. ("Thus we see women who are deprived and disgusting in all sorts of ways are esteemed in their lovers' eyes in highest honor. And some lovers will even deride others, and even exhort them to propitiate Venus because they are afflicted by some disgusting infatuation—but these wretches won't even reflect upon their own misery! (Or, at least, not often). To them, a dark-skinned girl is 'honey-skinned,' a dirty and unwashed one is simply 'disorganized,' a gray-eyed girl is a 'little Minerva,' a nervous and strung-out girl is a 'little gazelle,' a gross little dwarf is 'one of the Graces,' and the epitome of style; a great big giant is a 'stunner,' and full of dignity; if she stutters but won't stop talking, she 'twitters like a bird,' and the silent one is simply modest; if she's all fired up with loathsome talk, she's made his 'little torch.' The thin girl is made his 'little lover,' even though she is too thin to live; 'slender' means almost dead with the cough. If she's fat and big-breasted she is Ceres herself after giving birth to Iacchus, a flat-nosed girl is a satyr or silena, and a full-lipped girl 'all kisses.' It would take an awful long time to go through the whole list").

39. *Nil nimium studeo, Caesar, tibi velle placere, / nec scire utrum sis albus an ater homo.* ("I'm not minded to care about you, Caesar, whether you're a man black or white"); for discussion, see Dee 2004: 157.

40. *nonne fuit satius tristis Amaryllidis iras / atque superba pati fastidia? nonne Menalcan, / quamuis / ille niger, quamuis tu candidus esses? / o formose puer, nimium ne crede colori: / alba ligustra cadunt, uaccinia nigra leguntur* ("Was it not enough to endure the anger and the pompous aversion of sad Amaryllis? Or Menaclas, although he is dark, and you are fair? Oh lovely boy, don't put excessive trust in color; the white privets fall, and the dark hyacinths are plucked").

41. *Si quis forte mihi possit praestare roganti, / Audi, quem puerum, Flacce, rogare velim. / Niliacis primum puer hic nascatur in oris: / Nequitias tellus scit dare nulla magis. / Sit nive candidior: namque in Mareotide fusca / Pulchrior est, quanto rarior, iste color. / Lumina sideribus certent mollesque flagellent / Colla comae: tortas non amo, Flacce, comas. / Frons brevis atque modus leviter sit naribus uncis, / Paestanis rubeant aemula labra rosis.* ("Hear me out, Flaccus, about what type of boy I'd like—if it's at all possible to fulfil my request. This boy here was born on the banks of the Nile; no land knows how to make worthlessness more than Egypt. No, let mine be whiter than snow; for even in the mud of Lake Mareotis that color stands out, if rarer by far. Let his eyes rival the stars, and soft hair dangle down his neck; you know I don't

like curly hair, Flaccus. Let his brow be short and let there be some measure to the curve of his nose; let his lips burn red like Paestum roses").

42. *Candida me doCuit nigras / OdIsse Pvellas; odero; sepotero; sed non InvItus / Amabo / Scripsit Venus Fiscia Pompeiana* ("A pale woman taught me to hate dark women; I would hate them if I could; but not unwilling, I will love them"). Cf. Haley 2021: 136.

43. *Quisquis amat nigra(m) nigris carbonibus artet / Nigra(m) cum video mora libenter <a>ed<e>o* ("Whoever loves a dark woman burns with dark coals; when I see a dark woman, I gladly eat blackberries"). Cf. Haley 2021: 136.

44. Heng 2018: 3.

45. E.g. Tuplin 1999: 47; Bérard 2000: 394; Isaac 2004: 37; Bagnall 2006 [1997]: 230; Gruen 2011: 197; Hunt 2018: 28; Harrison 2020: 153.

46. Seth 2020: 357–58.

47. ἐσθῆτά τε γὰρ οὐδὲν βελτίων ὁ δῆμος αὐτόθι ἢ οἱ δοῦλοι καὶ οἱ μέτοικοι καὶ τὰ εἴδη οὐδὲν βελτίους εἰσίν.

48. Gould 1996 [1981]: 51.

49. Boys-Stones 2007: 74 n. 119.

50. E.g. Frank 1916; Nilsson 1921 (retracted by Nilsson 1939); Myres 1930: 23–24; Diller 1937; Blegen 1940; Angel 1943; on this topic, see Saura 2014; K. Fields and B. Fields 2012: 4–11; McCoskey 2022: 261–71; Parmenter 2024a, Duray forthcoming.

51. Barkan 1992: 341–49; Brattain 2007: 1386–90.

52. E. Williams 1994 [1944]: 7–29.

53. Robinson 2000 [1983]: 9.

54. Keita 1993: 299.

55. Barkan 1992: 287.

56. Barth 1998 [1969]; see J. M. Hall 1997: 19–32; 2002: 9–19; Malkin 1998: 55–61.

57. Barkan 1992: 184; McCoskey 2003: 104; 2012: 27–29; Lape 2010: 37; McInerney 2014: 1.

58. Parmenter 2021a; Keita 2023; cf. Angel 1946.

59. Duster 2003.

60. E.g. Lazaridis et al. 2022; for critique, see Hakenbeck 2019; Maran 2022; Parmenter 2024b.

61. J.M. Hall 1997: 44–46; 2002: 9–19; 2015: 25.

62. E. Hall 1989a: 103.

63. Ros. Thomas 2000: 75–79.

64. E.g. Hartog 1988 [1980]; Bérard, Lissarrague, et al. 1989a [1984]; Lissarrague 1990; E. Hall 1989; Cartledge 1997; Vasunia 2001. The obvious debt to Edward Said [1978] in this work was rarely acknowledged; see Vasunia 2003. Summaries of this scholarship can be found in Luraghi 2014: 213–15; Harrison 2020: 139–45. The beginnings of the backlash against the "Other" can be found in Davidson 2002.

65. Malkin 2011: 9–15; Vlassopoulos 2013: 19–32.

66. Important early work includes C. Morgan 1991; Malkin 1998; essays collected in Malkin 2001; McInerney 1999; essays collected in Dougherty and Kurke 2003. A mere sample of important later publications would include Luraghi 2008; Dietler 2010; Malkin 2010; Demetriou 2012; Skinner 2012; essays collected by McInerney 2014; Vlassopoulos 2013, 2015; Mac Sweeney 2013, 2017; Porucznik 2021.
67. Hall (2002: 4) and Malkin (quoted in Shani 2014) highlight European integration as reason for such optimism; on the optimistic tendencies of the ethnicity paradigm, see Harrison 2020: 156–58.
68. Skinner 2012: 21–22.
69. E.g. Gruen 2011: 3.
70. Harrison 2020: 153.
71. Θρᾷττά τις ἐμμελὴς καὶ χαρίεσσα θεραπαινίς.
72. Plat. *Ap.* 20c1: "I congratulate Euenos if it's really the case that he has this skill—and teaches it so cheaply" (καὶ ἐγὼ τὸν Εὔηνον ἐμακάρισα εἰ ὡς ἀληθῶς ἔχοι ταύτην τὴν τέχνην καὶ οὕτως ἐμμελῶς διδάσκει). Enslaved Thracians famously drew low prices; see Alexianu 2011.
73. Lesher 1992: 3.
74. Trans. after Lesher 1992: 25.
75. Snowden 1971: 104; E. Hall 1989a: 185; Skinner 2012: 95.
76. Cf. Murray 2021. My formulation differs from Lape (2010), who theorizes that Classical Athenians saw themselves as a "race."
77. E.g., Goldenberg 1998; essays in J. J. Cohen 2000; Beidler and Taylor 2005.
78. Isaac 2004: 37; Eliav-Feldon, Isaac, and Ziegler 2009. For critique, see Haley 2005; McCoskey 2006; McInerney 2006.
79. Wheeler 2000: 28–33; Block 2016: 10–34.
80. Although scholars point to various earlier precedents, the first work squarely identifiable in adopting a Critical Race approach in the United States is Derrick Bell's legal casebook, *Race, Racism, and American Law* [1973]). Other important studies of this era include Centre for Contemporary Cultural Studies 1982; Robinson 2000 [1983]; Omi and Winant 2015 [1985]; H. L. Gates 1986; Gilroy 2010 [1987]; Crenshaw 1989; Rutherford 1990 [legible interview with Homi K. Bhabha]. CRT is an extremely slippery label; certain scholars expressed discomfort with the moniker even before its recent weaponization against scholars whose work even peripherally touches race (Kennedy 2022: 1). For an attempt at definition, see Delgado and Stefancic 2017 [2001]: 28–43.
81. K. Fields and B. Fields 2012: 17.
82. J. Murray 2021: 144.
83. K. Fields and B. Fields 2012: 17.
84. E.g., Omi and Winant (2015 [1986]: 7, 13): "a social structure deeply rooted . . . in institutions, fundamental patterns of inequality, social geography, and the exercise of political power [. . .] [through which] human bodies are visually read, understood, and narrated by means of symbolic meanings and associations."

85. Current literature on race in antiquity stems from the rise of Classical Reception as a major subdiscipline of Classical Studies in the late 2000s; for thematic discussions, see Rankine 2006: 22–34; Goff and Simpson 2007: 39–77; and Greenwood 2009, 2010: 1–19; and for a recap see Parmenter 2023. The 2010s saw a renewed interest in questions of race in the disciplinary history of Classical Studies and its related disciplines; see especially Tanner 2010; McCoskey 2012; and contributions to Orrells, Bhambra, and Roynon 2011; Matić 2018.
86. Seth 2020.
87. Heng 2018: 19: "Race-making thus operates as specific historical occasions in which strategic essentialisms are posited and assigned through a variety of practices and pressures, so as to construct a hierarchy of peoples for differential treatment... race is a structural relationship for the articulation and management of human differences, rather than a substantive content."
88. Reed 2013: 49.
89. Hendricks 2019.
90. Padilla Peralta 2021: 157.
91. Pinney 1983: 134; Hedreen 1991: 325–28; on the date of the poem, see M. L. West 2003: 1.
92. Lissarrague (1990: 247–93) compiles a list of 696 individuals, the bulk dating between 510 and 490 BCE. On the interpretive issues behind identifying a "Scythian," see M. Miller 1991: 59; Ivantchik 2006: 199.
93. Najee Olya's forthcoming monograph will compile a similar list.
94. Snowden 1976: 158, fig. 181.
95. Reyes 2001: 34–40.
96. Parmenter 2021a: 11–18.
97. Skinner 2012: 47.
98. E.g., Gruen 2011.
99. Olya 2021.
100. Snowden 1971, 1976. Snowden is the central figure in the study of Blackness in antiquity during the twentieth century. His influence cannot be fully captured here; see however Chapter 3 below for additional discussion. Well connected in both academia and politics, Snowden was shaped by his participation in moderate civil-rights activism, Republican patronage politics, and the project of anticommunism. For critical discussion of Snowden and his legacy, see Tanner 2010: 2–12, 27–38; Parmenter 2021a: 1–11; Derbew 2022: 23–25.
101. Snowden 1971: 4.
102. Lissarrague 1990: 1–2, "images sont en effet porteuses de significations—à travers un type de discours autre que le discours de la langue."
103. Derbew 2022: 48.
104. Eaverly 2013: 83–130; Skuse 2018.
105. Mintz 1985: 157; cf. Hopkins and Wallerstein 1977.

106. The consequences of this were dramatically illustrated in the African American artist Kara Walker's monumental installation, A Subtlety (2014), which depicted a pornographically anthropomorphic sphinx with the head of a Black woman constructed out of sugar sprayed onto Styrofoam blocks. The didactics written for Walker's installation explicitly refer to Mintz's research; see Creative Time 2014. For discussion, see Barnard 2017: 178–85.
107. Gikandi 2011: 3.
108. "Mr. Cheselden has given us a very curious story of a boy who had been born blind, and continued so until he was thirteen or fourteen years old; he was then couched for a cataract, by which operation he received his sight … some time after, upon accidentally seeing a negro woman, he was struck with great horror at the sight. The horror, in this case, can scarcely be supposed to arise from any association. The boy appears by the account to have been particularly observing and sensible for one of his age; and therefore it is probable, if the great uneasiness he felt at the first sight of black had arisen from its connection with any other disagreeable ideas, he would have observed and mentioned it" (Burke 1887: [1757] 177).
109. Jefferson (1998 [1785]: 145) asks, was there "not a greater share or less share of beauty in the two races? ... are not the fine mixtures of red and white ... preferable to the eternal monotony, which reigns in the countenances, that immoveable veil of black which covers all the emotions of the other race?"
110. Derbew 2019: 336.
111. "As to the physiognomy of the negro, the difference is no doubt astonishing if you put an ugly negro (and there are ugly negroes as well as ugly Europeans) exactly opposite the Greek ideal. […] there is no so-called savage nation under the sun which has distinguished itself by such examples of perfectibility and original capacity for scientific culture, and thereby attached itself so closely to the most civilized nations of the earth, *as the Negro*" (Blumenbach 1865 [1795]: 306, 312).
112. Cugoano (1999 [1787]: 12) would respond by challenging the assumption of white beauty: "and if their complexion be not what I may suppose, it is at least the nearest in resemblance to an infernal hue."
113. Lawrance and Roberts 2019: 173–77.
114. I. Morris 2004: 710–12; Ober 2010: 247–49.
115. Foxhall 1998: 298–300; Kurke 1999: 74–75; Dietler 2010: 138–45.
116. Appadurai 1986; Kopytoff 1986; I. Morris 1986a; Langdon 2001; Gunter 2009; Feldman 2014.
117. J.-P. Wilson 1997–98, Lamont 2023.
118. Briant and Descat 1998: 73.
119. In a 2018 survey of kitchen wares recovered from seventh- and sixth-century shipwrecks, Greene (2018: 138–40) finds evidence that certain ships—and perhaps crews—habitually sailed the same long-distance routes.
120. For comparative cases, see Trivellato 2009; Aslanian 2011; Kowalzig (2018) and Villing (2019) apply this model to Archaic trade.

121. Greene, Lawall, and Polzer 2008: 706. Cf. also the "Dymas, famed in ships" in *Od.* 6.22.
122. *P.Sapph.Obbink*; see Obbink 2014. There has been recent speculation whether Obbink, who was arrested for antiquities theft in Oxford in 2019, might have forged the Charaxos poem; see Higgins 2020. In 2020, Brill retracted the venue for Obbink's final publication (Bierl and Lardinois 2016). Regardless of Obbink's character, misdeeds, or alleged criminality, I personally consider it unlikely to be a forgery.
123. Names marked † can be looked up in Appendix 2.
124. To these might be added Demaratos of Corinth, the legendary founder of the Tarquin dynasty who made enormous profits exporting ceramics to Etruria (Dion. Hal. *AR* 3.46); one tradition (*Ps.-Aristot. Ath. Pol.* 11.2) even made †Solon of Athens a merchant who traded with Egypt.
125. Torelli 1982: 318. Torelli's argument is cautiously endorsed by Johnston (2010, 2015a, 2019) and Demetriou (2012: 128–34). New evidence for Sostratos comes from sixth-century Vougliameni, Attica, where a recently published *graffito* depicts a merchant ship labelled "I am Sostratos"; see van de Morteel and Langdon 2017: 400, fig. 17.
126. In the 1990s, Kurke (1999) and Morris (1996, 2000) made class conflict a central fixture of Archaic Greece: foreign trade destabilized existing hierarchies of value in (largely agrarian) EIA Greece, leading to the birth of the egalitarian *polis*. For critique, see Seaford 2002: 156–60; Hammer 2004; more recent critics have found the class conflict narrative overdetermined (Duplouy 2018: 45–46; Arrington, Spyropoulos, and Brellas 2021: 233–34, 267–69).
127. Similar anti-merchant thinking might be found in Solon fr. 13 West; Euenos *El.* 2 West = Theog. 667–82 West.
128. Κριοὺς μὲν καὶ ὄνους διζήμεθα, Κύρνε, καὶ ἵππους / εὐγενέας, καὶ τις βούλεται ἐξ ἀγαθῶν / βήσεσθαι· γῆμαι δὲ κακὴν κακοῦ οὐ μελεδαίνει / ἐσθλὸς ἀνήρ, ἤν οἱ χρήματα πολλὰ διδῷ / [. . .] χρήματα μὲν τιμῶσι· καὶ ἐκ κακοῦ ἐσθλὸς ἔγημε / καὶ κακὸς ἐξ ἀγαθοῦ· πλοῦτος ἔμειξε γένος.
129. Hopkins and Wallerstein 1977: 128.
130. Braund 1994: 46; Kallet 2007: 81–85; Lewis 2015b.
131. ἐπεσέρχεται δὲ διὰ μέγεθος τῆς πόλεως ἐκ πάσης γῆς τὰ πάντα, καὶ ξυμβαίνει ἡμῖν μηδὲν οἰκειοτέρᾳ τῇ ἀπολαύσει τὰ αὐτοῦ ἀγαθὰ γιγνόμενα καρποῦσθαι ἢ καὶ τὰ τῶν ἄλλων ἀνθρώπων.
132. Braund 1994: 46; Kallet 2007: 81–85.
133. καὶ πλείω τούτων ἀπολαύει ὁ ὄχλος ἢ οἱ ὀλίγοι καὶ οἱ εὐδαίμονες.
134. Hartog 1988 [1980]: 7.
135. Taylor 2001: 34.
136. Kurke 1999: 223.
137. K. Fields and B. Fields 2012: 17.
138. Hendricks 2019.
139. An earlier version of this chapter is Parmenter 2020.

CHAPTER 1

1. Kuhrt 2007: 2.697, KV2:21–22.
2. Colburn 2018: 76–81; van Alfen 2020: 67.
3. This chapter converts Greek currency to metric weights following the Late Period custom of using coinage as silver bullion. On conversions between Greek and Achaemenid standards in the Elephantine document, see Briant and Descat 1998: 75–78; van Alfen 2020: 52–58.
4. Our earliest reference to grain exports is Bacc. fr. 20b.14–16 in the mid-fifth century: "grain ships on the wine-dark sea bear the greatest wealth from Egypt" (πυροφόροι δὲ κατ' αἰγλάεντα πόντον / νᾶες ἄγουσιν ἀπ' Αἰγύπτου μέγιστον / πλοῦτον); see Villing 2015a: 4–8. For a catalogue of all attested Egyptian exports in the Classical Period, see van Alfen 2006: 280–85 tbs. 12.1–2.
5. Hermippus fr. 63.12–13 K-A: "From Egypt ropes, rigging, and sails" (ἐκ δ' Αἰγύπτου τὰ κρεμαστὰ / ἱστία καὶ βύβλους).
6. Agut-Labordère 2019. One of the Demotic epics depicts the Egyptian independence hero Pemu (who, like Aḥiqar, was thought to have lived in Assyrian times) wearing a cloak of "Milesian wool"; see Rutherford 2016: 89 n. 25.
7. Hdt. 3.6; on amphorae in Late Period tombs, see Bareš 1999: 88–89, 97–99.
8. One ship registered in the Elephantine document (GV3:1) delivered fifty-three old oars among its cargoes; see van Alfen 2020: 46.
9. "Samian earth" (šmwš) listed in *TAD* C3.7 GR2.25 and GR3.4, FR1.18; despite its name, this commodity might come from the Levant (Briant and Descat 1998: 2; van Alfen 2002: 147–50; Photos-Jones and Hall 2011: 57–61; Villing 2015b: 238). This commodity is also mentioned by Theophr. *On Stones* 64.
10. Grafe 2012: 63.
11. This arithmetic is laid out in Appendix 1. I argue that Egypt exported something in the region of 1,000 tons of natron annually in exchange for c. 30 kg of silver in export duties. (Egypt also collected 95.3 kg of silver and 2.82 kg gold in import duties; see van Alfen 2020: 52–53, tb. 1.) Deep uncertainty surrounds Herodotus' numbers; see Monson 2015: 12; Colburn 2018: 79.
12. Mintz 1985: xxiii.
13. Gunter 2009: 70–79; Loar, MacDonald, and Padilla Peralta 2017: 3–5; Lopez-Ruiz 2021: 65–67.
14. Yardeni 1994: 67.
15. The document was originally published by Porten and Yardeni (1986–99: 3, no. C3.7); for analysis, see Yardeni 1994; Briant and Descat 1998; van Alfen 2020; Folmer 2021. A new edition is being prepared by James D. Moore. Dating remains uncertain. Yardeni (1994: 67) preferred 475 BCE; Briant and Descat (1998: 61–62) and Moore are open to 454 BCE (Artaxerxes). In a 2018 conference presentation, Damien Agut-Labordère advocated for 412 BCE (Darius II) on the basis of paleography.
16. See Shortland et al. 2006: 523; Boardman 2013; and Bresson 2016: 353. Other commentators are less certain; see Porten and Yardeni 1986–99: 3.xx; Briant

and Descat 1998: 91; Villing 2015a: 6. Van Alfen (2020: 44) suggests Thonis-Herakleion; Moore (pers. comm.) believes it is Saqqara.
17. On this identification, see Briant and Descat 1998: 63. The identification of tiny Phaselis as the Ionian merchants' home port has puzzled scholars. Bresson's suggestion (2000: 68–73) that Phaselis offered a "flag of convenience" allowing Greek merchants to operate in the Achaemenid Empire during or after the wars of 499–49 BCE is generally accepted; see Malkin 2011: 72.
18. Folmer (2021: 282–86: tb. 1) offers a complete breakdown.
19. Folmer 2021: 275–76.
20. Folmer 2021: 274–75.
21. Pliny describes a process of treating natron with sulfur, melting it, and molding it into vessels (*NH* 31.46.111). This narrative is generally regarded as misleading; see Lucas and Harris 1962: 266; Bresciani 1998; Shortland et al. 2011: 926–27; Jackson et al. 2018: 1179–81.
22. Natron was occasionally used in conjunction with earths: Pliny *NH* 31.46.117–18 recommends mixing it with "Samian" and "Kimolian" earths. For general discussions, see Theophr. *On Stones* 62–64 with Caley and Richards 1956: 208–22; Photos-Jones and Hall 2011: 17–21.
23. Hence Horden and Purcell (2000: 344): "Many of the characteristic products of Mediterranean lands are common and widespread . . . the changing history and geography of connectivity enable the produce of a particular area to become a recognizable commodity even if its source is less elusive than the entrepreneurs who gain from its exportation might claim."
24. On "Kimolian earth," Theophr. *On Stones* 62–63; Caley and Richards 1956: 208–22; Photos-Jones and Hall 2011: 68–70.
25. Totelin 2009: 125–28.
26. ὅσων εἶεν αἱ πηγαὶ ἐκ πετρέων . . . ἢ ἐκ γῆς ὅκου θερμὰ ὕδατά ἐστιν, ἢ σίδηρος γίγνεται, ἢ χαλκὸς, ἢ ἄργυρος, ἢ χρυσός, ἢ θεῖον, ἢ στυπτηρίη, ἢ ἄσφαλτον, ἢ νίτρον.
27. Ἀλλὰ γὰρ ψευσάμενοί εἰσιν οἱ ἄνθρωποι τῶν ἁλμυρῶν ὑδάτων πέρι δι' ἀπειρίην.
28. Totelin 2009: 193–95. Forms of νίτρον appear fifty-seven times in the Hippocratic corpus; λίτρον appears twenty-three times.
29. Sonnini and Denon 1815: 360–61.
30. Said 1978: 84.
31. A few years after Sonnini and Denon, the English sea captain Henry A. S. Dearborn (1819: 2.258) noted that "[The Wadi Natrun] is dry nine months in the year; but in winter, there oozes from the earth, a water of a reddish violet colour, which fills the lakes to the height of five or six feet; the return of the great heats causing this to evaporate, leaves the ground covered with a salt sediment, two feet thick, that is chrystalized and hardened by the sun. The thickness of this layer of salt, varies according to the longer or shorter continuance of the waters on the ground. It is procured principally in the month of August."
32. Lucas 1932; Harris 1961: 192; Lucas and Harris 1962: 263–68.

33. See Sonnini and Denon 1815: 359–60; Dearborn 1819: 2.358–59; G. O. Wilkinson 1843.
34. G. O. Wilkinson, surveying the Wadi el-Natrun in 1842, came upon the remains of several of what he termed Roman "glasshouses" near the no-longer-extant village of Zakuk: "The glass-house was probably of Roman times. It is built of stone and the scoria of common green glass; and pieces of the fused substance attached to the stones sufficiently indicate its site as the rounded summits the form of three distinct ovens" (1843: 117). See locations of two "glasshouses" on Wilkinson's map; these locations are now underneath the town of Bîr Hooker. A rescue survey conducted ahead of land reclamation in 1958 found several matching structures in the "southwestern quarter" of the Wadi el-Natrun, and samples of industrial crucibles and glass ovens found there were taken to Cairo for analysis (Saleh, George, and Helmi 1972: 168–69); other glass kilns have recently been excavated there as well (see Nenna 2003 and Shortland et al. 2011: 917–18).
35. See Coulson and Leonard 1981: 69–70; Wilson and Grigoropoulos 2009: 160–64; Kenawi 2014: 142–56; and Jackson et al. 2018.
36. On the techniques of preindustrial salt-drying, see Lovejoy 1986: 88–93. Salt evaporation is known from documents, but not the archaeological record, at LBA Ugarit (Potts 1984) and Archaic Ephesos (*I.Eph.* 1).
37. Segal and Smith 1983 no. 24
38. Parkinson 1991; see also Fabre 2004: 158.
39. Teeter 2011: 32–34; Quack 2013a.
40. On the lexicography of natron, see Birwood 1911; J. R. Harris 1961: 193–94; Lucas and Harris 1962: 267–68; van Alfen 2002: 153 n. 153.
41. J. R. Harris (1961: 186) suggests that alum also circulated as *bd*, a rare word for natron.
42. Warburton 1997: 143–45.
43. Caminos (1954: 78) glosses "*P3-ḥr* waters" as "a canal or body of water"; Erman and Grapow (WB s.v.) define *P3-ḥr* as "art Fisch."
44. This was the analogous situation in the Sudan, where salts were produced far too widely to be effectively regulated (Lovejoy 1986: 13). Homemade salt was a frequent target of enforcement by state agents defending the salt, and likely natron, monopolies in Ptolemaic Egypt; see McGing 2002: 45–46 on *TCD Pap. Gr.* 273, Adams 2013: 272–75. The state monopoly in Ottoman Mesopotamia has left a similar record of oppression; see Potts 1984: 42–45.
45. On scribal imaginaries, see Warburton 1997: 133; Kemp 2006 [1991]: 330.
46. "You go down to your ship of fir-wood, (fully) manned from bow to stern, and you reach your beautiful villa, the one which you have built for yourself. Your mouth is full of wine and beer, of bread, meat and cake. Oxen are slaughtered and wine is opened, and melodious singing is before you. Your overseer of anointers anoints with ointment of gum. Your chief of inundated lands bears wreaths. Your overseer of fowlers brings *wrd*-birds. Your fisherman brings fish. Your ship is come

from Khor loaded with all manner of good things" (trans. Caminos 1954: no. 5, 3.7–11).

47. καὶ τότε νῆα θοὴν ἅλαδ' ἑλκέμεν, ἐν δέ τε φόρτον /ἄρμενον ἐντύνασθαι, ἵν' οἴκαδε κέρδος ἄρηαι.

48. Roger Bagnall (2005) has explored the disciplinary separation of Egypt from the economic rhythms of the Mediterranean. The records of wealthy Egyptian households, epitomized by the archive of the twelfth-dynasty landowner Hekanakht (Allen 2002), show frequent market activity and the spread of the family's productive assets across a wide geographical area to distribute risk; see Kemp 2006 [1991]: 323 for discussion.

49. Natron lakes produce various evaporite minerals depending on conditions, including trona ($Na_2CO_3 \cdot NaHCO_3 \cdot 2H_2O$), thermonatrite ($Na_2CO_3 \cdot H_2O$), nahcolite ($Na[HCO_3]$), thenardite, also known as Glauber's salt (Na_2SO_4), and halite, or table salt ($NaCl$); see Lovejoy 1986: 33–39; Shortland et al. 2011: 916–17; Jackson et al. 2018.

50. See Yardeni 1994: 69 tb. 2; Briant and Descat 1998: 72; see Goitein 1967–93: 1.298 and Fabre 2004: 25 on delta navigation in low water. Dearborn (1819: 2.339) reports depth differences as much as 30 feet between flood and drought. Low water on the Nile matched the general winter slowdown in sea traffic; see Horden and Purcell 2000: 142–43; McCormick 2001: 450–54.

51. Cf. an anonymous Roman-era poet (*AP* 9.383): "Mecheir bids sailors prepare for a voyage" (σημαίνει πλωτῆρσι Μεχεὶρ πλόον ἀμφιπολεύειν).

52. Horden and Purcell 2000: 178.

53. Appendix 1 attempts to quantify this labor.

54. Stronk (2010) interprets †Herostratos' rough passage as an early season voyage.

55. Demetriou 2010: 79.

56. ἑλκέμεν ἐς πόντον φόρτον τ' ἐς πάντα τίθεσθαι·

57. Horden and Purcell 2000: 178.

58. Rauh, Dillon, and McClain 2008.

59. Abramzon and Tunkina 2018.

60. S. Bujskikh 2006.

61. Kirigin et al. 2009.

62. Greene 2018: 138–40: fig. 6.2. Analysis of coroplastics dedicated at seventh-century Ionian sanctuaries indeed suggest a substantial traffic in artists and other specialists between Cyprus and southeast Asia Minor; see Henke 2019: 250–51.

63. The substantivist tradition of interpreting the ancient economy labels cities like Naukratis as "ports of trade": these were sites that allowed limited, and closely monitored, interaction between natives and foreigners (Möller 2000: 19–25). Indeed, there were periodic attempts by the Saite and Achaemenid governments to limit the movement of Greek traders within Egypt. (One Aramaic letter, dated to the fifth century [Segal and Smith 1983: no. 26], instructs an official that "you will not permit [the Ionians and Carians] to go out in a forward direction . . . of

the barrier ... carrying bags of the tanner's work"). But, in general, Greeks do appear to have traded and dispersed widely within Egypt by the fifth century (Hdt. 2.39.2, 2.41.3). Thonis-Herakleion and Naukratis might better be interpreted as "bottlenecks" that confined this movement for the purpose of taxation; see Purcell 2005: 203–6; Demetriou 2012: 16–23; Agut-Labordère 2013: 1004–6; Muhs 2016: 186–87.

64. Villing 2015a: 9.
65. Villing 2015a: 8.
66. *PSI* 5.488, l. 9–19, dating to the fourth century, mentions Syro-Persian and Carian quarters next to the temple of Ptah in Memphis.
67. Ἦν δὲ τὸ παλαιὸν μούνη Ναύκρατις ἐμπόριον καὶ ἄλλο οὐδὲν Αἰγύπτου.
68. Dietler (2010: 138–55) emphasizes the ubiquity of a "floater" trade conducted at roadsteads, promontories, and other impermanently inhabited sites.
69. Yoyotte 1991/92: 637; Villing 2019: 206.
70. Hermitage 2962; see Agut-Labordère 2013: 1004–6, Muhs 2016: 186–87.
71. Vittmann 2003: 220–21, fig. 111.
72. BM 1885,1101.110; see Villing 2015b: 232.
73. Yoyotte 1992/93: 684; Spencer 2011: 33–37.
74. Villing 2019: 218–30.
75. Henke 2019: 259.
76. Pendlebury 1930: 82.
77. Johnston 2015a, 2019.
78. Rauh, Dillon, and McClain 2008: 220.
79. On storage structures in Egyptian temples and state buildings, see Kemp 2006 [1991]: 257–60; Muhs 2016: 193–95; on the Tell Dafana casemate structure, see Leclère and Spencer 2014: 6–24.
80. Kemp 2006 [1991]: 351–60; see also von Bomhard 2012: 6; Muhs 2016: 178–79; Villing 2019: 232.
81. *O.Gardiner* 28; see Fabre 2004: 141; Pino 2005: 95–96.
82. Villing and Thomas 2015: 9; Villing 2019: 231–32.
83. Kemp 2006 [1991]: 256–61; Muhs 2016: 178–80.
84. For the Nitocris adoption stela, see Caminos 1964; on the foundation of the Saite dynasty, see Kitchen 1986: 399–410; Kahn 2006.
85. Objects bearing the names of three of these men have found their way to Western museums: the possibly half-Greek †Neferpre-sa-Neith, son of *Grḫs* (Hermitage 8499); Psamtik-sa-Neith (Penn 42-9-1); Ahmes-sa-Neith (BM 1885,1101.110).
86. Von Bomhard 2015: 104–5.
87. Agut-Labordère 2016: 320–21.
88. Folmer 2021: 288.
89. Ἦν δὲ τὸ παλαιὸν μούνη Ναύκρατις ἐμπόριον καὶ ἄλλο οὐδὲν Αἰγύπτου ("In the old days, Naukratis was the only trade port in Egypt—and no other").
90. Folmer 2021: 268.

91. Oppenheim 1967: 248 n. 64.
92. Raaflaub 2016: 138–39; Bowie 2016: 161–63.
93. YOS 6.168, PTS 2098, TCL 12.84; see interpretation in Oppenheim 1967: 236–37.
94. The rejection of Wenamun's credentials in Tyre (Goedicke 1975: 152 sec. 13) long predates the period examined in this chapter, but harassment at the border is a universal phenomenon.
95. Goitein 1967–93.1: 314; Horden and Purcell 2000: 140–43; McCormick 2001: 425–26.
96. Janssen 1961.
97. On šwty, see Janssen 1961: 101–3; Castle 1992: 250–53; Fabre 2004: 141–42; Pino 2005: 101–2; Kemp 2006 [1991]: 332–33.
98. TAD A2.6 = Porten 6 = Porten 6 = Porten 6 = Porten 6 = Porten 6 = Porten et al. 2011 no. B6.
99. TAD A2.4 = Porten 4 = Porten 4 = Porten 4 = Porten 4 = Porten 4 = Porten et al. 2011 no. B4.
100. TAD A2.5 = Porten 5 = Porten 5 = Porten 5 = Porten 5 = Porten 5 = Porten et al. 2011 no. B5.
101. The "translators" of Hdt. 2.154 might be the same group described elsewhere as "Karomemphitai" (Polyaen. 7.3) and "Hellenomemphitai" (Hdt. 2.112); see Vittmann 2003: 227; Malkin 2011: 89–90; Kaplan 2015: 401.
102. Strattis fr. 33 K-A, dating to the late fifth century, lampoons one Δεινίας ἀγύπτιος as a wealthy merchant infamous for his use of perfume. This is very likely the same person. For the reading of Αἰγ[as "from Aegina," see Figueira 1988: 543–44.
103. Rothman 2009: 773–75; Ferreira 2012: 132–33; Sparks 2014: 199–209.
104. Neither of these names are attested elsewhere in *LGPN*; for discussion, see Piccolo 2019: 168–72.
105. On the events of 570 BCE, see Leahy 1988: 189–93. On Egyptian attitudes toward migration, see O'Connor 2003: 167–74; Kemp 2006 [1991]: 37–42.
106. Ray 1998; Vittmann 2003: 155–79. See prosopographical entries for †Pirapia, son of *Khaa-s-n-Mut*, †*Pdrwihy* (?), son of *'Ipdy*, †Itoana.
107. Graffiti carved on the leg of Ramesses II at the funerary chapel of Abu Simbel (M-L 7), dating to the campaign of Necho II against Nubia in 591/0 BCE, provides the earliest substantial proof of a Greek mercenary presence in Egypt. Individuals who signed their names as †Psammetichos and †Psammetes have been argued to be mixed-descent children of Greeks and Egyptians. Odysseus' journey to Egypt loomed large in the memory of seventh- and sixth-century merchants. Dillon (1997) argues that the †Peleqos, son of Eudamos (Oudamos), who carved his name at Abu Simbel, was riffing off Odysseus' identification as *Me Tis* ("nobody") to the cyclops Polyphemus at *Od.* 9.366. Ancient authors are unanimous in highlighting the place of mercenaries in the early Greek community in Egypt; see Hdt. 2.151–54; Diod. 1.66.10–12; Strabo 17.1.18; Polyaen. 7.2.
108. This is translated from the German text of Zaghloul 1985: 23–24 no. 1.

109. Kemp 2006 [1991]: 358.
110. Moyer 2011: 57.
111. Kemp 2006 [1991]: 375–81.
112. E.g., Juvenal 15.8: "a whole village worships a dog, but no one worships Diana!" (*oppida tota canem uenerantur, nemo Dianam!*). See Isaac 2004: 364; Shumate 2006: 130.
113. Moyer 2011: 34.
114. Kurke 1999: 4. She discusses her methodology in depth in 1999: 23–32.
115. Kurke 1999: 223.
116. See Kemp 2006 [1991]: 376 fig. 131.
117. von den Driesch, Kessler, Steinmann, Berteaux, and Peters 2005; on the condition of the animals, Kemp 2006 [1991]: 380.
118. Descriptions by Herodotus and Diodorus are the only known sources for the process of mummification. Their descriptions have inspired a century or more of debate, but are now generally understood to have been filtered through an ideological lens; see Lucas and Harris 1962: 281–83; Garner 1979: 19; and Colombini, Silvano, and Onur 2000: 19.
119. Grandet 1994–97: 2.94.
120. See von den Driesch, Kessler, Steinmann, Berteaux, and Peters 2005: 210–12; Kemp 2006 [1991]: 379.
121. Herodotus' description of Scythian burials was famously treated as a narratological exercise by Hartog (1988 [1980]: 144–51); see Ivantchik 2011.
122. For general discussions on embalming in ancient Egypt, see Lucas and Harris 1962: 270–326; Garner 1979; and Colombini, Silvano, Onur 2000: 19–20.
123. Thus the new pharaoh in the *Tale of Sinuhe* is able to persuade Sinuhe to return from exile in the Levant to avoid dying without access to eternal life (Pritchard 1969: 30–21 secs. 185–200).
124. See Janssen and Pestman 1968; on funerary expenditures and private demand, see Warburton 1997: 63–64; Kemp 2006 [1991]: 308–10.
125. Kemp 2006 [1991]: 313–14.
126. Warburton 1997: 106–7 on unmarked *shabtis*. On BM EA10800, see Edwards 1971; Poole 2005.
127. van Heel 1996.
128. This is shared in other Greek descriptions of mummification; see Lucas and Harris 1962: 283.
129. Davidson 1998: 3–11.
130. Kurke 1999: 89–100.
131. Lucas and Harris 1962: 78.
132. On the lexicography of natron, see J. R. Harris 1961: 190–97.
133. Mintz 1985: 175–76.
134. Stringfellow 2014 and Pacific Coast Borax Company 1915: 19.

CHAPTER 2

1. Mintz 1985: xxiv.
2. Marx 1867: 1.85 (Das Geheimnisvolle der Warenform besteht also einfach darin, daß sie den Menschen die gesellschaftlichen Charaktere ihrer eignen Arbeit als gegenständliche Charaktere der Arbeitsprodukte selbst, als gesellschaftliche Natureigenschaften dieser Dinge zurückspiegelt, daher auch das gesellschaftliche Verhältnis der Produzenten zur Gesamtarbeit als ein außer ihnen existierendes gesellschaftliches Verhältnis von Gegenständen. Durch dies Quidproquo werden die Arbeitsprodukte Waren, sinnlich übersinnliche oder gesellschaftliche Dinge).
3. Hobsbawm 1983: 1.
4. These practices were selectively taken up by the people they encountered in mainland Italy, Sardinia, North Africa, and Spain; for a summary, see Hölbl 1981; Fletcher 2004; Pappa 2012; Sossau 2012. Including so-called exotica in graves was a very ancient practice that appears sporadically in the Mediterranean as early as the second millennium BCE; see Wengrow 2010; S. Murray 2018b.
5. López-Ruiz 2021: 193.
6. Luraghi 2006: 25.
7. Webb (2015a: 21–24; 2016: 10) and Masson-Berghoff (2018: 82–86) date the heyday of Greek *aegyptiaca* to 650–570 BCE with residual production as late as 525 BCE.
8. On the end of *aegyptiaca*, see Skon-Jedele 1994: xxi; Webb 2015a: 31; Masson-Berghoff 2018: 82–86.
9. For distribution maps, see Hölbl 1979: 1, k. 1; Webb 1978: 8 fig. 3; Pardó i Parcerisa 1980–95: 1 map 3; Gorton 1996. For regional outlines of *aegyptiaca*, see Hölbl 1979 (peninsular Italy), 1986 (Sardinia); Pardo i Parcerisa 1980–95 (Mediterranean Spain); Reyes 2001 (Cyprus); Hölbl 2007 (Ionia); Skon-Jedele 1994 (mainland Greece and islands); Parmenter 2019 (the north Black Sea).
10. On east Greek faience, including the hypothesized workshop, see Webb 1978: 2–3; on Naukratis, Gorton 1996: 91–131; Masson-Berghoff 2018. Archaeometric analysis, conducted via XRF and PIXE, has laid bare how little we know about the production of Greco-Egyptian faience. Meek et al. (2016: 98–9) argue for discernable difference in composition of faience *aegyptiaca* assigned stylistic provenance from Rhodes or Naukratis held at the Louvre and British Museums. But Belfiore et al. (2021), who analyze a heterogenous assemblage of faience with archaeological context from EIA Sicily, emphasize that these differences are slight and based on a small sample size. Their testing finds considerably greater variety in composition (2021: 67).
11. This chapter follows the convention of referring to all low-fired vitreous substances—including frit, paste, Egyptian blue, and glazed steatite—as "faience." On the technical differences between these materials, see Webb 1978: 5; 2016: 1–4; Peltenberg 1987: 11–15; Clerc 1991: 1–3; P. Nicholson 2012: 13; Masson-Berghoff 2018: 13–15.

12. Whitehouse 2002: 193; Shortland et al. 2006: 522.
13. Kolesnychenko and Kiosak 2021: 90.
14. Our understanding of the so-called Orientalizing phase of the eighth–seventh centuries BCE draws heavily on the Homeric poems; see Winter 1995; Gunter 2009: 61–70; Arrington 2022: 43–45.
15. Ogundiran 2014: 70.
16. Arrington 2015: 24; Skuse 2021: 61–64.
17. Skuse 2021: 40–43.
18. Masson-Berghoff 2018: 30–31.
19. σκευαστὸς δ' ὁ Αἰγύπτιος. καὶ οἱ γράφοντες τὰ περὶ τοὺς βασιλεῖς καὶ τοῦτο γράφουσι, τίς πρῶτος βασιλεὺς ἐποίησε χυτὸν κύανον μιμησάμενος τὸν αὐτοφυῆ, δῶρά τε πέμπεσθαι παρ' ἄλλων τε καὶ ἐκ Φοινίκης φόρον κυάνου, τοῦ μὲν ἀπύρου τοῦ δὲ πεπυρωμένου.
20. Henderson 2013: 13.
21. Jackson, Nicholson, and Gneisinger 1998.
22. This is also the case for faience in found in mainland Greece during the LBA; see J. Davis et al. 2018: 623–29.
23. Shortland et al. 2006: 522–33; Tite et al. 2007: 1577–79; Henderson 2013: 54–55; Meek et al. 2016: 96–97; Masson-Berghoff 2018: 13.
24. Lloyd 1983: 243–45. Shortland (2000: fig. 5-5) provides a useful flow chart of faience's commodity chain.
25. On the natron/plant ash transition at the end of the first millennium CE, see Whitehouse 2002; Zimmermann 2011: 105–14; Henderson 2013: 54–55; Phelps et al. 2016.
26. Jackson et al. 2016.
27. Shortland et al. 2011: 925; Jackson et al. 2018. Garner (1979: 22) found that much of the "natron" used in mummification contained as little as 20 percent natron.
28. On this distinction, see Webb 1978: 2–3; 2016: 5–9; Clerc 1991: 1–3; Masson-Berghoff 2018: 13–15.
29. See Masson-Berghoff (2018: 13) with notes on recent work; Lucas and Harris (1962: 177–78) on their experiments.
30. Wengrow 2010: 148.
31. For a summary of faience *aegyptiaca* found the mainland during the LBA, see S. Murray 2018b: 223–24. A faience ring has recently been discovered at Pylos; see J. Davis et al. 2018: 623–29. The crew of the Uluburun ship was carrying a few small pendants; see Bass, Pulak, Collon, and Weinstein 1989: 20–24. On the Knossos house models, see Momigliano et al. 2014.
32. S. Murray 2018a: 34.
33. Using numbers from S. Murray 2017: 117 tb. 2.9, 126 tb. 2.12.
34. López-Ruiz 2021: 48–50.
35. See Smithson 1968: 114–15 nos. 78–78f; Skon-Jedele 1994: 13–15, 67–69 no. 14+; on the question of value, see Arrington 2015: 7. On *aegyptiaca* from Geometric contexts in Athens, see Skon-Jedele 1994: 12–32, 46 tb 1; S. Murray 2017: 109.

36. I. Morris 1986b; 2000: 171–78. Hints of this attitude might be found in the Homeric dismissal of amber beads as "trinkets" (ἀθύρματα, *Od.* 15.460) sold by Phoenicians.
37. Crielaard 2018: 196–202, S. Murray 2018a: 55–58.
38. The practice of using *aegyptiaca* as grave goods continued through the sixth century on Rhodes; for objects from the necropolis at Ialysos and Makri Langoni, see Skon-Jedele 1994: 2337–54 nos. 4311–4353; Webb 2019a: 331–35. A handful of scarabs and amulets come from graves on Aegina (Skon-Jedele 1994: 960–61 nos. 1342–43) and Samos (Skon-Jedele 1994: 1631–34 nos. 2721–25; Webb 2016: 99 nos. 167–72). Including *aegyptiaca* in graves continues at Greek settlements in Sicily (Hölbl 2001: 37–40), South Italy, (Hölbl 1979: 2.174–259), and around the northern Black Sea (Parmenter 2019) through the sixth century.
39. On the Eretria faience, see Verdan 2013: 135.
40. On the difficulties surrounding pinpointing "origins" for this material, see Kourou 2012: 220; S. Murray 2017: 127 n. 196. For early *aegyptiaca* assemblages at Peloponnesian sanctuaries, see S. Murray 2017: 103–5, tb. 2.6.
41. See Bammer 1990: 150–53; Hölbl 2007: 452.
42. Gjerstad et al. 1935: 824; Reyes 2001: 33.
43. Cypriot votary sculptures often portray worshippers wearing seal necklaces; see Lagarce 1976: 168–74; Beer 1994 pls. 1–3, 8–38.
44. Cook and Nicholls 1998: 22–26, pls. 20 and 21.
45. On the Samian Heraion, see Skon-Jedele 1994: 1429–38; for specific deposits, see Skon-Jedele 1994: 1463–67; Webb 2016: 195–206; 2021: 6–7 with plans in 2016: xvi fig. 1, 2021: 3–4 figs. 1–2. On the phenomenon of temple cleaning in general, see Osborne 2004.
46. Furtwängler, Fiechter, and Thiersch 1906: 386; Skon-Jedele 1994: 917–18.
47. James (1962: 464–66) valiantly attempts to provide location data using Payne's publication (1940: 118) and Pendlebury's notes, but nearly half the objects from Perachora come from no known context; see Skuse 2021: 43–50.
48. Blinkenberg 1931: 1.335.
49. On the Argive Heraion, see Skon-Jedele 1994: 700; citing Waldstein 1905: 1.39 and archival work; on Sounion, Skon-Jedele 1994: 143, Theodoropoulou-Polychroniadis 2015: 23–28.
50. Hölbl 2007: 457; 2014: 184–85; on the finds generally, see Hölbl 1999.
51. For instance, stone scarabs far outnumber faience on Cyprus; see Gorton 1996: 175–77; Reyes 2001: 41–44.
52. For the bronzes, see Skon-Jedele 1994: 1489–1558 nos. 1687–1815; Ebbinghaus 2006.
53. For the inlays, see Skon-Jedele 1994: 2355–73 nos. 4354–74; Kousoulis and Morenz 2007: 184–88 figs. 2–4; Kousoulis 2017: 35 εικ. 2; for the *senet* set, see Skon-Jedele 1994: 2583–87 nos. 4824–4827.
54. Webb 1978: 7–9; 2016: 10–12; 2019b: 44–51.

55. The chronology for Webb's phasing is partially based on the existence of imitation LPC aryballoi at Kameiros; see Webb 1978: 108; 2015b: 5–6.
56. The earliest group of scarabs produced in the Greek world appear during the mid-seventh century; these are called by Hölbl (1979) the "Typus Perachora-Rodos"; Skuse (2021: 41), however, problematizes this label. Perachora-Rhodes scarabs recirculate a tight repertoire of ten hieroglyphs, including Gardiner A40/B1 (seated deity); F35 (*nfr*); I12 (uraeus); M17 (*i*); N5 (*rʿ*); N35 (*n*); S34 (*ʿnkh*); V30 (*nb*); X1 (*t*); and D58 (*b*). Amulets of the Egyptian gods Bes, Sekhmet, and Nefertum were widely popular in the Cypro-Phoenician world, and indeed are found in quantity at Rhodian sanctuaries, where mass dedication of *aegyptiaca* took root earlier than elsewhere in the Aegean; see Webb 2021: 37.
57. Parmenter 2021b.
58. Vercoutter 1945: 354–56.
59. Masson-Berghoff 2018: 84.
60. Pendlebury 1930: 82.
61. Skuse 2021: 47.
62. E.g. Pendlebury 1930: 109; James 1962: 480 no. D56, which could not possibly carry a cartouche of Akhenaten as Pendlebury believed.
63. Critiques of what was originally Pendlebury's position—now generalized in the scholarship—have recently been made by Wengrow (2010: 143), Arrington (2015: 4), S. Murray (2018b: 221), and Skuse (2021: 53–55). Aaron Brody (1998, 2008), who has studied religious practices among sailors in the eastern Mediterranean, finds only intermittent evidence for amulet usage. The best-known instances are the Bes amulets on the LBA Uluburun ship; see Bass, Pulak, Collon, and Weinstein 1989: 20–24.
64. Webb 2015a: 30–31; 2015b: 5–6; 2019b: 59–66; Masson-Berghoff 2018: 5.
65. Petrie 1886: 36.
66. Petrie's excavation of the "scarab factory" has been revisited several times due to its importance in the site's chronology; see Boardman 1980 [1964]: 126–29; Gorton 1996: 91–131; Möller 2000: 152–54; James 2003: 252–58. For discussion in light of the recent excavations, see Webb 2015a: 31; 2015b: 6; 2019b; Masson-Berghoff 2018: 5–30.
67. Petrie 1886: 36. This became the prevailing interpretation; see Gorton 1996: 94 ("It is obvious that they are imitations which must have looked strange to an Egyptian accustomed to the traditional clarity and symmetry in the writing of hieroglyphs").
68. Webb 2015a: 2; Masson-Berghoff 2018: 23. On Petrie's colonial model, see Villing 2019: 209.
69. E.g., Edgar in Hogarth, Edgar, and Gutch 1898–99: 48–50.
70. For Aegina, see Furtwängler, Fiechter, and Thiersch 1906: 386–90; for Argos, see Lythgoe 1905; for Ephesus, see Hogarth 1908: 202–8; for Artemis Orthia, see Dawkins 1929: 378–86; for Sounion, see Stais 1917: 195–97; and for Lindos, see Blinkenberg 1931: 334–91.

71. Lythgoe 1905: 368; Hogarth 1908: 207; Blinkenberg 1931.1: 374–75. For detailed discussion about Naukratite typology, see Hölbl 1979: 1.202–4; Gorton 1996: 91–131. Though its definition remains problematic, it has been upheld in recent years; see Webb 2015a: 29–31; Masson-Berghoff 2018: 17–23; Skuse 2021: n. 56.
72. These views are earliest attested in Furtwängler's publication of faience material from the sanctuary of Aphaia on Aegina (Furtwängler, Fiechter, and Thiersch 1906: 386) and in Stais' publication of Sounion (1917: 196–97), both of which quote von Bissing's personal correspondence. Pendlebury's lack of engagement with continental scholarship was immediately identified by Scharff (1931: 536).
73. Cf. Arrington (2022: 44–47), who notes the marginalization of Egypt, Assyria, and other eastern Mediterranean regions in scholarship on Greek ceramics after the turn of the twentieth century.
74. On the role of Phoenicians in transporting early *aegyptiaca* to Greece, see Gunter 2009: 66 (summarizing previous scholarship); Sherratt 2010: 126; Kourou 2012: 227; Feldman 2014: 168–69; López-Ruiz 2021: 52–54. Memphite triad amulets are especially common at Lefkandi and the Rhodian sanctuaries at Ialysos, Kameiros, and Lindos; see Fletcher 2004: 71–74 app. 2; Hölbl 2015: 243; Apostola 2018.
75. Fabre 2004: 200; de Ruiter 2020: 8–9.
76. V. Wilson 1975: 81.
77. On Amun Re in Naukratis, see Yoyotte 1991/92: 637; 1992/93: 684; for Psamtik I's grant of landholdings in the western delta to Thebes, see Caminos 1964: 100, tb. 1.
78. "It dominates in the Naukratis corpus if we accept most cryptic readings of the god's name" (Masson-Berghoff 2018: 30). Cryptographic renderings of the name of Amun are well known among Egyptologists; for instance, Drioton (1957) draws attention to the wordplay between the name of Amun (*i-mn-n*) and the word "to hide" (*imn*) represented by the determinative A5. He lays out a complete scheme of phonetic correspondences for other hieroglyphs to represent the "hidden" name of Amun; for further discussion, see Bolshakov and Ilyna 1988; Dan 2011; Lohwasser 2014. The play on words between *i-mn-n* and *imn* was already recognized by Hecataeus of Abdera in the third century (Plut. *de Iside* 354c–d = *FGrHist* 264 F 4), raising the possibility that even earlier Greek writers were aware of cryptography.
79. Masson-Berghoff 2018: 30.
80. Shortland 2000: 63–77; Vanthuyne 2012/13: 414; Webb 2016: 66 n. 403.
81. Clerc (1991: 97–114) summarizes possible roles filled by the Egyptian gods on Cyprus in her publication of the *aegyptiaca* from Amathus; for the childbirth thesis, see Hölbl 1981; Kousoulis 2017: 39.
82. Wengrow 2010: 145; Arrington 2015: 20.
83. In this usage, the article indicates "son of"; see Masson 1977: 61–63.
84. I. Morris 2000: 184.
85. E.g., Hammer's critique (2004), which largely dwells on Kurke's reading of Althusser.
86. Corner 2010: 353–57.

87. Arrington 2015: 4; S. Murray 2018b: 221–22.
88. Arrington 2021: 7.
89. The social production of trust is a major topic of inquiry among those who study merchant diasporas; for instance, see Greif (2002) and Trivellato (2009), who problematize the assumption that trust is simply the byproduct of family, ethnic, or religious ties. Adopting a Bourdieuian framework, Aslanian (2011: 166–201) contextualizes trust as a form of social capital generated and circulated through relationships.
90. Purcell 2005: 203–6; Bresson 2016: 286–90.
91. Some of the hazards of entering port are shown in a lead letter from Berezan, c. 550–50 BCE (*CGP* 25). Its writer is seized as a slave by local merchant in a case of what might be deliberately "mistaken" identity; for discussion, see Chapter 4 and entry for *Achillodoros in Appendix 6. That citizenship came with definite economic rights is the position of I. Morris (2004: 731–36) and Ober (2010: 271, 75). Bresson (2000: 250) and Duplouy (2018: 41) see citizenship predicated on the successful performance of rights.
92. Malkin 2011: 72.
93. Horden and Purcell 2000: 349.
94. χοΐσκον is the diminutive of χοῦς, a volumetric unit equivalent to 3.27 l. The specific gravity of natron is 1.42 cc./g.
95. *IG* 11.2 144, *IG* 11.2 161, *IG* 11.2 203, *IG* 11.2 205, *IG* 11.2 234, *ID* 290, *ID* 316, *ID* 338, *ID* 354, *ID* 396.
96. Separately, Rask (2020: 127–30) argues that the overwhelming "sameness" of votive assemblages acted as part of an "aesthetic of accumulation" that enabled participation in a larger group identity.
97. This fragment has been attributed to the early fifth century poet Euenos of Paros; see Bowie 2006.
98. Kurke 1999: 75.
99. Παύροισιν πίσυνος μεγάλ' ἀνδράσιν ἔργ' ἐπιχείρει, / μή ποτ' ἀνήκεστον, Κύρνε, λάβῃς ἀνίην. / Πιστὸς ἀνὴρ χρυσοῦ τε καὶ ἀργύρου ἀντερύσασθαι.
100. Κύρνε, σοφιζομένωι μὲν ἐμοὶ σφρηγὶς ἐπικείσθω / τοῖσδ' ἔπεσιν, λήσει δ' οὔποτε κλεπτόμενα, / οὐδέ τις ἀλλάξει κάκιον τοὐσθλοῦ παρεόντος·.
101. Ps.-Aristotle (*Ath. Pol.* 44.1) reports that the Prytanis in Athens had access to a "state seal" (δημοσίαν σφραγῖδα). These are known in the Achaemenid world; see Villing 2015b: 6 fig. 4.
102. Most sealings from pre-Classical Greece appear to be the result of curiosity, rather than to mark property. Boardman (2001 [1972]: 112, 418) lists four sealings from EIA-Archaic Greece. To these can be added four more from Corinth, one from Perachora, and two from Naukratis, one of which is an Egyptian cartouche; see Pfaff 1988: 39–40; Papadopoulos 1994: 453; Stubbings 1962: 432 no. A112; Johnston 2015a: 8–9. That Theognis is referring to commercial sealing is usually taken for granted by critics (e.g., Pratt 1995).

103. See Villing 2015a: 14 fig. 15 for the seal of Amasis-Sa-Neith at Naukratis, dating to the pharaoh Amasis.
104. Ogundiran 2014: 72–85.
105. "And strange it was to see the great allteration it made in a few years amonge the Indeans them selves; for all the Indeans of these parts, & the Massachusets, had none or very little of it [wampampeake], but the sachems & some spetiall persons that wore a litle of it for ornamente. [. . .] But after it grue thus to be a comoditie in these parts, these Indeans fell into it allso, and learne how to make it. . . and it hath now continued a current comoditie aboute this 20. years, and it may prove a drugg in time. In the mean time it maks the Indeans of these parts rich & power full and also prowd thereby; and fills them with peeces, powder, and shote, which no laws can restraine, by reasone of the bassnes of sundry unworthy persons, both English, Dutch, & French, which may turne to the ruine of many" (Bradford 1962 [1897]: 139).
106. Becker 2008.
107. Matory 2005: 89–92; see also Parés 2005: 148–50; Reis 2013: 70.
108. On Branco, see Matory 2005: 95–99; Parés 2005: 149–50; on Bomfim and Sousa, see Parés 2005: 149–50.
109. Matory 2005: 99.
110. Burkert 1992 [1984]: 128; S. Morris 1993: 124–39; López-Ruiz 2010: 190–95; 2021: 68.
111. Martin 1993: 109.
112. Fabre 2004: 193–95.
113. Goedicke 1975: 152 sec. xviii.
114. Trans. Caminos 1954 no. 5, 3.7–11.
115. Hartog 2001 [1996]: 41–77; Vasunia 2001: 121–26. For general discussion of genealogy and Greek ethnicity, see J. M. Hall 2002: 30–36; Mac Sweeney 2009.
116. On Kadmos myths, see S. Morris 1993: 133–49; Gruen 2011: 233–26.
117. See Mac Sweeney 2013: 68–69. Both Douris of Samos *FGrHist* 76 F74 and Maiandros *FGrHist* 492 F 17 cite Herodotus in claiming Thales' descent from Kadmos.
118. Hdt. 1.37.3–4 = *FGrHist* 489 F1; see S. Morris 1993: 146. Thus Almagor 2016 *BNJ* s.v. "Among the shadowy figures who populate Jacoby's opus, Kadmos of Miletus seems to hold a place of honour."
119. *FGrHist* 545 F 1. See Mac Sweeney 2017: 409 n. 126. This claim is repeated Simon. Gen., *FGrHist* 8 F2 in the fourth century.
120. The earliest reference to Kadmos is Hom. *Od.* 5.333; he might also appear as Phoenix, father of Europa, in Hom. *Il.* 14.321–22. Three fragments exist of a cyclic *Danais*; see M. L. West 2013: 3–4. Pelops appears in Hom. *Il.* 2.100–108 and Tyrtaeus fr. 2 Diehl. For a discussion of early references, see E. Hall 1989a: 32–38; S. Morris 1993: 131–49; Gruen 2011: 227–43.
121. See Panyassis fr. 25K Matthews; this claim is summarized by Apoll. *Bib.* 3.14.4.

122. Polyzalos of Rhodes *FGrHist* 521 F 1 and Zenon of Rhodes *FGrHist* 523 F 1, both cited in the Lindian chronicle (Higbie 2003: 72 sec. 16–17 and 131 sec. 90–91); see also Diod. Sic. 5,58; S. Morris 1993: 133.
123. S. Morris 1993: 133–35; cf. López-Ruiz 2010: 25–27.
124. Indeed Danaos is the least popular of the "barbarian" culture heroes; his earliest reference might be Hecataeus *FGrHist* 1 F 119. On dramatic treatments of Danaos and the Danaids, see Vasunia 2001: 33 n. 1; for general discussion see E. Hall 1989a: 36–37; M. L. West 1997: 446–47; Gruen 2011: 229–33. Kadmos is sometimes called Egyptian; for the latter, see Bacc. 18.39–40 Snell and Pherecydes *FGrHist* 3 F 21.
125. E.g., Pennington 1841: 22. Today, the conquests of Sesostris are largely associated with Martin Bernal, who literally credited him with the prehistoric conquest and settlement of Greece (1987–2006: 2.187–273). Bernal never acknowledged the use of this myth in the Black historical counternarrative; see Daniels 2019.
126. Manetho (*BNJ* 609 F 3) equates Sesostris to Senusret III, the third king of the twelfth dynasty. Herodotus and other Greek writers seem to equate Sesostris with the deeds of several New Kingdom pharaohs; see Lloyd 1982: 38; Ryholt 2010: 431, Quack 2013b: 64.
127. These monuments are now known to be neo-Hittite monuments with inscriptions in Luwian hieroglyphs. The inscription between Ephesus and Phocaea has not been identified, but the inscription between Smyrna and Sardis is likely the Karabel relief. Other neo-Hittite reliefs in the region are found at Akpınar, Torbalı, and Suratkaya. See Ivantchik 1999: 401–3, Mac Sweeney 2017: 389 map 1.
128. Τὰ δὴ καὶ μετεξέτεροι τῶν θεησαμένων Μέμνονος εἰκόνα εἰκάζουσί μιν εἶναι, πολλὸν τῆς ἀληθείης ἀπολελειμμένοι ("Other observers claim they are signs left by Memnon, veering greatly from the truth").
129. †τέαρε[.....]δεύειετ τὴν ἐπὶ Σμύρνης / ἰθὺ διὰ Λυδῶν παρὰ τὸν Ἀττάλ<εω> τύμβον / καὶ σῆμα Γύγ<εω> καὶ [Σεσώ]στρ[ιος] στήλην / καὶ μνῆμα Τωτος Μυτάλιδι πάλμυδος, / πρὸς ἤλιον δύνοντα γαστέρα τρέψας: "follow the road to Smyrna, go on through Lydia past the tomb of Attales, the barrow of Gyges and Sesostris' stele, and the †μνήματ' ώτοςt, lord at Mutalis, turning your belly towards the setting sun." On this emendation, see Ivantchik 1999: 404; Dale 2013: 49. [Σεσώ]στρ[ιος] is still accepted by West, but codd. offer the possibly non-Greek word μεγάστρυ.
130. Ivantchik 1999: 401.
131. Vasilescu 2007: 121–22; Rung and Gablenko 2019: 92.
132. The earliest evidence for the Demotic cycle independent of Herodotus is the fifth century Sheik el-Fadl *dipinto* from Thebes; for the text, see Porten and Yardeni 1986-99 D23.1. For a list of texts and proposed chronologies, see Hoffmann 2009: 355–59, Jay 2016: 127–31. On Herodotus as a source, see Hoffmann 2009: 352–64; Quack 2013b.
133. For general discussion, see Jay 2016: 127–210; Rutherford 2016: 99–100.
134. Ivantchik 1999: 441.

135. Hölbl 1999/2000: 12–13.
136. Kitchen 1986: 359, 369; Hölbl 1999/2000: 18; Lohwasser 2014: 179.
137. Lohwasser 2014: 184.
138. For scarabs with praenomen of Senusret III, see Skon-Jedele 1994 no. 1186 (Artemis Orthia); Skon-Jedele 1994 no. 3797 (Lindos); Skon-Jedele 1994 no. 4557 (Ialysos); and Vercoutter 1945 no. 19 (Carthage).
139. Ryholt 2010: 436.
140. Kitchen 1986: 141–43, 376–77; Markiewicz 2008: 326.
141. Two major examples are known from Italy. For the Bocchoris scarab from Pithekoussai, see and De Salvia 1993: 779 no. 325-16; Ridgway 1999: 152 no. 325–16. For the Bocchoris vessel from Tarquinia, see Sannibale 2014: 318–19 no. 187.
142. See Manetho *FGrHist* 609 F 3c; Hecataeus of Abdera *FGrHist* 264 F 25 = Diod. 1.79.1; Tac. *Hist.* 5.3; Ael. *de nat.* 12.3.
143. Gill and Vickers (1996) date the appearance of the tradition to as early as the seventh century. Their chronological argument has been dismissed by Ridgway (1999) and Hölbl (1999/2000), but Markiewicz (2008) has revived a Saite date for the appearance of a mythology surrounding Bocchoris.
144. On the use of hieroglyphs in Egyptian decorative schemes, see R. Wilkinson 1992.
145. Skuse 2021: 61.
146. Skon-Jedele 1994: 1380.
147. Taranto grave 1 on Via Nitti between Corso Umberto and Via di Palma was excavated by G.F. Lo Porto between 30 June and 4 July 1960. It is dated by ceramics to 545–40 BCE. See Hölbl 1979: 1.130–42, 1979: 2.219–37 nos. 1065–1221.
148. ἔστι πόλις Ἐφύρη μυχῷ Ἄργεος ἱπποβότοιο, / ἔνθα δὲ Σίσυφος ἔσκεν, ὁ κέρδιστος γένετ' ἀνδρῶν
149. Ephyra also appears in the *Odyssey* (1.259–65) as a land of poisons. Although *Il.* 6.154–55 states Sisyphos was king of Ephyra, the association between Sisyphos and Corinth per se is first attested in Eumelos *EGEF* fr. 24. For discussion, see M.L. West 2002: 119; Ziskowski 2014: 85; Tsagalis 2017: 95.
150. Our basic knowledge about Eumelos' *Korinthiaka* remains shaky, and there is some reason to think it might have been an inference by Hellenistic scholiasts. The earliest equation between Ephyra and Corinth are Eumelos *EGEF* frs. 16 and 17. Ziskowski (2014: 86–87) argues that the *Iliad* is already drawing off Corinthian traditions, but this is not accepted by M. West (2002: 119, 2013: 65) and Tsagalis (2017: 82–85), who place the poem in the sixth century.
151. On this passage, see Powell 1991: 198–200; Ceccarelli 2013: 59–62.
152. Papadopoulos 2016: 1239–45; López-Ruiz 2021: 226–36.
153. The earliest reference to 'Phoenician letters' is *SEG* 60.986 (Eltyna, Crete) τὰ] ποινικήια (l. 2), dating to 600–550 BCE; see Kritzas 2010. Subsequent references include *SEG* 27.631(Aphrati, Crete) ποινικάζεν (l. A.5), dating to 500 BCE and *SEG* 31.985 (Teos, Ionia) [φ]- / οινικογρα- / φέων (l. D.19–20), dating to 480–50 BCE; see W. West 2015: 60 n. 20.

154. Herodotus states that the 'Phoenician' Gephyraios family claim to come from Eretria (5.57.1). Herodotus disputes this with the claim that they are 'Phoenician,' reasoning that they must have actually come from Boeotia; see López-Ruiz 2021: 235.
155. Papadopoulos 2016: 1239.
156. Theories of Phoenician settlement have long attended Corinth. Dow (1942) proposed three points of evidence for an early Phoenician presence: a syncretism between Melikertes-Palaimon, the child hero of Isthmia, and the Phoenician Melqart; the cult of Athena Phoinike; and the month of Phoinikaios. Subsequently, S. Morris and Papadopoulos (1999) argue that the origins of the Protocorinthian style can be found in a population of Phoenician immigrants who worshipped at some tentatively identified stele shrines in the Potters' Quarter; cf. Papadopoulos 2016: 1241, "indeed, the evidence for immigrant craftsmen at . . . Corinth is clear." These arguments have been accepted by Ziskowski (2016: 99–100) and most robustly by López-Ruiz (2021: 53, 186–87, 191–95, 197), who sees the scarab assemblage at Perachora as evidence for a Phoenician presence. This argument remains difficult, given how little is known about Archaic Corinth in general. The presence of Egyptian(-izing) material culture or an interest in styles from the Eastern Mediterranean cannot be taken as proof of a resident community of Phoenicians. In fact, Corinth has attracted its fair share of 'migration' theories; de Salvia (1985) argued for resident Egyptians. Skuse (2021: 51–60) presents a robust argument against migration-based models of stylistic diffusion in Archaic Corinth.
157. The earliest writing at Corinth is a short inscription on an LG Kotyle from the Potter's Quarter (inv. no. KP 1335), followed by a much longer of MPC date (KP 1336a + b). That only 30 or so stone inscriptions are known from the entirety of the Archaic Period in Corinth is probably due to issues of survival (compare with the 130 *dipinti* known through the sixth century), but even these numbers pale with elsewhere. For survey, see Powell 1991: 132–34; Ziskowski 2010: 235–44.
158. On local scripts and identity, see Luraghi 2010. For the diffusionist model, see foldout in Kirchhoff (1887) with discussion in Salmon (1984: 145); Jeffery and Johnston (1990: 42); Luraghi (2010: 83–84).
159. Hölbl 1979: 1.212; Skon-Jedele 1994: 291–99; Gorton 1996: 72.
160. The *aegyptiaca* from Perachora have only rarely been discussed in print since their 1962 publication by James. Major discussions of the sanctuary at Perachora and Corinthian religion in general by Sinn (1990), C. Morgan (1994), Menadier (1995), and Novaro-Lefèvre (2000) have all but left them out. *Aegyptica* from Perachora are currently being republished by Matthew Skuse (cf. Skuse 2021).
161. Traces of this debate are appear in late compilers. Souda φ 787 and Photius φ 652 s.v. Φοινικήια γράμματα both claim there was an early debate between "Lydians and Ionians" and Cretans over foreign vs. domestic origins. What Jeffrey called a "theory of division," where authors allow polygenous origins for the alphabet, appears as early as the fourth century; this appears in Pliny *NH* 7.56.192. See Jeffrey

1967: 155; Ceccarelli 2013: 68. Some foreign attributions, including Assyrians (Anon. *FGrHist* 468 F 1 = Diod. 5.73.1) and the Egyptian god Thoth (Phaidros 274c-275a, Diod. 1.16.1) are not traceable before the late fourth century.
162. For a summary of competing traditions about the invention of the alphabet, see Jeffreys 1967; Węcowski 2010 s.v. 9 F 1; Pownall 2013 s.v. *BNJ* 1 F 20; Ceccarelli 2013: 64–68; Almagor 2014.
163. Jeffrey 1967: 152; ἐν δετέρωι τῆς Ὀρεστείας ... τὸν Παλαμήδην φησὶν εὑρηκέναι [τὰ γράμματα] ("In the second book of his *Oresteia* ... he says Palamedes discovered letters").
164. Ceccarelli 2013: 66.
165. Πυθόδωρος (IV) δὲ [ὡς] ἐν τῶι Περὶ στοιχείων καὶ Φίλλις ὁ Δήλιος (II) ἐν τῶι Περὶ Χρόνων πρὸ Κάδμου Δαναὸν μετακομίσαι αὐτὰ φασιν. ἐπιμαρτυροῦσι τούτοις καὶ οἱ Μιλησιακοὶ συγγραφεῖς Ἀναξίμανδρος (9 F 3) καὶ Διονύσιος (III) καὶ Ἑκαταῖος, οὓς καὶ Ἀπολλόδωρος ἐν Νεῶν καταλόγωι (II) παρατίθεται. ("Pythodorus in his On Letters and Phillis of Delos in his On Time say that Danaus brought them [letters] instead of Cadmus. The Milesian writers Anaximander, Dionysius, and Hecataeus provide witness, which Apollodorus cites in his Catalogue of Inventions").
166. See Lloyd 1975: 55–60; Salmon 1984: 225–26; Skon-Jedele 1994: 208–12. Some editors correct his father's name to the Gorgos, brother of Periander, referred to in Plut. *Sept. Sap. Conv.* 17.
167. Ure 1922: 213.
168. This is especially the case for Chian and south Ionian wares. At Corinth, 34 out of a total 36 Chian vessels were chalices; 25 out of the total 66 south Ionian vessels were black glazed cups or bowls. At Perachora, 55 east Greek vessels are known in total; slightly over the majority of these are open sympotic shapes, and all 18 Chian vessels are either cups or chalices. For east Greek ceramics from Perachora, see Dunbabin 1962: 373–78; for Corinth, see Siegel 1978: 64–217, 296–351.
169. See Catling 1973/74: 7–8; Williams, MacIntosh and Fisher 1973: 14–24; Pfaff 2003: 138 n. 202; for Chian and south Ionian wares from the building, see Siegel 1978: 74, 166–67.
170. Corinthian pottery at Naukratis has long been thought to be carried by Aeginetans; see Ure 1922: 215; Salmon 1984: 144; Bergeron 2015: 269–73.

CHAPTER 3

1. Wilkerson 2010: 97–98. Excerpt from *The Warmth of Other Suns: The Epic Story of America's Great Migration* by Isabel Wilkerson, copyright © 2010 by Isabel Wilkerson. Used by permission of Random House, an imprint and division of Penguin Random House LLC. All rights reserved.
2. Wilkerson 2010: 36–46.
3. Blackmon 2008: 267–69, 74–75.

4. Nightingale 2012: 295–332.
5. Omi and Winant 2015 [1986]: 21–39.
6. Reed 2013: 49.
7. McCoskey 2022; Parmenter 2024a.
8. Matić 2018: 23–39.
9. Parmenter 2021a.
10. Derbew (2022: xiv–iv, 14) uses orthography to distinguish black people in antiquity from Blackness as a legal and social regime in modernity.
11. Derbew 2022: 16.
12. I follow Derbew (2022: 48) in not capitalizing "black" in reference to dark-skinned people in antiquity.
13. Snowden 1947: 290–92; 1948: 40; 1971: vii; 1976: 133–35; 1983: vii.
14. Snowden 1947: 268–82; 1948: 31–33; 1971: 1–21; 1983: 3–17.
15. Snowden 1947: 288; 1948: 41; 1971: 216–18; 1976: 242–45; 1983: 63–65.
16. Hock n.d.
17. Parmenter 2021a: 6.
18. L. Thompson 1989: 25–27; Bernal 1987–2006: 1.434–36.
19. E.g., Snowden's gratuitously aggressive review of L. Thompson 1989 (Snowden 1990b), which marginalized Thompson from the literature until very recently. There is no doubt that Isaac's book suffers from both a failure to engage very much with post-1945 literature on race, and a lack of interest in ancient views toward Blackness (McCoskey 2006: 254–54). The latter is what Haley (2005: 452), Betancourt (2020: 177), and Derbew (2022: 19–21) articulate as erasure.
20. Figure 3.1, A comes from Berezan, Ukraine, but was very likely manufactured at Naukratis; see Parmenter 2019: 20 n. 13.
21. Snowden 1976: 140.
22. See Parmenter 2021a: 15–16 ns. 70–71; this practice continues even in recent publications (e.g., Masson-Berghoff 2018: 8–10; Apostola and Kousoulis 2019: 16). Both Gaither et al. (2020) and Derbew (2022: 34) note the tendency for scholars to identify representations as "Black" or "African" without much reflection.
23. Petrie 1886: 36.
24. Although speculations about "Africans" in ancient authors appear sporadically in writers as far back as the Enlightenment, concerted scholarly interest only emerged after World War I. For bibliographical review, see Beardsley 1929: v–vi; Snowden 1970: 1–2, ns. 1–5; Isaac 2004: 8–13. Other major studies of the 1920s include Seltman 1920; Beazley 1929. Beardsley's primary supervisor, D. M. Robinson (1880–1958), collected "Negroid" figurines (Fraser 1929: 426). Although Robinson was famous for plagiarizing his female graduate students (Kaiser 2015), he appears to have never stolen from Beardsley.
25. McCoskey 2022: 252.
26. The department disinvited the American Philological Association's several Black members from attending the 1908 and 1920 annual meetings it hosted in

27. Frank 1916.
28. Baltimore's Black population grew 27.1% between 1910 and 1940; see US Census Bureau 2012.
29. On migration panics and the socialization of Anglo-American Classics, see Padilla Peralta 2015; 2021: 158–59; cf. comments in Posner 2021.
30. Beardsley 1929: 21.
31. Derbew 2022: 23–25.
32. Brewer 1929: 534.
33. Du Bois 1947: x.
34. A Google Scholar search (surely incomplete) finds only ten citations of Beardsley between 1929 and 1980, subtracting her book's initial reviews, as well as Snowden's rebuttals.
35. Letter from Frank M. Snowden to unidentified correspondent, June 14, 1932. W. E. B. Du Bois Papers, Special Collections and University Archives, University of Massachusetts Amherst Libraries.
36. McManus 2020.
37. Parmenter 2021a: 7–11.
38. McCoskey 2012: 180.
39. Lissarrague 1990: 1–2.
40. Lissarrague 1995: 4; Bérard 2000: 395.
41. Heng 2018: 19.
42. Hemelrijk 1984.
43. The earliest versions of the Busiris narrative appear in the early fifth-century writers Pherecydes (Σ Ap. Rhod. 4.1396) and Panyassis (Ath. 4.172d) Panyassis' nephew Herodotus (2.45) declares the story an attempt to smear Egyptians as barbarous; see Vasunia 2001: 185–93.
44. Olya 2021.
45. Eaverly 2013: 113–17.
46. As Derbew (2022: 22) notes, Furtwängler and Reichhold's 1904 watercolor of the Busiris hydria appeared on the cover of Isaac's *Invention of Racism* (2004), visually modified as to make Herakles' skin black. The vase is otherwise only tangentially discussed in Isaac's book.
47. Skuse 2018: 235.
48. Snowden 1971: 159–60.
49. E. Hall 1989a: 172.
50. Snowden 1971: 19; 1983: 56; 1990a: 162.
51. "He was round-shouldered, dark of skin, and curly-haired, and his name was Eurybates; and Odysseus honored him above his other comrades, because he was like-minded with himself" (γυρὸς ἐν ὤμοισιν, μελανόχροος, οὐλοκάρηνος, / Εὐρυβάτης δ' ὄνομ' ἔσκε· τίεν δέ μιν ἔξοχον ἄλλων / ὧν ἑτάρων Ὀδυσεύς, ὅτι οἱ φρεσὶν ἄρτια ᾔδη).

52. Dee 2004: 161; cf. J. Murray 2021: 154.
53. See Skinner's different perspective (2012: 96).
54. This volume was published by the Houston-based Menil Foundation, which had funded the original Harvard University Press *Image of the Black in Western Art* (1976–1994) series. It is favorably reviewed by Snowden 1990a.
55. Snowden 1976: 140; Karageorghis 1988: 22–31.
56. Derbew 2022: 66–97.
57. William Shakespeare, *The Tempest* 1.2.397–405.
58. *Od.* 4.128–32, quoted by Gunter (2009: 68–69).
59. Rask 2020: 138–40.
60. Papalexandrou 2010: 43–45; 2016: 42–52.
61. ἀλλ' ἤ τοι πρώτιστα λέων γένετ' ἠϋγένειος, / αὐτὰρ ἔπειτα δράκων καὶ πάρδαλις ἠδὲ μέγας σῦς· / γίνετο δ' ὑγρὸν ὕδωρ καὶ δένδρεον ὑψιπέτηλον.
62. Courtois 1984: 114–34; Lassen 2000: 233–35.
63. For human head-shaped weights, Schaeffer 1936: 147 fig. 12, B (Ugarit); Bossert 1951: 21 no. 306 (no provenance); Maier 1971 pl. XX.4–6 (Kouklia); Courtois 1983: 123 no. 11 (Kalavasos-Ayios Dhimitrios); 1984: 57 no. 511 (Enkomi).
64. For the weight set from Kalavasos-Ayios Dhimitrios, see Courtois 1983 nos. 5–15; Lassen 2000: 235–36; for a weight set with balance from Ugarit, Schaeffer 1936: 147–50, pl. XXIV.
65. Crielaard 2018: 198–99.
66. S. Murray 2018a: 55–58.
67. On head seals in Cyprus, see Zazoff 1983: 170–71; Karageorghis 1988: 14–19; Clerc 1991: 20–21, 116–17; Boardman 1991: 162; Reyes 2001: 34–40; the Levant, Stern 1976: 116–17; Giveon 1978: 90–91; and North Africa, Vercoutter 1945: 195–99 with pl. XIII.
68. For instance, Amathus T.232 where an "Assyrian" and a headdress-wearing pendant appear on the same necklace; see Clerc 1991: 15–17, 64–68; Boardman 1991: 159–62.
69. Appendix 5.2 no. 19, Amathus T.242; see Clerc 1991: 24–26, 72–75.
70. Appendix 5.2 nos. 38–41, Amathus T.297; see Boardman 1991: 162; Reyes 2001: 34–36.
71. E.g., the necklaces in Amathus T.142 ("Assyrian" center pendant); a necklace from Taranto with an "African" center pendent (Appendix 5.4 no. 69; Hölbl 1979: 2 no. 1220) offers a similar case. On seal-wearing votaries, see Lagarce 1976: 168–74 and Beer 1994 pls. 1–3, 8–38. Heads are used as center pendants in the necklaces from Amathus tombs 142 (Clerc 1991: 5–9; Boardman 1991: 162) and 550 (Karageorghis 1973).
72. The seventeen amulets listed in Appendix 5.1 without provenance, three (nos. 11, 13, 15) certainly come from Cyprus, while others have been assigned Cypriot origin by curators.
73. Marconi 2004; Gunter 2009: 126–28; Papalexandrou 2010.
74. J. Smith 2009: 15.

75. Rask 2020: 138–40.
76. Skon-Jedele 1994: 879 only lists scarab B (no. 1246).
77. See Masson-Berghoff 2018: 27–28. On the use of decorative hieroglyphs generally, see R. Wilkinson 1992: 9–12. On Nilotic vegetation in Cypro-Phoenician art, see Markoe 1985: 55 with no. E12; Reyes 2001: 94.
78. Markoe 1985: 320–23 no. G4; on city-siege scenes, see Markoe 1985: 51–52.
79. For examples from Italy, see Markoe 1985: nos. E3, E5–7, E8–9, E11, and E13.
80. This is perhaps notable because David Robinson, who published scarab C (1949), was Beardsley's doctoral advisor.
81. E.g., Boardman and Hayes 1966: 165 no. 92; Karageorghis 1988: 15–16 nos. 6–7; Webb 2016: 99 no. 167; Masson-Berghoff 2018: 8–10, all describing objects in this shape.
82. Masson-Berghoff 2018: 10, fig. 13.
83. O'Connor 2000: 97–99; Tubb 2014: 44 no. 10.
84. Sørensen 2013; the bulk of these are Gjerstad type IV/V Bichrome and White Painted vessels, dating to CAI (700–600 BCE).
85. See Wachsmann 2000: 115, figs. 6.13–15, 17–19.
86. Assyrian records from as early as the reigns of Tiglath-pileser III (738–32 BCE) mention *Iamanaja* "who live in the midst of the sea" harassing the borders of empire (for phrase, see Sargon II's accounts in Luckenbill 1927: 2.80, 92, 99, 118). Much has been made of references to "Ionian" raiders in this period; for a summary of views, see Braun 1982: 14–21; Luraghi 2006: 30–35; Hale 2013: 180–84; Rollinger 2001, however, urges caution.
87. Ebbinghaus 2006: 210–12; Luraghi 2006: 38–40; Apostola 2018: 120.
88. Both Gunter (2009: 124–28) and Feldman (2014: 161–70) employ a contextual reading of reinscribed north Syrian horse trappings dedicated at Eretria, Samos, and Miletos to express doubts on the mercenary thesis. Guralnick (2004: 219) and Niemeier (2014: 296) have argued for the trade in scrap metal as a major source for dedications.
89. Lanfranchi 2011: 225–30.
90. Sørensen 2013: 168.
91. Bahrani 2006: 55–57; see also Aruz and de Lapérouse 2014: 145–56. On the imitation in Assyrian ivory carving, see Gunter 2009: 117–23; Feldman 2014: 11–18.
92. Quoted on Lehmann and Tallis 2019: 35.
93. Thomas Clarkson, *History of the Rise, Progress, and Abolition of the* African Slave Trade (1968 [1808]: 191–92).
94. For an accounting, see Aptheker 1970; Guyatt 2000: 97–98. Although enslaved Africans are ubiquitous in eighteenth-century British art, representations of slaves in pain only begin to appear around 1770; see Bindman 1994: 76–79.
95. D. B. Davis 1975: 113–19.
96. Mintz 1985: 68–70.
97. Lawrance and Roberts 2019: 173.

98. Webb 2015a: 21–25; Webb 2019b: 50.
99. Jenkins 2001: 168; Webb 2015a: 4.
100. See Webb 2015a: 19; 2016: 122, 131.
101. Webb 2015a: 7–8.
102. Webb 2015a: 19 fig. 9 and 18 fig. 27.
103. These are published as Webb 1978 nos. 381 and 405 respectively.
104. Webb 2021: 28.
105. Frankfurter 1998: 104.
106. Webb 1978: 102–3, nos. 628–37.
107. Webb 2016: 196–200; 2021: 17–22.
108. The stratigraphy of the Aphrodite sanctuary is not known; see Webb 2015a: 13–14. Webb has located twelve male *aulos*-players at the sanctuary.
109. Webb 2015a: 15–16; Ross Thomas 2015b: 5. These fourteen figurines are those published by Webb 1978.
110. Petrie (1886: 62 nos. 532 and 531 respectively) was quick to restore sherd inscriptions as Σαφ[or Ῥοδ[, proving that luminaries like Sappho or Rhodopis had been present at the Greek sanctuaries; for further examples of this logic, see Gardner 1888: 64.
111. The existence of Archaic-Classical "taverns" or "brothels" has been argued for at Corinth (C. H. Morgan 1953); long debate has followed Building Z in the Athenian Keremeikos. On the physical space of taverns, see Kurke 1999: 72–80; Davidson 1998: 53–61. Rauh, Dillon, and McClain (2008: 197–208) offer a contextual reading of a Hellenistic building with a similar argued function near the docks on Delos. The best-attested brothel in Late Archaic/Early Classical Greece appears to have been near the quayside at Thasos, as attested by part of a fragmentary law dated c. 480 BCE (*SEG* 42.785). The lines in question (l. 30–35) read: ἐπὶ τõ τέγεος τῶν | κατ᾽ οἰκιῶν τῶν δημοσίων τῶν ἐν τῆι ὁδῶι τ— | αὐτηι: θῆς ἕνεκεν μηδὴς ἀναβαινέτω: μηδ— | ἐ γυνὴ δ᾽ ἐ[κ] τῶν θυρίδων θήσθω· ὅ τι ἄν τούτ— | ων ποιῆι: στατῆρα κατ᾽ ἕκαστον ὁ ἐνοικέων |ὀφελέτω τῆι πόλι. ("Let no climb up onto the roof of the public houses [Graham translates 'brothels'] on this street for the purpose of being seen; let no woman peek out from the windows; whoever does this, let the inhabitant owe a stater to the city each time"). See Graham 1998; Henry 2002.
112. There has been some ambivalence whether the women of the Naukratis inscriptions were sex workers. The assumption that they were by early excavators (e.g., Gardner 1888: 64) has made later scholars rightfully wary; see Demetriou 2010: 69; 2012: 141.
113. Beazley (1927: 352) accompanied his description with a fictional dialog between the two.
114. *Dipinti* are relatively rare in *Lieblingsinschriften*; Lang 1971: 11–15, publishing examples from the Athenian Agora, does not find a single one.

115. Ethnonyms were typically slave names (Vlassopoulos 2010: 116). Perhaps the most vivid example is a late fifth-century Attic cup from the Agora inscribed Σικέλα καταπύγ(αινα); see Lang 1971: 14 no. C27. Aigyptia is attested as a name for enslaved women in fourth-century Athens from three funerary stelae, as well as a name inscribed on a manumission bowl (*IG* 2² 1567.3). For a survey of the evidence, see Bäbler 1998: 209–11 nos. 4–7.
116. Petrie 1886: 36. For recent re-evaluations of the "scarab factory," see Masson-Berghoff 2018: 23; Webb 2019b: 66–67; Parmenter 2021a: 11–18.
117. Masson-Berghoff 2018: 9, ch. 3.
118. Some head scaraboids clearly predate the Naukratis "scarab factory." Two physiognomic scaraboids from Perachora (Appendix 5.4 cat. nos. 60–61) date before 600 BCE; see James 1962: 466. Four head scaraboids from Kameiros (Appendix 5.4 cat. nos. 16–18, 53) date to the seventh century as well.
119. There remains some disagreement between scholars on which represent "Bes" and which are "Black Africans"; see Gorton 1996: 97; Masson-Berghoff 2018: 4 n. 8.
120. Villing 2019: 209.
121. Mason-Berghoff 2018: 86–88.
122. van Oppen 2020: 8.
123. For the relationship between masking and head pendants in the Phoenician world, see Stern 1976: 116. On masking rituals on Cyprus, see Averett 2015. Snowden himself identified the preponderance of representations of "Ethiopians" in the western Mediterranean; see Snowden 1976: 148 figs. 161–62, 149 fig. 163, 158–59, figs. 181–83.
124. Karageorghis, Mertens, and Rose 2000: 197–98 nos. 326–28.
125. On Egyptian portrayals of non-Egyptians, see O'Connor 2003; Bahrani 2006.
126. Webb 1978: 122; on production contexts, see Webb 1978: 108; 2015b: 5–6.
127. Webb 1978: 130–31 nos. 874–83. Of these, no. 876 is certainly not janiform; see Parmenter 2021b. Subsequently published examples include Figures 3.18, A, B, D, E.
128. A few examples, including Figure 3.18, C (and likely also the origins of Webb 1978 nos. 875, 883) come from tombs, albeit from uncontrolled excavations. Figure 3.18, B came from a controlled but unstratigraphic excavation at a sanctuary; see Parmenter 2021b.
129. Reger 2005: 254–57.
130. Simon 1970: 17.
131. Biers 1994.
132. A. Smith 2018.
133. Lissarrague 2015.
134. E.g., Snowden 1971; Gruen 2011.
135. Lissarrague 1995: 4.
136. Derbew 2022: 37.

137. Hobden 2013: 66–116.
138. Derbew 2022: 42.
139. Lesher 1992: 90–95; Skinner 2012: 96.
140. Mintz 1985: xxiv.

CHAPTER 4

1. This chapter draws heavily on Madalina Dana's magisterial new edition of the letters (2021), henceforth abbreviated *CGP*. The original version of this chapter (published as Parmenter 2020) followed the edition of Ceccarelli (2013). Earlier checklists of the letters can be found in Dana 2007, Eidinow and Taylor 2010. The initial discovery of the letters in the 1970s encouraged scholars, beginning with Bravo (1974), to vouch for the literacy of traders in Archaic Greece; see also J.-P. Wilson 1997–98. A recent discussion of the lead letters in their wider epigraphic context can be found in Lamont 2023.
2. Hartman 2008: 11.
3. J. Morgan 2021.
4. Finley 1980: 9.
5. K. Fields and B. Fields 2012: 17.
6. Hunt 2018: 28.
7. E.g. McKeown 2002: 31; F. H. Thompson 2003: 104; Gruen 2011: 210; Pandey 2020: 18. On the historiography of this debate, see Parmenter 2024a.
8. Finley 1980: 18.
9. Smallwood (2007), Rediker (2007), and Lindsay and Sweet (2014) have used the reconstructed life histories of slaves to explore the workings of the Atlantic slave trade. Purcell (2013: 85–88) proposes a similar approach for studying life histories in the ancient Mediterranean. Harrison (2019) explores connections between Greek ethnography and the slave trade. A previous version of this chapter was Parmenter 2020.
10. Some exceptions: Forsdyke 2012; Padilla Peralta 2017.
11. Finley 1980: 108. Finley's legacy in shaping narratives of slavery in antiquity has recently been examined by Bodel (2018) and Lenski and Cameron (2018).
12. See Stampp 1956; Curtin 1969; Fogel and Engerman 1974; Mintz 1985.
13. See Blassingame 1972; Genovese 1974; Patterson 1982.
14. Finley 1981 [1959]: 114; see discussion by Descat 2006: 22.
15. Finley (1980: 86–87); Garlan (1988: 37–40); and Patterson (1991: 78) adopt this narrative.
16. Finley's argument for an abrupt phase-change in the Solonic period had already been challenged by Fisher (1993: 14–21), Rihill (1996: 95–96), and Descat (2006: 32–33).
17. On the politics of Finley's binaries, see Nafissi 2015; on Finley and global slaveries, see Lenski 2018: 19–24.

18. This is the position taken by Arist. *Pol.* 1.6, 1255a, who sees the enslavement of Greeks as accidents contrary to nature. On this principle see Finley 1980: 118; Fisher 1993: 86–89; Fynn-Paul 2009: 4.
19. Captive laborers have long been assumed to be an important export from the Black Sea; see, e.g., Minns 1913: 436–48. The current dialog about the impact of slavery in the region begins after World War II. See Blavatskiy 1954; Finley 1981 [1962]; Velkov 1964, 1967; Pippidi 1966, 1975; Khazanov 1975; Braund and Tsetskhladze 1989; Hind 1994; Vinogradov 1998; Heinen 2001a; Taylor 2001; Gavriljuk 2003; Braund 2007b, 2011; Avram 2007; Tsetsklhadze 2007a; Lewis 2011; Fischer 2016.
20. The demography of Athenian slavery has been constructed on the basis of three slave lists—*IG* I^3 421–30 (415/4 BCE), *IG* I^3 474–76 (412 BCE), and *IG* I^3 1032 (410–400 BCE)—and a collation of fourth-century Laurion funerary inscriptions by Lauffer (1979 [1956]); these are collected by Lewis (2011: 111–13). Demographic evidence from elsewhere is sporadic; for additional epigraphical lists, see Robert 1935: 459 (Chios, late fifth century), *SEG* 23.381 = *IG* 9.1^2 4.1778 (Rheneia, third century BCE; for discussion see Pippidi 1966), and *IG* 12^1 881 (Lindos, Hellenistic; for discussion see Bresson 1997), as well as the synthetic list of slaves from Hellenistic Lokris collected by Blavatskaja 1972: 60–62 (see also Lewis 2018: 277–82). The value of onomastics in determining slave ethnicity is a topic of fierce debate; see Pritchett and Pippin 1956; Pippidi 1966; Velkov 1967; Tsetskhladze 2007a; Robertson 2008; Vlassopoulos 2010; Braund 2011; Lewis 2011. For ancient perspectives on using names to determine the origin of slaves, see Pl. *Cra.* 384b and Varro *Ling.* 8.9 with Braund and Tsetskhladze 1989: 119; Avram 2007: 242; Fischer 2016: 56; Harrison 2019: 45.
21. Phrygia was another region consistently depicted as a source of slaves by Greek writers; see Lewis 2011, 2015; Andreeva 2017.
22. Harrison (2019: 37–39) recently notes this dynamic in Greek ethnographies of the Black Sea. On the role of the slave trade in European ethnographies of the African "slave coast" in the seventeenth and eighteenth centuries, see Rediker 2007: 73–107; Smallwood 2007: 102–9.
23. Hind 1994: 154; Braund 2011: 180; Alexianu 2011; Lewis 2015.
24. On fifth-century depictions of this region, see Hartog 1988 [1980]; Romm 1992: 60–77; Ros. Thomas 2000: 54–71; S. West 2003; Harrison 2019. On the centrality of slavery behind Herodotus' depictions, see Heinen 2001a: 489; Taylor 2001: 34–35; Braund 2007b.
25. Horden and Purcell 2000: 133–34; Dietler 2010: 49–50.
26. Lewis 2015 n. 47 citing Pollux 7.14 and Harpokration s.v.
27. J. C. Miller 2014.
28. Hartman 2008; cf. J. Morgan 2021.
29. Lindsay and Sweet 2014: 5.
30. Vlassopoulos (2016: 12) echoes Miller's call "to shift our focus from slavery as an ahistorical institution to slaving as a historically dynamic agglomeration of processes that involved various agents alongside slaves and masters."

31. This closely follows the interpretation of Bravo 2001; for another interpretation see L. Dubois (1996: 55), whose downdating to c. 400 BCE has not been accepted.
32. In this case, I follow the text and translation of Ceccarelli (2013: 339 no. A6) over Dana's new edition in *CGP* 28.
33. On the long-distance cult networks of the region's Milesian colonies, see Rusjaeva 1986; Burkert 1994; Greaves 2004; Braund 2007a; Herda 2016. The Greek colonization of the region was characterized by the foundation of many Greek settlements in clusters, with some early attempts abandoned within a generation; see A. Bujskikh 2013; Schlotzhauer and Zhuravlev 2014; Giaime et al. 2016.
34. For the hypothesized Ionic temple on Leuke, see Rusjaeva 2003; for Istros, see Alexandrescu 2005: 159–67; Bîrzescu 2018: 261–64; for Phanagoria, see Kuznetsov and Abramzon 2021: 40.
35. A. Bujskikh 2015: 226.
36. These doubts are expressed by Tsetskhladze 2007a, 2007b. A. Bujskikh (2015: 246) argues for the mobility of architects between cities of the region; on coin hoards, see Bresson 2007. Parmenter 2019 discusses the spread of Egyptianizing votives.
37. The 1920 *Black Sea Pilot* notes that Black Sea currents slack in late summer, allowing for opportunistic trips against the prevailing current; see US Hydrographic Office 1920: 126–28.
38. Maximowa 1959: 106; Hind 2001: 25. Herodotus' voyage of three days and two nights indicates how slow this crossing was against the wind; he claims this is the sea's widest point, when in fact it is the narrowest. Dearborn (1819: 2.15) gives the direct passage between the Bosporus and Sevastopol as fifty hours with a south wind during the winter.
39. See Dearborn 1819: 2.2–3; Hobbs 1847: 13; on the three-month itinerary, see Hobbs 1847: 16. The fourth-century Athenian shipping contract preserved in Ps.-Dem. 35.10 requires the contracted merchants to exit the Bosporus by the middle of September or incur a greater rate of interest; see Bresson 2016: 280–85; Russell 2017: 25–37. Sultan Selim III opened the Black Sea to western navigators after the Treaty of Küçük Kaynarca in 1774; on the massive expansion of foreign trade in the years following, see Özveren 1996: 84–87.
40. On the foundation of Chersonesos, see Klenina 2015: 38–39. Chersonesos was formally colonized by Dorians from Heraclea Pontica in 422/1 BCE (Ps.-Skymnos 850), but Milesian settlers were on the scene a century earlier; Milesian names are known from late Archaic ostraca there, while the existence of a fifth-century sherd inscribed with the opening lines of the cyclic *Little Iliad* (Vinogradov and Zolotarev 1988: 109 no. IV) might point to the existence of Achilles cult. Although Maximowa (1959: 106–9) and Arnaud (1992: 62–63) doubt much deep-sea travel between Sinope, Crimea, and Olbia before the end of the fifth century, two *ateleia* decrees are known at Olbia (*IGDOP* 1 and 5) for individuals from Sinope c. 450 BCE.

41. See Tsetskhladze 1998b: 44–47; Solovyev 1998: 29–30; Kryzhitskiy 2007: 107–8. This seems also to have been the case in Aegean Thrace; see Ilieva 2017. The Danube Delta, on the other hand, was clearly inhabited when Greeks arrived: see Avram 2006; Bîrzescu 2018: 252–53.
42. On Herodotus' Scythian interlocutors and his geography of the interior, see Braund 2007a: 349; Ivantichik 2011: 93. On the large concentration of Scythian tombs in this region, see Tsetskhladze 1998b: 24–25; Ivantchik 2011: 93.
43. On Belskoye, see Shramko 1987; on questions surrounding its identification, see Tsetskhladze 1998b: 50. On slaving in the forest-steppe, see Taylor 2001; Gavriljuk 2003; Avram 2007. On early modern slaving in the region, see Kołodziejczyk 2006.
44. For the half-Greek Kallipidai see Hdt. 4.17; for the "Helleno-Scythian" Gelonoi, Hdt. 4.108–9.
45. See Hdt. 4.62, 66, and 70 and Braund 2007b: 3–5. On the earliest Greek imports in the region, see Tsetskhladze 1998b: 10–15; Rusjaeva 1999; and Vakhtina 2007, whose ongoing project is publication of the large assemblage from Nemirovo.
46. On the Peshchannoe canoe, see Tsetskhladze 1998b: 65.
47. Diodoros (5.26.3) notes the existence of a trade in slaves for wine up the Rhône Valley between Greeks and Romans on the coast and Celts in interior Gaul. This has been used to explain spectacular finds of Greek imports in western Europe, such as at Heuneburg in Germany; see Wells 1980: 63–70; Taylor 2001: 28–29; Fentress 2019: 153. Dietler (2010: 48–49) expresses caution on this reading.
48. Boltrik and Fialko 2007.
49. On this dynamic, see Eidinow and Taylor 2010: 38. For letters written in this scenario, see *CGP* 23, 25, 27, 36, 38, 49.
50. For the Achillodoros letter, see *CGP* 25; for the Gorgippa letter, see *CGP* 54.
51. Zavojkina and Pavlichenko 2016, now *CGP* 48. A dialectical variant of this term (ἀνδράποτον) is also used in a newly published lead letter from Myrmekeion on the Crimean side of the Kerch Straits, dating to the mid-fourth century BCE; see *CGP* 46.
52. For Herodotus on slaves in Scythian society, see 4.2–3; on gender, see 4.26 ("the women have equal power with the men," ἰσοκρατέες δὲ ὁμοίως αἱ γυναῖκες τοῖσι ἀνδράσι); for the transgender Enarees (οἱ δὲ ἐνάρεες οἱ ἀνδρόγυνοι), see 4.67. The gender structure of historical slave populations varies widely; in the seventeenth century, the English Royal African Company supplied enslaved Africans to West Indian plantations at a ratio of 2:1 male to female (Smallwood 2007: 164). On the other hand, four-fifths of Crimean slaves exported by the Venetians and Genoese to Italy during the fourteenth century were women (Quirini-Popławska 2017).
53. Over five hundred dugout houses have been excavated at Olbia, Berezan, and their surrounding countryside; see Solovyev 1998: 28–43; A. Bujskikh 2015: 246–47. A small number of dugouts have been discovered elsewhere, including at Istros and Orgame; see Bîrzescu 2018: 249–51.

54. Hylaia and Tendra appear in Hdt. 4.55. On Beikush, see Hedreen 1991: 315–18; S. Bujskikh 2006; and Burgess 2009; for the disks, see S. Bujskikh 2006: 126 pl. 32.
55. For the Tendra sanctuary, see Tunkina 2006, 2007. At least three Classical shipwrecks have been found along the stretch of coast between the Kinbrun Spit and Zmeinyy; see Table 5.1 below. For the Achilles cult at Tyras, see Hupe 2006. On Akkerman as a slaving fortress, see Kołodziejczyk 2006: 154.
56. See Hedreen 1991: 319–22. On the site's Ionic architecture, see Rusjaeva 2003: 7–12.
57. Hedreen 1991: 320; Burgess 2009: 126. For the Steisichoros fragments, see Garner 1993. Proclus' summary of the *Aithiopis* by Arktinos of Miletos claims that the poem depicted Achilles' transfer to Leuke, but it is not clear that it was located in the Black Sea. Euripides' two references to Leuke (*Andr.* 1260–62 and *IT* 435–38) seem to conflate Leuke with Tendra. The most extensive ancient description of Leuke is in Arrian *Periplus* 21.
58. Abramzon and Tunkina 2018 catalog some two hundred coins of the over one thousand found in the nineteenth-century excavations on Zmeinyy.
59. Hobbs 1847: 19.
60. S. Bujskikh 2006: 148–49; Burgess 2009: 128; for reference to the cult, see Ath. 2.43d. The cyclic *Aithiopis* was written by a Milesian author, but the city has few other associations with Achilles; see Bujskhikh 2006: 131; Braund 2007a: 53.
61. ἀκτῇ ἔπι προὐχούσῃ, ἐπὶ πλατεῖ Ἑλλησπόντῳ, / ὥς κεν τηλεφανὴς ἐκ ποντόφιν ἀνδράσιν εἴη. See Hedreen 1991: 313; Burgess 2009: 113.
62. Posamentir (2006) notes that three-quarters of the early sixth-century pottery from Berezan is North Ionian. For veneration of Achilles in the Troad, see Burgess 2009: 112–18.
63. M. L. West 2003.
64. Hupe 2006: 155–57.
65. Hartog 1988 [1980]; Ivantchik 2011.
66. See Heinen 2001b: 10–15 and Braund 2007a: 52–53. C. Meyer (2013: 202–3) doubts this identification.
67. Dearborn 1819: 2.15.
68. These myths culminated in the fifth-century linkage drawn between the Artemis cults in Halai in Attica and at Tauris in Euripides' *Iphigenia in Taurus*. Kowalzig (2013) argues that this connection reflects a longstanding cultic network between the north shore of Attica, the Euboean Gulf, the North Aegean, and the Crimea. This route was the same one that was heavily travelled between the Bosporan Kingdom and Athens in the late fifth and fourth centuries; see Ps.-Dem. 34 and 35.
69. *CGP* 38. Vinogradov (1991: 509–19) proposed that Greek cities were under a Scythian protectorate in the fifth century, but this idea is currently doubted; see Kryzhitskiy 2007 and Braund 2007b: 6.
70. The region on both sides of the straits was densely settled in the first century of Greek presence in the region. Many of the earliest harbor settlements were abandoned within generations due to sedimentation; see Schlotzhauer and Zhuravlev

71. Patterson 1982: 14.
72. For depictions of the Heniochoi, see also Ov. *Pont.* 4.10.25–56 and Strabo 11.2.12–14 with Asheri 1998 and Hind 2012. On Greek characterizations of the Black Sea, see S. West 2003.
73. Arrian (*Periplus* 9) expressly observes this to the emperor Hadrian.
74. See Stronk 1986–87; on navigating the "false entrance," see Hobbs 1847: 15–16. On the local Thracians, see Hipponax fr. 115 West = Archil. fr. 79 Diehl; Aesch. *PB* 726–27; Xen. *An.* 7.5.12; Ps.-Skymnos 723; Strabo 7.6.1; Diod. Sic. 14.37.2–3.
75. *CGP* 25; *CGP* 26. *CGP* 32, an incompletely-published epigraphic letter dating to the fourth century BCE, appears to present a similar case.
76. This poem was attributed to Archilochus by Diehl as fr. 79; see Stronk 1986–87: 66.
77. ὥσπερ αὐλῶι βρῦτον ἢ Θρέϊξ ἀνὴρ / ἢ Φρὺξ ἔμυζε· κύβδα δ' ἦν πον<εο>μένη.
78. *CGP* 25; translation after Ceccarelli 2013: 335 no. A1, slightly modified for clarity.
79. On the origin of Matasys' name, see Bravo 1974: 55–56.
80. Bravo (1974: 150; 1980: 882–83) and J.-P. Wilson (1997–98: 38) argue that Achillodoros actually is a free agent employed by Anaxagoras, mistaken for a slave; this is dismissed by E. M. Harris 2013: 115. The extensive literature on this issue is summarized by Dana 2021: 383–91.
81. *CGP* 26; translation after Ceccarelli 2013: 338–40 no. A5, slightly modified for clarity.
82. On *sulan* see Bravo 1980 and Lintott 2004. J.-P. Wilson (1997–98: 38) describes *sulan* as "a way of getting what you felt was rightfully yours without going to law," but this mischaracterizes: if *Achillodoros or Apatorios felt they could resist without consequences, surely they would have.
83. *SEG* 54.694 advocates the male name Thathaiēn in the accusative; Dana (2007: 76) argues it is a dialectical form of the female name Tataiê, while Santiago and Gardeñes (2006: 61) advocate the non-Greek woman's name Oathaiê.
84. After his family was sold at Olbia, Bion was bought by a *rhētor* "on account of [his] youth and graciousness" (νεώτερον ὄντα καὶ εὔχαριν, Diog. Laert. 4.46), instructed in philosophy, freed, and allowed to emigrate to Athens to make a living.
85. Solon fr. 36 West. Retroactive denationalization and enslavement is a prospect raised in Ps.-Arist. *Ath. Pol.* 42.1, but is a topic we know very little about. *Ath. Pol.* 26.4 claims that the Periclean citizenship laws were passed to reduce the number of citizens, but it is unclear whether the mass denationalization claimed to have taken place in the mid-fifth century by Plutarch (*Per.* 37.3–5) ever happened; see Ogden 1996: 59–64.
86. Phillips 2012: 42. For false claims of citizenship, see *Ps.*-Dem. 49.66–67, 59.16–17, and 59.51–53; for denationalization and enslavement at age eighteen, see *Ps.*-Arist. *Ath. Pol.* 49.2.

87. Zelnick-Abramovitz 2005: 274–92. E. Meyer (2010) takes the opposite stance, arguing that these were prosecutions of metics for failing to pay the metic tax; see further comments by E. M. Harris 2012.
88. Zelnick-Abramovitz 2005: 292–300; for the case of heirs challenging a manumission, see Isaeus fr. 15 Thalheim. Both were common in colonial America; for instances of both in the same court case, see Sweet 2003: 228–39.
89. E. M. Harris (2013: 115) argues that *Achillodoros was looking for someone to "bring him to freedom." The nature of these proceedings is little known; see Zelnick-Abramovitz 2005: 292–300. For their use in preventing testimony, see Isoc. 17.15–16.
90. It seems to have been a real possibility for some lucky captives to be redeemed by their families at home. Several *freedmen accompanied by Herodes on a ship from Athens to Ainos in Thrace in the fifth century were freed in this way (Antiph. 5.20).
91. This possibility is explored and rejected by J.-P. Wilson (1997–98: 37). Vlassopoulos (2010: 119) notes the frequency of theophoric names among the slave population of Classical Athens. A search of *LGPN* s.v. Ἀχιλλ- finds that theophoric names based on Ἀχιλλεύς are relatively rare (forty-seven total) and mostly confined to the Black Sea; Vinogradov (1971: 97) and Bravo (1974: 135) note the obvious allusion to the regional Achilles cult.
92. Zavojkina and Pavlichenko 2016: 235 n. 47.
93. *SIG*³ 4; see Lewis 2015.
94. Kryzhitskiy 2007.
95. *Ps.*-Arist. *Oec.* 2, 1346b. On the onomastics of Byzantion, see Dana 2016: 49–51.
96. Ferreira 2012: 52–87.
97. Sparks 2014.
98. Seven short fragments of Aristeas have generated a large bibliography. See Phillips 1955, 1957; Bowra 1956; Bolton 1960; Huxley 1986; Ivantchik 1993; Mayor and Heaney 1993; S. West 2004; Skinner 2012: 64–68. The Suda (*FGrHist* 35 T 1a) dates Aristeas to the late sixth century BCE, contemporary with Hipponax.
99. This reading was first proposed by Bowra (1956: 5).
100. Fr. 11 Bernabé; translation mine.
101. Diog. Laert. 1.103–104; see Romm 1992: 75.
102. E.g., Hurston 2018 [1931]: 55.
103. Aelian fr. 74a–h Domingo-Foraste; translation mine.
104. Kurke 2011: 10; Forsdyke 2012: 42.

CHAPTER 5

1. Quoted in Behrendt 2010: 140.
2. Behrendt 2010: 160 n. 110.

3. The issue of documentation—and whose voices are preserved in it—came to the fore in the study of the Transatlantic Slave Trade since the publication of the *TASTD* by Eltis et al. in 1999. The *TASTD* preserves a colossal amount of data, allowing intricate reconstruction of transatlantic slaving voyages from c. 1495 through the end of the nineteenth century—and with them, the journeys of over 12 million enslaved people. On the one hand, this mass of data has enabled scholars to track individuals between archives, demonstrating the diversity of fates met by people caught up in the institution of slavery (Lindsay and Sweet 2018). But scholars have become increasingly bothered with how this abundance of documentation reproduces the logic of slavery, focusing on the marketable aspects of captives (name, age, origin, and price) at the expense of other data usually recoverable from archives. For general discussion, see Smallwood 2007: 2–5; Hartman 2008; Berry 2017: 5–9; J. Morgan 2021: 21–23.
4. Handler (2002: 27 tb. 1) collects fifteen accounts of the Middle Passage written by African survivors in any language. Of these, only Olaudah Equiano relates a detailed description of the voyage. Equiano's account is problematic; see Rediker 2007: 109 ns. 2–3.
5. *TASTD* 82258.
6. Behrendt 2010: 160 n. 110.
7. Finley 1999 [1973]: 24. The counterargument to Finley began with Bravo 1974, 1977. For key recent discussion about the complexity of trade in Archaic and Classical Greece, see J.-P. Wilson 1997–98; Dietler 2010: 138–47; Bresson 2016: 345–51; Dana 2021: 363–91; Lamont 2023: 7–11.
8. *TAD* C3.7; for most discussion see van Alfen 2020: 50–59.
9. *Ps.*-Dem. 35.10–13.
10. Dana 2021 = *CGP*.
11. Rostovtzeff 1922.
12. As Purcell notes (2012: 206–20), centralized data collection is rare in the Mediterranean until the end of the Middle Ages. Even Athenian figures are impressionistic. For instance: Demosthenes (20.32) reports that Athens imported 400,000 *mendimioi* of grain annually in 355–54 BCE, but provides no sourcing for this curiously round figure. Likewise, Strabo reports that the Bosporan king Leukon (r. 389–49 BCE) donated some 2,100,000 *mendimioi* from the port of Theodosia in Crimea between 359–44 BCE. For discussion and attempts to rationalize these figures, see Moreno 2007: 207; Bresson 2016: 402–14.
13. Such expressions are widespread. Thus Thucydides' Pericles (2.38.2): "All things from all parts of the earth are imported here, and we no less enjoy the commodities of all other nations than our own." A half century later, Isocrates (4.42) voiced a similar opinion: "And since no land is truly independent from another's commodities—i.e. some come up in short and others produce more than they need—and since there was great confusion where some could dispose the surplus and others fill their needs, our city these needs. It established the Piraeus, a market

in the middle of Greece, which has such abundance that whatever it is difficult to find—something from here, one thing from there—all of it are easy to get your hands on." See Bresson (2016: 339–43) on the idea of a "balance of trade" in Greek political economy.

14. *IG* I³ 61 (Methone decree), *IG* I³ 1453 (Coins, Weights, and Measures decree), *Ps.-Xen. Ath. Pol.* 2.11–13, Thuc. 1.88.2. For detailed discussions of Athenian "mercantilist" policies in the fifth century, see Kallet 2007: 87–90; Kallet and Kroll 2020: 111–19.
15. Moreno 2007: 242–51; Bresson 2016: 317–25.
16. On the metaphor of the household in fourth century political economy (e.g., Xen. *Oec.* 1.4), see Nelsestuen 2017.
17. This passage is often taken as a simple explanation the premodern slave trade; e.g., Taylor 2001: 28–29; Gavriljuk 2003: 79–80; Braund 2011: 121; Fentress 2019: 153. Dietler (2010: 48–49) expresses caution on this reading.
18. "The things imported here from Pontus are quite different" (ἐκ δὲ τοῦ Πόντου ἕτερά ἐστιν ἃ εἰσάγεται δεῦρο).
19. In particular, Grafe (2012: 58–80) explores the use of third commodities to finance long-distance trade.
20. This approach began in earnest with the publication of Michael McCormick's *Origins of the European Economy* (2001, esp. 319–90). For similar studies, see Hind 1994, Taylor 2001; Braund 2011; Fentress 2019; Mata 2019; Raffield 2019.
21. US Hydrographic Office 1920: 233; on ancient sailing routes, see Saprykin 2017: 253. Strabo (7.4.3) claims that both Crimea and Anatolia could be seen from the halfway point of the voyage.
22. Højte 2005: 138.
23. Iron is indeed listed as a trade good in a badly fragmented merchant letter (*CGP* 27) that dates to the early fifth century BCE. But it is not attested elsewhere in literary or documentary sources. That Greeks came to the Black Sea in search of bulk commodities—such as those forged by the Chalybes—is a chestnut of Soviet and post-Soviet scholarship, which have strong materialist tendencies (e.g., Tsetskhladze 1998b: 65–68; Solovyev 1998: 53). But its earliest iteration (Minns 1913: 440) is both pre-revolutionary and non-eastern European. Scholars working on Greek colonization elsewhere express considerable doubt about the commodities thesis; see Horden and Purcell 2000: 133–34; Dietler 2010: 49–50
24. Vnukov et al. 2020: 8. For initial publication of the ceramics, see Olkhovsky 2018: 250 tb. 1.
25. Olkhovsky 2018: 249. Vnukov et al. (2020: 15) doubt the latter position.
26. Rostovzteff 1922; for discussion, see Tunkina 2003; Meyer 2013: 39–94; Mordvintseva 2017.
27. Early analysis pointed to Sinope as source for the clay (Vnukov et al. 2020: 10). But more recently, media report (https://web.archive.org/web/20220601220110/http://www.jinr.ru/posts/jinr-studies-unique-artifact-found-in-kerch-strait/) that

Eduard Greshnikov and Wael Badawy raise the more likely possibility of manufacture in Puglia.
28. Kashkharov et al. 2021: 171.
29. The late fifth-century elegiac poet Critias (fr. 2.13–14 West) praises Athens as exporter of ceramics. Bresson and de Callataÿ (2008: 22–23) characterize ancient ceramics markets as neither fully integrated nor disintegrated.
30. On decorated ceramics as cargoes in Archaic and Classical shipwrecks, see Dietler 2010: 134; as a trade item in the Black Sea region, see Moreno 2007: 206 n. 293; in Black Sea shipwrecks, see Tershenko 2013: 71–72.
31. Gill and Vickers 2001; van der Wilt 2018.
32. Blavatskiy and Peters 1969: 151; Tereshenko 2013: 69–73, fig. 3; Gerasimov et al. 2018: 190.
33. Stos-Gale and Gale 2009; Vaxevanopoulos et al. 2022 tb. 1.
34. "They [the Athenians] have a spring of silver . . . they are neither slaves nor servants of any mortal" (ἀργύρου πηγή τις αὐτοῖς ἐστι, θησαυρὸς χθονός [. . .] οὔτινος δοῦλοι κέκληνται φωτὸς οὐδ' ὑπήκοοι) (Aes. Pers. 238, 242).
35. Writers ancient and modern treat silver mining in the Lavreotiki euphemistically. Hence Xenophon (Mem. 3.6.12), who calls it a "hard country" (λέγεται βαρὺ τὸ χωρίον εἶναι); Lauffer (1979 [1956]: 121) and Kakavoyiannis (2001: 376) actually vouch for their health and safety to excuse the Athenians. (Lauffer was a former Nazi official). But Mussche, who worked in the region for nearly forty years, notes (1998: 2) that in his youth "the symptoms of poisoning [in the Lavreotiki] could indeed be clearly observed amongst the local inhabitants and animals."
36. Enslavers regularly rotated miners in and out of the mining region (Andoc. 1.38, Xen. Poroi 4.22). Was this done to limit lead exposure? Due to later disturbances to the archaeological record, the bioarchaeology of the mining region in the Archaic and Classical Period has not been adequately explored. Ian Morris (2011) identifies a site containing 219 individuals interred between 470-40 BCE with few grave goods, excavated by Salliora-Oikonamakou (1991), as a burial of enslaved laborers. Other scholars have adopted Morris' criteria to identify further burials (e.g. Van en Eijnde, Pieters, Van Wijk, and Docter 2021; Janot and Munaro 2021). A manacled ankle currently held in Freiburg, Germany is said to have been come from a disturbed burial from Kamariza near Lavrio prior to 1914 (S. Morris 2018). But at present, no remains survive in a condition to explore issues of pathology.
37. The three largest slaveholders of Classical Athens were Nicias (who enslaved 1,000 people), Hipponikos (600), and Philemonides (300). All three of these men contracted enslaved labor to the mines (Xen. Por. 4.14). But even private individuals (Andoc. 1.38) are attested leasing enslaved laborers to mine concessionaries by ones or twos. On the economics of labor in the Athenian mining industry, see G. Davis 2014: 270.
38. Hipponikos was mocked by Cratinus (fr. 492 K-A) and Eupolis (fr. 20 K-A) for being red-faced like a Scythian; Aristophanes (Ecc. 427–29) remembers Nicias for his pale face (λευκός), another stereotypically Scythian trait.

39. ἀλλὰ μὴν καὶ τοῖς ἐμπόροις ἐν μὲν ταῖς πλείσταις τῶν πόλεων ἀντιφορτίζεσθαί τι ἀνάγκη· νομίσμασι γὰρ οὐ χρησίμοις ἔξω χρῶνται· ἐν δὲ ταῖς Ἀθήναις ... ἢν δὲ μὴ βούλωνται ἀντιφορτίζεσθαι, καὶ [οἱ] ἀργύριον ἐξάγοντες καλὴν ἐμπορίαν ἐξάγουσιν.
40. Scheidel 2005: 11. Even the everyman protagonists of Aristophanes' comedies usually enslave multiple people; see Lewis 2018: 183–86.
41. *IGCH* 1082, discovered in 1824 in what is now Tokarevka, Kazakhstan.
42. The Bosporan Kingdom granted generous privileges to Athenian traders; see Dem. 31.32–33; Isoc. 17.57.
43. Lines 8–10 of the Coins, Weights, and Measures decree (*IG* I^3 1453) come from a fragment discovered in Olbia (*IG* I^3 1453f), now in Odessa. Osborne and Rhodes (2017: 337) hesitate to date more specifically than c. 425–14 BCE.
44. The earliest attestation for the stater as common currency in the Black Sea comes in a commercial letter from Olbia, dated to the late sixth century BCE; see *CGP* 26. For other letters documenting use of the stater, see *CGP* 20, 26, 29, 48. Weights for converting the drachma to the stater are known from the Black Sea as early as the 420s BCE; see Meyer and Moreno 2007; Kroll 2018; Kallet and Kroll 2020: 120–21. Athenian customs points along the Turkish Straits are attested in the 420s (Aristoph. *Vesp.* 235–37; Eupolis fr. 247 K-A; Xen. *Hell.* 2.2.1–2). Athens accepted the Cyzicene stater for payment of tribute (*IG* I^3 259); the stater was also used for long-distance trade within the Aegean (Lys. 12.10–11). See Kallet and Kroll 2020: 42.
45. Kuznetsov and Abramzon 2021: 20.
46. *IGDOP* 14, Moreno 2008: 702–3, no. I2. Olbia was successful in attracting foreign currencies that included Cyzicene staters; for a list of finds from the Agora up to 2003, see Karyshkovsky 2003: 302–8.
47. Olbia's bronze coinage was uniquely casted in the shape of bronze arrowheads and, later, dolphins. For an overview, see Korshenko 2001; Talmatchi and Papuc 2007.
48. Kuznetsov and Abramzon 2021: 35.
49. Blavatskiy 1954: 38–39; cf. Gavriljuk 2003: 79–80.
50. Men. fr. 891 K-A; Pollux 7.14; see Alexianu 2011.
51. Khotylev and Olkhovsky 2020.
52. Rung and Gabelko 2019: 115.
53. A. Bujskikh 2015: 245.
54. σκέψασθε δέ· εἰ γὰρ ἦμεν νησιῶται, τίνες ἂν ἀληπτότεροι ἦσαν;
55. Horden and Purcell 2000: 115.
56. Transshipment at Byzantion, Cyzicus, Tenedos, and other ports in the Propontis region is known from early on. For Cyzicus, see *SIG*^{3} 4 (sixth cent. BCE); Byzantion, Ps.-Dem. 33.5; 35.13. The complex hydrology of the Bosporus was well known even in antiquity; for overviews, see Moreno 2008: 663–66; Russell 2017: 25–37.
57. In the 1980–90s, both western and eastern European scholarship swung toward a minimalist interpretation of the grain trade; see reviews in Whitby 1996: 102–3; Tsetskhladze 1998b: 58–63; Gavriljuk 2003: 75. Current scholarship emphasizes

the dynamism of ancient cities' food strategies; see Horden and Purcell 2000; Moreno 2007; Oliver 2007; Bresson 2016.
58. Gavriljuk (2003: 78–80) uses pricing data extrapolated from Xenophon's *Poroi* to argue that slaves were a more remunerative export for Pontic cities than grain. This conclusion deserves caution: all of our Classical slave prices (in the *Poroi* and auction list *IG* I³ 421) come from Athens and not the Black Sea; even these yield too few individual numbers to extrapolate much. Gavriljuk's argument likewise assumes that slave-catching was an activity without seasonality.
59. Demosthenes' labelling of Lampis as enslaved (οἰκέτῃ) is probably a smear attempt; see Lewis 2022: n. 3.
60. The disposal of human remains at sea has generated extensive discussions ancient (Lindenlauf 2003) and modern (Rediker 2007: 38–39). But finds of human remains at ancient shipwreck sites remain extremely rare. On human remains from the early Hellenistic wreck off Eregli, Turkey, see D. Davis et al. 2018: 72–73.
61. For bankers funding voyages to the Pontus, see Isoc. 17.5; for private individuals, see Dem. 37.6, *Ps.*-Dem. 35.3. Phormion would later become a financier himself; he and other freedmen, including Pasion and Kittos, worked together closely, and the amount of litigation they received has made it possible to track their respective careers from slavery to freedom: see McArthur 2019.
62. *IG* 2³ 1.1315 (176/75 BCE) honors a merchant who stopped in Athens on the way to the Pontus from an unspecified port and sold his cargo of oil there during a time of shortage rather than carrying it to the north.
63. Braund 2011: 123.
64. Ἔοικε δὲ τοῦτο ὥσπερ οἱ Σκύθαι ποιέουσιν ἐκ τοῦ ἱππείου γάλακτος· ἐγχέοντες γὰρ τὸ γάλα ἐς ξύλα κοῖλα σείουσι· τὸ δὲ ταρασσόμενον ἀφριῇ καὶ διακρίνεται, καὶ τὸ μὲν πῖον, ὃ βούτυρον καλέουσιν, ἐπιπολῆς διίσταται τοῦτο, ἐλαφρὸν ἐόν· τὸ δὲ βαρὺ καὶ παχὺ κάτω ἵσταται, ὃ καὶ ἀποκρίναντες ξηραίνουσιν· ἐπὴν δὲ παγῇ καὶ ξηρανθῇ, ἱππάκην μιν καλέουσιν·
65. A second form of butter mentioned in the passage, known as ἱππάκην, also appears in the canonical Hippocratic discussion of the Scythian diet in *AWP* 18. See Ros. Thomas 2000: 57–58.
66. Hadjidaki 1996.
67. Dem. 34.10.
68. *Ps.*-Dem. 35.31.
69. Gerasimov et al. 2018.
70. Tereshenko 2013.
71. Lund and Gabrielsen 2005: 164
72. D. Davis et al. 2018.
73. Hadjidaki 1996: 588.
74. Tereshenko 2013: 74–75, figs. 1, 2, 4. The actual number might approach 3,000.
75. Tzochev 2016: 89–97.

76. The chronology of Thasian amphorae is much better known than other North Aegean wine ports, including Mende, Skione, and Skopelos. For the issues at stake here, see Lawall 2003: 37–53; for a general overview, see Monakhov and Kuznetsova 2017: 70–76.
77. Epigraphic correspondence between Black Sea merchants, usually inscribed on lead tablets, is overwhelmingly concerned with intraregional trade; see Dana 2021: 367. Shipwreck evidence suggests an uptick in intraregional trade after the eclipse of Athens in the late fourth century; assemblages from the Kinbrun Spit wreck (Gerasimov et al. 2018: 181) and the Eregli wreck (D. Davis et al. 2018: 62–63) show a great diversity of amphora types, with Black Sea manufactures dominating.
78. The correct reading of the text is disputed. Lewis argues that the Oxford text's emendation of the victims to πλέον ἢ τριάκοντα σώματα ἐλεύθερα χωρὶς τῶν ἄλλων ("more than thirty free people aside from the others") is unjustified given the MSS, which give πλέον ἢ τριακόσια σώματα χωρὶς τῶν ἄλλων ("more than three hundred slaves aside from the others").
79. Fifteenth-century export records from Genoese Caffa (mod. Feodosia) show wild variation from year to year: for instance fifteen captives in 1420 CE and over 200 in 1423 (Stello 2017: 384, fig. 2).
80. Grafe 2012: 63.
81. Lund and Gabrielsen 2005: 163–66; Højte 2005: 135–56; Lytle 2016: 2–6; Lamont 2023: 9–10.
82. Hdt. 4.54, Diog. Laert. 4.46.
83. ἔσπετε νῦν μοι Μοῦσαι Ὀλύμπια δώματ' ἔχουσαι, / ἐξ οὗ ναυκληρεῖ Διόνυσος ἐπ' οἴνοπα πόντον, / ὅσσ' ἀγάθ' ἀνθρώποις δεῦρ' ἤγαγε νηὶ μελαίνῃ [. . .] ἐκ δ' Ἑλλησπόντου σκόμβρους καὶ πάντα ταρίχη·.
84. Lytle 2016: 7.
85. Davidson 1998.
86. Stolba 2005: 121–24.
87. Mani Hurter and Liewald 2002: 25, nos. 12a–b.
88. On Herodotus' use of the flail as a cultural symbol in this passage, see Dovatur, Kallistov, and Shishova 1982: 205–6. Scythian archers appear as municipal slave-catchers in at least two comic passages: Aristoph. *Lys.* 463–65 (Lysistrata taunting a Scythian archer "what did you expect? Did you imagine that we were slaves, or did you think that women can't show courage?") and Eupolis *Officers* fr. 273 K-A, where a speaker calls for archers to drag a female character offstage to be auctioned.
89. Athenaeus glosses θρᾶττα as a fish name in several passages quoting from Old Comedy (7.120; 7.128; 7.138; 9.67). Harassing slaves named Thra(i)tta is a comic trope; see *Acharn.* 273, *Vesp.* 828, *Pax* 1138 and Cratinus frs. 73–89 K-A with Velkov 1967: 75; Bäbler 1998: 183–87; Davidson 1998. Thra(i)tta does appear to have been a common name for real enslaved sex workers; see *Ps.*-Dem. 59.35, 120.
90. "chickling, wheat, hulled barley, spelt, rice-wheat, wheat-flour, and darnel" (ἀράκους, πυρούς, πτισάνην, χόνδρον, ζειάς, / αἴρας, σεμίδαλιν).

91. "plain mackerel, coly mackerel, scaly saltfish, mully, perch, tunafish" (σκόμβροι, κολίαι, μύλλοι, σαπέδραι, θυννίδες).
92. "bowls, kneading-troughs, cake-stands" (σκαφίδας, μάκτρας, μοσσυνικὰ μαζονομεῖα).
93. Vakhtina 2018: 214–21.
94. E.g., Hdt. 4.62, 66, 70; see Braund 2011: 125.
95. Boltrik and Fialko 2007.
96. This exchange is most vividly illustrated by the Peshchannoe canoe, found during the construction of a hydroelectric dam on the Dnieper in the 1960s. Here, several fourth-century Athenian gilded vessels—as well as two bodies—were uncovered in a logboat preserved in the muck of the river (Tsetskhladze 1998b: 65). Such vessels are becoming better known. The submerged remains of an Iron Age logboat have been found in the harbor of Apollonia Pontica in Bulgaria; see Georgieva 2021: 94.
97. J. Morgan 2021: 6.
98. Lewis forthcoming.
99. I. Morris 2004: 710; Ober 2010: 279; 2015: 115.

CHAPTER 6

1. There remains debate whether this was actually true; see Canevaro 2018: 101–2.
2. Plutarch (*Dem.* 4.1–3) presents this as questionable, but it was quite certain to Demosthenes' rivals. On the question of Demosthenes' birth, see Ober 1989: 268–69.
3. This claim is repeated in Aesch. 2.78, 180; Dein. 1.15, 95.
4. Indeed, the Athenians had a specific court for adjudicating these claims (*Ps.*-Aristot. *Ath. Pol.* 59.3–5). Accusing rich Athenians of being foreigners was common stuff of Old Comedy, much of which was only written at a generation's remove from the 451/50 BCE law; see Lape 2010: 64–70. A short list would include Exekestides (Aristoph. *Birds* 765, 1527), Kephisodemos (Aristoph. *Acharn.* 703), Cleon (Aristoph. *Knights*), Cleophon (Platon fr. 65 K-A), and Hyperbolus (Platon fr. 185 K-A, Polyzelos fr. 5 K-A). Aeschines' attack on Demosthenes (2.76) explicitly refers to the questions surrounding Kleophon's citizenship. Demosthenes himself accuses at least three people of foreign ancestry; see Dem. 18.130, 21.149–50, 45.71.
5. Compiled as early as the 1830s, LSJ glosses γένος (s.v. A) as "race, stock, kin" before moving onto other definitions. (This reflects the expansive lexical range of 'race' in nineteenth century English; see Lape 2010: 32 n. 116.) Recent lexica are more cautious: *BDAG* offers "race, stock, family (as kinship)" only as a subsidiary definition (s.v. B).
6. Lape 2010: 186–239.
7. Lape 2010: 192.
8. Cratinus (fr. 492 K-A): "Cratinus calls Hipponikos 'Scythian' because of his redness" (Κρατῖνος Σκυθικὸν ἔφη τὴν Ἱππόνικον, διὰ τὸ πυρρὸν εἶναι).

9. Eupolis (fr. 20 K-A): "Eupolis in his *Nanny-Goats* mocks Hipponikos as red-faced" (Εὔπολις Αἰξὶν Ἱππόνικον σκώπτων ὡς ἐρυθρὸν τῆι ὄψει).
10. In Aristoph. *Ecc.* 427–29, Chremes describes "an attractive young man, white like Nicias" getting up to speak in the assembly. (εὐπρεπὴς νεανίας / λευκός τις ἀνεπήδησ' ὅμοιος Νικίᾳ / δημηγορήσων). Since the play was performed in 411 BCE, two years after Nicias' death in Sicily, scholars have assumed this is Nicias' grandson; Kirchner (*PA* 10809) presents this identification as tenuous.
11. K. Fields and B. Fields 2012: 17.
12. Ober 1989: 267; Lape 2010: 71. Cf. Aesch. 1.114, where he blames Athens' various defeats on false citizens.
13. Reed 2013: 49.
14. Hipp. *AWP* 20; Hdt. 4.64.3; *Ps.*-Aristot. *Phys.* 812a13–14.
15. Xenophanes fr. 14 Diehl; Hipp. *AWP* 20; Cratinus fr. 492 K-A; Eupolis fr. 298.3 K-A; *Ps.*-Aristot. *Phys.* 812a13–14; *Ps.*-Aristot. *Prob.* 38.2.966b.
16. Hdt. 5.6.1; Hermippus fr. 63.19 K-A; Eupolis fr. 298.2 K-A; Clearchus ap. Ath. 12.524c1–f4; see Kamen 2010: 96 n. 8.
17. Aristoph. *Thes.* 838, Pl. 1 *Alc.* 120b, Clearchus ap. Ath. 12.524c1–f; see, Bäbler 1998: 24–25.
18. Aristot. *Gen. an.* 5.782b30–35, *Ps.*-Aristot. *Physiog.* 806b16–18.
19. *Ps.*-Xen. *Ath. Pol.* 1.10, Aristoph. *Lys.* 1155.
20. σπεῖραν ἔχει τριχῶν πυρρῶν, ἀνατέταται τὰς ὀφρῦς, συνάγει τὸ ἐπισκύνιον . . . ὁ δὲ κάτω τριχίας ἀναφαλαντίας ἐστὶ καὶ πυρρόθριξ, ἐπηρμένος τὰς ὀφρῦς.
21. Pritchett (1953: 232–34) dates *IG* i³ 421–30 to early fall due to their reference to harvested crops. Meiggs and Lewis (1969: 245) prefer a date of 414 over 415 BCE due to the period of only a few months between spring, when the purges began, and early fall.
22. For a summary of the prosecutions of 415–14 BCE, see Furley 1996.
23. The extent to which evidentiary torture (βάσανος) was used as a formal process to elicit slave testimony in Athenian courts remains cloudy. Athenian courts appear to have had a legal process to "cure" slave testimony, which began with a formal challenge (πρόκλησις) made by a litigating slaveholder to his opponent. While Mirhady (1991, 1996) regards challenges for evidentiary torture as evidence for a type of non-judicial arbitration otherwise unattested in surviving legal sources, Thür (1977, 1996) and P. DuBois (1991) take the consensus position, itself vouched by Aristotle (*Rhet.* 1.15.1376b) that slave testimony could only be introduced after a formal process of evidentiary torture. It is worth noting that the debate over evidentiary torture has tended to be short-sighted at best: even though, as is frequently repeated, no slaves in the Attic oratorical corpus are ever *actually* tortured for evidence via Aristotle's procedure (Gagarin 1996: 4), there are many instances where slaves were tortured for evidence *outside* the official process, for instance by their own enslavers (Ant. 1.20, 5.30; Dem. 48.16–18, Lys. 1.18), a plaintiff acting out of order (Dem. 37.42), or the city in a time of crisis, as in 415–14 BCE (And. 1.22; And. 1.64).

The near-instance of evidentiary torture in Isoc. 17.15–makes it pretty clear that Aristotle's procedure was a reality. For full accounting, see Table 6.1.
24. Furley 1996: 31.
25. Furley 1996: 65–66.
26. Patterson 1982: 38. Enslaved families were only weakly protected in ancient Greece. While they were recognized in the Gortyn Law Code (Willetts 1967: 41, col. III.41–55), the only protection they appear to have had in Athens was a cultural inhibition against separation. (*IG* I³ 422 195–99, for instance, appears to list a family being sold together; see Osborne and Rhodes 2017: 444). Regardless, slaves and other household property could be sold off or divided up piecemeal during probate (Dem. 38.7, *Ps*.-Dem. 40.15), bankruptcy (*Ps*.-Dem. 47.57), or marriage (Dem. 45.28). In a recently recovered speech, Hyperides lambastes "slave dealers and merchants" (ἀνδραποδοκάπηλ[οι] καὶ ἔμποροι) who (legally) split up families; see Jones 2008: 19–20. Even in the antebellum south, where slaveholders widely subscribed to paternalist ideology, 25% of marriages between enslaved people were broken by sale, often upon the death or bankruptcy of an owner (Johnson 1999: 19). On how fear of sale shaped enslaved life, see Berry 2017: 19–31.
27. K. Fields and B. Fields 2012: 17.
28. For textual evidence, see Wycherley 1957: 145–46; Camp and Mauzy (2015 [2010]): 119–22) locate trial courts in a square peristyle in the Agora's northeast corner.
29. The use of physical geography and building morphologies to reinforce enslaved status has been explored in a Roman context by Fentress (2005), Joshel and Petersen (2014), and Padilla Peralta (2017).
30. μὴ γὰρ εἰ Σύρος ἢ Μάνης ἢ τίς ἕκαστος ἐκείνων, οὗτος δὲ Φορμίων· ἀλλὰ τὸ πρᾶγμα ταὐτό· δοῦλοι μὲν ἐκεῖνοι, δοῦλος δ' οὗτος ἦν, δεσπόται δ' ὑμεῖς, δεσπότης δ' ἦν ἐγώ.
31. I follow Greenwood (2022b: 337–48) in emphasizing Aristotle's use of the indefinite pronoun τι as a mark of uncertainty.
32. It is on this basis that Monoson (2011a: 265–66; 2011b: 140–44) argues that Aristotle's argument is fundamentally non-racial. Monoson's definition of race here is narrowly premised on "visibly discernible physical 'marks' of slave and free nature" (2011a: 266).
33. βαρβάρων δ'Ἕλληνας ἄρχειν εἰκός.
34. For instance, Antiphon (fr. 5 Gernet): ἐν τ[ο]ύτῳ γὰρ πρὸς ἀλλή[λους] βεβαρβαρώ[με]θα, ἐπεὶ φύσει πάντα πάντ[ες] ὁμοίως πεφύκ[α]μεν καὶ βάρβαροι καὶ Ἕλην[ες] εἶναι ("This means we have become barbarians in relation to each other, for by nature we are all equally equipped in every respect to be barbarians or Greeks"). See Fisher 1993: 89–90; Isaac 2004: 173.
35. The sophist Alkidimas: ἐλευθέρους ἀφῆκε πάντας θεός, οὐδένα δοῦλον ἡ φύσις πεποίηκεν ("God made all men fee, and nature has made no slave"); quoted in Σ Aristot. *Rhet.* 1373b18. See Garnsey 1996: 75–76.
36. In Bäbler's catalog of 136 funerary monuments dedicated to foreigners in fifth- and fourth-century Athens, 35 are easily identified as enslaved by the addition of this

adjective (1998: 207–95). If lone ethnonyms like "Thracian" or "Phrygian" without a name are added to the list, the number rises considerably.

37. Ἕλληνα μὲν ἀντὶ βαρβάρου . . . γνώριμον δ' ἀντ' ἀνδραπόδου.

38. Very few ancient buildings have proven as elusive as the slave market. Fentress (2005) presents an interesting exercise in determining what buildings *might* have served as slave markets in Roman cities; for critique, see Trümper (2009) and response by Roth (2010). Purpose-built markets are relatively uncommon even in slave societies; for rare exceptions, see Johnson 1999: 2–3 (nineteenth-century New Orleans); Barker 2019: 93–94 (Medieval Alexandria). On the politics of identifying slave markets in a historical context, see Goldstein 2012.

39. On platforms, see Aristoph. fr. 903 K-A. A context for slave sales that is less known are rural fairs, as attested under the Roman Empire; see Garlan 1988 [1980]: 54; Swain 2013: 271; Padilla Peralta 2017: 334.

40. For creditors seizing slaves from a ship, see *Ps.*-Dem. 33.1; from a farm, *Ps.*-Dem. 48.53–56; for prisoners coffled from foreign lands, Men. *Asp.* 36–37, 89; see Konstan 2013: 145–46.

41. The closest person to a professional slave trader in Classical Athens might have been one Mnesikles, who ran a business leasing slaves to mine concessionaries and was contracted as a professional torturer (βασανιστής); see Dem. 37.4, 40. Epigraphic documents from elsewhere, such as the Archaic Black Sea coast (for references, see Parmenter 2020: 83–86) or Roman Pompeii (Bodel 2005: 185–86), show slaves typically being traded in ones or twos alongside other commodities.

42. Johnson 1999: 12–14; Barker 2019: 98–104.

43. Our earliest evidence for slave markets as institutions comes from commercial letters sent between slave traders working along the northern coast of the Black Sea (*CGP* 25). By the last quarter of the century, Cyzicus on the Propontis granted a slave trader named Manes immunity on all taxes except a 25% levy on the sale of slaves (*SIG*[3] 4; see Lewis 2015: 320). In the mid-fifth century, the law code of Gortyn on Crete incentivized slave buyers to buy from traders in the public marketplace by imposing a sixty-day warranty on sales (Willetts 1967: 45 coll. VII.10–15). Evidence for regulated slave markets in Athens is roundabout, but they seem likely. Plato (*Leg.* 11.916a) calls for warranties of between six and twelve months in his ideal city. Disputes over market transactions—and presumably transactions over enslaved people—were adjudicated in Athens by magistrates known as the Eisagogues; see *Ps.*-Ar. *Ath. Pol.* 52.2.

44. Σ Aristoph. *Eq.* 43 (slaves); *Vesp.* 169–71 (livestock); Pollux 10.18 (agricultural implements); in general, see Pollux 7.11; Harp. s.v. Lewis (2015: 324) notes three slaves named Nomenios ("Monthly") in the *IG* I[3] 1032 slave list (lines 254, 350, 389). For further discussion, see Braund 2011: 122.

45. On slaves in comedy, see Tordoff 2013: 41–42; Hunt 2018: 180–86.

46. ἀνδραπόδα πέντε, πωλικὸν ζεῦγος βοῶν.

47. ἐγὼ μὲν ἤδη μοι δοκῶ, νὴ τοὺς θεούς, ἐν τοῖς κύκλοις ἐμαυτὸν ἐκδεδυκότα ὁρᾶν κύκλῳ τρέχοντα καὶ πωλούμενον.
48. οἴμοι κακοδαίμων τῆς τόθ᾽ ἡμέρας, ὅτε εἶπέν μ᾽ ὁ κῆρυξ οὗτος ἀλφάνει.
49. ἐχθὲς ἐωνημένος ἄνθρωπος.
50. On "slave" as an insult, see Rosivach 1999: 148–49.
51. Langdon 1991: 65–66.
52. The speaker of *Ps.*-Dem. 25.57 accuses one Aristogeiton of kidnapping a metic woman and taking her to the Poleterion to be sold.
53. "These lists are rather like the heads of executed criminals which once adorned London Bridge" (Furley 1996: 45).
54. My use of the phrase "evidentiary torture" encompasses any act of torture against an enslaved person used to elicit evidence, rather than the formal process outlined by Gagarin (1996: 2–4) or Thür (1996: 132–33). Despite contemporary debates over the extent to which evidentiary torture actually occurred, the orators certainly treated it as a reality; speakers in the corpus extoll evidentiary torture as trustworthy (Ant. 1.11, 2.2, Isae. 8.12, Dem. 30.36–37, *Ps.*-Dem. 47.9, Lyc. 1.29), except when they do not (Ant. 5.39–42, Aes. 2.128, Dem. 29.14; cf. Aristot. *Rhet.* 1.15.1376b). Twenty-eight formal or informal solicitations for evidentiary torture are preserved in the Attic corpus; of these six (22%) are actually carried out, while five (18%) are averted at the last moment. For full accounting, see Table 6.1.
55. E.g., Lys. 1.16, Dem. 29.25, *Ps.*-Dem. 46.21, 47.6, 59.120–25. The speaker of Antiphon's *On the Murder of Herodes* (5.30) reports the torture of an enslaved witness for evidence at sea. The victim is murdered by his owner soon after.
56. The first step of evidentiary torture was determining whether a victim was eligible to be tortured on the basis of either enslaved status (Lys. 4.14, Ant. 2.3, Dem. 29.39, *Ps.*-Dem. 49.53–55) or race (Lys. 13.27, 59): "Indeed, certain people did not want him tortured since he was a pure Athenian" (τοῦτον μέντοι ὡς οὐ καθαρῶς Ἀθηναῖον ὄντα ἐβούλοντό τινες βασανισθῆναι).
57. For indemnities in case a slave is disabled, see *Ps.*-Dem. 59.124.
58. Mirhady (1996: 121) does not regard this as legally possible. Thürr (1977: 190–92) does.
59. Wycherly 1957: 149–50; Camp and Mauzy 2015 [2010]: 176–78.
60. For professional slave torturers, see also Dem. 37.40; for torture by state officials, Dem. 53.23, Aes. 2.126.
61. For torture agreements, see Dem. 37.40–42, 45.61, Aristoph. *Ran.* 618–25.
62. Thompson and Griswold 1963.
63. Γένος is included for eighteen of the forty-four slaves, while thirty-one had names identifiable as foreign; see Pritchett and Pippin 1956: 278.
64. *plerumque enim natio servi aut provocat aut deterret emptore.* Trans. after Watson, who translates *natio* as nationality.
65. Pl. *Cra.* 384c10–d8, Var. *DLL* 8.9, Strb. 7.3.12.

66. On Medieval Arab slave trade ethnographies, see Ghersetti 2007: 294–96; Swain 2013: 70–79; Barker 2019: 39–60; Harrison 2019: 37–43; for eighteenth- and nineteenth-century examples, see Rediker 2007: 73–107; Smallwood 2007: 102–9; Fett 2017: 30–39.
67. Harrison 2019: 43–46.
68. Robertson 2008: 83–95; Wrenhaven 2012: 33–36.
69. Ps.-Ar. Oec. 1.5.6.1344b19–20.
70. Three slaves in *IG* I³ 421–30 are listed as οἰκογενής ("born at home"); see Pritchett and Pippin 1956: 280 no. 30; Vlassopoulos 2010: 130.
71. Lape 2010: 186–239.
72. Finley 1980: 118.
73. A few years earlier, Mavis Campbell had made a nearly identical point (1974: 290) regarding Aristotle's doctrine of natural slavery in the Black Studies journal *Race*. But there is little to suggest that Finley ever encountered this article, which would never be cited by an ancient historian. See Parmenter 2024a: 321–22.
74. This argument partially came from Black scholars; Snowden (1971: x), for instance, followed Eric Williams (e.g., 1994 [1944]: 7–29]) in seeing racism as a phenomenon of modernity. But the first historian of ancient slavery to squarely mark antiquity off from modernity was Finley's very conservative doctoral supervisor, William Westermann, whose 1935 *Pauly-Wissowa* article (1935: 910, 940, 1051) and subsequent monograph (1955: 1) dismissed any notion that race could have operated in antiquity.
75. E.g., McKeown 2002: 31; F. H. Thompson 2003: 104; Gruen 2011: 210; Hunt 2018: 28.
76. Bäbler 1998: 21.
77. Isaac 2004: 37; Seth 2020: 359.
78. Dee 2004: 162; Eaverly 2013: 105. This becomes clear in Pollux's list of Old Comedy slave masks, where enslaved men are consistently identified as πυρρός (4.150) while young women are λευκή (4.152).
79. Πυρρὸν δὲ τὸ γένος ἐστὶ τὸ Σκυθικὸν διὰ τὸ ψύχος, οὐκ ἐπιγιγνομένου ὀξέως τοῦ ἡλίου· ὑπὸ δὲ τοῦ ψύχεος ἡ λευκότης ἐπικαίεται καὶ γίγνεται πυρρή.
80. Tragedy mainly uses λευκ- and its cognates to describe women's bodies, and it is extremely common to find it paired with χροιά (skin, e.g., Eur. *Bacc.* 457), δειρή (neck, e.g., Eur. *Hipp.* 775), or other body parts. But this is not the case in comedy, where it is more often used as an effeminizing term of abuse for men, e.g., Aristoph. *Thes.* 191–92, or to describe a drunk person, e.g., *Frogs* 1092.
81. Like most Greek authors, Aristophanes' use of γένος is in fact very rich: we have "race of old men" (τὸ γένος ... τῶν γερόντων) (*Wasps* 223–24), "the manliest race" (ἀνδρικώτατον γένος) (*Wasps* 1077), "the race of the gods" (γένος ἀθανάτων) (*Birds* 700), "race of birds" (ὀρνίθων γένος) (*Birds* 1707, 1727). Aristophanes' use of the term here to indicate ancestry is charged by the politics of Athenian citizenship; see Lape 2010: 101–5.

82. On this usage, see Storey 2003: 272.
83. Pollux's types are: the leader of slaves; the curly haired slave; and stock characters named Maison and Tettix. Of these, all are identified as πυρρός except Tettix, who is μέλας.
84. Wrenhaven 2012: 83. Baldness and cross-eyedness are not popular tropes, but they do turn up: see Pollux 4.149–50.
85. Robertson 2008: tb. 5.2.
86. Vlassopoulos 2010: 130.
87. Kamen 2010: 96–97; Wrenhaven 2012: 63–71.
88. Ruffell 2000: 490–92; cf. Cratinus fr. 223 K-A (c. late 420s BCE), which provides a tantalizing mention of a "city of slaves" (πόλιν δούλων) in the desert beyond the Phoenicians. Ruffell's reading is questioned by Storey (2003: 270).
89. E. Hall 1989a: 47–48.
90. οὐ γῆς ἀνάσσει βαρβάροισι βάρβαρος, *IT* 31. γῆ βάρβαρος also appears in Aristoph. *Thes.* 1098.
91. Wrenhaven 2012: 83–86.
92. Storey 2003: 190–91; Olson 2016: 94–95.
93. Isaac 2004: 37; Wrenhaven 2012: 52; Hunt 2018: 31.
94. Barkan 1992: 83–87; Reed 2013: 50.
95. Wheeler 2000: 28–33; Block 2016: 10–34
96. Ghersetti 2007: 285–306; Barker 2019: 53–59.
97. Gleason 1996: 55.
98. Isaac 2004: 101–9; Block 2016: 17–19; Jablonski 2021: 440.
99. Physiognomy existed as a *mode* of writing long before it was a distinct *genre*. So although Boys-Stones (2007: 20 n. 4) separates Plato and other writers from the mainstream of the physiognomical tradition, I see them clearly working in reference to it.
100. Swain 2007: 131.
101. McLean 2007: 67–75.
102. Boys-Stones 2007: 23.
103. Ghersetti 2007: 282.
104. *qui se profitebatur hominum mores naturasque ex corpore, oculis, vultu, fronte pernoscere* (*Tusc.* 81).
105. διὰ νόσον μακρὰν ἢ διὰ καῦμα.
106. "The skin of the coward changes color (χρὼς ἄλλυδις) one way or another" (*Il.* 13.279); cf. Aristoph. *Lys.* 127, "Why is your skin changing color?" (Τί χρὼς τέτραπται;).
107. ὅτι μὲν οὖν γίγνονται διὰ πάθος πολλαὶ μεταβολαὶ χρωμάτων, δῆλον· αἰσχυνθείς γάρ τις ἐρυθρὸς ἐγένετο καὶ φοβηθεὶς ὠχρός.
108. Boys-Stones 2007: 74 n. 119.
109. Διὰ τί περὶ τὴν τῶν σιτίων ἐργασίαν, οἱ μὲν περὶ τὰς κριθὰς ἄχροοι γίνονται;
110. On the archaeology of bakeries, see Joshel and Petersen 2014: 125–28; on the bioarchaeology of grain-grinding, see Üstündağ 2020: 39–42.

111. For other mention of enslaved grain grinders in comedy, see Aristophanes fr. 427 K-A; Pherecrates fr. 10 K-A.
112. Wrenhaven 2012: 51.
113. ἀνδρόγυνος. ἡμεῖς μόνοι / οἱ Θρᾷκές ἐσμεν ἄνδρες· οἱ μὲν δὴ Γέται, / Ἄπολλον, ἀνδρεῖον τὸ χρῆμα· τοιγαροῦν / γέμουσιν οἱ μυλῶνες ἡμῶν.
114. Ros. Thomas 2000: 4–9.
115. Taylor 2001: 34; Harrison 2019: 43–44; Parmenter 2020: 72–73; cf. Chapter 4 above.
116. "Agamemnon the lord of men left them lying there and their pale (παμφαίνοντας) bodies showing, since he had stripped off their tunics" (*Il.* 11.99–100); "From violent hands the numerous thrown spears were driven, some deep in the bodies of quick-stirring young men, while many in the space between before they had got to the white skin (χρόα λευκὸν) stood fast in the ground, though they had been straining to reach the bodies" (*Il.* 15.314–17).
117. The most notorious instance of this is in 3.12, where Herodotus argues that Egyptians have thick skulls because they shave their heads and do not wear hats. Ros. Thomas (2000: 31–32) sees Herodotus' answer here as evidence of a his thought process: Herodotus provides an explanation and moves on, whether that explanation is credible or not.
118. δέρμα δὲ ἀνθρώπου καὶ παχὺ καὶ λαμπρὸν ἦν ἄρα, σχεδὸν δερμάτων πάντων λαμπρότατον λευκότητι.
119. Ros. Thomas 2000: 94–95. The strongest attestation of heredity appears to be Aristot. *Gen. an.* 722a10–14, which explicitly refers to the child of a Greek woman and an Ethiopian. Other writers are more ambivalent, e.g., Ps.-Plato's question why the qualities of parents *do not* pass to children (1 *Alc.* 118a–119a).
120. Hdt. 5.6.1, Thuc. 2.97.5, Aristot. *Gen. An.* 748a25–28.
121. Ros. Thomas 2000: 142.
122. Braund 2005: 25–30.
123. Kobylina's drawing (Figure 6.4) represents the original restoration of the Leoxos inscription by V.V. Latyshev (*SEG* 3.594 = *IOSPE* I² 270 suppl.): A: [Ἐνθάδε σῆμ' ἔστ]ηκα· λέ[γ]ω δ' ὅτι τῆλε πόλε[ώς που] / [ἐν Σκυθίηι? κεῖτ]αι Λέωξος ὁ Μολπαγόρεω. B: [Μνῆμ]ά εἰ|[μι Λεώξου τοῦ Μολπαγόρ]εω ("A: I set up a monument here; I say that Leoxos, son of Molpagores, lies in Scythia, far from the city. B: I am the monument of Leoxos, son of Molpagores").
124. Vinogradov 1991: 509. Vinogradov's theory of a "Scythian protectorate" around Olbia has now largely faded from the literature; see Moreno 2007: 154–55.
125. J. Fornasier and K. Fornasier 2004: 166; J. Fornasier 2016: 88; cf. Skinner 2012: 173–74.
126. Hartog 1988 [1980]: 4.
127. Hobsbawm 1983: 1.
128. Porucznik 2021: 9–13; cf. Trigger 1989: 225–27. But we should be hesitant to push this reading too far. As Ivan Ladynin notes (2016: 28), although dialectical materialism was *important* to Soviet archaeology, much of its apparatus continued with the premises of turn-of-the-century cultural historicism.

129. Hartog's *Mirror of Herodotus* (1988 [1980]) is usually blamed for taking an aporetic attitude toward the archaeology of the Pontic steppe. But as Ivantchik (2011: 71–74) argues, Hartog has been maligned unfairly; after all, he rather explicitly acknowledges Soviet archaeology at the start of his monograph (1988 [1980]: 6). The assumption that Herodotus was writing fiction is better associated with Fehling (1989 [1971]) and Armayor (1978).

130. The high-water mark of this was Mikhail Rostovzteff's (1870–1952) 1922 synthesis, *Iranians and Greeks in South Russia*, which posited that Russia was a fusion of European and Asiatic civilizations. Rostovzteff was part of a wider circle of St. Petersburg intellectuals to hold these views on the eve of the revolution; also worth citing here is Alexander Blok's (1880–1921) 1918 poem, "Scythians" (Скифы), which deploys an uncomfortably racialist vocabulary to make a similar point (Meyer 2013: 39). Soviet authorities were ambivalent toward this so-called Eurasianism, whose loudest advocates were always exiles like Rostovzteff or dissidents like Lev Gumilyov (1912–92). Regardless, it always had a constituency. It is no mistake that A. I. Dovatur, A. P. Kallistov, and I. A. Shishova's monumental 1982 commentary of Herodotus' fourth book is titled, *The Peoples of Our Country in the Histories of Herodotus* (Народы нашей страны в «Истории» Геродота).

131. Torbakov 2021: 80–81.

132. Крымчан... продиктованный самой историей - быть вместе с Россией (Putin 2021: 6).

133. Heinen 2010: 104–18; Ladynin 2016: 18–19. Marx himself was notoriously unclear about antiquity's mode of production; see Alston 2011: 3–8.

134. This position was widely agreed upon; see Khazanov 1975: 114; Nadel 1976: 199–200.

135. Blavatskiy 1954: 47–48.

136. Braund 2007a: 3.

137. See Dovatur, Kallistov, and Shishova 1982: 203–4 n. 126–27. Their unusual method of milking, involving sticking a tube up a mare's anus, is also discussed in Hipp. *De Morbis* 4.14; this practice was observed in the Russian far east in the early twentieth century.

138. οἱ δέ εἰσι Σκύθαι ἐγγενέες· οὗτοι γὰρ θεραπεύουσι τοὺς ἂν αὐτὸς ὁ βασιλεὺς κελεύσῃ, ἀργυρώνητοι δὲ οὐκ εἰσί σφι θεράποντες.

139. In fact, these were almost always young men; see Daragan 2016: 116.

140. Daragan 2016: 118–29.

141. Jacobson 1995: 72–73; Meyer 2013: 210–11.

142. Meyer 2013: 95–118.

143. Meyer 2013: 211. Women do appear elsewhere in the Scythian repertoire; on women and sympotic imagery in Scythian stone-carving, see Vlassova 2001.

144. Ivantchik 2011: 77 map 3.1.

145. Meyer 2013: 209.

146. On the cup from Tolstaya Mogila, see Meyer 2013: 207. Despite the lack of social gradation on the cup, excavators have noted that Tolstaya Mogila closely resembles Herodotus' description of a Scythian burial; see Rolle 1989: 35.
147. Lissarrague 1990: 247–73. Scythians appear only sporadically on the Black Figure ceramics of the sixth century; the earliest is on the François Vase, c. 570 BCE (Florence 4209). On Scythians in Black Figure, see Skinner 2012: 72.
148. M. Miller 1991: 59; Bäbler 1998: 165–68; Porucznik 2021: 143.
149. Ivantchik 2006: 199.
150. M. Miller 1991: 61–62.
151. Von Bothmer 1957: 94.
152. Lissarrague 1990: 7.
153. E.g., Anacreon fr. 356b West, Theog. 825–30, Hdt. 6.84.3; see Hobden 2013: 73–83.
154. M. Miller 1991: 66–69; Skinner 2012: 68–69.
155. Porucznik 2021: 146.
156. Rolle 1991; Meyer 2013: 227–29.
157. M. Miller 1991; Porucznik 2021: 146.
158. Bäbler 1998: 262–63 no. 89.
159. Aristoph. *Acharn.* 703; see Bäbler 2005: 115.
160. Bäbler 2005: 121.
161. ἀλλὰ τί γὰρ ᾤου; πότερον ἐπὶ δούλας τινὰς / ἥκειν ἐνόμισας, ἢ γυναιξὶν οὐκ οἴει / χολὴν ἐνεῖναι;
162. "Won't one of the archers quickly take her away and auction her off for whatever she may fetch?" (trans. Storey 2011) (Οὐ θᾶττον αὐτὴν δεῦρό μοι τῶν τοξοτῶν / ἄγων ἀποκηρύξει τις, ὅ τι ἂν ἀλφάνηι;)
163. Aristophanes' mockery has, in fact, been used in reconstructions of the Scythian language; see Hall 1989b: 39–40; Mayor, Sanders, and Colrusso 2014: 464.
164. Storey 2011: 55.
165. δοῦλοι μὲν ἐκεῖνοι ... δεσπόται δ' ὑμεῖς.
166. K. Fields and B. Fields 2012: 17.

POSTSCRIPT

1. Gleason 1996: 56. Barker (2019: 45–59) locates the mobilization of physiognomics as a theory of race in late Medieval slave markets.
2. Gould 1996 [1981]: 404–5; Jablonski 2021: 440.
3. E.g., E. Williams 1994 [1944]: 7–29.
4. Parmenter 2021a.
5. Heng 2018: 3.
6. E.g., Omi and Winant 2015 [1986]: 7, 13.
7. Seth 2020: 348.
8. For a catalogue, see Seth 2020: 359–60.

9. Seth 2020: 361.
10. πολλοὺς δ' Ἀθήνας πατρίδ' ἐς θεόκτιτον / ἀνήγαγον πραθέντας, ἄλλον ἐκδίκως, / ἄλλον δικαίως, τοὺς δ' ἀναγκαίης ὑπὸ / χρειοῦς φυγόντας, γλῶσσαν οὐκέτ' Ἀττικὴν / ἱέντας, ὡς δὴ πολλαχῆι πλανωμένους· / τοὺς δ' ἐνθάδ' αὐτοῦ δουλίην ἀεικέα / ἔχοντας, ἤθη δεσποτ<έω>ν τρομ<εο>μένους, / ἐλευθέρους ἔθηκα.
11. Finley 1980: 118.
12. Isaac 2004: 37.
13. *Somerset vs. Stewart* (1772) [98 ER 499].
14. Finley's ambivalence about his Jewishness (which he ultimately "made respectable" by changing his name) is well known (e.g., Schwartz 2013: 34–44). But his academic biographers have tended to overlook how vulnerable his Jewish identity made him to the McCarthy purges—an oversight given the nakedly anti-Semitic character of American anticommunism in the 1950s. See Parmenter 2024a: 321–22.
15. Isaac 2004: 165.
16. Isaac 2004: 16.
17. Snowden 1971: 169.
18. Hartog 2016: 72–73.
19. Heng 2018: 4.
20. Westermann 1935: 910, 940, 1051. This is surely the mark of Finley's activism: he worked under Franz Boas when he was at Columbia in the 1930s and was involved in an anti-racist pamphleting campaign; see Tompkins 2013: 13–20.
21. Reed 2021: 5.
22. Beardsley 1929: 36.
23. Challis 2013: 129–48; Samuels 2014; Matić 2018; Davies 2019–20.
24. L. Thompson 1989: 27; cf. Snowden 1971: 218.
25. Padilla Peralta 2017: 359; 2021: 164–65.
26. Haley (1993: 29) noted the widespread casual assumption that America's race dynamic was universal when teaching Hellenistic Egypt in the late 1980s: "We had been told if we had one Black ancestor, we were Black. Films and plays have reinforced this idea. Our family histories and photographs proved this to us . . . even as a 'Greco-Egyptian,' Cleopatra was a product of miscegenation. How is she not Black? My grandmother and students were being logical; they were applying to Cleopatra the social decoding typically applied to them."

APPENDIX 1

1. See Bresson 2016: 353–58 with his earlier appraisal in 2000: 67–73.
2. Locally available substances included stale wine, urine, alum-rich clays, and "fuller's earths." On this topic, see Photos-Jones and Hall 2011: 66–67; Wasserman 2013; Spantidaki 2016: 91–92.

3. See Volgelsang-Eastwood 2000: 280; Bresson 2016: 354. On the high variability of natural natron deposits, see Lovejoy 1986: 33–39; Shortland et al. 2011: 917.
4. On alum as mordant, see Lucas and Harris 1962: 154; Vogelsang-Eastwood 2000: 275; on alum in Pylos, Firth 2007; Nakassis 2013: 99–100; in Linear B texts generally, Perna 2005. The texts are Pylos (PY Un 443 and PY An 53), Tiryns (TI X 6), and Knossos (KN X 986). Designated alum workers, probably related to textiles, are known from neo-Assyria (*SAA* 12.83).
5. *I.Priene*² 417 with Bresson 2016: 254.
6. Lucas and Harris 1962: 258; Picon, Vichy, and Ballet 2005: 43–47. On evaporation in Greece, Photos-Jones and Hall 2011: 32–54
7. Picon, Vichy, and Ballet 2005: 45–46.
8. Horden and Purcell 2000: 344–51, 361.
9. Grafe 2012: 45–48.
10. Horden and Purcell 2000: 77–80.
11. McCormick 2001: 86–92.
12. Briant and Descat 1998: 88–90.
13. "Even economic historians," Morley writes (2005: 45), "do not have a choice about their dependence on narratives . . . there is no rhetoric-free means of communication available to them." Quantification became popular among historians of the ancient economy in the late 1990s to address the apparent contradiction between its high degree of development but uneven integration; see Saller 2002: 258–60.
14. The numbers that follow in Table A1.1 are based on Ada Yardeni's original publication of *TAD* C3.7, which used infrared photographs taken in the early 1990s. Some figures—particularly outliers and incomplete values—are products of speculation. James D. Moore's forthcoming edition of *TAD* C3.7, which is based on new photography and includes additional fragments, promises to clarify the picture. I thank Moore for his comments here.
15. Total exports for the month were taxed 49 karsh, 1 shekel, and 28 hallurs, converted at the following rates: 1 karsh = 84 g.; 1 shekel = 8.4 g.; 1 Hallur = 0.21 g. See Briant and Descat 1998: 67 and Kuhrt 2007: 2.700 n. 9 for conversions. Georgian conversions for the Egyptian month differ by pharaoh; these are calculated using http://aegyptologie.online-resourcen.de/latePeriod.
16. Total exports for the month were taxed 16 or 26 karsh, 27 hallurs, and 2 quarters.
17. Total exports for the month were taxed at least 22 karsh.
18. *P.Cairo* 65739 reports a 100:1 copper to silver ratio in the twentieth dynasty; see Janssen 1975a: 101–2, 440–41.
19. 0.002 kg silver per 27.264 kg. natron. This is calculated using the specific gravities of halite (2.16 cc./g.) and natron (1.42 cc./g.).
20. *P.Mich* 5.245; see Drexhage 1991: 39–41.
21. 1 obol = 0.72 g; 1 artaba = 27.13 l.
22. Garner 1979: 22.

23. From 137 to 10.2:1. The value of copper to silver collapsed to 350:1 in the Hellenistic period; see Janssen 1975a: 100–101.
24. Janssen 1975b: 177; Kemp 2006 [1991]: 319–25.
25. For a list of early hoards, see Colburn 2018: 82–83 tb. 4.1; see also Monson 2015: 13; Muhs 2016: 185. On monetization in the Ptolemaic period, see von Reden 2007: 70–71.
26. Briant and Descat 1998: 78.
27. Export taxes of 50%, 33.3%, and 25% are attested at Pelousion in 259 BCE; see *P.Cairo.Zen.* 59012 with Briant and Descat 1998: 84; Bresson 2016: 293.
28. See Briant and Descat 1998: 66–69. Our knowledge of the size of ships in this period is intermittent. Six shipwrecks are known from the eastern Mediterranean dating between c. 750 and 600 BCE, the largest weighing 25 tons. Ship size appears to expand rapidly over the following century, with ships of almost 140 tons known by the middle of the fifth century (Hadjidaki 1996). On the other hand, Egyptian river barges, built for far less demanding conditions, had reached the area of 60 tons during the Bronze Age; see Castle 1992: 240; Bresson 2016: 84–88. Emily Wilson, who has usefully synthesized this data (2018: 87–95 with chart 1), notes that the practice of loading ships with standardized containers of oil and wine had already set in in the eastern Mediterranean gyre by the end of the eighth century. We will never know if any of our six eastern Mediterranean wrecked ships carried water-soluble blocks of natron or alum.
29. Kemp 2006 [1991]: 255.
30. See Drexhage 1991: 39–41 on *P.Mich.* 5.245, McGing 2002: 45–46 on *SB* 28.16851, and Adams 2013: 272–75.
31. Kemp 2006 [1991]: 317–18 and fig. 111.
32. Warburton 1997: 319; Kemp 2006 [1991]: 256; Grandet 2009: 8.
33. The size of the pharaoh's holdings is a topic of some uncertainty. Grandet (1994–97: 1.88–89) estimates that his grants of *khato* land to the temples represent 20,000 km^2, or about 15% of all agricultural land in Egypt; this would imply that his real holdings were larger. Warburton (1997: 311) argues that the pharaoh's holdings were much smaller.
34. Brewster 1812: 394.
35. On the natron trade between Alexandria and Venice see Dearborn 1819.1: 358. On the end of natron glass in Europe, see Scott and Degryse 2015: 21–22.
36. Dearborn 1819.2: 358–59. Conversions are given by Dearborn (1819: 2.409), with 1 quintal = 44 oke, 1 oke = 200 drachms, and 1 drachm = 64 grains. This yields 36.52 kg. per quintal.
37. Lucas and Harris 1962: 258. 1 kantar = 45.02 kg.
38. Kostick 1998: 15–17. These techniques were quickly superseded by brine pumping in the west and synthetic production in the east. US national production reached 329,000 tons by 1900; see Porter, Kostick, and Bolen 2017.
39. Lovejoy 1986: 88–93.

APPENDIX 2

1. Some 154 individual names are known from inscribed ceramic dedications at Naukratis; see Johnston 2015a: 51–52. Only a handful have been catalogued here, either on the basis of multiple attributions or significance in the literature.
2. 42 ships are known from the Elephantine palimpsest with perhaps 41 captains. The 19 listed here are those with partially or fully preserved names.

APPENDIX 3

1. Data assembled from Skon-Jedele (1994) unless noted otherwise. Numbers presented with a greater than sign (>) represent an absolute minimum gleaned from preliminary publications.
2. The categories used to categorize scarab inscriptions at Greek sanctuaries were first developed by T. G. H. James (1962) in his publication of scarabs from Perachora. Although out of date, it has been repurposed by Masson-Berghoff (2018: 31).

APPENDIX 4

1. E.g., two large scarabs from Perachora (James 1962 D 435 and D541) appear to display close resemblance to this group based on photographs. They are published without measurement or close analysis. On the problems of dating objects from the Perachora excavations, see Skuse 2021.
2. On glazed steatite, see Henderson 2013: 13; Masson-Berghoff 2018: 13–17.
3. For the scheme in A see Perdrizet 1908: 26; for D, Cambitoglou et al. 1988: 235. Similar hieroglyph border scheme is found on a pair of glazed steatite scarabs from seventh-century Cyprus; see Clerc et al. 1976: 96 no. Kit. 1005 (Kition), Clerc 1991: 5–6 T. 142/2 (Amathus).
4. Increasingly common in Late Period Egyptian scarabs; Jaeger 1982: 29; Lohwasser 2014: 178.
5. Markoe 1985: 55; Reyes 2001: 94; on bowls and glyptic, Markoe 1985: 87–89.
6. R. Wilkinson 1992: 113; on Cypriot scarabs, see Lagarce 1976 nos. 482, 776.
7. On the name of Menkepherre in first millennium scarabs, see Jaeger 1982; R. Wilkinson 1992: 113; Lohwasser 2014.
8. Phoenician: Maspero quoted in Perdrizet 1908: 26; Robinson 1949: 311; Greco-Phoenician or Cypriot: Amandry 1944: 50; imitation: Cambitoglou et al. 1988: 109.
9. See J. Gates 2002: 118–20; Gunter 2009: 117–23; Feldman 2014: 178–80. On Cypriot and Levantine imagery in Aegean seals, see Boardman 2001 [1970]: 384. On Cyprus and Egypt, Reyes 2001: 17–18, 137–39; the Levantine coast and Egypt, Boschloos 2012: 178–79; Cyprus and the Levantine coast, Markoe 1985: 6–8; on Cyprus and Assyria, Gunter 2009: 21–28.

10. Other regions, such as Phrygia, have been consistently underestimated as a route; see Gunter 2009: 144; Feldman 2014: 169. Notably, there is at least one head seal from Gordion; see Dusinberre 2005 cat. no. 23 fig. 147a–b.
11. Robinson 1949: 311; Langdon 1993: 189.
12. An additional large glazed steatite scarab has been found in a LG pithos burial on Odos Palaistriou 7 in Aigio on the Corinthian Gulf in an assemblage including bronze fibulae, amber beads, a polished stone scarab, an amber pendant, and an unspecified ceramic vessel. It is publicly displayed in Aigio Archaeological Museum.
13. A was erroneously published as "*En contre-bas monument des Epigones*" (Perdrizet 1908: 25); see Amandry 1944: 36; Skon-Jedele 1994: 868.
14. Squares H9565-H9560-H9555-J0060 (Cambitoglou et al. 1988: 178).
15. Cambitoglou et al. 1988: 235 no. 1324; Skon-Jedele 1994: 983 no. 1394.

APPENDIX 5

1. Descriptions of obverses are drawn from previous bibliography. In a few cases where legible drawings or photographs are available, I have attempted to read hieroglyphic phrases. On the use of hieroglyphs in visual schemes in Egyptian art, see R. Wilkinson 1992; on cryptographic readings of scarab impressions, see Masson-Berghoff 2018.

Works Cited

Abramzon, Mikhail G., and Irina V. Tunkina. 2018. "Гости Острова Левки (Античные Монеты По Неизданным Рисункам Н.Н. Мурзакевича)" [Guests Of Leuke Island (Ancient Coins After Unpublished Drawings By N. N. Murzakevitch)]. *VDI* 78.1: 52–87.
Adams, Colin. 2013. "Natural Resources in Roman Egypt Extraction, Transport, and Administration." *BASP* 50: 265–81.
Agius, Dionisius A. 2017. "Red Sea Folk Beliefs: A Maritime Spirit Landscape." *Northeast African Studies* 17.1: 131–62.
Agut-Labordére, Damien. 2012. "Plus que des mercenaires! L'intégration des hommes de guerre grecs au service de la monarchie saite." *Pallas* 89: 293–306.
Agut-Labordére, Damien. 2013. "The Saite Period: The Emergence of a Mediterranean Power." In *Ancient Egyptian Administration*, ed. J.-P. García: 965–1028. Leiden: Brill.
Agut-Labordére, Damien. 2016. "Beyond the Persian Tolerance Policy: Great Kings and Egyptian Gods during the Achaemenid Period." In *Religion in the Achaemenid Persian Empire: Emerging Judiasms and Trade*, ed. D. Edelman, A. Fitzpatrick-McKinley, and P. Guillaume: 319–28. Tübingen: Mohr Siebeck.
Agut-Labordére, Damien. 2019. "The Wool of Naukratis: About the Stela Michigan Kelsey Museum 0.2.5803." *British Museum Studies in Ancient Egypt and Sudan* 24: 91–104.
Akrigg, Ben, and Rob Tordoff, eds. 2013. *Slaves and Slavery in Ancient Greek Comic Drama*. Cambridge: Cambridge University Press.
Akurgal, Ekrem. 1983. *Alt-Smyrna: Wohnschichten und Athenatempel*. Ankara: Türk Tarhi Kurumu Basımevi.
Alexandrescu, Petre. 2005. "Le temple d'Aphrodite." In *La zone sacrée d'époque grecque. Histria* vol. 7, ed. P. Alexandrescu: 159–86. Bucharest: Editura Academiei Române.
Alekseeva, E. M. 1975. *Античные бусы Северного Причерноморья* [Ancient Beads of the Northern Black Sea Region]. Moscow: Academy of Sciences of the U.S.S.R.
Alexianu, Marius. 2011. "Lexicographers, Paroemiographers, and Slaves-for-Salt Barter in Ancient Thrace." *Phoenix* 65.3/4: 389–94.
Allen, James P. 2002. *The Heqanakht Papyri*. New York: Metropolitan Museum of Art.
Almagor, Eran. 2014. "Dionysios of Miletos (687)." In Worthington 2007-ongoing. https://scholarlyeditions.brill.com/bnjo/.

Almagor, Eran. 2016. "Kadmos of Miletos (489)." In Worthington 2007-ongoing. https://scholarlyeditions.brill.com/bnjo/.

Alston, Richard. 2011. "Introduction: Rereading Ancient Slavery." In Alston, Hall, and Proffitt: 1–33.

Alston, Richard, Edith Hall, and Laura Proffitt, eds. 2011. *Reading Ancient Slavery*. London: Bristol Classical Press.

Amandry, Pierre. 1944. "Petits objets de Delphes." *BCH* 68–69: 36–74.

Amitai, Reuven, and Christoph Cluse, eds. 2017. *Slavery and the Slave Trade in the Eastern Mediterranean (c. 1000–1500 CE)*. Turnhout: Brepols.

Andreeva, Evgeniia N. 2017. "*Sero sapivnt Phryges:* Образ Фригийца в античной литературе." [*Sero sapivnt Phryges:* Image of Phrygians in Classical Literature]. *VDI* 77.3: 599–614.

Angel, J. Lawrence. 1943. "A Racial Analysis of the Ancient Greeks: An Essay on the Use of Morphological Types." *American Journal of Physical Anthropology* 2.4: 329–76.

Angel, J. Lawrence. 1946. "Race, Type, and Ethnic Group in Ancient Greece." *Human Biology* 18.1: 1–32.

Apostola, Electra. 2018. "Representations of the Demon-God Bes in Rhodes and Samos during the 7th and 6th Centuries BC and Their Influence on Popular Religious Beliefs: Bes and the 'Fat-Bellied Demons.'" In *Popular Religion and Ritual in Prehistoric and Ancient Greece and the Eastern Mediterranean*, ed. G. Vavouranakis, K. Kopanias, and C. Kanellopoulos: 113–24. Oxford: Archeopress.

Apostola, Electra, and Panagiotis Kousoulis. 2019. "Aegyptiaca in Archaic Greece: Preliminary Remarks on Scarabs and Scaraboids from the Sanctuary of Ialysus (Rhodes)." *Göttinger Miszellen* 258: 9–20.

Appadurai, Arjun, ed. 1986. *The Social Life of Things: Commodities in Cultural Perspective*. Cambridge: Cambridge University Press.

Aptheker, Herbert. 1970. "Anti-Slavery Medallions in The Martin Jacobowitz Collection." *Negro History Bulletin* 33.5: 114–21.

Armayor, O. Kimball. 1978. "Did Herodotus Ever Go to the Black Sea?" *HSCP* 82: 45–62.

Arnaud, P. 1992. "Les relations maritimes dans le Pont-Euxin d'après les données numériques des géographes anciens." *RÉA* 94.1–2: 57–77.

Arrington, Nathan T. 2015. "Talismanic Practice at Lefkandi: Trinkets, Burials, and Belief in the Early Iron Age." *CCJ* 61: 1–30.

Arrington, Nathan T. 2021. *Athens at the Margins: Pottery and People in the Early Mediterranean World*. Princeton, NJ: Princeton University Press.

Arrington, Nathan T. 2022. "The Persistence of Orientalising." *Ancient West and East* 21: 37–59.

Arrington, Nathan T., Georgios Spyropoulos, and Demetrios J. Brellas. 2021. "Glimpses of the Invisible Dead: A 7th-Century B.C. Burial Plot in Northern Piraeus." *Hesperia* 90.2: 233–79.

Aruz, Joan, and Jean-François de Lapérouse. 2014. "Nimrud Ivories." In Aruz, Graff, and Rakic: 141–51.

Aruz, Joan, Sarah B. Graff, and Yelena Rakic, eds. 2014. *Assyria to Iberia at the Dawn of the Classical Age*. New Haven, CT: Yale University Press.

Asheri, David. 1998. "The Achaeans and the Heniochi: Reflections on the Origins and History of a Greek Rhetorical Topos." In Tsetskhladze: 265–86.

Aslanian, Sebouh D. 2011. *From the Indian Ocean to the Mediterranean: The Global Trade Networks of Armenian Merchants from New Julfa*. Berkeley: University of California Press.

Averett, Erin Waleck. 2015. "Masks and Ritual Performance on the Island of Cyprus." *AJA* 119.1: 3–45.

Avram, Alexandru. 2006. "The Territories of Istros and Kallatis." In *Surveying the Greek Chora: The Black Sea Region in a Comparative Perspective*, ed. P. Bilde and V. Stolba: 59–80. Aarhus: Aarhus University Press.

Avram, Alexandru. 2007. "Some Thoughts about the Black Sea and the Slave Trade before the Roman Domination (6th–1st Centuries BC)." In *The Black Sea in Antiquity: Regional and Interregional Economic Exchanges*, ed. P. Gabrielsen and J. Lund: 239–52. Aarhus: Aarhus University Press.

Babin, Boris. 2020. "Sanction Policy of Ukraine and Cultural Heritage of Crimea." Accessed February 28, 2022. https://culture.voicecrimea.com.ua/en/monitoring-of-violations-of-international-humanitarian-law-regarding-the-preservation-of-cultural-heritage-in-the-temporarily-occupied-territory-of-the-autonomous-republic-of-crimea-and-the-city-of-se/

Bäbler, Balbina. 1998. *Fleissige Thrakerinnen und wehrhafte Skythen: Nichtgriechen im klassischen Athen und ihre archäologische Hinterlassenschaft*. Stuttgart: B. G. Teubner.

Bäbler, Balbina. 2005. "Bobbies or Boobies? The Scythian Police Force in Classical Athens." In *Scythians and Greeks: Cultural Interactions in Scythia, Athens, and the Early Roman Empire*, ed. D. Braund: 114–22. Exeter: University of Exeter Press.

Bagnall, Roger. 2005. "Egypt and the Concept of the Mediterranean." In W. V. Harris: 339–47.

Bagnall, Roger. 2006 [1997]. "Decolonizing Ptolemaic Egypt." In *Hellenistic and Roman Egypt: Sources and Approaches*, ed. R. Bagnall: 225–41. Burlington, VT: Ashgate.

Bahrani, Zainab. 2006. "Race and Ethnicity in Mesopotamian Antiquity." *WorldArch* 38.1: 48–59.

Bammer, Anton. 1990. "A 'Peripteros' of the Geometric Period in the Artemision of Ephesus." *Anatolian Studies* 40: 137–60.

Baralis, Alexandre, Krastina Panayotova, and Dimitar Nedev. 2019. *Apollonia du Pont. Sur les pas des archéologues. Collections du Louvre et des musées de Bulgarie*. Paris: Musée de Louvre.

Bareš, Ladislav. 1999. *The Shaft Tomb of Udjahorresnet at Abusir*. Prague: Karolinum Press.

Barkan, Elazar. 1992. *The Retreat of Scientific Racism: Changing Concepts of Race in Britain and the United States between the World Wars.* Cambridge: Cambridge University Press.

Barker, Hannah. 2019. *That Most Precious Merchandise: The Mediterranean Trade in Black Sea Slaves, 1260-1500.* Philadelphia: University of Pennsylvania Press.

Barnard, John Levi. 2017. *Empire of Ruin: Black Classicism and American Imperial Culture.* Oxford: Oxford University Press.

Barth, Fredrik. 1998 [1969]. *Ethnic Groups and Boundaries: The Social Organization of Culture Difference.* Long Grove, IL: Waveland Press.

Bass, George F., Cemal Pulak, Dominique Collon, and James Weinstein. 1989. "The Bronze Age Shipwreck at Ulu Burun: 1986 Campaign." *AJA* 93.1: 1–29.

Beardsley, Grace Hadley. 1929. *The Negro in Greek and Roman Civilization.* Baltimore, MD: Johns Hopkins University Press.

Beazley, J. D. 1927. "Some Inscriptions on Vases." *AJA* 31.3: 345–53.

Beazley, J. D. 1929. "Charinos." *JHS* 49.1: 38–78.

Becker, Marshall Joseph. 2008. "Small Wampum Bands Used by Native Americans in the Northeast: Functions and Recycling." *Material Culture* 40.1: 1–17.

Beer, Cecilia. 1994. *Temple Boys: A Study of Votive Sculpture on Cyprus.* Jonsered: Paul Åströms Förlag.

Behrendt, Stephen D., A. J. H. Latham, and David Northrup. 2010. *The Diary of Antera Duke: An Eighteenth-Century African Slave Trader.* Oxford: Oxford University Press.

Beidler, Philip D., and Gary Taylor, eds. 2005. *Signs of Race: Writing Race in the Atlantic World, Medieval to Modern.* London: Palgrave Macmillan.

Bekker-Nielsen, Tønnes, ed. 2005. *Ancient Fishing and Fish Processing in the Black Sea Region.* Aarhus: Aarhus University Press.

Belfiore, Cristina M., Paolo Mazzoleni, Angela M. Manenti, Maria A. Mastelloni, Valentina Corsale, and Germana Barone. 2021. "Non-Destructive XRF Analysis of *Aegyptiaca* from Sicilian Archaeological Sites." *Mediterranean Archaeology and Archaeometry* 21.1: 37–69.

Bell, Derrick. 2008 [1973]. *Race, Racism, and American Law.* 6th ed. New York: Aspen Publishers.

Bérard, Claude. 2000. "The Image of the Other and the Foreign Hero." In B. Cohen: 390–412.

Bérard, Claude, Christiane Bron, Jean-Louis Durand, Françoise Frontisi-Ducroux, François Lissarrague, Alaine Schnapp, and Jean-Pierre Vernant. 1989 [1984]. *A City of Images: Iconography and Society in Ancient Greece.* Trans. D. Lyons. Princeton, NJ: Princeton University Press.

Bergeron, Marianne. 2015. "Pots and People: Greek Trade and Votive Rituals at Naukratis." In Robinson and Goddio: 267–82.

Bernal, Martin. 1987–2006. *Black Athena: the Afro-Asiatic Origins of Greek Civilization.* 3 vols. New Brunswick, NJ: Rutgers University Press.

Bernand, André and Olivier Masson. 1957. "Les inscriptions grecques d'Abou-Simbel." *RÉG* 70.329–30: 1–46.

Berry, Daina Ramey. 2017. *The Price for Their Pound of Flesh: The Value of the Enslaved, from Womb to Grave, in the Building of a Nation.* Boston: Beacon Books.

Betancourt, Roland. 2020. *Byzantine Intersectionality: Sexuality, Gender, and Race in the Middle Ages.* Princeton, NJ: Princeton University Press.

Bierl, Anton, and André Lardinois, eds. 2016. *The Newest Sappho: P.Sapph.Obbink and P.GC inv. 105, Frs. 1–4.* Leiden: Brill.

Biers, William R. 1994. "Mass Production, Standardized Parts, and the Corinthian 'Plastic' Vase." *Hesperia* 63.4: 509–16.

Bindman, David. 1994. "Am I Not a Man and a Brother? British Art and Slavery in the Eighteenth Century." *RES* 26: 68–82.

Birwood, George. 1911. "The Etymology of Natron." *Journal of the Royal Society of Arts* 59.3072: 1061.

Bîrzescu, Iulian. 2018. "Archaeological Research on the Western Black Sea Coast from the Archaic Period until the Roman Conquest: An Overview." In *Essays on the Archaeology and Ancient History of the Black Sea Littoral*, ed. M. Manedolakis, G. Tsetskhladze, and I. Xydopoulos: 243–71. Leuven: Peeters.

Blackmon, Douglas A. 2008. *Slavery by Another Name: The Re-enslavement of Black Americans from the Civil War to World War II.* New York: Anchor Books.

Blassingame, John W. 1972. *The Slave Community: Plantation Life in the Antebellum South.* Oxford: Oxford University Press.

Blavatskiy, V. D. 1954. "Рабство и его источники в античных государствах северного Причерноморья" [Slavery and its sources in ancient states of the northern Black Sea coast]. *SovArch* 20: 31–56.

Blavatskiy, V. D., and B. G. Peters. 1969. "Кораблекрушение конца iv - начала iii вв. До н. Э. Около Донузлава" [Shipwreck of the late fourth/early third century BC near Donuzlav]. *SovArch* 35.3: 151–58.

Blegen, Carl W. 1940. "Athens and the Early Age of Greece." *HCSP* 51 supp. 1: 1–9.

Blinkenberg, Christian. 1931. *Lindos: Fouilles de l'Acropole, 1902–14.* 2 vols. Berlin: De Gruyter.

Block, Sharon. 2016. *Colonial Complexions: Race and Bodies in Eighteenth-Century America.* Philadelphia: University of Pennsylvania Press.

Blumenbach, Johann Friedrich. 1865 [1795]. "On the Natural Variety of Mankind." In *The Anthropological Treatises of Johann Friedrich Blumenbach*, ed., trans. T. Bendyshe: 145–276. 3rd ed. London: Longman, Green, Longman, Roberts, and Green.

Boardman, John. 1980 [1964]. *The Greeks Overseas.* 2nd ed. London: Thames and Hudson.

Boardman, John. 1991. "Cypriot, Phoenician, and Greek Seals and Amulets." In Karageorghis, Picard, and Tytgat: 159–70.

Boardman, John. 2001 [1972]. *Greek Gems and Finger Rings.* 2nd ed. London: Thames and Hudson.

Boardman, John. 2013. "Why Naukratis?" *Ancient West and East* 12: 265–67.

Boardman, John, and John Hayes. 1966. *Excavations at Tocra: 1963–65. The Archaic Deposits I*. London: Thames and Hudson.

Bodel, John. 2005. "*Caveat emptor:* Towards a Study of Roman Slave-Traders." *JRA* 18: 181–95.

Bodel, John. 2018. "Ancient Slavery and Modern Ideologies: Orlando Patterson and M. I. Finley among the Dons." *Trajectories* 30.1: 3–6.

Bolshakov, Andrei O., and I.Y. Ilyna. 1988. "Египетские скарабеи с острова Березань" [Les scarabée égyptiens de l'île de Berezan']. *VDI* 3 (186): 51–67.

Bolton, J. D. P. 1960. *Aristeas of Proconnesus*. Oxford: Oxford University Press.

Boltrik, Y. V., and E. E. Fialko. 2007. "Trakhtemirov: A Fortified City Site on the Dnieper." In Braund and Kryzhitskiy: 103–119.

Borgard, Phillipe, Jean-Pierre Brun, and Maurice Picon, eds. 2005. *L'alun de Méditerranée*. Aix-en-Provence: Diffusion de Boccard.

Bosanquet, R. C. 1899. "Some Early Funeral Lethykoi." *JHS* 19: 169–84.

Boschloos, Vanessa. 2012. "Egyptian and Egyptianizing Scarab-Shaped Seals in Syria and Lebanon." *Bibliotheca Orientalis* 69.3–4: 175–81.

Bossert, Helmuth. 1951. *Altsyrien: Kunst und Handwerk in Cypern, Syrien, Palästina, Transjordanien und Arabien von den Anfängen bis zum völligen aufgehen in der griechisch-römischen Kultur*. Tübingen: Verlag Ernst Wasmuth.

Bowie, Ewen. 2006. "Evenus of Paros." In *Brill's New Pauly*, ed. H. Cancik et al. Leiden: Brill. https://referenceworks.brill.com/display/package/bnpo.

Bowie, Ewen. 2016. "How Did Sappho's Songs Get into the Male Sympotic Repertoire?" In Bierl and Lardinois: 149–64.

Bowra, C. M. 1956. "A Fragment of the *Arimaspea*." *CQ* 6.1/2: 1–10.

Boys-Stones, George. 2007. "Physiognomy and Ancient Psychological Theory." In Swain: 19–124.

Bradford, William. 1962 [1897]. *Of Plymoth Plantation*. Edited by H. Wish. New York: Capricorn Books.

Bradley, Keith. 1987 [1984]. *Slaves and Masters in the Roman Empire*. Oxford: Oxford University Press.

Bradley, Keith, and Paul Cartledge, eds. 2011. *The Ancient Mediterranean World. The Cambridge World History of Slavery*, vol. 1. Cambridge: Cambridge University Press.

Brattain, Michelle. 2007. "Race, Racism, and Antiracism: UNESCO and the Politics of Presenting Science to the Postwar Public." *American Historical Review* 112.5: 1386–1413.

Braun, T. F. R. G. 1982. "The Greeks in the Near East." In Boardman and Hammond, *The Cambridge Ancient History* 2nd ed., vol. 3.3: 1–31. Cambridge: Cambridge University Press.

Braund, David. 1994. "The Luxuries of Athenian Democracy." *Greece and Rome* 41.1: 41–48.

Braund, David. 2005. "Neglected Slaves." *VDI* 4 (254): 24–45.

Braund, David. 2007a. "Greater Olbia: Ethnic, Religious, Economic, and Political Interactions in the Region of Olbia, c. 600–100 BC." In Braund and Kryzhitskiy: 37–78.

Braund, David. 2007b. "Royal Scythians and the Slave-Trade in Herodotus' Scythia." *Antichthon* 42:1–19.

Braund, David. 2008. "Scythian Laughter: Conversations in the Northern Black Sea Region in the 5th Century BC." In *Meetings of Cultures in the Black Sea Region: Between Conflict and Coexistence*, ed. P. Bilde and H. Petersen: 346–67. Aarhus: Aarhus University Press.

Braund, David. 2011. "The Slave Supply in Classical Greece." In Bradley and Cartledge: 112–33.

Braund, David, and Sergei D. Kryzhitskiy, eds. 2007. *Classical Olbia and the Scythian World: From the Sixth Century BC to the Second Century AD*. Oxford: Oxford University Press.

Braund, David, and Gocha Tsetskhladze. 1989. "The Export of Slaves from Colchis." *CQ* 39.1: 114–25.

Bravo, Benedetto. 1974. "Une lettre sur plomb de Berezan': colonisation et modes de contact dans le Pont." *Dialogues d'histoire ancienne* 1: 111–87.

Bravo, Benedetto. 1977. "Remarques sur les assises sociales, les formes d'organisation et la terminologie du commerce maritime à l'époque archaïque." *Dialogues d'histoire ancienne* 3: 1–59.

Bravo, Benedetto. 1980. "Sulân: Représailles et justice privée contre des étrangers dans les cités grecques (Étude du vocabulaire et des institutions)." *Annali della Scuola Normale Superiore di Pisa* 10.3 (serie III): 675–987.

Bravo, Benedetto. 2001. "Luoghi di culto nella chora di Olbia Pontica." In *Problemi della chora coloniale dall'Occidente al Mar Nero*, ed. A. Stazio and S. Ceccoli: 221–66. Taranto: Istituto per la storia e l'archeologia della Magna Grecia.

Bresciani, Edda. 1998. "Plinio, il natron e le navi del Mediterraneo." In *Alle soglie della classicità il Mediterraneo tra tradizione e innovazione studi in onore di Sabatino Moscati*, ed. E. Acquaro: 59–61. Pisa: Instituti Editoriali e Poligrafici Internazionali.

Bresson, Alain. 1997. "Remarques préliminaires sur l'onomastique des esclaves dans la Rhodes antique." In *Schiavi e dipendenti nell'ambito dell' 'oikos' e della 'familia': Atti del xxii Colloquio GIREA Pontignano (Siena), 19-20 novembre 1995*, ed. M. Moggi, G. Cordiano, and M. Pettinato: 117–26. Pisa: Edizioni ETS.

Bresson, Alain. 2000. *La cité marchand*. Bordeaux: Ausonius.

Bresson, Alain. 2007. "La construction d'un espace d'approvisionnement: les cités égéennes et le grain de mer Noire." In Bresson, Ivantchik, and Ferrary: 49–68.

Bresson, Alain. 2016. *The Making of the Ancient Greek Economy: Institutions, Markets, and Growth in the City States*. Trans. S. Rendall. Princeton, NJ: Princeton University Press.

Bresson, Alain, Askhold Ivantchik, and Jean-Louis Ferrary, eds. 2007. *Une koinè pontique. Cités grecques, sociétés indigènes et empires mondiaux sur le littoral nord de la Mer Noire (VIIe s. a. C. – IIIe s. p. C.)*. Bourdeaux: Ausonius.

Bresson, Alain, and François de Callataÿ. 2008. "The Greek Vase Trade: Some Reflections about Scale, Value and Market." In *Pottery Markets in the Ancient World (8th–1st Centuries BCE)*, ed. A. Tsingarida and D. Viviers: 21–24. Brussels: CReA-Patrimoine.

Brewer, William M. 1929. Review of Beardsley 1929. *Journal of Negro History* 14.4: 531–37.

Brewster, David. 1812. "Of the Detergent, and Other Substances Used in Bleaching." *Belfast Monthly Magazine* 9.52: 394–403.

Briant, Pierre, and Raymond Descat. 1998. "Un registre douanier de la satrapie d'Égypte à l'époque achéménide (*TAD C3.7*)." In *Le commerce en Égypte ancienne*, ed. B. Grimal and G. Menu: 59–104. Cairo: Institut français d'archéologie orientale.

Brody, Aaron, J. 1998. *"Each Man Cried Out to His God": The Specialized Religion of Canaanite and Phoenician Seafarers*. Atlanta: Scholars' Press.

Brody, Aaron, J. 2008. "The Specialized Religions of Ancient Mediterranean Seafarers." *Religious Compass* 2.4: 444–54.

Brückner, Helmut, Alexander Herda, Michael Kerschner, Marc Müllenhoff, and Friederike Stock. 2017. "Life Cycle of Estuarine Islands—From the Formation to the Landlocking of Former Islands in the Environs of Miletos and Ephesos in Western Asia Minor (Turkey)." *Journal of Archaeological Science: Reports* 12: 876–95.

Bujskikh, Alla B. 2013. "О греческой колонизации северо-западного Причерноморья(Новая модель?)" [Greek colonization of the northwestern Pontic area (A new model?)]. *VDI* 1 (284): 21–39.

Bujskikh, Alla B. 2015. "The Southern *Temenos* in Pontic Olbia (Preliminary Results of the Investigation)." *Ancient Civilizations from Scythia to Siberia* 21: 222–50.

Bujskikh, Sergei B. 2006. "Kap Bejkuš—Kap des Achilleus: eine Kultstätte des göttlichen Heros im Mündungsgebiet des Bug." In Hupe: 111–54.

Burgess, Jonathan S. 2009. *The Death and Afterlife of Achilles*. Baltimore, MD: Johns Hopkins University Press.

Burke, Edmund. 1887 [1757]. *A Philosophical Enquiry into the Origin of Our Ideas of the Sublime and Beautiful*. In *Burke's Writings and Speeches*. 12 vols.: 67–262. London: John C. Nimmo.

Burkert, Walter. 1992 [1984]. *The Orientalizing Revolution: Near Eastern Influence on Greek Culture in the Early Archaic Age*. Trans. M. E. Pinder and W. Bukert. Cambridge, MA: Harvard University Press.

Burkert, Walter. 1994. "Olbia and Apollo of Didyma: A New Oracle Text." In *Apollo: Origins and Influences*, ed. J. Solomon: 49–60. Tucson: University of Arizona Press.

Caley, Earle R., and John F. C. Richards. 1956. *Theophrastus: On Stones*. Columbus: Ohio State University Press.

Cameron, Alan. 1995. *Callimachus and His Critics*. Princeton, NJ: Princeton University Press.

Caminos, Ricardo A. 1954. *Late-Egyptian Miscellanies*. London: Oxford University Press.

Caminos, Ricardo A. 1964. "The Nitocris Adoption Stela." *JEA* 50: 71–101.

Campbell, Mavis. 1974. "Aristotle and Black Slavery: A Study in Race Prejudice." *Race* 15.3: 283–301.

Canevaro, Mirko. 2018. "The Public Charge for Hubris against Slaves: The Honour of the Victim and the Honour of the *Hubristēs*." *JHS* 138: 100–26.

Cambitoglou, Alexander. 1981. *Archaeological Museum of Andros*. Athens: Archaeological Museum of Andros.

Cambitoglou, Alexander, Ann Birchall, J. J. Coulton, and J. R. Green. 1988. *Excavation of a Geometric Town on the Island of Andros; Excavation Season 1969, Study Season 1969–70. Zagora* vol. 2. 2 vols. Athens: Athens Archaeological Society.

Cartledge, Paul. 1997. *The Greeks: a Portrait of Self and Others*. Oxford: Oxford University Press.

Catling, H. W. 1973/74. "Archaeology in Greece, 1973–74." *AR* 20: 3–41.

Castle, Edward W. 1992. "Shipping and Trade in Ramesside Egypt." *JESHO* 35.3: 239–77.

Ceccarelli, Paula. 2013. *Ancient Greek Letter Writing: A Cultural History (600–150 B.C.)*. Oxford: Oxford University Press.

Centre for Contemporary Cultural Studies, ed. 1982. *The Empire Strikes Back. Race and Racism in 70s Britain*. London: Hutchinson.

Challis, Debbie. 2013. *The Archaeology of Race: The Eugenic Ideas of Francis Galton and Flinders Petrie*. London: Bloomsbury.

Clarkson, Thomas. 1968 [1808]. *History of the Rise, Progress, and Abolition of the African Slave Trade*. London: F. Cass and Company.

Clarysse, Willy. 1991. *The Petri Papyri: Second Edition (P. Petrie^2)*. Brussels: Koninklijke Academie.

Clerc, Gisèle. 1991. "Aegyptiaca." In Karageorghis, Picard, and Tytgat: 1–158.

Clerc, G., V. Karageorghis, E. Lagarce, and J. Leclant. 1976. *Objets égyptiens et égyptisants. Fouilles de Kition*, vol. 2. Nicosia: Republic of Cyprus Department of Antiquities.

Cohen, Ada, 2011. "The Self as Other: Performing Humor in Ancient Greek Art." In *Cultural Identity in the Ancient Mediterranean*, ed. E. Gruen: 465–490. Los Angeles: Getty Publishers.

Cohen, Beth, ed. 2000. *Not the Classical Ideal: Athens and the Construction of the Other in Greek Art*. Leiden: Brill.

Cohen, Jeffrey Jerome, ed. 2000. *The Postcolonial Middle Ages*. New York: Palgrave Macmillan.

Colburn, Henry P. 2018. "The Role of Coinage in the Political Economy of Fourth Century Egypt." In *Ptolemy I Soter and the Transformation of Egypt*, ed. P. McKechnie and J. A. Cromwell: 70–119. Leiden: Brill.

Colombini, Maria Perla, Flora Silvano, and Massimo Onor. 2000. "Characterization of the Balm of an Egyptian Mummy from the Seventh Century B.C." *Studies in Conservation* 45.1: 19–29.

Cook, J. M., R. V. Nicholls, and D. M. Pyle. 1998. *Old Smyrna Excavations: The Temple of Athena*. London: British School at Athens.

Corner, Sean. 2010. "Transcendent Drinking: The Symposium at Sea Reconsidered." *CQ* 60.2: 352–80.

Coulson, W. D. E., and A. Leonard, Jr. 1981. *Cities of the Delta, Part I: Naukratis. Preliminary Report on the 1977–78 and 1990 Seasons*. Malibu, CA: Udena Publications.

Courtois, Jacques-Claude. 1983. "Le trésor de poids de Kalavassos-*Ayios Dhimitros* 1982." *RDAC* 1983: 117–30.

Courtois, Jacques-Claude. 1984. *Alasia III: Les objets des niveaux stratifies d'Enkomi (Fouilles C.F.-A. Schaeffer 1947–1970). Mission archeologique d'Alasia*, vol. 6. Paris: Éditions Recherche sur les Civilisations.

Creative Time. 2014. "Creative Time Presents Kara Walker's *A Subtlety*." http://creativetime.org/projects/karawalker/.

Crenshaw, Kimberle. 1989. "Demarginalizing the Intersection of Race and Sex: A Black Feminist Critique of Antidiscrimination Doctrine, Feminist Theory and Antiracist Politics." *University of Chicago Legal Forum* 1.8: 139–67.

Crielaard, Jan Paul. 2018. "Hybrid Go-Betweens: The Role of Individuals with Multiple Identities in Cross-Cultural Contacts in the Late Bronze Age and Iron Age Central and Eastern Mediterranean." In *Change, Continuity, and Connectivity: North-Eastern Mediterranean at the Turn of the Bronze Age and in the early Iron Age*, ed. L. Niesiołowski-Spanò and M. Węcowski: 196–220. Wiesbaden: Harrasowitz Verlag.

Crosby, Margaret. 1950. "The Leases of the Laureion Mines." *Hesperia* 19.3: 189–297.

Cugoano, Quobna Ottobah. 1999 [1787]. *Thoughts and Sentiments on the Evil of Slavery*. Ed. V. Carretta. Penguin: New York.

Curtin, Phillip D. 1969. *The Atlantic Slave Trade: A Census*. Madison: University of Wisconsin Press.

Dale, Alexander. 2013. "Hipponax fr. 42 *IEG* 2 = 7 Degani." *ZPE* 187: 49–51.

Dan, Anca. 2011. "Deux scarabées d'Orgame/Argamum." *Dialogues d'histoire ancienne* 37.1: 9–40.

Dana, Dan. 2016. "Onomastique indigène à Byzance et à Cyzique." In *Identité régionale, identités civiques autour des Détroits des Dardanelles et du Bosphore: Ve siècle av. J.-C. - IIe siècle apr. J.-C. Dialogues d'histoire ancienne* Supp. 15, ed. M. Dana and Prêteux: 47–68.

Dana, Madalina. 2007. "Lettres grecqués dialectales nord-pontiques (sauf *IGDOP* 23-26)." *RÉA* 109.1: 67–97.

Dana, Madalina. 2021. *La correspondance grecque privée sur plomb et sur tesson*. Munich: C.H. Beck.

Daniels, Megan. 2019. "Black Athena, 30 Years On." *Eidolon* February 27. https://eidolon.pub/black-athena-30-years-on-5a78253028cc.

Daragan, Marina N. 2016. "Scythian Internecine Feuds." *Ancient Civilizations from Scythia to Siberia* 22.1: 96–140.

Davidson, James. 1998. *Courtesans and Fishcakes: The Consuming Passions of Classical Athens*. New York: St. Martin's Press.

Davidson, James. 2002. "Too Much Other?" *Times Literary Supplement* April 19 (issue 5168): 13–14.

Davies, Vanessa. 2019–20. "W.E.B. Du Bois, a New Voice in Egyptology's Disciplinary History." *ANKH* 28/29: 19–29.

Davis, Dan, Michael L. Brennan, Andrei Opait, and Jared S. Beatrice. 2018. "The Ereğli E Shipwreck, Turkey: An early Hellenistic Merchant Ship in the Black Sea." *IJNA* 47.1: 57–80.

Davis, Gil. 2014. "Mining Money in Late Archaic Athens." *Historia* 63.3: 257–77.

Davis, Jack L., Sharon Stocker, Andreas Karydas, Vasiliki Kantarelou, and Maria Kaparou. 2018. "The Gold Necklace from the Grave of the Griffin Warrior at Pylos." *Hesperia* 87.4: 611–32.

Dawkins, R. M. 1929. *The Sanctuary of Artemis Orthia at Sparta*. London: Society for the Promotion of Hellenic Studies.

Dearborn, Henry A. S. 1819. *A Memoir of the Commerce and Navigation of the Black Sea and the Trade and Maritime Geography of Turkey and Egypt*. 2 vols. Boston: Wells and Lily.

Dee, James H. 2004. "Black Odysseus, White Caesar: When Did 'White People' Become 'White?'" *CJ* 99.2: 157–67.

Degryse, P., ed. 2015. *Glass Making in the Greco-Roman World: Results of the ARCHGLASS Project*. Leuven: Leuven University Press.

Delgado, Richard, and Jean Stefancic. 2017 [2001]. *Critical Race Theory: An Introduction*. New York: New York University Press.

Demetriou, Denise. 2010. "Τῆς πάσης ναυτιλίης φύλαξ: Aphrodite and the Sea." *Kernos* 23: 67–89.

Demetriou, Denise. 2012. *Negotiating Identity in the Ancient Mediterranean: The Archaic and Classical Greek Multiethnic Emporia*. Cambridge: Cambridge University Press.

DePauw, Mark. 2011. "Physical Descriptions, Registration, and εἰκονίζειν with New Interpretations for P. Par. 65 and P. Oxy. I 34." *ZPE* 176: 189–99.

Derbew, Sarah. 2019. "(Re)membering Sara Baartman, Venus, and Aphrodite." *Classical Receptions Journal* 11.3: 336–54.

Derbew, Sarah. 2022. *Untangling Blackness in Greek Antiquity*. Cambridge: Cambridge University Press.

De Salvia, Fulvio. 1993. "Catalogo." In *Pithekoussai, La necropoli: tombe 1-723, scavate dal 1952 al 1961*, ed. G. Buchner and D. Ridgway: 775–811. Rome: Giorgio Bretschneider.

Descat, Raymond. 2006. "Argyronetos: Les transformations de l'échange dans la Grèce archaïque." In *Agoranomia: Studies in Money and Exchange Presented to John H. Kroll*, ed. P. van Alfen: 21–36. New York: American Numismatic Society.

Dietler, Michael. 2010. *Archaeologies of Colonialism: Consumption, Entanglement, and Violence in Ancient Mediterranean France*. Berkeley: University of California Press.

Diller, Aubrey. 1937. *Race Mixture among the Greeks before Alexander*. Urbana: University of Illinois Press.

Dillon, Matthew P. J. 1997. "A Homeric Pun from Abu Simbel (*Meiggs & Lewis* 7A)." *ZPE* 118: 128–30.

Docter, R. F., and M. Webster, eds. 2021. *Thorikos: Reports and Studies*, vol. 12. Leuven: Peeters.

Dougherty, Carol, and Leslie Kurke, eds. 2003. *The Cultures within Ancient Greek Culture*. Cambridge: Cambridge University Press.

Dovatur, A. I., D. P. Kallistov, and I. A. Shishova. 1982. *Народы нашей страны в «Истории» Геродота (Текст, перевод, комментарий)* [The peoples of our country in the *Histories* of Herodotus: texts, translation, comments]. Moscow: Nauka.

Dow, Sterling. 1942. "Corinthiaca I: the Month Phoinikaios." *AJA* 46.1: 69–72.

Drexhage, Hans-Joachim. 1991. *Preise, Mieten/Pachten, Kosten und Löhne im römischen Ägypten bis zum Regierungsantritt Diokletians*. Vorarbeiten zu einer Wirtschaftsgeschichte des römischen Ägypten I. St.-Katharinen, Germany: Scripta Mercuriae Verlag.

Drioton, E. 1957. "Trigrammes d'Amon." In *Festschrift Hermann Junker: zum 80. Geburtstag gewidmet von seinen Freunden und Schülern*, ed. G. Thausing: 11–33. Vienna: Selbstverlag des Orientalistischen Institutes.

DuBois, Laurent. 1996. *Inscriptions grecques dialectales d'Olbia du Pont*. Geneva: Librairie Droz.

DuBois, Paige. 1991. *Torture and Truth*. London: Routledge.

Du Bois, W.E.B. 1947. *The World and Africa: An Inquiry into the Part which Africa Has Played in World History*. New York: Viking.

Dunbabin, T. J., ed. 1962. *Pottery, Ivories, Scarabs, and Other Objects from the Votive Deposit of Hera Limenia. Perachora: The Sanctuaries of Hera Akraia and Limenia. Excavations of the British School of Archaeology at Athens, 1930–1933*, vol. 2. Oxford: Oxford University Press.

Duray, Anne. Forthcoming. "Racial Discourses in Aegean Prehistory ca. 1900: The Case of the Cupbearer Fresco at Knossos." *EJA* forthcoming.

Duplouy, Alain. 2018. "Pathways to Archaic Citizenship." In *Defining Citizenship in Archaic Greece*, ed. A. Duplouy and R. W. Brock: 1–49. Oxford: Oxford University Press.

Dusinbere, Elspeth R. M. 2005. *Gordion Seals and Sealings: Individuals and Society*. Philadelphia: University Museum.

Duster, Troy. 2003. "Buried Alive: The Concept of Race in Science." In *Genetic Nature/Culture*, ed. A. H. Goodman, D. Heath, and M. S. Lindee: 258–77. Berkeley: University of California Press.

Eaverly, Mary Ann. 2013. *Tan Men/Pale Women: Color and Gender in Archaic Greece and Egypt*. Ann Arbor: University of Michigan Press.

Ebbinghaus, S. 2006. "Begegnungen mit Ägypten und Vordasien im archaischen Heraheiligtum von Samos." In *Stranieri e non cittadini nei santuari greci*, ed. A. Naso: 187–229. Florence: Grassina.

Edgar, C. C. 1907. "Notes from the Delta, II. Inscribed potsherds from Naukratis." *Annales du Service des Antiquités de l'Égypte* 8: 157.

Edwards, I. E. S. 1971. "Bill of Sale for a Set of Ushabtis." *JEA* 57: 120–27.
Eidinow, Esther, and Claire Taylor. 2010. "Lead-Letter Days: Writing, Communication and Crisis in the Ancient Greek World." *CQ* 60.1: 30–62.
Eisen, Gustavus A. 1940. *Ancient Oriental Cylinder and Other Seals with a Description of The Collection of Mrs. William H. Moore*. Chicago: University of Chicago Press.
Eliade, Mircea, and Willard R. Trask. 1972. "Zalmoxis." *History of Religions* 11.3: 257–302.
Eliav-Feldon, Miriam, Benjamin Isaac, and Joseph Ziegler, eds. 2009. *The Origins of Racism in the West*. Cambridge: University of Cambridge Press.
Eltis, David, et al. 1999–ongoing. *Transatlantic Slave Trade Database*. http://www.slavevoyages.org/.
Fabre, David. 2004. *Seafaring in Ancient Egypt*. London: Periplus.
Fantalkin, Alexander, and Ephraim Lytle. 2016. "Alcaeus and Antimenidas: Reassessing the Evidence for Greek Mercenaries in the Neo-Babylonian Army." *Klio* 98.1: 90–117.
Fehling, Detlev. 1989 [1971]. *Herodotus and His "Sources": Citation, Invention, and Narrative Art*. Trans. Howie. Leeds: Francis Cairns.
Feldman, Marian H. 2014. *Communities of Style: Portable Luxury Arts, Identity, and Collective Memory in the Iron Age Levant*. Chicago: University of Chicago Press.
Fentress, Elizabeth. 2005. "On the Block: *catastae*, *chalcidica*, and *cryptae* in Early Imperial Italy." *JRS* 18: 220–34.
Fentress, Elizabeth. 2019. "The Domitii Ahenobarbi and Tribal Slaving in Gaul." In *Una lezione di archeologia globale. Studi in onore di Daniele Manacorda*, ed. M. Modolo, S. Pallecchi, G. Volpe, and E. Zanini: 149–55. Bari: Edpuglia.
Ferreira, Roquinaldo. 2012. *Cross-Cultural Exchange in the Atlantic World: Angola and Brazil in the Era of the Slave Trade*. Cambridge: Cambridge University Press.
Fett, Sharla M. 2017. *Recaptured Africans: Surviving Slave Ship, Detention, and Dislocation in the Final Years of the Slave Trade*. Chapel Hill: University of North Carolina Press.
Fields, Barbara J., and Karen E. Fields. 2012. *Racecraft: The Soul of Inequality in American Life*. New York: Verso.
Figueira, Thomas J. 1988. "Four Notes on the Aeginitans in Exile." *Athenaeum* 66: 523–51.
Finley, Moses I. 1980. *Ancient Slavery, Modern Ideology*. New York: Viking.
Finley, Moses I. 1981 [1959]. "Was Greek Civilisation Based on Slave Labour?" In Shaw and Saller: 97–115.
Finley, Moses I. 1981 [1962]. "The Slave Trade in Antiquity: The Black Sea and Danubian Regions." In Shaw and Saller: 167–75.
Finley, Moses I. 1999 [1973]. *The Ancient Economy*. 3rd ed. Berkeley: University of California Press.
Fischer, Josef. 2013. "Zum Sklavenhandel im römischen Ephesos." In *Kultur(en)—Formen des Alltäglichen in der Antike. Festschrift für Ingomar Weiler zum 75. Geburtstag*, ed. P. Mauritsch and C. Ulf: 553–66. 2 vols. Graz: Leykam Verlag.
Fischer, Josef. 2016. "Der Schwarzmeerraum und der antike Sklavenhandel: Bemerkungen zu einigen ausgewählten Quellen." In *Akten des 15. Österreichischen Althistorikertages*, ed. M. Frass, H. Graßl, and G. Nightingale: 53–71. Salzburg: Diomedes.

Fisher, N. R. E. 1993. *Slavery in Classical Greece*. Bristol: Bristol Classical Press.
Fletcher, Richard. 2004. "Sidonians, Tyrians, and Greeks in the Mediterranean: The Evidence from Egyptianising Amulets." *Ancient West and East* 3: 51–77.
Fogel, Robert William, and Stanley Engerman. 1974. *Time on the Cross: The Economics of American Negro Slavery*. Boston: Little and Brown.
Folmer, Margaretha. 2021. "Taxation of Ships and Their Cargo in an Aramaic Papyrus from Egypt (*TAD* C3.7)." In *Taxation in the Achaemenid Empire*, ed. K. Kleber: 261–300. Wiesbaden: Harrasowitz Verlag.
Fornasier, Jochen. 2016. *Die griechische Kolonisation im Nordschwarzmeerraum vom 7. bis 5. Jahrhundert v. Chr.* Bonn: Habelt Verlag.
Fornasier, Jochen, and Kristen Fornasier. 2004. "*Monumentum publicum* oder steppen nomadischer Kultureinfluß? Zur Leoxos-Stele aus der Nekropole von Olbia." In *Bildergeschichte: Festschrift Klaus Stähler*, ed. J. Gebauer, E. Grabow, F. Jünger, and D. Metzler: 151–67. Möhnesee: Bibliopolis.
Forsdyke, Sara. 2012. *Slaves Tell Tales: And Other Episodes in the Politics of Popular Culture in Ancient Greece*. Princeton, NJ: Princeton University Press.
Foxhall, Lin. 1998. "Cargoes of the Heart's Desire: The Character of Trade in the Archaic Mediterranean World." In *Archaic Greece: New Approaches and New Evidence*, ed. N. Fisher and H. van Wees: 295–309. Swansea: Classical Press of Wales.
Fraenkel, Max. 1891. *Antike Denkmaeler*, vol 1. Berlin: Kaiserlich Deutschen Archaeologischen Institut.
Frank, Tenney. 1916. "Race Mixture in the Roman Empire." *American Historical Review* 21.4: 689–708.
Frankfurter, David. 1998. *Religion in Roman Egypt: Assimilation and Resistance*. Princeton: Princeton University Press.
Fraser, A. D. 1929. Rev. of Beardsley 1929. *Art Bulletin* 11.4: 426–27.
Furley, William D. 1996. *Andokides and the Herms: A Study of Crisis in Fifth-Century Athenian Religion*. London: Institute of Classical Studies.
Furtwängler, Adolf, Ernst R. Fiechter, and Hermann Thiersch. 1906. *Aegina: Das Heiligtum der Aphaia*. Munich: Bayerische Akademie der Wissenschaften.
Furtwängler, Adolf, and Karl Reichhold. 1904–32. *Griechische Vasenmalerei: Auswahl hervorragender Vasenbilder*. 3 vols. Munich: F. Bruckmann.
Fynn-Paul, Jeffrey. 2009. "Empire, Monotheism and Slavery in the Greater Mediterranean Region from Antiquity to the Early Modern Era." *Past & Present* 205: 3–40.
Gagarin, Michael. 1996. "The Torture of Slaves in Athenian Law." *CP* 91.1: 1–18.
Gaither, Paula, Elisa McAtee, Kenneth Lapatin, and David Saunders. 2020. "Rethinking Descriptions of Black Africans in Greek, Etruscan, and Roman Art." https://blogs.getty.edu/iris/rethinking-descriptions-of-black-africans-in-greek-etruscan-and-roman-art/.
Gallavotti, Carlo. 1990. "Revisione di testi epigrafici." *Bollettino dei classici* 11: 155–59.
Gardner, Ernest A. 1888. *Naukratis II*. London: Trübner & Son.

Garlan, Yvon. 1988 [1985]. *Slavery in Ancient Greece*. Trans. J. Lloyd. Ithaca, NY: Cornell University Press.

Garner, R. 1979. "Experimental Mummification." In *Manchester Museum Mummy Project: Multidisciplinary Research on Ancient Egyptian Mummified Remains*, ed. A. R. David: 19–24. Manchester: Manchester University Press.

Garner, Richard. 1993. "Achilles in Locri: *P.Oxy.* 3876 frr. 37–77." *ZPE* 96: 153–65.

Garnsey, Peter. 1996. *Ideas of Slavery from Aristotle to Augustine*. Cambridge: Cambridge University Press.

Gates, Henry Louis, Jr., ed. 1986. *"Race," Writing, and Difference*. Chicago: University of Chicago Press.

Gates, Jennifer E. 2002. "The Ethnicity Name Game: What Lies behind 'Graeco-Persian'?" *Ars Orientalis* 32: 105–32.

Gavriljuk, Nadezda. 2003. "The Graeco-Scythian Slave-Trade in the 6th and 5th Centuries BC." In *Black Sea Studies 1: The Cauldron of Ariantas: Studies Presented to A.N. Sceglov on the Occasion of His 70th Birthday*, ed. P. Bilde, J. Højte, and V. Stolba: 75–85. Aarhus: Aarhus University Press.

Genovese, Eugene D. 1974. *Roll, Jordan, Roll: The World the Slaves Made*. New York: Vintage.

Georgieva, Zdravka H. 2021. "Logboats from the Bulgarian Black Sea Coast." *IJNA* 50.1: 87–96.

Gerasimov, Vyacheslav, Roman Reyda, Oleksandr Smyrnov, and Piotr Prejs. 2018. "The Ancient Ship Wreck of the Late 4th/Early 3rd Century BC at Kinburn Spit, Black Sea (Ukraine)." *Skillis* 18.2: 186–94.

Ghersetti, Antonella. 2007. "The Semiotic Paradigm: Physiognomy and Medicine in Islamic Culture." In Swain: 281–308.

Giaime, M., S. Avnaim-Katav, C. Morhange, N. Marriner, F. Rostek, A. V. Porotov, A. Baralis, D. Kaniewski, H. Brückner, and D. Kelterbaum. 2016. "Evolution of Taman Peninsula's Ancient Bosphorus Channels, South-west Russia: Deltaic progradation and Greek Colonization." *Journal of Archaeological Science: Reports* 5: 327–35.

Gikandi, Simon. 2011. *Slavery and the Culture of Taste*. Princeton, NJ: Princeton University Press.

Gill, David, and Michael Vickers. 1996. "Bocchoris the Wise and Absolute Chronology." *Romische Mitteilungen* 103: 1–9.

Gill, David, and Michael Vickers. 2001. "Laconian Lead Figurines: Mineral Extraction and Exchange in the Archaic Mediterranean." *BSA* 96: 229–36.

Gilroy, Paul. 2010 [1987]. *There Ain't No Black in the Union Jack*. 2nd ed. London: Routledge.

Giustozzi, Nunzio, ed. 2016. *Guide to the Egyptian Collection at the MANN*. Trans. R. Sadlier. Naples: Museo archeologico nazionale di Napoli.

Giveon, Raphael. 1978. *The Impact of Egypt on Canaan: Iconographical and Related Studies*. Göttingen: Universitätsverlag Freiburg Schweiz.

Gjerstad, Einar, John Lindros, Erik Sjöqvist, and Alfred Westholm. 1935. *Finds and Results of the Excavations in Cyprus 1927–1931. The Swedish Cyprus Expedition* vol. 2. Stockholm: Swedish Cyprus Expedition.

Gleason, Maude W. 1996. *Making Men: Sophists and Self-Presentation in Ancient Rome.* Princeton, NJ: Princeton University Press.

Greaves, Alan M. 2004. "The Cult of Aphrodite in Miletos and Its Colonies." *AnatSt* 54: 27–33.

Goedicke, Hans. 1975. *The Report of Wenamun.* Baltimore: Johns Hopkins University Press.

Goff, Barbara, and Michael Simpson. 2007. *Crossroads in the Black Aegean: Oedipus, Antigone, and Dramas of the African Diaspora.* Oxford: Oxford University Press.

Goitein, Shelomo Dov. 1967-93. *A Mediterranean Society: The Jewish Communities of the Arab World as Portrayed in the Documents of the Cairo Geniza.* 6 vols. Berkeley: University of California Press.

Goldenberg, David M. 1998–99. "The Development of the Idea of Race: Classical Paradigms and Medieval Elaborations." *International Journal of the Classical Tradition* 5.2: 561–70.

Goldstein, Holly Markovitz. 2012. "St. Augustine's "Slave Market": A Visual History." *Southern Spaces* September 28. https://southernspaces.org/2012/st-augustines-slave-market-visual-history/.

Gorton, Andrée Feghali. 1996. *Egyptian and Egyptianizing Scarabs: A Typology of Steatite, Faience and Paste Scarabs from Punic and Other Mediterranean Sites.* Oxford: Oxbow.

Gould, Stephen Jay. 1996 [1981]. *The Mismeasure of Man.* 2nd ed. New York: W.W. Norton.

Grafe, Regina. 2012. *Distant Tyranny: Markets, Power, and Backwardness in Spain, 1650–1800.* Princeton, NJ: Princeton University Press.

Graham, A. J. 1998. "The Woman at the Window: Observations on the 'Stele from the Harbour' of Thasos." *JHS* 118: 22–40.

Grallert, Silke. 2001. "Akkulturation im ägyptischen Sepulkralwesen—Der Fall eines Griechen in Ägypten zur Zeit der 26. Dynastie." In *Naukratis: Die Beziehungen zu Ostgriechenland, Ägypten und Zypern in archaischer Zeit,* ed. U. Höckmann and D. Kreikenbom: 185–95. Möhnesee, Germany: Bibliopolis.

Grandet, Pierre. 1994-97. *Le Papyrus Harris I (BM 9999).* 3 vols. Cairo: Institut français d'archéologie orientale.

Grandet, Pierre. 2009. "Early to Mid-20th Dynasty." In *UCLA Encyclopedia of Egyptology,* W. Wendrich et al. https://escholarship.org/uc/item/0d84248t.

Greene, Elizabeth S. 2018. "Shipwrecks as Indices of Archaic Mediterranean Trade Networks." In Knappett and Leidwanger: 132–62.

Greene, Elizabeth, Mark L. Lawall, and Mark E. Polzer. 2008. "Inconspicuous Consumption: The Sixth-Century B.C.E. Shipwreck at Pabuç Burnu, Turkey." *AJA* 112.4: 685–711.

Greenwood, Emily. 2009. "Re-rooting the Classical Tradition: New Directions in Black Classicism." *Classical Receptions Journal* 1.1: 87–103.

Greenwood, Emily. 2010. *Afro-Greeks: Dialogues between Anglophone Caribbean Literature and Classics in the Twentieth Century.* Oxford: Oxford University Press.

Greenwood, Emily, ed. 2022a. "Classical Philology, Otherhow." Special issue, *AJP* 143.2.

Greenwood, Emily. 2022b. "Reconstructing Classical Philology: Reading Aristotle, *Politics* 1.4 after Toni Morrison." *AJP* 143.2: 335–57.

Greif, Avner. 2022. "Institutions and Impersonal Exchange: From Communal to Individual Responsibility." *Journal of Institutional and Theoretical Economics* 158.1: 168–204.

Gruen, Erich. 2011. *Rethinking the Other in Antiquity.* Princeton, NJ: Princeton University Press.

Gunter, Anne. 2009. *Greek Art and the Orient.* Cambridge: Cambridge University Press.

Guralnick, Eleanor. 2004. "A Group of Near Eastern Bronzes from Olympia." *AJA* 108: 2: 187–222.

Guyatt, Mary. 2000. "The Wedgwood Slave Medallion: Values in Eighteenth-Century Design." *Journal of Design History* 13.2: 93–105.

Hadjidaki, Elpida. 1996. "Underwater Excavations of a Late Fifth Century Merchant Ship at Alonnesos, Greece: the 1991–1993 Seasons." *BCH* 120.2: 561–93.

Hakenbeck, Susanne E. 2019. "Genetics, Archaeology and the Far Right: An Unholy Trinity." *WorldArch* 51.4: 517–527.

Hale, John R. 2013. "Not Patriots, Not Farmers, Not Amateurs: Greek Soldiers of Fortune and the Origins of Hoplite Warfare." In *Men of Bronze: Hoplite Warfare in Ancient Greece*, ed. D. Kagan and G. Viggiano: 179–93. Princeton, NJ: Princeton University Press.

Haley, Shelley. 1993. "Black Feminist Thought and the Classics: Re-membering, Re-claiming, and Re-empowering." In *Feminist Theory and the Classics*, ed. N. S. Rabinowitz and A. Richlin: 23–42. New York: Routledge.

Haley, Shelley. 2005. Review of Isaac 2004. *AJP* 126.3: 451–54.

Haley, Shelley. 2021. "Race and Gender." In McCoskey: 119–36.

Hall, H. R. 1913. *Catalogue of Egyptian Scarabs, Etc., in the British Museum.* London: British Museum.

Hall, Edith. 1989a. *Inventing the Barbarian: Greek Self-definition through Tragedy.* Oxford: Oxford University Press.

Hall, Edith. 1989b. "The Archer Scene in Aristophanes' *Thesmophoriazusae*." *Philologus* 133: 38–54.

Hall, Jonathan M. 1997. *Ethnic Identity in Greek Antiquity.* Cambridge: Cambridge University Press.

Hall, Jonathan M. 2002. *Hellenicity: Between Ethnicity and Culture.* Chicago: University of Chicago Press.

Hall, Jonathan M. 2015. "Ancient Greek Ethnicities: Towards a Reassessment." *BICS* 58.2: 15–29.

Hammer, Dean. 2004. "Ideology, the Symposium, and Archaic Politics." *AJP* 125.4: 479–512.

Handler, Jerome S. 2002. "Survivors of the Middle Passage: Life Histories of Enslaved Africans in British America." *Slavery and Abolition* 23.1: 25–56.

Harris, Edward M. 2012. "Homer, Hesiod, and the 'Origins' Of Greek Slavery." *RÉA* 114.2: 2–22.

Harris, Edward M. 2013. "Were There Business Agents in Classical Greece? The Evidence of Some Lead Letters." In *The Letter: Law, State, Society and the Epistolary Format in the Ancient World: Proceedings of a Colloquium Held at the American Academy in Rome 28–30.9.2008*, U. Yiftach-Firanko: 105–124. Wiesbaden: Harrasowitz Verlag.

Harris, Edward M., David Lewis, and Mark Woolmer, eds. 2015. *The Ancient Greek Economy: Markets, Households, and City States*. Cambridge: Cambridge University Press.

Harris, J. R. 1961. *Lexographical Studies in Ancient Egyptian Minerals*. Berlin: Akadamie Verlag.

Harris, W. V., ed. 2005. *Rethinking the Mediterranean*. Oxford: Oxford University Press.

Harris, W. V., ed. 2013. *Moses Finley and Politics*. Leiden: Brill.

Harrison, Richard J. 1988. *Spain at the Dawn of History: Iberians, Phoenicians, and Greeks*. London: Thames and Hudson.

Harrison, Thomas. 2019. "Classical Greek Ethnography and the Slave Trade." *ClassAnt* 38.1: 36–57.

Harrison, Thomas. 2020. "Reinventing the Barbarian." *CP* 115: 139–63.

Hartman, Saidiya. 2008. "Venus in Two Acts." *small axe* 26: 1–14.

Hartog, François. 1988 [1980]. *The Mirror of Herodotus: The Representation of the Other in the Writing of History*. Trans. J. Lloyd. Berkeley: University of California Press.

Hartog, François. 2001 [1996]. *Memories of Odysseus: Frontier Tales from Ancient Greece*. Trans. J. Lloyd. Chicago: University of Chicago Press.

Hartog, François. 2016. *Regimes of Historicity: Presentism and the Experience of Time*. Trans. S. Brown. New York: Columbia University Press.

Hedreen, Guy. 1991. "The Cult of Achilles in the Euxine." *Hesperia* 60.3: 313–30.

Heinen, Heinz. 2001a. "Sklaverei im nördlichen Schwarzmeerraum: Zum Stand der Forschung." In *Forschungen zur antiken Sklaverei an der mainzer Akademie 1950–2000: Miscellanea zum Jubiläum*, ed. H. Bellen and H. Heinen: 487–503. Stuttgart: Franz Steiner Verlag.

Heinen, Heinz. 2001b. "Greeks, Iranians, and Romans on the North Shore of the Black Sea." In Tsetskhladze: 1–24.

Heinen, Heinz. 2010. "Aufstieg und Niedergang der sowjetischen Sklavereiforschung: Eine Studie zur Verbindung von Politik und Wissenschaft." In *Antike Sklaverei: Rückblick und Ausblick: neue Beiträge zur Forschungsgeschichte und zur Erschliessung der archäologischen Zeugnisse*, ed. H. Heinen: 95–138. Stuttgart: Franz Steiner Verlag.

Hemelrijk, Jaap M. 1984. *Caeretan Hydriae*. 2 vols. Mainz: Philipp von Zabern.

Henderson, Julian. 2013. *Ancient Glass: An Interdisciplinary Exploration*. Cambridge: Cambridge University Press.

Hendricks, Margo. 2019. "Coloring the Past, Rewriting Our Future: RaceB4Race." https://www.folger.edu/institute/scholarly-programs/race-periodization/margo-hendricks.

Heng, Geraldine. 2018. *The Invention of Race in the Middle Ages*. Cambridge: Cambridge University Press.

Henke, Jan-Marc. 2019. "Cypriot Terracotta Figurines in the East Aegean as Evidence for a Technical and Cultic Innovation Transfer?" *British Museum Studies in Ancient Egypt and Sudan* 24: 248–80.

Henry, A. 2002. "Hookers and Lookers: Prostitution and Soliciting in Late Archaic Thasos." *BSA* 97: 217–21.

Herda, Alexander. 2016. "Megara and Miletos: Colonising with Apollo: A Structural Comparison of Religious and Political Institutions in Two Archaic Greek Polis States." In *Mégarika: Nouvelles recherches sur Mégare, les cités de la Propontide et du Pont-Euxin*, ed. A. Robu and I. Bîrzescu: 15–127. Paris: Éditions de Boccard.

Higbie, Carolyn. 2003. *The Lindian Chronicle and the Greek Creation of their Past*. Oxford: Oxford University Press.

Higgins, Charlotte. 2020. "A Scandal in Oxford: The Curious Case of the Stolen Gospel." *The Guardian*, January 9. https://www.theguardian.com/news/2020/jan/09/a-scandal-in-oxford-the-curious-case-of-the-stolen-gospel.

Hind, John G. F. 1994. "The Trade in Getic Slaves and the Silver Coins Of Istria." In *Thracica Pontica V: Les ports dans la vie de la thrace ancienne*, ed. M. Lazarov and C. Angelova: 153–58. Sozopol: Centre d'archéologie subaquatique.

Hind, John G. F. 2001. "A Sea 'Like a Scythian Bow' and Herodotus' 'Rugged Peninsula' (*Hist*. 4.99)." In Tsetskhladze: 25–32.

Hind, John G. F. 2012. "Milesian and Sinopean Traders in Colchis (Greeks at Phasis and the Ransoming of Shipwrecked Sailors." In *The Black Sea, Paphlagonia, Pontus, and Phrygia in Antiquity: Aspects of Archaeology and Ancient History*, ed. G. Tsetskhladze, E. Lafli, J. Hargrave, and W. Anderson: 105–8. Oxford: Archeopress.

Hobbs, J. S. 1847. *New Sailing Directions for the Dardanelles, Sea of Marmara, Bosphorus, Black Sea, and the Sea of Azov*. London: Charles Wilson.

Hobden, Fiona. 2013. *The Symposium in Ancient Greek Society and Thought*. Cambridge: Cambridge University Press.

Hobsbawm, Eric. 1983. "Introduction: Inventing Tradition." In *The Invention of Tradition*, ed. E. Hobsbawm and R. Ranger: 1–14. Cambridge: Cambridge University Press.

Hock, Rudolph. N.d. "Snowden, Frank Martin, Jr." Database of Classical Scholars. https://dbcs.rutgers.edu/all-scholars/9133-snowden-frank-martin-jr.

Hoffmann, Friedhelm. 2009. "Die Entstehung der demotischen Erzählliteratur Beobachtungen zum überlieferunggeschichtlichen Kontext." In *Das Erzählen in frühen Hochkulturen*, ed. J. Assmann and H. Roeder: 351–84. Munich: Wilhelm Fink.

Hogarth, David George. 1908. *Excavations at Ephesus: the Archaic Artemisia*. London: British Museum.

Hogarth, D. G., C. C. Edgar, and Clement Gutch. 1898-99. "Excavations at Naukratis." *BSA* 5: 26–97.

Højte, Jacob Munk. 2005. "The Archaeological Evidence for Fish Processing in the Black Sea Region." In Bekker-Nielsen: 133–60.

Hölbl, Günther. 1978. *Zeugnisse ägyptischer Religionsvorstellungen für Ephesus*. Leiden: Brill.

Hölbl, Günther. 1979. *Beziehungen der Ägyptischen Kultur zu Altitalien*. 2 vols. Leiden: Brill.

Hölbl, Günther. 1981. "Die Ausbreitung ägyptischen Kulturgutes in den ägäischen Raum um 8. bis zum 6. Jh. v. Chr." *Orientalia* 50.2 (n.s.): 186–92.

Hölbl, Günther. 1985. "Aegyptiaca aus vorhellenistischen Fundzusammenhängen im Bereich der türkischen Mittelmeerküste." In *Lebendige Altertumswissenschaft: Festgabe zur Villendung des 70. Lebensjahres von Hermann Vetters*, ed. M. Kandler: 38–42. Vienna: Holshausen.

Hölbl, Günther. 1986. *Ägyptisches Kulturgut im Phönikischen und Punischen Sardinien*. 2 vols. Leiden: Brill.

Hölbl, Günther. 1999. "Funde aus Milet VIII: die Aegyptiaca vom Aphroditetempel auf dem Zeytintepe." *AA*: 345–71.

Hölbl, Günther. 1999/2000. "König Bokchoris und die Aegyptiaca mit Königsnamen bei den Griechen." *Egyptian Society of Greek and Roman Studies* 4: 11–29.

Hölbl, Günther. 2001. "I rapporti culturali della Sicilia orientale con l'Egitto in età arcaica visti attraverso gli *Aegyptiaca* del territorio siracusano." In *La Sicilia antica nei rapporti con l'Egitto*, ed. C. Basile and A. di Natale: 31–47. Siracusa: Quaderni del Museo del Papiro.

Hölbl, Günther. 2007. "Ionien und Ägypten in archaischer Zeit." In *Frühes Ionien eine Bestandsaufnahme*, Milesische Forschungen 5, ed. J. Cobet, V. von Graeve, W.-D. Niemeier, and K. Zimmermann: 447–61. Mainz: Verlag Philipp von Zabern.

Hölbl, Günther. 2014. "Ägyptisches Kulturgut in Ionien im 7. Jh. v. Chr.: der Beitrag Milets zu einem religionshistorischen Phänomen." In *Der Beitrag Kleinasiens zur Kultur- und Geistesgeschichte der griechisch-römischen Antike*, ed. J. Fischer: 181–209. Vienna: Österreichischen Akademie der Wissenschaften.

Hölbl, Günther. 2015. "Die ägyptische Götterwelt in den rhodischen Votivdepots von Kameiros." In *Sapientia Felicitas: Festschrift für Günter Vittmann zum 29. Februar 2016*, ed. S. Lippert, M. Schentuleit and M. Stadler: 217–54. Montpellier: Cahiers de l'ENiM.

Holmes, George Frederick. 1850. "Observations on a Passage in the *Politics* of Aristotle Relative to Slavery." *Southern Literary Messenger* 16.4: 193–205.

Hopkins, T., and I. Wallerstein. 1977. "Patterns of Development of the Modern World System." *Review (Fernand Braudel Center)* 1.2: 11–145.

Horden, Peregrine, and Nicholas Purcell. 2000. *The Corrupting Sea: a Study of Mediterranean History*. Malden, MA: Blackwell.
Hunt, Peter. 2018. *Ancient Greek and Roman Slavery*. Malden, MA: Wiley Blackwell.
Hupe, Joachim, ed. 2006. *Der Achilleus-Kult im nördlichen Schwarzmeerraum vom Beginn der griechischen Kolonisation bis in die römische Kaiserzeit*. Rahden, Germany: Verlag Marie Leidorf.
Hupe, Joachim. 2006. "Der Achilleus-Kult in Tyras." In Hupe: 155–60.
Hurston, Zora Neale. 2018 [1931]. *Baracoon: The Story of the Last "Black Cargo."* Ed. Plant. New York: Harper Collins.
Ilieva, Petya. 2017. "Thracians on the Northern Aegean Islands: Written *Testimonia* and Current Archaeological Evidence." *Thracia* 22: 253–70.
Isaac, Benjamin. 2004. *The Invention of Racism in Classical Antiquity*. Princeton, NJ: Princeton University Press.
Ivantchik, Askhold I. 1993. "La datation du poème l'Arimaspée d'Aristéas de Proconnèse." *AntCl* 62: 35–67.
Ivantchik, Askhold I. 1999. "Eine griechische Pseudo-Historie. Der Pharao Sesostris und der skytho-ägyptische Krieg." *Historia* 48.4: 395–441.
Ivantchik, Askhold I. 2006. "'Scythian' Archers on Archaic Attic Vases: Problems of Interpretation." *Ancient Civilizations from Scythia to Siberia* 12.3–4: 197–271.
Ivantchik, Askhold I. 2011. "The Funeral of Scythian Kings: The Historical Reality and the Description of Herodotus (4.71–72)." In *The Barbarians of Ancient Europe: Realities and Interactions*, ed. L. Bonfante: 71–104. Cambridge: Cambridge University Press.
Jablonski, Nina G. 2021. "Skin Color and Race." *American Journal of Physical Anthropology* 175: 437–47.
Jacobson, Esther. 1995. *The Arts of the Scythians: the Interpenetration of Cultures at the Edge of the Hellenic World*. Leiden: Brill.
Jackson, C. M., P. T. Nicholson, and W. Gneisinger. 1998. "Glassmaking at Tell el-Amarna: An Integrated Approach." *JGS* 40: 11–23.
Jackson, C. M., S. Paynter, M.-D. Nenna, and P. Degryse. 2018. "Glassmaking Using Natron from el-Barnugi (Egypt); Pliny and the Roman Glass Industry." *Archaeological and Anthropological Sciences* 10.5: 1179–91.
Jaeger, Bertrand. 1982. *Essai de classification et datation des scarabées Menkhéperrê*. Orbis Biblicus et Orientalis, Series Archeologica 2. Göttingen: Vendenhoeck & Ruprecht.
James, T. H. G. 1962. "The Egyptian-type objects." In Dunbabin: 461–515.
Janot, F., and P. Munaro. 2021. "Observations on Individual T13-1-15 from the South-East Necropolis at Thorikos." In Docter and Webster: 145–50.
Janssen, Jac J. 1961. *Two Ancient Egyptian Ship's Logs: Papyrus Leiden I 350 Verso and Papyrus Turin 2008 + 2016*. Leiden: Brill.
Janssen, Jac J. 1975a. *Commodity Prices from the Ramessid period: an Economic Study of the Village of Necropolis Workmen at Thebes*. Leiden: Brill.

Janssen, Jac J. 1975b. "Prolegomena to the Study of Egypt's Economic History during the New Kingdom." *Studien zur Altägyptischen Kultur* 3: 127–85.

Janssen, Jac J., and P. W. Pestman. 1968. "Burial and Inheritance in the Community of the Necropolis Workmen at Thebes (*Pap. Bulaq* X and *O.Petrie* 16)." *JESHO* 11: 137–70.

Jay, Jacqueline E. 2016. *Orality and Literacy in the Demotic Tales*. Leiden: Brill.

Jeffrey, Lilian. 1967. "Αρχαία Γράμματα: Some Ancient Greek Views." In *Europa: Studien zur Geschichte und Epigraphik der Frühen Aegaeis*, ed. W.C. Brice: 152–62. Berlin: De Gruyter.

Jefferson, Thomas. 1998 [1785]. *Notes on the State of Virginia*, ed. F. Shuffleton. New York: Penguin.

Jeffery, Lilian Hamilton, and Alan W. Johnston. 1990. *The Local Scripts of Archaic Greece: a Study of the Origin of the Greek Alphabet and its Development from the Eighth to the Fifth Centuries B.C.* 2nd ed. Oxford: Oxford University Press.

Jenkins, Ian. 2001. "Archaic Kouroi in Naucratis: The Case for Cypriot Origin." *AJA* 105.2: 163–79.

Johnson, Walter. 1999. *Soul by Soul: Life inside the Antebellum Slave Market*. Cambridge, MA: Harvard University Press.

Johnston, Alan W. 2010. "Trading Families?" In *Onomatologos: Studies in Greek Personal Names Presented to Elaine Matthews*, ed. R. Catling and F. Marchand: 470–77. Oxford: Oxbow.

Johnston, Alan W. 2015a. "Ceramic inscriptions." In Villing et. al. 2013–19. https://webarchive.nationalarchives.gov.uk/20190801123859/https://www.britishmuseum.org/pdf/johnston_ceramic_incriptions_new.pdf.

Johnston, Alan W. 2015b. "Greek and Latin inscriptions on stone." In Villing et. al. 2013–19. https://webarchive.nationalarchives.gov.uk/20190801125430/https://www.britishmuseum.org/pdf/Johnston_Stone_inscriptions.pdf.

Johnston, Alan W. 2019. "Votive Inscriptions from Naukratis." *British Museum Studies in Ancient Egypt and Sudan* 24: 105–17.

Jones, Christopher. 2008. "Hyperides and the Sale of Slave Families." *ZPE* 164: 19–20.

Joshel, Sandra R., and Lauren Hackworth Petersen. 2014. *The Material Life of Roman Slaves*. Cambridge: Cambridge University Press.

Kahn, Dan'el. 2006. "The Assyrian Invasions of Egypt (673–663 B.C.) and the Final Expulsion of the Kushites." *Studien zur Altägyptischen Kultur* 34: 251–67.

Kaiser, Alan. 2015. *Archaeology, Sexism, and Scandal: The Long-Suppressed Story of One Woman's Discoveries and the Man Who Stole Credit for Them*. Lanham, MD: Rowman and Littlefield.

Kakavoyiannis, Evangelos. 2001. "The Silver Ore-Processing Workshops of the Lavrion Region." *BSA* 96: 365–80.

Kallet, Lisa. 2007. "The Athenian Economy." In *The Cambridge Companion to the Age of Pericles*, ed. L. Samson: 70–95. Cambridge: Cambridge University Press.

Kallet, Lisa, and John H. Kroll. 2020. *The Athenian Empire: Using Coins as Sources*. Cambridge: Cambridge University Press.

Kamen, Deborah. 2010. "A Corpus of Inscriptions: Representing Slave Marks in Antiquity." *Memoirs of the American Academy in Rome* 55: 95–110.

Kaplan, Philip. 2003. "Cross-cultural Contacts among Mercenary Communities in Saite and Persian Egypt." *Mediterranean Historical Review* 18.1: 1–31.

Kaplan, Philip. 2015. "Sojourner in the Land: The Resident Alien in Late Period Egypt." In *Walls of the Prince: Egyptian Interactions with Southwest Asia in Antiquity: Essays in Honour of John S. Holladay, Jr.*, ed. J. S. Holladay, T. Harrison, E. B. Banning, and S. Klassen: 396–413. Leiden: Brill.

Karageorghis, Vassos. 1973. "Chronique des fouilles et découvertes archéologiques à Chypre en 1972." *BCH* 97.2: 601–89.

Karageorghis, Vassos. 1988. *Blacks in Ancient Cypriot Art*. Houston: Menil Foundation.

Karageorghis, Vassos. 1989. "Chronique des fouilles et découvertes archéologiques à Chypre en 1988." *BCH* 113.2: 789–853.

Karageorghis, Vassos, Joan R. Mertens, and Marice E. Rose. 2000. *Ancient Art from Cyprus: The Cesnola Collection at the Metropolitan Museum of Art*. New York: Metropolitan Museum of Art.

Karageorghis, V., O. Picard, and C. Tytgat, eds. 1991. *La nécropole d'Amathonte tombes 110–385 (Études chypriotes XIII)*. Nicosia: A.G. Leventis.

Karyshkovsky, P.O. 2003. Монетное Дело и Денежное Обращение Ольвии (VI В. До Н.Э. - VI В. Н.э.). [Coinage and Money Circulation of Olbia (6th Century B.C.–6th Century A.D.). Odessa: AD. Friedman.

Kashkharov, P. K., M. V. Kovalchuk, N. A. Makarov, E. B. Yatsishina, E. A. Greshnikov, A. A. Antsiferova, P. A. Volkov, L. I. Govor, S. V. Olkhovsky. N. N. Presniakova, and R. D. Svetogorov. 2021. "Provenance Study of the Lead Detected in the Antique Ceramic Sculpture from the Kerch Bay." *Crystallography Reports* 66.1: 165–73.

Keita, Shomarka O. Y. 1993. "*Black Athena*: 'Race,' Bernal, and Snowden." *Arethusa* 26.3: 293–314.

Keita, Shomarka O. Y. 2023. "Seeing and Not Seeing Bias/Racism in Science and Society, Inconsistencies and Legacies of Charles Seligman and Ashley Montagu in Anthropological and Genetics Research on Africa." *American Anthropologist* 125.4: 797–808.

Kemp, Barry J. 2006 [1991]. *Ancient Egypt: Anatomy of a Civilization*. 2nd ed. London: Routledge.

Kenawi, Mohamed. 2014. *Alexandria's Hinterlands: Archaeology of the Western Nile Delta, Egypt*. Oxford: Archeopress.

Kennedy, Rebecca Futo. 2022. "Teaching Race in Greco-Roman Antiquity: Some Considerations and Resources." *Classical Outlook* 97.1: 2–8.

Khazanov, A. 1975. "Caractère de l'esclavage chez les Scythes." In *Formes d'exploitation du travail et rapports sociaux dans l'Antiquité Classique*, ed. J. Annequin, M. Clavel-Lévêque, and F. Favory: 111–28. Paris: Critique.

Khotylev, Alexey, and Sergey Olkhovsky. 2020. "Geological Studies as a Source of Data on the Maritime Trade between the Cimmerian Bosporus and the Mediterranean in the 1st Millennium BCE." *Skillis* 20: 97–107.

Kirchhoff, Adolf. 1887. *Studien zur Geschichte des griechischen Alphabets*. Berlin: F. Dümmler.

Kirigin, Branko, Alan Johnston, Marko Vučetić, and Zvonimir Lušić. 2009. "Palagruža—The Island of Diomedes—And Notes on Ancient Greek Navigation in the Adriatic." In *A Connecting Sea: Maritime Interaction in Adriatic Prehistory*, ed. S. Forenbaher: 137–55. Oxford: Archeopress.

Kitchen, K. A. 1986. *The Third Intermediate Period in Egypt, 1100-650 B.C.* Warminster: Aris & Phillips.

Klein, Wilhelm. 1898. *Die griechischen Vasen mit Lieblingsinschriften*. Leipzig: Veit.

Klenina, E. K. 2015. "The Dorian Colony of Chersonesos in Taurica: Historical and Economic Aspects of the Development in the Hellenistic Period." In *Greek Colonisation: New Data, Current Approaches: Proceedings of the Scientific Meeting Held in Thessaloniki (6 February 2015)*, ed. P. Adam-Belene: 37–57. Athens: Alpha Bank.

Knappett, Carl, and Justin Leidwanger, eds. 2018. *Maritime Networks in the Ancient Mediterranean*. Cambridge: Cambridge University Press.

Kołodziejczyk, Dariusz. 2006. "Slave Hunting and Slave Redemption as a Business Enterprise: The Northern Black Sea Region in the Sixteenth to Seventeenth Centuries." *Oriente Moderno* 25(86).1 (n.s.): 149–59.

Kolesnychenko, Anzhelika, and Dmytro Kiosak. 2021. "The Ancient Glass-Workshop of Yahorlyk Settlement in the Northern Pontic Region." In *Annales du 21e congrès de l'Association Internationale pour l'Histoire du Verre*, ed. O. Sevindik: 81–94. Istanbul: Association Internationale pour l'Histoire du Verre.

Konstan, David. 2013. "Menander's Slaves: The Banality of Violence." In *Slaves and Slavery in Ancient Greek Comic Drama*, ed. B. Akrigg and R. Tordoff: 144–58. Cambridge: Cambridge University Press.

Kopytoff, Igor. 1986. "The Cultural Biography of Things: Commoditization as Process." In Appadurai: 64–91.

Korshenko, A. N. 2001. Дельфины Ольвии [The Dolphins of Olbia]. Volgoda: MDK.

Koshelenko, G. A., I. T. Kurglikova, and V. S. Dologorukov. 1984. *Античные государства Северного Причерноморья* [Ancient States of the Northern Black Sea Region]. Moscow: Nauka.

Kostick, Dennis. 1998. "The Origin of the U.S. Natural and Synthetic Soda Ash Industries." In *Proceedings of the First International Soda Ash Conference*, ed. J. Dyni and R. Jones: 43–56. 2 vols. Laramie: Wyoming State Geological Survey.

Kourou, Nota. 2012. "Cypriots and Levantines in the Central Aegean during the Geometric Period: the Nature of Contacts." *MeditArch* 25: 215–27.

Kousoulis, Panagiotis. 2017. "Ροδιακά Αιγυπτιακά: Μια εισαγωγή στις αιγυπτιακές εκφάνσεις της οικουμένης του 7ου και 6ου αιώνα π.X. [Rhodian *aegyptiaca*: An introduction to the Egyptian expressions of the world in the seventh and sixth centuries B.C.]. *Θέματα Αρχαιολογίας* 1.1: 34–45.

Kousoulis, Panagiotis, and Ludwig Morenz. 2007. "Ecumene and Economy in the Horizon of Religion: Egyptian Donations to Rhodian Sanctuaries." In *Das Heilige und die Ware zum Spannungsfeld von Religion und Ökonomie*, ed. M. Fitzenreiter: 179–92. London: Golden House.

Kowalzig, Barbara. 2013. "Transcultural Chorality: *Iphigenia in Tauris* and Athenian Imperial Economics in a Polytheistic World." In *Choral Mediations in Greek Drama*, ed. R. Gagné and M. Hopmann: 178–210. Cambridge: Cambridge University Press.

Kowalzig, Barbara. 2018. "Cults, Cabotage, and Connectivity: Experimenting with Religious and Economic Networks in the Greco-Roman Mediterranean." In Knappett and Leidwanger: 93–131.

Kroll, John H. 2018. "Two Fifth-Century Lead Weights of Kyzikos on the Commercial Standard of Athens." In *Proceedings of the Second International Congress on the History of Money and Numismatics in the Mediterranean World, 5-8 January 2017*, ed. Oğuz Tekin: 85–90. Antalya: Koç Üniversitesi.

Kritzas, C. 2010. "Φοινίκηια γράμματα: νέα αρχαϊκή επιγραφή από την Ελτύνα" [Phoenician letters: a new Archaic inscription from Eltyna]. In *Το γεωμετρικό νεκροταφείο της Ελτύνας* [The Geometric cemetery of Eltyna], ed. G. Rethemiotakis and M. Egglezou: 1–16. Iraklio: Archaeological Institute of Cretological Studies.

Kryzhitskiy, Sergei D. 2007. "Criteria for the Presence of Barbarians in the Population of Early Olbia." In Braund and Kryzhitskiy: 17–22.

Kuhrt, Amélie. 2007. *The Persian Empire: A Corpus of Sources from the Achaemenid Period*. London: Routledge.

Kurke, Leslie V. 1999. *Coins, Bodies, Games, and Gold: the Politics of Meaning in Archaic Greece*. Princeton, NJ: Princeton University Press.

Kurke, Leslie V. 2011. *Aesopic Conversations: Popular Tradition, Cultural Dialogue, and the Invention of Greek Prose*. Princeton, NJ: Princeton University Press.

Kuznetsov, Vladimir D., and Mikhail G. Abramzon. 2021. *The Beginning of Coinage in the Cimmerian Bosporus (A Hoard from Phanagoria)*. Leuven: Peeters.

Lacaze, Ginette, Olivier Masson, and Jean Yoyotte. 1984. "Deux documents memphites copies par J.M. Vansleb au XVIIe siècle." *RÉg* 35: 127–37.

Ladynin, I. A. 2016. "Особенности ландшафта: (насколько марксистской была «советская древность»?" [Features of the Landscape (How Marxist was the "Soviet Antiquity?")]. *Вестник Университета Дмитрия Пожарского* [Bulletin of Dmitry Pozharsky University] 2.4: 9–32.

Lagarce, E. 1976. "Remarques sur l'utilisation des scarabées, scaraboides, amulettes et figurines de type égyptien a Chypre." In Clerc, Karageorghis, Lagarce, and Leclant: 167–82.

Lamont, Jessica. 2023. "Trade, Literacy, and Documentary Histories of the Northern Black Sea." *JHS* 143: 1–23.

Lanfranchi, Giovanni. 2011. "The Expansion of the Neo-Assyrian Empire and its peripheries: Military, Political and Ideological Resistance." In *Lag Troia in Kilikien? Der aktuelle Streit um Homers Ilias*, ed. C. Ulf and R. Rollinger: 219–33. Darmstadt: Wissenschaftliche Buchgesellschaft.

Lang, Mabel. 1971. *Graffiti and Dipinti. The Athenian Agora*, vol. 21. Princeton, NJ: American School of Classical Studies at Athens.

Langdon, Merle K. 1991. "Poletai Records." In *Inscriptions. The Athenian Agora*, vol. 19, ed. G. V. Lalonde, M. K. Langdon, and M. B. Walbank: 53–144. Princeton, NJ: The American School of Classical Studies at Athens.

Langdon, Susan. 1993. *From Pasture to Polis: Art in the Age of Homer*. Columbia: University of Missouri Press.

Langdon, Susan. 2001. "Beyond the Grave: Biographies from Early Greece." *AJA* 105.4: 579–606.

Lape, Susan. 2010. *Race and Citizen Identity in the Classical Athenian Democracy*. Cambridge: Cambridge University Press.

Lassen, Hanne. 2000. "Introduction to Weight Systems in the Bronze Age East Mediterranean: The Case of Kalavasos-Ayios Dhimitrios." In *Metals Make the World Go Round: The Supply and Circulation of Metals in Bronze Age Europe*, ed. C. Pare: 233–46. Oxford: Oxbow.

Lauffer, Siegfried. 1979 [1956]. *Die Bergwerkssklaven von Laureion*. 2nd ed. Wiesbaden: Franz Steiner Verlag.

Law, Robin, and Kristin Mann. 1999. "West Africa in the Atlantic Community: The Case of the Slave Coast." *William and Mary Quarterly* 56.2: 307–34.

Lawall, Mark. 2003. "Negotiating Chronologies: Aegean Amphora Research, Thasian Chronology, and Pnyx III." In *Chronologies of the Black Sea Area in the Period C. 400-100 BC*, ed. V. Stolba and L. Hannestead: 31–67. Aarhus: Aarhus University Press.

Lawrance, Benjamin N., and Richard L. Roberts. 2019. "Viral Video 'Blood Chocolate' Activism, Millennial Anti-trafficking, and the Neoliberal Resurgence of Shaming." *Slavery & Abolition* 40.1: 168–98.

Lazaridis, Iosif, et al. 2022. "A Genetic Probe into the Ancient and Medieval History of Southern Europe and West Asia." *Science* 377: 940–51.

Leclère, François, and Jeffrey Spencer, eds. 2014. *Tell Dafana Reconsidered: the Archaeology of an Egyptian Frontier Town*. London: British Museum Press.

Leclant, Jean. 1980. "Fouilles et travaux en Égypte et au Soudan, 1978–1979." *Orientalia* (n.s.) 49.4: 346–420.

Lehmann, Manuela, and Nigel Tallis. 2019. "Esharhaddon in Egypt: An Assyrian-Egyptian Battle Scene on Glazed Tiles from Nimrud." *British Museum Studies in Ancient Egypt and Sudan* 25: 1–100.

Lenski, Noel. 2018. "Framing the Question: What Is a Slave Society?" In Lenski and Cameron: 15–57.

Lenski, Noel, and Catherine M. Cameron, eds. 2018. *What Is Slavery: The Practice of Slavery in Global Perspective*. Cambridge: Cambridge University Press.

Lesher, J. H. 1992. *Xenophanes of Colophon: Fragments*. University of Toronto Press: Toronto.

Lewis, David M. 2011. "Near Eastern Slaves in Classical Attica and the Slave Trade with Persian Territories." *CQ* (n.s.) 61: 91–113.

Lewis, David M. 2015a. "The Market for Slaves in the Fifth and Fourth Century Aegean: Achaemenid Anatolia as a Case Study." In Harris, Lewis, and Woolmer: 316–36. Cambridge: Cambridge University Press.

Lewis, David M. 2015b. "Commodities in Classical Athens: The Evidence of Old Comedy." In Harris, Lewis, and Woolmer: 381–98.

Lewis, David M. 2018. *Greek Slave Systems in their Eastern Mediterranean Context: c. 800–146 BC*. Oxford: Oxford University Press.

Lewis, David M. 2022. "A Cargo of Slaves? Demosthenes 34.10." *Mariner's Mirror* 108.2: 135–48.

Lewis, David M. Forthcoming. "Slave Families, Reproduction, and the Market: Towards a Study of the Ancient Greek Slave Supply." In *Familles d'esclaves / esclaves dans la famille*, ed. S. Maillot. Clermont Ferrand.

Lindenlauf, Astrid. 2003. "The Sea as a Place of No Return in Ancient Greece." *WorldArch* 35.3: 416–33.

Lindsay, Lisa A., and John Wood Sweet, eds. 2014. *Biography and the Black Atlantic*. Philadelphia: University of Pennsylvania Press.

Lintott, Andrew. 2004. "*Sula*: Reprisal by Seizure in Greek Inter-Community Relations." *CQ* 54.2 (n.s.): 340–53.

Lissarrague, François. 1990. *L'autre guerrier: archers, peltastes, cavaliers dans l'imagerie attique*. Rome: École française de Rome.

Lissarrague, François. 1995. "Identity and Otherness: the Case of Attic Head Vases and Plastic Vases." *Source* 15.1: 4–9.

Lissarrague, François. 2015. "Corps à corps: épisèmes anthropomorphiques dans la céramique attique." In *Bodies in Transition: Dissolving the Bounds of Embodied Knowledge*, ed. D. Boschung, A. Shapiro, and F. Wascheck. Wiesbaden: Harrasowitz Verlag.

Lloyd, Alan B. 1975. "Were Necho's Triremes Phoenician?" *JHS* 95: 45–61.

Lloyd, Alan B. 1982. "Nationalist Propaganda in Ptolemaic Egypt." *Historia* 31.1: 33–55.

Lloyd, Alan B. 1983. "The Late Period, 664–323 BC." In *Ancient Egypt: A Social History*, ed. B. G. Trigger, B. J. Kemp, D. O'Connor, and A. B. Lloyd: 279–348. Cambridge: Cambridge University Press.

Loar, Matthew, Carolyn MacDonald, and Dan-el Padilla Peralta, eds. 2017. *Rome, Empire of Plunder: The Dynamics of Cultural Appropriation*. Cambridge: Cambridge University Press.

Lohwasser, Angelika. 2014. "Neue Skarabäen mit *mn-khpr-rʿ* aus der 25. Dynastie." In *Skarabäen des 1. Jahrtausends*, ed. A. Lohwasser: 175–98. Göttingen: Academic Press Fribourg.

López-Ruiz, Carolina. 2010. *When the Gods Were Born: Greek Cosmogonies and the Near East*. Cambridge, MA: Harvard University Press.

López-Ruiz, Carolina. 2021. *Phoenicians and the Making of the Mediterranean*. Cambridge, MA: Harvard University Press.

Lovejoy, Paul E. 1986. *Salt of the Desert Sun: a History of Salt Production and Trade in the Central Sudan*. Cambridge: Cambridge University Press.

Lucas, A. 1932. "The Occurrence of Natron in Ancient Egypt." *JEA* 18.1/2: 62–6.

Lucas, A, and J. R. Harris. 1962. *Ancient Egyptian Materials and Industries*. 4th ed. London: Edward Arnold.

Luckenbill, Daniel David. 1927. *Ancient Records of Assyria and Babylon*. 2 vols. Chicago: University of Chicago Press.

Lund, Peter, and Vincent Gabrielsen. 2005. "A Fishy Business: Transport Amphorae of the Black Sea Region as a Source for the Trade in Fish and Fish Products in the Classical and Hellenistic Periods." In Bekker-Nielsen: 161–69.

Luraghi, Nino. 2006. "Traders, Pirates, Warriors: the Proto-history of Greek Mercenary Soldiers in the Eastern Mediterranean." *Phoenix* 60.1: 21–47.

Luraghi, Nino. 2008. *The Ancient Messenians: Constructions of Ethnicity and Memory*. Cambridge: Cambridge University Press.

Luraghi, Nino. 2010. "Local Scripts from Nature to Culture." *ClassAnt* 29.1: 68–91.

Luraghi, Nino. 2014. "The Study of Greek Ethnic Identities." In McInerney: 213–27.

Lythgoe, Albert Morton. 1905. "Egyptian, or Graeco-Egyptian, Objects." In Waldstein: 2.367–74.

Lytle, Ephraim. 2016. "Chaerephilus & Sons: Vertical Integration, Classical Athens, and the Black Sea Fish Trade." *Ancient Society* 46: 1–26.

Mac Sweeney, Naoise. 2009. "Beyond Identity: The Overlooked Diversity of Group Identities." *JMA* 21.1: 101–26.

Mac Sweeney, Naoise. 2013. *Foundation Myths and Politics in Ancient Ionia*. Cambridge: Cambridge University Press.

Mac Sweeney, Naoise. 2017. "Separating Fact from Fiction in the Ionian Migration." *Hesperia* 86.3: 379–421.

Maier, F. G. 1971. "Excavations at Kouklia (Palaepaphos). Fifth Preliminary Report: Season 1970." *RDAC* 21: 43–48.

Malkin, Irad. 1998. *The Returns of Odysseus: Colonization and Ethnicity*. Berkeley: University of California Press.

Malkin, Irad. 2001, ed. *Ancient Perceptions of Greek Identity*. Washington: Center for Hellenic Studies.

Malkin, Irad. 2011. *A Small Greek World: Networks in the Ancient Mediterranean*. Oxford: Oxford University Press.

Mani Hurter, Silvia, and Hans-Joachim Liewald. 2002. "Neue Münztypen der Kyzikener Elektronprägung." *Schweizerische numismatische Rundschau* 81: 21–39.

Manzano, Annalisa. 2013. *Harvesting the Sea: The Exploitation of Marine Resources in the Roman Mediterranean*. Oxford: Oxford University Press.

Maran, Joseph. 2022. "Archaeological Cultures, Fabricated Ethnicities and DNA Research: 'Minoans' and 'Mycenaeans' as Case Examples." In *Material, Method, and Meaning: Papers in Eastern Mediterranean Archaeology in Honor of Ilan Sharon*, ed. U. Davidovich, N. Yahalom-Mack, and S. Matskevich: 7–25. Münster: Zaphon.

Marconi, Clemente. 2004. "Kosmos: The Imagery of the Archaic Greek Temple." *RES* 45: 211–24.

Markoe, Glenn. 1985. *Phoenician Bronze and Silver Bowls from Cyprus and the Mediterranean*. Berkeley: University of California Press.

Mata, Karim. 2019. *Iron Age Slaving and Enslavement in Northwest Europe*. Oxford: Archeopress.

Martin, Richard. 1993. "The Seven Sages as Performers of Wisdom." In *Cultural Poetics in Archaic Greece: Cult, Performance, Politics*, ed. C. Dougherty and L. Kurke: 108–30. Cambridge: Cambridge University Press.

Marx, Karl. 1867. *Das Kapital: Kritik der politischen Oekonomie*. Hamburg: Verlag von Otto Meissner.

Masson, Olivier. 1977. "Quelques bronzes égyptiens à inscription grecque." *RÉg* 29: 53–67.

Masson, Olivier, and Jean Yoyotte. 1988. "Une inscription ionienne mentionnant Psammétique Ier." *Epigraphica Anatolica* 11: 171–80.

Masson, Olivier, Geoffrey Thorndike Martin, and Richard Vaughan Nicholls. 1978. *Carian inscriptions from North Saqqâra and Buhen*. London: Egyptian Exploration Society.

Masson-Berghoff, Aurélia. 2018. "Scarabs, Scaraboids, and Amulets." In Villing et al. 2013-19. https://webarchive.nationalarchives.gov.uk/20190801123440/https://www.britishmuseum.org/pdf/Masson_Scarabs_and_amulets.pdf.

Matić, Uroš. 2018. "De-colonizing the Historiography and Archaeology of Ancient Egypt and Nubia. Part 1. Scientific Racism." *Journal of Egyptian History* 11: 19–44.

Matory, J. Lorand. 2005. *Black Atlantic Religion: Tradition, Transnationalism, and Matriarchy in the Afro-Brazilian Candomblé*. Princeton, NJ: Princeton University Press.

Maximova, Maria. 1959. "Der kurze Seeweg über das Schwarze Meer im Altertum." *Klio* 37: 101–18.

Mayor, Adrienne, and Michael Heaney. 1993. "Griffins and Arimaspeans." *Folklore* 104.1/2: 40–66.

Mayor, Adrienne, John Colrusso, and David Saunders. 2014. "Making Sense of Nonsense Inscriptions Associated with Amazons and Scythians on Athenian Vases." *Hesperia* 83.3: 447–93.

McArthur, Millis. 2019. "Kittos and the *Phialai Exeleutherikai*." *BSA* 114: 263–91.

McCormick, Michael. 2001. *Origins of the European Economy: Communications and Commerce, A.D. 300–900*. Cambridge: Cambridge University Press.

McCoskey, Denise Eileen. 2003. "By Any Other Name? Ethnicity and the Study of Ancient Identity." *Classical Bulletin* 79.1: 93–109.

McCoskey, Denise Eileen. 2006. "Review: Naming the Fault in Question: Theorizing Racism among the Greeks and Romans." *International Journal of the Classical Tradition* 13.2: 243–67.
McCoskey, Denise Eileen. 2012. *Race: Antiquity and Its Legacy*. London: I.B. Tauris.
McCoskey, Denise Eileen, ed. 2021. *A Cultural History of Race in Antiquity*. Bloomsbury: London.
McCoskey, Denise Eileen. 2022. "Basil Gildersleeve and John Scott: Race and the Rise of American Classical Philology." *AJP* 143.2: 246–71.
McGing, Brian C. 2002. "Illegal Salt in the Lycopolite nome." *ArchPF* 48: 42–66.
McInerney, Jeremy. 1999. *The Folds of Parnassos: Land and Ethnicity in Ancient Phokis*. Austin: University of Texas Press.
McInerney, Jeremy. 2006. Review of Isaac 2004. *Social History* 31.1: 84–87.
McInerney, Jeremy, ed., 2014. *A Companion to Ethnicity in the Ancient Mediterranean*. London: John Wiley & Sons.
McKeown, Niall. 2002. "Seeing Things: Examining the Body of the Slave in Greek Medicine." In *Representing the Body of the Slave*, ed. T. Wiedemann and J. Gardner: 29–40. London: Frank Cass.
McLean, Daniel R. 2007. "The Socratic Corpus: Socrates and Physiognomy." In *Socrates from Antiquity to the Enlightenment*, ed. M. B. Trapp: 65–85. Aldershot, UK: Ashgate.
McManus, Stuart M. 2020. "Frank M. Snowden, Jr. and the Origin of *The Image of the Black in Western Art*." Unpublished conference paper, Society for Classical Studies Meeting, Washington, DC.
Meek, Andrew, Ann Bouquillon, Patrice Lehuédé, Aurélia Masson, Alexandra Villing, Geneviève Pierrat-Bonnefois, and Virginia Webb. 2016. "Discerning Differences: Ion Beam Analysis of Ancient Faience from Naukratis and Rhodes." *Technè* 43: 94–101.
Meiggs, Russel, and David Lewis. 1969. *A Selection of Greek Historical Inscriptions to the End of the Fifth Century B.C.* Oxford: Oxford University Press.
Menadier, Blanche. 1995. "The Sixth Century BC Temple and the Sanctuary and Cult of Hera Akraia, Perachora." Dissertation, University of Cincinnati.
Meyer, Caspar. 2013. *Greco-Scythian Art and the Birth of Eurasia: From Classical Antiquity to Russian Modernity*. Oxford: Oxford University Press.
Meyer, E. A. 2010. *Metics and the Athenian Phialai-Inscriptions: A Study in Athenian Epigraphy and Law*. Stuttgart: Franz Steiner Verlag.
Meyer, H.-C., and A. Moreno. 2007. "A Greek Metrological Koine: A Lead Weight from the Western Black Sea Region in the Ashmolean Museum, Oxford." *OJA* 23.1: 209–16.
Miller, Joseph C. 2014. "A Historical Appreciation of the Biographical Turn." In Lindsay and Sweet: 19-47.
Miller, Margaret C. 1991. "Foreigners at the Greek Symposion?" In *Dining in a Classical Context*, ed. W. J. Slater: 59–81. Ann Arbor: University of Michigan Press.

Minns, Ellis H. 1913. *Scythians and Greeks: A Survey of Ancient History and Archaeology on the North Coast of the Euxine from the Danube to the Caucasus.* Cambridge: Cambridge University Press.

Mintz, Sidney W. 1985. *Sweetness and Power: the Place of Sugar in Modern History.* New York: Penguin.

Mirhady, David Cyrus. 1991. "The Oath-Challenge in Athens." *CQ* 41: 78–83.

Mirhady, David Cyrus. 1996. "Torture and Rhetoric in Athens." *JHS* 116: 119–31.

Möller, Astrid. 2000. *Naukratis: Trade in Ancient Greece.* Oxford: Oxford University Press.

Momigliano, Nicoletta, Laura Phillips, Michela Spataro, Nigel Meeks, and Andrew Meek. 2014. "A Newly Discovered Minoan Faience Plaque from the Knossos Town Mosaic in the Bristol City Museum and Art Gallery: a Technological Insight." *BSA* 109: 97–110.

Monakhov, Sergei I., and Elena V. Kuznetsova. 2017. "Overseas Trade in the Black Sea Region from the Archaic to the Hellenistic Period." In *The Northern Black Sea in Antiquity: Networks, Connectivity, and Cultural Interactions*, ed. V. Kozlovskaya: 59–99. Cambridge: Cambridge University Press.

Monson, Andrew. 2015. "Egyptian Fiscal History in a World of Warring States, 664–30 BCE." *Journal of Egyptian History* 8: 1–36.

Monoson, S. Sara. 2011a. "Recollecting Aristotle: Pro-Slavery Thought in Antebellum America and the Argument of *Politics* Book 1." In *Ancient Slavery and Abolition: From Hobbes to Hollywood*, ed. E. Hall, R. Alston, and J. McConnell: 247–77. Oxford: Oxford University Press.

Monoson, S. Sara. 2011b. "Navigating Race, Class, Polis, and Empire: The Place of Empirical Analysis in Aristotle's Account of Natural Slavery." In *Reading Ancient Slavery*, ed. R. Alston, E. Hall, and L. Proffitt: 133–51. London: Bristol Classical Press.

Mordvintseva, Valentina I. 2017. "The Aetiological Myth of the Russian Empire and the Study in Russia of Cultural Changes in the North Pontic Region from the 3rd Century BC to the 3rd Century AD (Prior to the 1920s)." *Ancient Civilizations from Scythia to Siberia* 23: 255–49.

Moreno, Alfonso. 2007. *Feeding the Democracy: The Athenian Grain Supply in the Fifth and Fourth Centuries B.C.* Oxford: Oxford University Press.

Moreno, Alfonso. 2008. "Hieron: The Ancient Sanctuary at the Mouth of the Black Sea." *Hesperia* 77.4: 655–709.

Morgan, Catherine. 1991. "Ethnicity and Early Greek States: Historical and Material Perspectives." *PCPS* 37: 131–63.

Morgan, Catherine. 1994. "The Evolution of a Sacral 'Landscape:' Isthmia, Perachora, and the Early Corinthian State." In *Placing the Gods: Sanctuaries and Sacred Space in Ancient Greece*, ed. S. Alcock and R. Osborne: 143–60. Oxford: Oxford University Press.

Morgan, Charles H. 1953. "Investigations at Corinth, 1953—A Tavern of Aphrodite." *Hesperia* 22.3: 131–40.

Morgan, Jennifer L. 2021. *Reckoning with Slavery: Gender, Kinship, and Capitalism in the Early Black Atlantic.* Durham, NC: Duke University Press.

Morley, Neville. 2005. "Narrative Economy." In *Ancient Economies, Modern Methodologies: Archaeology, Comparative History, Models, and Institutions,* ed. P. Bang, M. Ikeguchi, and H. Ziche: 27–47. Bari: Edipuglia.

Morris, Ian. 1986a. "Gift and Commodity in Archaic Greece." *Man* (n.s.) 21.1: 1–17.

Morris, Ian. 1986b. "The Use and Abuse of Homer." *ClassAnt* 5.1: 81–138.

Morris, Ian. 1996. "The Strong Principle of Equality and the Archaic Origins of Greek Democracy." In *Dêmokratia: A Conversation on Democracies, Ancient and Modern,* ed. C. Hendrick and J. Ober: 19–48. Princeton, NJ: Princeton University Press.

Morris, Ian. 2000. *Archaeology as Cultural History: Words and Things in Iron Age Greece.* London: Bloomsbury.

Morris, Ian. 2004. "Economic Growth in Ancient Greece." *Journal of Institutional and Theoretical Economics* 160.4: 709–42.

Morris, Ian. 2011. "Archaeology and Greek slavery." In Bradley and Cartledge: 176–93.

Morris, Sarah P. 1993. *Daidalos and the Origins of Greek Art.* Princeton, NJ: Princeton University Press.

Morris, Sarah P. 2018. "Looking for Slaves? The Archaeological Record: Greece." In *The Oxford Handbook of Greek and Roman Slaveries,* ed. S. Hodkinson, M. Kleijwegt, and K. Vlassopoulos. Oxford: Oxford University Press.

Morris, Sarah, and John Papadopoulos. 1999. "Phoenicians and the Corinthian Pottery Industry." In *Archäologische Studien in Kontaktzonen der antiken Welt,* ed. R. Rolle, K. Schmidt, and R. Docter: 251–62. Göttingen: Vandenhoeck und Ruprecht.

Morton, Samuel George. 1842. *Crania Aegyptiaca, or, Observations on Egyptian Ethnography Derived from Anatomy, History and the Monuments.* Philadelphia: John Pennington.

Moyer, Ian. 2011. *Egypt and the Limits of Hellenism.* Cambridge: Cambridge University Press.

Muhs, Brian. 2016. *The Ancient Egyptian Economy: 3000–30 BCE.* Cambridge: Cambridge University Press.

Murray, Jackie. 2021. "Race and Sexuality: Racecraft in the *Odyssey*." In McCoskey: 137–56.

Murray, Sarah C. 2017. *The Collapse of the Mycenaean Economy: Imports, Trade, and Institutions 1300-700 BCE.* Cambridge: Cambridge University Press.

Murray, Sarah C. 2018a. "Imported Exotica and Mortuary Ritual at Perati in Late Helladic IIIC East Attica." *AJA* 122.1: 33–64.

Murray, Sarah C. 2018b. "Imported Objects in the Aegean beyond Elite Interaction: A Contextual Approach to Eastern Exotica on the Greek Mainland." In Niesiołowski-Spanò and Węcowski: 221–34.

Mussche, Herman. 1998. *Thorikos: A Mining Town in Ancient Attica. Fouilles de Thorikos / Opgravingen an Thorikos* vol. 2. Ghent: École archéologique belge en Grèce.

Myres, J. L. 1930. *Who Were the Greeks?* Berkeley: University of California Press.

Nadel, B. 1976. "Slavery and Related Forms of Labor on the North Shore of the Euxine in Antiquity." In *Actes du colloque 1973 sur l'esclavage. Besançon 2-3 mai 1973*: 197–233. Besançon: Presses Universitaires de Franche-Comté.

Nafissi, Mohammad. 2015. "Between Utopia and Dystopia: Moses Finley and the Athenian Democracy versus Moses Finley and the Ancient Economy." *BICS* 58.2: 107–44.

Nails, Debra. 2002. *The people of Plato: a Prosopography of Plato and Other Socratics*. Indianapolis: Hackett.

Nakassis, Dimitri. 2013. *Individuals and Society in Mycenaean Pylos*. Leiden: Brill.

Nelsestuen, Grant A. 2017. "*Oikonomia* as a Theory of Empire in the Political Thought of Xenophon and Aristotle." *GRBS* 57: 17–104.

Nenna, Marie-Dominique. 2003. "Les ateliers égyptiens à l'époque gréco-romaine." In *Coeur de verre: production du verre antique*, ed. D. Foy: 32–33. Lyon: Gollion.

Nicholson, Paul L. 2012. "'Stone . . . That Flows:' Faience and Glass as Man-Made Stones in Egypt." *JGS* 54: 11–23.

Niesiołowski-Spanò, Łukasz, and Marek Węcowski, eds. 2018. *Change, Continuity, and Connectivity: North-Eastern Mediterranean at the turn of the Bronze Age and in the early Iron Age*. Wiesbaden: Harrasowitz Verlag.

Niemeier, Wolf-Dietrich. 2014. "The Heraion at Samos." In Aruz, Graff, and Rakic: 295–312.

Nightingale, Carl. 2012. *Segregation: A Global History of Divided Cities*. Chicago: University of Chicago Press.

Nilsson, M. P. 1921. "The Race Problem in the Roman Empire." *Hereditas* 2.3: 370–90.

Nilsson, M. P. 1939. "Über Genetik und Geschichte." *Hereditas* 25: 210–23.

Novaro-Lefèvre, Daniela. 2000. "Le culte d'Héra à Pérachora (viii e - vi e s.): essai de bilan." *REG* 113.1: 42–69.

Obbink, Dirk. 2014. "Two New Poems by Sappho." *ZPE* 189: 32–49.

Ober, Josiah. 1989. *Mass and Elite in Democratic Athens*. Princeton, NJ: Princeton University Press.

Ober, Josiah. 2010. "Wealthy Hellas." *TAPA* 140.2: 241–86.

Ober, Josiah. 2015. *The Rise and Fall of Classical Greece*. Princeton, NJ: Princeton University Press.

O'Connor, David. 2000. "The Sea Peoples and the Egyptian Sources." In Oren: 85–102.

O'Connor, David. 2003. "Egypt's Views of 'Others.'" In *Never Had the Like Occurred': Egypt's View of Its Past*, ed. J. Tait: 155–82. London: Routledge.

Ogden, Daniel. 1996. *Greek Bastardry in the Classical and Hellenistic Periods*. Oxford: Oxford University Press.

Ogundiran, Akinwumi. 2014. "Cowries and Rituals of Self-Realization in the Yoruba Region, ca. 1600–1860." In *Materialities of Ritual in the Black Atlantic*, ed. A. Ogundiran and P. Saunders: 68–86. Bloomington: Indiana University Press.

Oliver, Graham J. 2007. *War, Food, and Politics in Early Hellenistic Athens*. Oxford: Oxford University Press.

Olkhovsky, S. B. 2018. "Подводные исследования на она «бухта Ак-бурун» (Республика Крым, Керченская Бухта)" [Underwater research in OAS area "Bukhta Akburun" (Republic of Crimea, Kerch Bay)]. In *Города, селища, могильники. Раскопки 2017* [Cities, settlements, burial grounds: Excavations, 2017], ed. A. V. Engovatova: 246–51. Moscow: Institute of Archaeology, Russian Academy of Science.

Olya, Najee. 2021. "Herakles in Africa: Confronting the Other in Libya and Egypt." *Ancient World Magazine.* https://www.ancientworldmagazine.com/articles/herakles-africa/.

Olson, S. Douglas. 2016. *Eupolis: Translation and Commentary.* 3 vols. Mainz: Verlag Antike.

Omi, Michael, and Howard Winant. 2015 [1986]. *Racial Formation in the United States.* 3rd ed. London: Routledge.

Oppenheim, A. Leo. 1967. "Essay on Overland Trade in the First Millennium B.C." *JCS* 21: 236–54.

Oren, Eliezer D., ed. 2000. *The Sea Peoples and Their World: a Reassessment.* Philadelphia: University Museum.

Orrells, Daniel, Gurminder K. Bhambra, and Tessa Roynon, eds. 2011. *African Athena: New Agendas.* Oxford: Oxford University Press.

Osborne, Robin. 2004. "Hoards, Votives, Offerings: The Archaeology of the Dedicated Object." *WorldArch* 36.1: 1–10.

Osborne, Robin, and P. J. Rhodes. 2017. *Greek Historical Inscriptions, 478–404 BC.* Oxford: Oxford University Press.

Özveren, Y. Eyüp. 1996. "A Framework for the Study of the Black Sea World, 1789–1915." *Review (Fernand Braudel Center)* 20.1: 77–113.

Pacific Coast Borax Company. 1915. *The Magic Crystal.* Chicago: Pacific Coast Borax Company.

Pacheco-Ruiz, Rodrigo, Jonathan Adams, Felix Pedrotti, Michael Grant, Joakim Holmlund, and Chris Bailey. 2019. "Deep Sea Archaeological Survey in the Black Sea—Robotic Documentation of 2,500 Years of Human Seafaring." *Deep-Sea Research Part I* 152: 103087.

Padilla Peralta, Dan-el. 2015. "Barbarians Inside the Gate, Part I. Fears of Immigration in Ancient Rome and today." *Eidolon* November 9. https://eidolon.pub/barbarians-inside-the-gate-part-i-c175057b340f.

Padilla Peralta, Dan-el. 2017. "Slave Religiosity in the Roman Middle Republic." *ClassAnt* 36.2: 317–69.

Padilla Peralta, Dan-el. 2021. "Anti-Race: Anti-racism, Whiteness and the Classical Imagination." In McCoskey: 157–71.

Pandey, Nandini B. 2020. "The Roman Roots of Racial Capitalism." *The Berlin Journal* 34: 16–20.

Papalexandrou, Nassos. 2010. "Are There Hybrid Visual Cultures? Reflections on the Orientalizing Phenomena in the Mediterranean of the Early First Millennium BCE." *Ars Orientalis* 38: 31–47.

Papalexandrou, Nassos. 2016. "The MultiCorporeality of Beings and Objects in the Mediterranean During the Orientalizing Period (7th c. BCE)." In *Hybrid and Extraordinary Beings: Deviations from "Normality" in Ancient Greek Mythology and Modern Medicine*, ed. P. N. Soucacos, A. Garztiou-Tatti, and M. Paschopoulos: 41–54. Athens: Konstantaras Iatrikes.

Papadopoulos, John. K. 1994. "Early Iron Age Potters' Marks in the Aegean." *Hesperia* 63.4: 437–507.

Papadopoulos, John, K. 2016. "The Early History of the Greek Alphabet: New Evidence from Eretria and Methone." *Antiquity* 90.353: 1238–54.

Pappa, Eleftheria. 2012. "Oriental Gods but Domestic Elites? Religious Symbolism and Economic Functions of Phoenician–Period Cult Loci in South Iberia." In *Sanctuaries and the Power of Consumption: Networking and the Formation of Elites in the Archaic Western Mediterranean World*, ed. E. Kistler, B. Öhlinger, M. Mohr, and M. Hoernes: 43–62. Wiesbaden: Harrasowitz Verlag.

Pardó i Parcerisa, Josep. 1980-95. *Egyptian-Type Documents from the Mediterranean Littoral of the Iberian Peninsula before the Roman Conquest*. 3 vols. Leiden: Brill.

Parés, Luis Nicolau. 2005. "The Birth of the Yoruba Hegemony in Post-Abolition Candomblé." *Journal de la Société des américanistes* 91.1: 139–59.

Parkinson, R. B. 1991. *The Tale of the Eloquent Peasant*. Oxford: Griffith Institute.

Parmenter, Christopher Stedman. 2019. "Egypt on the Steppe: A Gazetteer of Sixth Century *Aegyptiaca* from the North Black Sea." *Bibliotheca Orientalis* 76.3-4: 13–24.

Parmenter, Christopher Stedman. 2020. "Journeys into Slavery along the Black Sea Coast, c. 550–450 BCE." *ClassAnt* 39.1: 57–94.

Parmenter, Christopher Stedman. 2021a. "'A Happy Coincidence': Race, the Cold War, and Frank M. Snowden, Jr.'s *Blacks in Antiquity*." *Classical Receptions Journal* 13.4: 485–506.

Parmenter, Christopher Stedman. 2021b. "Egyptianizing Faience from the Sanctuary of Apollo Hylates, Kourion, Cyprus." *Journal of Ancient Egyptian Interconnections* 29: 39–51.

Parmenter, Christopher Stedman. 2023. Review of Derbew 2022. *Journal of Eastern Mediterranean Archaeology and Heritage Studies* 11.2: 124–28.

Parmenter, Christopher Stedman. 2024a. "'But They Were a Race of Whites:' Race and the Makings of 'Ancient Slavery in the Anglophone World, 1785-1980." *TAPA* 154.1: 295–330.

Parmenter, Christopher Stedman. 2024b. "'The Twilight of the Gods?' Genomic History and the Return of Race in the Study of the Ancient Mediterranean." *History and Theory* 63.1: 45–70.

Patterson, Orlando. 1982. *Slavery and Social Death: A Comparative Study*. Cambridge, MA: Harvard University Press.

Patterson, Orlando. 1991. *Freedom: Freedom in the Making of Western Culture*. New York: Basic Books.

Payne, Humfry. 1940. *Architecture, Bronzes, Terracottas. Perachora: The Sanctuaries of Hera Akraia and Limenia. Excavations of the British School of Archaeology at Athens, 1930–1933*, vol. 1. Oxford: Oxford University Press.

Peltenberg, E. J. 1987. "Early Faience: Recent Studies, Origins, and Relations with Glass." In *Early Vitreous Materials*, ed. M. Bimson and I. Freestone: 5–29. London: British Museum.

Pennington, James C. 1841. *A Text Book of the Origin and History, &c &c, of the Colored People*. Hartford: L. Skinner.

Perna, Massimo. 2005. "L'alun dans les documents en linéaire B." In Borgard, Brun, and Picon: 39–42.

Pfaff, Christopher A. 1988. "A Geometric Well at Corinth: Well 1981-6." *Hesperia* 57.1: 21–80.

Pfaff, Christopher A. 2003. "Archaic Corinthian Architecture, ca. 600–480 B.C." In *The Centenary: Corinth* vol. 20, ed. C. Williams and N. Bookidis: 94–140. Princeton, NJ: American School of Classical Studies at Athens.

Pendlebury, John D. S. 1930. *Aegyptiaca: a Catalogue of Egyptian Objects in the Aegean Area*. Cambridge: Cambridge University Press.

Perdrizet, P. 1908. *Monuments figurés, petits bronzes, terres cuites, antiquités diverses. Fouilles de Delphes* vol. 5. Paris: École Français d'Athènes.

Perry, Ben E. 1952. *Aesopica: A Series of Texts Relating to Aesop or Ascribed to Him*. Urbana: University of Illinois Press.

Petrie, William Matthew Flinders. 1886. *Naukratis I*. London: Trübner & Son.

Phelps, Matt, Ian C. Freestone, Yael Gorin-Rosen, and Bernard Gratuze. 2016. "Natron Glass Production and Supply in the Late Antique and Early Medieval Near East: The Effect of the Byzantine-Islamic Transition." *Journal of Archaeological Science* 75: 57–71.

Phillips, David D. 2012. *The Law of Ancient Athens*. Ann Arbor: University of Michigan Press.

Phillips, E. D. 1955. "The Legend of Aristeas: Fact and Fancy in Early Greek Notions of East Russia, Siberia, and Inner Asia." *Artibus Asiae* 18.2: 161–77.

Phillips, E. D. 1957. "A Further Note on Aristeas." *Artibus Asiae* 20.2/3: 159–62.

Photos-Jones, Effie, and Allan J. Hall. 2011. *Lemnian Earth and the Earths of the Aegean: An Archaeological Guide to Medicines, Pigments, and Washing Powders*. Glasgow: Potingair Press.

Piccolo, Alessandro. 2019. "Pedon, Son of Amphinnes. A game of Donors?" *Aegyptus* 99: 163–80.

Picon, Maurice, Michèle Vichy, and Pascale Ballet. 2005. "L'alun des oasis occidentales d'Égypte: Recherches sur le terrain et recherches en laboratoire." In Borgard, Brun, and Picon: 43–57.

Pinney, Gloria F. 1983. "Achilles, Lord of Scythia." In *Ancient Greek Art and Iconography*, ed. W. G. Moon: 127–47. Madison: University of Wisconsin Press.

Pino, Cristina. 2005. "The Market Scene in the Tomb of Khaemhat (TT 57)." *JEA* 91: 95–105.

Pippidi, D. M. 1966. "Sclavi « histrieni » la Rheneia?" *Studii Clasice* 8: 232–35.

Pippidi, D. M. 1975. *Scythica Minora: Recherches sur les colonies grecques du littoral roumain de la mer Noire*. Bucharest: Editura Academei Române.

Poole, Federico. 2005. "'All that has been done to the Shabtis:' Some Considerations on the Decree for the Shabtis of Neskhons and P.BM EA 10800." *JEA* 91: 165–70.

Porten, Bezalel, and Ada Yardeni, eds. 1986–99. *Textbook of Aramaic Documents from Ancient Egypt*. 4 vols. Winona Lake, IN: Eisenbrauns.

Porten, Bezalel, J. Joel Faber, Cary J. Martin, Günter Vittmann, Leslie S. B. MacCoull, Sarah Clackson, Simon Hopkins, and Ramon Katzoff, eds. 2011. *The Elephantine Papyri in English: Three Millenia of Cross-Cultural Continuity and Change*. 2nd ed. Leiden: Brill.

Porter, K. E., D. S. Kostick, and W. P. Bolen. 2017. "Soda Ash (Sodium Carbonate) Statistics." Washington: US Geological Survey.

Porucznik, Joanna. 2021. *Cultural Identity within the Northern Black Sea Region in Antiquity: (De)constructing Past Identities*. Leuven: Peeters.

Posamentir, Richard. 2006. "The Greeks in Berezan and Naukratis: A Similar Story?" In *Naukratis: Greek Diversity in Egypt*, ed. A. Villing and U. Schlotzhauer: 159–68. London: British Museum.

Posner, Rachel. 2021. "He Wants to Save Classics from Whiteness. Can the Field Survive?" *The New York Times* February 2. https://www.nytimes.com/2021/02/02/magazine/classics-greece-rome-whiteness.html.

Potts, Daniel. 1984. "On Salt and Salt Gathering in Ancient Mesopotamia." *JESHO* 27.3: 225–71.

Powell, Barry B. 1991. *Homer and the Origin of the Greek Alphabet*. Cambridge: Cambridge University Press.

Pownall, Frances. 2013. "Hekataios of Miletos (1)." In Worthington 2007-ongoing. https://scholarlyeditions.brill.com/bnjo/.

Pratt, Louise. 1995. "The Seal of Theognis, Writing, and Oral Poetry." *AJP* 116.2: 171–84.

Pritchard, James B., ed. 1969. *Ancient Near Eastern Texts Relating to the* Old Testament. 3rd ed. Princeton: Princeton University Press.

Pritchett, W. Kendrick. 1953. "The Attic Stelai, Part I." *Hesperia* 22.4: 225–99.

Pritchett, W. Kendrick, and Anne Pippin. 1956. "The Attic Stelai: Part II." *Hesperia* 25.3: 178–328.

Purcell, Nicholas. 2005. "The Ancient Mediterranean: the View from the Customs House." In W. V. Harris: 200–34.

Purcell, Nicholas. 2012. "*Quod Enim Alterius Fuit, Id Ut Fiat Meum, Necesse Est Aliquid Intercedere* (Varro): The Anthropology Of Buying And Selling In Ancient Greece And Rome: An Introductory Sketch." In *Antiquité et anthropologie. Bilans et perspectives*, ed. P. Payen and E. Sheid: 81–98. Turnhout.

Purcell, Nicholas. 2013. "Tide, Beach, and Backwash: The Place of Maritime Histories." In *The Sea: Thalassology and Historiography*, ed. P. Miller: 84–108. Ann Arbor: University of Michigan Press.

Putin, Vladimir V. 2021. "Приветственное слово президента российской федерации В.В. Путина" [Welcome speech by the President of the Russian Federation V. V. Putin]. In *История Севастополя. Том I. Юго-Западный Крым с древнейших времен до 1774 года* [History of Sevastopol, Vol. 1. The South-East Crimea from Antiquity to 1774], ed. J. A. Petrova and E. B. Altabaevoj: i. Moscow.

Quack, Joachim Friedrich. 2013a. "Conceptions of Purity in Egyptian Religion." In *Purity and the Forming of Religious Traditions in the Ancient Mediterranean World and Ancient Judaism*, ed. C. Frevel and C. Nihan: 115–58. Leiden: Brill.

Quack, Joachim Friedrich. 2013b. "Quelques apports récents des études démotiques à la compréhension du livre II d'Hérodote." In *Hérodote et l'Égypte regards croises sur le livre II de l'enquête d'Hérodote*, ed. L. Coulon, P. Giovannelli-Jouanna, and F. Kimmel-Clauzet: 63–88. Lyon: Maison de l'Orient et de la Méditerranée.

Quirini-Poplawska, Danuta. 2017. "The Venetian Involvement in the Black Sea Slave Trade (Fourteenth-to-Fifteenth Centuries)." In Amitai and Cluse, 255–99.

Raaflaub, Kurt. 2016. "The Newest Sappho and Archaic Greek-Near Eastern Interactions." In Bierl and Lardinois: 127–47.

Raffield, Ben. 2019. "The Slave Markets of the Viking World: Comparative Perspectives on an 'Invisible Archaeology.'" *Slavery and Abolition* 40.4: 682–705.

Rankine, Patrice. 2006. *Ulysses in Black Ralph Ellison, Classicism, and African American Literature*. Madison: University of Wisconsin Press.

Rask, K. A. 2020. "Familiarity and Phenomenology in Greece: Accumulated Votives as Group-made Monuments." *Archiv für Religionsgeschichte* 21–22.1: 127–51.

Rauh, Nicholas K., Matthew J. Dillon, and T. Davina McClain. 2008. "*Ochlos Nautikos*: Leisure Culture and Underclass Discontent in the Roman Maritime World." In *The Maritime World of Ancient Rome. MAAR* Supplement 6, ed. R.L. Hohlfelder: 197–242. Rome: American Academy in Rome.

Ray, John D. 1998. "Aegypto-Carica." *Kadmos* 37: 125–36.

Rediker, Marcus. 2007. *The Slave Ship: a Human History*. New York: Viking.

Reed, Adolph, Jr. 2013. "Marx, Race, and Neoliberalism." *New Labor Forum* 22.1: 49–57.

Reed, Adolph, Jr. 2021. *The South*. New York: Verso.

Reger, Gary. 2005. "The Manufacture and Distribution of Perfume." In *Making, Moving and Managing: The New World of Ancient Economies, 323–31 BC*, ed. Z. Archibald, M. Davies, and J. Gabrielsen: 253–97. Oxford: Oxbow.

Reis, João José. 2013. "African Nations in Nineteenth-Century Salvador, Bahia." In *The Black Urban Atlantic in the Age of the Slave Trade*, ed. J. Cañizares-Esguerra, M. Childs, and J. Sidbury: 63–82. Philadelphia: University of Pennsylvania Press.

Reyes, A. T. 2001. *The Stamp-Seals of Ancient Cyprus*. Oxford: Oxford School of Archaeology.

Ridgway, David. 1999. "The Rehabilitation of Bocchoris: Notes and Queries from Italy." *JEA* 85: 143–52.

Rihill, Tracey. 1996. "The Origin and Establishment of Ancient Slavery." In *Serfdom and Slavery: Studies in Legal Bondage*, ed. M. Bush: 89–111. London: Routledge.

Robert, L. 1935. "Sur les Inscriptions de Chios." *BCH* 59: 453–70.

Robertson, Bruce. 2008. "The Slave-Names of *IG* I³ 1032 and the Ideology of Slavery at Athens." In *Epigraphy and the Greek Historian*, ed. C. Cooper: 79–115. Toronto: University of Toronto Press.

Robinson, Cedric. 2000 [1983]. *Black Marxism: The Making of the Black Radical Tradition*. 2nd ed. Chapel Hill: University of North Carolina Press.

Robinson, David M. 1949. "The Robinson Collection of Greek Gems, Seals, Rings, and Earrings." In *Commemorative Studies in Honor of Theodore Leslie Shear*. *Hesperia* supp. 8: 305–23. Princeton, NJ: American School of Classical Studies at Athens.

Robinson, Damian, and Franck Goddio, eds. 2015. *Thonis-Heracleion in Context*. Oxford: Oxford Centre for Maritime Archaeology.

Rolle, Renate. 1989 [1980]. *The World of the Scythians*. Trans. F. G. Walls. Berkeley: University of California Press.

Rolle, Renate. 1991. "Haar- und Barttracht der Skythen." In *Gold der Steppe Archäologie der Ukraine*, ed. R. Rolle, M. Müller-Wille and K. Schietzel: 115–26. Neumünster: Karl Wachholtz Verlag.

Rollinger, Robert. 2001. "The Ancient Greeks and the Impact of the Ancient Near East: Textual Evidence and Historical Perspective (ca. 750–650 BC)." In *Mythology and Mythologies: Methodological Approaches to Intercultural Influences: Proceedings of the Second Annual Symposium of the Assyrian and Babylonian Intellectual Heritage*, ed. R. Whiting: 233–64. Helsinki: Neo-Assyrian Text Corpus Project.

Romm, James. 1992. *The Edges of the Earth in Ancient Thought: Geography, Exploration, and Fiction*. Princeton, NJ: Princeton University Press.

Rostovzteff, Michael. 1922. *Iranians and Greeks in South Russia*. Oxford: Oxford University Press.

Roth, Ulrike. 2010. Rev. of Trümper 2009. *Bryn Mawr Classical Review*, December 20. https://bmcr.brynmawr.edu/2010/2010.12.20/.

Rothman, E. Natalie. 2009. "Interpreting Dragomans: Boundaries and Crossings in the Early Modern Mediterranean." *Comparative Studies in Society and History* 51.4: 771–800.

Ruffell, I. 2000. "The World Turned Upside Down: Utopia and Utopianism in the Fragments of Old Comedy." In *The Rivals of Aristophanes*, ed. D. Harvey and J. Wilkins: 473–506. London: Duckworth.

Rung, Eduard, and Oleg Gabelko. 2019. "From Bosporus . . . to Bosporus: a New Interpretation and Historical Context of the Old Persian Inscription from Phanagoreia." *Iranica Antiqua* 54: 83–125.

Rusjaeva, Anna S. 1986. "Милет - Дидимы - Борисфен - Ольвия. Проблемы Колонизации Нижнего Побужья" [Miletus – Didyma – Borysthenes – Olbia: The Colonization of the Lower Bug Region]. *VDI* 2 (177): 25–64.

Rusjaeva, Anna S. 1999. "Проникновение эллинов на территорию украинской лесостепи в архаическое бремя" [The Problem of the Hellenic Penetration in the Area of the Ukrainian Forest-Steppe in Archaic Times]. *VDI* 4 (231): 84–97.

Rusjaeva, Anna S. 2003. "The Temple of Achilles on the Island of Leuke in the Black Sea." *Ancient Civilizations from Scythia to Siberia* 9.1–2: 1–16.

Rusjaeva, A. S., and J. G. Vinogradov. 1991. "Der 'Brief des Priesters' aus Hylaia." In *Gold der Steppe: Archäologie der Ukraine*, ed. R. Rolle, M. Müller-Wille, and K. Schietzel: 201–2. Neumünster: Karl Wachholtz Verlag.

Russell, Thomas. 2017. *Byzantium and the Bosporus: A Historical Study, from the Seventh Century BC until the Foundation of Constantinople*. Oxford: Oxford University Press.

Rutherford, Ian. 2016. "The Earliest Cross-Cultural Reception of Homer? The Inaros-Narratives of Greco-Roman Egypt." In *Greco-Egyptian Interactions: Literature, Translation, and Culture, 500 BC–AD 300*, ed. I. Rutherford: 83–100. Oxford: Oxford University Press.

Rutherford, Jonathan. 1990. "The Third Space: Interview with Homi Bhabha." In *Identity: Community, Culture, Difference*, ed. J. Rutherford: 207–21. London: Lawrence and Wishart.

Ryholt, Kim. 2010. "A Sesostris Story in Demotic Egyptian and Demotic Literary Exercises (*O. Leipzig* UB 2217)." In *Honi soit qui mal y pense: Studien zum pharaonischen, griechisch-römischen und spätantiken Ägypten zu Ehren von Heinz-Josef Thissen*, ed. H. Knuf, C. Leitz, and D. von Recklinghausen: 429–38. Leuven: Peeters.

Sahin, Çetin. 1987. "Zwei Inschriften aus den südwestlichen Kleinasien." *Epigraphica Anatolica* 10: 1–4.

Said, Edward. 1978. *Orientalism*. New York: Pantheon.

Saleh, Ahmed Saleh, Adel Wageih George, and Fatma Helmi. 1972. "Study of Glass and Glass-Making Processes at Wadi el-Natrun, Egypt in the Roman Period 30 B.C. to 359 A.D. Part 1. Fritting Crucibles, Their Technical Features and Temperature Employed." *Studies in Conservation* 17.4: 143–72.

Saller, Richard. 2002. "Framing the Debate over Growth in the Ancient Economy." In *The Ancient Economy*, ed. W. Scheidel and S. von Reden: 251–69. New York: Routledge.

Salliora-Oikonomakou, M. 1991. "Αρχαιο νεκροταφειο στο Λαυριο" [An ancient cemetery at Lavrio]. *ArchDelt* 40.1: 90–132.

Salmon, J. B. 1984. *Wealthy Corinth: A History of the City to 338 BC*. Oxford: Oxford University Press.

Salzmann, Auguste. 1875. *Nécropole de Camiros : Journal des fouilles exécutées dans cette nécropole 1858-65 par Aug. Salzmann*. Paris: Detaille.

Samuels, Tristian. 2014. "The Elephant in the Room: Confronting Petrie's Racism." *Eras* 16.2: 101–6.

Sannibale, Maurizio. 2014. "Levantine and Orientalizing Luxury Goods from Etruscan Tombs." In Aruz, Graff, and Rakic: 313–29.

Santiago, R. A., and M. Gardeñes. 2006. "Algunas observaciones a la 'Lettre d'Apatorios a Léanax.'" *ZPE* 157: 57–69.

Saprykin, S. 2017. "Ancient Sea Routes in the Black Sea." In *The Sea in History— The Ancient World*, ed. P. de Souza, P. Arnaud, and C. Buchet: 345–61. Woodbridge: Boydell & Brewer.

Saura, Annsi. 2014. "A Tale of Two Papers." *Hereditas* 151: 119–22.

Scarborough, William Sanders. 2005. *The Autobiography of William Sanders Scarborough: An American Journey from Slavery to Scholarship*. Ed. M. V. Ronnick. Oxford: Oxford University Press.

Schaeffer, Claude F.-A. 1936. "Fouilles de Ras Shamra-Ugarit. Huitième campagne (printemps 1936)." *Syria* 18.2: 125–54.

Scharff, A. 1931. Rev. of Pendlebury 1930. *Gnomon* 7.10: 535–37.

Scheidel, Walter. 2005. "Real Slave Prices and the Relative Cost of Slave Labor in the Greco-Roman World." *Historia* 53.1: 1–17.

Schlotzhauer, Udo, and Denis Zhuralev. 2014. "Greek Colonization in the Cimmerian Bosporus: Russian-German Interdisciplinary Investigations in Southern Russia." In *Tyritake: Antique Site at Cimmerian Bosporus*, ed. A. Twardecki: 203–19. Warsaw: National Museum.

Schwartz, Seth R. 2013. "Finkelstein the Orientalist." In W. V. Harris: 31–48.

Scott, R. B., and P. Degryse. 2015. "The Archaeology and Archaeometry of Natron Glass Making." In Degryse: 15–26.

Seaford, Richard. 2002. "Reading Money: Leslie Kurke on the Politics of Meaning in Archaic Greece." *Arion* 9 (3rd s.): 145–69.

Segal, J. B., and H. S. Smith. 1983. *Aramaic Texts from North Saqqâra with Some Fragments in Phoenician*. London: Egyptian Exploration Society.

Seipel, Wilfried, ed. 2008. *Das Artemision von Ephesos: Heiliger Platz einer Göttin*. Vienna: Phoibos Verlag.

Seltman, Charles T. 1920. "Two Heads of Negresses." *AJA* 24.1: 14–26.

Seth, Vanita. 2020. "The Origins of Racism: A Critique in the Theory of Ideas." *History and Theory* 59.3: 343–68.

Shani, Ayelett. 2014. "'The Nation-state is Increasingly Losing its Relevance:' 'Fast talk' with historian Irad Malkin." *Hareetz*, June 9. https://www.haaretz.com/the-nat ion-state-is-losing-its-relevance-1.5251206.

Shaw, Brent D., and Richard P. Saller, eds. 1981. *Economy and Society in Ancient Greece by M.I. Finley*. London: Chatto & Windus.

Sherratt, Susan. 2010. "Greeks and Phoenicians: Perceptions of Trade and Traders in the Early First Millennium BC." In *Social Archaeologies of Trade and Exchange: Exploring Relationships among People, Places, and Things*, ed. A. Bauer and A. Agbe-Davies: 119–42. New York: Taylor & Francis.

Shortland, Andrew J. 2000. *Vitreous Materials at Amarna: the production of glass and faience in 18th Dynasty Egypt*. Oxford: Archeopress.

Shortland, Andrew, Lukas Schachner, Ian Freestone, and Michael Tite. 2006. "Natron as a flux in the Early Vitreous Materials Industry: Sources, Beginnings and Reasons for Decline." *Journal of Archaeological Science* 33: 521–30.

Shortland, A. J., P. Degryse, M. Walton, M. Geer, V. Lauwers, and L. Salou. 2011. "The Evaporitic Deposits of Lake Fazda (Wadi Natrun, Egypt) and Their Use in Roman Glass Production." *Archeometry* 53.5: 916–29.

Shramko, B. A. 1987. *Бельское городище скифской эпохи (город Гелон)* [The city of Belskoe in the Scythian period (city of Gelon)]. Kiev: Institute of Archaeology, Academy of Sciences of the Ukrainian SSR.

Siegel, Laura B. 1978. "Corinthian Trade in the Ninth through Sixth Centuries B.C." Dissertation, Yale University.

Simon, Erika. 1970. "Aphrodite Pandemos auf attischen Münzen." *SNR* 49: 5–19.

Sinn, Ulrich. 1990. "Das Heraion von Perachora : eine sakrale Schutzzone in der Korinthischen Peraia." *AM* 105: 53–116.

Skinner, Joseph, 2012. *The Invention of Greek Ethnography: From Homer to Herodotus*. Oxford: Oxford University Press.

Skon-Jedele, Nancy J. 1994. "Aigyptiaka: A Catalogue of Egyptian and Egyptianizing Objects Excavated from Greek Archaeological Sites, ca. 1100–525, with Historical Commentary." Dissertation, University of Pennsylvania.

Skuse, Matthew L. 2018. "The Arcesilas Cup in Context: Greek Interactions with Late Period Funerary Art." *BSA* 113: 221–49.

Skuse, Matthew L. 2021. "*Aegyptiaca* in Action: Assessing the Significance of Scarabs and Other Egyptian and Egyptianizing 'Amulets' at Perachora and Beyond." *Journal of Ancient Egyptian Interconnections* 32: 39–81.

Shumate, Nancy. 2006. *Nation, Empire, Decline: Studies in Rhetorical Continuity from the Romans to the Modern Era*. London: Duckworth.

Smallwood, Stephanie E. 2007. *Saltwater Slavery: A Middle Passage from Africa to American Diaspora*. Cambridge, MA: Harvard University Press.

Smith, Amy C. 2018. "The Left Foot Aryballos Wearing a Network Sandal." In *Shoes, Slippers, and Sandals: Feet and Footwear in Classical Antiquity*, ed. S. Pickup and S. White: 190–210. New York: Routledge.

Smith, Joanna S. 2009. *Art and Society in Cyprus from the Bronze Age into the Iron Age*. Cambridge: Cambridge University Press.

Smithson, Evelyn Lord. 1968. "The Tomb of a Rich Athenian Lady, ca. 850 B.C." *Hesperia* 37.1: 77–116.

Snowden, Frank M., Jr. 1947. "The Negro in Classical Italy." *AJP* 68.3: 266–92.

Snowden, Frank M., Jr. 1948. "The Negro in Ancient Greece." *American Anthropologist* 50.1: 31–44.

Snowden, Frank M., Jr. 1971. *Blacks in Antiquity: Ethiopians in the Greco-Roman Experience*. Cambridge, MA: Harvard University Press.

Snowden, Frank M., Jr. 1976. "Iconographical Evidence on the Black Populations in Greco-Roman Antiquity." In *The Image of the Black in Western Art*, vol. 1, ed. L. Bugner: 133–245. Cambridge, MA: Harvard University Press.

Snowden, Frank M., Jr. 1983. *Before Color Prejudice: the Ancient View of Blacks*. Cambridge, MA: Harvard University Press.

Snowden, Frank M., Jr. 1990a. Rev. of Karageorghis 1988. *AJA* 94.1: 161–62.

Snowden, Frank M., Jr. 1990b. Rev. of Thompson 1989. *AJP* 111.4: 543–57.

Snowden, Frank M., Jr. 1992. "Asclepiades' Didyme." *GBRS* 32.3: 239–53.

Solovyev, Sergei L. 1998. *Ancient Berezan: The Architecture, History, and Culture of the First Greek Colony in the Northern Black Sea*. Leiden: Brill.

Solovyev, Sergei L. 2005. *Березань–Борисфен: начало античной эпохи в Северном Причерноморье. Каталог выставки* [Borysthenes – Berezan: the 120th Anniversary of Archaeological Investigations of the Ancient Settlement on Berezan Island]. St. Petersburg: State Hermitage Museum.

Sonnini, C. S., and Vivant Denon. 1815. *Travels in Upper and Lower Egypt during the Campaigns of Buonaparte, Interspersed with Notes and Observations Geographical, Commercial, and Philosophical*. Glasgow: Edward Khull and Co.

Sørensen, Lone Wriedt. 2013. "'Head Hunting' in Cyprus." In *Vessels and Variety: Aspects of Ancient Pottery*, ed. H. Thomasen, A. Rathje, and K. Hohannsen: 149–74. Copenhagen: Museum Tusculum Press.

Sossau, Veronika. 2012. "The Cultic Fingerprint of the Phoenicians in the Early Iron Age West?" In *Sanctuaries and the Power of Consumption: Networking and the Formation of Elites in the Archaic Western Mediterranean World*, ed. E. Kistler, B. Ohlinger, M. Mohr, and M. Hoernes: 21–40. Wiesbaden: Harrasowitz Verlag.

Spantidaki, Stella. 2016. *Textile Production in Classical Athens*. Oxford: Oxbow.

Sparks, Randy J. 2014. *Where the Negroes are Masters: an African Port in the Era of the Slave Trade*. Cambridge: Harvard University Press.

Spencer, A. J. 2011. "The Egyptian Temple and Settlement at Naukratis." *British Museum Studies in Egypt and Sudan* 17: 31–49.

Stais, Valerios. 1917. "Σουνίου ἀνσκαφαί." *ArchEph* 1915: 168–213.

Stampp, Kenneth M. 1956. *The Peculiar Institution: Slavery in the Ante-Bellum South*. New York: Vintage.

Stello, Annika. 2017. "Caffa and the Slave Trade during the First Half of the Fifteenth Century." In Amitai and Cluse: 375–400.

Stern, E. 1976. "Phoenician Masks and Pendants." *PEQ* 108: 109–18.

Storey, Ian C. 2003. *Eupolis: Poet of Old Comedy*. Oxford: Oxford University Press.

Storey, Ian C. 2011, ed. *The Fragments of Old Comedy*. Loeb Classical Library. Cambridge, MA: Harvard University Press.

St.-Pierre Hoffmann, Catherine, and Thomas Brisart. 2010. "Les offrandes orientales et orientausantes dans les sanctuaires grecs. Compétition et idéal communautaire." In *La Méditerranée au VIIr' siècle av. J.-C. (Essais d'analyses archéologiques)*, ed. R. Etienne, A. Esposito, and L. Costa: 249–73. Paris: de Boccard.

Stringfellow, Kim. 2014. "Borax: the Magic Crystal." In *The Mojave Project*, ed. K. Stringfellow. https://mojaveproject.org/dispatches-item/borax-the-magic-crystal/.

Stolba, Vladimir F. 2005. "Fish and Money: Numismatic Evidence for Black Sea Fishing." In Bekker-Nielsen: 115–32.

Stos-Gale, Zofia Anna, and Noël H. Gale. 2009. "Metal Provenancing Using Isotopes and the Oxford Archaeological Lead Isotope Database (OXALID)." *Archaeological and Anthropological Science* 1: 195–213.

Stronk, Jan P. 1987–87. "Wreckage at Salmydessos." *Talanta* 63–75.

Stronk, Jan P. 2010. "Polycharmos (640)." In Worthington 2007-ongoing. https://scholarlyeditions.brill.com/bnjo/.

Stubbings, J. M. 1962. "Ivories." In Dunbabin: 403–51.

Swain, Simon, ed. 2007. *Seeing the Face, Seeing the Soul: Polemon's Physiognomy from Classical Antiquity to Medieval Islam.* Oxford: Oxford University Press.

Swain, Simon. 2013. *Economy, Family, and Society from Rome to Islam: A Critical Edition, English Translation, and Study of Bryson's Management of the Estate.* Cambridge: Cambridge University Press.

Sweet, John Wood. 2003. *Bodies Politic: Negotiating Race in the American North, 1730–1830.* Philadelphia: University of Pennsylvania Press.

Talmatchi, Gabriel, and Gheorghe Papuc. 2007. "The Arrow-Monetary Signs Hoard, Founded in Constanta (Constanta County)." In *Coin Hoards of Dobruja* I, ed. G. Custurea, M. Dima, G. Talmatchi, and A. Velter: 11–36. Constanta: Ex Ponto.

Tanner, Jeremy. 2010. "Introduction to the New Edition: Race and Representation in Ancient Art: *Black Athena* and After." In *The Image of the Black in Western Art*, vol. 1. 2nd ed., ed. D. Bindman, H. L. Gates, Jr., and C. C. Dalton: 1–39. Cambridge, MA: Harvard University Press.

Taylor, Timothy. 2001. "Believing the Ancients: Quantitative and Qualitative Dimensions of Slavery and the Slave Trade in Later Prehistoric Eurasia." *WorldArch* 33.1: 27–43.

Teeter, Emily. 2011. *Religion and Ritual in Ancient Egypt.* Cambridge: Cambridge University Press.

Tereshenko, O. I. 2013. "Античне торговельне судно Зміїний-Патрокл (склад продукції)" [Ancient Greek Merchant Ship "Zmiinyi-Patroclus" (cargo composition)]. *Археологія* [Archaeology] 2013.3: 69–88.

Theodoropoulou-Polychroniadis, Zetta. 2015. *Sounion Revisited: the Sanctuaries of Poseidon and Athena at Sounion in Attica.* Oxford: Archeopress.

Thomas, Rosalind. 2000. *Herodotus in Context: Ethnography, Science, and the Art of Persuasion.* Cambridge: Cambridge University Press.

Thomas, Ross I. 2015a. "Naukratis, 'Mistress of Ships,' in Context." In Robinson and Goddio: 247–66.

Thomas, Ross I. 2015b. "Cypriot figures in terracotta and limestone." In Villing et al. 2013-19. https://webarchive.nationalarchives.gov.uk/20190801125419/https://www.britishmuseum.org/pdf/Thomas_Cypriot_Figures.pdf.

Thompson, F. H. 2003. *The Archaeology of Greek and Roman Slavery.* London: Duckworth.

Thompson, Lloyd A. 1989. *Romans and Blacks.* London: Routledge.

Thompson, Dorothy Burr, and Ralph E. Griswold. 1963. *Garden Lore of Ancient Athens*. Princeton, NJ: American School of Classical Studies at Athens.

Thür, Gerhard. 1977. *Beweisführung vor den Schwurgerichtshöfen Athens. Die Proklesis zur Basanos*. Vienna: Österreichische Akademie der Wissenschaften.

Thür, Gerhard. 1996. "Reply to D. C. Mirhady: Torture and Rhetoric in Athens." *JHS* 116: 132–34.

Tompkins, Daniel P. 2013. "Moses Finkelstein and the American Scene: The Political Formation of Moses Finley, 1932–1955." In W. V. Harris: 5–30.

Torbakov, Igor. 2021. "On 'Nostalgia for the Empire: The Politics of Neo-Ottomanism' by M. Hakan Yavuz." *Sociology of Islam* 9: 76–83.

Tordoff, Rob. 2013. "Introduction: Slaves and Slavery in Ancient Greek Comedy." In *Slaves and Slavery in Ancient Greek Comic Drama*, ed. B. Akrigg and R. Tordoff: 1–62. Cambridge: Cambridge University Press.

Torelli, Mario. 1982. "Per la definizione del commercio greco-orientale: il caso di Gravisca." *La Parola del Passato* 37: 304–25.

Totelin, Laurence M. V. 2009. *Hippocratic Recipes: Oral and Written Transmission of Pharmacological Knowledge in Fifth- and Fourth-Century Greece*. Leiden: Brill.

Touraïeff, B. 1911. "Objets égyptiens et égyptisants trouvés dans la Russie méridionale." *RA* 18 (4th s.): 20–35.

Trigger, Bruce. 1989. *A History of Archaeological Thought*. Cambridge: Cambridge University Press.

Trivellato, Francesca. 2009. *The Familiarity of Strangers: the Sephardic Diaspora, Livorno, and Cross-cultural Trade in the Early Modern Period*. New Haven, CT: Yale University Press.

Trümper, Monika. 2009. *Graeco-Roman Slave Markets: Fact or Fiction?* Oxford: Oxbow.

Tsagalis, Christos. 2017. *Early Greek Epic Fragments I: Antiquarian and Genealogical Epic*. Berlin: De Gruyter.

Tsetskhladze, Gocha, ed. 1998a. *The Greek Colonization of the Black Sea Area: Historical Interpretation of Archaeology*. Stuttgart: Franz Steiner.

Tsetskhladze, Gocha. 1998b. "Greek Colonization of the Black Sea Area: Stages, Models, and Native Population." In Tsetskhladze: 9–68.

Tsetskhladze, Gocha. 2001, ed. *North Pontic Archaeology: Recent Discoveries and Studies*. Leiden: Brill.

Tsetskhladze, Gocha. 2007a. "Pontic Slaves in Athens: Orthodoxy and Reality." In *Antike Lebenswelten: Konstanz-Wandel-Wirkungsmacht*, ed. P. Mauritsch, W. Petermandl, R. Rollinger, and C. Ulf: 309–20. Wiesbaden: Harrasowitz.

Tsetskhladze, Gocha. 2007b. "'Grain for Athens.' The view from the Black Sea." In *Feeding the Ancient City*, ed. R. Alston and O. van Nijf: 47–62. Leuven: Peeters.

Tubb, Jonathan. 2014. "Sea Peoples and Philistines." In Aruz et al.: 38–45.

Tunkina, Irina V. 2003. "The Formation of a Russian Science of Classical Antiquities of Southern Russia in the 18th and Early 19th Century." In *The Cauldron of Ariantas*.

Studies Presented to A.N. Ščeglov on the Occasion of His 70th Birthday, ed. P. G. Bilde, J. M. Højte, and V. F. Stolba: 303–64. Aarhus: Aarhus University Press.

Tunkina, Irina V. 2006. "Archivmaterialien aus dem ersten Drittel des 19. Jhs. über das Achilleus-Heiligtum auf der Landzunge von Tendra." In Hupe: 89–110.

Tunkina, Irina V. 2007. "New Data on the Panhellenic Achilles Sanctuary on the Tendra Spit (Excavation of 1824)." In Bresson, Ivantchik, and Ferrary: 225–240.

Tuplin, Christopher. 1999. "Greek Racism? Observations on the Character and Limits of Greek Ethnic Prejudice." In *Ancient Greece: West and East*, ed. G. R. Tsetskhladze: 47–76. Leiden: Brill.

Tzochev, Chavdar. 2016. *Amphora Stamps from Thasos. The Athenian Agora* vol. 37. Princeton, NJ: American School of Classical Studies at Athens.

United States Census Bureau. 2012. "The Great Migration, 1910–1970." https://www.census.gov/dataviz/visualizations/020/.

U.S. Hydrographic Office. 1920. *The Black Sea Pilot: The Dardanelles, Sea of Marmara, Bosporus, Black Sea, and Sea of Azov*. Washington, DC: Government Printing Office.

Ure, Percy Neville. 1922. *The Origin of Tyranny*. Cambridge: Cambridge University Press.

Üstündağ, Handan. 2020. "Entheseal Changes in the Hellenistic-Roman Population of Boğazköy, Turkey: Evidence for Gender Division of Labor?" *Bioarchaeology of the Near East* 14: 27–49.

Vakhtina, Marina J. 2007. "Greek Archaic Orientalising Pottery from the Barbarian Sites of the Forest-steppe Zone of the Northern Black Sea Coastal Region." In *The Black Sea in Antiquity: Regional and Interregional Economic Exchanges*, ed. P. Gabrielsen and J. Lund: 23–37. Aarhus: Aarhus University Press.

Vakhtina, Marina J. 2018. "Греческая керамика из раскопок Немировского городища" [Greek pottery from the excavations of Nemirovo]. In *Городище Немиров на реке Южный Буг* [Nemirov Hill Fort on South Bug River], ed. G. I. Smirnova, M. J. Vakhtina, M. T. Kashuba, E. G. Starkova: 193–222. St. Petersburg: Nauka.

Van Alfen, Peter. 2002. "*Pant'agatha:* Commodities in Levantine-Aegean Trade During the Persian Period, 6-4th c. B.C." Dissertation, University of Texas.

Van Alfen, Peter. 2006. "Aegean-Levantine Trade, 600–300 BCE: Commodities, Consumers, and the Problem of *Autarkeia*." In *The Ancient Greek Economy: Markets, Households, and City-States*, ed. E. Harris, D. Lewis, and L. Woolmer: 277–98. Cambridge: Cambridge University Press.

Van Alfen, Peter. 2020. "The Role of Coinage in Archaic Aegean-Egyptian Overseas Trade: Another Look at *TAD* C.3.7." In *Money Rules! The Monetary Economy of Egypt, from Persians until the Beginning of Islam*, ed. T. Faucher: 43–67. Cairo: Institut français d'archéologie orientale.

Van de Moortel, Aleydis, and Merle K. Langdon. 2017. "Archaic Ship Graffiti from Southern Attica, Greece: Typology and Preliminary Contextual Analysis." *IJNA* 46.2: 382–405.

Van den Eijnde, F., T. Pieters, R. Van Wijk, and R.F. Docter. 2021. "Excavations in a Terrace on the South-East Velatouri at Thorikos and the Discovery of a Slave Burial." In Docter and Webster: 99–108.

Van Heel, Koenraad Donker. 1996. "Abnormal Hieretic and Early Demotic Texts Collected by the Theban Choachytes in the Reign of Amasis." Dissertation, University of Leiden.

Van Oppen de Ruiter, Branko. 2020. "Lovely Ugly Bes! Animalistic Aspects in Ancient Egyptian Popular Religion." *Arts* 9.51: 1–27.

Vanthuyne, Bart. 2012/13. "Amarna Factories, Workshops, Faience Moulds and their Produce." *Ägypten und Levante/Egypt and the Levant* 22/23: 395–429.

Vasunia, Phiroze, 2001. *The Gift of the Nile: Hellenizing Egypt from Aeschylus to Alexander*. Berkeley: University of California Press.

Vasunia, Phiroze, 2003. "Hellenism and Empire: Reading Edward Said." *Parallax* 9.4: 88–97.

Vaxevanopoulos, Markos, Janne Blichert-Toft, Gillan Davis, and Francis Albarède. 2022. "New Findings of Ancient Greek Silver Sources." *Journal of Archaeological Science* 137, 105474.

Velkov, Velizar. 1964. "Zur Frage der Sklaverei auf der Balkanhalbinsel während der Antike." *Études balkaniques* 1: 125–38.

Velkov, Velizar. 1967. "Рабы-Фракийцы в античных полисах Греции VI—II ВВ. ДО Н. Э." [Thracian Slaves in Ancient Greek Cities, 6th-2nd centuries BC]. *VDI* 4 (102): 70–80.

Venit, Marjorie Susan. 1988. *Greek Painted Pottery from Naukratis in Egyptian Museums*. Winona Lake, IL: Eisenbaums.

Vercoutter, Jean. 1945. *Les objets égyptiens et égyptisants du mobilier funéraire carthaginois*. Paris: Librairie Orientaliste Paul Geuthner.

Verdan, Samuel. 2013. *Le sanctuaire d'Apollon Daphnéphoros à l'époque géométrique. Eretria* vol. 22. Athens: École Suisse d'archéologie en Grèce.

Villing, Alexandra. 2015a. "Naukratis, Egypt and the Mediterranean world: a port and trading city." In Villing et al. 2013–19. https://webarchive.nationalarchives.gov.uk/20190801151053/https://www.britishmuseum.org/PDF/Naukratis_ORC_Port_Trading_City_Villing.pdf.

Villing, Alexandra. 2015b. "Egyptian-Greek Exchange in the Late Period: The View from Nokradj-Naukratis." In Robinson and Goddio: 229–46.

Villing, Alexandra. 2019. "Naukratis: Religion in a Cross-cultural Context." *British Museum Studies in Ancient Egypt and Sudan* 24: 204–47.

Villing, Alexandra, and Ross Thomas. 2015. "The Site of Naukratis: Topography, Buildings and Landscape." In Villing et al. 2013–19. https://webarchive.nationalarchives.gov.uk/20190801124830/https://www.britishmuseum.org/pdf/Naukratis_ORC_Topography_Villing_Thomas.pdf.

Villing, Alexandra, M. Bergeron, G. Bourogiannis, A. Johnston, F. Leclère, A. Masson-Berghoff, and R. Thomas, eds. 2013–19. *Naukratis: Greeks in Egypt*. Online research catalogue, British Museum. https://webarchive.nationalarchives.gov.uk/2019080 1105436/https://www.britishmuseum.org/research/online_research_catalogues/ng/naukratis_greeks_in_egypt.aspx.

Vinogradov, Yuri A. 1971. "Древнее грейсское писание с острой Березань" [A Greek Letter from Berezan]. *VDI* 4 (118): 74–100.

Vinogradov, Yuri A. 1991. "Die Stele des Leoxos, Molpagores' Sohn, aus Olbia und die Skythisch-Griechischen Beziehungen im frühen 5. Jh. V. Chr." *AA* 1991: 499–510.

Vinogradov, Yuri A. 1998. "The Greek Colonization of the Black Sea Region in Light of Private Lead Letters." In Tsetskhladze: 153–78.

Vinogradov, Y. A., and M. Zolotarev. 1988. "La Chersonèse de la fin d'archaïsme." In *Le Pont-Euxin vu par les Grecs: Sources écrites et archéologie*, ed. O. Lordkipanidzé and P. Lévêque: 85–120. Paris: Belles Lettres.

Vittmann, G. 2003. *Ägypten und die Fremden Im Ersten Vorchristlichen Jahrtausend*. Mainz: Philipp von Zabern.

Vives y Escudero, Antonio. 1917. *Estudio de arqueología Cartaginesa: La necrópolis de Ibiza*. Madrid: Blass y Cia.

Vlassopoulos, Kostas. 2010. "Athenian Slave Names and Social History." *ZPE* 175: 113–44.

Vlassopoulos, Kostas. 2013. *Greeks and Barbarians*. Cambridge: Cambridge University Press.

Vlassopoulos, Kostas. 2015. "Ethnicity and Greek History: Re-examining Our Assumptions." *BICS* 58.2: 1–13.

Vlassopoulos, Kostas. 2016. "Does Slavery Have a History? The Consequences of a Global Approach." *Journal of Global Slavery* 1: 5–27.

Vlassova, E. V. 2001. "The Scythian Drinking-Horn." In *North Pontic Antiquities in the State Hermitage Museum*, ed. J. Boardman, S. Solovyov, and G Tsetskhladze: 71–112. Leiden: Brill.

Vnukov, S. J., T. A. Ilyina, M. B. Muratov, S. V. Olkhovsky, A. V. Smokotina. 2020. "Терракотовая мужская голова из бухты у мыса Ак-Бурун: Предварительные результаты исследования и новые вопросы" [The terracotta male head from the bay near Cape Ak-Burun: preliminary results of research and new questions]. *Краткие сообщения Института археологии* [Brief Reports from the Institute of Archaeology] 258: 7–18.

Volgelsang-Eastwood, Gillian. 2000. "Textiles." In *Ancient Egyptian Materials and Technology*, ed. P. Nicholson and I. Shaw: 268–98. Cambridge: Cambridge University Press.

Vollenweider, Marie-Louise. 1983. *Catalogue raisonné des sceaux, cylindres, intailles et camées: La collection du révérend dr. V.E.G. Kenna et d'autres acquisitions et dons récents*. Mainz: Philipp von Zabern.

Von Bomhard, Anne-Sophie. 2012. *The Decree of Sais: the Stelae of Thonis-Heracleion and Naukratis*. Oxford: Oxford School of Archaeology.

Von Bomhard, Anne-Sophie. 2015. "The Stela of Thonis-Heracleion: Economic, Topographic, and Epigraphic Aspects." In Robinson and Goddio: 101–20.

Von Bothmer, Dietrich. 1957. *Amazons in Greek Art*. Oxford: Oxford University Press.

Von den Driesch, Angela, Dieter Kessler, Frank Steinmann, Veronique Berteaux, and Joris Peters. 2005. "Mummified, Deified and Buried at Hermopolis Magna—the Sacred Birds from Tuna el-Gebel, Middle Egypt." *Ägypten und Levante* 15: 203–44.

Von Reden, Sitta. 2007. *Money in Ptolemaic Egypt: from the Macedonian Conquest to the End of the Third Century BC*. Cambridge: Cambridge University Press.

Waldstein, Charles. 1905. *The Argive Heraeum*. 2 vols. New York: Houghton, Mifflin, and Company.

Warburton, David. 1997. *State and Economy in Ancient Egypt: Fiscal vocabulary of the New Kingdom*. Freiburg: Universitätsverlag.

Wachsmann, Shelley. 2000. "To the Sea of the Philistines." In Oren: 103–43.

Walters, H. B. 1926. *Catalogue of the Engraved Gems and Cameos, Greek, Etruscan, and Roman in the British Museum*. London: British Museum.

Wasserman, Nathan. 2013. "Treating Garments in the Old Babylonian Period: 'At the Cleaners' in a Comparative View." *Iraq* 75: 255–77.

Webb, Virginia. 1978. *Archaic Greek Faience: Miniature Scent Bottles and Related Objects from East Greece, 650–500 B.C.* Warminster: Aris and Phillips.

Webb, Virginia. 2015a. "Archaic Mixed Style Faience Figures." In Villing et. al. 2013–19. https://webarchive.nationalarchives.gov.uk/20190801135657/https://www.britishmuseum.org/pdf/Webb_faience_figures.pdf.

Webb, Virginia. 2015b. "Archaic Mixed Style Faience Vessels." In Villing et. al. 2013–19. https://webarchive.nationalarchives.gov.uk/20190801143001/https://www.britishmuseum.org/pdf/Webb_Faience_vessels_SF_AV.pdf.

Webb, Virginia. 2016. *Faience Material from the Samos Heraion Excavations*. Wiesbaden: Reichert Verlag.

Webb, Virginia. 2019a. "The Significance of Faience in the Religious Practices at Naukratis and Beyond." *British Museum Studies in Ancient Egypt and Sudan* 24: 312–40.

Webb, Virginia. 2019b. "Faience Finds from Naukratis and Their Implications for the Chronology of the Site." *British Museum Studies in Ancient Egypt and Sudan* 24: 41–70.

Webb, Virginia. 2021. "Faience Found in the Recent Excavations to the East of the Great Altar in the Samos Heraion." *AA* 2020/21: 1–62.

Węcowski, Marek. 2010. "Anaximander the Younger (9)." In Worthington 2007-ongoing. https://scholarlyeditions.brill.com/bnjo/.

Weil, Simone. 1965 [1940–41]. "The *Iliad*, or the Poem of Force." Trans. McCarthy. *Chicago Review of Books* 18.2: 5–30.

Wells, Peter S. 1980. *Culture Contact and Culture Change: Early Iron Age Central Europe and the Mediterranean World*. Cambridge: Cambridge University Press.

Wengrow, David. 2010. "The Voyages of Europa: Ritual and Trade in the Eastern Mediterranean, circa 2300–1850 BC." In *Archaic State Interaction: the Eastern Mediterranean in the Bronze Age*, ed. W. Parkinson and M. Galaty: 141–60. Santa Fe: School for Advanced Research.

West, Martin L. 1997. *The East Face of Helicon: West Asiatic Elements in Greek Poetry and Myth*. Oxford: Oxford University Press.

West, Martin L. 2002. "'Eumelos': A Corinthian Epic Cycle?" *JHS* 122: 109–33.

West, Martin L. 2003. "'Iliad' and 'Aethiopis.'" *CQ* 53.1 (n.s.): 1–14.

West, Martin L. 2013. *The Epic Cycle: A Commentary on the Lost Troy Epics*. Oxford: Oxford University Press.

West, Stephanie. 2003. "'The Most Marvelous of All Seas:' The Greek Encounter with the Euxine." *Greece and Rome* 50.2: 151–67.

West, Stephanie. 2004. "Herodotus on Aristeas." In *Pontus and the Outside World: Studies in Black Sea History, Historiography, and Archaeology*, ed. C. Tuplin: 43–67. Leiden: Brill.

West, William C. III. 2015. "Learning the Alphabet: Abecedaria and the Early Schools in Greece." *GBRS* 55: 52–71.

Westermann, William L. 1935. "Sklaverei." In *Paulys Real-Encyclopädie der classischen Altertumswissenschaft* supp. 6, ed. G. Wissowa and W. Kroll: 894–1068. Stuttgart: J. B. Metzlersche Verlagsbuchhandlung.

Westermann, William L. 1955. *The Slave Systems of Greek and Roman Antiquity*. Philadelphia: American Philosophical Society.

Wheeler, Roxann. 2000. *The Complexion of Race: Categories of Difference in Eighteenth-Century British Culture*. Philadelphia: University of Pennsylvania Press.

Whitehouse, David. 2002. "The Transition from Natron to Plant Ash in the Levant." *JGS* 44: 193–96.

Wilkerson, Isabel. 2010. *The Warmth of Other Suns: The Epic Story of America's Great Migration*. New York: Vintage.

Wilkinson, G. O. 1843. "Some Account of the Natron Lakes of Egypt; In a Letter to W. R. Hamilton, Esq." *Journal of the Royal Geographical Society of London* 13: 113–18.

Wilkinson, Richard H. 1992. *Reading Egyptian Art: A Hieroglyphic Guide to Ancient Egyptian Painting and Sculpture*. London: Thames and Hudson.

Willetts, Ronald F. 1967. *The Law Code of Gortyn*. Berlin: Walter de Gruyter & Co.

Williams, Charles K. II, Jean MacIntosh, and Joan E. Fisher. 1973. "Excavation at Corinth, 1973." *Hesperia* 43.1: 1–76.

Williams, Dyfri. 2013. "Greek Potters and Painters: Marketing and Movement." In *Pottery Markets in the Ancient Greek World (8th–1st centuries BC)*, ed. A. Tsingarida and D. Viviers: 39–60. Brussels: CReA Patrimoine.

Williams, Eric. 1994 [1944]. *Capitalism and Slavery*. Chapel Hill: University of North Carolina Press.

Wilson, Emily Sarah. 2018. "What's in a Name? Trade, Sanctuaries, Diversity and Identity in Archaic Ionia." PhD dissertation, University of Chicago.

Wilson, Jean-Paul. 1997–98. "The 'Illiterate Trader?'" *BICS* 42: 29–56.

Wilson, Veronica. 1975. "The Iconography of Bes with Particular Reference to Cypriot Evidence." *Levant* 7.1: 77–103.

Wilson, Penelope, and Dimitrios Grigoropoulos. 2009. *The West Nile Delta Regional Survey, Beheira and Kafr el-Sheikh Provinces*. London: Egyptian Exploration Society.

Winter, Irene. 1995. "Homer's Phoenicians: History, Ethnography, or Literary Trope? (A Perspective on Early Orientalism)." In *The Ages of Homer: A Tribute to Emily Townsend Vermeule*, ed. J. B. Carter and S. Morris: 247–71. Austin: University of Texas Press.

Worthington, Ian, ed. 2007–ongoing. *Brill's New Jacoby*. 2nd ed. https://scholarlyeditions.brill.com/bnjo/. Leiden: Brill.

Wrenhaven, Kelly L. 2012. *Reconstructing the Slave: The Image of the Slave in Ancient Greece*. London: Bloomsbury.

Wycherley, R. E. 1957. *Literary and Epigraphical Testimonia. The Athenian Agora* vol 3. Princeton, NJ: The American School of Classical Studies at Athens.

Yardeni, Ada. 1994. "Maritime Trade and Royal Accountancy in an Erased Customs Account from 475 B.C.E. on the Ahiqar Scroll from Elephantine." *BASOR* 293: 67–78.

Yiftach, Uri. 2019. "The Rise of the Flexible Template: Patterns of Change in Identification Methods between the Ptolemaic and Roman Period." In *L'identification des personnes dans les mondes grecs*, ed. R. Guicharrousse, P. Ismard, M. Vallet, and A. Veïsse: 77–89. Paris: Éditions de la Sorbonne.

Yoyotte, Jean. 1991/92. "Naucratis, ville égyptienne." *Annuaire du Collège de France* 92: 634–44.

Yoyotte, Jean. 1992/93. "Les contacts entre Égyptiens et Grecs (VIIe-VIe siècles avant I.C.): Naucratis, ville égyptienne (1992–1993, 1993–1994)." *Annuaire du Collège de France* 93: 679–92.

Zaghloul, El-Hussein Omar M. 1985. *Frühdemotische Urkunden aus Hermupolis*. Cairo: Ain Shams University.

Zavojkina, N. V., and N. A. Pavlichenko. 2016. "Письмо на Свинцовой Пластине из Патрея" [A letter on a lead tablet from Patrasys]. In *Фанагория. Результаты Археологических Исследований* [Phanagoria: Results of Archaeological Research], vol. 4, ed. V. D. Kuznetsov: 230–49. Moscow: Institute of Archaeology, Russian Academy of Science.

Zanovello, S. L. 2018. "Some Remarks on Manumission and Consecration in Hellenistic Chaeronea." *Journal of Global Slavery* 3: 129–51.

Zazoff, Peter. 1983. *Die antiken Gemmen*. Munich: C.H. Beck'sche Verlagsbuchhandlung.

Zelnick-Abramovitz, R. 2005. *Not Wholly Free: The Concept of Manumission and the Status of Manumitted Slaves in the Ancient Greek World*. Leiden: Brill.

Zimmermann, Martin. 2011. "Natronhandel und Glasherstellung im Frühmittelalter." *Sudhoffs Archiv* 95.1: 94–114.

Ziskowski, Angela. 2010. "The Construction of Corinthian Identity in the Early Iron Age and Archaic Period." Dissertation, Bryn Mawr College.

Ziskowski, Angela. 2014. "The Bellerephon Myth in Early Corinthian History and Art." *Hesperia* 83.1: 81–102.

Ziskowski, Angela. 2016. "Networks of Influence: Reconsidering Braudel in Archaic Corinth." In *Across the Corrupting Sea: Post-Braudelian Approaches to the Ancient Eastern Mediterranean*, ed. N. Concannon and L. Mazurek: 91–110. London: Routledge.

Index

For the benefit of digital users, indexed terms that span two pages (e.g., 52–53) may, on occasion, appear on only one of those pages.

Tables and figures are indicated by *t* and *f* following the page number

Achilles, 14–15, 131, 139–41
Achillodoros, 138–39, 142–44, 145–48, 154
aegyptiaca
    Amun Re and, 56, 66–67, 66*f*, 77
    as background for genealogical tales, 74–82
    Bellerophontes narrative and, 82–85
    biographies of faience and, 59–63
    circulation of myths outside of Egypt and, 78–79
    class-conflict interpretation of, 68–69
    colonialism and, 71–73
    commodity biography and, 53–54
    cowries and, 71–72
    cultural heroes and, 74–82
    dating of, 55
    dedication of Melanthios to "Theban Zeus" and, 67–68, 68*f*
    dedicators and, 64, 67, 71, 79
    definition of, 54
    development of, 53–57, 58, 59–63
    Egyptianizing cults and, 56–57, 75–76, 77
    Elephantine document and, 55, 69
    Ephesian Artemision and, 61
    epigraphy and, 77–80, 78*f*
    examples of, 55*f*, 63*f*, 64*f*
    foreign production of, 55
    as graveyard of scholarly ambition, 56
    Greek awareness of Egyptian background of, 67
    Ile Axe Opo Afonja and, 72, 73*f*
    inscriptions and, 64–65, 67, 74, 77–80
    invented traditions and, 54, 75–76
    lack of Greek cultural reference to faience and, 59–60, 81–82
    makeup of faience and, 57, 58*f*
    mass production and, 62–63
    meanings of, 55–56
    as miniaturization and popularization of eastern import, 70
    natron and, 57–58
    Naukratis scarabs and mold and, 64–67, 64*f*
    necklace of faience and, 59, 60*f*
    negotiation with the past and, 79
    as oddity in history of Greek religion, 55–56
    overview of, 53–57, 85
    Pendlebury's model and, 63–68
    Phoenician alphabet and, 83–84
    racialized commodities and, 14–15
    religious networks and, 74
    sailors and scarabs and, 63–68, 64*f*, 66*f*
    Samian Heraion and, 61–62
    sanctuaries and, 62*f*, 64–70, 73–74, 79–80, *81*, 233*t*

aegyptiaca (cont.)
   scholarship on, 55–56, 64–65, 67
   script of the heroes and, 82–85
   secondary contexts and, 61
   shell currencies and, 71–72
   in situ discovery of, 60–61
   spiritscapes and, 74
   Taranto scarab necklaces and, 79–80, 80*f*
   three-stage typology for categorizing faience and, 62–63, 63*f*
   on the trail of Sesostris and, 74–82
   translation and, 79
   trust generated through circulating trinkets and, 69–71
   uniformity in assemblages and, 61–62
   voyaging with the gods and, 68–74
   wampumpeag and, 71
   wandering charismatics and, 72–73
Aegyptiaca (Pendelbury), 63, 85
Aelian, 150–51
Aeschines, 171–72, 179
Aeschylus, 5–6, 19–20, 75, 83–84
Aesop, 127–28, 150–51
Against Aphobos (Demosthenes), 171
Against Lacritus, 161–62, 166–67
Aigyptis, 113–14
Airs, Waters, Places, 5–6, 30–31, 190, 192
Aithiopis (Arktinos of Miletus), 14–15, 140
Ak-Burun head, 156–59, 157*f*
Alcaeus, 140, 178–79
Amasis, 14–15, 38–39, 41, 45, 50, 69–70
Amenophis III, 77
Amun Re, 56, 66–68, 66*f*, 73
Anacharsis, 148
Anaxagoras, 144
Ancient Slavery and Modern Ideology (Finley), 183, 209
Andocides, 175–77, 203
Andomachos, 175–76
Apatorios, 142, 144–45, 146
Apollos, 44
Archaeology as Cultural History (Morris), 68–69
Archilochus, 18, 97, 142–43

Aristeas, 147–48
Ariston, 44–45, 46, 48–49, 50–51
Aristonymos, 146–47
Aristonymos' slave, 135, 138–39
Aristophanes, 30–31, 130, 167–68, 171–72, 185, 186, 203
Aristotle
   barbarians and, 7
   natural slaves and, 7, 129–30, 177–78, 182, 184, 207
   physiognomy and, 7, 184
   Scythians and, 142
   skin color and, 188–89
   slave as breathing piece of property and, 177–78
   trade routes and, 129–30
Arktinos of Miletus, 14–15
Arrington, Nathan, 55–56, 67–69
aryballoi, 62–63, 117–20, 118*f*, 119*f*
Asclepiades of Samos, 6
Ashurbanipal, 106–7
Athenian Black Figure vase painting, 14–15, 14*f*, 94–96, 96*f*, 117–18, 121, 201
Ayia Irini, 61

Bagnall, Roger, 271n.48
Bahrani, Zainab, 106–7
Bakenranef, 78–79
Bammer, Anton, 60–61
barbarians, 2, 4, 5–6, 7, 9–10, 14–15, 75, 128–29, 141–42, 170–72, 177–78, 186, 195–96, 204
Barth, Fedrik, 8–9
Beardsley, Grace Hadley
   criticism of, 92–93
   education of, 92
   Great Migration and, 93
   head scarabs and, 91–92, 115–16
   influences on, 92
   lack of evidence for positions of, 210
   overview of, 91–92
   Snowden and, 92–93
Belfiore, Cristina, 275n.10
Bell, Derrick, 264n.80
Bellerophontes narrative, 82–85

Bergk, 76–77
Bernal, Lloyd Thompson, 90
Bernal, Martin, 75–76, 90
Bes, 65–67, 114–18
Bewer, William M., 92
Bion of Borysthenes, 145–46
Bissing, F. W. von, 65
Blackness, 15, 88–89, 93, 97, 120–22, 173–74
Blavatskiy, V. D., 197
Blumenbach, Johann Friedrich, 16
Boas, Franz, 186–87
Bomfim, Martiniano Eliseu de, 72
Bomhard, Anne-Sophie, 40–41
Bradford, William, 71
Bradley, Keith, 128
Branco, Joaquim Francisco Devodê, 72
Bravo, Benedetto, 292n.1
Brisart, Theodore, 70
Bujskikh, Alla, 135
Burke, Black, 16
Burrows, John, 152
Busiris Painter, 14–15, 94, 95*f*, 109–10

Cameron, Alan, 261n.32
Candomblé, 72
Capitalism and Slavery (Williams), 8, 128
Cargo Ships (Aristophanes), 167–68
catalogue of enslaved journeys, 255–177
catalogue of Greeks in Egypt (7th to early 5th centuries BCE), 225–32
Catalogue of Women, 97, 108–9
Ceccarelli, Paula, 292n.1
Charaxos of Lesbos, 17–18, 37, 41, 73–74, 113
Civil Rights Movement, 183
Clarkson, Thomas, 108
Clearchus, 130, 192–94
Colchian girl, 131–33, 149–51
commodity biography, 18, 21, 28, 53–54, 121–22
Corrupting Sea (Hordern and Purcell), 214–15
Cratinus, 171–72, 204
Crielaard, Jan-Paul, 99–100
Critias, 18–19
Critical Race Theory (CRT), 12, 207

Cugoano, Ottobah, 16

Damoxenos, 44
Dana, Madalina, 292n.1
Danaos, 75–76, 83–84
Darius I, 76–77, 201–3
Davidson, James, 50, 167
dedicators, 39–40, 64, 67, 71, 79, 98–99, 100–1, 113
Deinias, 44
Demosthenes of Paiania
    barbarians and, 171, 174, 178, 195–96, 204
    birth of, 195–96
    enemies of, 171–72
    father of, 171
    fortune inherited by, 171
    Meidias charged with hubris by, 171–72
    racialized commodities and, 196, 199–201
    as Scythian, 184, 194, 195–96
    slave auctions and, 178–79, 182
    Stephanos prosecuted by, 177
Denon, Vivant, 31
Derbew, Sarah, 15, 88, 118–20
Dillon, Matthew, 273n.107
Dio, 162–63
Diodorus Siculus, 153
Diogenes Laertius, 145–46, 148
Diomedes, 82
Dionisius Agius, 74
Dionysius Thrax, 83–84
double-standard interpretation of racism, 12, 20, 126, 172–73, 176–77, 182, 188–89, 190–91, 204–5
Dow, Sterling, 284n.156
Du Bois, W. E. B., 92
Duke, Antera, 152–53
Duster, Troy, 9

Egypt. *See aegyptiaca*; Ethiopians; natron
Egyptianizing cults, 56–57, 75–76, 77
eikonismos, 260n.21
Elephantine document
    aegyptiaca and, 55, 69
    creation of, 29–30
    discovery of, 29–30

Elephantine document (*cont.*)
    letters of Makkibanit in, 43
    narratives of trade and, 37
    natron and, 27–28, 29–30, 34–37
    overview of, 21
    port stays and, 42–43, 42*t*
    seasonality and, 35–36
    significance of, 27–28
    tension between supply and demand in, 34–35, 35*f*
Engels, Friedrich, 197
enslaved journeys. *See* journeys into slavery
Esarhaddon, 106–7
Ethiopians
    aesthetic of migration and, 97–108
    anti-Black racism and, 88
    anti-slavery medallions and, 108–9
    aryballoi and, 117–20, 118*f*, 119*f*
    Blackness and, 88–89, 93, 97, 120–22
    Busiris Painter and, 94, 95*f*, 109–10
    consuming the body and, 108–20
    as dark-skinned, 5–6, 10–11, 85
    double hermeneutic of interaction and, 110–12
    Egyptians and, 94–97
    ethnicity in literary world of the heroes and, 96–97
    Exekias and, 93–96, 96*f*, 109–10, 121
    faience and, 89–94
    as flat-nosed, 5–6, 11, 15
    Great Migration and, 87–88, 92–93
    Greek belief in being Egyptian and, 94
    head amulets and, 100–1, 100*f*, 107–8
    head scarabs and, 90–92, 91*f*, 101–8, 102*f*, 103*f*, 104*f*, 105*f*, 106*f*, 107*f*, 114–17, 115*f*, 116*f*, 120
    head vessels and, 117–18, 118*f*
    head weights and, 99–100, 99*f*
    Herodotus on, 85
    iconography of, 10
    ideological basis of racism and, 88
    imaginings of the body and, 108–20
    inscriptions and, 106–7, 113–14, 114*f*
    janiform and quadform vessels and, 117–20

    Jim Crow and, 88
    lack of association between diversity and culture and, 98–99
    mixed-style figures and, 110–15, 111*f*, 112*f*, 120
    natron and, 109–10
    Other and, 88–89, 93–94, 114–15, 119–20
    overview of, 87–89, 121–22
    racialized commodities and, 4, 88–89, 93–94, 108–9
    sanctuaries and, 98, 112–14, 234
    scarcity of depictions prior to sixth century of, 97
    segregation and, 88
    sex workers and, 113–14
    spectrum of people, beasts, and gods and, 121–22
    Transatlantic Slave Trade and, 93
    vase painting and, 14–15
    vector of images of the "Ethiopian" body and, 117
    white supremacy and, 88
    as wooly-haired, 7, 15, 85, 97
Euclides, 1
Euenos, 17–18
Eupolis, 185–86, 204
Euripides, 139–40, 177–78, 186, 203
Eurybates, 96–97
Exekias, 14–15, 22, 93–96, 96*f*, 109–10, 121

faience. *See also* aegyptiaca
    afterlife of, 89–94
    biographies of, 59–63
    Ethiopians and, 89–94
    lack of Greek cultural reference to, 59–60
    makeup of, 57, 58*f*
    natron and, 57–63
    racialized commodities and, 4, 14–15, 17–18, 17*f*
    three-stage typology for categorizing, 62–63, 63*f*
Falconbridge, Alexander, 152–53
Federal Writers' Project, 128
Ferreira, Roquinaldo, 147
Fields, Barbara, 12–13, 126, 172

Index

Fields, Karen, 12–13, 126, 172
Finley, Moses, 126–27, 128–30, 183, 209–10
Fornasier, Jochen, 194–95
Fornasier, Kirsten, 194–95
Frank, Tenney, 92
Frogs (Aristophanes), 184
Fynn-Paul, Jeffrey, 129, 147–48

Gavriljuk, Nadia, 131
Gikandi, Simon, 15–16
Gildersleeve, Basil, 92
Gladney, Ida Mae, 87–88
Glaphyros, 42, 45–46
Glaucus, 82
Gleason, Maude, 187
Golden Race (Eupolis), 185
Grafe, Regina, 28, 214–15
Great Migration, 87–88, 92–93
Greeks in Egypt catalog (7th to early 5th centuries BCE), 225–32
Greene, Elizabeth, 37–38
Gruen, Erich, 10

Haley, Shelley, 210–11
Hall, Edith, 96–97
Hall, Jonathan M., 9–10
Harris, Edward, 129
Harris, J. R., 31–32, 34, 58
Hartman, Saidiya, 126, 133
head amulets, 100–1, 100*f*, 107–8
head scarabs, 90–92, 91*f*, 101–8, 102*f*, 103*f*, 104*f*, 105*f*, 106*f*, 107*f*, 114–17, 115*f*, 116*f*, 120, 242
head vessels, 117–18, 118*f*
head weights, 99–100, 99*f*
Hecataeus of Miletus, 83–84
Heflin, James "Cottom Tom," 92
Hendricks, Margo, 13, 20–21
Heng, Geraldine, 13, 207
Hermippus, 18–19
Hermotimos of Pedasos, 150
Herodotus
   aegyptiaca and, 69–70, 75
   animal worship and, 46–49
   Blackness and, 97

   Black Sea Basin and, 135–37
   body modification and, 191
   business of slavery and, 193–94
   Busiris Painter and, 94
   commodity encounters and, 50–51
   Egyptian difference and, 29, 45, 46–49
   Ethiopians and, 85
   ethnographic knowledge and, 22–23, 196–97
   genealogical claims and, 75
   Helleno-Scythian settlements and, 137–38
   Isis festival rituals and, 110–13
   mummification and, 49–51
   natron and, 29
   natural slaves and, 19
   Naukratis and, 38–39, 41
   origins of the alphabet and, 83
   relentlessly material logic of, 20
   sanctuaries and, 75–76, 98
   Scythians and, 19, 137–39, 140–42, 146–48, 167, 191–94, 197–99
   Sesostris and, 76–79
   slavery among the Scythians and, 197–99
   steppe culture and, 196–98, 204
   Thracians and, 19, 130, 150, 193–94
   translators and, 44
Herostratos of Naukratis, 36–37
Hesiod, 34, 37–38, 59–60, 75–76, 142–43, 201
Hippocrates, 184, 186–87, 190–91
Hipponax, 76–77, 131, 142–43
Hipponikos, 171–72, 184, 204
Hirophos, 134
Homer
   Bellerophontes narrative and, 82–83, 84
   Ethiopians and, 88, 96–97
   Eurybates and, 98–99
   faience not mentioned by, 59–60
   Iliad, 83–84, 105–6, 140–41
   journeys into slavery and, 129
   Odyssey, 98–99, 108–9, 121, 140
   Scythians and, 201
   skin color and, 188–89, 190–91
Horden, Peregrine, 16–17, 35–36, 37–38
Hunt, Peter, 126

Ilê Axé Opô Afonjá, 72, 73*f*
Iliad (Homer), 83–84, 105–6, 140–41
Image of the Black in Western Art (Snowden), 91
Inaros, 46
inscriptions, 64–65, 67, 74, 77–80, 106–7, 114*f*, 235
inventing whiteness
  abuse of slaves and, 171
  ancient slavery as double-standard based on ancestry, 172–73, 176–77, 183, 188–89, 190–91, 204–5
  Athenian citizenship and, 172–73, 176–77, 182
  barbarians and, 177–78, 186
  differential treatment and, 174–82
  enslaved archers from Scythia and, 203
  foreignness and, 172
  imagining the steppe and, 194–204
  lack of biodeterminism in theater tropes and, 186–87
  law courts and slave markets juxtaposed and, 177
  millwork and, 190
  natural history and, 188–89
  nomad attire worn by Athenians and, 201–3
  overview of, 170–74, 204–5
  physiognomy and, 187–89, 194
  purges in Athens and, 175–77
  racialized commodities and, 172–208
  "redness" concept and, 184, 196
  servile "whiteness" and, 173–74, 190–91
  skin color interpretations and, 182–94
  slave sales and evidentiary torture and, 175–82, 176*f*, 180*t*
  social structure in ancient Pontic steppe and, 196–97
  somatic terms and, 184–85
  Soviet archaeology and, 196–97
  tattoos and, 186
  theater and, 185–88
  training athletes amphora and, 201, 202*f*
  Transatlantic Slave Trade and, 186–87
  "whiteness" concept and, 173–74, 191, 196

Invention of Racism in Classical Antiquity, The (Isaac), 90, 209
Isaac, Benjamin, 12, 209
Ivantchik, Askold, 76–77, 201

James, T. G. H., 64
janiform and quadform vessels, 117–20
Jefferson, Thomas, 16
Jim Crow, 6–7, 88, 90, 207, 209–10
journeys into slavery
  Achilles cults and, 139–41
  alien space in Greek thought and, 142
  attested or likely slave markets and, 131, 132*t*
  barbarian violence as driver of slave supply and, 141–42
  binary between enslavable and non-enslavable and, 147–48
  biographical turn in scholarship and, 128–34
  Black Sea Basin and, 135–37
  catalogue of, 255–177
  commodity hunger explanations of slavery and, 131
  development of Greek slavery and, 128–31
  from document sources, 255–173
  double-standard interpretation of racism and, 126
  enslavement of non-citizens and, 145–46
  Greek fear of falling into slavery and, 142–43
  hatred of locals toward ships and, 148
  intraregional mobility and, 134–41
  from literary sources, 256–177
  litigation use to entrap people into slavery and, 145–47
  map of routes taken by enslaved captives and, 135, 136*f*
  navigational knowledge and, 135
  overview of, 127–28, 149–51
  Priest's Letter and, 135
  racialized commodities and, 125–27
  reconstructing historical lived experience and, 126
  reenslavement and, 145–46

shipwrecks and law courts and, 141–48
short-distance trade routes and, 131
slavery as backdrop to racial imaginaries and, 128
social history and, 126
Transatlantic Slave Trade and, 126, 128, 133

Karageorghis, Vassos, 97, 116–17
Kemp, Barry, 40
Kittos, 180–81
Kolaios of Samos, 17–18
Kom el-Barnugi, 31–32
Kowalzig, Barbara, 74, 296n.68
Kurke, Leslie, 20, 48, 70–71

Lampis, 162–66
Lape, Susan, 172
Leoxos, 194–97, 195f, 199–203
Lewis, David M., 129, 165–66
Lindsay, Lisa, 133
Linnaeus, Carolus, 206
Lion (ship), 152–53
Lissarrague, François, 93–94, 117–18, 119–20, 201
Longinus, 147–48
López-Ruiz, Carolina, 54, 72–73, 284n.156
Lucas, Alfred, 31–32, 58
Lydos, 175–76, 181–82
Lykaon, 131, 140–41
Lysistrata (Aristophanes), 203

Making of the Ancient Greek Economy, The (Bresson), 213
Malkin, Irad, 9–10, 69, 74
Marx, Karl, 53–54
Masson-Berghoff, Aurélia, 66–67, 115–16
Matasys, 144, 146–47
Matory, J. Lorand, 72–73
McCoskey, Denise, 93
Meek, Andrew, 275n.10
Melas' enslaved woman, 135, 138–39, 147–48
Memnon, 121
Menelaus, 98–99
Mentes of Taphos, 17–18
Metrophanes, 134

Miller, Joseph C., 133
Mintz, Sidney, 15–16, 28–29, 51, 53–54, 121–22
mixed-style figures, 110–15, 111f, 112f, 120
modern concept of race. *See* racialized commodities
Morely, Neville, 215
Morgan, Jennifer, 168–69
Morris, S., 284n.156
Morris, Sarah, 75–76
Moyer, Ian, 79, 110–12
Murray, Jackie, 12
Murray, Sarah, 59, 68–69

natron. *See also* quantifying the natron trade
aegyptiaca and, 57–58
ancient understanding of, 30–31
animal worship and, 46–49
buying and selling of, 36–42
cabotage and, 37–38
colonial interest in, 31–32
commodity encounters and, 27–28, 45–51
demand and supply of, 29–36
earliest reports in trade of, 41
Egyptian understanding of, 33–34
Elephantine document and, 27–28, 29–30, 34–37
Ethiopians and, 109–10
faience and, 57–63
geography of production of, 31–32
Greek understanding of Egypt and, 28–29, 51
integration of Greeks into Egyptian culture and, 45
logic of connoisseurship and, 34
as loss leader, 28
mariners and, 37–38
mixed marriages and, 44–45
mummification and, 49–51
narratives of trade and, 36–37
Naukratis and, 38–39
opportunistic rather than systematic use of, 31–32
overview of, 27–29, 51–52
port stays and, 42–43, 42t

natron (cont.)
   racialized commodities and, 54
   risk of porting without temple backing and, 43
   seasonality of, 31–32, 34–35
   soda-evaporation complex and, 31–32, 32f
   sources for analysis of, 29–34
   temples and, 40–43
   tension between supply and demand and, 34–35, 35f
   ties that bind and, 42–45
   trade routes and, 37–39, 38f
   translators and, 44
   ubiquity in Egypt of, 33–34
   uses of, 27–28
   variation in cargo of, 35
Naukratis
   Achaemenid invasion of, 40–41
   aegyptiaca and, 64–67, 64f, 69–70
   dedicators in, 39–40
   Egyptian temple at, 40–41
   Ethiopians and, 109–13
   founding of, 38–39
   head scarabs and, 114–16, 116f
   as house of the port, 39
   infrastructure built by Greeks in, 39
   inscriptions and, 113–14, 114f
   mixed-style figures and, 110–15, 111f
   natron and, 38–39
   Othered bodies and, 114–15
   scarab factory at, 114–17, 115f
   sex workers and, 113–14
   significance of, 39–42
Neferpre-sa-Neith, 39, 44–45, 46, 49
Negro in Greek and Roman Civilization (Beardsley), 210
Nicias, 171–72, 184

Odyssey (Homer), 98–99, 108–9, 121, 140
Officers (Eupolis), 203
O.Gardiner 28, 34, 73–74
Ogundiran, Akinwumi, 55–56
Oreos, 165–66
the Other, 21–22, 88–89, 93–94, 114–15, 119–20, 141–42

Pairisades, 162–63
Palamedes, 83–84
Panionios, 150
Papadopoulos, John, 284n.156
Patroklos, 140–41
Patterson, Orlando, 141–42
Pdrwihy, 49
Pendlebury, John, 63, 67
Peoples of the Historic Slave Trade (PHST), 133
Periander, 84
Persians (Aeschylus), 19–20
Petrie, W. M. F., 64–65, 91, 114–16
Phaedo of Elis, 188
Phaedrus, 1
P.Harris 1, 48–49
Phaylles, 125, 126–27, 131, 135, 137, 139, 141, 147–48
Phocylides, 18
Phormion, 177–78
Physiognomica, 7, 187, 189–90
physiognomy
   definition of, 2–3, 187
   inventing whiteness and, 187–89, 194
   legacy of, 206
   popularity of, 206
   racialized commodities and, 2–3, 7, 15, 187
   slavery and, 189
Pindar, 139–40
Plato
   faces, beauty, and ugliness as framing devices for, 2
   lack of writing on slave origins and, 129–30
   noble lie and, 7
   social and political context of, 1
   Thracians and, 10–11
   use of dead persons in works of, 1
Pliny the Elder, 30, 31–32, 34
Politics (Aristotle), 177–78, 184
Pollux, Julius, 2, 6, 172, 185, 187–88
Polybius, 129–30, 150, 153
Porten, Bezalel, 29–30
premodern concept of race. *See* racialized commodities

Problems, 186–87, 190–91
Proclus, 140
Protokles, 28–30, 42, 45–46, 56–57
Psammetichos II, 38–39
Psamtik II, 39, 41, 44–45
Ps.-Skylax, 135–37
Ptolemy II Philadelphus, 6
P.Turin 1887, 50–51
P.Turin 2008 + 2016, 43
Purcell, Nicholas, 16–17, 35–36, 37–38
Putin, Vladimir, 196–97
Pythermos, 67

quantifying the natron trade
  borax harvesting and, 222–23, 222*f*
  challenges to, 214–15, 217
  estimating production and, 220–23, 221*t*
  lack of hard data and, 214–15
  metrics used for, 214–20, 215*t*, 216*t*, 216*t*, 218*t*, 218*t*, 218*t*, 219*t*, 219*t*, 219*t*, 220*t*
  natron and alum and, 214
  overview of, 213

racialized commodities. *See also* Ethiopians; Scythians; Thracians
  aegyptiaca and, 4, 14–15
  aggregative logic of Greek ethnicity and, 9–10
  artistic representations and, 14–15, 14*f*
  atlas of the body and, 5–8
  barbarians and, 4, 7, 9–10
  Blackness and, 15, 88–89, 93, 97, 120–22, 173–74
  cabotage and, 16–17
  caution for scholarship on, 13
  commodity biography and, 18, 21
  contributions of current volume on, 11–13, 21–23
  Critical Race Theory and, 12, 207
  depictions of slaves and, 2, 3*f*
  double-standard interpretation of racism, 12, 20, 126, 172–73, 176–77, 182, 188–89, 190–91, 204–5
  Ethiopians and, 4, 88–89, 93–94, 108–9
  ethnic imaginaire and, 14–15
  from ethnicity to race and, 8–13
  ethnographic discourse and, 5–6
  faience and, 4, 14–15, 17–18, 17*f*
  familiarity is recognition and, 208–11
  form and ugliness and, 1–3
  gender and, 5–7
  Greek identity and, 9–10
  horizons of trade and, 13–21
  inventing whiteness and, 172–208
  journeys into slavery and, 125–27
  lexicon to describe human diversity and, 5–8
  mining and, 19–20
  modern concept of race and, 2–3, 6–7, 8–13, 88–89, 206–7
  mythology of prolepsis and, 6–7, 207
  natron and, 54
  overview of, 1–4, 206–8
  path forward on, 211
  Persian Wars and, 9
  physiognomy and, 2–3, 7, 15, 187
  premodern concept of race and, 4, 12–13, 93–94, 207
  professionalization and, 210
  proto-racism and, 12, 209
  race as product of Transatlantic Slave Trade and, 4, 8, 207
  race turn in scholarship and, 3–4
  racialism paradigm and, 9, 22
  scholarship on race and, 3, 8–13
  Scythians and, 126, 174, 187, 199–201
  slavery and, 4, 5–6, 11–12, 15–16, 18–19
  social construction of race and, 8
  somatic terms and, 5
  specialists in trade and, 17–18
  structure of current volume on, 4
  summary of chapters of current volume on, 21–23
  systemic racism and, 3–4, 12
  theater and, 6, 19–20
  theory of race and, 184, 186–87
  Thracians and, 126, 174, 187, 199–201
  Transatlantic Slave Trade and, 4, 8, 15–17, 207
  usefulness of race concept and, 13–21
  visuality of Black bodies and, 16

"redness" concept, 23, 184, 196
Reed, Adolph, Jr., 88, 209–10
Republic (Plato), 5, 11, 187–88
Rhodopis/Doricha, 113–14, 150–51
Ricardo, David, 213
Robinson, Cedric, 3, 8

Samian Heraion, 61–62, 83–84, 112–13
Sappho, 17–18, 113
scarab heads, 90–92, 91*f*, 101–8, 102*f*, 103*f*, 104*f*, 105*f*, 106*f*, 107*f*, 114–17, 115*f*, 116*f*, 120, 234*t*
scarabs from LG Greece
   catalogue of, 239
   context and dating of, 238
   style of, 237–38
Scyles, 146–47
Scythians
   Athenian Scythians, 204
   body modification and, 191
   burial mounds and, 199
   business of slavery and, 193–94
   as dim-witted, 4, 126, 181–82
   enslaved archers and, 203
   as enslavers of Thracians, 174, 193–94, 199–201
   fertility of, 192–93
   Herodotus on, 19, 137–39, 140–42, 146–48, 167, 191–94, 197–99
   human sacrifice and, 198, 198*f*
   iconography of, 10
   imagining the steppe and, 194–204
   as light-skinned, 4, 5–6, 10, 184, 186–87, 190–92
   physiognomy and, 187
   purported rituals of, 142, 163, 193
   racialized commodities and, 4, 126, 174, 187, 199–201
   as red, 184, 190–91
   scalped heads and, 191, 192*f*
   self-portrayal of, 201–3
   slave mode of production and, 197–99
   slavery as backdrop to imagining, 11, 126, 128, 130
   as straight-haired, 7

   Thracians and, 174, 193–94, 199–201
   vase painting and, 201–3
Senusret III, 77–78, 79
Sesostris, 56–57, 74–82
Seth, Vanita, 6–7, 207
Skinner, Joseph, 10, 14–15
Skinner, Quentin, 207
Skuse, Matthew, 55–56
slave journeys. *See* journeys into slavery
slavery and racialization. *See* racialized commodities
slavery and the balance of trade
   Ak-Burun head and, 156–59, 157*f*
   amphorae and, 165
   classical shipwrecks and, 163–65, 164*t*, 166*f*
   currency exchanges and, 158–59
   dismissiveness toward the periphery and, 154
   financing a surplus and, 155–61
   lack of documentation on Greek slave trade and, 153
   lead and, 158–59
   likening of fish trade to enslaved captives and, 167
   literary narratives and, 153–54, 163–65
   map of fourth-century trade and, 159, 160*f*
   metals, minerals, and currency and, 155–61
   overview of, 152–55, 168–69
   silver and, 158
   staples in trade and, 161–68
   Stater of Cyzicus and, 167, 168*f*
   wine, oil, grain, and fish and, 161–68
slave sales and evidentiary torture, 175–82, 176*f*, 180*t*
slave trade (Transatlantic). *See* Transatlantic Slave Trade
Snowden, Frank M., Jr.
   ancient multiracialism and, 89–90, 109–10
   Busiris Painter and, 96–97
   career of, 89
   Civil Rights movement and, 92–93
   criticism of, 90

education of, 92–93
family and upbringing of, 92–93
government work of, 90
Great Migration and, 92–93
head scarabs and, 90–92, 91*f*, 107–8, 115–17
Homer and, 96–97
influence of, 90, 207
as member of talented tenth, 92–93
Naukratis and, 91, 93, 109–10
overview of, 89
terminology employed by, 91
tripartite thesis on ancient concept of race and, 89–90, 109–10
upbringing of, 90
Society for Effecting the Abolition of the Slave Trade, 108
Socrates, 1–2, 5
Sokydides, 67
Solokha comb, 199, 200*f*
Solomon, 72–73
Solon, 72–73, 128–29, 131, 146, 208–9
Sonnini, C. S., 31
Sørensen, Lone Wriedt, 106–7
Sostratos of Aegina, 17–18
Souza, Filisberto AmErico, 72
Spivak, Gayatri Chakravorty, 126
St.-Pierre Hoffmann, Catherine, 70
Strabo, 31–32, 129–30, 142, 150, 154
Stringfellow, Kim, 51
Subtlety, A (Walker), 266n.106
Suppliants (Aescheylus), 75
Sweet, John Wood, 133
Sweetness and Power (Mintz), 15–16, 121–22

Taharqa, 106–7
Tale of Sinhue, 77–78
Tale of the Eloquent Peasant, 33, 45–46
Tamumos, 113–14
Teale, Isaac, 16
Terpsion, 1
"textual" scarab inscriptions, 235
Thales, 10–11, 65
Thathaie(s), 146–47
Theaetetus, 1–2

Theaetetus (Plato), 1, 10, 20
theater, 6, 19–20, 185–88
Theocritus of Syracuse, 6
Theodorus of Cyrene, 1–2
Theognis, 70–71, 185
Theophrastus, 30–31, 57
Thesmophoria (Euripides), 203
Thracians
    business of slavery and, 193–94
    cultural practices as result of slave raiding and, 192–93
    as dim-witted, 4, 126, 181–82
    as enslavable by Scythians, 174, 193–94, 199–201
    as gray-eyed, 184
    Herodotus on, 19, 130, 150, 193–94
    as light-skinned, 4, 5–6, 10, 174, 190–91
    as most populous nation, 130
    as opposite of Greeks, 19
    racialized commodities and, 4, 126, 174, 187, 199–201
    as red-haired, 174
    as ruddy, 184
    Scythians and, 174, 193–94, 199–201
    as selling children into slavery, 19, 130, 181–82
    slavery as backdrop to imagining, 11, 126, 128, 130, 142
    as straight-haired, 7
    vase painting and, 14–15
Thucydides, 18–19, 169
Totelin, Laurence, 30–31
Transatlantic Slave Trade
    biographical turn and, 133
    Blackness and, 93
    data sets for research on, 133
    Ethiopians and, 93
    Federal Writers' Project and, 128
    inventing whiteness and, 186–87
    journeys into slavery and, 126, 128, 133
    lack of relevant documentation on, 128, 152–53
    race as product of, 4, 8, 207
    racialized commodities and, 4, 8, 15–17, 207

Transatlantic Slave Trade (*cont.*)
   reconstruction of, 152–53
   slave psychology and, 128
   theory of race and, 186–87
   visuality of Black bodies and, 15–16
Transatlantic Slave Trade Database (TASTD), 133, 152–53
Traysians, 19
Tuthmosis III, 77
Tymnes, 146–47

Ulpian, 181–82
Ure, Percy, 84

Vinogradov, Y. G., 131, 194–95, 196–97

Wahibre-em-achet, 44–45, 46, 49
Warmth of Other Suns (Wilkerson), 87–88
Webb, Virginia, 62–63, 110, 117
Wedgwood, Josiah, 16, 108–9
Wenamun, 73–74
Westermann, William, 209–10
white ground lekythos, 2, 3*f*
whiteness. *See* inventing whiteness
white supremacy, 88, 183
Williams, Eric, 3, 8
Women at the Thesmophoria (Aristophanes), 203, 260n.25

Xanthos, 150
Xenophanes of Kolophon, 11–12, 15, 88–89, 121–22, 184
Xenophon, 1, 7, 131

Yardeni, Ada, 29–30

Zekerba'al, 73–74
Zelnick-Abramowitz, R., 145–46
Ziskowski, Angela, 284n.156
Zopyros the Thracian, 188, 196, 204